EMPLOYMENT, DISABILITY, AND
THE AMERICANS WITH DISABILITIES ACT

Employment, Disability, and the Americans with Disabilities Act

Issues in Law, Public Policy, and Research

Edited by Peter David Blanck

NORTHWESTERN UNIVERSITY PRESS
EVANSTON, ILLINOIS

Northwestern University Press
Evanston, Illinois 60208-4210

Printed in the United States of America

ISBN 0-8101-1688-X (cloth)
ISBN 0-8101-1689-8 (paper)

Library of Congress Cataloging-in-Publication Data

    Employment, disability, and the Americans with Disabilities Act:
issues in law, public policy, and research / edited by Peter David Blanck
       p.   cm.
    Includes bibliographical references and index.
    ISBN 0-8101-1688-X (cloth : acid-free paper) — ISBN 0-8101-1689-8 (pbk : acid-free paper)
       1. Handicapped—Employment—Law and legislation—United States. 2. Discrimination in employment—Law and legislation—United States. 3. Handicapped—Legal status, laws, etc.—United States. I. Blanck, Peter David, 1957-.
KF3469.E48   2000
344.7301'59—dc21   00-008840

Contents

Figures and Tables

Preface

> Work is a basic ingredient in our culture. . . . The individual with a
> disability frequently presents a unique employment problem. If his
> impairment makes it impossible for him to meet the performance
> requirements of occupations for which he is otherwise qualified . . .
> retraining or job-restructuring might be necessary to permit his
> entering the society of the work force. If the disabled person is barred
> from employment because of the assumptions or fears of those who can
> withhold or grant employment, then community re-education is
> indicated.
>
> —Esco Obermann (1965, p. 23)

Since Dr. Obermann's seminal work, *A History of Vocational Rehabilitation in America,* and particularly during the past twenty-five years, disability law, culture, and policy, as reflected most directly by the passage of the Americans with Disabilities Act of 1990 (ADA), have undergone a dramatic shift toward the equal employment of persons with disabilities. Title I of the ADA, embodying the ADA's employment provisions, is playing a central role in enhancing the labor force participation of qualified persons with disabilities and in reducing their dependence on governmental entitlement programs (Blanck 1998, 1997, this volume).

Yet, on the tenth anniversary of the ADA, systematic information from multiple scholarly disciplines on the work lives of persons with disabilities was lacking (Burris and Moss, this volume). The promise of the ADA and related laws to integrate into society millions of Americans makes this lack of information troubling. Dramatic positive changes affecting the work lives of persons with disabilities are occurring in public attitudes and behavior toward individuals with disabilities in employment, governmental services, telecommunications, and public accommodations (Blanck 1998).

In 1998 the United States Supreme Court decided its first case under the ADA, *Bragdon v. Abbott,* involving interpretation of the scope of the definition of disability under the law (Blanck, this volume; Olick, this volume). In 1999 the Supreme Court ruled in five more cases interpreting the ADA, each having important implications for the law's definition of disability and its relation to other federal laws. Among other issues, the 1999 cases involved the ADA and the provision of social security benefits and community-based services for persons with disabilities. The importance of these and other developments is discussed throughout the book, with analysis from multiple disciplines of the implications for people with disabilities (Wilkinson and Frieden, this volume).

Documentation of ADA implementation from the perspectives of multiple disciplines is necessary to address the growing attitudinal backlash against disability law and policy implementation (Miller 1997; Stein, this volume). Some critical of the ADA have stated that the law should be rewritten to protect only people with "genuine" disabilities (Blanck 1998). Others argue that there is little definitive evidence that disability law and policy have resulted in larger numbers of qualified persons with disabilities participating in the workplace (Rosen 1991; Willborn, this volume).

This volume addresses these and related issues through an examination of employment, disability, and implementation of the ADA. The contributions to the volume are reflective of the recent paradigm shift in disability policy and law toward individual and civil rights, equal participation in the democratic process, empowerment, and self-determination (Blanck 2000).

Substituting Information for Myths about Disability

One goal of this volume is to substitute information for the prevalent myths and misconceptions about persons with disabilities, particularly in the realm of employment (Blanck 1998). Researchers estimate that people with disabilities make up approximately 20 percent of the total U.S. population, excluding persons living in nursing homes or other institutions (McNeil 1997). According to Jack McNeil's 1997 report, *Americans with Disabilities,* which is based on U.S. Census Bureau data collected between October 1994 and January 1995, approximately 54 million Americans reported some level of disability. Approximately 26 million people described their disability as severe.

Recent data from the U.S. Census Bureau suggest that the employment rate for people ages 21 to 64 without a disability was 82 percent and 77 percent for those with nonsevere disabilities (reviewed in Blanck 1998). In comparison, only 26 percent of those with severe disabilities were employed. The presence of a disability is associated with lower earnings. The median monthly earnings were $2,190 for men ages 21 to 64 without disabilities and $1,470 for comparable women. For those with nonsevere disabilities, the median monthly earnings were $1,857 for men and $1,200 for women. For those with severe disabilities, the median monthly earnings dropped substantially to $1,262 for men and $1,000 for women.

Thus, the presence of a disability is related to a lower likelihood of being employed, and, when employed, to a substantially lower level of income. People with disabilities who want to work and who are capable of working also are less likely to be able to work because affordable private health insurance is not available to them (Blanck 1998).

Communicating Information about Disability and Employment

Communicating information from multiple disciplines about people with disabilities is critical to effective ADA implementation in the future. It is instrumental to the evaluation of employment integration and economic opportunity for all Americans (Blanck 1998). Policy makers, researchers, employers, courts, and members of the disability community benefit from this information.

The need to inform ADA stakeholders of the progress toward achieving equal employment opportunity for all qualified Americans is not unlike that faced after the landmark 1954 Supreme Court school desegregation decision in Brown v. Board of Education. After the Supreme Court's decision, extensive study was conducted on attitudes and behavior toward school desegregation policies. Scholars from many disciplines took up the challenge—social psychologists, political scientists, economists, and sociologists—examining the links between historically rooted prejudicial attitudes and social behavior (Blanck 1998).

An analogous body of multidisciplinary research on employment integration under ADA implementation is needed. The passage of the ADA alone has significantly changed biased and unfounded attitudes toward persons with disabilities in American society. This has resulted from the government's recognition of disabled persons' civil rights and the acknowledgment of the prejudice and segregation historically faced by many qualified individuals with disabilities (Baynton, this volume). Beyond these effects, practical knowledge of employment integration under ADA Title I is needed (Moss, this volume).

Central Goals of the Present Volume

Employment integration during the initial stages of ADA implementation poses many challenges that may be addressed through the systematic study of people with disabilities who grapple with the law on a daily basis (Hall and Hall 1994). The present investigation has three related goals:

1. to foster multidisciplinary dialogue and research about employment, disability, and economic opportunity for persons with disabilities;
2. to raise awareness of the work capabilities and qualifications of people with different disabilities; and
3. to enhance the effective implementation of ADA law and disability policy by providing information to improve communication about employment integration, workplace accommodations, and related areas.

To date, the literature has not adequately addressed these issues. Although criticism of the ADA and disability policy by the press and academia is abundant, little effort has been devoted to communicating their importance to the future of American society. This volume examines employment, disability, and the ADA implementation from the premise that multidisciplinary analysis is crucial to complement knowledge about individual civil rights in these areas.

There is no denying that employment, disability, and ADA implementation warrant careful attention. The ADA is the most comprehensive federal civil rights law addressing discrimination against people with disabilities in all aspects of their daily lives (Baldwin, this volume; Morin 1990). The Civil Rights Act of 1964 does not address discrimination on the basis of a disability. The Rehabilitation Act of 1973 prohibits discrimination against persons with disabilities by federal contractors and recipients of federal grants but does not apply to providers of public accommodations or to private-sector employers. The Individuals with Disabilities Education Act (IDEA) is meant to ensure an equal and appropriate education to children and young adults with disabilities. Unlike these prior laws, the ADA prohibits discrimination against persons with disabilities in employment, governmental and local services, public accommodations, insurance, telecommunications, and public transportation (Wilkinson and Frieden, this volume).

Overview of This Volume

This volume presents an examination of emerging issues in employment, disability, and ADA implementation. It grew out of the 1997 University of Iowa Obermann Seminar of the same title. The Obermann Seminar brought together leading researchers, policy makers, employers, members of the disability community, and others to discuss and examine the issues.

Although many scholars and policy makers have described the import of the ADA in general (Blanck 1998), prior to the Obermann Seminar little if any attention had been devoted to multidisciplinary analysis of issues related to employment, disability, and ADA implementation. Yet these issues have been the subject of particular discussion and debate, particularly as they relate to recent welfare and health care reforms (Blanck, this volume). Today, some employers vigorously lobby Congress to limit the reach of Title I, in terms of the types of persons covered by the law and the remedies available under the law. Others oppose provisions that allow for jury trials in cases of employment discrimination and for compensatory and punitive damages when employers intentionally discriminate against workers with disabilities. Some critics express concern over what they characterize as economically inefficient, vague, and undefined terms and obligations of the employment provisions of the ADA.

As is the case with any new legislation, questions about ADA Title I implementation may be raised in terms of its impact on the citizens it is designed to serve and on those responsible for complying with and enforcing it. This is why the development of information from multiple perspectives relating to the implementation of the law in practice is crucial. Independent of the civil rights guaranteed by the ADA, this information helps to define the parameters of the law. It enables ADA stakeholders — persons with disabilities, employers, and others — to attempt proactive interpretations that make business sense and that transcend minimal compliance with the law (Chirikos, this volume; Scheid, this volume).

The volume is divided into five parts designed to explore pressing issues in the area of employment, disability, and the ADA. The parts examine, respectively,

1. a "road map" to future multidisciplinary study of employment, disability, and the ADA;
2. legal interpretations of the implementation and enforcement of the ADA;

3. economic analysis of employment, disability, and the ADA, and related issues in the area of employment and wage discrimination and the provision of workplace accommodations;
4. research applications on employment, disability and the ADA, exploring areas such as genetic discrimination, professional licensing, and the use of technology in the workplace; and
5. the analysis of the impact of culture and society on employment, disability, and the ADA.

The varying audiences for the volume include:

• scholars, graduate students, and undergraduate students in the areas of economics, law, medicine, sociology, history, rehabilitation counseling, organizational behavior, and psychology;
• law school teachers and students studying federal and state disability law and policy;
• policy makers, persons in government, and advocates in the areas of welfare, work, and health care reform;
• employers and human resource professionals; and
• employment and labor law practitioners and scholars.

As our society enters the new millennium, these and other individuals will face critical questions about the workforce of the twenty-first century, increasingly comprised of workers with disabilities. Such pressing issues addressed by the contributors to this volume include:

• will our increasingly diversified and aging workforce include millions of qualified persons with disabilities? (Baldwin, Stein, Thunder-McGuire, Willborn chapters)
• what will be the characteristics, capabilities, and qualifications of this workforce? (Baldwin, Hirsch, Scheid, Walz and Boucher chapters)
• what types of workplace accommodations and job supports will be available to employees of this emerging workforce? (Blanck, Chirikos, Zwerling et al. chapters)
• how will the dramatic changes that have occurred in the last quarter of the twentieth century in areas such as disability law, culture, public policy, and assistive technology shape the emerging workforce of the next century? (Baynton, Berven and Blanck, Olick chapters)

Discussion of these and many other questions are needed to help define future legal, research, and policy approaches in the area. Dialogue and study from multiple disciplines are needed to raise awareness and understanding of the complex issues that underlie attitudes and behavior toward workers with disabilities.

This volume benefited greatly from the dedication and support of members of the Center for Advanced Studies at the University of Iowa, directed by Jay Semel, who were responsible for the Obermann Seminar series. I am grateful for the additional support for this project that was provided by the University of Iowa College of Law Foundation and subgrants from the National Institute on Disability and Rehabilitation Research (NIDRR) and the Social Security Administration.

This volume is dedicated to the late Esco Obermann, who taught the Obermann Fellows that "you can learn a lot from a cornfield."

As always, my work in this particular corn field could not have been accomplished without the loving support of my wife, Wendy, and our four children, Jason, Daniel, Albert, and Caroline.

—Peter David Blanck

References

Americans with Disabilities Act of 1990, 42 U.S.C. § § 12101–12113.

Blanck, Peter David. 1991. The Emerging Work Force: Empirical Study of the Americans with Disabilities Act. *J. Corp. L.* 16:693.

———. 1992a. Empirical Study of the Employment Provisions of the Americans with Disabilities Act: Methods, Preliminary Findings and Implications. *N.Mex. L. Rev.* 22:119.

———. 1992b. On Integrating Persons with Mental Retardation: The ADA and ADR. *N. Mex. L. Rev.* 22:259.

———. 1994. Employment Integration, Economic Opportunity, and the Americans with Disabilities Act: Empirical Study from 1990–1993. *Iowa L. Rev.* 79(4):853–923.

———. 1997. The Economics of the Employment Provisions of the Americans with Disabilities Act: Part 1: Workplace Accommodations. *DePaul L. Rev.* 46:877–914.

———. 1998. *The Americans with Disabilities Act and the Emerging Workforce.* Washington, D.C.: American Association on Mental Retardation.

———. 2000. Civil War Pensions, Civil Rights, and the ADA. Forthcoming.

Blanck, Peter David, and Mollie W. Marti. 1997. Attitudes, Behavior, and the Employment Provisions of the Americans with Disabilities Act. *Villanova L. Rev.* 42:345–407.

Bragdon v. Abbott. 524 U. S. 624 (1998).

Brown v. Board of Education. 347 U.S. 483 (1954).

Civil Rights Act of 1964, Title VII, 42 U.S.C. §§ 2000e–2000e-17.

Hall, Francine S., and Elizabeth L. Hall. 1994. The ADA: Going beyond the Law. *Acad. Mgmt. Exec. J.* 8:17.

Individuals with Disabilities Education Act, Pub. L. 101–476.

McNeil, Jack. 1997. *Americans with Disabilities: 1994–95.* U.S. Census Bureau— Household Economic Studies Current Population Reports, P70-61 (Sept. 16).

Miller, Paul Steven. 1997. The Americans with Disabilities Act in Texas: The EEOC's Continuing Efforts in Enforcement. *Hous. L. Rev.* 34:777, 778.

Morin, Elizabeth C. 1990. American with Disabilities 1990: Social Integration through Employment. *Cath. U. L. Rev.* 40:189, 201-2.

Obermann, C. Esco. 1965. *A History of Vocational Rehabilitation in America.* Minneapolis, Minn.: T. S. Denison.

Rehabilitation Act of 1973, Pub. L. 93–112.

Rosen, Sherwin. 1991. Disability Accommodation and the Labor Market. In *Disability and Work: Incentives, Rights, and Opportunities,* ed. Carolyn L. Weaver, pp. 18, 22. Washington, D.C.: AEI Press.

Employment, Disability, and the Americans with Disabilities Act

Introduction

The Evolving ADA

PAUL STEVEN MILLER

The work of today is the history of tomorrow, and we are its makers.
—Juliette Low, founder of the Girl Scouts

The passage of the Americans with Disabilities Act of 1990 (ADA) marked a victory in the ongoing struggle of over 49 million people with disabilities to overcome the barriers that prevent their full participation in American society.[1] Since its enactment, the ADA has provided a powerful means to increase workplace equality, promote social integration, and enhance the fundamental dignity of people with disabilities. Yet the work necessary to fulfill the objectives of this landmark law is only beginning.

Federal agencies and the courts need to continue providing guidance to employers and employees through technical assistance, enforcement activities, and the development of case law. These efforts, in tandem with research, education, and advocacy from the disability community, will gradually begin to change attitudes about people with disabilities.

This book represents the first major discussion and compilation of employment, disability policy, and the ADA from *multiple* research disciplines. In his preface to this volume, Peter David Blanck has delineated the primary goals of this book: to substitute information from multiple perspectives for myths about disability, to communicate this information to ADA stakeholders, and to enhance the implementation of the employment provisions of the ADA. To help examine these issues, my task in this introduction is to highlight the evolution of the ADA after the law's tenth anniversary.

Employment, Disability Policy, and the ADA

The ADA is about independence, empowerment, and integration for disabled people. Like women, people of color, and religious minorities, people with disabilities have had to fight for the recognition of their civil rights, battle to get legal protections, and struggle to become integrated in society. Nowhere is this challenge more visible than in their efforts to enter and succeed in the workplace (Burris and Moss, this volume). The goal of the ADA is to allow qualified people with disabilities to be hired, promoted, retained, and treated equally, instead of being excluded from work based upon the fears, myths, and stereotypes associated with their disabilities.

Gradually, the ADA is changing attitudes about people with disabilities and recasting public policy and case law to reflect a different concept of disability (Marti and Blanck, this volume). Where once a medical model of disability based on pity and charity guided public policy, now gradually public policy is being guided by a civil rights model of disability based on ability, value, and pride (Walz and Boucher, this volume). As a result, people with disabilities are becoming more fully integrated into American life and society.

Today, nearly a quarter century after the enactment of Section 504 of the Rehabilitation Act and ten years since the passage of the ADA, many physical and attitudinal barriers are crumbling, and people with disabilities are increasingly valued for their abilities instead of pitied for being different.[2] Public policy no longer equates difference with uselessness. Since the passage of the ADA, more and more people with disabilities are moving off government benefits, entering the workforce, and becoming taxpayers. According to the Census Bureau, in 1994, two years after the ADA's employment provisions took effect, approximately 800,000 more severely disabled individuals were working than were working in 1991.[3] In addition, as educational laws and policies have become more inclusive, greater numbers of people with disabilities have prepared for and pursued higher education.[4] As a result, more qualified individuals with disabilities are entering the job market today than in previous years.

Despite the gains made since the passage of the ADA, people with disabilities continue to have higher unemployment rates, and a greater percentage live in poverty than any other group in American society.[5] Almost all disabled people are interested in and willing to work, and many have job skills. Yet discrimination and prejudice are still cited most often by disabled people as the reason they do not have a job (Baldwin, this volume).[6] Despite legal protections, prejudice and bias continue to exist and have a tremendous influence on people with disabilities' ability to work and succeed.[7] The ADA requires that employment decisions be made based upon the merits of an individual's qualifications, regardless of disability.

The high unemployment rate for people with disabilities is a complex problem with multiple causes. In addition to the problem of discrimination and bigotry in the workplace, many people with disabilities must contend with inaccessible job sites and public transportation systems. While the ADA addresses the issue of accessibility in public accommodations,[8] public transportation,[9] and access to the telephone system for people who are deaf, hard of hearing, or have speech disabilities,[10] modification of those systems is taking place over time. While future changes in the infrastructure mark positive steps forward, they will not help somebody who is looking for a job today. Equally important is the inability of many disabled people to acquire adequate and affordable health care from an employer or in the private marketplace. Often, qualified disabled people who want to work choose not to enter the job market because they fear giving up or not being able to replace their Medicare or other government health benefits (Bristo, this volume).

The Need for Diverse Study of Employment, Disability, and the ADA

The ADA removes many barriers which have previously excluded people with disabilities from the workplace; it contains broad language prohibiting discrimination against a "qualified individual with a disability" in hiring, promotion, discharge, compensation, and other terms and conditions of employment.[11] An "individual with a disability" is defined as a person with a physical or mental impairment that substantially limits him or her from performing a major life activity; a person with a record of such an impairment; or a person who is regarded as having such an impairment (Wilkinson and Frieden, this volume).[12] The ADA requires that a covered employer provide "reasonable accommodations" for qualified individuals with disabilities if such accommodations do not impose an undue hardship on the employer.[13]

The ADA's duty of reasonable accommodation has allowed many people with disabilities to gain and maintain employment without causing much difficulty for employers (Blanck, this volume). The vast majority of reasonable accommodations are inexpensive.[14] The President's Committee on Employment of People with Disabilities reports that the cost of making an accommodation averages around $200 per employee with a disability, with many accommodations costing less than $50.[15] Providing a reasonable accommodation does not mean that an employer must hire a second person to do the disabled person's job. The key to making a reasonable accommodation work is often creativity and common sense, not cost (Chirikos, this volume). Inherent in implementing the ADA is the creation of new ways of thinking and new practices. Studies indicate that disabled employees perform as well on the job as nondisabled employees.[16] Yet despite the relative ease and low cost of most accommodations, many employers harbor stereotypes and fears over the cost of reasonable accommodations and the perception that they will disrupt the workplace.

An employer's responsibility to provide an accommodation to a worker with a disability is limited by "undue hardship."[17] Implied in this notion is the fact that the employer will need to bear the cost in providing the accommodation, as long as it does not impose an undue burden on the employer after considering the size and financial resources of the business. Accommodations that may create an undue hardship for a small auto parts shop may not create an undue hardship for General Motors.

The ADA's contextual definitions of disability, reasonable accommodation, and undue hardship lie at the core of the statute's ability to respond to discrimination on an individualized basis. The flexibility embraced by the ADA is necessary to take into account the wide range of different disabilities, and the different financial resources of employers to pay for such accommodations. Not every disability is manifested in the same way, and different disabilities may require different accommodations depending on the degree of limitation and the job in question.

The ADA is structured to take into account the factual circumstances of each case in order to address the underlying discrimination encountered by the individual. The law does not lay out an all-inclusive list of disabilities that are covered by its provisions since such a list would have to be based on assumptions, which may be incorrect or inapplicable, about how those disabilities may affect an individual's ability to function. Rather, the law's coverage is extended to all individuals who fit within one of the three prongs of the definition of disability.[18] The fluidity of this definition requires employers as well as judges to set aside their preconceived notions about individuals with disabilities and evaluate each person based on his or her own abilities and circumstances. And yet the law's flexible structure is sometimes blamed for failing to provide clear answers to all situations (Willborn, this volume).

The ADA has been criticized for not offering easy solutions and for being difficult to interpret, because of its apparent lack of clear definitions about who is covered by the law and what is required as reasonable accommodation. However, because different disabilities create different accommodation needs, definitiveness is simply not possible or feasible as a way of responding to the kind of discrimination that disabled people face. Similarly, every job has unique essential functions. The lack of a simplistic "one size fits all" approach to many aspects of the ADA has led courts to grapple with issues of implementation (Burris and Moss, this volume).

The implementation of the ADA is at a crucial stage right now. It is important that courts seek to embrace the underlying vision of the ADA. Yet, in the absence of a sound research base, courts are often construing the ADA far too narrowly and excluding from its protection many victims of real disability discrimination.[19] There has been much litigation and case law concerning the threshold question of whether an employee has a disability that is covered by the law.[20] The definitional issue of showing that one is "disabled" is critical because, without such a showing, one is not protected by the law and thus not entitled to any accommodation. Some courts are finding that people with various types of cancer, diabetes, specific learning disabilities, major depression, and other significant impairments fall outside the definition of "individual with a disability" and are unprotected by the ADA.[21]

Similarly, some courts have interpreted the term "qualified" in an equally narrow manner. For example, despite the statute's clear language, which applies the ADA to the "terms, conditions, and privileges" of employment, including employee benefits,[22] courts have nonetheless thrown out cases challenging discrimination in post-employment benefits like disability insurance and health insurance.[23]

By narrowing the ADA's scope, disabled people who want to work and need reasonable accommodations are excluded from protection. Would-be disabled plaintiffs are put in a catch-22 situation. On the one hand, if an individual is functioning *too* well on the job, he or she may be found to fall outside the ADA's definition of disability, and thereby be unprotected. On the other hand, if an individual proves that his or her impairment is severe enough to get over the hurdle of qualifying for protection, he or she may be deemed to be *so impaired* as not to be "qualified" to perform the essential functions of the job. Similarly, the evidence the individual submits to establish that he or she is disabled may be used improperly against the individual in determining whether or not he or she is qualified, and vice versa.

Future Study of Employment, Disability, and the ADA

Despite its growing pains, the ADA has provided much-needed relief to people with disabilities in the workplace. The U.S. Equal Employment Opportunity Commission (EEOC), which is responsible for enforcing the job discrimination sections of the ADA, has engaged in an aggressive yet commonsense program of administrative and judicial enforcement. The EEOC's enforcement efforts have produced substantial relief for thousands of aggrieved individuals, including monetary benefits of almost $186 million in the administrative process alone since July 26, 1992, the effective date of the statute.

Between July 26, 1992, when the EEOC began enforcing the ADA, and December 31, 1997, the EEOC received 95,117 ADA charges (cf. Moss, this volume). The majority of charges (52.3 percent) allege that the employee was discharged because of his or her disability. Failure to provide the charging party with reasonable accommodation for his or her disability comprises 29.1 percent of the charges; harassment due to disability comprises 12.7 percent; and failure to hire makes up 9.3 percent. Although the EEOC avoided going to court in all but 252 cases, just in the administrative process, the commission has achieved positive results for over 8,500 individuals seeking to enforce their rights under the law. Moreover, those cases pursued in court have produced overwhelmingly successful results.

For example, the EEOC settled a case on behalf of a plaintiff who was employed for twelve years as a laboratory technician in a chemical production facility.[24] After being diagnosed with bipolar disorder and being put on lithium, the plaintiff requested that he be permitted to work a nonrotating shift in accordance with his physician's instructions. His request was granted on a temporary basis and his performance was satisfactory. Subsequently, the employer required him to go back to a rotating shift. As a result, the plaintiff was forced to discontinue his medications, used up all of his vacation and sick leave, and, eventually, was terminated. In settling the case, the employer agreed to pay the employee $120,000. In this case, the employer could have avoided court and retained a long-term employee by using some common sense and recognizing the necessity and reasonableness of the requested accommodation. Instead, the employer dug in its heels and engaged in a legal battle that ended up costing it much more than it would have to simply reassign the plaintiff.

In another case, a federal jury awarded a New Mexico man with one arm $150,000 in punitive damages against Wal-Mart after determining that the store made illegal medical inquiries and did not hire him because of his disability. This case was the largest award ever involving unlawful pre-employment medical inquiries.[25] In that case, plaintiff John Otero applied for a stocker's job in the night receiving department and was asked during the interview, "What current or past medical problems might limit your ability to do the job?" Although Wal-Mart had issued its own manual citing a nearly identical question as an example of an unlawful inquiry, Wal-Mart did not follow its own policy and had taken no steps to implement its directives or train employees on the ADA.

Another case of note is the Complete Auto Transit case, in which the EEOC obtained a jury verdict of $5.5 million for a man with epilepsy who was unfairly terminated because of his employer's baseless fears about his ability to perform his job safely.[26] Although Complete Auto Transit only involved one employee and one employer, the size of the verdict has sent a message to employers and their attorneys across the country that taking action against an employee on the basis of an unsubstantiated stereotype can be hazardous to their business's financial health.[27]

These cases underscore the fact that compliance with the ADA is not difficult and not expensive, but noncompliance may prove very costly. Independent of civil rights considerations, an employer's best interests are served by determining how to retain a long-term employee who develops a disability, just as an interviewer's best interests are served by keeping the interview focused on an applicant's ability to do the job. Although success in enforcing the ADA is important, striving to create a workplace in which litigation never occurs is even more essential.

During its 1997–98 term, the U.S. Supreme Court delivered its first decision on an ADA issue in *Bragdon v. Abbott* (Blanck, preface, this volume).[28] Although Bragdon is not an employment case, the decision has implications in the employment context.[29] In *Bragdon,* the Supreme Court concluded that the ADA protects individuals with asymptomatic HIV. The Supreme Court, reversing a growing trend of some courts setting up barriers to ADA coverage, applied a more commonsense view of who is covered by the ADA (Olick, this volume).

In addition, some courts have trapped disabled plaintiffs in another catch-22 situation, the judicial estoppel dilemma. This situation arises if an individual is fired for what he or she perceives to be discriminatory reasons and applies for public disability benefits, worker's compensation, or private long-term disability insurance benefits, which he or she may be entitled to and need in order to survive. To receive such benefits, the person must assert under oath that he or she is "totally" or "permanently" disabled. As a result, such individuals have been found by some courts to be "estopped" or prevented from challenging the termination or layoff under the ADA. This has occurred even in circumstances where the benefit program uses a definition of "disabled" and "unable to work" different from those found in the ADA, even one which does not account for the possibility of a reasonable accommodation (cf. Zwerling et al., this volume).

The EEOC appears to have arrested this development of the law pertaining to the judicial estoppel dilemma.[30] Recently, in *Swanks v. Washington Metropolitan Area Transit Authority*,[31] the court endorsed the EEOC's position that an individual's eligibility for disability benefits under the Social Security Act does not bar the individual from proceeding with a claim of employment discrimination under the ADA. Since that critical ruling, courts have begun to allow individuals to apply for disability benefits while preserving a possible ADA claim.[32]

The ADA only defines public policy; it does not assure its acceptance or practice. It is important to challenge old stereotypes about disability to ensure that they do not become embodied in the developing case law (Stein, this volume). The EEOC, through the development of policy guidance, has tried to help courts, attorneys, and employers understand the ADA. For instance, the EEOC has issued guidance on the "Definition of the Term Disability" under the ADA;[33] on pre-employment disability-related questions and medical examinations of applicants under the ADA (Herr, this volume);[34] on the interplay between the ADA and worker's compensation programs;[35] on disability-related and service-related retirement plans under the ADA;[36] on the effect of representations made in the application for benefits on the determination of whether a person is a "qualified individual with a disability" under the ADA;[37] and on the ADA and psychiatric disabilities.[38]

The EEOC's guidance on psychiatric disabilities and the ADA sought to respond to many of the stereotypes about workers with psychiatric disabilities and to answer many of the questions posed by employers about how the principles of the ADA apply in the context of employees with mental and psychiatric disabilities (Scheid, this volume).[39] The guidance makes clear that ADA does not require an employer to accept conduct that is a direct threat to the health and safety of the employee or others in the workplace. The guidance also clarifies that many employees with psychiatric disabilities function perfectly well in their jobs with little, if any, accommodation. For instance, employers can accommodate employees with psychiatric disabilities by allowing an employee with difficulty concentrating to take periodic breaks during the day, changing the schedule of an employee who needs time off for therapy appointments, or providing training to all employees to sensitize them to issues confronting coworkers with mental disabilities. Even though the EEOC has promulgated guidance on a number of different topics under the ADA, its guidance does not have the force and effect of a statute and has not been followed by all courts.

Evolving ADA Law, Policy, and Study

The ADA, like all civil rights laws, strengthens business and strengthens America, many times in ways unanticipated when the law was enacted (Blanck, this volume; Berven and Blanck, this volume). It ensures that employers, businesses, and public accommodations look at an individual's ability, free from stereotypes, biases, or preconceived notions made about that person due to his or her disability. The ADA offers America a valuable tool to pursue workplace equality and to promote the dignity of all people, including people with disabilities. Like the Civil Rights Act of 1964,[40] the ADA signals a unique opportunity for all individuals to join together in breaking down long-standing myths about disabilities and building more inclusive communities.

The ADA is much more than an antidiscrimination statute. The ADA and the principles embodied in it represent an important paradigm policy shift in how society views people with disabilities (Baynton, this volume). No longer does the law exclude a disabled person because there is something "wrong" with him or her. Rather, the law recognizes that inherent in the physical environment and societal attitudes are bigotries, myths, and fears that exclude disabled people from the workplace and social life. The solution to these problems lies in modifying the environment and documenting and studying changing attitudes. Discrimination against people with disabilities is a social phenomenon that the ADA only begins to address (Hirsch, this volume; Thunder-McGuire, this volume). Only through implementing and embracing the ADA will the true vision of an equal society be realized.

Justin Dart, one of the fathers of the disability civil rights movement, once stated:

> Our forefathers and mothers came to this country because we offered unique legal guarantees of equal opportunity. They got rich, and America got rich. Every time we expanded our civil rights guarantees to include another

oppressed minority, America got richer. America is not rich in spite of civil rights. America is rich *because* of civil rights.[41]

Implementation of the ADA will allow America to prosper—people with disabilities will benefit from the dignity found in work, and employers will thrive by tapping into an underutilized source of good employees. Society will flourish as it becomes more inclusive and diverse, and, through research efforts such as those identified in this volume, we will systematically replace our myths, fears, and stereotypes about people with disabilities with recognition and understanding.

Notes

1. Americans with Disabilities Act of 1990, 42 U.S.C. §12101.

2. See 29 U.S.C. §794 (1994).

3. See *Employment Rate of People with Disabilities Increases under the Americans with Disabilities Act* (President's Committee on Employment of People with Disabilities, Washington, D.C.), July 22, 1996.

4. See, e.g., Individuals with Disabilities Education Act, 104 Stat. 1103 (1990).

5. See Robert L. Burgdorf, Jr., The Americans with Disabilities Act: Analysis and Implications of a Second-Generation Civil Rights Statute, *Harvard C. R.-C. L. L. Rev.* 26 (1991): 413, 422 (stating that the rate of poverty among people with disabilities is more than twice that of other Americans).

6. International Center for the Disabled (ICD), *The ICD Survey II: Employed Disabled Americans* (1987).

7. For example, it is ironic that the highest incidence of disability is psychiatric, and yet psychiatric disability promotes the greatest prejudice. The National Institute of Mental Health estimated that there are over 3 million adults aged 18 to 69 who have a serious mental illness, of whom 70–90 percent are unemployed. There has been an enormous growth in the social security rolls; over the last ten years, this nation has spent $72 billion on cash assistance for people with mental illness. As a result of fears, myths, and stereotypes, people with mental disabilities continue to find themselves discriminated against in all facets of life. Moreover, in another poll done by Lou Harris, 47 percent of those surveyed were very comfortable with people who are blind, and 59 percent of those surveyed were very comfortable with people who use a wheelchair, while only 19 percent of the people surveyed were very comfortable with people with mental illness (National Organization on Disability, "Public Attitudes toward People with Disabilities," survey conducted by Louis Harris and Associates, Inc. 1991). These public fears continue to be fueled through a media that overwhelmingly portrays persons with mental disabilities as violent. A Robert Wood Johnson Foundation study found that 87 percent of the American public say they get their information about

mental illness from the media ("Public Attitudes toward People with Chronic Mental Illness," prepared for the Robert Wood Johnson Foundation Program on Mental Illness, April 1990). This is troubling given the fact that approximately 70 percent of media and film references to persons with mental disabilities portray violent behavior. Yet the great majority of people with psychiatric disabilities and mental illness, like people with physical disabilities, want to work and can work with appropriate accommodations.

8. See 42 U.S.C. § 12182(a).

9. See 42 U.S.C. §§ 12141-65.

10. 42 U.S.C. § 12182(b)(2)(A)(iii).

11. See id. § 12112(a).

12. See id. § 12102(2).

13. 42 U.S.C. §§ 12111-12117. A reasonable accommodation is a modification or adjustment to the work environment that enables a qualified individual with a disability to perform the essential functions of the job. 42 U.S.C. § 12112 (b)(5)(A). Examples of possible reasonable accommodations include making existing facilities used by employers readily accessible and usable by people with disabilities, job restructuring, modifying work schedules, the acquisition or modification of equipment or devices, or providing interpreters, to name only a few. 42 U.S.C. § 12111(9). In addition, the term "reasonable accommodation" includes modifications or adjustments to a job application process for applicants or modifications or adjustments that enable an employee with a disability to enjoy equal benefits and privileges of employment enjoyed by employees without disabilities. 29 C.F.R. § 1630.2 (o)(ii)-(iii).

14. The typical accommodation cost is $200. See President's Committee on the Employment of People with Disabilities, *Report to Congress on the Job Accommodation Network* (July 26, 1995) at http://janweb.icdi.wvu.edu/english/congress.htm (visited May 27, 1998) (hereafter President's Committee, *Report to Congress*).

15. See id.

16. International Center for the Disabled, *The ICD Survey II: Employed Disabled Americans* (1987).

17. 42 U.S.C. §12111(10)(A).

18. See id. § 12112(b)(4).

19. A recent study done by the American Bar Association found that employers win most disability employment discrimination lawsuits. The study found that employers won 92 percent of ADA Title I cases filed, while employees won only 8 percent of the cases (Associated Press, "ABA Study Shows Employers Win Most Disability Discrimination Suits," June 17, 1998).

20. An employee has a "disability" for purposes of the ADA if he or she (1) has a physical or mental impairment that substantially limits a major life activity, (2) has a record of such an impairment, or (3) is regarded as having such an impairment. See 42 U.S.C. §12112(b)(4).

21. See, e.g., *Ellison v. Software Spectrum Inc.*, 85 F.3d 187 (5th Cir. 1996)(a woman with breast cancer was not an individual with a disability under the ADA because she

managed to keep working while she was undergoing chemotherapy); *Gilday v. Mecosta County*, 920 F. Supp. 792 (W.D. Mich. 1996) (a diabetic firefighter was not disabled under the ADA); *Kelly v. Drexel University*, 94 F.3d 102, 106 (3d Cir. 1996) (an individual who suffered from degenerative hip disease was not substantially limited in his ability to walk); *Szymanska v. Abbot Laboratories*, 1994 WL 118154 (N.D. Ill. 1994) (an individual who returned to work during treatment of a cancerous kidney tumor was not disabled under the Rehabilitation Act).

22. See, e.g., *Ellison v. Software Spectrum Inc.*, 85 F.3d 187 (5th Cir. 1996).

23. *EEOC v. CNA Insurance Companies*, 96 F.3d. 1039 (7th Cir. 1996); *Gonzales v. Garner Food Services, Inc.*, 89 F.3d. 1523 (11th Cir. 1996); *Ford v. Schering Plough Corp.*, 1998 WL 258386 (3rd Cir. (NJ)).

24. *EEOC v. Union Carbide*, Civil Action No. 94-0103, E.D. La., settled on April 15, 1996.

25. *EEOC v. Wal-Mart*, D.C. N. Mex., 95-1199, February 21, 1997.

26. *EEOC v. Complete Auto Transit, Inc.*, Civil Action No. 95-73427, E.D. Mich. The jury award was later reduced to $491,931, plus costs and attorney's fee.

27. See id.

28. *Bragdon v. Abbott*, No. 97-156, 1998 WL 332958, at *5-11 (U.S. June 25, 1998).

29. Sidney Abbott, who has asymptomatic HIV, was refused office treatment by her dentist, Dr. Randon Bragdon. Abbott sued Bragdon under Title III of the ADA.

30. See EEOC Enforcement Guidance on the Effect of Representations Made in Applications for Benefits on the Determination of Whether a Person Is a "Qualified Individual with a Disability" under the Americans with Disabilities Act of 1990 at 7-10 (1997). The guidance describes why an assertion of "total disability" or "permanent disability" for purposes of qualifying for a government benefits program should never act as an absolute bar to pursuing a claim under Title I of the ADA. Government benefits programs use a different definition of "disabled" than the ADA's definition of a "person with a disability." Moreover, benefits programs, such as Social Security, exclude the application of reasonable accommodations in determining whether a person is unable to work. The EEOC thus concludes that it is inappropriate to take assertions made for purposes of qualifying for such programs as a categorical admission of an inability to work under any circumstances. The guidance does indicate that statements made about a disability in an application for disability benefits may be relevant to an analysis of whether an individual is "qualified" for a particular job under the ADA. However, such statements must be taken in context, and must not act as an absolute bar to a Title I claim.

31. 116 F.3d 582 (D.C. Cir. 1997).

32. See, e.g., *Johnson v. State of Oregon*, 1998 WL 181297 (9th Cir.); *Blanton v. INCO Alloys International, Inc.*, 123 F.3d 916 (6th Cir. 1997).

33. See *U.S. Equal Employment Opportunity Commission Compliance Manual*, vol. 2, EEOC Order 915.002, Section 902: Definition of the Term "Disability" (Mar. 1995).

34. See U.S. Equal Employment Opportunity Commission, ADA Enforcement Guidance: Preemployment Disability-Related Questions and Medical Examinations (Oct. 1995).

35. See U.S. Equal Employment Opportunity Commission, ADA Enforcement Guidance: Workers' Compensation and the ADA (Sept. 1996).

36. See *U.S. Equal Employment Opportunity Commission Compliance Manual,* vol. 2, EEOC Order 915.002: Disability and Service Retirement Plans under the ADA (May 1995).

37. See U.S. Equal Employment Opportunity Commission, ADA Enforcement Guidance on the Effect of Representations Made in Applications for Benefits on the Determination of Whether a Person Is a "Qualified Individual with a Disability" under the Americans with Disabilities Act of 1990 (Feb. 1997).

38. See U.S. EEOC Enforcement Guidance: The Americans with Disabilities Act and Psychiatric Disabilities at 2–5 (Mar. 1997).

39. See U.S. EEOC Enforcement Guidance: The Americans with Disabilities Act and Psychiatric Disabilities at 2–5 (Mar. 1997).

40. See 42 U.S.C. § 2000e-4.

41. Testimony July 26, 1995, Senate Labor Disability Policy: Americans with Disabilities Forum, 104th Cong. (1995) (testimony of Justin Dart).

Part One
Road Map to ADA Title I

Chapter I

A Road Map for ADA Title I Research

Scott Burris and Kathryn Moss

I. Introduction

In a frequently cited work, the Congressional Office of Technology Assessment (U.S. Congress, Office of Technology Assessment 1994) described the Americans with Disabilities Act (ADA) as a "watershed in the history of disability rights, . . . the most far-reaching legislation ever enacted against discrimination of people with disabilities." Pfeiffer and Finn (1995), Blanck (1994a), Gostin and Beyer (1993), and Burgdorf (1991), among many others, have agreed and noted that the ADA is the most significant civil rights law since the Civil Rights Act of 1964.

At the same time, the ADA has been criticized as having confusing goals and being hard to interpret (Weaver 1991). Parry (1993) points out that this sort of criticism tends to be aimed at most important social legislation, and that the ADA makes a justifiable trade-off between the fairness of individualized remedies and the uncertainty of broadly defined terms. Regulations, interpretive guidance, and reference to prior practice under the Rehabilitation Act of 1973 have also reduced the ambiguity of the statute itself. Critics are right, however, that there is still a diversity of opinion about precisely what the statute was intended to accomplish.

We believe that this ambiguity creates a serious problem both for researchers and policy makers. Without a clear account of what the law is supposed to accomplish, and for whom, it is difficult to figure out whether it is succeeding, where enforcement needs to be directed, and how to make enforcement succeed as well as possible given available resources (Collignon 1997). Getting clear answers to these questions is both more important and more difficult in an atmosphere of political dispute over the ADA and government regulation more generally. If, for example, the ADA's "goal" is viewed as fully integrating all people with disabilities into all aspects of social life, it would be much easier to declare it a failure than if the goal were perceived as merely reducing discriminatory behavior against people with disabilities who are able to participate in employment or programs with minor accommodation or no accommodation at all.

For those of us interested in answers to important empirical questions about the ADA, ambiguity in defining its parameters is related to a second difficulty: research about the ADA is inevitably conducted in a variety of fields whose practitioners rarely talk to each other or read each other's work, let alone subscribe to the same set of more or less ambiguous ideas about the ADA or theories about law and human behavior more generally. The discussions we shared with our colleagues at the Obermann Center seminar that gave rise to this book were extremely useful in delineating these two problems, and encouraged us to attempt to provide some useful conceptual tools for Title I research. At the outset, however, the discussions required us to scrutinize the practices within our own fields.

Interest in the outcome of policies has grown steadily in recent years in the field of policy research (Moss, Johnsen, and Ullman, in press; Susser et al. 1997; Hoagwood, Jensen, and Petti 1996; Kutash and Rivera 1996; Armstrong et al. 1995; Bruininks et al. 1992; Burchard et al. 1991). Beginning in the 1960s, outcome research has been undertaken for a variety of reasons: to assess whether or not policies produce their intended effects; to judge unintended consequences of policies; to satisfy the accountability requirements of program funders and other interested parties; and to advance substantive and methodological social science knowledge (Rossi and Freedman 1993).

Since the early 1970s, numerous studies have also been concerned with the all-too-frequent gap between the intent of public policies and their implementation (Pressman and Wildavsky 1973; Murphy 1974; Van Meter and Van Horn 1975; Pressman 1975; Bardach 1977; Montjoy and O'Toole 1979; Moss 1997, 1992, 1987, 1985, 1984; Wilson 1989; Percy 1993; Blumrosen 1993). The motivation for the early implementation studies was that there had been, in the study of public policy, a "missing link" between the concern with policy making and the assessment of policy outcomes (Hargrove 1975; Ham and Hill 1984). Initially, implementation researchers viewed laws as clear-cut, controversial entities, whose implementation could be studied quite separately from the policy making and policy outcome processes (Ham and Hill 1984). In reality, however, implementation is a complex administrative and political process, strongly affected by the negotiations and compromises leading to legislation and covering the period from the enactment of legislation through policy transformation activities that produce outcomes (Percy 1989). Thus, it is increasingly recognized that any attempt to analyze policy implementation requires giving sufficient thought to the definition of the problem that a policy is meant to solve.

In sociolegal studies, a split arises between behaviorists, who study and largely define law in terms of what people do, and interpretivists, who focus on how law emerges in people's belief systems (Tamanaha 1997). Work in the behaviorist tradition, exemplified by the research of Donald Black (1989) and of the Law and Economics School, is oriented toward identifying and testing "laws" of human behavior in relation to law, and tends to be quantitative in its methods. Work in the interpretivist school has centered on the notion of "legal consciousness," which has developed using qualitative methods of an anthropological sort (Sarat and Kearns 1993). While this scheme is, of course, somewhat overdrawn — there are many works, like Tyler's (1990) important study of obedience to law, that are concerned with both behavior and beliefs — it does capture a real split in sociolegal scholarship.

Thinking about how to assess Title I demonstrates the need to draw upon all these divergent approaches within our own disciplines, as well as for general interdisciplinary cross-fertilization. The problems the ADA addresses, how it is implemented, and its outcomes need to be better understood in terms of how people who are affected by the law feel and what they do. The law may be successful if it changes attitudes, even if it does not as effectively change short-term behavior. It needs to be assessed by the study of outcomes, but its effectiveness can be improved only by the study of the process through which the outcomes are achieved, including how it influences the knowledge, attitudes, and beliefs of people with disabilities and their employers.

In this chapter, we offer not prescriptions about the meaning or purposes of the ADA, nor a single or unifying theory of law or human behavior within which the statute should be studied; rather, we offer a set of conceptual tools designed to assist scholars and policy makers to (1) locate Title I research within a coherent topography of issues relating to disability; (2) identify important questions for research; and (3) facilitate coordination among different disciplines in this research.

II. Dimensions of Title I Research and Policy

Title I is a statute prohibiting employment discrimination, but it may equally well be seen as the linchpin of the nation's effort to improve the lives of people with disabilities. While both views are perfectly reasonable, each depends on assumptions and has implications for research and policy that are not always made explicit. In the discussions at the Obermann Seminar, we encountered several comparable alternative characterizations of Title I's mechanisms and goals. During the discussions, participants found that key assumptions about Title I, nurtured within our own disciplines, were not shared outside of them. Figure 1 portrays several "dimensions" of ADA research and policy that emerged in the Obermann discussions of Title I. Each represents a range of reasonable constructions of Title I or its mechanisms or goals, portrayed as continua rather than as dichotomies.

Figure 1: Dimensions of ADA Title I Policy and Research

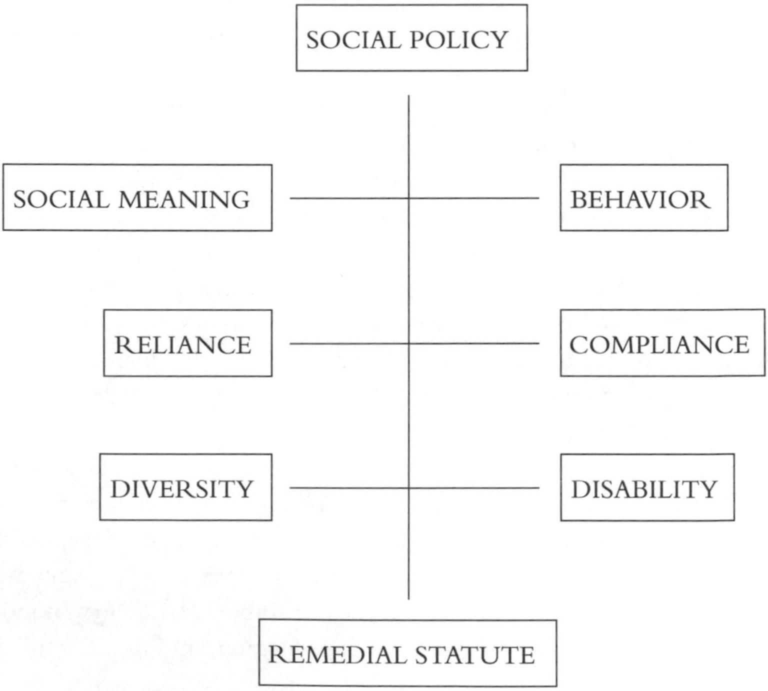

FROM REMEDIAL STATUTE TO SOCIAL POLICY

Title I serves both what Congress called "the nation's goals" of "equality of opportunity, full participation, independent living, and economic self-sufficiency" for individuals with disabilities (ADA 1991: § 12101) and the more limited purpose of eliminating discrimination in employment. Although Congress elided the distinction, it is quite important in assessing the statute's success, and also tends to influence both scholarly and political debate about the law.

Placing the ADA squarely within a larger social policy of improving the lot of people with disabilities tends to be associated with other assumptions or interests. Such a broad social policy is concerned with all people with disabilities, and looks to the full range of social and physical barriers they face. The goal of the policy is a change in the social conditions that harm individuals with disabilities. This goal is, by definition, a collective one, from which we all benefit and which society is seen as enforcing by collective means. As a *social* policy, it is furthered by a broad range of actors, including not only lawyers but also opinion leaders, clergy, educators, philanthropies, advocacy organizations, and so on.

At the other end of the continuum is a focus on Title I as a specific remedial statute. By its terms, it does not provide legal protection to all people with disabilities, but only those who meet its definition of a "qualified person with a disability." While Title I may contribute to meeting the goal of "full participation," it does so only through providing "equality of opportunity." Even this is subject to the caveat that equal opportunity is only guaranteed for those who meet the statute's qualification requirements.

In this latter view, Title I addresses directly the problem of discrimination (defined as disparate treatment of two functionally equivalent people), not the broader inequalities faced by the disabled. It does so within a form and rhetoric of civil rights, which are often perceived as benefiting an individual (increasingly said in political discourse to be enjoying "special rights") whose advancement, if not a zero-sum game with the employer, is at least not an automatic benefit for society. In this view, enforcement is an administrative and judicial process, triggered by the individual and largely conducted by or under the auspices of lawyers.

Observing this spectrum has a number of practical consequences, most notably two having to do with the assessment of the law in research and political debate. Consider the prime question of whether the ADA has "failed" because it has not raised the overall socioeconomic status of the disabled population as a whole. As we will discuss more in part V, Title I only protects those who are, as it were, eligible to suffer discrimination: those qualified individuals with disabilities who are in the workforce or trying to enter it. It does nothing, at least directly, for people with disabilities who are unable or unwilling to enter the workforce. Congress's broad policy goals to the contrary, Title I is simply not written to affect people who are kept out of the workplace by factors other than discrimination in its most narrowly defined forms.

Two conclusions follow. First, research on the socioeconomic benefits of the statute must distinguish between people with disabilities who are in a position to benefit directly from the law—people who are qualified to do the job with or without reasonable accommodation—and those who are not. To the extent that the question is whether Title I as a remedial statute is protecting those individuals to whom, by its terms, it actually provides protection, lack of impact on overall population status is, at most, fodder for an argument that the statute *should have been* written to apply more broadly.

Second, when Title I is judged according to its contribution to a social policy of enhancing the status of individuals with disabilities generally, it should be assessed within a model that accounts for other complementary and countervailing social policies, such as a system of transfer payments that creates incentives for some classes of people to stay out of the workforce. Its lack of impact on those it does not protect must be assessed in light of its contribution to the status of those it does reach.

REGULATING SOCIAL MEANING AND REGULATING INDIVIDUAL BEHAVIOR

Law works by changing both individual behavior and the cultural determinants of behavior—a process legal scholars have lately come to call "the regulation of social meaning" (Lessig 1995; Sunstein 1996). Both the goals and the effects of Title I may be portrayed as occupying a spectrum between changes in behavior among employers and changes in the social meaning of disability, qualification, reasonable accommodation, and other concepts, which in turn lead to both employers and people with disabilities behaving differently. The two processes are linked, part of the same continuum, and, indeed, part of a feedback loop across time. Yet both research and policy look very different from the two ends of the spectrum.

A focus on behavior tends to be a focus on the people whose behavior is being regulated—in this case, employers. Enforcement "works" if it directly coerces some employers to comply with the law and deters others from noncompliance. An emphasis on directly regulating the behavior of employers is associated with a focus on state enforcement. Administrative and judicial enforcement, designed to coerce individual noncompliers and deter others from noncompliance, is seen as the main mode of enforcing individual behavior change and advancing general deterrence.

In contrast, a focus on changing the social meaning of disability looks to the culture in which the behavior of both employers and people with disabilities is formed. The theory is that if the prevailing attitudes, beliefs, and norms about disability change in a community, behavior in the community will change. Individual employers will now have different beliefs, because they are more frequently exposed to people with disabilities or because they feel social pressure to conform (Lessig 1995; Sunstein 1996). Changes in social meaning, therefore, offer the prospect of what one commentator has called "compliance without enforcement" (Kagan and Skolnick 1993). A concern for social meaning leads one to emphasize tools beyond law enforcement, such as social marketing campaigns that use the techniques of advertising to "sell" new attitudes and behaviors to the public (Kotler and Roberto 1989). A concern for social meaning entails the pursuit of high profile, highly sympathetic or dramatic "impact" litigation over routine enforcement. The current strategies of the Equal Employment Opportunity Commission (EEOC) actually reflect both views to some extent: while it continues to process many tens of thousands of cases each year, it has instituted a system to identify particularly strong cases with greater potential impact for expedited handling and litigation by the EEOC itself. Still, neither the federal nor the state enforcement agencies have so far pursued a strong program of social meaning change outside the legal arena. Social marketing to offer more accurate images of people with disabilities remains an untapped possibility.

RELIANCE AND COMPLIANCE

The "reliance-compliance" dimension of figure 1 pertains to the mechanism of the law's effect. "Compliance" is the study of if and why people obey the law. Compliance studies undertaken by implementation scholars focus on the degree of conformity between a policy's requirements and its implementation. Another emphasis in the work of implementation scholars is the identification of factors that facilitate and obstruct compliance. There are numerous factors implementation scholars cite to explain compliance prospects. The specificity of policy language, inter- and intra-organizational characteristics of implementation actors, support by constituency groups for policies, and the sufficiency of resources allocated for compliance are just a few (Moss 1987).

Compliance is also the terrain of classic sociolegal scholarship based on an identification of law with social control. The focus here is on the nature and determinants of obedience. Almost by definition, studies of compliance focus on the attitudes and behavior of those of whom the law demands compliance. They ask whether those regulated view the law or the law-giving institutions as legitimate, or the process of lawmaking or enforcement as fair, or how they assess the risks of punishment. This complements a view of the law focused on individual behavior change and tends to lead in turn to an analysis of the law in terms of its relation to the noncompliant—in other words, at administrative and judicial enforcement—and an assumption that measuring compliance is the same as measuring the effectiveness of the law (Tamanaha 1997, pp. 150–52). The people protected by the law come into the analysis, if at all, as instigators of enforcement: plaintiffs or victims. Compliance certainly deserves considerable attention given the importance of the behavior of employers in the problem of discrimination, and it is an important short-term indicator of longer-term policy outcomes, but it should not be the sole inquiry.

What we are calling "reliance" is the study of how individuals formally protected or empowered by law actually integrate legal protection into their thinking and strategic behavior in relation to the activities the law purports to protect. The notion of "empowerment" embedded in the ADA requires attention to how, precisely, the law gives people with disabilities more options or a better bargaining situation. It requires attention to the many factors, such as education, wealth, race, or gender, that may influence the individual's ability or willingness to use law in this way (Burris 1998).

As we will discuss further in part V, a focus on reliance leads to an examination of the impact of Title I that is systematically different from one that focuses on compliance. It recognizes that there are many points in the process of a dispute over discrimination at which an individual with disabilities may choose to rely or not rely on the protection of Title I. For example, people's knowledge of the law, or their attitudes toward the legal system as a source of help, may influence their decision to seek work, to recognize and complain of discrimination, or to pursue formal over informal remedies. Individuals who cannot find lawyers will not be able to pursue cases after the EEOC issues a "right to sue" letter. Others may fear retaliation should they file a claim. In contrast to compliance, then, reliance focuses on the attitudes and behavior of people with disabilities, who are seen as important agents in the influence of law on discrimination, and who are deploying law as part of their strategy for living with a disability (Engel and Munger 1996; Kritzer, Bogart, and Widmar 1991; Felstiner, Abel, and Sarat 1980–81).

DIVERSITY AND DISABILITY

During the Obermann Seminar, we frequently discussed different notions and aspects of disability as well as of the ADA. The statute's broad definition of disability encompasses, according to Congress, something like a fifth of the population, which Congress refers to as a homogeneous "discrete and insular minority." It is easy to forget that people with disabilities have genders, ages, races, incomes, and other characteristics that significantly influence how they are treated by others, including employers. It is also easy to forget how problematic the very notion of disability is.

The ADA embodies important commitments to changing physical environments and allowing full participation by individuals with disabilities. Some have argued that it was intended not simply to guarantee equality, but "to redefine what equality means" (Weber 1997, pp. 874–75). In many respects, however, it still can be seen as relying on the perspective of the "abled," a perspective from which disability is usually conceived of as a negative deviation from the norm. Title I's concept of the "qualified individual with a disability," including the concept of "reasonable accommodation," still requires an evaluation of the disabled *as compared to* the normally abled. The question is whether, with or without an accommodation, the individual with a disability can match the performance of a nondisabled person. Moreover, the notion of reasonable accommodation, some people with disabilities may point out, carries not only a policy determination as to the amount of money to spend integrating people with disabilities, but also the notion that a workplace designed with the abled in mind makes sense and that changing that environment is a kindness. Although the statute states "full participation" as a goal, the employment provisions offer, at best, equal opportunity to be judged by substantially abled norms. As important as it is to remedying the traditional inequality faced by individuals with disabilities, the ADA still defines equality against a norm of abled performance, privileging abled standards and leaving behind disabled people who cannot meet those standards in an environment designed for the abled.

The "discrete and insular minority" model also has its limitations. While it implies an analogy to other traditionally marginalized populations, a view that treats so many people as meaningfully "the same" obviously misses a great deal of important difference, not just in the disabilities of individuals, or their impact upon function, but also in their social settings. Can we really assume that disability in the professions is the same sort of barrier as it is in the trades? That disability is viewed and accommodated the same way in rural and urban areas? That race and gender or class are unimportant?

It has also been observed that "disability" itself can be a disabling concept. There are other ways of conceptualizing the range of human abilities and their importance in identity. For example, Scotch and Schriner (1997) have argued for a model of human variation in which difference itself is the norm and the able-bodied are not analytically privileged at the outset. In contrast, the diversity model suggested by Tucker (1997) emphasizes the common characteristics of both the abled and the disabled, the differences among people with disabilities, the intersectionality of disability with other traits such as race and gender, and the fact that people with disabilities have many different visions of the goals of the disability movement.

III. A Model of Title I Research

Figure 2 suggests four general areas about which research needs to be conducted: the problem to be solved by the statute, which may also be thought of in terms of its goals; the mechanisms through which Title I will operate to achieve the goals; the range of other policies that will interact with the ADA in influencing various outcomes; and the sorts of outcomes that would define overall success.

Figure 2 emphasizes three important points. First, Title I operates in concert with other policies that affect people with disabilities, and both Title I and these policies operate within a set of social attitudes and practices that also affect people with disabilities. While a model of all these forces is beyond the scope of this chapter, ADA research needs to include a larger view of how people with disabilities function in society.

The second point is closely tied to the first. Title I needs to be assessed both in terms of its immediate influence on employment and its larger contribution to the lives of all Americans with disabilities. It becomes crucial, therefore, to match appropriate research outcomes with particular goals, and to keep in mind the extent to which Title I can itself directly promote particular goals. Title I is the principal statute protecting the employment rights of people with disabilities, but it is not the only relevant statute. Nor is it the only policy that influences employability. Whether people obey it or vigorously enforce it may

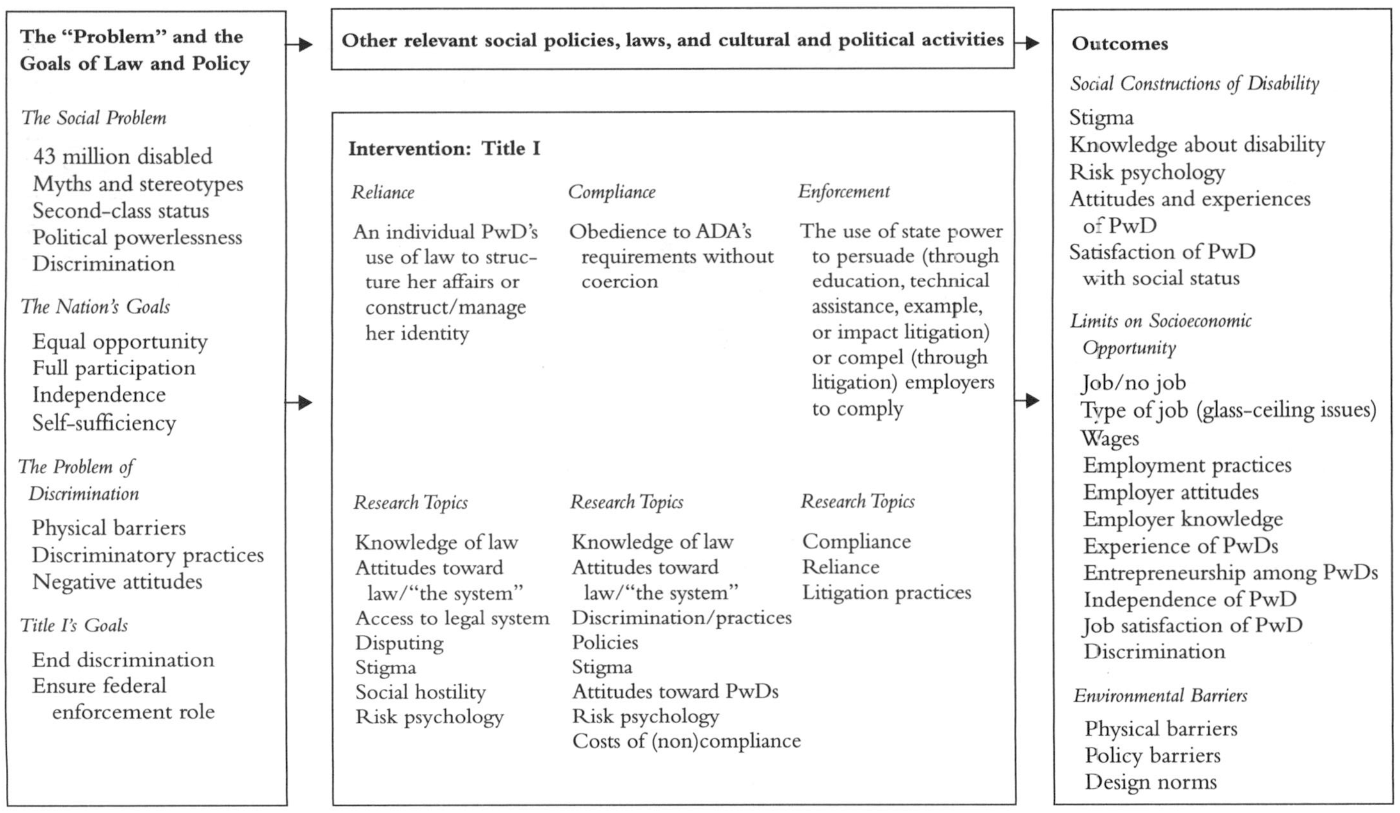

The "Problem" and the Goals of Law and Policy

The Social Problem

43 million disabled
Myths and stereotypes
Second-class status
Political powerlessness
Discrimination

The Nation's Goals

Equal opportunity
Full participation
Independence
Self-sufficiency

The Problem of Discrimination

Physical barriers
Discriminatory practices
Negative attitudes

Title I's Goals

End discrimination
Ensure federal enforcement role

→

Other relevant social policies, laws, and cultural and political activities

↑

Intervention: Title I

Reliance

An individual PwD's use of law to structure her affairs or construct/manage her identity

Research Topics

Knowledge of law
Attitudes toward law/"the system"
Access to legal system
Disputing
Stigma
Social hostility
Risk psychology

Compliance

Obedience to ADA's requirements without coercion

Research Topics

Knowledge of law
Attitudes toward law/"the system"
Discrimination/practices
Policies
Stigma
Attitudes toward PwDs
Risk psychology
Costs of (non)compliance

Enforcement

The use of state power to persuade (through education, technical assistance, example, or impact litigation) or compel (through litigation) employers to comply

Research Topics

Compliance
Reliance
Litigation practices

↑

Outcomes

Social Constructions of Disability

Stigma
Knowledge about disability
Risk psychology
Attitudes and experiences of PwD
Satisfaction of PwD with social status

Limits on Socioeconomic Opportunity

Job/no job
Type of job (glass-ceiling issues)
Wages
Employment practices
Employer attitudes
Employer knowledge
Experience of PwDs
Entrepreneurship among PwDs
Independence of PwD
Job satisfaction of PwD
Discrimination

Environmental Barriers

Physical barriers
Policy barriers
Design norms

↑

Figure 2: A Heuristic Model of Multidisciplinary Title I Research

PwD = person with disability

depend in part upon factors that have little to do with disability—for example, a broader political agenda opposing discrimination laws generally.

The third point is the importance of understanding the mechanism through which Title I has its effect. The ability to show how Title I has a particular impact is the best, if not the only, way to distinguish the effect of Title I from the effect of other policies. The study of how the statute works is also the best way to improve its utility. If, for example, research finds that many employers are unwilling to employ people with disabilities because they fear the costs of accommodation, efforts to publicize findings showing that costs are low could be as effective as more lawsuits (Blanck 1994a).

Overall, the model can be useful in promoting multidisciplinary coordination by identifying generic empirical questions and placing them in their proper relation. Scholars from a wide variety of fields may find useful data specifying the level of knowledge that employees and employers have of Title I. Research on the psychology of the hiring decision (whether, for example, employers tend systematically to overestimate the costs of hiring the disabled) should be as useful to economists modeling information problems as to sociologists directly observing the hiring process (Blanck and Marti 1996). In the remainder of the chapter, we discuss research needs in the principal domains identified in the model.

IV. The ADA's Characterization of the Problem and the Remedial Goals

The ADA is many things to many people. Although there is no "correct" characterization of its goals or of the values upon which it rests, it is important for anyone assessing the law to make clear his or her standpoint. Here we present ours, which we hope accommodates the broad range of opinions prevalent in ADA research and policy.

The statute's first section, "Findings and purposes," begins with the assertion that "43,000,000 Americans have one or more physical disabilities, and this number is growing as the population as a whole is growing older" (ADA 1991: § 112101(a)). Congress then describes the "problem" of their place in civil society like this: People with disabilities have historically been subject to negative stereotypes that bear little relation to their actual impairments or abilities. As a result, they have been isolated, segregated, and subjected to discrimination in virtually all aspects of life. They have been politically powerless;

disadvantaged vocationally, socially, economically, and educationally; and thrust into an inferior status in society. Unlike people subjected to arbitrary discrimination based on race, national origin, religion, gender, or age, individuals with disabilities have had almost no legal protection.

At the end of its findings, Congress identifies "the Nation's proper goals regarding individuals with disabilities [which] are to assure equality of opportunity, full participation, independent living, and economic self-sufficiency for such individuals" (ADA 1991: § 12101(a)(8)). These ambitious national goals are recognized in the *findings,* as legislative facts. Congress sets out what it calls the *purposes* of the statute in the next subsection: "(1) to provide a clear and comprehensive national mandate for the elimination of discrimination against individuals with disabilities; (2) to provide clear, strong, consistent, enforceable standards addressing discrimination against individuals with disabilities; (3) to ensure that the Federal Government plays a central role in enforcing the standards established in this Act on behalf of individuals with disabilities; and (4) to invoke the sweep of congressional authority, including the power to enforce the fourteenth amendment and to regulate commerce, in order to address the major areas of discrimination faced day-to-day by people with disabilities" (ADA 1991: § 12101(b)).

The distinction between the nation's goals and the statute's purpose strongly suggests that, although Congress took a broad view of society's mistreatment of people with disabilities, the ADA itself is aimed at "discrimination." The ADA cannot, and was evidently not intended to, *by itself,* assure equality of opportunity, full participation, independent living, and economic self-sufficiency for individuals with disabilities. Although it was no doubt intended to help move the nation toward these goals, the immediate goals of the statute are narrower: leaving aside the technical language required by Supreme Court precedent to invoke Congress's regulatory authority, by itself the ADA's goals are twofold: (1) to eliminate discrimination against individuals with disabilities, and (2) to ensure active federal enforcement of the Act's provisions.

The last necessary question is what Congress meant by "discrimination." Just as the purposes of the statute are not the same as the nation's goals regarding people with disabilities, the "problem" of discrimination the statute addresses does not seem to be simply the sum total of socioeconomic disadvantage identified in the findings. Looking at the ADA as a whole, Congress's view of discrimination appears to be consistent with the prevailing account in the disability literature, an account that divides the phenomenon of disability discrimination into three interrelated elements: (1) physical barriers, (2) discriminatory practices, and (3) negative stereotypical attitudes. In the remainder of this chapter, we will treat these three phenomena as the "problem" the statute is addressing.

We know rather less about discrimination than we ought. Evidence that people with disabilities are less likely to be employed and are paid less than conventionally abled people is important (Baldwin 1997), but it does not tell us enough about the social processes through which these outcomes are generated. We need more qualitative data about how discrimination occurs. What information do employers deploy in making decisions about people with disabilities? Is it accurate? How do stigma and prejudice influence the decision (e.g., personal distaste versus perceived customer preference)? "Testing," or the experimental use of trained applicants or simulated applications to measure actual employer behavior (Ayres 1991; Ravraud, Madiot, and Ville 1992); studies of employer attitudes and practices (Louis Harris and Associates 1995, 1987; Edelman 1992); and interviews with and surveys of people with disabilities (Engel and Munger 1996; Burris 1996) can all be used to better explain who discriminates and why. Research into discrimination must be as subtle as the phenomenon itself, which is increasingly accomplished through the repertoire of social means summed up in the term "glass ceiling."

V. A Flow Chart of Title I

Figure 3 illustrates the process through which an individual with a disability uses Title I to secure or maintain employment. The boxes represent significant actions or events in the process. Six "barriers," depicted by horizontal double lines, represent the material and psychosocial conditions necessary for an individual to move forward in the process. The identification and study of these conditions provide the context for understanding Title I's behavioral impact and its limitations.

The process is divided into three important phases. In the compliance-reliance phase, there is no legal dispute; the employer and the employee are operating in the shadow of law, which helps to shape their expectations and actions in ways of which they may not even be aware (Mnookin and Korn-hauser 1979). Individuals who suffer or believe they have suffered a legal injury because of a disability enter the disputing phase; figure 3's portrayal is drawn directly from the disputing literature, which explores the factors that determine how people respond to legally cognizable injuries (Kritzer, Bogart, and Widmar

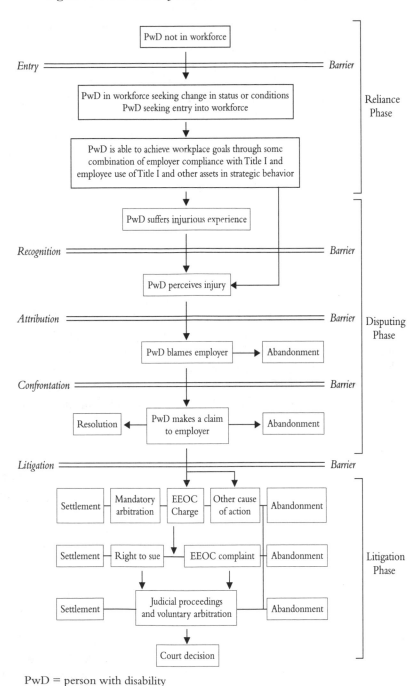

Figure 3: Flow Chart of Individual Law Use under Title I

PwD = person with disability

1991). At the bottom of the figure is the enforcement phase, in which the injured person with a disability triggers formal legal process.

Two important characteristics of the process are *not* captured in figure 3. The disputing process is often graphically portrayed as a pyramid, in which a broad base of injuries tapers more or less sharply to a small number of disputes entering the legal system. We have no reason to believe that the barriers suppressing litigation rates generally will not have the same effect in the realm of Title I. We expect that only a small proportion of people with disabilities in the workforce will ever be involved in a formal legal dispute in reliance on Title I. Figure 3 also does not portray the feedback effects of earlier disputes and litigation on the individuals going through the disputing and litigation process. For example, a series of decisions limiting the definition of disability may lead fewer employees who perceive discrimination to claim the protection of the law, and fewer employers to comply.

COMPLIANCE AND RELIANCE

We begin with the compliance-reliance phase. Although the least studied, this is the most important of the three phases. Title I's success in enhancing the status and opportunities of people with disabilities in private employment depends on voluntary obedience on the part of employers. This may be stimulated in whole or in part by changed demands, higher expectations, or strategic invocation of legal rights by people with disabilities and their allies in the workplace. Understanding how Title I is incorporated into the "everyday life" of American work is essential to assessing and properly administering the statute (Engel and Munger 1996).

When a person with a disability applies for employment or promotion, an employer may either comply with the statute or not. As long as the employer does not discriminate (because of the law or for other reasons), the goals of Title I are achieved and the individual with a disability will ordinarily have no need to proceed toward disputing or enforcement. Compliance, like other key questions arising from the ADA, can be studied according to many theoretical traditions. In sociolegal theory, for example, compliance is generally theorized to depend upon some combination of fear of sanctions, social pressure, and "legitimacy"—the belief that obedience is due because of attributes of the lawmaker, the law enforcer, or the law-making or law-enforcing process (Tyler 1990). In economic theory, one would say that an employer will comply with the ADA whenever the expected costs of sanctions exceed the benefits of satisfying a taste for discrimination or of employing a more productive worker at the same price.

Figure 3 portrays compliance as requiring the crossing of information barriers, thus emphasizing that virtually all theoretical perspectives will be informed by data about employers' knowledge of the ADA and their attitudes and beliefs about people with disabilities. Although Scheid (1997) found a high degree of awareness of the statute among a sample of employers, it remains unclear what most employers actually know about the law, how much they know, and whether they accept it as legitimate. Sources of ADA knowledge are also important, given evidence that the way in which legal information is diffused influences how people feel about the law as well as how much they know about it (Givelber, Bowers, and Blitch 1984). It also is essential to study how employers implement the law: there is an abundance of evidence showing a frequent gap between the implementation of policy by organizations and what lawmakers may have had in mind (Moss 1997, 1992, 1987, 1985; Edelman 1992; Bardach 1977; Pressman 1975; Pressman and Wildavsky 1973).

We also need to focus more research efforts on how myths and stereotypes influence the decision-making process of employers. We know that stigma varies among disabilities, but not enough about how stigma operates in different employment settings. Research on discrimination by dentists against people with HIV, for example, suggests that personal feelings of distaste or fear are less important in the dentist's decision to treat than anxiety about the reaction of other clients (Burris 1996). The same may apply for employers who fear their customers' reactions to employees with disabilities. Conversely, it is possible that some employers believe that employing people with disabilities has a positive impact on business, but if so we know little about the settings in which this positive incentive arises or how strong an influence it is. Particularly promising is the prospect of applying the extensive psychological literature on decision-making heuristics to the employment decision. Stereotypes work in a negative synergy with psychological strategies for assessing the risks of economic or physical harm from employing a person with a disability, leading employers to systematically overestimate the costs and risks of employing people with disabilities (Blanck and Marti 1996). If a considerable amount of discrimination can be described as an information problem, this literature offers a powerful way of analyzing, studying, and potentially remedying employers' misconceptions.

The concept of reliance pertains to how individuals with disabilities perceive and deal with the threat of discrimination. More specifically, it asks how law influences individuals' perceptions of discrimination and associated attitudes, and how, if at all, law enters into their strategies for dealing with these problems. People may "use" law to structure their decision making even when they do not invoke it in disputes—for example, when an employee uses the existence of law as a chip in bargaining over benefits or practices (Engel and Munger 1996). Reliance is rooted, theoretically, in the sociolegal work on "legal consciousness," which recognizes that law both shapes and is shaped by social expectations and understandings of what law is and does (Ewick and Silbey 1998; Engel and Munger 1996; Sarat 1990). People's understandings of law influence whether and how they have disputes and how they structure their relations in areas law is seen to potentially influence. While it comes from the interpretivist tradition in modern legal theory, this focus on law as it is lived by individuals offers considerable insight to any work on the influence of law. It restores proper attention to the individual as a "player" in the game of law, particularly in the use of law outside the formal legal system. As Macaulay (1963) long ago established in his classic article on contracts, people often ignore or adapt "law on the books" to meet the needs of daily life and business. The legal consciousness perspective suggests that major legislation, like Title I, that aims at least in part to regulate social meaning may, if it succeeds, change people's expectations and self-perceptions. It is here, rather than in the courts, that we might expect to find that people with disabilities become empowered. In all, then, the concept of reliance highlights the need for both qualitative and quantitative work to detect the influence of Title I on how people with disabilities perceive themselves in relation to law and how they use law to better their lot in seeking employment, promotion, or accommodations.

Figure 3 shows the many points at which it will be the employee, as much or more than the employer, who will determine whether or how law will influence the handling of an actual or perceived instance of discrimination, but also that the employee's options depend on the ability or willingness to pass through several barriers. At the outset (at the top of the figure), an individual with a disability will either be in the workforce seeking to remain there or advance, or will not be in the workforce. There are many barriers to entry that prevent millions of people with disabilities from relying on the statute. For reasons ranging from lack of transportation to medical and social insurance practices that may make work economically less favorable than unemployment, people with disabilities often will not even seek work. Stigma, demoralization, or the legacies of a poor education may also prevent an individual from seeking work or promotion. The concept of barriers to entry suggests the need to examine whether and how Title I influences people who are not in the workforce to try and get work, and what effects it has on the behavior of people already working.

DISPUTING

One will not rely deliberately and actively on Title I without sufficient knowledge of the law and the interpersonal skills to deploy that knowledge in some sort of strategy to overcome resistance in the workplace. Workers who are able to overcome these information and capacity barriers may often achieve their employment goals, and, of course, others will benefit from employer compliance. But some people with disabilities will suffer injuries to their employment rights that could be remedied by legal action, which moves them into the disputing phase of law use.

What sociolegal scholars call "disputing" is the process through which people with a potential legal dispute do or do not become plaintiffs in a formal legal proceeding. In the classic article in the field, Felstiner, Abel, and Sarat (1980–81) found that a legal dispute emerges in three steps: "naming," when an "unrecognized perceived injurious experience" gets recognized as such—for example, the asbestos worker finding out he has lung cancer; "blaming," which "occurs when a person attributes an injury to the fault of another individual or social entity" and comes to believe that something might be done about it; and "claiming," "when someone with a grievance voices it to the person or entity believed to be responsible and asks for some remedy." A claim is transformed into a dispute when it is rejected by the allegedly responsible person.

Figure 3's recognition barrier illustrates that some disabled people will not "name" their injury, and so may never move into the disputing phase. They will bear their loss without legal remedy. This may tend to arise especially among job applicants, and among people in the workforce encountering a glass ceiling or other forms of covert mistreatment. Individuals in these situations will often be unable to tell whether the failure to be hired or promoted is due to their disability or some other plausible factor. Equally important are the instances in which a person perceives an injury that has not occurred—believes, for example, that she is deliberately being assigned second-class tasks when she is not—or claims an injury mendaciously to gain some leverage in an employment dispute having nothing to do with disability. Some of these cases may constitute the group labeled as "frivolous." This type of case should also be seen, however, as an indicator of the degree to which individuals with disabilities perceive hostility and stigma in the workforce. One of the problems with the discrimination model is its difficulty in capturing the many subtle ways employers may isolate people with disabilities within the social networks of the workplace, and in so doing effectively depriving them of the information or opportunities necessary for advancement. There is a need to study not just incidents of potentially chargeable discrimination but the workplace environment as a whole, particularly if one uses the overall satisfaction and quality of life of workers with disabilities as a measure of Title I's success.

"Blaming" is the point at which the individual with a disability would invoke the term "discrimination," a step that requires the recognition of an injury and its attribution to a wrongdoer. People who for one reason or another cannot blame the employer for their injury are left to "lump it." The disputing literature has emphasized the psychological complexity of the blaming process. The tendency to blame oneself, or impersonal forces beyond one's control, has been identified as a major "attribution barrier" to pursuing a dispute (Coates and Penrod 1980–81). It is important to note as well that the blaming individual has to be aware of his "rights," of the existence of law labeling the behavior wrongful, and that he be comfortable with seeing himself as disabled.

Finally, "claiming" is the injured individual's demand for redress of the wrong to the blamed employer. It entails what may be for many a problematic decision to assert one's rights and pursue a dispute rather than simply take one's lumps. Unlike naming and blaming, it is not a necessary step, for a person can simply move on to formal legal process. It is, however, common for an injured person to make some sort of grievance to the employer, and this is therefore important as the final point at which the formal legal process may be avoided by some sort of settlement.

ENFORCEMENT

Only at the end of the disputing phase do some individuals actually initiate formal legal procedures under the ADA by filing a claim with the EEOC or a state or local fair employment practice agency. Figure 3 identifies the numerous paths litigation may follow, about many of which little is known. The "litigation barrier" represents the conditions of willingness to sue or complain, and knowledge of and access to legal services, that are necessary to pursue enforcement. Again, much remains to be learned about the height and permeability of this barrier: we have little data on the extent to which people with disabilities are aware of the existence or role of the EEOC, whether they have faith in its ability to deliver a remedy, and so on.

Enforcement poses two questions: what happens in the enforcement process, and what is its relation to reliance, compliance, and disputing. The former question has been investigated by Moss and is discussed in chapter 5. The question is nevertheless complicated by the lack of easily accessible data about even such apparently straightforward matters as the number of ADA complaints filed in the federal courts. Are Title I complainants able to find lawyers? What are the outcomes of mandatory arbitration? What proportion of cases are without merit? Are cases without merit disproportionately represented at any particular stage? What relation do litigated and decided cases bear to disputes that are settled without judicial process? The answers to these questions are politically important, given claims from some quarters that the ADA has become a source of groundless litigation and an unfair burden on employers.

The relationship between enforcement, reliance-compliance, and disputing is important for its potential insights into making enforcement more effective in changing individual behavior. It is important also to develop a more nuanced account of how compliance and reliance influence the apparent outcomes of enforcement. A recent survey of decided cases in federal courts found plaintiffs losing some 92 percent of the time (American Bar Association 1998). As Fiss (1984) warned, a legal system that promotes settlement may also foster a cycle of increasingly prodefendant court decisions: settlements in cases where the violation is clear will tend to produce a litigation pool made up of weak cases; these, in turn, will tend to produce more decisions in favor of defendants, decisions narrowing the scope of protection, which in turn will make more cases marginal and so on over time. Differing compliance in "clear" and more marginal cases may have a similar effect (Mudrick 1997). If employers are attentive to case outcomes, the cycle will conclude with employers adopting a narrower view of their obligations. Hence it is also important to study the extent to which employees and employers are aware of and influenced by settlement and litigation trends.

We are truncating our discussions of the administrative charge handling process under Title I because it has been covered in depth by Moss in chapter 5. In addition to those issues covered by Moss, perhaps the most pressing concern is what happens to complaints that result in what the investigating agencies call "administrative closures." Figure 3 highlights the fact that a court decision is not the only or even the most likely outcome of litigation. It also shows that individuals may drop out of the process even after completing the process at the EEOC or a state or local fair employment practice agency. Between July 21, 1992, and January 30, 1995, the EEOC and cooperating state and local agencies logged over 80,000 complaints of disability discrimination in employment. These agencies issued administrative closures or no cause findings in 78 percent of the resolved cases (n = 44,762). In all such cases, the file is closed as far as the agency is concerned. Further action will depend upon the charging party, which has the option of filing a suit in court. We have no data on what has happened to those cases (Moss 1997). Similarly, courts in recent years have increasingly signaled acceptance for clauses in employment contracts requiring binding arbitration of civil rights claims. We know very little about the extent and results of this practice under the ADA.

FOUR OVERARCHING QUESTIONS ABOUT LAW USE

Figure 3 suggests the need to investigate several basic questions about people's use of Title I, questions that would seem to arise in almost any model of how the law influences their behavior or attitudes.

1. Do people know about the law?

From the decision to seek work or promotion, to the moment an injured person decides to complain to the EEOC, using the legal rights conferred by Title I in any deliberate fashion requires knowledge about the law and the institutions that enforce it. We know very little about the extent to which those who are protected by the law are aware of and understand its provisions.

2. Do people feel entitled to protection?

Contrary to the myth of American litigiousness, empirical research suggests that people often simply accept their injuries without complaint (Kritzer, Bogart, and Widmar 1991), and rarely take up the opportunity to sue (Weiler et al. 1991). People with disabilities may blame themselves for the injuries they receive at the hands of employers or may in some more general sense regard them as inevitable. Research among people with HIV, for example, has detected a tendency toward self-blame in the face of mistreatment and an unwillingness to sue, suggesting the need for more research on the factors that lead people to see themselves as protected and entitled to use the legal process (Weitz 1989; Musheno 1995; Burris 1996).

One important element of this issue goes to how people who legally qualify for protection feel about taking on the label of "disabled." Here Engel describes the feelings of parents going through the classification process of the federal law governing educational rights for children with disabilities: "They are cognizant of the stigmatizing effects of everyday categories of disability, and they often display uneasiness about the tendency to reify such categories through the types of disabilities listed in the Act. . . . They need the classification for their children, but they chafe under the necessity of participating in the same process of categorization whose stigmatizing effects they are attempting to mitigate" (Engel 1993, p. 141).

3. Do people believe they have access to "the system"?

The skill necessary to identify relevant legal rules and invoke them in relationships with others is not evenly distributed throughout society. A decision to use law in managing the social and employment consequences of a disability would, presumably, reflect some more or less conscious evaluation of one's capacity in this respect, which may be probed directly or measured more indirectly in such items as one's level of confidence in one's legal knowledge, perceived access to legal help, and so on. One's sense of whether one could get a lawyer, indeed, whether one would know how to begin to look for a lawyer, may also be good indicators of one's sense of access to legal relief. The most complex aspect of this inquiry is the individual's attitude toward the system as a source of help. We would expect that people who believe that "law is on their side" will be more likely to rely on it than those who do not, and that degrees of comfort with the law will have a proportional impact on reliance.

4. Do people perceive the law to be effective?

To place serious reliance on the law in managing disability, one presumably must believe that law will be effective in the uses to which it is put. One might consider such factors as the degree to which people who might discriminate or otherwise pose a social risk are aware of the law and willing to obey it; the degree to which the law is being enforced by government or private litigants; and the degree of success of enforcement, including the size of monetary awards and the severity of nonmonetary sanctions. Also significant is the degree to which the individual believes that a legal remedy would be timely and would adequately compensate him for the injuries he anticipates. Of course, "consideration" of these factors may be based on inaccurate information and biased heuristics.

VI. Outcomes

This section addresses the outcomes that need to be measured in assessing the consequences of Title I. By outcomes we mean *what* should be measured, rather than how to measure what should be measured. Identifying measurement indicators is, of course, critical in evaluating the impact of Title I, but these indicators will often differ substantially among disciplines, and identifying them is beyond the scope of this chapter. We confine ourselves to the first step, selecting what needs to be measured in examining the success of Title I.

The outcomes that we discuss stem directly from the immediate goal of Title I: the prevention of employment discrimination against individuals with disabilities. As will be clear, however, the outcomes vary considerably in the closeness of their connection to this goal. Many of the outcomes will also have relevance in assessing the extent to which the ADA is having a positive impact on broader disability policy goals. We focus on outcomes that are important in evaluating Title I's immediate effect on the employment of qualified people with disabilities.

The discussion in this section is organized around three general outcome areas that correlate with the three commonly identified components of discrimination: *social constructions of disability, environmental barriers, and limitations on socioeconomic opportunity.* We debated whether to include satisfaction of people with disabilities as a fourth outcome area or to integrate satisfaction under the three primary outcome areas. We elected to take the latter approach but to do so in a way that would highlight the importance of satisfaction as an outcome.

SOCIAL CONSTRUCTIONS OF DISABILITY

The major premise of the ADA is that the circumstances of people with disabilities stem more from society's attitudes and practices with respect to disability than from any deficiencies of individuals with disabilities themselves. Our society devalues and disparages people with disabilities, and these negative attitudes are both caused by and contribute to widespread ignorance about the needs and abilities of people with disabilities. Employers, of course, share society's prejudicial attitudes. Their myths and stereotypes about the capabilities of people with disabilities have closed many employment opportunities. This account of disabling social attitudes is familiar (*School Board of Nassau County v. Arline* 1987).

It is also extremely important to address how individuals with disabilities themselves participate in the construction of disability. On the one hand, people with disabilities may often share negative attitudes toward themselves or people with disabilities generally. It is, for example, a defining characteristic of stigma that the stigmatized share the negative assessment of the characteristic, or, at least, are unable to fully reject it (Goffman 1963). Moreover, even the individual who rejects the stigma of the trait he or she carries may have more stereotypical views of other disabilities (as the individual with paraplegia who has strongly negative attitudes toward HIV). On the other hand, people with disabilities may reject and work against negative attitudes in themselves and in society. They may, and in fact do, band together to manage and combat stigma. They may distinguish between stigma (a relationship of "spoiled identity" in which the disabled person participates) and what we may call "social hostility," a set of myths and prejudices about disability that people with disabilities accurately perceive in their social interactions but which they do not share (Burris 1997). A deaf person, for instance, may reject the stigma of her disability, and take pride in a distinct deaf culture, while still recognizing that the hearing population is prejudiced toward deaf people (Tucker 1997).

All this suggests three main outcomes for investigation. The first pertains to changes in the attitudes of people with disabilities themselves. There has been much more study of stigmatizing attitudes about people with disabilities than there has been of stigmatizing attitudes among them. Research focusing on the experience of stigma finds that it may not be as powerful a force in the minds of people with disabilities as attitudes of the nondisabled would suggest (Admi 1996; Cahill and Eggleston 1995; Susman 1994), but additional study is needed.

More generally, focusing on the disabled as *victims* of stigma may tend to obscure the extent to which people with disabilities may and do individually and collectively engineer their own empowerment. Given the probable importance of how people with disabilities determine whether they will seek work or promotion or make use of law when opportunities are denied, research here will shed important light not simply on whether the ADA is helping to enhance the self-esteem of people with disabilities but on whether and why they will rely on the ADA to assert their legal rights.

The second important outcome area is change over time in employer attitudes. In recent years, there have been many important contributions to research on employer attitudes (Scheid 1997; Louis Harris and Associates 1995, 1987; Kregel and Tomiyasu 1994; Blumrosen 1993). Continued efforts are necessary, however, since the impact of large-scale reform legislation like the ADA is felt slowly. Such work should, moreover, pay attention to attitudes and sources of knowledge about the law, and should include qualitative research that focuses on how legal knowledge, attitudes, and beliefs conform with employers' other values and influence behavior toward people with disabilities.

Finally, it will be important to assess employers' attitudes about people with different types of disabling conditions. One theme that emerges from research on negative attitudes toward individuals with disabilities is that the severity of negative attitudes varies across different kinds of impairments (Baldwin 1997; Albrecht, Walker, and Levy 1982; Tringo 1987). The recent research on employer attitudes, however, has tended either not to distinguish between different kinds of impairments or to focus only on one type of impairment. Efforts are needed now to track changes in employer attitudes about different types of disabling conditions following the reforms mandated by Title I.

Research must also address the relationship between prejudiced attitudes and information about the group subject to prejudice (Blanck and Marti 1996). Economists sometimes explain discrimination based on group stereotypes as a means of overcoming the lack of information about individual applicants, while the conventional explanation of discrimination points to the problem of "myths and stereotypes" about disability. Researchers have been studying various aspects of employer knowledge of accommodating people with disabilities (Blanck 1994b; Hendricks et al. 1994; Fabian et al. 1993; Mancuso 1993). Research has also been conducted on the influence of employer size, with findings suggesting that the larger the company, the more informed it is likely to be about the ADA (Buys 1994). We do not know, however, the extent to which top managers, EEO officers, and line managers of large companies vary with respect to their knowledge of disability-related issues. Nor do we know the extent to which top managers, EEO officers, line managers, and small business managers need more information on particular types of disabilities now and over time, let alone how knowledge is integrated into action through psychological processes.

ENVIRONMENTAL OBSTACLES

Environmental obstacles constitute another aspect of discrimination against people with disabilities. Environmental obstacles are mostly thought of in terms of architectural and physical barriers, such as the lack of a ramp or an accessible bathroom for a person in a wheelchair. In the workplace, of course, these present major obstacles to individuals becoming employed or advancing in employment. But barriers beyond the workplace, in, for example, transportation and communication, also affect employment. In a broader sense, the environment is social as well as physical. Social policies and practices, such as insurance and benefit programs, or the system of educating and training the disabled, will also have a pervasive effect on employment. Similarly, the social environment includes attitudes and practices about race, gender, and age that interact with disability in ways that may influence employment. Research on the environmental barriers to employment must, therefore, extend beyond the workplace, and should attend to how disabled people experience and cope with the full range of conditions that make it harder to work.

SOCIOECONOMIC OPPORTUNITY

While the mandate of Title I is to prevent employment discrimination, the ADA is premised on the same basic assumption underlying other civil rights laws: that the elimination of discrimination will assist the targets of discrimination to improve their socioeconomic circumstances. Researchers and analysts have put much effort into studying the socioeconomic circumstances of people with disabilities, and have found that people with disabilities have high unemployment rates (Louis Harris and Associates 1994; Wehman 1993). It would also be useful to characterize socioeconomic opportunities of people with disabilities on the basis of other objective and subjective outcomes such as: satisfaction of people with disabilities with their jobs, careers, and income; attainment of "good" and permanent versus stereotyped, "dead end," or temporary jobs; and the accommodation practices of employers toward people with disabilities. Research findings about the influence of job skills and training on the employment experience of people with disabilities; the comparative experiences of workers in the paid labor force, in the home, and in volunteer activities; the perceptions of people with disabilities concerning opportunity in the workforce; and entrepreneurship among people with disabilities would all add significantly to our assessment of whether and how the statute is achieving its and the nation's goals.

VII. Summary

Title I may be seen as a statute to remedy employment discrimination against qualified people with disabilities and as an important tool to achieve a larger set of policy goals. It is important to keep these two characterizations distinct, because the two different roles demand very different research approaches. Precisely because the actual scope of the statute itself is so narrow relative to the full range of the disabled population and their possible social states, it is important to identify outcomes that meaningfully can be used to evaluate the statute's immediate goals, such as increasing employment among marginally employable individuals. We have identified three general outcome areas for assessing Title I: *social constructions of disability, environmental barriers,* and *limitations on socioeconomic opportunity.* Specific outcome measures will vary among disciplines, but should in every case be selected in light of the researcher's explicit account of the purposes of Title I.

While research on employer attitudes and behaviors will continue to be important in assessing the employment effects of Title I, researchers throughout the social sciences need to devote more attention to the impact of the law on the behavior and attitudes of the protected class and to integrate interpretive and behavioral analyses. The concept of reliance may be useful in directing research toward the legal consciousness and legal decision making of people with disabilities. Researchers should distinguish between stigma and the perception of social hostility, which may influence the behavior of people with disabilities who reject the social stigma of their disability. Research should recognize the heterogeneity of the population of people with disabilities, as well as the problem that a statutory system judging individuals with disabilities from an abled perspective may itself be the most significant and pervasive form of "discrimination." "Discrimination" is a complex phenomenon, about which more data are required, both as to its nature and its prevalence.

References

Admi, H. 1996. Growing Up with a Chronic Health Condition — a Model of an Ordinary Lifestyle. *Journal of Qualitative Health Research* 6:163–83.

Albrecht, G. L., V. G. Walker, and L. J. Levy. 1982. Social Distance from the Stigmatized: A Test of Two Theories. *Social Science and Medicine* 16:1323.

American Bar Association. Commission on Mental and Physical Disability Law. 1998. Study Finds Employers Win Most ADA Title I Judicial and Administrative Complaints. *Mental and Physical Disability Law Reporter* 22:403–7.

Armstrong, M. L., et al. 1995. Of Mutual Benefit: The Reciprocal Relationship between Consumer Volunteers and the Clients They Serve. *Psychiatric Rehabilitation Journal* 19:45–49.

Ayres, I. 1991. Fair Driving: Gender and Race Discrimination in Retail Car Negotiations. *Harvard L. Rev.* 104:817–72.

Baldwin, M. L. 1997. Can the ADA Achieve Its Employment Goals? *Annals of the American Academy of Political and Social Science* 549:37–52.

Bardach, E. 1977. *The Implementation Game.* Berkeley: University of California Press.

Black, D. 1989. *Sociological Justice.* New York: Oxford University Press.

Blanck, P. D. 1994a. *Communicating the Americans with Disabilities Act, Transcending Compliance: A Case Report on Sears, Roebuck and Co.* Washington, D.C.: Annenberg Washington Program in Communications Policy Studies of Northwestern University.

———. 1994b. Employment Integration, Economic Opportunity, and the Americans with Disabilities Act: Empirical Study from 1990–1993. *Iowa L. Rev.* 79:853–923.

Blanck, P. D., and M. W. Marti. 1996. Genetic Discrimination and the Employment Provisions of the Americans with Disabilities Act: Emerging Legal, Empirical, and Policy Implications. *Behavioral Sciences and the Law* 14:411–32.

Blumrosen, A. W. 1993. *Modern Law, the Law Transmission System, and Equal Employment Opportunity.* Madison: University of Wisconsin Press.

Bruininks, R. H., et al. 1992. Components of Personal Competence and Community Integration for Persons with Mental Retardation in Small Residential Programs. *Research in Developmental Disabilities* 12:127–42.

Burchard, S. N., et al. 1991. An Examination of Lifestyle and Adjustment in Three Community Residential Alternatives. *Research in Developmental Disabilities* 12:127–42.

Burgdorf, R. L., Jr. 1991. The Americans with Disabilities Act: Analysis and Implications of a Second-Generation Civil Rights Statute. *Harvard Civil Rights/Civil Liberties L. Rev.* 26:413–522.

Burris, S. 1996. Dental Discrimination against the HIV-Infected: Empirical Data, Law and Public Policy. *Yale Journal on Regulation* 13:1–104.

———. 1997. "Driving the Epidemic Underground?" A New Look at Law and the Social Risk of HIV Testing. *AIDS and Public Policy Journal* 12:66–78.

———. 1998. Law and the Social Risk of Health Care: Lessons from HIV Testing. *Albany L. Rev.* 61:831–95.

Cahill, S. E., and R. Eggleston. 1995. Reconsidering the Stigma of Physical Disability: Wheelchair Use and Public Kindness. *Sociological Quarterly* 36:681–98.

Coates, D., and S. Penrod. 1980–81. Social Psychology and the Emergence of Disputes. *Law and Society Review* 15:655.

Collignon, F. 1997. Is the ADA Successful? Indicators for Tracking Gains. *Annals of the American Academy of Political and Social Science* 549:129–47.

Edelman, L. B. 1992. Legal Ambiguity and Symbolic Structures: Organizational Mediation of Civil Rights Law. *American Journal of Sociology* 9:1531–76.

Engel, D. M. 1993. Law in the Domains of Everyday Life: The Construction of Community and Difference. In *Law in Everyday Life,* ed. A. Sarat and T. R. Kearns, pp. 123–70. Ann Arbor: University of Michigan Press.

Engel, D. M., and F. W. Munger. 1996. Rights, Remembrance and the Reconciliation of Difference. *Law and Society Review* 30:7–53.

Ewick, P., and S. Silbey. 1998. *The Common Place of Law.* Chicago: University of Chicago Press.

Fabian, E., et al. 1993. Reasonable Accommodations for Workers with Serious Mental Illness: Type, Frequency, and Associated Outcomes. *Psychosocial Rehabilitation Journal* 17:163–72.

Felstiner, W. L. F., R. L. Abel, and A. Sarat. 1980–81. The Emergence and Transformation of Disputes: Naming, Blaming, Claiming. *Law and Society Review* 15:631–54.

Fiss, O. 1984. Against Settlement. *Yale Law Journal* 93:1073–90.

Givelber, D. J., W. J. Bowers, and C. L. Blitch. 1984. *Tarasoff*, Myth, and Reality: An Empirical Study of Private Law in Action. *Wis. L. Rev.* 1984: 443–97.

Goffman, E. 1963. *Stigma: Notes on the Management of Spoiled Identity.* Englewood Cliffs, N.J.: Prentice-Hall.

Gostin, L. O., and H. A. Beyer. 1993. *Implementing the Americans with Disabilities Act: Rights and Responsibilities of All Americans.* Baltimore: Brookes.

Ham, C., and M. Hill. 1984. *The Policy Process in the Modern Capitalist State.* Brighton, Sussex: Wheatsheaf Books.

Hargrove, E. C. 1975. *The Missing Link.* Washington, D.C.: Urban Institute.

Hendricks, D., et al. 1994. Real-Life Issues in Job Accommodation: Employers' and Employees' Perspectives. *Journal of Vocational Rehabilitation* 4:174–82.

Hoagwood, K., P. S. Jensen, and T. Petti. 1996. Outcomes of Mental Health Care for Children and Adolescents: A Comprehensive Conceptual Model. *Journal of the American Academy of Child and Adolescent Psychiatry* 35:1055–63.

Kagan, R. A., and J. H. Skolnick. 1993. Banning Smoking: Compliance without Enforcement. In *Smoking Policy: Law, Politics and Culture*, ed. R. L. Rabin and S. D. Sugerman, pp. 69–94. New York: Oxford University Press.

Kotler, P., and E. L. Roberto. 1989. *Social Marketing: Strategies for Changing Public Behavior.* New York: Free Press.

Kregel, J., and Y. Tomiyasu. 1994. Employers' Attitudes toward Workers with Disabilities: Effect of the Americans with Disabilities Act. *Journal of Vocational Rehabilitation* 4:165–73.

Kritzer, H., W. Bogart, and N. Widmar. 1991. The Aftermath of Injury: Cultural Factors in Compensation Seeking in Canada and the United States. *Law and Society Review* 25:499–543.

Kutash, K., and V. R. Rivera, eds. 1996. *What Works in Children's Mental Health Services? Uncovering Answers to Critical Questions.* Baltimore: Brookes.

Lessig, L. 1995. The Regulation of Social Meaning. *University of Chicago L. Rev.* 62:943–1045.

Louis Harris and Associates. 1987. *The ICD Survey II: Employing Disabled Americans: A Nationwide Survey of 920 Employers.* Conducted for ICD-International Center for the Disabled. New York: Louis Harris and Associates.

———. 1994. *The N.O.D./Harris Survey of Americans with Disabilities.* New York: Louis Harris and Associates.

———. 1995. *The N.O.D./Harris Survey on Employment of People with Disabilities.* New York: Louis Harris and Associates.

Macaulay, S. 1963. Non-Contractual Relations in Business: A Preliminary Study. *American Sociological Review* 28:55–67.

Mancuso, L. 1997. *The Successful Employment of Consumers in the Public Mental Health Workforce.* An unpublished report available from the California Institute for Mental Health, 1119 K Street, 2d Floor, Sacramento, CA 95814.

Mancuso, L. L. *Case Studies on Reasonable Accommodations for Workers with Psychiatric Disabilities.* Washington, D.C.: Washington Business Group on Health.

Mnookin, R., and L. Kornhauser. 1979. Bargaining in the Shadow of Law: The Case of Divorce. *Yale Law Journal* 88:950–97.

Montjoy, R., and L. O'Toole. 1979. Toward a Theory of Policy Implementation: An Organizational Perspective. *Public Administration Review* 39:456–76.

Moss, K. 1984. Institutional Reform through Litigation. *Social Service Review* 58:421–33.

———. 1985. The Catalytic Effect of a Federal Court Decision on a State Legislature. *Law and Society Review* 19:147–57.

———. 1987. The "Baby Doe" Legislation: Its Rise and Fall. *Policy Studies Journal* 15:629–51.

———. 1992. *Implications of Employment Complaints Filed by People with Mental Disabilities.* Washington, D.C.: Mental Health Policy Resource Center.

———. 1997. The ADA Employment Discrimination Complaint Process: How Does It Work and Whom Is It Benefiting? Paper presented at the 1997 Obermann Center Faculty Research Seminar, University of Iowa.

Moss, K., M. Johnsen, and M. Ullman. In press. Assessing Employment Discrimination Charges Filed under the Americans with Disabilities Act. *Journal of Disability Policy Studies.*

Mudrick, N. R. 1997. Employment Discrimination Laws for Disability: Utilization and Outcome. *Annals of the American Academy of Political and Social Science* 549:53–70.

Murphy, J. 1974. *State Educational Agencies and Discretionary Funds.* Lexington, Mass.: Lexington Books.

Musheno, M. C. 1995. Legal Consciousness on the Margins of Society: Struggles against Stigmatization in the AIDS Crisis. *Identities* 2:102–22.

Parry, J. 1993. Title I—Employment. In *Implementing the Americans with Disabilities Act: Rights and Responsibilities of All Americans,* ed. L. O. Gostin and H. A. Beyer, pp. 57–74. Baltimore: Brookes.

Percy, S. L. 1989. *Disability, Civil Rights, and Public Policy: The Politics of Implementation.* Tuscaloosa: University of Alabama Press.

Pfeiffer, D., and J. Finn. 1995. Survey Shows State, Territorial, Local Public Officials Implementing ADA. *Mental and Physical Disability Law Reporter* 19:537–40.

Pressman, J. L. 1975. *Federal Programs and City Politics.* Berkeley: University of California Press.

Pressman, J. L., and J. Wildavsky. 1973. *Implementation.* Berkeley: University of California Press.

Ravraud, J. F., B. Madiot, and I. Ville. 1992. Discrimination towards Disabled People Seeking Employment. *Social Science and Medicine* 35:951–58.

Rossi, P. H., and H. E. Freeman. 1993. *Evaluation: A Systematic Approach.* Newbury Park, Calif.: Sage.

Sarat, A. 1990. ". . . The Law Is All Over": Power, Resistance and the Legal Consciousness of the Welfare Poor. *Yale Journal of Law and Humanities* 2:343–79.

Sarat, A., and T. R. Kearns. 1993. Beyond the Great Divide: Forms of Legal Scholarship and Everyday Life. In *Law in Everyday Life,* ed. A. Sarat and T. R. Kearns, pp.
21–62. Ann Arbor: University of Michigan Press.

Scheid, T. L. 1997. Compliance with the ADA and Employment of Those with Mental
Disabilities. Paper presented at the 1997 Obermann Center Faculty Research
Seminar, University of Iowa.

School Board of Nassau County v. Arline. 480 U.S. 273 (1987).

Scotch, R., and K. Schriner. 1997. Disability as Human Variation: Implications for Policy. *Annals of the American Academy of Political and Social Science* 549:148–59.

Sunstein, C. R. 1996. Social Norms and Social Roles. *Columbia L. Rev.* 96:903–68.

Susser, E. 1997. Preventing Recurrent Homelessness among Mentally Ill Men: A
"Critical Time" Intervention after Discharge from a Shelter. *American Journal of
Public Health* 87:256–62.

Susman, J. 1994. Disability, Stigma and Deviance. *Social Science and Medicine* 38:15–22.

Tamanaha, B. Z. 1997. *Realistic Socio-Legal Theory: Pragmatism and a Social Theory of Law.*
Oxford: Clarendon Press.

Tringo, J. L. 1987. The Hierarchy of Preference toward Disability Groups. *Journal of
Special Education* 4:300.

Tucker, B. P. 1997. The ADA and Deaf Culture: Contrasting Precepts, Conflicting
Results. *Annals of the American Academy of Political and Social Science* 549:24–36.

Tyler, T. 1990. *Why People Obey the Law.* New Haven, Conn.: Yale University Press.

U.S. Congress. Office of Technology Assessment. 1994. *Psychiatric Disabilities, Employment, and the Americans with Disabilities Act.* Washington, D.C.: U.S. Government
Printing Office.

Van Meter, D. S., and C. E. Van Horn. 1975. The Policy Implementation Process: A
Conceptual Framework. *Administration and Society* 6:445–88.

Weaver, C. L. 1991. Disabilities Act Cripples through Ambiguity. *Wall Street Journal,*
January 31, p. 16.

Weber, M. C. 1997. Foreword: A Symposium on Individual Rights and Reasonable
Accommodations under the Americans with Disabilities Act. *DePaul L. Rev.*
46:871, 874–75.

Wehman, P. 1993. Employment Opportunities and Career Development. In *The ADA
Mandate for Social Change,* ed. P. Wehman, pp. 45–86. Baltimore: Brookes.

Weiler, P. C., et al. 1991. *A Measure of Malpractice: Medical Injury, Malpractice Litigation,
and Patient Compensation.* Cambridge, Mass.: Harvard University Press.

Weitz, R. 1989. Uncertainty and the Lives of Persons with AIDS. *Journal of Health and
Social Behavior* 30:270–81.

Wilson, J. Q. 1989. *Bureaucracy: What Government Agencies Do and Why They Do It.*
New York: Basic Books.

Chapter II

Employing People with Disabilities

Some Cautionary Thoughts for a Second-Generation Civil Rights Statute

Michael Ashley Stein

The 1990 passage of the Americans with Disabilities Act (ADA)[1] was heralded as an "emancipation proclamation" for people with disabilities.[2] Ten years later, two questions must be addressed. First, how far have the disabled been emancipated? And, second, what (if anything) can be done to secure their future advancement? One gauge of empowerment, the subject of this year's Obermann Center for Advanced Studies Summer Research Seminar and thus the following essay, is employment among the disabled.

I. The Lessons of History

The thrust of ADA Title I, arguably the thrust of the entire statute, was to create employment opportunities for people with disabilities currently outside the workforce. This assertion is supported by several factors. The first is the careful consideration Congress placed in drafting Title I as an employment section[3] wherein it included the definition of disability.[4] Second is the compelling evidence submitted to Congress of the need for a national civil rights law banning disability-based discrimination in the workplace.[5] Last was the manner in which Congress—and implicitly business interests—were lobbied to accept the ADA as economically viable, the statute's advocates maintaining that the overall costs would be offset by benefits associated with increased employment among the disabled.[6]

Nevertheless, available data culled by the United States Census Bureau indicates that post-ADA employment among people with disabilities has increased only marginally.[7] Although this assertion comes with several caveats,[8] the census reports that the overall employment rate of people with disabilities improved only 0.3 percent during the period 1991–94, rising from 52.0 percent in 1991 to 52.3 percent in 1994.[9] Over this same period the overall employment rate for nondisabled individuals increased 1.6 percent, from 80.5 percent in 1991 to 82.1 percent in 1994.[10] Consequently, employment advances made by the disabled seem modest by comparison.[11]

Because these figures are moderately encouraging, especially in view of their time frame,[12] I am not (yet) sounding an alarm about Title I's ineffectiveness.[13] Nevertheless, I wish to provoke a discussion on how to utilize the ADA in a manner that will avoid the path trodden by African-Americans, who, more than three decades after passage of Title VII of the Civil Rights Act of 1964,[14] continue to occupy a position economically subordinate to the general population.[15]

Bearing in mind the old adage that "those who do not learn the lessons of history are doomed to repeat them," I have chosen in this essay to utilize some of the excellent scholarship on the economic empowerment experiences of blacks to raise concerns regarding Title I and the employment of people with disabilities.

SEEING PARALLELS

In analogizing from the experiences of African-Americans to that of the disabled community, I do not mean to imply that the situation of these groups is identical, but rather that similarities exist from which people with disabilities can learn.[16] In brief,[17] both groups have historically been viewed as biologically inferior; blacks are seen as lazy and unintelligent, while the disabled are characterized as feeble, incapable, and are often objectified.[18]

Where the groups differ is that subsequent discrimination against blacks is based mainly on animus. By contrast, inspired mostly[19] by pity,[20] mainstream society tends to treat the disabled in a patronizing manner.[21] Superficially it would seem that people with disabilities have a lesser preconception to overcome than blacks. Regardless, I would aver that while racism involves at least a marginal awareness of being socially unacceptable, pity expresses itself as the desire to help an affecting individual and thus registers as a laudable, socially acceptable activity.[22] As such, pity can be as insidious as animus.[23]

In practical terms, I would add that while blacks may be consciously excluded from given situations, including the disabled is not among the considered possibilities. While a private club may overtly prevent African-American membership, when the club was built in a physically inaccessible venue, the founders did not even think of a disabled member.[24]

This assertion may be demonstrated by a real-life example. During my judicial clerkship, I discovered that the only wheelchair-inaccessible parts of the immense federal courthouse building in Philadelphia were the judges' private elevator and the judicial benches. The inference to be drawn is that while a person with a disability might be a party to a suit, or even a lawyer, no one involved in designing the courthouse considered a physically disabled law clerk, let alone a judge.[25]

WHEN CIVIL RIGHTS STATUTES MAKE A DIFFERENCE

Prevailing scholarship on the effects of the Civil Rights Act of 1964 has concluded that promulgation of federal civil rights statutes and antidiscrimination provisions have not by themselves contributed to economic gains among African-Americans.[26] Instead, improvement in blacks' relative earnings has been realized because of the federal government's massive enforcement of antidiscrimination policies, including voting rights and school desegregation, that were concentrated on the South.[27]

Currently there exists no equivalent monumental federal government enforcement policy of employing or integrating the disabled.[28] Instead, efforts on behalf of people with disabilities by the Department of Justice (DOJ) and the Equal Employment Opportunity Commission (EEOC) — laudable and necessary as they are — mirror earlier enforcement on behalf of the African-American community.

Applying the conclusions drawn from prolonged black disempowerment, prospects would appear dim for the disabled. This is so despite the efforts of organizations that, like their predecessors in the African-American community, have been actively working to increase employment opportunities through interaction with employers. These include the Job Accommodation Network (JAN) established by the President's Committee on Employment of People with Disabilities, as well as ten regional disability and business technical assistance centers founded by the National Institute on Disability and Rehabilitation Research.[29] How much inroad these programs can make without simultaneous federal action (if only in the guise of immense funding) remains to be seen.

Finally, given the relative dearth of federal policy enforcement, it might be useful to focus efforts on understanding why certain employers voluntarily comply with Title I.[30] This information, which does not appear in census statistics or EEOC complaints, could significantly help disability-employment organizations such as JAN replicate these underdescribed successes.

UNCONSCIOUS DISCRIMINATION

Some notable black legal scholars posit a continuing economic disparity between the races due to unconscious racism. A seminal statement of this position is made by Charles Lawrence, who offers two different psychological explanations for unconscious racism.[31] Kimberle Crenshaw takes Lawrence's critique further, arguing that in addition to unconscious thought, racism forms a hegemonic force in American society, one in which blacks have been created as a subordinated "other."[32]

Similar expressions have been made regarding how mainstream America views the disabled.[33] For example, Justin Dart, one of the central proponents of the ADA, asserts, "Our society still is infected by an insidious, now almost subconscious, assumption that people with disabilities are less than fully human and therefore not entitled to the respect, the opportunities, and the services and support systems that are available to other people as a matter of right."[34] However, unlike blacks, disabled Americans were empowered by civil rights legislation prior to a general raising of social consciousness.[35] Absent the exposure afforded by an "I Have a Dream" speech or a march on the capital, the challenge of obtaining equality from an unprepared society seems equally daunting to that encountered by African-Americans.

This is especially so in view of the fact that apart from two very notable exceptions—a 1977 San Francisco sit-in to protest delay in promulgating Section 504 regulations[36] and passage of the ADA[37]—the history of disability rights advocacy has been one of uncoordinated activity among disparate disability-specific groups.[38] Thus, the disabled have neither a nationally recognized figure (such as the late Dr. Martin Luther King, Jr., or currently the Reverend Jesse Jackson) nor an established[39] central political congress (like the NAACP) through which to voice their concerns and desires.

Compounding these difficulties is the lamentable reality that insufficient knowledge about the ADA has been disseminated to people with disabilities. A joint 1994 survey by Louis Harris and Associates and the National Organization for the Disabled revealed that only 40 percent of the disabled people interviewed had either read or heard about the ADA (and by implication Title I).[40]

This problem, which is particularly acute among minorities with disabilities,[41] needs to be quickly remedied. As eloquently stated by John Donohue and Peter Siegelman, "To raise a bona fide claim of employment discrimination, a worker must first perceive that discrimination has occurred."[42]

Despite this gloomy portrait, three factors work in favor of Americans with disabilities. The first, present also for blacks, is that even though passage of civil rights statutes may not effect immediate changes in legal treatment, they often change attitudes.[43] As described by Lauren Edelman, this is achieved through "a process of institutionalization, whereby new forms of compliance are diffused among organizations and gradually become ritualized elements of organizational governance."[44]

The second, which exists to a lesser degree for African-Americans, is the process of mainstreaming. As reported to Congress by the ICD Survey, in the year prior to the ADA's enactment nearly two-thirds of individuals with disabilities did not attend either movies or sporting events, whereas three-fourths had not frequented live theater or music performances.[45] As these egregious percentages decrease over time due to physical changes (such as accessible public transportation) brought about by ADA Titles II and III, the disabled will become a more recognizable and therefore "normal" constituency to their fellow citizens.[46] To borrow Crenshaw's terminology,[47] they will lose some degree of "otherness."

The third determinant, a variant of mainstreaming, involves the transmogrification of able-bodied individuals into people with disabilities.[48] Among minority groups this phenomenon is unique to the disabled community[49] and also contributes to reducing "otherness." It is because of this factor that I am opposed to efforts to narrow Title I's definition of disability to the "truly" disabled,[50] even though to date the largest category of people asserting Title I claims are able-bodied individuals who conceive back-related maladies.[51] Although grounded in anecdote, I believe that when a known and valued able-bodied employee transmogrifies into a known and valued employee with a disability, the disabled community as a whole benefits.

BACKLASH

Despite continuing black economic disparity, eradication of superficial racial barriers (like segregated lunch counters) has led some neoconservative critics of civil rights to maintain that the causes of racism no longer exist[52] and that continuing imbalances are attributable to African-Americans themselves.[53]

The prospect of backlash against disabled empowerment manifests itself in two ways. First, resentment against people with disabilities for sums expended through Titles II and III, especially for visibly expensive adaptions to public transit. This is demonstrated by a Louis Harris poll taken prior to enactment of the ADA's regulations, in which about one-fifth of those interviewed expressed indignation at "the special treatment disabled people receive."[54]

Second, as more tangible (and thus superficial) barriers to integration are ameliorated, the disabled will be open to the same criticisms currently leveled at blacks, which ascribe enduring inequities to self-inflicted culpabilities.[55] This fits in neatly with the myth I have described elsewhere of the disabled "overcoming" their disabilities:[56] after public funds have been expended to assist the disabled, persisting needs are their own fault.[57]

II. The Efficiency Trap

ECONOMIC ANALYSES OF TITLE I

Much of the debate over the ADA's implementation has been phrased in economic terms, specifically over the question of Title I's "efficiency."[58] With due respect to the authors of these evaluations, little weight can be accorded to their analyses for the simple reason that to date insufficient concrete data exists from which to draw solid conclusions.[59]

Lack of available information has been a recurring theme of disability rights advocates[60] as well as the participants in this seminar, several of whom are actively working to cull such data.[61] Thus, broad economic judgments of Title I's efficiency are for the most part premature,[62] especially if weight is given to Judge Richard Posner's conviction that oftentimes the efficacy of civil rights statutes are not readily knowable.[63] Certainly, polemics[64] that even prior to promulgation of Title I's regulations branded its "reasonable accommodation" requirement as "onerous"[65] and "overwhelming"[66] appear less than responsible.

In fact, what data has surfaced demonstrates the inapposite conclusion, that is, that implementation of Title I is economically efficient. For example, JAN reported that 69 percent of their facilitated accommodations cost less than $500, 81 percent less than $1,000, with companies realizing an average return of $28.69 in benefits for every dollar invested in accommodating employees.[67] Some 80,000 employers contacted JAN in fiscal year 1995. Of those who subsequently accommodated employees, 34 percent reported saving from $1 to $5,000, 16 percent saved between $5,001 and $10,000, 19 percent conserved $10,001 to $20,000, and 25 percent reported saving between $20,001 and $100,000.[68]

RETHINKING SOME OF THE ASSUMPTIONS UNDERLYING
ECONOMIC ANALYSES OF TITLE I

Economists have focused on the costs of Title I's requisite on employers to make reasonable accommodations as a crucible for measuring efficiency. This in itself is a valid means for appraising the ADA's efficacy. Nevertheless, as a matter of fairness some of the assumptions underlying these economic analyses ought to be reconsidered.

First is the erroneous presumption that in contrast to other civil rights statutes, it is only the ADA that engenders costs through enforcement. This supposition ignores parallel costs incurred by a desegregated all-white firm losing clients and members, a formerly all-male corporation having to build women's restroom facilities, or a uniformly (acknowledged) heterosexual company extending benefits to same-sex partners. To varying degrees, integration uniformly involves expenditure.

Second, existing economic analyses either exclude or give little weight to external benefits such as increased worker morale,[69] wider customer base,[70] a stronger national economy,[71] and the negative costs of having to train new employees for positions vacated when existing workers become disabled. By this objection I do not reject economic approaches, but propose instead an analysis in which greater consequence be given to factors not always acknowledged in determining the market value of a disabled worker's labor.[72]

Third, efficiency examinations work from the baseline proposition that existing physical barriers are the norm to which emendation adds expense. Consider instead a worldview where obstacles to a disabled-friendly environment are deemed abnormal, and inherently assume their retrofitting costs. Under this method of analysis, Title I accommodations would be viewed as corrective rather than as purely distributive.

Finally, because civil rights statutes are blueprints for social policy change, perhaps the proper means of evaluation is not that of economic efficiency,[73] but rather one of moral imperative.[74] Possibilities for this type of estimation include engendering employment through an autonomous right to work[75] or as a value of citizenship.[76] If this latter thought prevails, Title I advocates can adopt as a mantra Justin Dart's statement to Congress that "America is rich not in spite of civil rights. America is rich because of civil rights."[77]

III. Conclusion

Without doubt, much of what I have said will not sit well with certain members of the disability rights community. Notwithstanding this displeasure, and without in any way denigrating their admirable and hard-won efforts, I mean to provoke a discussion of how to better empower people with disabilities through their increased membership in the workforce. Viewing the experience of blacks over the last thirty-three years in combination with the findings of current studies and scholarship (including those in this volume),[78] my optimism about increasing employment for Americans with disabilities is guarded. Still, as Lawrence concluded when in a similar position, "[a] difficult and painful exploration beats death at the hands of the disease."[79]

Notes

1. 42 U.S.C. §§ 12101–12213 (Supp V 1993).

2. Two legislators are credited with this description. See 136 Cong Rec S9689 (daily edition July 13, 1990) (statement of Sen. Harkin); 135 Cong Rec S10,789 (daily edition Sept. 7, 1989) (statement of Sen. Kennedy). See also Michael Ashley Stein, From Crippled to Disabled: The Legal Empowerment of Americans with Disabilities, *Emory L. J.* 43 (1994): 245 (hereafter From Crippled to Disabled); Joseph P. Shapiro, *No Pity: People with Disabilities Forging a New Civil Rights Movement* (1993) (hereafter *No Pity*).

3. In contrast to the later sections that address access to state and local government services (Title II), physical locations (Title III), and telecommunications (Title IV). There is also an omnibus section (Title V) that, among other things, applies the ADA to Congress. For a general overview of the ADA, see Robert L. Burgdorf, Jr., The Americans with Disabilities Act: Analysis and Implications of a Second-Generation Civil Rights Statute, *Harvard C. R.–C. L. L. Rev.* 26 (1991): 413. It is to Burgdorf that the phrase "second-generation civil rights statute" is owed.

4. As a "physical or mental impairment that substantially limits one or more of the major life activities of [an] individual." 42 U.S.C. § 12102(2) (Supp V 1993).

5. See Stein, From Crippled to Disabled, pp. 247–49. Among the testimony presented was near-verbatim citation of a 1986 Louis Harris and Associates poll finding that two-thirds of disabled Americans between the ages of 16 and 64 were unemployed despite yearning for work. In practical terms, this meant that 8.2 million citizens couldn't find a job. See Louis Harris and Associates, *ICD Survey of Disabled Americans: Bringing Disabled Americans into the Mainstream* 47 (1986) (hereafter *ICD Survey*).

6. See Developments in the Law: Employment Discrimination, *Harvard L. Rev.* 109 (1996): 1568, 1603 (Congress passed the ADA in part due to finding that discrimination against the disabled annually cost the United States billions of dollars); Tom Harkin, The Americans with Disabilities Act: Four Years Later—Commentary on Blanck, *Iowa L. Rev.* 79 (1994): 935, 937 (indicating as legislatively attractive, savings from increased disabled employment and attendant decrease in social welfare costs,

greater consumer goods purchases, and increased tax revenue); 42 U.S.C. § 12101(a)(9) (Supp V 1993) (citing the "unnecessary expenses resulting from dependency and non-productivity"). See also Signing of the Americans with Disabilities Act by President George Bush, South Lawn, The White House, Fed. News Serv., July 26, 1990 (LEXIS, News library, Wires file) (the President commenting that "when you add together federal, state, local and private funds, it costs almost $200 billion annually to support Americans with disabilities").

7. Unless otherwise noted, all population data cited in this essay are derived from either the Survey of Income and Program Participation (SIPP) or the Current Population Survey (CPS) disability-related data website, available on-line at http://www.census.gov/hhes/www/disable.html. Requests for disability-related census information can be made by e-mailing the bureau at hhes-info@census.gov. All the cited statistics are for individuals aged 16 to 64.

8. First, that any conclusion might be premature because Title I's regulations did not come into effect until July 26, 1992, with a further deferral until July 26, 1994, for employers of between fifteen and twenty-five workers. See 42 U.S.C. § 12111(5)(A) (Supp V 1993). Thus, any measurement of employment during the period 1990–94 is necessarily limited in scope, especially when one considers the necessary time lag for administrative enforcement by the Equal Employment Opportunity Commission (EEOC) and Department of Justice (DOJ), and in particular when these subsequently involve judicial adjudication. Moreover, much of the published census data is not up to date, the SIPP to a greater degree than the CPS.

Second, the definition of disability used by the census in garnering its figures probably overestimates the number of people with disabilities as defined by the ADA, because it relies on self-identification. As a result, the actual employment figures might be more favorable. However, like all statistics, it is subject to interpretive differences.

Third, there are studies of disabled individuals which indicate some progress among specific groups. The most noteworthy of these analyses was a study conducted by Peter David Blanck of a group of mentally disabled workers in Oklahoma. Blanck concluded that the fall in unemployment among participants from 39 percent in 1990 to 21 percent in 1994 signaled an "encouraging advance." See Peter David Blanck, Empirical Study of the Americans with Disabilities Act: Employment Issues from 1990 to 1994, *Behavioral Sciences and L.* 14 (1996): 5 (hereafter Empirical Study); Peter David Blanck, Assessing Five Years of Employment Integration and Economic Opportunities under the Americans with Disabilities Act, *Mental and Physical Disability L. Rep.* 19 (1995): 384 (hereafter Assessing Five Years); Peter David Blanck, Employment Integration, Economic Opportunity, and the Americans with Disabilities Act: Empirical Study from 1990–1993, *Iowa L. Rev.* 79 (1994): 853 (hereafter Employment Integration).

Finally, following submission of this essay two studies appeared which indicate that the post-ADA employment rate of workers with disabilities has declined moderately relative to that of workers without disabilities. See Daron Acemoglu and Joshua Angrist, *Consequences of Employment Protection? The Case of the Americans with Disabilities Act* (National Bureau of Economic Research Working Paper No. 6670) (1998); Thomas DeLeire, The Wage and Employment Effects of the Americans with Disabilities Act (University of Chicago unpublished mimeograph) (1997). These empirical studies are challenged for a number of technical reasons in two publications: Susan Schwochau and Peter David Blanck, The Economics of the Americans with Disabilities Act: Part II: Does the ADA Disable the Disabled? *Berkeley J. Emp. & Lab. L.* 21 (1999): 271–313; John J. Donohue III and Michael Ashley Stein, *Evaluating Post-ADA Employment Effects on People with Disabilities.*

Despite these reservations, because it applies constant variables over a national population base, to my knowledge the census statistics provide the best broad source of information we have available.

9. This rise was mostly due to a 2.8 percent elevation in the employment rate among people classified as having "severe" disabilities, which increased from 23.3 percent in 1991 to 26.1 percent in 1994. In practical terms, this translates into jobs for 800,000 of the hardest to employ among the disabled population. While this figure is in itself laudable, one must wonder whether the increase was due to new entries of disabled people into the workforce or the "severe" disablement of existing able-bodied workers. Because the percentage of all employed workers who are identified as disabled increased 0.2 percent during the period 1991–94, it is plausible, at least in part, to conjecture the latter.

10. Stated conversely, the unemployment rate among people with disabilities decreased from 48 percent in 1991 to 47.7 percent in 1994, while the incidence of unemployment among the nondisabled population dropped from 19.5 percent in 1991 to 17.9 percent in 1994.

11. Two Louis Harris and Associates polls taken eight years apart demonstrate an opposite trend. Compare *Louis Harris and Associates/National Organization for the Disabled Survey of Americans with Disabilities* 37 (1994) (68 percent of surveyed people with disabilities were unemployed) (hereafter *LH/NOD Survey*), with *ICD Survey,* p. 47 (66 percent of disabled people surveyed were unemployed).

12. Discussed in n. 8.

13. Assertions of ineffectiveness have been made, with varying motivation, by others. Compare Blanck, Employment Integration (urging further study as a means of inducing more productive implementation), with Walter Olson, *The Excuse Factory* (1997), pp. 85–140 (hereafter *Excuse Factory*) (decrying failure of the ADA).

14. Pub. L. No. 88-352, §§ 701-16, 78 Stat. 241, 253–66 (codified as amended at 42 U.S.C. §§ 2000e to 2000e-17 [1994]) (prohibiting discrimination on the basis of race, color, sex, religion, or national origin in both the public and private sectors).

15. See generally Richard Butler and James J. Heckman, The Government's Impact on the Labor Market Status of Black Americans: A Critical Review, in *Equal Rights and Industrial Relations,* ed. Leonard J. Hausman (1977), p. 235 (setting forth historical differential in employment rates between blacks and whites) (hereafter Government's Impact).

16. I am not alone in this contention. See generally Harlan Hahn, Antidiscrimination Laws and Social Research on Disability: The Minority Group Perspective, *Behav-*

ioral Sciences and L. 14 (1996): 41; Leonard Kriegel, Uncle Tom and Tiny Tim: Some Reflections on the Cripple as Negro, *Am. Scholar* 38 (1969): 412; S. A. Richardson and J. Royce, Race and Handicap in Children's Preference for Other Children, *Child Dev.* 39 (1968): 467.

17. The relationship between people with disabilities and other minority groups is among my current research interests and will be analyzed in greater detail in a future article.

18. See generally Alan Gartner and Joe Tom, *Images of the Disabled, Disabling Images* (1987); Claire H. Liachowitz, *Disability as a Social Construct* (1988); Marilynn J. Phillips, Damaged Goods: Oral Narratives of the Experience of Disability in American Culture, *Soc. Sci. Med.* 8 (1990): 30. See also Douglas C. Baynton, Bodies and Environments: The Cultural Construction of Disability (this volume).

19. I qualify this remark because the inclusion of HIV-positive individuals as disabled within the definitions of the ADA has added an element of fear (often irrational) to the traditional perspective of pity. Recently decided by the Supreme Court is a case involving refusal by a dentist to treat an asymptomatic HIV-positive patient. See *Bragdon v. Abbott,* 524 U.S. 624 (1998).

20. See Louis Harris and Associates, *Public Attitudes towards People with Disabilities* 13 (1991) (74 percent of Americans felt pity toward disabled individuals) (hereafter *Public Attitudes*).

21. Several areas of scholarship continue to interpret the source and manifestation of mainstream society's interaction with the disabled. For a sociological approach, see generally M. Oliver, *The Politics of Disablement: A Sociological Approach* (1990); L. M. Coleman, Stigma: An Enigma Demystified, in *The Dilemma of Difference: A Multidisciplinary View of Stigma,* ed. S. C. Ainlay, G. Becker, and L. M. Coleman (1986), p. 211; R. W. English, Correlates of Stigma toward Physically Disabled Persons, *Rehab. Res. and Pract. Rev.* 2 (1971): 1; N. Goodman, S. A. Richardson, and S. M. Dornbush, Variant Reactions to Physical Disabilities, *Am. Soc. Rev.* 28 (1963): 429; S. A. Richardson, N. Goodman, A. H. Hastorf, and S. M. Dornbusch, Cultural Uniformity in Reaction to Physical Disabilities, *Am. Soc. Rev.* 26 (1961): 241.

22. See generally J. Crocker and B. Major, Social Stigma and Self-Esteem: The Self-Protective Properties of Stigma, *Psych. Rev.* 96 (1989): 608; Harlan Hahn, Paternalism and Public Policy, *Society* 20 (1983): 36.

23. Especially because when not treated with pity, disabled people are commonly expected to fulfill the often unachievable dichotomous role of inspirational "supercrip." See Stein, From Crippled to Disabled, pp. 249–52.

24. The effects of legal choices relating to inclusion form the basis of Martha Minow's insightful and wise scholarship. See Martha Minow, *Making All the Difference: Inclusion, Exclusion, and American Law* (1990); Martha Minow, When Difference Has Its Home: Group Homes for the Mentally Retarded, Equal Protection, and Legal Treatment of Difference, *Harvard C. R.–C. L. L. Rev.* 22 (1987): 111; Martha Minow, Beyond State Intervention in the Family: For Baby Jane Doe, *U. Mich. J. L. Ref.* 18 (1985): 933.

25. See Michael Ashley Stein, When Justice Is Blind: Appointing Vision-Impaired Individuals to the Bench, *Minority L. J.* 5 (1992): 1; Stein, From Crippled to Disabled, pp. 267–69. In 1995, the first visually impaired judge was appointed to the federal bench.

26. One of the more outspoken and persuasive black legal scholars to assert that civil rights empowerment without concomitant economic gains is an impotent endowment is Derrick Bell. See Derrick Bell, *Faces at the Bottom of the Well: The Permanence of Racism* (1992); Derrick Bell, Forward: The Civil Rights Chronicles, *Harvard L. Rev.* 99 (1985): 4.

27. See John J. Donohue III and James Heckman, Continuous versus Episodic Change: The Impact of Civil Rights Policy on the Economic Status of Blacks, *J. of Ec. Lit.* 29 (1991): 1603; James J. Heckman and Brook S. Poyner, Determining the Impact of Federal Antidiscrimination Policy on the Economic Status of Blacks: A Study of South Carolina, *Am. Econ. Rev.* 79 (1989): 138, 167–73; David L. Rose, Twenty-five Years Later: Where Do We Stand on Equal Opportunity Employment Law Enforcement? *Vanderbilt L. Rev.* 42 (1989): 1121, 1169; Butler and Heckman, Government's Impact, p. 235.

28. Although an aggressive job program was unsuccessfully sponsored by former Senate majority leader Bob Dole. See Bob Dole, Are We Keeping America's Promises to People with Disabilities?—Commentary on Blanck, *Iowa L. Rev.* 79 (1994): 925, 929 (describing plan to raise level of employment among disabled to that of nondisabled population by the year 2000).

29. In addition to providing a wealth of its own information, the JAN website is linked with many other disability-related websites, and is available at http://janweb.icdi.wvu.edu/.

30. For example, Blanck has examined ADA compliance at a large national corporation. See Peter David Blanck, Communicating the Americans with Disabilities Act, Transcending Compliance: 1996 Follow-up Report on Sears, Roebuck and Co., *Annenberg Washington Program Reports* (1996); Peter David Blanck, Communicating the Americans with Disabilities Act, Transcending Compliance: A Case Report on Sears, Roebuck and Co., *Annenberg Washington Program Reports* (1994) (hereafter 1994 Sears Report).

31. See Charles R. Lawrence III, The Id, the Ego, and Equal Protection: Reckoning with Unconscious Racism, *Stanford L. Rev.* 39 (1987): 317 (hereafter The Id, The Ego). The first, a psychoanalytic theory, posits that racial antagonism finds its source in the unconscious and is then repressed in order to make the feeling more palatable. The second, cognitive psychological theory, views human behavior, including racial prejudice, as growing out of the individual's attempt to understand his relationship with the world while at the same time preserving his personal integrity. Through the processes of categorization, assimilation, and the search for coherence, attitudes are tacitly learned and the individual is not aware that he has been taught racial beliefs.

32. See Kimberle Williams Crenshaw, Race, Reform, and Retrenchment: Transformation and Legitimation in Antidiscrimination Law, *Harvard L. Rev.* 101 (1988):

1331. Under Crenshaw's theory, formal reforms such as civil rights statutes merely act to repackage racism, eliminating the symbolic manifestations of racial oppression while allowing the perpetuation of material subordination.

A more forceful approach is that of Alan David Freeman, who asserts that civil rights statutes are actually used by the white majority to legitimate the very racial inequality and oppression they were meant to remedy. See Alan David Freemen, Legitimizing Racial Discrimination through Antidiscrimination Law: A Critical Review of Supreme Court Doctrine, *Minn. L. Rev.* 62 (1978): 1049.

33. See the sources in nn. 21–22.

34. Justin W. Dart, Jr., The ADA: A Promise to Be Kept, in *Rights and Responsibilities of All Americans,* ed. Lawrence O. Gotsin and Henry A. Beyer (1993), p. xxi (hereafter *Rights and Responsibilities*).

35. See generally Shapiro, *No Pity.*

36. See generally Richard K. Scotch, *From Good Will to Civil Rights: Transforming Federal Disability Policy* (1984), pp. 111–16; Shapiro, *No Pity,* pp. 64–70.

37. See generally Arlene Mayerson, The History of the ADA: A Movement Perspective, in *Rights and Responsibilities,* p. 17; Sara D. Watson, A Study in Legislative Strategy: The Passage of the ADA, p. 26 (id.); Jonathan C. Drimmer, Cripples, Overcomers, and Civil Rights: Tracing the Evolution of Federal Policy and Social Policy for People with Disabilities, *UCLA L. Rev.* 40 (1993): 1341.

38. See generally Stein, From Crippled to Disabled, pp. 255–59; Shapiro, *No Pity,* passim.

39. In nascent stage is the American Association of People with Disabilities, which may be contacted via e-mail at aapd@aapd.com and whose website may be accessed at http://www.aapd.com.

40. *LH/NOD Survey,* p. 122.

41. See *ADA Watch Year One: A Report to the President and Congress on Progress, in National Council on Disability, Implementing the Americans with Disabilities Act* (1993), p. 5 ("Minorities with disabilities . . . are significantly under-reached by current ADA information and technical assistance efforts"). This knowledge gap corresponds to employment differentials within the disabled community. See William J. Hanna and Elizabeth Rogovsky, On the Situation of African-American Women with Physical Disabilities, *J. Applied Rehab. Counselling* 23 (1992): 39–45 (comparing the situation of the 25 percent of African-American women with disabilities that were fully employed with that of the 44 percent of white women, 57 percent of African-American men, and 77 percent of white men with disabilities).

42. John J. Donohue III and Peter Siegelman, The Changing Nature of Employment Discrimination, *Stanford L. Rev.* 43 (1991): 983, 993.

43. See id. at 993 (knowing what is discriminatory allows worker expectation of equal treatment); John J. Donohue III, Further Thoughts on Employment Discrimination Legislation: A Reply to Judge Posner, *U. Pa. L. Rev.* 136 (1987): 523, 539 (attitudinal changes brought about by Title VII over time reduce discrimination); John J. Donohue III and James J. Heckman, Re-evaluating Federal Civil Rights Policy, *Geo.*

L. J. 79 (1991): 1713, 1717 (observing that the Civil Rights Act of 1964 "at first, may not have changed the attitude, but it appears to have altered the behavior, of discriminatory employers").

44. Lauren B. Edelman, Legal Ambiguity and Symbolic Structure: Organizational Medication of Civil Rights Law, *Am J. of Soc.* 97 (1992): 1531, 1545.

45. *ICD Survey,* pp. 37, 39.

46. This empathy by identification was key to garnering nondisabled supporters of the ADA. See Stein, From Crippled to Disabled, pp. 258–59; Shapiro, *No Pity,* pp. 117–19, 124.

47. See text accompanying n. 32.

48. The rates of disability by age are 18–44 years: 13.6 percent; 45–64 years: 29.2 percent; 65–74 years: 44.6 percent; 75–84 years: 63.7 percent; 85 years and over: 84.2 percent.

49. A possible exception to this statement are individuals who through surgical and/or chemical means "change" genders. As with sexual orientation, I consider this a process of revelation rather than one of alteration.

50. See, e.g., John W. Parry, Executive Summary and Analysis, *Mental and Physical Disability L. Rep.* 19 (1995): 266 (criticizing the ADA for not benefiting the proper group of people with disabilities).

51. See Equal Employment Opportunity Commission, *Americans with Disabilities Act of 1990—Statistics* (Oct. 16, 1995) (reporting about 20 percent of individuals with back ailments). See also Gary J. Macfarlane, Elaine Thomas, Ann C. Papageorgiou, Peter R. Croft, Malcolm I. V. Jayson, and Alan J. Silman, Employment and Physical Work Activities as Predictors of Future Low Back Pain, *Spine* 22 (1997): 1143 ("Low back pain is one of the commonest causes of disability among people of working age"); Report to Congress on the Job Accommodation Network by Barbara Judy, Americans with Disabilities Forum, Senate Subcommittee on Disability Policy, 1995 WL 446714 (July 26, 1995) (noting that 48 percent of JAN inquiries involve motor impairments, especially back and carpal tunnel syndrome).

52. For example, see William Bradford Reynolds, The Reagan Administration's Civil Rights Policy: The Challenge for the Future, *Vanderbilt L. Rev.* 42 (1989): 993 ("The obvious and not-so-obvious barriers that once marked blacks as inferior and second-class citizens largely have been eliminated"). Reynolds served under President Reagan as the DOJ's Assistant Attorney General, Civil Rights Division.

53. See, e.g., Thomas Sowell, *Civil Rights: Rhetoric or Reality?* (1984) (averring that after so many years of empowerment racism is merely an excuse). Sowell is affiliated with Stanford's Hoover Institution.

54. See *Public Attitudes* at p. 13.

55. Both groups need to avoid the danger of acquiescing to these images, thus creating a self-fulfilling prophecy. See generally Martha Minow, Surviving Victim Talk, *UCLA L. Rev.* 40 (1993): 1411.

56. See Stein, From Crippled to Disabled, pp. 250–51, 261–64.

57. Marilynn Phillips describes this phenomena as the "Horatio Alger cripple story" (Damaged Goods, p. 250).

58. This debate is reviewed in detail in Peter David Blanck and Mollie Weighner Marti, Attitudes, Behavior, and the Employment Provisions of the Americans with Disabilities Act, *Villanova L. Rev.* 42 (1997): 345.

59. "Adequate economic data examining the effect of the population of young, qualified persons with disabilities able to join the work force is not available." Blanck, Employment Integration, p. 918. Peter David Blanck, The Economics of the Employment Provisions of the Americans with Disabilities Act: Workplace Accommodations (this volume) (most economic critiques made without recourse to data).

60. See, e.g., Achieving Independence: The Challenge for the Twenty-first Century—a Decade of Progress in Disability Policy Setting an Agenda for the Future (National Council on Disability 1996) (stressing the need for more information about people with disabilities); Edward H. Yelin, The Recent History and Immediate Future of Employment among Persons with Disabilities, *Milbank Q.* 69 (1991): 129, 143–46 (urging additional studies of ADA implementation).

61. See, e.g., in this volume, Thomas N. Chirikos, Employer Accommodation of Older Workers with Disabilities: Some Empirical Evidence and Policy Lessons (noting lack of hard data on which to make accurate evaluations about the ADA while also theorizing why some workers with disabilities are accommodated); Kathryn Moss, The ADA Employment Discrimination Charge Process: How Does It Work and Whom Is It Benefiting? (initiating, with colleagues, the first analysis of ADA employment complaint processes); Marjorie L. Baldwin, Estimating the Potential Benefits of the ADA on the Wages and Employment of Persons with Disabilities (estimating annual wage losses incurred by the disabled as $27 billion due to discrimination in employment and $10 billion because of discriminatory wages); Teresa L. Scheid, Compliance with the ADA and Employment of Those with Mental Disabilities (analyzing responses by employers in one metropolitan city to the ADA's mandates). See also Blanck, Empirical Study; Blanck, Assessing Five Years; Blanck, Employment Integration.

62. One exception is the question raised by Donohue of whether Title I structurally mandates affirmative action by requiring an otherwise profit-maximizing employer to hire or retain a worker requiring a reasonable accommodation, instead of an equally qualified worker requiring no such expenditure. See John J. Donohue III, Employment Discrimination Law in Perspective: Three Concepts of Equality, *Mich. L. Rev.* 92 (1994): 2583, 2608. See also Pamela S. Karlan and George Rutherglen, Disabilities, Discrimination, and Reasonable Accommodation, *Duke L. J.* 46 (1996): 1, 14 ("reasonable accommodation is affirmative action"). But see Chai R. Feldblum, The (R)evolution of Physical Disability Anti-discrimination Law: 1976–1996, *Mental and Physical Disability L. Rep.* 20 (1996): 613 (asserting that Title I's reasonable accommodation requirement "is not a remedy for discrimination in the way that various forms of affirmative action might" be). Because Title I does not require an employer to hire a lesser or equally capable "qualified" person with a disability, I agree with Feldblum's conclusion.

63. See Richard A. Posner, The Efficiency and Efficacy of Title VII, *U. Pa. L. Rev.* 136 (1987): 513, 519–20 (Title VII's effects are not readily knowable).

64. Some are more overtly political than others. See, e.g., Mark A. Schuman, The Wheelchair Ramp to Serfdom: The Americans with Disabilities Act, Liberty, and Markets, *St. John's J. Leg. Comm.* 10 (1995): 495 (incorrectly stating that "the ADA denies an employer the right to determine the qualifications and abilities relevant to a job"); Olson, *Excuse Factory,* pp. 85–140 (voicing blanket opposition to the ADA).

65. See Thomas H. Barnard, The Americans with Disabilities Act: Nightmare for Employers and Dream for Lawyers? *St. John's L. Rev.* 64 (1990): 229, 252.

66. See Steven F. Stuhlberg, Reasonable Accommodation under the Americans with Disabilities Act: How Much Must One Do Before Hardship Turns Undue? *U. Cin. L. Rev.* 59 (1991): 1311, 1320.

67. See President's Committee on Employment of People with Disabilities, *Costs and Benefits of Accommodations* (July 1996) (hereafter *Costs and Benefits*); President's Committee on Employment of People with Disabilities, *Job Accommodation Network (JAN) Reports* (Oct.–Dec. 1994).

68. See *Costs and Benefits.*

69. See John J. Donohue III, Advocacy versus Analysis in Assessing Employment Discrimination Law, *Stanford L. Rev.* 44 (1992): 1583, 1601 (reducing attitudinal discrimination can have economic gains for employers in terms of productivity of workers).

70. Then–Sears Chairman and CEO Edward Brennan opined that "when Sears hires, works with, and accommodates qualified employees with disabilities, Sears enhances its customer base." Blanck, *1994 Sears Report.*

71. See Louis Harris and Associates/National Organization on Disability, *1995 Survey of Corporate Executives of the ADA* (1995) (recounting that 79 percent of employers interviewed believed employing disabled workers improved the U.S. economy).

72. This theme is addressed in greater detail in Michael Ashley Stein, Labor Markets, Rationality, and Workers with Disabilities, *Berkeley J. Emp. & Lab. L.* (2000).

73. Peggy Radin has made this point with great persuasiveness in another context. See Margaret Jane Radin, Compensation and Commensurability, *Duke L. J.* 43 (1993): 56; Margaret Jane Radin, Property and Personhood, *Stanford L. Rev.* 34 (1982): 957.

74. See generally Tom Walz and Lea Anne Boucher, Avoiding Iron-Door Barriers to the Employment of Persons with Developmental Disabilities (this volume) (chronicling the satisfaction involved in hiring mentally disabled individuals).

75. See generally Gregory S. Kavka, Disability and the Right to Work, *Social Philosophy and Policy* 9 (1992): 262.

76. See generally Judith N. Shklar, *American Citizenship: The Quest for Inclusion* (1991).

77. Justin W. Dart, Jr., Testimony before the Senate Committee on Governmental Affairs, Apr. 28, 1994, LEXIS (Legis library, CNGTST file).

78. See, e.g., in this volume, Marjorie L. Baldwin, Estimating the Potential Benefits of the ADA on the Wages and Employment of Persons with Disabilities (annual wage losses incurred by the disabled were $27 billion due to discrimination in employment

and $10 billion because of discriminatory wages); Wendy Wilkinson and Lex Frieden, Glass-Ceiling Issues in Employment of People with Disabilities (describing discrimination against disabled work advancement); Steven L. Willborn, The Nonevolution of Enforcement under the ADA: Discharge Cases and the Hiring Problem (adumbrating legal doctrines utilized against people with disabilities); and Robert S. Olick, Genes in the Workplace: New Frontiers for ADA Law, Policy, and Research (considering the newest form of disability-based discrimination).

79. Lawrence, The Id, The Ego, p. 388.

Chapter III

Glass-Ceiling Issues in Employment of People with Disabilities

WENDY WILKINSON AND LEX FRIEDEN

Available data indicate that the rate of employment of people with disabilities in the workplace is still much lower than for any other group in our society. A number of factors contribute to this situation. Promoting employment among people with disabilities is a complex exercise because of the interconnectivity of variables that have an impact on social structures, political environments, and attitudinal milieus. The limited research available has begun to examine factors that influence employment status, particularly of people with disabilities who are or are becoming employed. Some studies have been industry-specific, some have sampled attitudinal climates, and others have assessed socioeconomic factors that affect the workplace and thus the employment status of people with disabilities.

One study, prepared for the federal Glass-Ceiling Commission by David Braddock and Lynn Bachelder from the University of Illinois (1994), indicates, not surprisingly, that people with disabilities face an invisible barrier that has confronted other groups once they have gained entrée into the workforce—that is, the "glass ceiling." The "term 'glass ceiling' refers to the invisible barriers, real or perceived, which appear to stymie advancement opportunities" (Dominguez 1991). This invisible barrier has a tremendous effect on people with disabilities with respect to both lateral and upward job mobility. It restricts them from accessing all of those opportunities they are qualified for because of factors unrelated to their ability to perform a job.

The glass ceiling for people with disabilities is influenced by many of the same factors that impede women and minorities in the workplace, but some are unique to people with disabilities. All these groups must negotiate through workplaces governed by facially neutral workplace "traditions" which, in effect, exclude or impede individuals with disabilities, minorities, and women. Our workplace does not reflect the diversity in our country, nor is it truly competitive, because large numbers of potential labor force participants are excluded from jobs for reasons unrelated to an ability to perform a job successfully. At this time, all groups seeking to assert their civil rights on any front are confronting an environment hostile to nondiscrimination laws.

People with disabilities, like other groups, are also tremendously impacted by factors exogenous to the workplace, which include limited access to health care, educational opportunities, and adequate housing and transportation, all of which severely restrict the ability of persons with disabilities to progress into and upward through the workforce. Successful employment outcomes do not occur in a vacuum; they are tremendously impacted by the progress of implementation of the Americans with Disabilities Act (ADA)[1] and other nondiscrimination laws which affect access to other areas of society.[2] This has been true for other groups as well. The status of people with disabilities in accessing other privileges and benefits of our system has a direct effect on their employment success. There is a great need for study to quantify the impact of each of the factors that affect people with disabilities in accessing and maintaining employment.

As the employment provisions of the ADA are litigated and the law develops, it is apparent that employers and the courts are struggling with the concept of disability. The issues that have surfaced in the cases brought to date highlight the barriers individuals with disabilities face not only in the workplace but in society as well. Apparent in many of these decisions and related commentary is limited societal understanding of disability and what nondiscrimination for this group means. They also illustrate the problems courts and employers are having reconciling the competing values the ADA embodies—the struggle among different conceptions of disability, a civil rights mandate balanced with cost considerations, misperceptions regarding the mandate of the ADA (affirmative action vs. nondiscrimination). Many of the cases also highlight the philosophical problem courts have trying to confine the ADA mandate to fit their experience with other civil rights statutes which require strictly equal treatment, instead of understanding that special treatment may be necessary to promote equal results under the ADA.

The nature of discrimination against individuals with disabilities manifests itself in different ways. Discrimination based on disability is often expressed through extensions of "charity," feelings of pity, or paternalism for those perceived to be unable to care for themselves. Our society still views people with disabilities as second-class citizens. There is no systematic, ongoing study regarding people with disabilities to help us paint a complete portrait of their true status. There is also no coordination or ongoing collection of the data and studies that do exist. Evidence indicates that the level of awareness and understanding of the ADA and disability is still very low. At this time a battle is being waged over legal interpretation of key parts of the ADA, which is compromising its power to make needed changes in the workplace.

In this chapter we will examine some of the factors that we believe contribute to the "glass ceiling" for people with disabilities. The progress of ADA implementation in the workplace will be explored to expose the issues that are arising in developing an equal opportunity mandate for people with disabilities in the workforce. We will also address the philosophical questions that arise with the implementation of any civil rights law, related to its efficacy, necessity, and the burdens some perceive it imposes as well.

Application of Civil Rights Legislation to Individuals with Disabilities

Implementing a nondiscrimination law that protects people with disabilities presents a new challenge for our society. It demands a different philosophical approach than is required in application of civil rights legislation protecting other groups. The desired outcome of civil rights laws is to achieve greater social integration and equity resulting in increased participation in social, political, and economic life. Equity is an abstract concept, difficult to define and thus measure. It incorporates both material and intangible factors. To achieve equity one must have access to the economic benefits our society offers. One must also have political freedom and autonomy. A law that promotes equality of opportunity does not necessarily guarantee that this will occur. There are numerous barriers that impede this outcome, especially when we try to eliminate employment barriers for individuals with disabilities. Equal outcomes for people with disabilities cannot occur if the law is applied as mandating only equal treatment.

Historic trends in workforce participation are difficult to change overnight. There are concentrations of women and minorities in certain types of occupations or industries. The limited evidence available suggests that people with disabilities are subjected to similar occupational segregation as well. Our workplace reflects, in many ways, the stratification that exists in our society. We are confined by workplace "traditions" that are influenced by political and social norms. Both women and people with disabilities are affected by apparently neutral job requirements which are, in effect, discriminatory because they screen out great numbers of "otherwise" qualified individuals. Women were traditionally excluded from many jobs because the jobs were designed and structured to accommodate males.[3] "Workforce traditions" become so ingrained that we don't question their validity. Their perpetuation impedes the entrée and mobility of many groups in the workforce.

Status of People with Disabilities

In our effort to understand the full range of barriers that people with disabilities face in the workplace, it is important to understand the history of people with disabilities in our society. The tremendous impact that decades of segregation, unemployment, and stigmatization have had must be acknowledged. Many people with disabilities have internalized their relegation to second-class citizenship to the extent that they have become so demoralized that they do not pursue educational opportunities or involve themselves in social, political, and other activities that would enhance their position in society and lead to expanded employment opportunities. The majority also exist at the lowest economic rung of society (West 1991). The 1986 Harris poll documented the link between disability, poverty, and unemployment, painting a compelling portrait of, perhaps, the most disenfranchised group in our society, existing at its fringes.[4]

One can only hypothesize as to the psychosocial effect that this societal conditioning has on people with disabilities who have been lucky enough to access the workplace. This conditioning may impede people with disabilities in a number of ways. Anecdotal evidence suggests that workplace pressure to conform makes individuals reluctant to request accommodations for fear of being singled out and appearing to demand special consideration (SWDBTAC). Many people with disabilities may be afraid to request accommodations because of a fear of having to disclose the existence of a disability. Others may be unaware of the law and their right to request accommodation. Hence, there may be significant numbers of people with disabilities in the workplace still trying to work within accepted norms that don't allow them to be as effective as they could be with an appropriate accommodation. Their performance as well as their opportunities for advancement may be significantly affected.

Society is still struggling with the notion that individuals with disabilities can contribute economically to society through employment. There remains a perception that people with disabilities cannot truly compete in the workplace unless they can be "cured" or rehabilitated. Historically, status in the workplace depended on the degree to which an individual could be "rehabilitated." Programs were developed to rehabilitate persons with disabilities so they could become economically productive and contribute to society in a way that was recognized and respected. The focus was placed completely on the individual, and the impact of traditional workplace structures and policies on the individual's abilities to perform in a job were not addressed. There was no recognition that most workplaces had been designed and jobs conceptualized with a "white, able-bodied male" as the role model. This model dictates the basis for workplace structures, values, and policies that exist today. Thus, it continues to be difficult for the significant numbers of individuals in our society who do not fit this model to join the workforce and, once there, progress latitudinally.

For those individuals with disabilities who could not fit into traditional workplace structures, other programs, designed to provide maintenance, were developed. As our society places a high value on economic productivity, those who are unable to contribute in this manner are devalued. The programs designed to provide income replacement for people with disabilities do little more than maintain them at the lowest rungs of society. The individuals accessing these programs are often viewed with pity—society has fulfilled its charitable obligation to these individuals through these programs.

These programs perpetuate historic conceptions of disability which focus on the medical and functional limitations of an individual (Drimmer 1993). The "medical model" conception of disability looks only at the individual; there is no evaluation of the effect of environment or societal attitudes on the disability. During the 1960s, a new concept of disability emerged, a product of the "independent living" movement (DeJong 1979). Sparked by other contemporary social and civil rights movements, the independent living movement revolutionized the historic conception of disability. The movement forced recognition of the societal and environmental barriers that prohibit people with disabilities from accessing all the opportunities and activities most other members of our society take for granted. This civil rights model "concentrates on the interactions between individuals and the environment" (Hahn 1993).

Although the independent living movement provided the impetus for official, legislative recognition of the civil rights of people with disabilities — the Americans with Disabilities Act being the most notable instance — it is not clear how much this movement has effected mainstream employers' conceptions of disability. Nor can we determine the extent to which its tenets have been internalized by, or even broadcast to, the majority of individuals with disabilities in the United States. How many of the estimated 54 million individuals with disabilities are aware of the movement? Far greater numbers of this group are exposed to more medically oriented portrayals of disability set forth in national disability-related telethons and other programs that do not have a civil rights focus. Thus, today societal perceptions of individuals with disabilities can range from being objects of pity to heroic "overcomers" or abnormal (Drimmer 1993).

A few studies provide some insight into the employment status of people with disabilities in the workforce. The primary source is the Current Population Survey from the Bureau of Census. Data gathered from other studies also indicate a low level of participation of people with disabilities in the workforce. Those that are present in the workplace are relegated principally to low income, manufacturing positions and are under-represented in professional and managerial occupations.

Attitudinal studies reveal that people with different types of disabilities are subjected to different kinds of discrimination (Fuqua, Rathbun, and Gade 1983). Individuals with physical disabilities are viewed more favorably than those with mental, communication, and other types of disabilities. One study showed a correlation between the type of disability and wages. Marjorie Baldwin, in discussing her study which documents the great losses people with disabilities sustain because of wage discrimination, hypothesizes that "prejudice is one important factor" in explaining the wage disparity people with disabilities experience (Baldwin, this volume).

Class Identification

Determining who is a covered person with a disability under Title I of the ADA can be a complex exercise. One cannot draw a bright line around the community of individuals entitled to protection under the ADA. In gender and race discrimination cases there is no question of coverage. People of a particular race or gender possess immutable traits. The same thing cannot be said of all individuals with disabilities. The individuals potentially defined as persons with disabilities under the ADA form an extremely heterogeneous group. It includes people with many different types of impairments which have varying degrees of impact on each individual. The manifestations of many types of disabilities are dynamic in nature, so the degree of impairment may fluctuate over time, which doesn't change the overall impact of the disability on the person but may cause confusion in others' perceptions of it. Within the overall population of people with disabilities there are numerous distinct subgroups. In addition, there are individuals with disabilities who are subjected to multiple forms of discrimination because of their gender and/or racial status.

Within the disability community itself there is stratification among individuals with different types of disabilities. Individuals with a certain type of impairment may make stereotypical assumptions concerning other types of impairments. Persons with disabilities are not immune from the influences that cause other people to make judgments about individuals with certain types of disabilities unfamiliar to them. People understand and accept those who are most like themselves (Henderson 1987, pp. 1620–30). Douglas Baynton takes note of the tensions that exist among different subgroups in the disability community: "Deaf people throughout the twentieth century have tried to distance themselves from the label of disability, while the tendency of those with less stigmatized disabilities to distance themselves from more stigmatized disabilities is a common phenomenon" (Baynton, this volume).

Persons with disabilities encounter different types and degrees of discrimination in the workplace relative to the type of impairment they have (Compton 1995). One study indicated that employers expressed considerably more doubt about the productivity of people with learning disabilities than they did about individuals with other types of disabilities (Gerber 1992). Another study revealed that individuals with visible, physical impairments are viewed more favorably than those with mental or sensory impairments (Fuqua, Rathbun, and Gade 1983). The hierarchy of acceptance depends on the particular type of disability. Individuals with hidden, unfamiliar, or more stigmatized disabilities face greater barriers in the workplace and in society. The unemployment rate among people with psychiatric disabilities is estimated to be 85 percent, significantly higher than the rate for individuals with physical disabilities (Mancuso 1990). Baldwin references studies of groups of individuals with different types of disabilities, noting, "studies of negative attitudes toward different impairment groups consistently find mental impairments eliciting the strongest prejudices" (Baldwin, this volume).

Another important factor related to "class identification" and definitional issues is the level of awareness, cohesiveness, and acculturation of persons with disabilities in our society. It is important to note that there may be significant numbers of people potentially covered by the law who are unaware of its existence. These may include individuals in the workforce. Many individuals, including both those who do not know about the ADA and those who are aware of its existence, may not consider themselves to be individuals with disabilities. As was noted earlier, many individuals who are deaf do not label themselves as individuals with disabilities; they consider themselves to be a part of a culture, linked together by a common language. Self-identification as belonging to a class is one key to breaking down employment barriers. The next step is educational: for people with disabilities to achieve social equity, they must first empower their own members and then "persuade others."

The individuals who do identify themselves as people with disabilities are not all politically active, "empowered" members of a class who are aware of the ADA's existence. Of those who are aware of its existence, few understand its mandate and possess the resources necessary to use it effectively. Perhaps this can be attributed, in part, to the nature of the legislative mandates with which people with disabilities are most familiar. The programs most people with disabilities have traditionally had access to are entitlement programs in nature, design, and perception. They have imbued many individuals with disabilities with a sense of powerlessness over their destiny. People with disabilities are faced with a tremendous learning curve. For years they have been conditioned to accept second-class citizenship. Individuals who have been segregated and who have existed at the lowest rungs of society for years cannot be expected to be able to develop a "civil rights conscience" overnight. Many may be afraid to exercise their civil rights for fear of losing access to the very programs that sustain them and provide them with access to medical care and related support services. This fear has not been proved unfounded, as we have seen a number of courts barring people utilizing disability support programs from bringing ADA claims.

Class or disability identification issues may also pose problems for proactive corporations wishing to develop equal opportunity or glass-ceiling initiatives for people with disabilities, which require some sort of monitoring to determine pay or promotion inequities. What instructions would they give executive search firms in recruiting efforts targeted to individuals with disabilities?

Developing Strategies for Addressing Disability Discrimination

Disability class–identification issues also create problems in application of theories of discrimination traditionally used in evaluating civil rights violations in other arenas. For instance, in disparate treatment and impact cases brought on the basis of gender or race, class identification is the first component of the case. Statistical evidence may be used to demonstrate systemic, occupational segregation. The four factors one must establish, as set forth by the Supreme Court in *McDonnell Douglas Corp. v. Green* (1973), to bring a disparate treatment suit under Title VII are: (1) the individual is a member of the protected class; (2) the individual did apply for a job for which he or she was qualified; (3) the individual was rejected by the employer; and (4) the employer kept the job open and continued to seek applicants with similar qualifications. If these conditions are met and the employer is able to set forth a legitimate reason for its decision, then the individual must bring forth evidence of discriminatory intent. Such evidence may include a demonstration that others not in his or her class were treated differently or that those in his or her class were treated in a different manner by the employer. Again, this evidence may include statistical information.

The need to develop theories to appropriately address disability discrimination presents a significant barrier for people with disabilities in the workforce. How does one demonstrate the existence of systemic discriminatory practices without determining whether the group passed over for jobs had disabilities? Obviously class membership is a given under Title VII. In a significant number of ADA cases brought to date, this has often been the only issue.

Definition of Disability Issues

Establishing one's status as an individual with a disability under the ADA has proven to be the greatest barrier to those seeking the protection of the Act. Under the ADA, an individual with a disability is one who currently has, possesses a record of, or is perceived as having a physical or mental impairment that substantially limits one or more major life activities. The first prong of the definition requires an individualized functional assessment of the impact of an impairment on one's ability to perform major life activities. The second and third parts of the definition cover individuals who do not actually have substantially limiting impairments but who are perceived as having such or who have a history of such.

It was clear from the very first cases brought under Title I that many judges were having great difficulty understanding the ADA concept of disability. Referencing the regulatory language of Title I, many individuals who clearly should have been covered were denied the protection of the ADA by the courts (*Ellison v. Software Spectrum, Inc.* 1996). Right from the start, individuals with mental disabilities encountered the greatest barriers. Apparently, courts are not immune from the tremendous bias that exists in our society toward individuals with mental impairments (*Dupre v. Harris County Hospital Dist.* 1998). Subsequent decisions continued to reflect a judiciary struggling with the concept of disability.

This struggle may be attributed to a number of different factors. Judges are not immune from the stereotypes and misconceptions about disability that are prevalent in our society. Perhaps mainstream exposure to disabilities, the manifestations of which are apparent and generally significant, restricts one's ability to understand impairments that are invisible and dynamic in nature. This limited exposure may also be causing some in the judiciary to implicitly compare disabilities they have had limited exposure to with "traditional" disabilities they have had more experience with. It is easy to evaluate the impact of impairments that clearly affect physical functioning. It is much more difficult to assess individuals' ability to care for themselves, think, concentrate, and interact with others, the life activities that are generally limited by mental impairments. In order to assess the true impact of psychiatric impairments, one must possess some depth of knowledge about the full range of impairments that fall under this "umbrella."

This identification with "traditional" disabilities has also made it difficult for individuals with "mitigated" disabilities to establish coverage. The regulations promulgated by the Equal Employment Opportunity Commission (EEOC) require that a disability be evaluated without reference to the mitigating measures that may ameliorate some of the manifestations of the disability, but have no effect on the nature and real impact of the disability on the individual. Unfortunately, many courts began rejecting this regulatory language and accompanying guidance, which is supported by the Act's legislative history, and evaluated the impact of an impairment on an individual after factoring in the effect of mitigating measures or medication. The Circuit Courts of Appeal split on the issue. Three cases centering around this issue, *Kirkingburg v. Albertson's Inc.,*[5] *Murphy v. United Parcel Service, Inc.,*[6] and *Sutton v. United Air Lines, Inc.*[7] eventually made their way to the United States Supreme Court.

On June 22, 1999, the Supreme Court issued its rulings in all three cases. The decisions drastically narrowed the scope of the definition of disability. In each case, the Court ruled that persons who can "correct" physical impairments with medication or some other type of corrective measure are not individuals with disabilities. These decisions will have a tremendous "chilling" effect on individuals with disabilities in the workplace. Persons who have impairments and need accommodations to do their jobs more effectively will be afraid to come forward and request them because they are uncertain whether the Act will protect them. A person who is terminated from a job or subjected to an adverse employment action because of an impairment may be unable to challenge either occurrence if he or she is taking medication or utilizing a prosthetic device, for instance, that ameliorates the disability. As Justices Stevens and Breyer stated in their dissent, "the court's holding means the act would not protect even those people who lost limbs in industrial accidents or perhaps in the service of their country in places like Iwo Jima." Will these decisions cause individuals in the workplace to forgo treatment, medication, and use of prosthetic devices, for example, in order to invoke the protection of the ADA?

In so ruling, the Supreme Court thwarted clear congressional intent to cover disabilities whether or not they were ameliorated by any corrective measure or medication. The legislative history of the Act states that the existence of an impairment is to be determined without regard to mitigating measures such as medicines or assistive or prosthetic devices. For example, an individual with epilepsy would be considered to have an impairment even if the symptoms of the disorder were completely controlled by medicine. Similarly, an individual with hearing loss would be considered to have an impairment even if the condition were correctable through the use of a hearing aid (Senate Report at 23, House Labor Report at 52, House Judiciary Report at 28).

Individuals who are alleging that they have a disability that substantially limits their ability to work are also encountering tremendous evidentiary burdens by having to establish that they are significantly restricted in their ability to perform a class or broad range of jobs. This is a surprisingly strict regulatory requirement that makes it exceedingly difficult for plaintiffs who have been subjected to an adverse employment action, because of a work disability, to establish the full range of jobs in which their performance would be restricted. This hurdle is especially difficult in cases where individuals allege that the employer regarded them as having a work disability. In these cases, they must not only prove that they were excluded from a range of jobs but also that the employer believed that there was a full range of jobs that these individuals were restricted from performing. So, individuals whose employer acts on a mistaken belief that they have a disability that impairs their job performance may have no recourse. The courts have taken this language and applied it very restrictively. Thus, individuals bringing forth evidence that their employer took the adverse action on the basis that the employer believed they could not perform their job have had a difficult time establishing coverage. This is because they were unable to prove the employer perceived them as unable to perform a full range of jobs.

"Qualified" Individual with a Disability

Under Title I of the ADA, a qualified individual with a disability is defined as "an individual with a disability who satisfies the requisite skill, experience, education and other job-related requirements of the employment position such individual holds or desires, and who, with or without reasonable accommodation, can perform the essential functions of such position." The legislative history, language of the act, and applicable case law[8] clearly indicate that the determination of whether or not one is a "qualified" individual should include an assessment of an individual's ability to perform essential job functions with *reasonable accommodations.*

Programs Providing Employment "Support"

Title VII of the Rehabilitation Act requires that states develop and implement statewide plans to provide services for individuals with the most severe disabilities. The act mandates that states "shall provide, at a minimum, for the provision of vocational rehabilitation services"[9] which are defined as "any goods or services necessary to render an individual with a disability employable."[10] Services provided are supposed to be directed toward removing barriers to education, employment, transportation, and recreation. For individuals with disabilities who qualify for Title VII services, these programs provide the greatest assistance in attaining employment. The act, however, does not provide specific guidance as to precisely what benefits must be provided, nor does it define the ultimate employment goal. The statutory language of the act appears to mandate the provision of some services, while the regulations seem to allow conditional provision of services. Thus, it is unclear how much discretion a state agency has over provision of "necessary" rehabilitation services. Hence, individuals may have no clear idea as to what rights they have in accessing these services. The ultimate employment goal is also unclear, which has resulted in some litigation. At issue has been the appropriate vocational goal level which the program must support. Should it be the "achievement of the highest vocational goals . . . or merely suitable employment"?[11]

For the most part, the programs developed by the Social Security Administration or through Title VII of the Rehabilitation Act do not follow the individual into the workplace. Once the employment goal has been attained, the individual's case will be closed or the individual will be deemed ineligible for further benefits. Some programs have been developed to allow for the transition into employment, but, for the most part, entrance into the workforce triggers a cut-off or phase-out of any assistance for disability-related expenses or health care. Many individuals with chronic health conditions or who need personal attendant services, which can be costly, are greatly restricted in their employment options because of these limitations. Many may have to choose unemployment or underemployment to remain qualified for services.

These programs came to life in different eras and are mired in antiquated notions of disability. The goals of these programs need to be refined and coordinated to correct perceptions of conflict. There must be recognition that many individuals with disabilities need basic supportive services if they are to access the social, political, and economic arenas like everyone else. The provision of supportive services must be understood as placing people with disabilities on a platform that allows them to access employment opportunities and compete like everyone else. These issues are some of the items which are on the agenda of the Disability Policy Panel of the National Academy of Social Insurance (*Preliminary Status Report*).

Limitations of ADA in Addressing Institutionalized Discrimination

Civil rights legislation provides important nondiscrimination mandates and gives discriminated-against individuals an avenue to seek redress. As with other groups, the barriers people with disabilities face in the workplace were erected decades ago and have become ingrained in our social fabric. Legislation simply cannot address all the behaviors which manifest themselves in the workplace as intolerance to difference. Numerous events can occur in the workplace which may not constitute actionable discrimination but which impact an individual's job performance, and the discomfort of coworkers or customers due to misperceptions of disability may significantly impede an individual's progress in the workplace.

The ADA, like other civil rights legislation, is limited in its ability to address institutionalized discriminatory practices in a comprehensive manner because it cannot address the full range of activities that impact employment discrimination. To date, enforcement efforts have focused on addressing discrimination at a micro level. Early Title VII enforcement efforts were targeted as well to addressing allegations of individualized discrimination. Soon after its enactment, this enforcement strategy was challenged because it did not address widespread, systematic employment discrimination (Graham 1990). In response, the EEOC developed the theory of disparate impact to address employment discrimination against a class. Strategies were developed utilizing statistical data to profile race disparities in the workplace. As discussed earlier, the difficulty of gathering data on people with disabilities in the workplace makes it difficult to use a traditional statistical approach in applying the disparate impact theory in the context of disability discrimination. New enforcement strategies need to be developed using other evidence to demonstrate prima facie evidence of disability class discrimination. Perhaps job applications, job descriptions, and company procedures that utilize discriminatory criteria could be used to demonstrate disparate impact. Once theories are developed, the next hurdle will be deciding what sort of corrective action, beyond eliminating the discriminatory criteria, should be required.

Nondiscrimination vs. Affirmative Action

The ADA is a civil rights act in the same tradition as Title VII in terms of desired outcomes, but it is different in its approach to achieving its nondiscrimination mandate. It asks that people with disabilities be treated differently. For instance, under Title VII, treating women or individuals from racial minorities differently constitutes discrimination. The ADA reasonable accommodation mandate asks that people with disabilities be allowed to perform job functions in a different manner or use other processes or approaches in accomplishing job tasks. The different route the reasonable accommodation mandate allows for individuals with disabilities to accomplish job tasks has given rise to debate over whether the ADA requires nondiscrimination or affirmative action. Many view the provision of an accommodation as an action that gives the individual with the disability an advantage: "under the civil rights statutes that protect women, blacks, or older workers, plaintiffs can complain of discrimination against them, but they cannot insist on discrimination in their favor; disabled individuals often can" (Karlan and Rutherglen 1996, p. 3). This debate is not new; Section

504 of the Rehabilitation Act of 1973 sparked similar discussion. In *Southwestern Community College v. Davis*,[12] the Supreme Court referred to reasonable accommodation at one point as an affirmative action requirement and later addressed it as a nondiscrimination mandate. In *Alexander v. Choate*,[13] the court clarified its analysis of reasonable accommodation, noting the criticism its earlier interpretation engendered, and found that it was a nondiscrimination mandate. The debate is circular, as either interpretation recognizes that nondiscrimination against people with disabilities requires more than mere acceptance. It also demands change in traditional workplace practices and structures which impose additional barriers.

Perhaps the ADA nondiscrimination model could be adapted by other groups,[14] as has been suggested by some, to alleviate the impact of sexist and racist practices. "We would not be protecting equality of opportunity if we simply ignored the impact of unfair social practices and formally made point-by-point comparisons of existing talents and skills" (Daniels 1997, pp. 284–85). Whether the arguments for expanding the model to other groups are as compelling or the justification on an equal par with the necessity for utilizing the model in disability discrimination cases is open to debate (Kavka 1992, p. 280).

Reasonable Accommodation Issues

Reasonable accommodation is not specifically defined in the act, but a list of potential accommodations is provided for guidance:

> The term reasonable accommodation may include: (A) making existing facilities used by employees readily accessible to and usable by individuals with disabilities; and (B) job restructuring, part-time or modified work schedules, reassignment to a vacant position, acquisition or modification of equipment or devices, appropriate adjustment or modifications of examinations, training materials or policies, the provision of qualified readers or interpreters, and other similar accommodations for individuals with disabilities.[15]

Tremendous barriers in the workplace remain because of traditional workplace culture and norms. Barriers are created by "routine personnel actions, policies, and procedures" (Compton 1995). Many employers are restricted by the "boundaries" of their workplace and their expectation of the type of individuals who can fit into the existing place of employment. It is clear from the statutory language and legislative history of the ADA that substantial changes in traditional workplace structures were anticipated. Many employers have very narrow views concerning the manner in which a job should be performed. Job descriptions often dictate the means which should be used to accomplish a particular job task instead of describing the "end result" desired. The ADA asks employers to reevaluate this practice and expand their conception of workforce requirements and the "ability" of the work environment to accommodate the various abilities of diverse individuals.

This struggle with workplace tradition reflects, in some ways, our judiciary's early struggle with gender-based discrimination issues that now seem comical. In one early case, *Phillips v. Martin Marietta Corp.,* the court held that Martin's refusal to hire women with preschool-age children was not discriminatory because employers were simply recognizing the different responsibilities of each sex, dictated by virtue of their sex, when they were establishing their employment policies. This requirement was found to be a neutral criterion. In ruling for the employer, the appellate court considered so-called normal gender roles in assuming child-care responsibilities.

The concept of reasonable accommodation has not been the subject of a great deal of litigation to date. In one important appearance in the judicial arena, the application of the concept was confined by traditional workplace policies and practices. In *Vande Zande v. State of Wisconsin Department of Administration,* at issue was the obligation of a state agency to accommodate an individual with paraplegia. In this case, the plaintiff, a program assistant, asked to be allowed to work at home. The court found "teamwork under supervision generally cannot be performed at home without a substantial reduction in the quality of the employee's performance." No objective data was cited for reaching this conclusion. It was also noted that the employer, a state agency, had no experience with this type of accommodation. In a subsequent case, *Anzalone v. Allstate Insurance Co.,*[16] working at home was found to be a reasonable accommodation. The court looked at the nature of the job and found it was not necessary that it be performed in one particular location. However, in this case, Allstate had allowed other employees to work at home for other reasons. It is important to remember that the ADA asks employers to look critically at traditional employment practices to avoid overruling a requested accommodation simply because it has not been made before.

Many unions view nondiscrimination laws as a threat to their core, guiding principles—job security and seniority. As in the aftermath of the passage of Title VII, conflicts with seniority clauses and the ADA have arisen. In the late 1960s women and minorities also faced collectively bargained seniority systems that were born in eras when they had no opportunity to join or be factors in the development of the systems, so the systems perpetuated discrimination (Behman 1976, pp. 490–93). Persons with disabilities are now confronting this same barrier. An employee with a disability who needs a reasonable accommodation in a unionized environment will find that her rights may be inextricably intertwined with the terms of a labor contract. Neither the statutory nor the regulatory language of the ADA provides detailed guidance concerning the interplay of collective bargaining agreements and employers' obligations under the ADA. However, it is clear from the regulatory language in the ADA that employers' obligations to provide reasonable accommodation should take precedence: "discrimination include[s] . . . participating in a contractual or other arrangement or relationship that has the effect of subjecting a covered entity's qualified applicant or employee with a disability to the discrimination prohibited by this title (such relationship includes a relationship with an employment or referral agency, labor union, an organization providing fringe benefits to an employee of the covered entity, or an organization providing training and apprenticeship programs)."[17] In unionized environments, it could be said that there is no such thing as a vacancy.

The ADA lists reassignment as one potential form of reasonable accommodation for current employees. Most courts have interpreted this provision to require employers to reassign qualified individuals with a disability to a vacant position only if the employer has a regular practice or policy of reassigning nondisabled employees to other positions. It appears that some courts are narrowing the scope of providing reasonable accommodation by holding that employers are not required to expand accommodation policies beyond what their existing policies allow. This interpretation, should it prevail, could prove to severely restrict reasonable accommodation options for many in the workplace by allowing employers to rely on existing policies and procedures.

Access to Other Areas of Society

A person's ability to successfully negotiate through the workplace is affected by a number of factors exogenous to the workplace. The 1986 Harris poll of people with disabilities identified a number of the external barriers that significantly impede their access in society. Included on the list were denials of educational opportunities, lack of access to public accommodations and transportation, and an inability to obtain health insurance. As with other groups, quality vocational training and education are extremely important factors in enhancing employment opportunities (Taylor 1985). Employers rely heavily on education and training as predictors of success in employment (Bowles, Gordon, and Weisskopf 1983). In addition, many jobs require testing, certification, or licensing by outside entities in order for individuals to advance in their careers.

Educational institutions at all levels are still struggling with their nondiscrimination obligations. The numbers of complaints against educational institutions alleging disability discrimination continue to rise, which suggests that individuals with disabilities continue to encounter significant barriers to education. According to the Department of Education Office for Civil Rights (OCR), the largest number of complaints have centered around the issues of accessibility, provision of auxiliary aids and services, and testing modifications.[18] Individuals with learning disabilities encounter the greatest barriers in accessing educational and testing opportunities as evidenced by the extensive documentation procedures required by state bar examiners, GED testing authorities, the types of complaints filed with OCR, and the case law involving educational institutions utilizing the ADA and Section 504 of the Rehabilitation Act of 1973. Documenting the existence and appropriate modification for an individual with a learning disability is difficult, as there is some controversy among experts concerning identifying and appropriately accommodating individuals with learning disabilities.

An individual's living situation and ability to access different forms of transportation and other societal benefits have tremendous impact on his ability to maintain employment as well. An early study of race discrimination demonstrated that equal employment outcomes cannot occur where there is unequal access to education and where individuals live in segregated communities (Loury 1981). People with disabilities have been subjected to pervasive discrimination in these arenas as well. Many people with disabilities are segregated by virtue of having severely limited housing options available to them. Many are institutionalized or live in de facto segregated housing because of the design of income support and state funded personal assistance programs as well as the lack of accessible, affordable housing. In addition, different groups of people with disabilities have had to fight battles with towns and cities over zoning ordinances that restrict their freedom to live in the community.

Other factors that impede progression in the workplace relate to the status of people with disabilities. Employers mirror societal attitudes in their workplace decisions. Many people with disabilities have been denied access to other areas of society and thus enter the workplace without common experiences to share with coworkers. The different socialization of men and women has been shown to affect the status of women in the workforce (Taub 1980). Many persons with disabilities have traveled a distinctly different route to the workplace than the able-bodied white males who dominate the upper echelons of most corporations. Many may also be at a distinct disadvantage in trying to participate in activities extracurricular to the workplace, which may be a factor in employment success.

Some groups of individuals with disabilities who have discontinuity in their work lives may be tremendously impacted, as women have been, in pursuing employment opportunities which offer the greatest returns. Discontinuous workforce participation has been shown to have a chilling effect on women's progression in the workforce (Polachek 1975).

Insurance

Lack of freedom of choice and difficulty in obtaining health care coverage limit employment autonomy for people with disabilities. It impedes their ability to progress longitudinally and latitudinally in the workforce. No strong nondiscrimination mandate exists that is applicable to insurance practices. Discriminatory health insurance practices impact the ability of individuals who have chronic health care needs, or are perceived as having such, from accessing the full range of employment opportunities available to others. A number of studies have been conducted into the status of people with disabilities in accessing health care, although we do not yet have complete understanding of the needs of the full range of people with disabilities. Acquiring more data on their status in accessing health care is a significant priority.

Keeping in mind the fragmented nature of these studies, one can still gather some valuable insights. It is clear that employment choices are tremendously impacted by health care concerns. In evaluating the results from existing studies, it is important to note the different variables which may have impacted the results of the studies. For example, disability and successful outcomes may have been defined differently in every study (Aday 1993).

A 1988 study concluded that there were 35.3 million Americans who were limited in a major life activity because of a health condition.[19] Thirty-four million Americans under the age of 65 have chronic medical conditions. Of the working-age population of individuals with disabilities with activity-limiting disabilities, one study found 15.6 percent had no health insurance (National Council on Disability 1993). Another study estimates that figure to be between

31 and 37 million and projects that millions more have inadequate insurance. An admittedly informal survey conducted by the Independent Living Research Utilization Program (1993) indicates that our current health care system is not working for individuals with disabilities. Twenty-six percent of the individuals who responded to the survey indicated they had been denied health insurance coverage, and 16 percent reported they had their insurance canceled.

It is important to understand the limitations of health care programs available to people with disabilities. Medicaid is a major source of health care coverage for individuals with disabilities.[20] A number of individuals with disabilities are forced to choose unemployment to retain Medicaid because it doesn't "follow" them into the workplace. Individuals with disabilities in the workplace may choose to remain in jobs which offer little upward mobility in order to retain access to health insurance. The experience of an identified group of individuals with disabilities, persons with HIV, provides a compelling portrait of what happens in our current system when someone develops a condition that requires significant medical care (Isbell 1993). Given the current state of our health care system, people who develop HIV travel a predictable route to inadequate health care and poverty. More than one-quarter of all individuals with HIV do not have any form of health coverage. People with HIV generally do not qualify for Medicaid until they have AIDS. Individuals with HIV also experience discrimination in accessing private insurance, as coverage for AIDS is often limited or nonexistent due to arbitrarily placed caps on coverage[21] and preexisting condition clauses.

Employer-provided benefit plans are governed either by state regulations or by the Employment Retirement Income Security Act (ERISA), depending on whether the plan is self-funded or purchased from an outside carrier. Self-funded plans are governed by ERISA, which does not prohibit disability-based discrimination. Under ERISA, employers may modify or terminate terms of employer-provided health plans. The act places few restrictions on employers. The only discriminatory actions prohibited are those motivated by a desire to retaliate against employees asserting rights under plans or any action that interferes with existing rights.

Section 501(c) of Title V of the ADA[22] states that the ADA should not be used to disrupt current, accepted insurance practices. Read together with the act's legislative history, it is clear that the ADA does not contain a strong, nondiscrimination mandate applicable to insurance practices.[23] The extent of an employer's obligation to assure any insurance it provides complies with the ADA's requirements is unclear and has been the subject of some litigation.

There is no doubt employers must provide insurance to their employees with disabilities as they do to others, however, it is not clear how extensive an inquiry must be made by the employer to assure the plan complies with the ADA. How many employers are qualified to assess the validity of risk classifications utilized by its insurer? The Disability Policy Panel recognized the importance of guaranteeing necessary health care, "independent of work, disability, health, or cash benefit status [and that this] would be a significant gain in . . . [e]nabling persons with disabilities to maximize their independence by remaining in or returning to the paid work force as well as participating in other productive activities" (*Preliminary Status Report*).

Understanding of the Law

One cannot underestimate the power of employer and societal perceptions of a law. The perception that those working with an accommodation are not truly "competing" like everyone else can lead to presumptions of incompetence: "the perceived suspension of ordinary and expected selection decision criteria provides impetus for the inference of incompetence" (Heilman, Block, and Lucas 1992, p. 536). To view providing the means of communicating with someone who is deaf in their language as a special privilege points up the tremendous barriers we are facing in battling this perception. In workplaces that have instituted affirmative action programs, a recent survey shows a significant number of employers believe these programs force them to promote and hire less qualified people.[24] Those that believe this are subscribing to a very narrow view of discrimination, focusing only on the issue of individual qualifications being suspect rather than stepping back and looking at how those qualifications are being assessed. What criterion is imposed during the review process? For instance, in *Price Waterhouse v. Hopkins*,[25] a well-known gender discrimination case, the plaintiff was told that if she wanted to be considered for partnership she should, "dress more femininely, wear make-up, have her hair styled, and wear jewelry." What sorts of employee "models" are being imposed on people with disabilities?

Societal perceptions of a law also impact its power to affect change. Some seem unwilling to understand the ADA as a civil rights law, instead attempting interpretation of the ADA as imposing a legal negligence theory and viewing an employer's nondiscrimination obligation as an imposition of liability on an employer who may not have discriminated intentionally (Karlan and Rutherglen 1996, p. 41). The ADA has also been the subject of negative debate and commentary. The media has spurred the negative views of the ADA through its persistence in focusing on a few isolated cases with sensational fact patterns. There is virtually no reporting of the inequities the ADA has remedied.

Implementation of civil rights legislation means that society will incur some costs, a fact which does not rest easily with many. Changing workplaces so they can accommodate the full range of individuals who exist in our society is necessary to assure nondiscrimination. Many costs will be short-term, as baseline changes are made. The costs of taking corrective action were recognized not only in the ADA's passage but also in cases eliminating gender discrimination.[26]

The perception of employers and individuals with disabilities regarding the government's commitment to enforcement is also an important factor in assessing workplace barriers. Can an employee with a disability be assured of accessing the protection of the law? Do employers perceive the law as one that is actively enforced? The government has the power to adjust the fulcrum. Does it appear that the government, through the ADA, is completely committed to ending workplace discrimination against people with disabilities?

Placing the Glass–Ceiling Issues of People with Disabilities on the Agenda

In addressing glass-ceiling issues for people with disabilities, perhaps the first thing that must be done is to acknowledge its existence and assure that discrimination against people with disabilities is recognized and placed on the same "platform of importance" that discrimination against other groups is. The Fourteenth Amendment to the Constitution includes the "equal protection" clause that is used to assure that all citizens are accorded equal protection of law. In analyzing whether or not a particular law violates the Fourteenth Amendment, a court looks at whether the group in question is part of a "suspect" class. Those who have been subjected historically to "invidious discrimination" receive "suspect class protection," meaning that "strict scrutiny" will be applied to any law or practice. The law in question will be found unconstitutional unless it serves a "compelling" state interest.

To date, race, national origin, and alienage have been granted suspect classification. Gender has been granted "quasi-suspect" classification which requires "heightened scrutiny."[27] The Supreme Court has yet to grant people with disabilities classification in either of these categories. In *City of Cleburne v.*

Cleburne Living Center[28] individuals with mental retardation were not placed in either classification, so the legislation at issue was analyzed only in terms of whether it was "rationally related" to a legitimate state interest.

It is clear from the findings Congress listed in the introductory section to the ADA that there was an intent to give people with disabilities suspect-class protection, as society has "tended to isolate and segregate individuals with disabilities, and, despite some improvements, such forms of discrimination against individuals with disabilities continue to be a serious and pervasive social problem . . . individuals with disabilities encounter many forms of discrimination, including outright intentional exclusion, architectural, transportation, and communication barriers,"[29] yet courts still have not accorded people with disabilities suspect-class protection.

People with disabilities are not included under the protections of the Equal Pay Act. The Equal Pay Act prohibits discrimination based on sex that results in unequal pay for equal work. Even if persons with disabilities were included in its protections, there could be problems in its application. The Act guarantees equal pay for similar work, which is defined as work that requires "equal skill, effort and responsibility." In assessing whether or not a job entails equal effort, an employer is supposed to weigh the amount of effort expended in performing the job.[30] Comparing jobs in terms of similar working conditions could prove problematic when jobs are being carried out with accommodations. At this time, another piece of wage discrimination legislation called the Fair Pay Act is being proposed. Race and national origin have been included as protected classes. People with disabilities are not mentioned.

The study we mentioned at the beginning of this chapter, conducted by Braddock and Bachelder, is one of a number of studies conducted under the auspices of the Glass-Ceiling Commission. However, that particular study is rarely mentioned in most of the literature that summarizes and synthesizes the outcomes of the different studies. Most references made to groups mention only women and minorities (Glass-Ceiling Commission 1995). In most of the commentary generated by the commission's work, again only women and minorities are referenced (Lukey 1996).

The issues of individuals with disabilities need to be placed on a par with those of other groups. Early on, the addition of women to the civil rights agenda was viewed by some in the minority community as a threat to their pursuit of racial justice. Although women's issues were viewed as important, they were not accorded as high a priority as those seeking racial justice (Bergmann 1985). Other groups may distance themselves from the disability rights movement because they are not immune from the influences that make them believe this is a "flawed" group and that association with this "less than able" community dilutes their cause. They may feel threatened by one more group demanding access to limited resources which they perceive as diminishing their share of the "pie."

Many in our society have no sense of the history of people with disabilities. In studies of racism, note has been made about the lack of inclusion of African-Americans in mainstream historical texts, translating into a general lack of knowledge of their culture or history. This contributes to the general lack of societal understanding and acceptance (Ashmore and Del Boca 1976, p. 98). Not only is there a distinct absence of people with disabilities in mainstream historical texts, but very few works exist which focus specifically on people with disabilities. In *Culture and Disability,* Karen Hirsch (1995) notes the lack of historical scholarship on disability in comparison to the number of studies on the history of African-Americans and women which impacted the civil rights movements for these groups. The lack of references and scholarship on disability in history further diminishes its importance to other groups: if it hasn't been documented how can its existence be recognized? This recognition is extremely important given studies that suggest that people with disabilities encounter more workplace discrimination than any other group (Johnson 1986).

People with disabilities, women, and minorities face some of the same types of barriers in the workplace, and membership in these groups is not mutually exclusive. We need to identify our common issues and understand that by coalescing we will have a better chance of making needed changes.

Conclusion

The glass ceiling that impedes the progress of people with disabilities in the workplace has been erected through decades of discrimination. As we contemplate this barrier, it is important that we understand that a recently implemented civil rights law cannot immediately tear down all barriers nor address all the factors that contribute to discrimination. We cannot forget how long our system has perpetuated this discrimination, how institutionalized it has become in all facets of our society. The ADA cannot address all the subtle forms of discrimination that affect the progress of people with disabilities in the workplace. Corporations need to scrutinize the factors or criteria they employ in assessing employee qualifications for advancement to expose those which impact people with disabilities in a different manner. It is far too soon to assess the ADA's impact, nor are all of its benefits subject to measurement. In our society we want quick results and outcome measures susceptible to accepted means of quantification. We find it easy to subscribe to the concept of civil rights in the abstract but shy away from societal commitment to real-world application (Yankelovich 1994).

The success of the ADA should be assessed in a number of different ways. We cannot ignore the economic costs which have been documented because, like other groups, we must "sell" the concept to the country. Baldwin noted losses of 27 billion due to employment discrimination and 10 billion attributable to wage discrimination (Baldwin, this volume). We must redefine how we quantify and assess the costs of discrimination versus compliance. Any assessment of the costs associated with ADA implementation should be compared with the societal cost of discrimination. Some of these costs are directly employment-related—discrimination diminishes the labor pool which can result in wage inflation, thus increasing the costs of goods and services. In addition, the costs to employers of having access to an arguably noncompetitive labor pool because it does not include all potentially qualified applicants should be included. Maintaining workforce traditions, the status quo, inhibits competition for jobs, as only those that can fit into the traditional design are allowed to compete. One can only guess how this affects the quality of the labor pool. Other costs of employment discrimination have more far-reaching implications for our society as a whole—the tremendous and ever-increasing costs of income replacement and disability benefit programs. Further costs are incurred as a result of the stratification of communities and the strain placed on family structures which have to bear the full weight of discrimination. As with some costs associated with gender discrimination, these cannot be quantified economically. Discrimination against women in the workplace has forced many women, in effect, to allow their jobs to dictate the timing and terms of their childbearing and child care. How do we quantify these costs? What about the costs to a family where one of its members has a disability? These should be weighed together with the benefits of having a truly competitive labor pool where employment options are not limited by gender, race, disability, age, or ethnic background.

Notes

1. Pub. L. No. 101–336, 104 Stat. 327 (1990).

2. For example, the Individuals with Disabilities Education Act (20 U.S.C. No. 1401 et seq.) and the Fair Housing Act (42 U.S.C. No. 3601 et seq.).

3. *Boyd v. Ozark Air Lines.*

4. Louis Harris and Associates, The ICD Survey of Disabled Americans: Bringing Disabled Americans into the Mainstream (1986).

5. 143 f.3d 1228 (9th Cir. 1998), 22 MPDLR 459, cert. granted, 1999 WL 5332 (Jan. 8, 1999).

6. (10th Cir. Mar. 11, 1998), 22 MPDLR 335, cert. granted, 1999 WL 5329 (Jan. 8, 1999).

7. 130 F.3d 893 (10th Cir. 1997) 22 MPDLR 53, cert. granted, 1999 WL 5326 (Jan. 8, 1998).

8. *Brennan v. Stewart,* 834 F.2d 1248 at 1262 (5th Cir. 1988).

9. In a significant number of the cases, the theory of judicial estoppel has been used to bar claims. "Under this doctrine, a party is bound by his judicial declarations and may not contradict them in a subsequent proceeding involving the same issues and parties. A party who by his pleadings, statements, or contentions, under oath, has assumed a particular position in a judicial proceeding is estopped to assume an inconsistent position in a subsequent action." *Black's Law Dictionary* 441 (5th ed. 1983).

10. In many of these cases the theory of judicial estoppel is being used to bar claims. *McNemar v. The Disney Store, Inc.,* 91 F.3d 610, 616–19 (3d Cir. 1996); *Kennedy v. Applause, Inc.,* 90 F.3d 1477, 1480B82 (9th Cir. 1996); *Baker v. ASARCO* (D. Ariz. 1995) 7 NDLR 395. The court found statements made in a disability application (under penalty of perjury) that individual's disability prevented him from doing his job proved conclusively that he was not otherwise qualified. *Kennedy v. Applause,* WL 426853 (9th Cir. 1996); *Smith v. Midland Brake, Inc.,* 911 F.Supp. 1351 (D. Kan. 1995), 7 NDLR 268. Plaintiff was not allowed to proceed on his ADA claim because the SSA had accepted his argument that he was totally disabled. *Nguyen v. IBP, Inc.,* 905 F. Supp. 1471 (D. Kan. 1994), 7 NDLR 214, judicial estoppel applied to an employee that had certified he was totally disabled in SSA proceedings. In *Bennett v. United Parcel Service,* 5 A.D. Cas. (BNA) 260 (S.D. Tex. 1995), an individual receiving SSDI benefits was estopped from pursuing an employment claim because the receipt of benefits was deemed to be an admission that the individual was not qualified to perform the job.

11. 120 F.3d 513 (5th Cir. 1997).

12. 29 U.S.C. § 721(a)(8).

13. 29 U.S.C. § 723(a).

14. *Matter of Polkabla v. Commission for Blind and Visually Handicapped of New York, State Department of Social Services,* 183 A.D.2d 575, 576, quoting S.Rep. No. 388, 99th Cong., 2d Sess. 5 (1986). See also *Schornstein v. New Jersey Division of Vocational Rehabilitation Services,* 519 F. Supp. 773 (D. N.J. 1981), aff'd., 688 F.2d 824 (3d Cir. 1982), a blanket policy which denied interpreter service to every deaf college student was in contravention of the act's requirement of providing individualized programs; *Scott v. Parham,* 422 F. Supp. 111 (D. Ga. 1976), a state guideline which provided financial support only to those individuals receiving vocational rehabilitation who lived inde-

pendently was unreasonable due to its failure to address the particular needs of each individual; *Marshall v. Switzer*, No. 92-CV-747 (FJS) (DNH) (N.D. N.Y. 1995), the act provides a framework within which states design and implement plans to provide individuals with vocational services in order to enable them to obtain "gainful employment to the extent of their capabilities. . . . The primary goal of the Rehabilitation Act is to enable states to provide rehabilitation services tailored to each individual client's needs"; *Romano v. Office of Vocational and Educational Services for Individuals with Disabilities*, 636 N.Y.S.2d 179 (1996), 7 NDLR 359, program not required "to sponsor every possible credential the individual desired. The advanced degree was not required to achieve the goal of social work. . . . The plaintiff wanted a master's degree to maximize her employment potential"; *Brooks v. Office of Vocational Rehabilitation (OVR)*, No. 1547, C.D. 1995, 8 NDLR 280, "It would be unreasonable and impractical to require the 'highest level of education achievable' be granted in every case of providing an individual with rehabilitation services."

15. 442 U.S. 397 (1979) at 410–12.

16. 469 U.S. 287 (1985).

17. "Perhaps an open-ended responsibility to enable all workers to enjoy equal education opportunities by taking account of the particular way in which their membership in a protected class has impaired their full participation in the economy would do more to end the continuing effects of past discrimination than the current combination of broad negative prohibitions and bureaucratic class-wide preferences" (Karlan and Rutherglen 1996, p. 41).

18. 42 U.S.C. § 12111(9).

19. *Anzalone v. Allstate Insurance Company*, 1995 U.S. District Lexus 588 (E.D. La. 1995).

20. 29 U.S.C. § 206(d).

21. *Hodgson v. Brookhaven General Hospital*, 436 F. 2d 719 (5th Cir. 1970).

22. 42 U.S.C. § 12112 (sec. 102(b)(2)). This provision is supported by language in the House Committee on Education and Labor Committee report which references the employment regulations for Section 504 of the Rehabilitation Act, 45 C.F.R. 8.11, which state obligations of a covered entity, a recipient of federal financial assistance, do not change because of an "inconsistent term of any collective bargaining agreement to which it is a party."

23. *National Disability Law Reporter* 7 (14): 4.

24. Sara Watson, A Reality Ignored: Health Reform and People with Disabilities, *Journal of American Health Policy* (Mar./Apr. 1993): 45–54.

25. Lambda at iii, "This is due to Medicaid eligibility rules. Even when individuals are able to access Medicaid, the treatment available is minimal at best."

26. These limitations on coverage of certain types of impairments have been challenged under the ADA. Also at issue in these cases has been the applicability of the ADA to the "contents" of insurance policies. *Carparts Distribution Center v. Automotive Wholesalers*, 37 F.3d 12 (1st Cir. 1994), provision of insurance was covered by Title III;

Doe v. Mutual of Omaha Ins. Co., 999 F. Supp. 1188 (N.D. Ill. 1998), "insurer's imposition of the caps violated Title III of the ADA."

27. 42 U.S.C. § 12201, 501(c). This provision states no provision in the act shall be construed to prohibit or restrict:

> (1) an insurer, hospital or medical service company, health maintenance organization, or any agent, or entity that administers benefit plans, or similar organizations from underwriting risks, classifying risks, or administering such risks that are based on or not inconsistent with State law; or (2) a person or organization covered by this Act from establishing, sponsoring, observing, or administering the terms of a bona fide benefit plan that are based on underwriting risks, classifying risks, or administering risks that are based on or not inconsistent with State law; or (3) a person or organization covered by this Act from establishing, sponsoring, observing or administering the terms of a bona fide benefit plan that is not subject to State laws that regulate insurance.
>
> Paragraphs (1), (2), and (3) shall not be used as subterfuge to evade the purposes of title[s] I and III.

28. U.S. Congress, House Committee on Education and Labor, The Americans with Disabilities Act of 1990, 101st Cong., 2d Sess., 15 May 1990, H.Rept. 101-485, pt. 2:136-37. The report noted the possible construction of the nondiscrimination language contained in Titles I, II, and III as they apply to insurance and added Section 501(c) to clarify this, the Act, would not disrupt the current insurance underwriting practices or the "current regulatory structure for self-insured employers or of the insurance industry in sales, underwriting pricing, administrative and other services, claims, and similar insurance-related activities based on classification of risks." However, the committee report does note insurers may not "refuse to insure, or refuse to continue to insure, or limit the amount, extent, or kind of coverage solely because of a physical or mental impairment, except where the refusal, limitation, or rate differential is based on sound actuarial principles or is related to actual or reasonably anticipated experience." The report also states risk classifications must be valid and not based on stereotypical perceptions of the costs of certain disabilities.

29. The study was conducted by Yankelovich Partners, the Public Broadcasting Systems (PBS) for the *Nightly Business Report*. This same survey indicates the attitudes of the employers surveyed vary greatly depending on the size of the company involved. A majority of large company employers (59 percent) favored affirmative action versus only 35 percent of small employers. Forty-seven percent of employers in large companies indicated a desire to eliminate affirmative action while 68 percent of small to medium size employers favored elimination of these programs.

30. 490 U.S. 228 at 235 (1989).

31. *UAW v. Johnson Controls, Inc.*, 111 S. Ct. 1196 (1991).

32. *Mississippi University for Women v. Hogan*, 458 U.S. 718, 733 (1982).

33. 473 U.S. 432, 440 (1985).

34. *More v. Farrier,* 984 F.2d, 269, 271 (8th Cir.), cert. denied, 144 S.Ct. 74 (1993); *Doe v. City of Chicago,* 1994 WL 792675, at 11 (N.D. Ill. Nov. 16, 1994).

Annotated References

Aday, Lu Ann. 1993. *At Risk in America: The Health and Health Care Needs of Vulnerable Populations in the United States.* Aday identifies individuals with chronic mental and physical conditions in her definition of "vulnerable" populations. "As with the system of providing and paying for services for the vulnerable, the conduct of research in this area is often categoric, fragmented, and not linked to other relevant bodies of research, and it fails to identify the issues that cut across different professional or service delivery domains" (p. 236). In citing the need for further research, the author summarizes the major difficulties with the data from the studies available:
- ambiguity in the definitions of the population;
- variability in the quality or completeness of information available on the population across data sources;
- changes in the definitions of the population or the availability of information over time;
- lack of demographic identifiers or details (i.e., race/ethnicity) for the comparison of subgroups within the population.

Ashmore and Del Boca. 1976. Psychological Approaches to Understanding Intergroup Conflicts. In *Towards the Elimination of Racism,* ed. Phyllis A. Katz. New York: Pergamon Press.

Behman. 1976. The Affirmative Action Position. *Labor Law Journal* 27 (8).

Bergmann. 1985. Is There a Conflict between Racial Justice and Women's Liberation? *Rutgers L. Rev.* 37 (4): 805.

Boyd v. Ozark Airlines, Inc., 419 F. Supp. 1061 (E.D. Mo. 1976), aff'd, 568 F.2d 50 (3rd Cir. 1977).

Braddock, David, and Lynn Bachelder. 1994. *The Glass Ceiling and Persons with Disabilities.* Public Policy Monograph Series, no. 56. This comprehensive report, initially prepared for the Glass-Ceiling Commission, U.S. Department of Labor, identifies and provides a comprehensive review of the barriers that people with disabilities face in the workforce.

Bowles, Gordon, and Weisskopf. 1983. *Hearts and Minds: A Social Model of Productivity Growth.* 2 Brookings Papers on Economic Activity.

Burgdorf, Robert, and Burgdorf. A History of Unequal Treatment: The Qualifications of Handicapped Persons as a "Suspect Class" under the Equal Protection Clause. *Santa Clara L. Rev.* 15:857–58.

Compton, C. 1995. Status of Deaf Employees in the Federal Government. *Volta Review* 95.

Daniels, N. 1997. Mental Disabilities, Equal Opportunity, and the ADA. In *Mental Disorder, Work Disability and the Law,* ed. Richard J. Bonnie and John Monahan. Chicago: University of Chicago Press.

DeJong. 1979. Independent Living: From Social Movement to Analytical Paradigm. *Arch. Phys. Med. Rehabil.* 60:435–46.

Dominguez. 1991. The Glass Ceiling and Workforce 2000. *Labor Law Journal* (Nov.).

Drimmer, Jonathan. 1993. Cripples, Overcomers, and Civil Rights: Tracing the Evolution of Federal Legislation and Social Policy for People with Disabilities. *UCLA L. Rev.* 40:1275, 1341–1408.

Dupre v. Harris County Hospital Dist., 13 NDLR & 150, No. H-96-3280 (S.D. 1998).

Ellison v. Software Spectrum, Inc., 85 F.3d 187 (5th Cir. 1996), 8 NDLR & 109. Although the radiation treatment made Ms. Ellison nauseated and tired and caused an allergic reaction to the radiation, the court found that her history of breast cancer was not a disability.

Ennis v. National Association of Business and Educational Radio, Inc. 53 F.3d 55, 58 (3rd Cir. 1995).

Fuqua, D., M. Rathbun, and E. M. Gade. 1983. A Comparison of Employer Attitudes toward the Worker Problems of Eight Types of Disabled Workers. *Journal of Applied Rehabilitation Counseling* 15 (1) (Spring).

Gerber, P. J. 1992. At First Glance: Employment for People with Learning Disabilities at the Beginning of the Americans with Disabilities Act. *Learning Disabilities Quarterly* 15.

Graham, Hugh Davis. 1990. *The Civil Rights Era: Origins and Development of National Policy 1960–1972.* New York: Oxford University Press.

Glass-Ceiling Commission. 1995. *A Solid Investment: Making Full Use of the Nation's Human Capital.* Final Report of the Glass-Ceiling Commission.

Hahn, Harlan. 1993. The Political Implications of Disability Definitions and Data. *Journal of Policy Studies* 4:41.

Heilman, M. E., C. J. Block, and J. A. Lucas. 1992. Presumed Incompetent? Stigmatization and Affirmative Action Efforts. *Journal of Applied Psychology* 77 (4): 536.

Henderson, C. 1987. Legality and Empathy. *Mich. L. Rev.* 85:1574.

Hirsch, Karen. 1995. Culture and Disability: The Role of Oral History. *Journal of the Oral History Association* 22 (1) (Summer).

The Independent Living Research Utilization Program (ILRU) *Insights.* 1993. Vol. 11, no. 5 (Sept.–Oct.). The survey conducted was part of the Robert Wood Johnson funded program, "Improving Service Systems for People with Disabilities." It was intended to elicit data on the health care coverage and concerns of individuals with disabilities connected to independent living centers. Survey forms were completed by independent living staff members, consumers, and center board members. Completion of the twelve-page, forty-nine-item survey was voluntary and 750 individuals responded. No self-identification was required. Survey results continue to be compiled and analyzed, but several preliminary findings have been released.

Following are some of the results: (1) Of those who had some kind of insurance, 27 percent had Medicare; 26 percent had Medicaid; 25 percent had employer-provided insurance; 16 percent had personal health insurance; 7 percent had Social Security Disability Insurance (SSDI); more than 3 percent had veterans' or military health care benefits. Total exceeds 100 percent as some individuals in the survey had coverage from more than one source. (2) Services covered by health insurance: 47 percent reported coverage for preventative services (i.e., mammography); 55 percent had coverage for health maintenance services (i.e., physical therapy, periodic examinations); 61 percent reported coverage for routine health problems and illness care; 64 percent reported coverage for acute care services; 39 percent had coverage for mental health services. (3) Impact of health coverage on survey respondents: 26 percent reported having been denied health insurance coverage; 16 percent reported having had their insurance canceled; 21 percent said they chose not to work to stay eligible for public health insurance; 35 percent reported they were afraid to change jobs because of limitations in health care coverage imposed by a new employer (i.e., no preexisting condition coverage); 24 percent reported they had been denied health services because of lack of insurance coverage; 46 percent said they had to forgo purchasing things they needed because of the necessity of paying for health care services; 21 percent reported developing disability-related problems because of inadequate or no health care; 16 percent said they experienced additional functional loss because of inadequate or no coverage; 23 percent reported being limited in working and other recreational activities because of inadequate or no health care. In addition, almost 25 percent of the respondents reported preexisting conditions were excluded in their coverage. Of those who indicated their policies did not contain exclusions, many noted waiting periods for preexisting condition coverage.

Isbell. 1993. *Health Care Reform: Lessons from the HIV Epidemic.* Lambda Legal Defense and Education Fund, Inc. (Mar.).

Johnson. 1986. The Rehabilitation Act and Discrimination against Handicapped Workers: Does the Cure Fit the Disease? In *Disability and the Labor Market*, ed. Monroe Berkowitz and Anne Hill. 242 at 245.

Karlan and Rutherglen. 1996. Disabilities, Discrimination, and Reasonable Accommodation. *Duke Law Journal* 6 (1): 3. The authors suggest adopting a reasonable accommodation approach for other groups should it be successful for addressing disability-based discrimination.

Kavka. 1992. Disability and the Right to Work. *Social Philosophy and Policy* 9 (1).

Loury. 1981. Is Equal Opportunity Enough? *J. Am. Econ. Assoc.* 71:122.

Lukey. 1996. The Multi-Layered Glass Ceiling: Why Does It Exist, and What Can We Do about It? *Maine Bar Journal* (July): 214–19.

Mancuso. 1990. Reasonable Accommodation for Workers with Psychiatric Disabilities. *Psychosocial Rehabilitation Journal* 14.

Martinson v. Kinney Shoe Corp. (3rd Cir. 1997).

McDonnell Douglas Corp. v. Green, 411 U.S. 792 (1973).

National Council on Disability. 1993. Sharing the Risk and Ensuring Independence: A Disability Perspective on Access to Health Insurance and Health-Related Services; A Report to the President and the Congress of the United States. Mar. 4. Of the general population, the Employee Benefit Research Institute estimates that 37 million Americans are uninsured (Fasser, p. 26).

Polachek. 1975. Discontinuous Labor Force Participation and Its Effects on Women's Market Earnings. In *Sex, Discrimination, and the Division of Labor,* ed. Cynthia B. Lloyd. New York: Columbia University Press.

Rethinking Disability Policy: The Role of Income, Health Care, Rehabilitation, and Related Services in Fostering Independence. 1994. *Social Security Bulletin* 57 (2): 59. "In its remaining work, the Panel is focusing on specific issues concerning disability policy, which is divided into nine necessarily overlapping categories:
- The definition of disability for DI and SSI eligibility, and its assessment in functional, medical, and vocational terms;
- Work and other incentives and disincentives for DI and SSI applicants and beneficiaries;
- Prospects for vocational rehabilitation and job placement for persons with significant disabilities;
- The coordination of health care and cash benefits for persons with disabilities;
- Provisions for personal assistance services and assistive devices for persons with significant functional limitations;
- The coordination of short-term and long-term disability income protection;
- Implementing and administering cash benefits and services for persons with disabilities;
- The relationship of disability and retirement policy, particularly in light of scheduled increases in the Social Security normal retirement age; and
- The special concerns of subgroups of persons with disabilities, including children and persons with severe mental illness.

In each area, we propose to develop what we believe to be the appropriate objectives of disability policy, to analyze the degree to which current public and private programs and processes accomplish those objectives, and to make recommendations for policy and administration that are consistent with the objectives as defined. As our work proceeds, we may decide that some of these categories require further disaggregation or that others are so interconnected that separate recommendations on those topics are unnecessary or unwarranted."

SWDBTAC, Southwest Disability and Business Technical Assistance Center, based at ILRU (Independent Living Research Utilization). Funded by a grant from the National Institute on Disability and Rehabilitation Research, the center is one of ten centers across the country providing training and technical assistance on the

ADA. The center fields, on average, 1,000 calls per month; the information gathered is based on interviews of personnel providing technical assistance to callers.

Taub, Nadine. 1980. Keeping Women in Their Place: Stereotyping Per Se as a Form of Employment Discrimination, 21 *B.C. L. Rev.* 345:350.

Taylor, L. 1985. The Crucial Role of Education in Achieving the Civil Rights Goals of the 1980's. *Rutgers L. Rev.* 4:961–75.

Tucker, Bonnie. 1989. Section 504 of the Rehabilitation Act after Ten Years of Enforcement: The Past and the Future. *U. Ill. L. Rev.* 4:845.

Vande Zande v. State of Wisconsin Department of Administration. 44 F.3d 538, 63cUSLW 2459 (1995).

West, Jane, ed. 1991. *The Social Policy of the Act in the Americans with Disabilities Act: From Policy to Practice.* New York: Milbank Memorial Fund. Fifty percent of adults with disabilities had household incomes of $15,000 or less, while only 25 percent of persons without disabilities had household incomes in this bracket.

Yankelovich. 1994. *How Changes in the Economy Are Reshaping American Values in Public Policy,* ed. H. J. Aaron, T. E. Mann, and T. Taylor. Washington, D.C.: Brookings.

Part Two
Implementing ADA Title I Law

Chapter IV

The Nonevolution of Enforcement under the ADA

Discharge Cases and the Hiring Problem

Steven L. Willborn

Enforcement under a newly enacted antidiscrimination law has an expected evolution. In the early years, members of the protected group use the law to gain entry into good jobs from which they historically had been excluded. As a result, in those early years, one would expect to see mostly cases alleging hiring discrimination. Eventually, however, obvious barriers to entry would be reduced and members of the protected group would begin to use the law to protect their status in those good jobs. As a result, over time one would expect to see cases alleging improper discharges to outnumber hiring discrimination claims.

Under Title VII, this story has been told twice. Donohue and Siegelman found that hiring charges filed with the Equal Employment Opportunity Commission (EEOC) exceeded termination charges by 50 percent in 1966, but that the ratio had reversed dramatically by 1985 with termination cases outnumbering hiring cases by a ratio of 6 to 1 (1991, p. 1015). Similarly, Ayres and Siegelman found that court cases alleging disparate impact discrimination in hiring exceeded termination cases by about 3 to 1 from 1970 to 1985, but the ratio reversed in 1986 and, since 1990, has been about 3 to 1 the other way (1996, pp. 1494–95).

Enforcement under the American with Disabilities Act (ADA) has deviated substantially from the expected pattern. Hiring cases under the ADA have never exceeded discharge cases. Rather, over the short life of the ADA, the ratio of discharge to hiring cases has been about 10 to 1, a ratio that is substantially higher than for Title VII cases even though the ADA is about three decades younger and, hence, should be at an earlier stage in its evolution.

This chapter will begin by describing the pattern of enforcement under the ADA. This study examined ADA court cases that resulted in published opinions. As indicated above, that data revealed an unexpected enforcement pattern. Section II will then consider possible reasons for this unexpected pattern: why does the pattern for ADA enforcement differ from the pattern for Title VII? Section III will discuss why this unexpected pattern is a cause for concern. Finally, section IV will suggest possible responses.

I. The Pattern of Enforcement under the ADA

Enforcement under the ADA follows the Title VII procedure (ADA § 107). To pursue claims, individuals with disabilities must first file a charge of discrimination with the EEOC. The EEOC has authority to investigate claims, to make preliminary determinations, to attempt to settle claims, and to file lawsuits on behalf of charging parties, but it has no authority to adjudicate claims or order employers to take actions to eliminate discrimination. The latter authority resides in the courts.

This study examined all published opinions of the federal district courts involving ADA employment claims from the time the ADA first became effec-

Figure 1: ADA Employment Cases

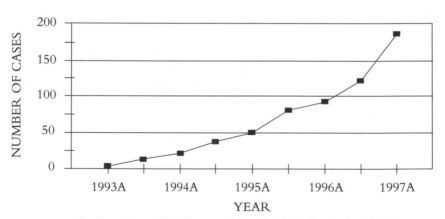

The data points are for half-year periods with *A* indicating the first half of the year.

tive on July 26, 1992, through June 30, 1997.[1] There were 605 opinions. Figure 1 plots the number of cases by semiannual period. The number of cases has been increasing every year. This was also the experience during the early years of Title VII (Donohue and Siegelman 1991, p. 986).

The cases were divided into three categories: hiring cases, discharge cases, and accommodation cases. Hiring cases were interpreted liberally; they include, for example, cases in which former employees were applying to be rehired (see *Thomas v. Mississippi State Dept. of Health* 1996; *Malek v. Martin Marietta Corp.* 1994). Discharge cases were also interpreted liberally to include any case in which the plaintiff was no longer employed by the defendant employer. Thus, the category included constructive discharge cases (see *Spillman v. Carter* 1996). The residual category was accommodation cases, those that were neither hiring cases nor discharge cases. The "accommodation cases" label is descriptive in that the cases generally involve current employees who were requesting some type of workplace accommodation, for example, the use of leave time (*Morton v. Haskell Co.* 1995; *Nelson v. Ryan* 1994). Obviously, however, many of the cases in the hiring and discharge categories also included requests for accommodations.

Figure 2 plots the hiring and discharge cases as a percentage of all ADA employment cases. The figure demonstrates a consistent and large gap between the percentage of hiring and discharge cases. Over the entire period, there were about ten discharge cases for every hiring case (408 discharge cases versus 39 hiring cases).

Figure 2 reports on data compiled from published legal opinions. This can lead to bias since the decision to write an opinion is not random, nor is the decision to publish a decision once written (Songer 1990; Siegelman and Donohue 1990). For several reasons, however, it is unlikely that the data presented in figure 2 are misleading. First, nonrandom selection would lead to bias only if the selection criteria (whether to write and publish a decision) are correlated with the variables of interest (hiring versus discharge cases). There is no obvious reason to think that such a correlation exists in this case (Ayres and Siegelman 1996, p. 1496). Second, the ratio of discharge to hiring cases reported in figure 2 is supported by independent sources from earlier points in the claim process. Moss (this volume) provides data on charges filed with the EEOC and state fair employment practice agencies. Those charges also exhibit a high ratio of discharge to hiring cases. Third, as indicated, Ayres and Siegelman (1996) conducted a similar study of published legal opinions in disparate impact cases. The results of their study were consistent with another study that used data from *filed* cases (Donohue and Siegelman 1991). Although the data on

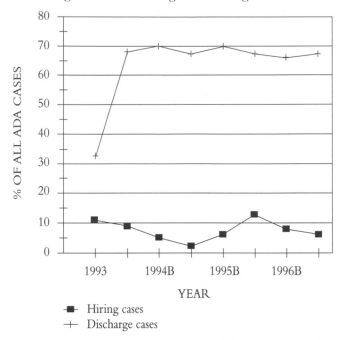

Figure 2: ADA Hiring and Discharge Cases

- ■ Hiring cases
- + Discharge cases

Because of small numbers, the cases for the two halves of 1993
have been combined. For all other years, the two data points are
for the first and second half of each year.

filed cases cannot be used to support the results of this study, the consistency
between the two Title VII studies indicates that relying on published legal
opinions does not lead to biased results for these purposes.

II. Why Does the Pattern of Enforcement under the ADA Differ from the Pattern under Title VII?

The ADA enforcement experience described in section I is dramatically different
from the experience under Title VII. Ayres and Siegelman, using essentially the
same technique as this study to compile their sample, found that disparate impact
hiring cases outnumbered discharge cases by about 3 to 1 until 1986. At that
point, discharge cases began to outnumber hiring cases and, since 1990, the ratio
in the other direction has been about 3 to 1 (1996, pp. 1494–95). Thus, during
the early years of Title VII, the discharge/hiring ratio was quite different and in

the opposite direction from the ratio during the early years of the ADA. Even during later years under Title VII, when the ratio was in the same direction as under the ADA, it has been about three times less severe. Why this difference?[2]

One possibility would be that hiring discrimination was less prevalent against individuals with disabilities when the ADA was enacted than it was against women and African-Americans when Title VII was enacted. Remember that the standard story for the switch in the ratio of discharge to hiring cases under Title VII is that protected groups under Title VII used the law first to gain entry to good jobs, and only later did they begin to use the law to protect their tenure in those jobs. If individuals with disabilities were already in good jobs when the ADA was enacted, the enforcement experience under the ADA may simply have begun at the second stage.

This possibility, however, seems highly implausible. The legislative history of the ADA provides strong evidence that individuals with disabilities were facing severe problems entering the workforce when the ADA was enacted, for example, that two-thirds of Americans with disabilities were not working at all and that only 23 percent of males with a disability were working full time (House Report 1990, p. 314). Similarly, Marjorie Baldwin's analysis (this volume) suggests that the hiring discrimination faced by individuals with disabilities at the time of the ADA's enactment was severe and, indeed, more severe than the wage discrimination faced by individuals with disabilities who had jobs.

Probable explanations for the difference in enforcement patterns between the ADA and Title VII fall into three interrelated categories. First, employers were more sophisticated about discrimination issues when the ADA was enacted. The early hiring cases under Title VII included many easy-to-win cases. Employers, for example, made explicitly discriminatory statements (see *Butta v. Anne Arundel Co.* 1979) or used hiring criteria that could easily be shown to have a disparate impact against a protected group (see *Griggs v. Duke Power Co.* 1971; *Albermarle Paper Co. v. Moody* 1975). These cases tended to be hiring cases because the attitude evidenced by the statements and the improper hiring criteria operated to exclude women and African-Americans from the workforce. Under Title VII, these kinds of cases diminished over time as employers either changed their hiring practices or learned to disguise them (Ayres and Siegelman 1996, p. 1492). When the ADA was enacted, with a two- to four-year lag between its enactment and the effective date of Title I, employers were able to call on their experience under Title VII to adjust (or hide) their practices and avoid the early period when hiring cases predominated.

Second, for several reasons, applicants under the ADA were in a weaker position than applicants under Title VII to bring suit. As already mentioned, applicants under the ADA were not presented with the same type of easy-to-win suits. When this happened to Title VII applicants, they began to mount statistics-based challenges to employer hiring practices (see *Hazelwood School District v. United States* 1977; see generally Paetzold and Willborn 1998). Statistics-based challenges to hiring practices, however, were not as appealing for ADA applicants. The courts tightened the standards for proving statistical cases during the late 1970s and 1980s, before the enactment of the ADA (see *New York City Transit Authority v. Beazer* 1979; *Wards Cove Packing Co. v. Atonio* 1989). In addition, while it was relatively easy for women or African-Americans to specify the protected and comparator groups for statistical analysis, that is considerably more difficult for the more diffuse group of individuals with disabilities.[3] Finally, applicants under the ADA were in a weaker position than Title VII applicants to bring suit because the same level of support from outside groups was not available. The National Association for the Advancement of Colored People (NAACP) and the National Organization for Women (NOW), among others, were available to assist Title VII applicants. While somewhat similar groups exist for those protected by the ADA, the groups tend to be more dispersed and less litigation-oriented.

Third, the difference in enforcement patterns may exist because current and discharged employees were *more* likely to sue under the ADA than under Title VII. Consider first the explicitly discriminatory employer. When Title VII was enacted, this type of employer was unlikely to have any women or African-Americans as employees. As a result, the only possible kind of Title VII suit was a hiring suit. But under the ADA, many categories of disabilities are "hidden." In addition, some employees who were not individuals with disabilities at the time of hire may have become such individuals during their work lives. Thus, when the ADA was enacted, this type of discriminatory employer, by definition the type most likely to violate the act, may already have employed individuals with disabilities and, hence, would have been subject to suit by a current or discharged employee.

Now consider the nondiscriminatory employer. Under Title VII, this employer would already have women and African-Americans in its workforce and would be treating them nondiscriminatorily. Since Title VII would merely require this type of employer to continue its nondiscriminatory practices, a Title VII suit by a current or discharged employee would be unlikely. Under the ADA, a nondiscriminatory employer would also have individuals with disabilities as employees. The ADA's conception of discrimination, however, may require an employer to do more than merely continue its prior nondiscriminatory practices. Before the ADA, for example, a nondiscriminatory employer may have employed an individual with disabilities so long as the employee paid for the cost of her own accommodations, for example, so long as a blind employee provided her own readers. After the ADA, the employer may be required by the reasonable accommodation requirement to provide readers out of its funds. Thus, under the ADA, even a "nondiscriminatory" employer may be subject to suit by an employee seeking to shift the cost of accommodations.[4] Stated more generally, a "nondiscriminatory" employer may be subject to an ADA lawsuit by a current or (if the dispute escalates) a discharged employee because of differences between the employer's prior understanding of nondiscrimination and the ADA's conception of it.

III. ADA Discharges and the Hiring Process

The pattern of enforcement under the ADA seems disconnected from one of the principal problems leading to its enactment. As indicated above, the legislative history of the ADA identified problems in obtaining employment as one of the major obstacles faced by individuals with disabilities (House Report 1990, p. 314). This finding has been confirmed by Baldwin (this volume). The pattern of enforcement, however, suggests that the act has been used little to address that problem. Instead of suits by applicants seeking fair access to the labor market, the ADA has been used very disproportionately by employees and former employees.

The issue posed by the pattern of enforcement under the ADA is more serious than one of mere underuse. The pattern of enforcement may actually aggravate the employment problem faced by individuals with disabilities. Two models of the hiring process suggest that the ADA's pattern of enforcement may actually cause employers to hire fewer individuals with disabilities than they would have if the ADA did not exist at all.

HIRING BY THE LITIGATION-CONSCIOUS EMPLOYER

Consider first an employer who is thinking of hiring an individual with a disability. If the employer hires the individual, there is obviously no possibility of a hiring discrimination suit and, hence, no possibility of ADA liability. On the other hand, if the employer fails to hire the individual, there is a possibility of a hiring discrimination suit and of ADA liability. Thus, at this level, the ADA increases the expected cost to the employer of failing to hire the individual. The employer's estimate of the expected cost would depend on a number of factors, such as the probability the individual would actually file suit, the probability the individual would win the suit, the costs of defending the suit, and the likely damages if the employer were found to have violated the ADA.

Viewed only at this level, then, the ADA would tend to increase the hiring of individuals with disabilities. The ADA does not affect the employer's estimate of costs if it hires the individual, but it increases the estimated costs if the employer fails to hire the individual. So, at the margin, the employer should hire more individuals with disabilities (or, stated more consistently with the example, fail to hire such individuals less often).

But even when hiring, the litigation-conscious employer is interested not only in ADA liability for *hiring* discrimination, but also in ADA liability for *firing* discrimination. For firing discrimination, the reverse set of incentives exists. If the employer never hires the individual, there is obviously no possibility of a firing discrimination suit and, hence, no possibility of that type of ADA liability. On the other hand, if the employer hires the individual, there is a possibility of a firing discrimination suit and of ADA liability. On this issue, the ADA increases the expected cost to the employer of *hiring* the individual with disabilities. As with hiring discrimination, the employer's expected cost from firing discrimination would depend on a number of factors, such as the probability the individual would later be fired, the probability the individual would bring suit, the probability the individual would win the suit, the costs of defending the suit, and the likely damages if the employer were found liable. But here, the employer anticipates no expected costs from firing discrimination if it never hires the individual, but does expect extra costs from firing discrimination if it hires. Consequently, liability for firing discrimination under the ADA *decreases* the likelihood that employers will hire individuals with disabilities.[5]

Because our litigation-conscious employer is concerned with the expected costs of both hiring and firing liability under the ADA, the key question is: what is the balance between those two types of expected costs at the hiring stage? Donohue and Siegelman estimated the balance under Title VII using a wide range of values for the factors that would influence expected cost (that is, factors such as the probability the individual would bring suit, the cost of defending the suit, damages if the suit were lost, etc.). They were estimating the balance under Title VII where they had found a ratio of discharge to hiring suits of 6 to 1. Their conclusion was that the 6-to-1 ratio produced a net *disincentive* to hire protected group members for every set of values. When they reestimated the balance using the same range of values for the relevant factors, but a 3-to-2 ratio with hiring cases predominating (a ratio they had found during the early years of Title VII), the act produced a net incentive to hire protected group members for every set of values (Donohue and Siegelman 1991, pp. 1024–28).

This suggests that the ADA is currently producing a net disincentive to hire individuals with disabilities. This study found a 10-to-1 ratio of discharge to hiring cases, a ratio significantly higher than the ratio under Title VII. Moreover, this ratio is likely to be an underestimate of the difference. Under Title VII, the discharge and hiring cases that are included in the ratio constitute virtually all of the caseload; only about 10 percent of Title VII cases are brought by current employees (Donohue and Siegelman 1991, p. 1031). Under the ADA, in contrast, a significantly higher proportion of cases is brought by current employees — about 26 percent of the cases in this study. For obvious reasons, these cases would be included with the discharge cases for our litigation-conscious employer making hiring decisions. If they are included, the ratio creating the disincentive to hire individuals with disabilities increases to more than 14 to 1.

The suggestion that the ADA provides a net disincentive to hire individuals with disabilities, obviously, should be interpreted cautiously. One shortcoming of the preceding analysis is that it relies heavily on a "litigation-conscious" employer. Employers are motivated by a variety of factors other than ADA litigation and those other factors may outweigh any net disincentive to hire individuals with disabilities. (On the other hand, the preliminary results by Scheid [this volume] indicate that employers, if anything, tend to overweight legal consequences.) An alternative model, however, which is not as dependent on litigation-consciousness, also suggests that the discharge-limiting aspects of the ADA may provide a net disincentive to hire individuals with disabilities.

PROBATIONARY HIRING

Employers operate with uncertainty when they hire employees. In particular, they are uncertain about the true productivity of prospective employees. Probationary hiring is a very common technique employers use to deal with this uncertainty (Holzer 1987; Groshen and Loh 1993). Employers hire employees temporarily, directly observe their productivity in the workforce, and then decide to retain or discharge the employees based on the new information.

Consider a very simplified and stylized version of the probationary hiring process.[6] An employer is presented with employees who have a true marginal productivity that the employer does not know. The employer makes its hiring decisions based on its best estimate of each employee's marginal productivity (MP^E) and a margin of error (e). Assume that e can take the same range of values in both directions from MP^E, is equally likely to be positive or negative, and will become known immediately upon hiring (but not before). In this simple world, the employer will obviously hire all employees for whom the wage (w) < MP^E – e. Even if the employer's estimate of marginal productivity erred on the wrong side, this employee will produce a profit for the employer. On the other side of the continuum, the employer will obviously refuse to hire employees for whom w > MP^E + e. Even if the employee meets the employer's best estimate, she will fail to produce a profit for the employer. But what about employees in the middle, those employees for whom the wage falls somewhere within the range provided by the employer's best estimate of marginal productivity surrounded by the margin of error (MP^E + e > w > MP^E – e)? Probationary employment provides a simple solution to this problem. The employer would hire all employees in the middle range, observe e upon hiring, and then retain or discharge employees depending on the observed e.

The ADA may interfere with the normal process of probationary employment. A large majority of ADA cases are discharge cases, so employers may worry about their ability to discharge probationary employees who fall within the protection of the ADA. What effect would this have on the employment of individuals with disabilities? Consider figure 3, which sets an individual with a disability above a wage line. The individual with a disability has an MP^E of 50 and an e of 10. The wage line illustrates an array of employers with jobs with wages ranging from 35 to 65.

In the absence of the ADA, the individual with a disability would be offered jobs by all employers with wages of less than 60. Of particular interest here, the individual would be offered jobs within the 51-to-60 wage range, even though that is above the individual's estimated marginal productivity,

Figure 3: Disabilities and the Wage Line

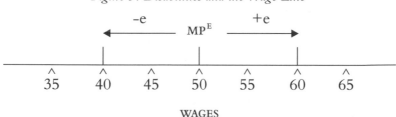

WAGES

because probationary employment permits the employer to reevaluate the employment decision after observing the individual's "true" marginal productivity. Thus, for example, an employer offering a job at the 55 wage level would be willing to hire the individual probationally, observe the individual's actual marginal productivity, and then make a decision to retain or discharge.

If, however, employers perceive the ADA as limiting their ability to discharge probationary employees, only employers with jobs with wages below 50 would be willing to offer jobs to the individual with disabilities. Since employers perceive that they cannot reevaluate later, they would hire based on their best prediction of *group* marginal productivity at the time of hire. Thus, an employer offering a job at the 55 level would not be willing to hire individuals like the one illustrated in figure 3, because, if it did, it would obtain (and, by assumption, be required to retain) employees with an *average* marginal productivity of 50, which would be insufficient.[7]

The imbalance of ADA discharge cases, then, may interfere with the probationary hiring process and, consequently, limit the range of jobs available to individuals with disabilities. The limitation would be especially problematic if, as seems plausible, employers provide a lower estimate of the marginal productivity of individuals with disabilities and a larger estimate of the margin of error.[8] Figure 4 illustrates that situation. The individual with disabilities (above the line) has an estimated marginal productivity of 45 and a margin of error of 15. The other applicant has an estimated marginal productivity of 50 and a margin of error of 10. With probationary hiring, employers at the very top of the wage range would be willing to hire both applicants. Without probationary hiring, the individual with disabilities would be offered jobs based on her estimated marginal productivity alone and, hence, be offered jobs only by employers with

Figure 4: Marginal Productivity and Margin of Error

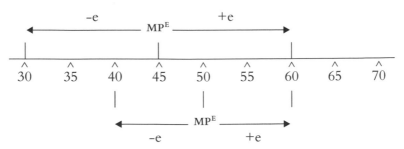

wages of 45 and below. The other applicant would be offered jobs by employers with wages up to 50. Indeed, if employers perceived that the limit on probationary hiring applied only to individuals with disabilities, the other applicant would still be offered jobs by employers with wages up to 60. Once again, this story suggests that the imbalance of discharge cases under the ADA may mean that the act not only fails to solve, but actually aggravates, the employment problems of individuals with disabilities.[9]

In sum, analysis based on both the litigation-conscious employer and on probationary employment suggests that the hiring/discharge imbalance in ADA cases may contribute to employment problems faced by individuals with disabilities. Both suggestions, however, must be interpreted cautiously for a number of reasons, for example, employer perceptions about the hiring/discharge ratio may differ from the results of this study, the highly simplifying assumptions made in the models of employer decision making may be misleading, or the effect of the ADA on employer decision making may be small relative to other factors at play. Further study must be conducted, especially empirical investigation, before firm conclusions can be reached.[10]

IV. Responses to the Pattern of Enforcement under the ADA

A complete analysis of possible responses to the pattern of enforcement under the ADA is beyond the scope of this paper. Nevertheless, the pattern suggests a problem and a brief review of possible responses would be appropriate.

Even if the ADA does not aggravate the employment problem of individuals with disabilities, the low proportion of hiring cases is problematic. Even though employment has been identified as one of the principal problems facing individuals with disabilities, the experience under the ADA is that the act has been used only sparingly to address it. For a number of reasons, discharged employees have greater incentives than frustrated applicants to file suit under the ADA.[11] This suggests several possible responses to the low number of hiring discrimination cases. First, to counterbalance the incentives of private litigants, the EEOC could focus its enforcement resources on hiring cases. It would certainly be appropriate for the principal *public* enforcement entity to skew its cases toward an area that may not be adequately enforced through the private litigation process. Second, public interest groups could also focus their enforcement resources on hiring cases. The NAACP has always been well known for pursuing a public agenda through its litigation program. Public interest groups interested in the welfare of individuals with disabilities could follow that model by focusing their efforts on hiring cases to address the otherwise underaddressed employment problem. Third, a variety of statutory amendments could be made to provide adequate incentives for possible victims of hiring discrimination to bring suit, such as enhanced damages or attorney's fees awards for plaintiffs who prevail in hiring (but not discharge) cases.

Notes

1. The sample was generated from the Westlaw federal district court database. The search request was "78I(B) & ADA "Americans with Disabilities Act" & [date restrictions]." Under West's Key Number System, 78I(B) captures all employment-related civil rights claims. "ADA" and "Americans with Disabilities Act" were used to segregate from that broader category those cases involving an ADA claim. The search was run separately for every six-month period from the effective date of Title I of the ADA through June 30, 1997.

2. A number of reasons might explain why there are more discharge than hiring cases under *both* Title VII and the ADA. For example, the endowment effect (Hovencamp 1991), rising wages over the life cycle (Brown 1989), and greater knowledge of potential comparators would all imply a higher proportion of discharge than hiring cases. The issue addressed in this section, however, is not that issue, but the issue of why there are more discharge cases under the ADA *relative to* Title VII.

3. Only one of the 605 cases in the sample was a class action, and that case did not involve statistical analysis (*Cramer v. Florida* 1995).

4. This example is based on *Nelson v. Thornburgh* (1983), a case in which blind employees, who had formerly paid for their own readers, were successful in requiring their employer to pay for them in the future.

5. This idea has been best explicated by Donohue and Siegelman (1991). It was first suggested by Posner (1987, p. 519).

6. This description of the probationary hiring process is a simplified version of the conceptualization provided by Ayres and Siegelman (1996, pp. 1498–1507).

7. This result is highly ironic. One of the oft-stated purposes of antidiscrimination laws, such as the ADA, is to limit stereotyping and statistical discrimination (*Price Waterhouse v. Hopkins* 1989; Donohue 1987, pp. 531–34). Probationary employment aligns well with that goal because it facilitates a very individualized evaluation of employees. This analysis suggests that the ADA may interfere with the probationary employment process and encourage employers to revert to a more group-based evaluation of applicants. If this is true, the ADA may perversely increase the extent of stereotyping and statistical discrimination.

8. Employers may provide a lower estimate of marginal productivity both because of the functional limitations required to fit within the category of individuals with

disabilities and because of the stigma associated with those limitations (Baynton, this volume). They may provide a larger estimate of the margin of error because of more limited experience with individuals with disabilities.

9. As this last example suggests, the consequences of any limitations on regimes of probationary employment are not limited to employment levels. To the extent the ADA imposes limits on probationary employment, the consequences may appear in different employment levels for individuals with disabilities, or they may appear in wage level differentials, or there may be some combination of employment and wage effects.

10. Preliminary empirical studies purport to show employment losses from the ADA that are consistent with the analysis of this paper (Acemoglu and Angrist 1998; DeLeire 1997). The studies, however, are by no means conclusive. (For a thoughtful critique of the studies, see Schwochau and Blanck 1999.) As a result, it is still premature to reach firm conclusions.

11. See note 2.

References

Acemoglu, Daron, and Joshua Angrist. 1998. *Consequences of Employment Protection? The Case of the Americans with Disabilities Act.* Cambridge, Mass.: National Bureau of Economic Research (Working Paper No. 6670).

Albemarle Paper Co. v. Moody. 422 U.S. 405 (1975).

Americans with Disabilities Act. 1994. 42 U.S.C. §§ 12101–12213.

Ayres, Ian, and Peter Siegelman. 1996. The Q-Word as Red Herring: Why Disparate Impact Liability Does Not Induce Hiring Quotas. *Texas L. Rev.* 74:1487–1526.

Brown, James N. 1989. Why Do Wages Increase with Tenure? On-the-Job Training and Life-cycle Wage Growth Observed within Firms. *American Economic Review* 79:971–91.

Butta v. Anne Arundel Co. 473 F. Supp. 83 (D. Md. 1979).

Cramer v. Florida. 885 F. Supp. 1545 (M.D. Fla. 1995).

DeLeire, Thomas. 1997. The Wage and Employment Effects of the Americans with Disabilities Act. Unpublished manuscript.

Donohue, John J., III. 1987. Further Thoughts on Employment Discrimination Legislation: A Reply to Judge Posner. *U. Pa. L. Rev.* 136:523–51.

Donohue, John J., III, and Peter Siegelman. 1991. The Changing Nature of Employment Discrimination Litigation. *Stanford L. Rev.* 44:983–1033.

Griggs v. Duke Power Co. 401 U.S. 424 (1971).

Groshen, Erica L., and Eng Seng Loh. 1993. What Do We Know about Probationary Periods? In *Industrial Relations Research Association Series: Proceedings of the Forty-fifth Annual Meeting,* ed. John F. Burton Jr., pp. 10–19. Madison, Wis.: Industrial Relations Research Association.

Hazelwood School District v. United States. 433 U.S. 299 (1977).

Holzer, Harry J. 1987. Hiring Procedures in the Firm: Their Economic Determinants and Outcomes. In *Human Resources and the Performance of the Firm,* ed. Morris M. Kleiner et al., pp. 243–74. Madison, Wis.: Industrial Relations Research Association.

House Report No. 101-485. 1990. *U.S. Code Congressional and Administrative News* 4, 267–565.

Hovenkamp, Herbert. 1991. Legal Policy and the Endowment Effect. *Journal of Legal Studies* 20:225–47.

Malek v. Martin Marietta Corp. 859 F. Supp. 458 (D. Kan. 1994).

Morton v. Haskell Co. 5 A.D. Cases 272 (M.D. Fla. 1995).

Nelson v. Ryan. 860 F. Supp. 76 (W.D.N.Y. 1994).

Nelson v. Thornburgh. 567 F. Supp. 369 1983), aff'd, 732 F.2d 146 (3d Cir. 1984), cert. denied, 469 U.S. 1188 (1985).

New York City Transit Auth. v. Beazer. 440 U.S. 568 (1979).

Paetzold, Ramona L., and Steven L. Willborn. 1998. *The Statistics of Discrimination: Using Statistical Evidence in Discrimination Cases.* Eagan, Minn.: West Group.

Posner, Richard A. 1987. The Efficiency and Efficacy of Title VII. *U. Pa. L. Rev.* 136:513–21.

Price Waterhouse v. Hopkins. 490 U.S. 228 (1989).

Schwochau, Susan, and Peter David Blanck. 1999. The Economics of the Americans with Disabilities Act: Part III: Does the ADA Disable the Disabled? *Berkeley J. Emp. & Lab. L.* 21:271–313.

Siegelman, Peter, and John J. Donohue III. 1990. Studying the Iceberg from Its Tip: A Comparison of Published and Unpublished Employment Discrimination Cases. *Law and Society Review* 24:1133–70.

Songer, Donald R. 1990. Criteria for Publication of Opinions in the U.S. Courts of Appeal: Formal Rules versus Empirical Reality. *Judicature* 73:307–13.

Spillman v. Carter. 918 F. Supp. 336 (D. Kan. 1996).

Thomas v. Mississippi State Dept. of Health. 934 F. Supp. 768 (S.D. Miss. 1996).

Wards Cove Packing Co. v. Atonio. 490 U.S. 642 (1989).

Chapter V

The ADA Employment Discrimination Charge Process

How Does It Work and Whom Is It Benefiting?

KATHRYN MOSS

Title I of the Americans with Disabilities Act (ADA) provides recourse to individuals who believe they have been discriminated against by an employer because of their disability.[1] Under Title I, the filing of an administrative charge of employment discrimination is the first avenue of recourse. Aggrieved individuals may also file a lawsuit, but they must first file an administrative charge.

The U.S. Equal Employment Opportunity Commission (EEOC) shares responsibility with state and local Fair Employment Practice Agencies (FEPAs) for receiving and investigating charges of employment discrimination. In general, an individual may file a charge either with the EEOC or a FEPA. If an individual files a disability-based charge with either the EEOC or a FEPA, the charge is "dual-filed," under both the ADA and the applicable state or local law.

This chapter presents data on the first three years of implementation of Title I. It addresses the following questions:

1. To what extent are people who file charges under Title I receiving beneficial outcomes?
2. What is the nature of the benefits?
3. Are some impairments associated with higher benefit rates than others?
4. Do demographic characteristics affect the awarding of benefits?
5. To what extent is there variation in beneficial outcomes among the various EEOC and FEPA offices?

6. Do people whose charges are processed by FEPAs fare better or worse than those whose charges are processed by the EEOC?

My focus on the outcomes of charges stems from a plethora of research showing that a considerable gap frequently exists between the intentions of laws and the results of their implementation (Pressman and Wildavsky 1973; Murphy 1974; Van Meter and Van Horn 1975; Pressman 1975; Bardach 1977; Montjoy and O'Toole 1979; Thompson 1981; Moss 1992, 1987, 1985; Wilson 1989; Blumrosen 1993).

In this chapter, I build on work that my colleagues and I already have conducted: a mostly qualitative examination of how the charge process works in five EEOC field offices (Moss 1996; Moss and Johnsen 1997) and a quantitative analysis of nationwide data on the outcome of ADA charges processed by the EEOC (Moss 1996; Moss, Johnsen, and Ullman, 1998).[2]

The research discussed in the chapter is designed to achieve two interrelated goals. The first is to examine what happens to people with disabilities who file charges in FEPA offices as compared with those who file in EEOC offices. The second is to develop a more general understanding of what happens to *all* discrimination charges filed under Title I of the ADA.

The results show that approximately 20 percent of all people who have filed a Title I charge have benefited from doing so. Moreover, individuals tend to experience different charge outcomes, depending on whether the EEOC or a FEPA processes their charge. They also may obtain different kinds and amounts of awards from beneficial charge closures, depending on *which* EEOC office or FEPA processes their charge.

The EEOC and FEPAs

The EEOC is responsible for administrative enforcement of Title I of the ADA as well as of four other laws: the Equal Pay Act, which prohibits employers from wage discrimination based on gender; Title VII of the Civil Rights Act of 1964, which prohibits employment discrimination based on race, color, religion, sex, or national origin; the Age Discrimination in Employment Act, which prohibits employers from discriminating against persons 40 years of age or older, and Section 501 of the Rehabilitation Act of 1973, which prohibits federal sector discrimination against persons with disabilities.

The EEOC has fifty field offices in thirty-three states and the District of Columbia. Individuals who believe they have been subject to employment discrimination may file a charge of discrimination with the EEOC in any one of the agency's fifty field offices.

The FEPAs enforce in states and localities laws that are similar to federal antidiscrimination statutes. Thus, usually an individual may file a charge either with the EEOC or a FEPA. Sometimes charges filed with a FEPA get transferred to an EEOC field office for investigation. Less frequently, charges filed with the EEOC get transferred to a FEPA for investigation.

The FEPAs are located in forty-eight states, the District of Columbia, Puerto Rico, and the Virgin Islands.[3] Under agreements between the EEOC and 125 FEPAs, the FEPAs contract to process a minimum number of charges at a fixed rate per charge. In fiscal year 1995, the EEOC paid the FEPAs (which then numbered eighty-nine) $24,414,350 to complete 48,486 dual-filed charge resolutions at $500 per charge and to conduct 2,067 initial charge interviews at $50 an interview.[4] EEOC policies and procedures require that FEPA investigations meet the EEOC's standards. Thus, the EEOC maintains oversight responsibility for the work performed by the FEPAs (State and Local Task Force 1995).

A Summary of the Earlier Research on Charges Investigated by the EEOC

ACCESS TO THE RESEARCH DATA

In March 1995, I obtained an Intergovernmental Personnel Act (IPA) position at the EEOC. This provides me with access to two types of data: (1) the EEOC's computerized data system which summarizes the charge-processing history of every charge the EEOC receives, including those which are filed also with FEPAs; and (2) investigative files that EEOC field offices maintain for all individuals whose charges are investigated by the EEOC. In working with the data and before publishing or disseminating the data or reports based on the data, I am subject to the confidentiality provisions of Title VII of the Civil Rights Act of 1964 as incorporated into the ADA.

THE RESEARCH

The earlier research dealt with all ADA charges processed by the EEOC, with emphasis on persons with psychiatric disabilities. It consisted of two interrelated studies, both of which focused on the time period from July 26, 1992 (the effective date of Title I implementation), through June 30, 1995.[5] The first study was an in-depth, mostly qualitative examination of how the charge process works in the EEOC field offices located in Charlotte, Greensboro, and Raleigh, North Carolina, as well as New York City and Boston (Moss 1996; Moss and Johnsen 1997).

Findings from the site visits showed that few charges get fully investigated and even fewer get closed in a reasonable amount of time. Inadequate and lengthy investigations were related to numerous problems facing EEOC offices. They have experienced enormous increases in new charges filed in recent years, even as most of them have experienced reductions in staff. Investigators were required to conduct intake interviews, leaving less time for investigating charges. There have been inadequate resources for training staff and conducting on-site investigations and interviews with witnesses. Until recently, investigators have been evaluated annually on standards which reward the number of cases closed with little regard for the quality of the investigation or its outcome. These factors, together with a recently discontinued policy requiring full investigations of all charges, contributed to a large increase in the EEOC's pending inventory of uninvestigated charges (Moss 1996; Moss and Johnsen 1997).

Using nationwide data, the second study was a quantitative analysis of the extent to which people who file charges under the ADA with the EEOC generally benefit from their charges, the kind of benefits received, and whether particular charge outcomes were associated with specific types of impairments, demographic characteristics, and alleged violations (Moss 1996; Moss and Johnsen 1997; Moss, Johnsen, and Ullman, 1998). The results showed that:

1. Of all ADA complainants whose charges were closed as of June 30, 1995, 16.2 percent received benefits of some type from filing a charge.
2. There was relatively little difference in the benefit rate of persons with psychiatric disabilities (14.9 percent) and those with all other types of disabilities (16.4 percent).
3. Among persons with psychiatric disabilities, type of psychiatric disability (self-reported) had little relation to benefit rates, with one notable exception: schizophrenia. Individuals with schizophrenia had a strikingly lower benefit rate (10.9 percent) than individuals with other types of psychiatric disorders, including manic depression (17.6 percent), depression (17.6 percent), anxiety (16.0 percent), and "other emotional/psychiatric impairments" (14.2 percent).
4. Of all disability groups, persons with mental retardation had the highest benefit rate (28.2 percent).

5. Other disability groups showing especially high benefit rates included persons with kidney impairments (24.2 percent); persons in a coding category that includes anemia, sickle cell, and lupus (22.9 percent); persons with asthma (20.9 percent); and persons with vision impairments (20.9 percent).

6. Disability groups having especially low benefit rates included chemical sensitivity (9.4 percent), schizophrenia (10.9 percent), and alcoholism (12.8 percent).

7. Average benefit rates of individual EEOC field offices ranged from 7 percent to 28 percent.

Methodology

DATA

I obtained the data for this study from the EEOC's Charge Data System (CDS). The CDS is used by the agency to monitor and track processing and investigation of charges, and to prepare informational, management, and statistical reports. It is operational in all EEOC offices. FEPAs also are linked to the CDS. Both EEOC field offices and FEPAs continuously enter and update information in the CDS. When data are entered and updated, one copy is stored in local CDS databases while another is transmitted to a computer at EEOC headquarters. The latter computer consolidates the transmitted data and forwards them for entry into the national database where data pertaining to discrimination charges are maintained (General Accounting Office 1989).

The EEOC requires its field offices and FEPAs to enter a standardized set of information about each charging party and charge into the CDS. This information includes the individual's impairment and usually his or her race, national origin, gender, and age. It documents the filing and closing dates of all charges and the EEOC office or FEPA where the charge was filed, investigated, and closed. It describes the issue(s) over which the charge was filed, the status of the charge (whether it is open or has been closed), and, if closed, whether there was a finding of "cause" or "no cause." For all charges closed, it records the specific charge outcome.

The EEOC could not provide the complete data set for all individual ADA records. For the current study, however, I obtained *population* level data in bivariate and multivariate form about charges filed with and processed by FEPAs. To be consistent with our earlier research, I again focused on the time period of July 26, 1992, through June 30, 1995. As of the latter date, there were eighty-nine FEPAs with which the EEOC had work-sharing agreements. For each of these eighty-nine offices I obtained data on the frequency of disability charges that were dual-filed under a state or local law and the ADA; the joint frequencies and percentages of all possible charge outcomes by type of impairment;[6] the joint frequencies and percentages of all possible charge outcomes by race, gender, and national origin; the number of individuals who received monetary benefits; the total amount of monetary benefits received; the number of individuals who received nonmonetary benefits; the average amount of time it took to investigate and close charges; and variation among FEPA offices in complainants' benefit rates. We had obtained these same data for the EEOC's fifty field offices in the earlier research.[7]

DATA ANALYSIS

Simple percentages were calculated in analyzing types of impairments most frequently cited in ADA charges, allegations cited in charges, and the extent to which charges resulted in benefits to charging parties. Simple percentages were also employed to compare the rates at which people with different impairments, with different demographic characteristics, and whose charges were processed by different offices received benefits from the charges that they filed. Difference of proportions tests and correlation analyses were used to compare the EEOC and FEPAs with respect to the outcomes of charges and possible relationships between type of impairment or demographic characteristics and benefit rates. Because the data obtained from the EEOC were provided in the form of bivariate and multivariate tables, not individual records, statistical procedures using individual cases as the unit of analysis could not be employed.

Results

NUMBER OF CHARGES FILED

As of June 30, 1995, 83,633 employment discrimination charges had been filed under the ADA. Of these, 59.8 percent (n = 49,974) had been filed with the EEOC and 40.2 percent (n = 33,659) had been filed with the FEPAs.

WHO IS FILING CHARGES

As table 1 indicates, of the charges filed with the EEOC, the four impairments most commonly cited were back impairments (n = 9,560; 19.1 percent), psychiatric disabilities (n = 5,872; 11.8 percent), neurological disorders (n = 5,839; 11.7 percent), and impairments related to extremities (defined by the EEOC as the loss of limbs or digits or nonparalytic orthopedic impairments of hands, legs, feet, and shoulders) (n = 4,044; 8.1 percent). Any one of the many other specific impairment classifications represented no more than 4.4 percent of all charges filed.

Table 1 shows that the situation was generally similar with charges filed with the FEPAs. The four impairments most commonly cited were back impairments (n = 4,468; 13.3 percent), psychiatric disabilities (n = 2,765; 8.2 percent), impairments related to extremities (n = 2,723; 8.1 percent), and neurological impairments (n = 2,229; 6.6 percent). Any one of the other specific impairment classifications represented 3.1 percent or less of all charges filed.

Table 1: Cases Received by Disability Type
July 26, 1992–June 30, 1995

Disability	EEOC		FEPA	
	Cases	% of Total Cases	Cases	% of Total Cases
Allergies	391	0.8	167	0.5
Asthma	880	1.8	379	1.1
Back impairment	9,560	19.1	4,468	13.3
Chemical sensitivity	170	0.3	66	0.2
HIV	903	1.8	385	1.1
Other blood disorders	413	0.8	195	0.6
Cancer	1,210	2.4	514	1.5
Diabetes	1,757	3.5	772	2.3
Disfigurement	201	0.4	102	0.3
Dwarfism	25	0.1	15	0.0
Anxiety	689	1.4	310	0.9
Depression	1,774	3.5	979	2.9
Manic depression	570	1.1	248	0.7
Schizophrenia	115	0.2	50	0.1
Other psychological	2,724	5.5	1,178	3.5
All psychiatric disabilities	5,872	11.8	2,765	8.2
Extremities	4,044	8.1	2,732	8.1
Gastrointestinal	428	0.9	243	0.7
Hearing impairments	1,507	3.0	849	2.5
Heart impairments	2,186	4.4	1,056	3.1
Kidney impairments	335	0.7	142	0.4
Mental retardation	191	0.4	98	0.3
Neurological	5,839	11.7	2,229	6.6
Cumulative trauma	395	0.8	346	1.0

	EEOC		FEPA	
Disability	Cases	% of Total Cases	Cases	% of Total Cases
Respiratory	459	0.9	232	0.7
Speech impairment	290	0.6	260	0.8
Alcoholism	1,148	2.3	659	2.0
Drug addiction	616	1.2	322	1.0
Vision impairment	1,378	2.8	714	2.1
Other	11,265	22.5	15,456	45.9
Record of disability	760	1.5	271	0.8
Regarded as disabled	2,580	5.2	1,133	3.4
Relationship	290	0.6	77	0.2
Retaliation	5,091	10.2	2,578	7.7
Net total cases	**49,974**		**33,659**	

The net total reflects the fact that charging parties may cite up to six types of disabilities when filing a charge.

There was one major difference between the EEOC and the FEPAs with respect to impairments cited in charges. Impairments not labeled in the CDS database, called "other impairments," represented 22.5 percent (n = 11,265) of the EEOC charges. In contrast, "other impairments" comprised 45.9 percent (n = 15,456) of FEPA charges.

NATURE OF ALLEGATIONS

Table 2 shows that the largest percentage of ADA charges filed with the EEOC consisted of individuals alleging they had been illegally terminated (n = 25,509; 51 percent). That is consistent with charges filed under the other laws enforced by the EEOC. Other alleged violations were failure to provide reasonable accommodations (n = 13,284; 26.6 percent), harassment (n = 5,575; 11.2 percent), hiring (n = 5,191; 10.4 percent), discipline (n = 3,812; 7.6 percent), and layoffs (n = 2,487; 5.0 percent). The many other classifications of allegations were each found in less than 5 percent of the charges.

The situation with the FEPAs was again similar. Table 2 reveals that the most commonly cited allegations in charges filed with a FEPA were job termination (n = 19,411; 57.7 percent), hiring (n = 3,343; 9.9 percent), harassment (n = 3,297; 9.8 percent), failure to provide reasonable accommodation (n = 2,797; 8.3 percent), discipline (n = 1,765; 5.2 percent), and layoffs (n = 1,316; 3.9 percent). The many other classifications of allegations were each found in less than 3.9 percent of the charges filed with the FEPAs.

Again, allegations not labeled at all in the CDS database constituted a large percentage of FEPA charges, especially relative to the percentage of unlabeled allegations cited in EEOC charges. Unlabeled allegations constituted 37.5 percent (n = 12,608) of FEPA charges, compared to 24.6 percent (n = 12,283) of EEOC charges.

Table 2: Nature of Allegation

	EEOC		FEPA	
Issue	Cases	% of Total Cases	Cases	% of Total Cases
Benefits	2,035	4.1	664	2.0
Discipline	3,812	7.6	1,765	5.2
Discharge	25,509	51.0	19,411	57.7
Harrassment	5,575	11.2	3,297	9.8
Hiring	5,191	10.4	3,343	9.9
Layoff	2,487	5.0	1,316	3.9
Promotion	1,935	3.9	1,073	3.2
Rehire	1,789	3.6	931	2.8
Accommodation	13,284	26.6	2,797	8.3
Suspension	1,123	2.2	682	2.0
Wages	1,762	3.5	949	2.8
Other	12,283	24.6	12,608	37.5
Net total cases	**49,974**		**33,659**	

The net total reflects the fact that charging parties may cite up to eight issues when filing a charge.

CHARGE CLOSURES

As of June 30, 1995, the EEOC had closed 57.7 percent (n = 28,826) of the 49,974 ADA charges that had been filed with the agency in the nearly three years since Title I took effect. During the same period of time, the FEPAs closed only 47.3 percent (n = 15,936) of the 33,659 disability-based charges that were dual-filed under state or local laws and the ADA.

OVERALL BENEFITS

ADA charges can be closed in six ways. The following three bring some type of direct benefit to charging parties. "Withdrawals with benefits" are non-written, informal agreements between employers and charging parties that typically resolve a charge before the EEOC or a FEPA has completed its investigation and determined the merits of the charge. "Settlements" are formal, written agreements between the employer and charging parties that resolve a charge before the EEOC or a FEPA has completed its investigation and determined the merits of the charge. "Conciliation agreements" are formal, written agreements between employers and charging parties that resolve a charge after an investigation indicates reasonable cause to think that discrimination occurred. Three other types of closures bring no direct benefits to charging parties. "Unsuccessful conciliations" are failures to achieve an agreement between employers and charging parties after an investigation indicates that there is reasonable cause to think that discrimination occurred. "No cause determinations" are determinations that there is not reasonable cause to think that discrimination occurred. "Administrative closures" are charges closed for other reasons without a determination of cause or no cause (e.g., a determination that the charging party is not a qualified individual with a disability, a decision that the employer is not a covered entity under the ADA, a request by the charging party for a right-to-sue letter 180 days after the charge was first filed even if the agency processing is not complete).[8]

Table 3 shows that of the 44,762 ADA charges that were closed either by the EEOC or a FEPA as of June 30, 1995, 8,907 (19.9 percent) brought some measure of benefit to charging parties. The data indicated, however, that charges investigated and closed by a FEPA were significantly more likely to benefit complainants in some way than charges investigated and closed by the EEOC. As table 3 reveals, 26.6 percent (n = 4,232) of the charges investigated and closed by a FEPA resulted in some sort of benefit, compared to 16.2 percent (n = 4,675) of the charges investigated and closed by the EEOC.

Table 3 also provides information about determinations by EEOC and FEPA investigators that there is reasonable cause to think that discrimination occurred. Referred to as "cause findings," these can result only from conciliations, either successful or unsuccessful. The rows describing successful and unsuccessful conciliations in table 3 represent only 1.2 percent of the total FEPA charge closures and 2.9 percent of the total EEOC charge closures. These low percentages are consistent with criticisms the EEOC frequently receives for making too few cause determinations (Selmi 1996; Seymour 1995, Blumrosen 1994, 1993; Norton 1992; General Accounting Office 1994, 1988, 1987), although withdrawal-with-benefit outcomes and formal settlements probably would have resulted in more "cause" determinations if their investigations had been concluded.

Table 3: Outcome of All ADA Employment Discrimination Charges Processed and Closed by EEOC and FEPA Offices through June 30, 1995

Type of Closure	Total		EEOC		FEPA	
	Closures	% of Total Closures	Closures	% of Total Closures	Closures	% of Total Closures
Withdrawal with benefits	4,508	10.9	2,643	9.2	1,865	11.7
Settlements	4,015	8.1	1,773	6.2	2,242	14.1
Successful conciliations	384	0.9	259	0.9	125	0.8
Total benefits	**8,907**	**19.9**	**4,675**	**16.2**	**4,232**	**26.6**
Unsuccessful conciliations	624	1.4	563	2.0	61	0.4
No cause determinations	17,678	39.5	10,130	35.1	7,548	47.4
Administrative resolutions	17,553	39.2	13,458	46.7	4095	25.7
Total nonbenefits	**35,855**	**80.1**	**24,151**	**83.7**	**11,704**	**73.5**
Total	**44,762**	**100.0**	**28,826**	**100.0**	**15,936**	**100.0**

Difference of proportions between EEOC and FEPA is significant at the .01 level.

AMOUNT OF BENEFITS

The EEOC's Charge Data System tracks three types of benefits resulting from charge closures. "Actual monetary benefits" can be provided by an employer to a charging party and/or a group of similarly situated employees through back pay, remedial relief, compensatory damages, or punitive damages. "Projected monetary benefits" are remedies to be provided by an employer during a one-year time period through hiring, promotion, reinstatement, or accommodations that would bring monetary returns. "Nonmonetary benefits" can be provided by employers also. Examples include providing a charging party with a positive job reference, referring a charging party to a job, providing a charging party or a group of similarly situated individuals with union membership, or posting antidiscrimination notices in an employment setting.

Before presenting data from the EEOC's Charge Data System, it is important to note that the benefit data include information both about how many charges are closed in each charge closure category as well as how many people receive each kind of closure. The number of charges and people may differ because in some instances one individual may file more than one charge and in other instances an individual charge may result in benefits to a class of similarly situated individuals. The EEOC field office data, for example, show 3,579 ADA charges resulting in benefits for 4,388 people.

In contrast, the FEPA data reveal 3,869 charges resulting in benefits for 151,362 people. Because this disparity appeared much too large to be explained by classwide benefits resulting from one or even more than one charge, I compared the number of charges and number of people receiving benefits for each FEPA. I found that in three of the FEPA offices, the number of individuals receiving benefits did not reasonably match the number of charges. In one case, the data showed 115 charges resulting in 94,316 individuals receiving nonmonetary benefits. In another case, 349 charges resulted in actual monetary benefits for 11,420 people. In that same case, 240 charges had resulted in nonmonetary benefits for 11,310 people. In the third case, 25 charges resulted in actual monetary benefits for 39,895 people.

It is possible that the disparities between charges and people might have been caused by charges resulting in classwide relief. Given the size of the disparities, however, it seemed at least as likely that they may have been caused either by data entry errors or misleading presentations about who benefited from charges. Because of this ambiguity, I omitted data for the three questionable FEPAs in assessing the amount of benefits received by Title I complainants. The resultant table 4 still reports data from eighty-six FEPA offices.

Table 4 shows the actual, projected, and nonmonetary benefits obtained by EEOC and FEPA offices. The percentage of people who received actual monetary and nonmonetary benefits was higher in FEPA offices than in EEOC offices. EEOC offices, however, showed a higher percent of projected monetary benefits. More important, individuals whose charges were processed by EEOC offices received distinctly higher average actual and projected monetary benefits than those whose charges were processed by FEPAs.

NEW JOBS AND REINSTATEMENTS

Many observers argue that the goal of increasing employment opportunities for people with serious disabilities has not been met (Auberger 1994; Redenbaugh 1994). I therefore analyzed the number and percentage of closed charges that resulted in new jobs and reinstatements. Table 5 presents the results of the analysis.

Table 4: Amount of Benefits

	Actual Monetary Benefits			Projected Monetary Benefits			Nonmonetary Benefits	
	Average per Person	Number of Persons	% of Total Persons Receiving Benefits	Average per Person	Number of Persons	% of Total Persons Receiving Benefits	Number of Persons	% of Total Persons Receiving Benefits
EEOC	$15,082	2,298	52.4	$23,630	1,152	26.3	2,413	55.0
FEPA	$3,812	3,369	61.5	$15,016	297	5.4	4,063	74.1

The computations for this table reflect all ADA-based charges that resulted in benefits. The percentages total to greater than 100 percent because individuals can receive more than one kind of benefit.

Table 5: New Jobs and Reinstatements Resulting from All ADA Employment Discrimination Charges Processed and Closed by EEOC and FEPAs through June 30, 1995

Closure Result	Total		EEOC		FEPA	
	Closures	% of Closures	Closures	% of Closures	Closures	% of Closures
New hires and reinstatements	982	2.2	735	2.5	247	1.5
All other closures	43,780	97.8	28,091	97.5	15,689	98.5
Total	**44,762**	**100.0**	**28,826**	**100.0**	**15,936**	**100.0**

Difference of proportions between the EEOC and FEPAs is significant at the .01 level.

The results of table 5 support the conclusions of those who argue that only a small percentage of charges result in increased employment opportunities for people with disabilities. They also show that although there was a statistically significant difference between individuals whose charges were processed and closed by the EEOC and those whose charges were processed and closed by a FEPA in obtaining new jobs or getting old jobs back, in terms of magnitude the former group of individuals was only negligibly more successful than the latter group of individuals. On the other hand, table 5 shows that nearly 1,000 individuals with disabilities who brought ADA employment discrimination charges were either hired into new jobs or had their old jobs reinstated. It can be argued that this is not a trivial result after only three years of Title I implementation.

CHARGE OUTCOMES AND TYPES OF IMPAIRMENTS

As noted previously in this chapter, my colleagues and I compared the benefit rates associated with each discrete impairment category for charges processed by the EEOC in our earlier research (Moss 1996; Moss, Johnsen, and Ullman 1998).[9] For this investigation, I compared the benefit rates associated with each discrete impairment category for charges processed by the EEOC and charges processed by the FEPAs.[10] Table 6 shows the results of the analysis.

As table 6 shows, there are different types of impairments associated with high and low benefit rates obtained by the EEOC and FEPAs. I analyzed the data to see if there was any correlation between the overall patterns of impairments associated with benefits for charges processed by the EEOC, on the one hand, and the overall patterns of impairments associated with benefits for charges processed by FEPAs, on the other hand. No significant correlation was found ($r = .20$; $p = 0.28$).

CHARGE OUTCOMES AND DEMOGRAPHIC CHARACTERISTICS

The EEOC does not require its field offices and FEPAs to enter information about ADA complainants' demographic characteristics into their databases. Nevertheless, about 90 percent of the EEOC records and 70 percent of the FEPA records contain information about race, national origin, and gender. The data were therefore analyzed to see if charge outcomes were associated with these variables (see table 7).

Table 6: Benefit Rate by Disability Type
Closed Cases July 26, 1992–June 30, 1995

Disability	EEOC		FEPA	
	Cases	Benefit Rate (%)	Cases	Benefit Rate (%)
Allergies	237	16.9	79	20.3
Asthma	478	20.9	147	32.7
Back impairment	5,450	16.2	1,911	28.0
Chemical sensitivity	64	9.4	15	26.7
HIV	703	18.6	207	37.7
Other blood disorders	210	22.9	70	24.3
Cancer	749	17.6	190	30.0
Diabetes	983	18.5	330	34.8
Disfigurement	128	14.8	52	17.3
Dwarfism	15	13.3	9	44.4
Anxiety	256	16.0	102	37.3
Depression	666	17.6	280	32.5
Manic depression	199	17.6	81	30.9
Schizophrenia	46	10.9	22	27.3
Other psychological	1,990	14.2	505	30.7
Extremities	1,872	17.0	1,096	27.6
Gatrointestinal	239	15.9	103	38.8
Hearing impairments	836	19.4	366	29.0
Heart impairments	1,338	16.3	440	32.5
Kidney impairments	182	24.2	73	32.9
Mental retardation	110	28.2	49	38.8
Neurological	3,487	17.3	981	29.7
Cumulative trauma	125	16.8	113	32.7
Respiratory	269	19.3	79	26.6
Speech impairment	172	15.7	128	21.9
Alcoholism	649	12.8	302	31.5
Drug addiction	391	14.6	166	22.3
Vision impairment	804	20.0	326	31.9
Other	7,432	14.2	8,149	24.5
Record of disability	272	17.6	85	32.9
Regarded as disabled	844	17.7	317	27.1
Relationship	114	7.9	22	31.8
Retaliation	2,558	15.3	1,098	23.8
Net total cases	**28,826**	**16.2**	**15,936**	**26.6**

The net total reflects the fact that charging parties may cite up to six types of disabilities when filing a charge.

Table 7: Benefit Rate by Race/Ethnicity and Gender

Race/Ethnicity and Gender	EEOC		FEPA	
	Cases	Benefit Rate (%)	Cases	Benefit Rate (%)
White males	11,680	16.1	4,354	23.6
White females	7,945	17.1	3,687	26.7
Black males	2,653	16.5	1,144	24.3
Black females	2,228	16.4	1,046	26.1
Hispanic males	1,024	13.0	572	25.5
Hispanic females	595	18.0	335	25.7
Total	**26,125**	**16.4**	**11,138**	**25.1**

The total number of cases and benefit rates reflects missing data on race/ethnicity and gender.

Table 7 reveals that compared to the average benefit rate of the EEOC (16.2 percent), the EEOC's average benefit rates for different demographic groupings were as follows: white males (16.1 percent), white females (17.1 percent), black males (16.5 percent), black females (16.4 percent), Hispanic males (13.0 percent), and Hispanic females (18.0). Compared to the average benefit rate of FEPAs (26.6 percent), the FEPAs' average benefit rates for different demographic groupings were as follows: white males (23.6 percent), white females (26.7 percent), black males (24.3 percent), black females (26.1 percent), Hispanic males (25.5 percent), and Hispanic females (25.7 percent).

These data show that differences in benefit rates among individuals of different races, national origins, and genders were minimal.

TIME IT TAKES TO PROCESS AND CLOSE AN ADA CHARGE

The length of time it takes to investigate and close charges is another measure of the service provided to charging parties. Long processing times delay closure and may influence the nature of the outcome. The longer it takes to investigate a charge, the more the potential for problems in locating witnesses and securing credible accounts from witnesses. This is in addition to the longer waits for victims of discrimination to obtain relief (General Accounting Office 1995).

The length of time it takes to process and close cases increased dramatically in both the EEOC and FEPAs during the first three years after Title I took effect. In 1993 it took the EEOC an average of 154 days to close a case; in the first three quarters of 1995 it took an average of 316 days. As for the FEPAs, it took an average of 142 days in 1993 to close a case but 310 days in the first three quarters of 1995.

VARIATION IN BENEFIT RATES WITHIN AND
BETWEEN EEOC AND FEPA OFFICES

There was considerable variation in benefit rates among field offices of the EEOC, with rates ranging from 7 to 28 percent, an average benefit rate of 16.2 percent, and a standard deviation of 4.6 percent. There was even more variation in benefit rates among the different FEPAs, with rates ranging from 0 to 100 percent, an average benefit rate of 26.6 percent, and a standard deviation of 21.5 percent. FEPAs with very low and very high benefit rates were usually very small FEPAs. Benefit rates for FEPAs that processed at least fifty charges during the study period ranged from 7.3 to 69.4 percent.

VARIATION IN OFFICE BENEFIT RATES AND UNUSUAL
PROPORTIONS OF IMPAIRMENTS ASSOCIATED WITH BENEFIT
RATES SIGNIFICANTLY ABOVE OR BELOW THE AVERAGE RATE

It seemed possible that if an office's workload involved unusual proportions of impairments whose average benefit rates were significantly above or below the average rate, this could account for the variation in benefit rates among offices. To test this possibility, all offices whose combined beneficial outcome rates fell significantly above or below the national average, and all offices whose rates fell between the extremes, were compared. Charge closures involving impairments associated with benefit rates significantly above or below the average rate, as well as all other charge closures, were grouped as "high," "low," and "intermediate" impairment type. These groups were then analyzed for their percent of all closures by the office groupings and the weighted[11] average rate of beneficial outcomes for the different impairment groupings. Results can be seen in tables 8 and 9.

These data show that many offices indeed received a lower percentage of "high benefit" impairments and a higher percentage of "low benefit" impairments than other offices. This general disparity could account for some of the difference noted in the overall beneficial outcome rates between offices. However, both tables 8 and 9 indicate that in all three impairment groupings, the low benefit offices had uniformly lower rates of beneficial outcomes than the average benefit offices. Similarly, the average benefit offices had uniformly lower

Table 8: High, Average, and Low Benefit EEOC Offices

A Comparison of Total Charges and Beneficial Outcomes of Closed Cases
in the Three Impairment Groupings, July 26, 1992–June 30, 1995

| Office Groupings | Total Charges | High Benefit Impairments | | Average Benefit Impairments | | Low Benefit Impairments | |
		% of Total Charges	% with Beneficial Outcomes	% of Total Charges	% with Beneficial Outcomes	% of Total Charges	% with Beneficial Outcomes
High benefits	7,117	27.8	25.5	59.5	21.6	33.2	20.9
Average benefits	12,158	27.7	18.1	55.2	16.3	34.4	13.7
Low benefits	9,514	25.6	14.3	52.0	12.3	38.0	10.1

The percentages of total charges in each office grouping add to more than 100 percent because more than one impairment may be included in a charge.

The total number of charges for the three office groupings add to slightly less than the net total of charges closed by the EEOC as of June 30, 1995 (n = 28,826), because a few of the cases have unspecified office information.

Table 9: High, Average, and Low Benefit FEPA Offices

A Comparison of Total Charges and Beneficial Outcomes of Closed Cases
in the Three Impairment Groupings, July 26, 1992–June 30, 1995

Office Groupings	Total Charges	High Benefit Impairments		Average Benefit Impairments		Low Benefit Impairments	
		% of Total Charges	% with Beneficial Outcomes	% of Total Charges	% with Beneficial Outcomes	% of Total Charges	% with Beneficial Outcomes
High benefits	4,650	36.3	45.1	35.1	44.3	45.8	43.5
Average benefits	3,894	22.7	28.5	31.5	27.4	52.7	25.8
Low benefits	7,383	16.3	17.1	27.3	14.3	68.6	15.8

The percentages of total charges in each office grouping add to more than 100 percent because more than one impairment may be included in a charge.

The total number of charges for the three office groupings add to slightly more than the net total of charges closed by the FEPAs as of June 30, 1995 (n = 15,936), because a few of the cases have unspecified office information.

rates of beneficial outcomes than the high benefit offices. The data make clear that operations and not just differences in complainants' impairments account for most of the differences in rates of beneficial outcomes. The operational differences have not been clarified.

Conclusions

This chapter discussed the ADA employment discrimination charge process. The analyses examined the kinds of impairments cited in charges, the allegations made, and the benefits obtained. The findings make a contribution to the ongoing debate about the efficacy and efficiency of Title I, but must be viewed with proper recognition of their limitations.

The finding that the two most frequently cited disabilities in Title I charges are back impairments and psychiatric disabilities might be fodder for critics who argue that the ADA is being used by individuals with "minor" disabilities instead of more "serious" or "traditional" disabilities such as vision or hearing impairments or paralysis. Arguably, this view indicates a misunderstanding of the nature of back and psychiatric impairments, and, given the Supreme Court's decision in *Bragdon v. Abbott* (1998), of the intended scope of the ADA. Many individuals with back impairments, psychiatric impairments, neurological impairments, and impairments related to extremities have substantially limiting disorders but can make very good employees with reasonable and inexpensive accommodations. Title I was designed to give those individuals who are qualified the opportunity to file a charge in order to improve their chance to work. The fact remains, however, that many individuals filing charges cite disabilities which are not commonly perceived as serious, which are difficult for employers to assess, or which raise concerns about coverage under the ADA.

The data also show that most charging parties receive nonbeneficial outcomes. Of the closed charges, only 2.3 percent (n = 1,008) resulted in determinations of cause and 19.9 percent (n = 8,907) brought benefits of any sort to those who filed them. A mere 2.2 percent of the charges that were resolved beneficially for complainants resulted either in new jobs or reinstatements. The average actual monetary award was only $8,382. Furthermore, 66 percent (n = 6,476) of the small group of individuals who received beneficial closures received nonmonetary benefits such as a positive job reference, a referral to a job, membership in a union, or the posting of an antidiscrimination notice in the charging party's employment setting.

Moreover, for the charging parties, results can be considerably different, depending on whether the charge is processed by the EEOC or a FEPA office. Individuals who rely on a FEPA to investigate their charge have a greater likelihood of receiving a beneficial outcome than individuals who rely on the EEOC. However, proportionately more individuals obtaining a beneficial outcome are likely to obtain monetary benefits from the EEOC than from a FEPA. Further, those who obtain beneficial outcomes will probably receive greater monetary benefits from charges handled by the EEOC than from those handled by a FEPA.

Do these findings support the claims of those who argue that the ADA's employment provisions are being used by the "wrong" people or are too frequently being abused by people without meritorious claims (Bovard 1995; Mathews 1995, 1993; Will 1996; Zuriff 1996; Olson 1997)? I believe not. First, any sweeping judgments about the success of Title I are premature. Implementation researchers have found repeatedly that translating important legislative and administrative policies into action proceeds slowly and requires years of adjustment, compromise, experience, and fine-tuning (Wilson 1989; Goldman et al. 1992; Blumrosen 1993). What this analysis points out is that 8,900 individuals with disabilities are better off in some way after only three years of Title I implementation. This includes almost 1,000 individuals with disabilities who have obtained new jobs or been reinstated into old jobs.

A more important reason for caution in assessing the overall success of the process by these findings is that Title I charges reflect an unknown, and probably small, fraction of the total number of instances in which the ADA influences an employment decision. They do not include situations in which individuals with disabilities encounter discrimination but take no action. More important, charge data do not address "compliance without enforcement," the voluntary nondiscriminatory behavior that would be the best measure of the overall success of the ADA (Burris and Moss, this volume). The existence of the ADA and the authority of the EEOC to enforce it present a powerful stimulus for employers to comply with its requirements. The need to respond to a charge, the chance of investigation by the EEOC or a FEPA, and the possibility of being the target of judicial proceedings motivate many employers who do not initially comply to seek settlements when disputes arise. There is a predominance of legal settlements and "withdrawal-with-benefit" resolutions among those who benefit from their ADA charges. The finding that 19 percent of beneficial outcomes out of a total of 19.9 percent are either withdrawal-with-benefit resolutions or formal settlements indicates that the presence of the law and the threat of administrative enforcement present a high motivational impact for employers. It is only in some cases resulting in withdrawal-with-benefit resolutions or formal settlements that EEOC or FEPA investigators actually are involved in the negotiations resulting in settlements.

In a similar interpretation of findings about the impact of the 1964 Civil Rights Act on African-American and female workers, Blumrosen (1993) discussed how the legislation encouraged employers to comply with the values contained in the law, notwithstanding demographic and political changes that have decreased the impact of employment discrimination in recent times. Blumrosen makes an important point: in assessing the impact of equal employment opportunity laws, statistics about charges and cases reveal only the "tip of the iceberg." The growing presence of knowledgeable and sophisticated human resource personnel in larger firms has meant an increase in the implementation of equal employment opportunity laws without direct government intervention (Edelman 1992). Corporations are adopting policies to educate managers and workers about ADA requirements and to assist them in achieving compliance without direct EEOC or FEPA intervention. Because of these additions to corporate structure and awareness, EEOC statistics about charges and lawsuits show only one aspect of the consequences of laws such as the ADA. Widespread compliance would be expected to generate a pool of charges in which it is less clear that the individual's claim is meritorious and that the impairments are "disabilities" as defined under the ADA.

There can be little doubt that many Title I charges involve frivolous claims. That does not mean, however, that the charge process is failing or even that it is being extensively abused. The administrative charge process is intended to provide a relatively quick and inexpensive means of resolving disputes between employers and employees. It is very easy for an employee who suspects discrimination to file a charge, even the employee who lacks hard evidence to support the claim (as is frequently the case even in ultimately meritorious cases). There is no fee, no lawyer is required, and charges can be filed by phone or mail or faxed to agencies. The initial screening of weak or malicious cases, which in standard litigation is performed by lawyers and court clerks, comes during the charge receipt process or after filing in the ADA charge system.

On the other hand, the data raise questions about the oversight by EEOC headquarters of FEPAs and EEOC offices. In 1995, an EEOC Task Force was created to assess EEOC's FEPA program and its relationship with the FEPAs. It found that the computers provided to some of the FEPAs by the EEOC were too small for their large volume of charges. Many FEPAs have data transmission problems due either to aging modem equipment or problems with phone lines. At least seven FEPAs must duplicate data entry, entering the data into their own system and again into CDS. Although many of the larger FEPAs have a staff person knowledgeable in computer matters who is responsible for the FEPA's overall data entry, many others have few or no staff sufficiently trained in computer procedures. According to the task force, these problems result in slow and inefficient data processing as well as inaccuracies (State and Local Task Force 1995: XII-3).

The results discussed in this chapter lend support to the task force's conclusions. In short, I found missing data, too much unlabeled data, and, for at least three FEPAs, overly large discrepancies between the number of charges and the number of people. It seems obvious that effective oversight and administration of EEOC and FEPA field offices depend heavily on accurate and timely data entry into the CDS.

Perhaps the most important finding in this study is an apparent need for more uniform implementation of the Title I charge process. People tend to have different charge outcomes, depending on whether the EEOC or a FEPA processes and closes a charge. They also may receive a different type and amount of award from a favorable charge resolution, depending on which particular EEOC office or FEPA processes their charge.

During the last several years, the EEOC has taken decisive action in dealing with some of the problems pertaining to charge processing. It has abandoned its long-standing policy of conducting full investigations of every charge. In its place is a policy that focuses investigative attention only on cases in which it appears likely that discrimination occurred. This may ensure more complete investigations of creditable charges. The EEOC has also begun to use mediation to achieve early settlement of individual cases, particularly where the charging party wants to keep working for an employer or to be reinstated in a former job.

This study's results showing that complainants' experiences vary widely depending on where their charge is processed suggest that firmer monitoring by EEOC headquarters is needed to produce a more equitable implementation of the ADA. This conclusion runs counter to a recent policy directive from EEOC headquarters giving EEOC field offices more, not less, autonomy (Cassellus 1995). It also runs counter to current campaigns aimed at reducing federal government authority generally and increasing the control of states and localities. Indeed, there have been recent calls by some to rethink the proper role and even the necessity of the EEOC (Gunderson 1995; Gunderson and Goodling 1995; Selmi 1996).

The EEOC remains the main enforcement agency for the ADA's Title I. The results presented here show that even in its early years of effort, the EEOC has in fact helped thousands of people with disabilities to receive benefits from their employment discrimination claims. The agency is still plagued with operational problems, many due to understaffing and underfunding. However, the combined effect of the presence of federal antidiscrimination employment laws, the enforcement activities of the EEOC and other federal and state agencies, and the threat of enforcement by the EEOC and other agencies has had positive effects beyond the benefits documented here. Larger companies and corporations have established offices charged with helping to bring employment practices into conformity with law. Small employers too know that discrimination can, and often will, be challenged.

In sum, the findings presented here suggest some correspondence between the promise of the ADA and actual outcome. They also generally support the concept of a federal agency monitoring and uniformly enforcing a federal law that remains much needed by individuals with disabilities. Furthermore, with the recent *Bragdon v. Abbott* Supreme Court decision liberalizing the definition of disability, the narrowing trend apparent during lower court ADA decisions in the past several years may reverse. After all, it is still early in the life of the ADA.

Notes

I am grateful to many people for their assistance with this chapter. Michael Ullman provided expert statistical help. Scott Burris and Steven Willborn read and commented on earlier drafts of the manuscript. Robert Merriam, my husband, is my faithful critic, editor, and supporter. Finally, my thanks go to Peter Blanck for providing me with the opportunity to participate in the 1997 Obermann Center's Faculty Research Seminar and to everyone who participated in the seminar for their suggestions about many of the ideas presented.

1. Title I's requirements apply to private employers who have fifteen or more employees, state and local governments, employment agencies, labor unions, and joint labor-management committees. For simplicity, this chapter uses the term "employers" to refer to all covered entities.

2. Since this chapter was submitted for publication, more recent investigations have been undertaken. For more updated findings, see Moss et al. (1999) and Moss et al. (in press).

3. Many states have more than one FEPA since both states and localities may have approved FEPAs.

4. This figure is greater than the $500 would imply because it includes the contract amounts for new FEPAs. In their first year of operation, new FEPAs are provided with additional money to help them with start-up costs.

5. Our more recent research (Moss et al. 1999, in press) extends the time period through March 31, 1998.

6. Joint frequency and percentage data focus attention on the description of two variables together.

7. For the earlier research, we also obtained individual records pertaining to the people whose charges were processed by the offices we visited. Additionally, we obtained a sample of 4,509 individual records to examine interrelationships among disability classifications, psychiatric disability codings, alleged violations, and charge outcomes as well as the length of time it took to process individual charges.

8. Some right-to-sue letters may eventually result in benefits for charging parties. In particular, a charging party or attorney may request a right-to-sue letter, even if the EEOC or a FEPA has not finished processing the charge, because the case seems very strong. In such cases, the nonbeneficial outcome received administratively may be a strong case where a beneficial outcome is received—not before the agency, but eventually in court. These cases are not included in the analysis for this paper because I do not have information about them. They most likely constitute a small group, however, because the cost of attorneys and the difficulty in getting attorneys to take ADA cases prevents most people from filing lawsuits. Furthermore, there has been an increasing tendency of federal courts to deny protection to individuals who bring ADA claims. It is also important to note that right-to-sue letters may also be issued when the EEOC or FEPA makes a no-cause determination or when conciliation attempts fail and EEOC decides not to sue on the charging party's behalf. Again, it is possible that some of these right-to-sue letters may eventually result in a judicially obtained beneficial outcome.

9. The EEOC's Charge Data System groups ADA charges according to twenty-eight discrete impairment categories.

10. In recording data for the CDS, FEPAs use the same categories of impairments as does the EEOC.

11. The simple average would have just totaled the benefit rates in each office in each grouping and then divided by the number of offices without accounting for the different number of cases in each office. The weighted average accounts for the different number of cases in each office.

References

Auberger, M. 1994. Cited in L. Kaufman-Rosen and K. Springen, Who Are the Disabled? *Newsweek,* Nov. 7. P. 80.

Bardach, E. 1977. *The Implementation Game.* Berkeley: University of California Press.

Blumrosen, A. W. 1993. *Modern Law: The Law Transmission System and Equal Employment Opportunity.* Madison: University of Wisconsin Press.

———. 1994. Testimony to U.S. House Committee on Education and Labor. Oversight Hearing on the Equal Employment Opportunity Commission: Hearing before the Subcommittee on Select Education and Civil Rights of the Committee on Education and Labor. 103d Cong., 2d Sess. July 26.

Bovard, J. 1995. The Disabilities Act's Parade of Absurdities. *Wall Street Journal,* June 22. P. A18.

Bragdon v. Abbott. 118 S. Ct. 2196 (1998).

Cassellus, Gilbert F. 1995. *Priority Charge Handling Procedures.* Washington, D.C.: U.S. Equal Employment Opportunity Commission. June.

Edelman, L. B. 1992. Legal Ambiguity and Symbolic Structures: Organizational Mediation of Civil Rights Laws. *American Journal of Sociology* 97:1531–76.

General Accounting Office. 1987. *EEOC Birmingham Office Closed Discrimination Charges without Full Investigation.* Report No. HRD 87-81.

———. 1988. *EEOC and State Agencies Did Not Fully Investigate Discrimination Charges.* Report No. HRD-89-11. Oct.

———. 1989. *ADP Systems: EEOC's Charge Data System Contains Errors But System Satisfies Users.* Report No. IMTEC-90-5. Dec.

———. 1994. *EEOC's Expanding Workload Increases in Age Discrimination and Other Charges: Call for New Approach.* Report No. HEHS-94-32. Feb.

———. 1995. Testimony by Linda G. Morra, Director, Education and Employment Issues, Health, Education, and Human Services Division to U.S. Senate Committee on Labor and Human Resources. Report No. T-HEHS-95-170. May.

Goldman, H. H., et al. 1992. Lessons from the Program on Chronic Mental Illness. *Health Affairs* (Fall): 51–68.

Gunderson, S. 1995. Testimony to U.S. House Committee on Economic and Educational Opportunities. Hearings on Departmental Reorganization. 104th Cong., 1st Sess. June 7.

Gunderson, S., and W. F. Goodling. 1995. A Proposal Submitted to U.S. House Committee on Economic and Educational Opportunities. Hearings on Departmental Reorganization. 104th Cong., 1st Sess.

Mathews, J. 1993. Having Doubts about Disabilities Act. *Washington Post,* Dec. 6. P. A21.

———. 1995. Disabilities Act Failing to Achieve Workplace Goals. *Washington Post,* Apr. 16. P. A18.

Montjoy, R., and L. O'Toole. 1979. Toward a Theory of Policy Implementation: An Organizational Perspective. *Public Administration Review* 39:456–76.

Moss, K. 1985. The Catalytic Effect of a Federal Court Decision on a State Legislature. *Law and Society Review* 19 (1): 147–57.

———. 1987. The "Baby Doe" Legislation: Its Rise and Fall. *Policy Studies Journal* 15 (4):629–51.

———. 1992. *Implications of Employment Complaints Filed by People with Mental Disabilities.* Washington, D.C.: Mental Health Policy Resource Center.

———. 1996. *Psychiatric Disabilities, Employment Discrimination Charges, and the ADA.* Silver Spring, Md.: National Rehabilitation Information Center.

Moss, K., and M. Johnsen. 1997. Employment Discrimination and the ADA: A Study of the Administrative Complaint Process. *Psychiatric Rehabilitation Journal* 21 (2): 111–21.

Moss, K., M. Johnsen, and M. Ullman. 1998. Assessing Employment Discrimination Charges Filed under the ADA. *Journal of Disability Policy Studies* 9 (1): 81–105.

Moss, K., et al. 1999. Different Paths to Justice: The ADA, Employment, and Administrative Enforcement by the EEOC and FEPAs. *Behavioral Sciences and the Law* 17:29–46.

Moss, K., et al. In press. From Employment Rights under the ADA to Actual Outcomes. *Psychiatric Services.*

Murphy, J. T. 1974. *State Educational Agencies and Discretionary Funds.* Lexington, Mass.: Lexington Books.

Norton, E. H. 1992. Testimony before the U.S. Senate Committee on Labor and Human Resources. Oversight on Activities of the Equal Employment Opportunity Commission (EEOC): Hearing before the Subcommittee on Employment and Productivity of the Committee on Labor and Human Resources. 102d Cong., 2d Sess. Apr. 28.

Olson, Walter. 1997. *The Excuse Factory.* New York: Free Press.

Pressman, J. L. 1975. *Federal Programs and City Politics.* Berkeley: University of California Press.

Pressman, J. L., and J. Wildavsky. 1973. *Implementation.* Berkeley: University of California Press.

Redenbaugh, R. 1994. Cited in L. Kaufman-Rosen and K. Springen, Who Are the Disabled? *Newsweek,* Nov. 7. P. 80.

Selmi, Michael. 1996. The Value of the EEOC: Reexamining the Agency's Role in Employment Discrimination Law. *Ohio State Law Journal* 57 (1): 1–64.

Seymour, Richard T. 1995. *Civil Rights Act and EEOC News.* Issue no. 19. May 8.

———. 1997. *Civil Rights Act and EEOC News.* Issue no. 28. Oct. 30.

State and Local Task Force. 1995. *State and Local Task Force Report.* An unpublished report prepared for EEOC Chairman Gilbert F. Casellas.

Thompson, F. 1981. *Health Policy and the Bureaucracy.* Cambridge, Mass.: MIT Press.

Van Meter, D. S., and C. E. Van Horn. 1975. The Policy Implementation Process: A Conceptual Framework. *Administration and Society* 6 (4): 445–88.

Will, G. 1996. Moral Defect or Medical Problem? *San Diego Union Tribune,* Apr. 4.

Wilson, J. Q. 1989. *Bureaucracy: What Government Agencies Do and Why They Do It.* New York: Basic Books.

Zuriff, G. E. 1996. Medicalizing Character. *Public Interest* (Spring): 94–99.

Chapter VI

Compliance with the ADA and Employment of Those with Mental Disabilities

Teresa L. Scheid

Introduction

This chapter reports on the response of the business community to the American with Disabilities Act (ADA) with specific focus on the employment of those with mental disabilities. The ADA is viewed as an important legal and normative demand to which businesses are expected to adapt or conform. Yet organizations comply with legal prescriptions in accordance with prior ideological constructions and belief sets (Scheid-Cook 1992): if employers do not view those with mental illnesses as employable, they will not make any realistic attempt to hire those with mental disabilities, despite the requirements of the ADA. In addition to requiring structural changes, workplace accommodations include the perceptions and attitudes of employers (Bonnie and Monahan 1997; Hall and Hall 1994).

As we are all painfully aware, mental disability is widely associated with social stigma (Link 1987; Link, Mirotznik, and Cullen 1991), which is itself a significant barrier to employment for individuals with mental disabilities. Hence, successful employment of those with mental disabilities must target the workplace itself (Yelin and Katz 1994), and organizational cultures must be modified to be more receptive to change and accepting of people with disabilities (Zuckerman 1994). Yet we know little about the impact that the ADA has had on employment practices, much less about employers' efforts to provide a supportive work environment.

In order to examine the response of businesses to the ADA, I collected two sets of data: (1) Study A: a focused in-depth interview with a small sample of employers (n = 14) who have employed individuals with severe, persistent mental illness via supported employment; and (2) Study B: a survey of a random sample of 117 businesses in a major metropolitan city. Study A explored the experience of employers who provided supported employment to individuals with severe mental illnesses. Study B examined the response of a random sample of businesses to the ADA, what factors contribute to compliance with the ADA, employment practices with regard to those with mental disabilities, the degree of stigma which exists regarding the "mentally ill," and the role played by stigma in the employment of those with mental disabilities. In addition, I asked questions about the work environment and attempts to create an organizational culture that is supportive of those with disabilities. The survey also asked which mechanisms businesses thought would help them employ more people with mental disabilities. Consequently, the data presented will add to the general understanding of whether or not businesses have hired those with mental disabilities, their experience with these employees, and what factors contribute to compliance with the ADA, and will address more pragmatic concerns about increasing the viability of the ADA with respect to those with mental disabilities.

Mental Illness, Employment, and Stigma

This research focuses specifically on those with severe, persistent mental illnesses because much attention has been focused on the employability of this population and on the potential impact of the ADA (thus the discussion eliminates those with developmental disabilities, mental retardation, or organic brain disorders). For ease of description, I refer to the target population of this research as individuals with mental disability because this terminology is consistent with the language of the ADA. When such individuals receive services from the mental health system they are generally referred to as consumers. Unlike many physical handicaps, mental disability is not easily discernible. In addition, mental illness is widely associated with stigma, which is itself a significant barrier to employment.

Difficulty maintaining steady employment is seen as a defining feature of severe mental illness (Gerhart 1990); many argue that psychiatric illness impairs work capacity (Dilling and Weyener 1980). Jobs that require low levels of skill and concentration are generally considered suitable for those with mental disability, yet these jobs are frequently low pay, low status, entry level, and involve menial labor (Anthony and Blanch 1987; Wansbrough and Cooper 1980). Such jobs may not result in the development of new skills or a sense of mastery and may negatively impact upon self-esteem as well as be a tangible source of psychological stress. Of course, unemployment is also associated with these same problems (Scheid 1993).

Increasing the employment opportunities of individuals with mental disability is consistent with the objectives of normalization whereby consumers are expected to resume normal lives in the community and reduce their dependence upon mental health services. Sullivan (1992) found that consumers most often mentioned vocational activity (85 percent) as central to their successful adaptation to community living. Consequently, many programs providing services to consumers have focused upon employment and offer skills training, workshops, some form of vocational rehabilitation, and transitional or supported employment (Lang and Cara 1989). Transitional employment refers to part-time, entry-level jobs that prepare consumers for permanent employment while supported employment is competitive (though limited to twenty hours a week) and provides ongoing supports such as job-site training, ongoing monitoring, or job coaches (Hirsch 1989).

In an exploratory study of ten consumers conducted in 1993 and 1994, Scheid and Anderson (1995) found that while mental illness had disrupted life trajectory and career plans, many consumers were able to work during times of emotional distress and exacerbation of the illness, although at reduced capacity. A key factor was a supportive work environment where employers and coworkers knew about the problems experienced by the consumer and made allowances for his or her special needs. Additional supports and backup (such as substitute workers, shortened work schedules, and shared jobs) are needed to help consumers cope with the problems of severe mental illnesses (Bachrach 1991). Employers providing low-level menial jobs generally have little incentive to provide a supportive work environment as the worker can be quickly and easily replaced.

Other researchers have also targeted the work environment as being critical in the ability of consumers to maintain employment (Cook 1992). Storey and Horne (1991) found that the characteristics of the job site may have had a greater impact on the social integration of thirty-seven adults with severe mental disabilities than the fact of supported employment itself. An earlier study of the first jobs of schizophrenics found that "noisome" job conditions may have been a factor in precipitation of the disorder (Link, Dohrenwend, and Skodol 1986, p. 256). It is not merely a matter of developing realistic expectations about the abilities of consumers (Bachrach 1991); in addition to preparing workers for employment, focus must be directed toward changing the expectations of the workplace (Midgley 1990; Zuckerman 1994).

One major barrier to the successful employment of those with mental disabilities is stigma. Stigma refers to the application of a negative trait to a group or an individual. Susman (1994) examines the influence of stigma on those with disabilities, which she defines as a loss or abnormality of psychological or physiological functions. Individuals are twice stigmatized by the labels of disability and mental illness; the labels of "mentally ill" and "disabled" override other personality traits and the individual is assigned a "spoiled identity" (Goffman 1961). The stereotypical view is that those with mental illnesses are unpredictable, irrational, slow, stupid, and unreliable. Mental illness is also associated with violence or dangerousness (Monahan 1992). Such labels are not generally associated with that of a desirable employee. Ravaud, Madiot, and Ville (1992) found employers did discriminate against physically disabled individuals; consequently, employment rates for the disabled are much lower than for the general population (Yelin and Katz 1994). Baldwin's chapter in this volume looks at the employment rates and costs of discrimination for individuals with mental disabilities. Manning and White (1995) found that employers hold stigmatized and ignorant attitudes toward those with mental disabilities and were reluctant to hire these individuals. Braddock and Bachelder (1994) also found that employers held false assumptions about job-related abilities and the costs of accommodations. In field experiments, researchers have demonstrated that a history of mental illness will lead to fewer job offers and more negative reactions from employers (Farina and Felner 1973; Webber and Orcutt 1984).

Not only does stigma result in such negative reactions as devaluation and discrimination, the labeled individual has also internalized these community attitudes and comes to anticipate rejection from others (Link 1987). Link found that psychiatric patients' expectations of rejection produced demoralization, as patients expected others to find them less able, less intelligent, and less worthy of trust. In comparing psychiatric patients (labeled mentally ill) and untreated community residents (not labeled mentally ill), Link reported that beliefs about devaluation and discrimination (a scale he developed to assess common stigmatizing beliefs about those with mental illness) had a significantly greater impact upon those labeled as mentally ill. Further, there was no association between the specific psychiatric conditions (schizophrenia and major depression) and the effect of the devaluation–discrimination measure, strengthening the claim that it is the *label* and not the underlying psychiatric condition that accounts for the negative effects of stigma.

Stigma was found to produce more than demoralization; stigmatized individuals in fact earned less income and were unemployed for greater periods of time (Link 1987). Individuals with mental disabilities face the dilemma of informing potential employers about their "illness" and risking the resultant stigmatized reaction, or else "passing" and thus being unable to ask for additional support during times when the illness may interfere with one's capacity to work. One of the purposes of the ADA was to provide some legal sanctions against the more overt forms of discrimination directed toward employees which results from the stigma of mental illness.

Understanding Business Response to the ADA: Ritual Conformity

The ADA is a legal and normative demand to which businesses are expected to conform. Hence the ADA is a feature of the institutional environment: those normative demands, societal preferences, and legal policies that impinge on organizational activity. Institutional theory (DiMaggio and Powell 1991; Scott 1991) is a theoretical paradigm that examines the relationship between organizations and their institutional environments. Organizations are expected to conform to institutional expectations and constraints if they are to maintain legitimacy; this is referred to as "ritual conformity," as the organization is both attempting to meet agreed-upon social definitions and expectations while also maintaining social beliefs about the purposes of the organization (Scott 1983). Employers seeking to conform to the ADA must meet expectations about hiring those with disabilities while also maintaining their reputations for efficient production or service.

The most direct and unambiguous forms of institutional influence are formal laws (Fligstein 1991; Scott 1991). Legal mandates are part of the organization's institutional environment and direct organizational activity via normative demands (termed rational myths) that can be clearly identified as constraints. Organizational conformity with rational myths is generally referred to as isomorphism, and it is postulated that structural responses to the same rational myth will be similar— referred to as the homogenization of organizational response (DiMaggio and Powell 1983). As described by DiMaggio and Powell, institutional isomorphism can take three forms: normative, mimetic, or coercive.

Normative isomorphism is associated with the social influence of professionalism and refers to the legitimating force of professional expertise as well as the growth of professional networks that increasingly influence organizational activities and meanings (DiMaggio and Powell 1983). That is, professionalization is the source of organizational meanings and taken-for-granted definitions of how things ought to be done. Normative isomorphism also consists of adaptations (or conformity) to wider social beliefs and expectations. For example, deinstitutionalism was not singularly a movement within the professional mental health community; it had strong ideological grounding in the wider society (as exemplified by such movies as *One Flew over the Cuckoo's Nest*).

Mimetic isomorphism is a standard response to the conditions of uncertainty (DiMaggio and Powell 1983) whereby the organization duplicates or copies the behavior of other organizations in its sector. The organization may be unaware that it is "copying"; rather, it may simply be using another organization as a source for practices it will implement.

Coercive isomorphism refers to direct pressures placed on an organization by its environment to comply with various types of institutional demands. Governmental mandates such as the ADA clearly call forth ritual conformity that can be characterized as coercive in that the organization is legally compelled to adopt the policies specified. Yet the relationship between a legal mandate and organizational activity cannot be adequately captured by coercive isomorphism. Previous research on organizational compliance to another legal policy relevant to those with mental disabilities (outpatient commitment) demonstrated that mental health organizations manipulated and in large part created (or enacted) the very legal constraints to which they then adapted (Scheid-Cook 1992). Businesses may utilize a variety of responses to the ADA, hence manifesting diverse forms of ritual conformity that might include normative, mimetic, or coercive isomorphism as well as avoidance, ignorance, and manipulation of the statutes.

The ADA represents a federal mandate to end discrimination against those with disabilities and requires that employers make reasonable accommodations for employees with mental disabilities (Crist and Stoffel 1992; Essex-Sorlie 1994; Reed 1992). One of the more revolutionary and contentious aspects of the 1990 ADA is its coverage of persons with a mental impairment (any mental or psychological disorder, including mental retardation, developmental disability, organic brain syndrome, emotional or mental illness, or specific learning disabilities). Excluded are those whose disability would pose a threat to the health and safety of those not covered by the ADA, an important qualification when considering mental disability and the attitudes of employers toward those with mental illnesses. Hantula and Reily (1996, p. 110) argue that mental illnesses are the "least

protected and most misunderstood disorders covered by the law." While employers with fifteen or more employees are required to make reasonable accommodations to individuals with a mental disability, if they can show the specific
accommodation would cause undue hardship, would be financially costly, or
would fundamentally alter the type of operations of the business, they are not
required to hire individuals covered by the ADA (Reed 1992). Employers are also
expected to complete a job analysis to determine the essential features of the job
and to rework job descriptions so that the position could be filled by a qualified
individual with a disability. This is referred to as a Title I Implementation Plan.

The impact of the ADA is particularly equivocal when considering the
employability of those with mental disabilities. Mental disabilities are the second most common charge of discrimination under the ADA filed with the
EEOC (9.9 percent of the cases) and constitute 12.5 percent of all EEOC
charges having to do with harassment on the job (Hall 1997, p. 257). Yet mental disabilities are viewed with more skepticism, and there is far less professional
consensus on the diagnosis and treatment of mental illnesses. Consequently, the
meaning of the terms "qualified individual with a disability" or "reasonable
accommodation" is even more ambiguous with reference to mental disabilities.
Mental disabilities primarily affect, and are affected by, interactions with others.
For these individuals the job environment consists not only of essential job
functions, but of employee and coworker attitudes toward those with mental
health problems (Crist and Stoffel 1992; Hall and Hall 1994). Yet it is very
difficult to modify the social relations of the workplace.

Another issue is stigma. The fact is that the stigma associated with mental
illness has limited the job opportunities of millions of Americans (Ravid and
Menen 1993) as employers simply do not believe such individuals can perform
a job. Indeed, as reported by Mancuso (1990), many individuals with mental
illness do experience problems with concentration, maintaining stamina, managing time pressures and deadlines, focusing on multiple tasks simultaneously,
and initiating interpersonal contact. In previous research it was found that consumers themselves found that feeling tired and slowed down (a side effect of
psychotropic medications) and difficulties dealing with coworkers and customers to be major handicaps in their ability to manage a full-time job (Scheid and
Anderson 1995). Yet this is not to deny that consumers are employable, simply
that special attention must be given to matching the individual to the job and
to ensuring that employers (and coworkers) are willing to provide a supportive
work environment whereby needed accommodations are made to allow those
with the aforementioned problems to work. This is difficult to do if the mental
disability is not acknowledged.

The ADA does not require the individual to disclose his or her mental disability "because of the stigma associated with mental health problems" (Crist and Stoffel 1992, p. 437). Yet if individuals do not disclose their disability, they are not entitled to any kind of accommodation. This constitutes a very difficult dilemma for both those with mental disabilities and mental health professionals seeking to place their clients in competitive employment. While employees who do disclose their mental disability may be better off (Hall 1997; Stone and Colella 1996), this may well have more to do with the employer's tolerance and openness in the first place (i.e., an employer that an employee feels comfortable discussing his mental disability with is more likely to be willing to make accommodations for such disabilities).

Rybski (1992) argues that organizations must take a proactive stance toward the hiring of those with mental disabilities and seek innovative ways of matching a given individual to a job; persons with disabilities must be seen as valued rather than as a handicap. It is anticipated that employers will need to be educated about the various accommodations that are needed. As mental illness is exhibited in behavior, more than the physical requirements of the job need to be modified; employers must be willing to modify the scheduling and supervision of work as well as policies governing interpersonal relations on the job (Hall 1997; Kaufmann 1993). While the meaning of "reasonable accommodation" for those with mental disability is unclear (Haimowitz 1991), some examples of typical accommodations include part-time or flexible work schedules; provision of unpaid leave days for illnesses, difficult times, or appointments with service providers; redelegation of work assignments; and the use of a job coach or shared jobs (Reed 1992). Other examples of workplace modifications for those with mental disabilities include breaking existing jobs into simpler components, providing written instructions so as to minimize misunderstandings, and daily planning sessions (Rybski 1992). Changes in supervisory relations and modifications of performance expectations may also be necessary (Hall 1997). Furthermore, extra tolerance for unusual behavior—such as muttering or social withdrawal—is needed (Kaufmann 1993).

Yet employers and businesses have no incentive to make these kind of accommodations, beyond their own altruism. It is not anticipated that merely prescribing, by law, that employers must make reasonable accommodations will produce the kinds of needed changes in the workplace which will lead to the employment of greater numbers of mentally handicapped individuals. The very meaning of the ADA will be constructed both by the reactions of employers as well as by the resulting legal interpretations of violations of the ADA. In order to understand what effect the ADA has had upon the employment of those with mental disabilities, I undertook an exploratory study of businesses in one metropolitan community.

Data Sources

This exploratory study of compliance with the ADA was conducted in a major Southern metropolitan area with a low unemployment rate (3.5 percent at the time of data collection) and a mental health system widely recognized to provide quality care. In the summer of 1995 I conducted personal, in-depth interviews with fourteen of the fifteen employers who had hired individuals with severe mental illnesses via supported employment (Study A). Interviews were conducted with the company representative who had direct responsibility for employment practices and policies; in the case of small businesses the CEO or owner was the source of information. These employers had been contacted by a vocational rehabilitation counselor (job coach) who worked for the local Psychosocial Rehabilitation Program and had agreed to work with one or more severely, persistently mentally ill clients. The fifteen businesses had employed twenty-six clients during the previous year. I asked these employers about their knowledge of the ADA, their experience with supported employment and the job coach, mental illness and how it affected the capacity of an individual to work, and to describe accommodations they had made for these employees. Employers also provided an assessment of their company's work environment. Interviews were conducted by the author at the business sites and generally took forty-five minutes to an hour to complete. Given the small sample and the open-ended nature of the interviews, techniques for qualitative data analysis were utilized (Strauss and Corbin 1990).

The information from the personal interviews was then used to construct a fixed choice questionnaire which could be administered over the telephone to a random sample of local businesses (Study B). Many questions from the *International Center for the Disabled Survey II: Employing Disabled Americans* (Louis Harris and Associates 1987) were modified to focus on mental disability. The questionnaire asks the personnel manager or appropriate company representative to provide information on the company's knowledge and awareness of the ADA, specific employment policies and practices, experience with past and current employees with a mental disability and any needed accommodations that were made, and the company's work environment. Company representatives are also asked to assess the efforts made by their companies to hire those with mental handicaps and to provide feedback on a list of proposed initiatives and policy changes which might help employ more people with a mental handicap. Finally, company representatives were asked to assess community attitudes toward the "mentally ill." The questionnaire was pretested on forty-three businesses and then modified. Respondents from another seventy-four businesses were interviewed for a total sample of 117. These interviews were conducted over the telephone by graduate assistants and generally took a half hour to complete. Interviewing began in the fall of 1995 and was completed in the spring of 1997.

The sample was drawn from the locally generated *Major Employers Directory*, which lists companies representing each industrial division in the Standard Metropolitan Statistical Area (SMSA). I eliminated those occupations that required some kind of specialized training (such as computer programming) or involved dangerous or hazardous work (such as chemical plants), and then systematically sampled a proportional number of businesses from each of the major employment categories: manufacturing, wholesale trade, retail trade (including restaurant chains and hotels), health services, construction, transportation, communication, utilities, business and social services, finance and insurance, and educational and governmental organizations (n = 160). Another thirty businesses that were owned by minorities (as identified by the city Black Pages and the minority business directory of a neighboring county) were also randomly selected for a total sample of 190 organizations.

As noted above, interviews were completed with forty-three company representatives to pretest the instrument. The questionnaire was revised, and questions were added to assess some of the reasons for business compliance (or lack thereof) with the ADA and to provide a better analysis of stigma. In terms of stigma, I added a series of questions asking respondents to evaluate the employability of potential employees. Generally the interviews were completed with either the human resources manager or the personnel director (63 percent), and the rate of refusals was low (8.9 percent). The difficulty was in getting the appropriate person on the phone and scheduling the interview. Voice mail has added to this difficulty. Table 1 contains more detailed information about the rate of response and refusals for each major employment division; we had an overall response rate of 61.6 percent. Company representatives answered all the questions about their employment policies quite readily, and only one expressed any discomfort with the questions about community attitudes toward the mentally ill. In fact, most enjoyed the interview and a few kept the interviewer on the phone for over an hour.

Table 1: Sample and Response Rate

Type of Business	Sample N	Completed	Refused	Response Rate (%)
Wholesale trade	15	9	4	60.0
Retail trade (including hotels)	31	24	2	77.0
Manufacturing	41	24	7	58.0
Construction and transportation*	13	3	2	23.0
Health services	16	10	0	62.0
Communication	3	2	0	67.0
Business and social services	14	6	1	43.0
Utilities	4	3	0	75.0
Finance and insurance	8	7	0	87.0
Educational	7	5	1	71.0
Governmental	8	8	0	100.0
Minority owned†	30	16	0	53.0
Totals	**190**	**117**	**17**	**61.6**

* We had a great deal of difficulty contacting anyone in these two types of business; one can only speculate that due to the nature of the business, no one was available.

† Minority-owned businesses are also classified as to what type of business they are; the majority are retail firms or small-business services having fewer than 100 employees.

The data presented in table 1 are primarily descriptive and focus on the response of businesses to the ADA. Comparisons are made between businesses that have complied with the ADA by either hiring individuals with mental disabilities or who have developed policies to hire such individuals. Statistical analyses consist of simple group comparisons, utilizing contingency table analysis (where the variable of interest is categorical), and comparison of group means (where the variable of interest is continuous).

Findings

STUDY A: SUPPORTED EMPLOYMENT

The employers who had hired individuals with severe mental disability via supported employment displayed a normative commitment to hiring such individuals and were largely unaware of the legal requirements of the ADA. Interviews were completed with fourteen businesses (out of fifteen) who had employed twenty-six individuals with severe mental disability. While some of these businesses were quite small, the majority employed over twenty-five workers and most of the jobs were in the service sector (fast food, grocery stores, retail, domestic work) with a few in the manufacturing industries.

In general, employers had very positive experiences with their employees with mental disability; eleven out of fourteen reported being very satisfied and having good overall experiences. The majority felt that these employees did face minor limitations in the work that they could do, and generally that these employees needed more time or worked more slowly than other employees. Most felt the degree of limitation depended on the specific individual or the nature of the job—indicating that levels of stigma were very low. Neither did the employers appear to have a preconceived notion of the mental illness or of the mentally ill in general; they seemed willing to judge each employee individually.

Several of the employers were not aware that they had hired an individual with a mental disability, though most were, and the majority had worked with a job coach. The experience with the job coach was very positive, though one employer noted that it was time-consuming to have to train the job coach as well as the employee. However, seven felt that the job coach had made a significant and positive contribution to the successful employment experience with the consumer. Many employers commented that they found it useful to be informed about the specific nature of the disorder experienced by the employee, and to have been provided with information about likely limitations or difficulty prior to employment so that the employer could be prepared to face an emergency (such as a seizure or a period of slowed energy or depression).

In general, the majority of the employers reported a positive work environment, in both large and small companies. Those businesses with a stressful work climate, or those weak in employee morale, also had less successful experiences with employees, and it is likely that these work environments are generally unsupportive of any employee with specific or unique needs.

While most of the employers did not feel that individuals with mental disabilities in general needed special workplace accommodations, they were asked to respond to a list of specific accommodations identified in the rehabilitation literature as necessary based upon their experience with these employees. The percentages indicate agreement that employees with mental disabilities need jobs where instructions are straightforward (77.8 percent), that involve interaction with others (66.7 percent), allow for frequent breaks (55.5 percent), and where the job requires simple, repetitive tasks (55.5 percent). Less important were close supervision (44.5 percent) and jobs described as relatively uncomplicated (44.4 percent) or requiring low skill levels (44.5 percent).

I also examined the job tenure of employees with mental disability, looking at placements with longer job tenure as "successful" and those with short tenures as "unsuccessful." The job characteristics of successful and unsuccessful placements were analyzed using information on the work environment obtained from the employers as well as the characteristics of specific occupations obtained from the *Dictionary of Occupational Titles*.

Jobs that were less successful for those with severe mental disabilities required higher education, more training, more intelligence, higher verbal ability, better sensory judgment, more dealings with people, more pressure, and greater variety and change. While there was a great deal of variability in the "successful" jobs, they were all low in skill level (dishwasher, file clerk, cleaning, simple repetitive tasks), low in educational requirements, and required fairly low-level worker functions (i.e., taking instructions, serving, or handling objects as opposed to precision working or manipulation). None of the successful jobs required abstract or creative work; all involved routine and concrete activities. Few of the successful jobs required variety and change, while all of the unsuccessful jobs did. Furthermore, the majority of the successful jobs did not require performance under stress, while most of the unsuccessful jobs did. Likewise, most of the successful jobs did not require that the employee deal with people, while most of the unsuccessful jobs did.

The data from the in-depth interviews with employers who had provided supported employment was useful in understanding the experience of employers with their employees with severe mental illnesses, and in providing information on the benefits (and weaknesses) of supported employment. Yet this data does not tell us much about the experiences of employers in general or of the effect of the ADA on hiring practices. A fixed choice questionnaire was constructed, pretested, revised, and administered to a random sample of businesses in order to gain a more general understanding of employers' compliance with the ADA. I turn now to a discussion of the findings from this data.

STUDY B: COMPETITIVE EMPLOYMENT

A majority (78.6 percent) of the 117 companies surveyed had received formal information about the ADA, while 20.5 percent had not received such information (table 2). The source of the information about the ADA was divided between internal channels (37.0 percent), external channels (34.0 percent), and the EEOC (26 percent). In terms of specific practices that indicated compliance with the mandates of the ADA, only 33.3 percent of the companies had a Title I implementation plan, 35.9 percent did not, and 30.8 percent were unsure whether they did or not. Only 15.4 percent of the companies had a specific policy for hiring those with mental disabilities; 67.5 percent stated they had no such policy. While half (n = 6) implemented this policy when the ADA went into effect, 33.3 percent (n = 4) had such policies before the ADA went into effect. Few of these companies (14.3 percent) had a specific person or department that oversaw the hiring of those with mental handicaps; when they did, the individual or department was generally the same one that oversaw the hiring of individuals with physical disabilities (91.7 percent). Only 27.4 percent indicated that their company had a program or distributed literature to help managers and employers learn to work with the mentally disabled. The survey compared hiring of those with mental handicaps to other "target" populations by asking if companies made a special effort to hire people from minority groups (68.4 percent reported yes), people with physical handicaps (41.0 percent reported yes), and people with mental handicaps (33.3 percent reported yes). I label those businesses who make special recruiting efforts to hire the mentally disabled as proactive businesses.

While a relatively small number of companies had specific policies or programs targeting the hiring of those with mental disabilities, in fact 37.6 percent

Table 2: Compliance with the ADA

Status	% of 117 Employers Responding Yes
Received Formal Information on the ADA	78.6
Compliance with the ADA	
Title I implementation plan	33.3
Specific policy for hiring mentally disabled	15.4
Program or literature distribution to managers	27.4
Effects on Employment Practices	
Special effort to hire minority groups	68.4
Special effort to hire people with physical handicaps	41.0
Special effort to hire people with mental handicaps (proactive)	33.3
Mentally disabled employee hired since ADA	37.6
Workplace accommodations needed	61.0
Cost of accommodations not at all expensive	79.2
Satisfied with Employees with Mental Disabilities	70.0

had hired such an employee since the ADA went into effect in January of 1992. Company representatives reported that many such employees (46.9 percent) came in on their own initiative (the most common route to employment) or had been referred to the company by external sources (either a government vocational rehabilitation agency, a private vocational rehabilitation agency, a state employment service, private employment services, or an agency which places those with mental disabilities). It is of course very likely that these companies have more employees with mental disabilities, but the company is unaware of the disability. Sixty-one percent of the companies had made specific accommodations, with the majority adjusting work hours, creating part-time jobs, or restructuring jobs; 79.2 percent reported that these accommodations were not expensive at all; 16.7 percent found them somewhat expensive; and only 4.2 percent found them very expensive. Seventy percent of the employers were satisfied with their employees with mental disabilities; only two expressed dissatisfaction. Companies that had not hired a mentally disabled employee had a wide variety of reasons; the most common were a lack of qualified applicants (27.6 percent), the perception that these employees would be a safety risk to themselves or others (20.7 percent), or an absence of job openings (15.3 percent).

We also asked if company representatives knew of any business that had been accused of an ADA violation, whether they thought it likely that violations would result in a suit, and how costly the consequences of such a suit would be. This question was in the revised questionnaire and consequently was answered only by seventy-four business respondents. While very few knew of any accusation of ADA violations (13.5 percent, and only half of these had resulted in a suit), 83.6 percent thought that if a company were to violate the ADA a suit would ensue; 69.8 percent thought the business would lose that suit; 83.4 percent thought the consequences of a successful suit would be costly; and 75.4 percent thought the consequences of an unsuccessful suit would be costly. We also asked an open-ended question to see what businesses thought some of the benefits of ADA compliance were; slightly over half articulated coercive rationales for compliance—to avoid negative legal sanctions or the costs of a lawsuit. Another 49 percent articulated normative rationales for compliance, stating "it's the right thing to do," "to promote equity," or to "give everyone an equal chance."

A majority (54.3 percent) of the companies surveyed felt they were doing enough now to employ those with mental disabilities; 19.8 percent indicated they should be doing more; and 49.5 percent indicated that they thought they actually would make a greater effort to hire such employees in the next three years. In terms of policies or procedures to help employ more individuals with mental disabilities, the greatest support was given to policies which placed responsibility on the mental health or rehabilitation community; companies indicated they thought using job coaches or having disability professionals provide assistance to companies and mentally disabled employees to be the most helpful policies (data not shown). Policies that targeted the company (i.e., establishing voluntary employment targets, providing internships or part-time jobs, awareness training) were perceived as less likely to result in the employment of more people with mental disabilities. Awareness training, either by the company or by an outside agency, was generally viewed as an effective strategy.

ANALYSIS OF FACTORS AFFECTING COMPLIANCE

In order to compare those businesses that had displayed compliance with the ADA with those that had not, those businesses that had hired a mentally disabled individual since the ADA went into effect were combined with those that had a proactive recruiting policy. These organizations are referred to as compliers. I then compared the fifty-eight (49.5 percent) compliers with the fifty-nine (50.5 percent) noncompliers. I begin here by first examining the type of organizations that complied with the ADA and then determine whether such compliance was a result of primarily mimetic, coercive, or normative conformity with the mandates of the ADA. Finally, I examine the effect on compliance of stigma, or discriminatory attitudes toward those with mental disabilities.

Compliance was significantly associated with receiving information about the ADA, the type of business, and organizational size (table 3). Compliers were more likely to be government or educational organizations, and noncompliers were more likely to engage in wholesale trade, although compliers were no more likely to be white-collar or for their employees to possess a college degree. Larger companies were significantly more likely to be in compliance with the ADA, which is consistent with previous research. Proactive policies toward hiring those from minority groups or those with physical disabilities were significantly related with compliance, although minority-owned businesses were less likely to be compliers (despite the fact that they were more likely to have proactive policies for hiring minorities). Six of the businesses in our sample belonged to an affiliation labeled the Business Advisory Council; their stated purpose is to help promote employment opportunities for minorities and the disabled. However, these businesses were not any more likely to be in compliance with the ADA in terms of their employment of those with mental disabilities.

Table 3: Organizational Factors Affecting Compliance

Organizational Characteristics	Noncompliers		Compliers	
	Number	%	Number	%
Received information on the ADA (p = .0114)				
Yes	40	69.0	52	88.1
No	18	31.0	7	11.9
Type of business (p = .0670)				
Wholesale trade	10	17.2	1	1.7
Retail trade	16	27.6	16	27.1
Manufacturing (transportation and construction)	12	20.7	15	25.4
Health services	5	8.6	5	8.5
Business, utilities, and communications	11	19.0	12	20.3
Education and government	4	6.9	10	16.9
% blue collar and manual employees (standard deviation)	54	(35)	60	(29)
% employees with college degree (standard deviation)	24	(22)	31	(27)
Size of business (p = .0042)				
< 100 employees	16	27.6	4	6.8
100–249	22	37.9	18	30.5
250–499	11	19.0	12	20.3
500–1000	3	5.2	10	16.9
> 1,000	6	10.3	15	25.3
Minority-owned business (p = .0064)				
Yes	13	22.4	3	5.1
No	45	77.6	56	94.9
Member of business advisory council				
Yes	4	6.9	2	3.4
No	54	93.1	57	96.6
Insurance coverage for mental illness (p = .0017)				
Yes	19	54.3	34	87.2
No	16	45.7	5	12.8

Organizational Characteristics	Noncompliers		Compliers	
	Number	%	Number	%
Employee assistance program (p = .0108)				
Yes	18	51.4	31	79.5
No	17	48.6	8	20.5
Orientation for working with mentally disabled (p = .0049)				
Yes	9	15.5	23	39.0
No	49	84.5	36	61.0
Department overseeing hiring of disabled (p = .0088)				
Yes	1	2.9	10	23.8
No	34	97.1	32	76.2

Indicators of Supportive Work Environment
(Scale of 1-10, with 10 Most Supportive)

	Mean	(Standard Deviation)	Mean	(Standard Deviation)
Employers and supervisors are supportive of one another's efforts	7.3	(1.7)	7.4	(1.7)
Improved performance by coaching or counseling emphasized	7.2	(1.7)	7.5	(1.4)
Supervisors are rewarded for developing talents and ability of subordinates	7.4	(1.5)	7.8	(1.3)
Employees try to get to know one another (p = .0930)	7.3	(1.8)	7.8	(1.5)
Emphasis is placed on social and communal responsibility	6.5	(2.1)	6.9	(1.7)

Table 4: Compliance Rationales

Status	Noncompliers		Compliers	
	Number	%	Number	%
Mimetic Conformity				
When interview completed				
Fall 1995	13	22.4	12	20.3
Spring 1996	10	17.2	8	13.6
Winter 1996–1997	11	19.0	20	33.9
Spring 1997	24	41.4	19	32.2
When information on ADA received				
Ongoing	20	51.3	28	56.0
When ADA passed	6	15.4	3	6.0
Within past 3 years	11	28.2	16	32.0
Within past year	2	5.1	2	6.0
Source of information on the ADA				
Internal	14	35.0	20	40.8
External	14	35.0	17	34.7
EEOC	12	30.0	12	24.5
Coercive Conformity				
Violations of ADA likely to result in complaint or lawsuit (p = .0072)				
Yes	25	71.4	36	94.7
No	10	28.6	2	5.3
Business likely to lose lawsuit if ADA violated (p = .0230)				
Yes	20	57.1	31	81.6
No	15	42.9	7	18.4
Normative Conformity				
Hired mentally disabled individuals prior to ADA (p = .0070)				
Yes	3	8.6	15	38.5
No	12	34.3	6	15.4
Not sure	20	57.1	18	46.2
Company engaged in systematic efforts to create a supportive culture (p = .0118)				
Yes	8	22.9	20	51.3
No or not sure	27	77.1	19	48.3

Providing insurance for mental illnesses and/or having an employee assistance program were also organizational features that were positively associated with compliance. Not surprisingly, compliers were also more likely to provide an orientation for their employees to learn to work with those with mental disabilities, and to have a specific person or department that oversees the hiring of those with disabilities. Yet compliers were not significantly likely to have a supportive work environment (although the mean scores are higher on all of the supportive measures), although they were more likely to be workplaces where their employees "try to get to know one another." We now turn to the motivations for this compliance by examining the indicators of mimetic, coercive, and normative conformity.

Mimetic conformity can be assessed by determining whether compliance increased over time. Since interviews were completed over close to a two-year period (fall 1995 to spring 1997), we can determine if compliance was motivated by a mimetic response to increased awareness and knowledge about the minimal costs of most accommodations. We also asked companies when they received information about the ADA. As we can see in table 3, time was not associated with compliance; organizations interviewed in the spring of 1997 were not significantly more likely to be in compliance with the ADA. Nor were those companies who received information about the ADA more recently more or less likely to be in compliance. Another indicator of mimetic conformity would be if the information about the ADA came from outside the company but not from the EEOC or other governmental agency. Once again, the source of the information received about the ADA had no relationship with compliance (table 4).

Coercive conformity is assessed by whether companies that had complied were concerned with negative sanctions. Those that had complied with the ADA were significantly more likely to feel that if a business were to violate the ADA it would be likely to be subject to a complaint or a lawsuit, and to feel that if subject to a lawsuit it would be likely to lose the lawsuit (table 4).

Normative conformity is indicated if the business had hired those with disabilities prior to the ADA or had engaged in systematic efforts to create an organizational culture supportive of those with special needs. Compliers were significantly more likely to have hired a mentally disabled individual prior to the ADA, and noncompliers were much less likely to engage in efforts to create an organizational culture supportive of those with special needs (table 4).

It was anticipated that discriminatory attitudes and stigma would play a role in an employer's compliance with the ADA. While most of the employers surveyed

(52.1 percent) felt that the limitations imposed by mental illness "depended" on the degree or nature of the illness, which indicates a relatively unstigmatizing attitude, 22.2 percent felt that mental disability did impinge on an individual's level of understanding and mental comprehension, and 7.2 percent felt mental illness negatively affected productivity. Another concern was dangerousness; employers felt that these employees should not be given jobs that were in any way "dangerous" (24.6 percent of the employers targeted dangerous jobs as unsuitable). Many of those employers who had not hired a mentally disabled individual stated concern that these employees would be a safety risk to themselves or others (20.7 percent). One employer gave the example of an employee on "Prozac; you wouldn't want to put that person on any machinery because of the side effects of the medication." Another employer expressed concern that "you have a responsibility to other employees to keep someone who might be unstable—that is, violent—from hurting other employees." How widespread are such stigmatizing attitudes and how do they affect the behavior of companies in hiring those with mental disabilities?

As we can see in table 5, employers were most uncomfortable with employees with a sporadic work history (which is common among those with mental disabilities), a juvenile criminal record for petty theft, a history of substance abuse, a previous mental hospitalization, or with those taking antipsychotic medications. While only 43.8 percent were uncomfortable with a potential employee in treatment for depression, they were more comfortable with someone with no prior work experience, someone with a learning disability or a physical handicap, or a high school dropout.

It is clear that employers do hold discriminatory attitudes against those with mental health problems. Furthermore, noncompliers are more likely to be uncomfortable with employees with a previous mental hospitalization, those taking antipsychotic medications, and with employees with physical handicaps. Stigma was also accessed by using items from Link's devaluation-discrimination index and items from the *Market and Opinion Research International Study: Public Attitudes toward Mental Illness* (Huxley 1993). The questions asked respondents to assess how "most people" would act toward those with mental disabilities (table 6). There is little difference between compliers and noncompliers (which may point to weaknesses in these measures for assessing discriminatory attitudes), except that compliers are more likely to believe employees should have to tell an employer if they have been mentally ill (which may indicate an openness to accommodations).

Table 5: Degree of Discomfort with Various Types of Employees
Would Your Company Be Uncomfortable or Very
Uncomfortable with This Person as an Employee?

Person	% of All Employers (n = 73)	% of Noncompliers (n = 34)	% of Compliers (n = 39)
Sporadic work history	83.3	88.6	79.5
No prior work experience	33.8	34.3	33.3
Juvenile criminal record for petty theft	71.6	77.1	66.7
In treatment for depression	43.8	44.1	43.6
History of substance abuse	68.9	71.4	66.7
Learning disability	24.3	31.4	17.9
Physical handicap (p = .04)	16.2	25.7	7.7
High school dropout	20.3	20.0	20.5
Previous mental hospitalization (p = .12)	52.1	61.8	43.6
Taking antipsychotic medication (p = .04)	67.1	79.4	56.4

Conclusions

These results are preliminary and, given the small number of organizations surveyed, should be interpreted with some caution. Those businesses that had provided supported employment positions for individuals with a severe, persistent mental illness displayed normative isomorphism. That is, they had contact with mental health professionals and had decided to offer employment to those with a mental disability. These employers were in general very satisfied with these employees, but the jobs that seemed to result in successful employment (as measured by job tenure) were generally low skill and low status.

In the survey of the random sample of 117 businesses, only one-third of the companies had a Title I implementation plan and only 15.4 percent had specific policies for hiring those with mental disabilities. However, 37.6 percent had indeed hired such an individual. Large companies were more likely to comply with the ADA and hire those with mental disabilities, which is contrary to the expectation that organizations which process people continually, or in large batches, are less likely to individuate and more likely to apply labels (Ashworth and Humphrey 1995). Yet this supports the counterclaim that smaller compa-

Table 6: Assessment of Stigma against Those with Mental Disabilities

Items about Discrimination and Devaluation	Noncompliers (n = 58)	Compliers (n = 59)
	Scale of 1–5, with 5 = More Stigma (Standard Deviation)	
Most people believe a person who has been in a mental hospital is just as intelligent as the next person	3.4 (.99)	3.3 (1.1)
Most people believe that a former patient is just as trustworthy as an average citizen	3.2 (1.0)	3.1 (1.2)
Most people would accept a fully recovered former patient as a teacher of young children in a public school	3.8 (.92)	3.8 (1.0)
Most people would not hire a former mental patient to care for their children, even if he or she had been well for some time	3.6 (.96)	3.7 (1.0)
Most employers would hire a former mental patient if he or she were qualified for the job	2.7 (.97)	2.6 (1.1)
Most employers would pass over the application of a former mental patient in favor of another applicant	3.4 (.89)	3.3 (1.0)
Employers have a responsibility for the mental health of their employees	2.5 (1.1)	2.2 (1.1)
People should not have to tell an employer if they have been mentally ill (p = .0182)	3.0 (1.1)	2.5 (.90)
Stress at work is a major cause of mental illness	3.0 (1.0)	2.8 (1.2)
Most people with mental illness are unpredictable	2.5 (.86)	2.5 (.79)

nies are more suspicious of the ADA and fear it will be costly. Receiving information on the ADA was a significant factor in compliance, and governmental and educational agencies were more likely to comply with the ADA. It is likely that larger companies were more likely to comply with the ADA because of centralized and well-codified employment divisions within the company. Hence, large companies are more likely to receive information about the ADA and to be aware of current EEOC practices and policies, as are agencies in the public sector.

Employers in this sample were uncomfortable with employees who do have mental health problems (those who are taking antipsychotic medication, have a previous mental hospitalization, or are in treatment for depression). Stone and Colella (1996, p. 336) argue that "in work organizations supervisors may infer that individuals with 'dangerous' disabilities (e.g., mental illness) may be unlikely to comply with norms or rules, be more likely to have performance problems, or more likely to make coworkers uncomfortable than those with disabilities that are not dangerous." We found a good bit of evidence in the responses to open-ended questions (as well as the relevant fixed-choice questions) that employers were concerned with the potential dangerousness of individuals with mental disabilities. This is an issue that needs to be explored further.

Stone and Colella (1996) also argue that the more the organization values flexibility, egalitarianism, social justice, and cooperation, the more likely they are to hire, mentor, and promote the disabled. Companies who had complied with the ADA were more likely to feel that compliance with the ADA is "the right thing to do," to have hired those with mental disabilities prior to the ADA, and to have engaged in systematic efforts to create an organizational culture supportive of those with special needs.

However, conformity to the ADA cannot be characterized as primarily normative. The threat of negative sanctions also played an important role in compliance with the ADA. Specifically, employers were concerned with lawsuits and the costs of such lawsuits. Compliance with the ADA can also be characterized as coercive isomorphism, which is consistent with the ADA's status as a legal mandate. Business respondents also felt that employment of those with mental disabilities was not their responsibility, and they supported increased efforts in the rehabilitation community as opposed to policies developed within companies. Research is needed to see how policies that affect the employment of those with mental disabilities are developed, implemented, and practiced.

While the threat of legal sanction was significantly related to compliance, the long-lasting impact of the ADA will be contingent upon its ability to change the conceptual categories and assumptions employers and the public have of mental disability. When more employers articulate normative rationales for compliance and no longer equate mental disability with cognitive and functional impairment or dangerousness, then employment opportunities will improve. Furthermore, everyone must be more tolerant and open to working with coworkers who are different. The policies and practices which are exhibited by coworkers will have the greatest impact on the successful employment of those with mental disabilities (Stone and Colella 1996). We need more information about the nature of the job itself as well as more in-depth studies of interactions between employees with mental disabilities, coworkers, and supervisors in order to fully understand how workplaces can be made more supportive.

We could all benefit from environments that are less stressful, open to flexible schedules, and tolerant of individual idiosyncrasies. Employers must not only decide what is "reasonable" for the individual with a disability but what is fair to their other employees as well. It is partly out of this wider concern with equity that those with disabilities are generally unwilling to ask for special accommodations, as this marks the individual as different and in need of special treatment (Engel and Munger 1996). The ADA may have a greater than intended impact by actually creating more open, equitable, and hospitable work environments for all of us.

At the same time, the ADA may not be fully effective for individuals with mental disabilities because it is limited to competitive employment (Bell 1997). As with other employment policies, such as affirmative action for minorities, the law will help those who are least in need (i.e., those who are fully competitive in the labor market). Many individuals with mental disabilities, especially severe mental illnesses such as schizophrenia, may need noncompetitive employment in order to survive and thrive. The contemporary workplace is characterized by competition, pressure, and control—as well as patronizing and discriminatory attitudes. It may be too much to change the nature of the workplace.

Following Hahn (1996), a minority group perspective of disability grants individuals the right to be different and is consistent with models of consumer empowerment and advocacy. The meaning of disability needs to be reconstructed so that such differences are not seen either as functional limitations or as dangerous. Rather, these differences become a valid and valued employee contribution. In reconstructing the meaning of disability, we must all work to challenge prevailing conceptual categories that stigmatize those who are disabled. We might also work to reconceptualize the workplace; we would all benefit.

Note

This research was conducted with support from the University of North Carolina at Charlotte, Faculty Research Development funding. I am grateful to Myra Brown, Audrey Crowder, Terna Robertson, Elizabeth Smith, Victoria Szfransky, Debra Wakefield, and Keith Woodling for assistance with data collection.

References

Anthony, W., and A. Blanch. 1987. Supported Employment for Persons Who Are Psychiatrically Disabled: An Historical and Conceptual Perspective. *Psychosocial Rehabilitation Journal* 11:5–23.

Ashworth, B. E., and R. H. Humphrey. 1995. Labelling Processes in the Organization: Constructing the Individual. *Research in Organizational Behavior* 17:413–61.

Bachrach, L. L. 1991. Perspectives on Work and Rehabilitation. *Hospital and Community Psychiatry* 42:890–91.

Bell, C. G. 1997. The Americans with Disabilities Act, Mental Disability, and Work. In *Mental Disorder, Work Disability, and the Law,* ed. R. J. Bonnie and J. Monahan, pp. 203–19. Chicago: University of Chicago Press.

Braddock, D., and L. Bachelder. 1994. *The Glass Ceiling and Persons with Disabilities.* Washington, D.C.: Glass-Ceiling Commission, U.S. Department of Labor.

Bonnie, R. J., and J. Monahan. 1997. *Mental Disorder, Work Disability, and the Law.* Chicago: University of Chicago Press.

Cook, J. A. 1992. Outcome Assessment in Psychiatric Rehabilitation Services for Persons with Severe and Persistent Mental Illness. Prepared for the National Institute of Mental Health, Contract No. 91MF234749O2D.

Crist, P. A. H., and V. Stoffel. 1992. The ADA of 1990 and Employers with Mental Impairments: Personal Efficacy and the Environment. *American Journal of Occupational Therapy* 46:434–43.

Dilling, H., and S. Weyener. 1980. Psychiatric Illness and Work Capacity. In *The Social Consequences of Psychiatric Illness,* ed. L. N. Robins, P. J. Clayton, and J. K. Wing, pp. 229–47. New York: Brunner/Mazel.

DiMaggio, P., and W. Powell. 1983. The Iron Cage Revisited: Institutional Isomorphism and Collective Rationality in Organizational Fields. *American Sociological Review* 48:147–60.

———. 1991. *The New Institutionalism in Organizational Analysis.* Chicago: University of Chicago Press.

Engel, D., and F. W. Munger. 1996. Rights, Remembrance, and the Reconciliation of Differences. *Law and Society Review* 30:7–53.

Essex-Sorlie, D. 1994. The American with Disabilities Act: I. History, Summary and Key Components. *Academic Medicine* 69:519–24.

Farina, A., and R. D. Felner. 1973. Employment Interviewer Reactions to Former Mental Patients. *Journal of Abnormal Psychology* 82:268–72.

Fligstein, N. 1991. *The Transformation of Corporate Culture.* Cambridge, Mass.: Harvard University Press.

Gerhart, U. C. 1990. *Caring for the Chronically Mentally Ill.* Itasca, Ill.: F. E. Peacock.

Goffman, E. 1961. *Asylums.* Garden City, N.Y.: Anchor Books.

Hahn, Harlan. 1996. Antidiscrimination Laws and Social Research on Disability: The Minority Group Perspective. *Behavioral Sciences and the Law* 14:41–59.

Haimowitz, S. 1991. ADA of 1990: Its Significance for Persons with Mental Illness. *Hospital and Community Psychiatry* 42:23–24.

Hall, F. S., and E. L. Hall. 1994. The ADA: Going beyond the Law. *Academy of Management Review* 8:17–26.

Hall, L. L. 1997. Making the ADA Work for People with Psychiatric Disabilities. In *Mental Disorder, Work Disability, and the Law,* ed. R. J. Bonnie and J. Monahan, pp. 241–80. Chicago: University of Chicago Press.

Hantula, D. A., and N. A. Reilly. 1996. Reasonable Accommodation for Employees with Mental Disabilities: A Mandate for Effective Supervision? *Behavioral Sciences and the Law* 14:107–20.

Hayden, M. J. 1992. Disability Awareness Workshop: Helping Business Comply with the ADA of 1990. *American Journal of Occupational Therapy* 46:461–65.

Hirsch, S. W. 1989. Meeting the Vocational Needs of Individuals with Psychiatric Disabilities through Supported Employment. *Journal of Rehabilitation* 55:26–31.

Huxley, P. 1993. Location and Stigma: A Survey of Community Attitudes to Mental Illness: Part I. Enlightenment and Stigma. *Journal of Mental Health* 2:73–80.

Kaufmann, C. L. 1993. Reasonable Accommodation for Mental Disabilities at Work: Legal Constructs and Practical Application. *Journal of Psychiatry and Law* (Summer): 153–74.

Lang, S. K., and E. Cara. 1989. Vocational Integration for the Psychiatrically Disabled. *Hospital and Community Psychiatry* 40:890–92.

Link, B. G. 1987. Mental Patient Status, Work, and Income: An Examination of the Effects of a Psychiatric Label. *American Sociological Review* 47:202–15.

Link, B. G., B. P. Dohrenwend, and A. E. Skodol. 1986. Socio-economic Status and Schizophrenia: Noisome Occupational Characteristics as a Risk Factor. *American Sociological Review* 51:242–58.

Link, B. G., J. Mirotznik, and F. T. Cullen. 1991. The Effectiveness of Stigma Coping Orientations: Can Negative Consequences of Mental Illness Labelling Be Avoided? *Journal of Health and Social Behavior* 32:302–20.

Louis Harris and Associates. 1987. *The ICD Survey II: Employing Disabled Americans. A Nationwide Survey of 920 Employers.* Louis Harris and Associates Study No. 864009.

Mancuso, L. L. 1990. Reasonable Accommodation for Workers with Psychiatric Disabilities. *Psychosocial Rehabilitation Journal* 14:3–19.

Manning, C., and P. D. White. 1995. Attitudes of Employers to the Mentally Ill. *Psychiatric Bulletin* 19:541–43.

Midgley, G. 1990. The Social Context of Vocational Rehabilitation for Ex-psychiatric Patients. *British Journal of Psychiatry* 156:272–77.

Monahan, J. 1992. "A Terror to Their Neighbors": Beliefs about Mental Disorder and Violence in Historical and Cultural Perspective. *Bulletin of the American Academy of Psychiatry and Law* 20:191–96.

Ravaud, J. D., B. Madiot, and I. Ville. 1992. Discrimination towards Disabled People Seeking Employment. *Social Science and Medicine* 35:951–58.

Ravid, R., and S. Menen. 1993. Guidelines for Disclosure of Patient Information under the ADA. *Hospital and Community Psychiatry* 44:280–81.

Reed, K. L. 1992. History of Federal Legislation for Persons with Disabilities. *American Journal of Occupational Therapy* 46:397–408.

Rybski, D. 1992. A Quality Implementation of Title 1 of the ADA of 1990. *American Journal of Occupational Therapy* 46:409–18.

Scheid, T. L. 1993. An Investigation of Work and Unemployment among Psychiatric Clients. *International Journal of Health Services* 23:763–82.

Scheid, T. L., and C. Anderson. 1995. Living with Chronic Mental Illness: Understanding the Role of Work. *Community Mental Health Journal* 31:163-76.

Scheid-Cook, T. L. 1992. Organizational Enactments and Conformity to Environmental Prescriptions. *Human Relations* 45:537-54.

Scott, W. R. 1983. From Technology to Environment. In *Organizational Environment,* ed. J. W. Meyer and W. R. Scott, pp. 3-17. Beverly Hills, Calif.: Sage.

————. 1991. Unpacking Institutional Arguments. In *New Institutionalism in Organizational Analysis,* ed. W. W. Powell and P. J. DiMaggio, pp. 164-82. Chicago: University of Chicago Press.

Stone, D. L., and A. Colella. 1996. A Model of Factors Affecting the Treatment of Disabled Individuals in Organizations. *Academy of Management Review* 21:352-401.

Storey, K., and R. H. Horne. 1991. Social Interactions in Three Supported Employment Options: A Comparative Analysis. *Journal of Applied Behavior Analysis* 24:349-60.

Strauss, A., and J. Corbin. 1990. *Basics of Qualitative Research.* Newbury Park, Calif.: Sage.

Sullivan, W. P. 1992. "It Helps Me to Be a Whole Person": The Role of Spirituality among the Mentally Challenged. *Psychosocial Rehabilitation Journal* 16:125-34.

Susman, J. 1994. Disability, Stigma and Deviance. *Social Science and Medicine* 38:15-22.

Yelin, E. H., and. P. P. Katz. 1994. Making Work More Central to Work Disability Policy. *Milbank Quarterly* 72:593-619.

Wansbrough, N., and P. Cooper. 1980. *Open Employment after Mental Illness.* London: Tavistock Publications.

Webber, A., and J. D. Orcutt. 1984. Employer's Reactions to Racial and Psychiatric Stigma: A Field Experiment. *Deviant Behavior* 5:327-36.

Zuckerman, D. 1994. Workplace Accommodations. In *Mental Disabilities and the ADA: A Practitioner's Guide to Employment, Insurance, Treatment, Public Access and Housing,* ed. John Parry. Washington, D.C.: American Bar Foundation.

Chapter VII

Professional Licensing, Screening for Disabilities, and the ADA

STANLEY S. HERR

I. Introduction

The Americans with Disabilities Act needs to be analyzed not only in terms of its impacts on the entire labor force, but on how different sectors of the economy have adjusted to entrants with disabilities. Persons with disabilities not only seek jobs, but increasingly vie for places in the more prestigious and well-compensated professions. As a threshold matter to gaining such employment, candidates for professional credentialing and subsequent licensing must pass through certain screens that inquire as to disabilities. Although the actual number of candidates denied entry is minuscule, the form and nature of these inquiries may discourage some from pursuing professional careers. While one court has treated the bar's licensing as the functional equivalent of an employment decision,[1] the better view is that discriminatory licensing decisions may be challenged under Title II of the ADA, which deals with state government. In any event, ensuring that the emerging workforce of learned professionals includes people with various types of disabilities entails reducing barriers — practical as well as perceived — to licensure.

    Professional licensing of candidates with disabilities is a lively battlefield under the Americans with Disabilities Act. With growing frequency, skirmishes occur around issues of testing accommodations for licensing examinations, personal questionnaires, so-called character interviews, medical releases, and the process of further inquiries for those compelled to disclose disabilities past or present.[2] These issues have received the greatest attention in the legal and medical professions but have surfaced in a variety of professions and licensed occupations. This chapter focuses on the question of how far into a candidate's sensitive past bar examiners can probe. It offers a case study of a recent law school graduate who had passed the bar examination but, because of her affirmative, and candid, answers to questions about past mental health and alcohol abuse treatment, felt that her application was in limbo. This chapter not only recounts her experience but suggests that applicants in many states and many occupations could experience similar difficulties if questionnaires and procedures are not reformed.

Although the Americans with Disabilities Act (ADA) was enacted in 1990,[3] some state bars still need to revise their questionnaires and take other steps to comply with the letter and the spirit of this law. The ADA applies to law examiners as state government entities under Title II of the act and as administrators of licensing examinations under Title III. Although the ADA has been hailed as a Magna Carta for the disability rights movement and an emancipation proclamation for its members (Harkin 1990; Tucker 1989), change has often been grudging and uneven. Professional credentialing in general and bar admission procedures in particular pose cases in point (McKenna 1995).

In the field of medical licensure, poorly formulated questions also act to maintain the stigma attached to mental illness. One recent study analyzed changes in questions about psychiatric illness on medical licensure applications between 1993 and 1996 (Hansen et al. 1998). It concluded that the ADA appears to be encouraging state medical boards to revamp their questionnaires. However, despite the presence of federal law outlawing disability discrimination, this study found that 16 percent of medical boards continued to ask stigmatizing questions that applied different standards to mental health conditions than to physical conditions. Although this number did represent a small decline from 1993, the researchers found that this decline was not sharp enough to be statistically significant. Thus, although the direction is positive, the ADA has been slow to reduce the number of medical licensure boards that employ suspect questions.

This chapter demonstrates that change can come not only through litigation but through fact-finding, negotiation, and the submission of petitions and legal memoranda to licensing authorities. In addition to state-by-state reforms, this topic deserves searching national attention as the legal and other professions burden thousands of their entrants with intrusive questions into their mental health histories with nary a rejection solely on mental health grounds. As a policy and humanistic matter, putting aside issues of legality, one can surely question whether this questioning game is worth the candle.

This chapter explores these issues and reform strategies in the setting of the legal profession. Part II places the issue in a national context of rising numbers of candidates with disabilities seeking bar admission, certain examiners' persistent defense of disability inquiries, and mounting critiques of such probes. It also features a survey of bar questionnaires that reveals wide disparities of approach among the states. Part III presents a case study of a candidate's experience in winning admission to the bar and the results of a call by her lawyers and other Maryland law professors for systemic reforms in bar admission procedures for candidates with disabilities or a history of past disabilities. Part IV analyzes the case law on alleged discrimination in such bar queries. Part V suggests some further reforms to avoid discrimination or the appearance of discrimination against candidates with disabilities — changes that could be achieved without resort to litigation. Finally, part VI calls for an end to the stigma and discrimination that generations of candidates with disabilities or treatment histories have faced.

II. The Issue in National Context

The issue of lawyers with disabilities seeking entry to the bar is of growing importance. First, the pool of law students with a current or past disability is rising. In 1987, nearly 9 percent of law students in the United States had some type of disability (Adams 1996). Although no precise data are currently available on law school enrollment, anecdotal information and statistics collected on students requesting testing accommodations suggest that their numbers are climbing (Henderson 1995; Stone 1996). Second, many of those law students have enjoyed reasonable accommodations and exercised other disability rights in their prior school and undergraduate careers and are increasingly assertive in the face of perceived disability discrimination (Bahls 1999; Henderson 1995). Third, the bar has an obligation to model compliance with all civil rights laws and to set an example for employers in general, and employers of lawyers in particular. Fourth, despite an increasing public awareness of the need to end disability discrimination, controversy lingers as to how far bar officials can go in soliciting information from candidates about their disability or treatment history.

IN CRITICISM OF INQUIRIES

A growing body of literature is critical of broad bar inquiries into a candidate's mental health and the rationales supporting this practice (Rhode 1985). Although sharing a uniform disapproval of broad bar inquiries, these commentators have differed in their opinion of how far inquiries should be limited under the ADA. Some critics argue that the only valid questions relate to current or relatively recent disabilities (or treatment for such disabilities) because such information bears on the applicant's ability to practice law. Procedural critiques, in turn, stress putting the "burden on bar examiners to prove unfitness," requiring that they be permitted to ask only questions they can "properly demonstrate are relevant in predicting current and future ability to practice" (Stone 1995, pp. 370–71).

Substantive critiques come from a variety of perspectives. Civil rights specialists suggest that in light of the ADA, any questions concerning mental disabilities or treatment for such disabilities are "inherently suspect" (Parry 1993). As one prominent clinical psychiatrist notes, "the prejudice arising from a history of psychiatric diagnoses or treatment far outweighs its value as a predictor of future competence as an attorney" (Eth 1996). Many bar applications still ask whether an applicant has (or had within the past five or ten years) a particular condition which could render him or her psychotic. Supporters of examiners using this question often assume that most applicants experiencing a psychotic episode would be incapable of practicing law in a competent manner (Parry 1993). Other commentators, however, would argue that this question violates the ADA because some people who manage their psychosis with appropriate regimens may still be competent to practice law (Commission on Disability Law 1994).

Experts also contend that these categories cut too wide a swath because they do not affect the ability to make good judgments (Aron 1996) and single out persons with mental illness as "a class suspected of being unfit to practice law, which is discriminatory, and for which there is no scientific basis and support" (Eth 1996). In addition, bar examiners could determine an individual's fitness to practice law by asking about specific behaviors which may demonstrate incompetence or misconduct that may reveal untrustworthiness, without resorting to a diagnostic label.[4] Questionnaires could also limit inquiry into episodic outpatient mental health treatment, or into behavior or conduct that occurred before an applicant's eighteenth birthday or more than five years in the past (Stone 1995). Finally, in response to the objection that an affirmative answer to a question does not disqualify one for admission but simply provokes an investigation, there is doubt that the candidate's own explanations or the "expert" opinion of a medical examiner can lead to accurate predictions of dangerous unfitness to practice law (Ennis and Litwack 1974).

Other arguments focus on the ineffectiveness and underinclusiveness of bar queries. Very few candidates answer affirmatively, and only in the rarest case is a candidate actually denied admission to the bar (Commission on Disability Law 1994). Moreover, many state bars do not ask questions about physical conditions that might pose a risk to fitness to practice, such as narcolepsy or chronic fatigue syndrome. Bar screening is also underinclusive in terms of the public's protection. If these questions truly served that purpose, then practitioners might have to periodically answer them to identify conditions that arose during the postadmission stage of a lawyer's career. These arguments suggest that the bar questionnaires ferret out few candidates, impose intrusions on the privacy of novices that their more senior and powerful colleagues do not bear, and single out mental health conditions for more stigmatizing examinations. Given the porousness of the screening process, the many double standards between entrants and veterans, between mental health conditions and physical conditions, and the risks of arbitrary handling of individual cases, critics will continue to ask if the benefits of the mental health questions justify their price.

As previously noted, criticism of questionnaires probing mental health issues is not unique to bar admissions. In November 1995, the federal government overhauled its security clearance procedures to narrow (1) the question as to a mental or emotional disorder affecting the employee's ability to perform the particular job; (2) the type of sensitive government positions for which any such questions could be posed; and (3) the number of follow-up questions that could be asked in the security investigation interview of an employee who had given an affirmative answer (Aron 1996). Employees working in security classified positions or holding high-level positions of public trust are no longer asked questions in terms of specific psychiatric diagnoses or required to sign general releases to permit investigators to freely examine their medical records or interrogate their therapists. If the government could adopt such changes in the face of security concerns about employees entrusted with the nation's secrets or nuclear arsenals, surely bar examiners can limit their fishing expeditions into a candidate's mental health status and any treatment records.

ENCOURAGING REFORM IN QUESTIONNAIRES

The American Bar Association (ABA) issued a strong call for reform in 1994. Acting on the report of a joint committee composed of representatives of the ABA Commission on Mental and Physical Disability Law, the ABA Section on Legal Education and Admission to the Bar, the National Conference of Bar Examiners (NCBE), and the Association of American Law Schools (AALS), the House of Delegates passed a resolution condemning broad inquiries into mental health and treatment as unnecessarily invasive of bar applicants' privacy interests (Turnbull et al. 1994). The ABA urged state bar examiners to adopt a narrower set of mental health questions that addressed only current rather than past disabilities (Turnbull et al. 1994).

Responding to this report, the NCBE decided to limit the scope and durational time period of its mental health inquiries by adopting a new set of questions. One question asks, "Within the past five years have you been diagnosed with or have you been treated for bipolar disorder, schizophrenia, paranoia, or any other psychotic disorder?" Another inquires, "Do you currently have any condition or impairment (including, but not limited to, substance abuse, alcohol abuse, or a mental, emotional, or nervous disorder or condition) which in any way currently affects, or if untreated could affect, your ability to practice law in a competent and professional manner?" While these changes would commendably narrow the scope and durational period of disability inquiries in some states, they have neither been universally adopted by the examiners nor accepted by the critics.

A NATIONAL SURVEY OF BAR QUESTIONNAIRES

A national survey reveals great disparity in the approaches the states take in inquiries as to a candidate's disabilities. The author requested the bar questionnaires of the fifty states, the District of Columbia, Guam, the Marianna Islands, and Puerto Rico. Forty-one states and territories responded. This survey categorizes the bars' approaches under the following three categories: states with very intrusive inquiries, states with moderately intrusive inquiries, and states with no or nonintrusive inquiries.

1. States with Intrusive Inquiries

Questionnaire intrusiveness refers to a combination of the breadth of the inquiry and the length of the period for which responses are sought. Thus, bar applications included in this category compelled answers to questions that were both broad in scope and far-reaching in time.

The Kansas application is a prime example of such a sweeping bar questionnaire. Kansas's mental disability queries deal with substance abuse and other mental disabilities. The substance abuse questions are fairly straightforward but reach far back into the applicant's past. In contrast, the mental disability questions are breathtakingly open-ended. Question 15 (c) asks the applicant whether he has "ever been hospitalized or institutionalized for reasons of mental health" and question 15 (d) inquires into whether the applicant has "ever been adjudged a mentally incapacitated or disabled person . . . or declared a ward of the Court for any reason." Both questions are ambiguous and unlimited in scope. The bar examiners never state what the terms "mental health" or "mental disability" mean, leaving it to the applicant to determine whether his hospitalization resulted from a mental health problem. Moreover, the application does not define how long a period the candidate has to be hospitalized or institutionalized before reporting becomes mandatory. Finally, the bar examiners place no time limits on this inquiry, allowing the questions to intrude deeply into the applicant's history.

2. States with Moderately Intrusive Inquiries

States with moderately intrusive approaches delve into mental health problems that may range from the current to the relatively remote in time. Some of these states ask fairly detailed and far-ranging questions about the prospective candidate's mental health. For example, Kentucky unleashes a barrage of mental and physical health questions that could require extensive details about the past five years of an applicant's life.[5]

Other states seek information about an applicant's mental health nearer to the time of application. New Jersey, for instance, asks whether the applicant currently has an emotional, mental, or nervous disorder that would adversely affect the ability to practice law.[6] It also asks whether the individual has been admitted to a hospital "or other facility" for treatment of any psychotic disorder within the past twelve months. Washington state similarly leaves the applicant with the latitude to answer in the negative if past treatment does not affect current fitness to practice.

3. States with No or Minimal Disability Inquiries

Several states find it unnecessary to ask any questions about mental disabilities. Illinois, for example, does not make any inquiries into the mental disabilities of bar applicants. Other states are sparing in the scope of questions asked, focusing primarily on substance abuse.

The Pennsylvania bar application is a prototype for this type of questionnaire. Its drafters admirably avoid mental disability questions and only ask whether the applicant is currently "addicted to or dependent upon narcotics, intoxicating liquors, and other substances."[7] Other questions properly focus on conduct and behavior, such as the applicant's confrontations with an employer, supervisor, or teacher about truthfulness, competence, or safeguarding of confidential information.

Hawaii is another state that has taken a very enlightened and nonintrusive approach on its bar questionnaire. Hawaii limits its drug history question to only the previous year and does not include a specific "mental health" question. Instead, it asks, "Do you know of any factors that would impair your ability to competently practice law or to carry out your ethical responsibilities to clients or as an officer of the court?"[8] Such questions do not conflict with the ADA.

4. Summary of the Questionnaire Analysis

In contrast to earlier surveys, this data suggests that inquiries concerning outpatient treatment and inpatient hospitalization are becoming narrower and less widespread. For instance, a 1994 survey reported that over three-fourths of the responding bars asked about the applicant's outpatient mental health treatment and nearly 96 percent asked about such inpatient treatment (Stone 1995). Even more striking, over two-thirds of these bars placed no time limit on how far back these questions reached (Stone 1995). In this analysis, only fourteen of the thirty-five states that reported fell into the very intrusive category. Ten states and the District of Columbia fell into the moderately intrusive category, and twelve states fell into the less intrusive category. Thus, despite a lack of consensus, the prevailing trend across the country is toward less intrusive disability-related inquiries.

In summary, of the states responding to this survey, fourteen requested mental health information from ten or more years ago. Eleven states inquired about information dating back between five and nine years, and twelve states restricted their inquiries to fewer than five years. Of these twelve states, other than asking about a candidate's current functioning, ten made no probes at all into a history of psychiatric disability.

Although many states still include mental heath inquiries on their applications for admission to the state bar, some states have eliminated these inquiries completely. Their elimination of these unnecessarily intrusive questions, along with the methods which other states have employed to narrow the focus of their questions, effectively undermines the argument that comprehensive life-long inquiries about mental health are necessary to protect the public's safety. Other states offer the applicant some explanation of the kind of information a mental health inquiry is, or is not, trying to elicit. States like Oklahoma, Alabama, and Nebraska, for example, have adopted similar preambles to their mental health questions which explain that these questions are not intended to address information "that is fairly characterized as situational counseling." The preamble details examples of situational counseling as "stress counseling, domestic counseling, grief counseling and counseling for eating or sleeping disorders," which are not to be reported. Preambles such as these represent a significant protection against overly intrusive inquiries.

A further sign of flux is the frequency of change in some questionnaires. For example, in Maryland, over a span of two years, the relevant time period has plummeted from ten years, to five years, to the "present," and the questions as a whole have become increasingly less intrusive. The trend in Maryland, achieved through self-assessment by the bar as well as outside recommendations, is consistent with nationwide litigation in the area of bar questionnaires. Maryland's evolutionary experience provides instructive lessons for examiners and reformers alike. It also permits the often abstractly debated effects of the questioning process to be placed in a human perspective.

III. A Candidate's Quest for Admission and Reform

FINDING LEGAL COUNSEL

"Can you represent a woman whose bar admission is on hold because of her mental health history?" With that call for help from a former student in search of counsel for a graduate of another law school, my clinical students and I began to learn about the plight of Jane Doe. The essential facts of Ms. Doe's case seemed straightforward. She had passed the written bar examination held in the summer of 1994. Because she had answered in the affirmative to questions about mental health treatment and alcohol abuse, however, as of the fall of 1995 a bar of Maryland character committee was still deciding whether or not she possessed the fitness to practice law. We agreed to interview her and determine if she could become a client of Maryland Law School's Clinical Law Office.

The decision to accept Jane Doe as a client was influenced by her compelling story: she was a person who had overcome many obstacles to attend and graduate from law school and had successfully represented clients as part of her own law school's clinical program. She had reached a point of despair as the months wore on after the once happy news of passing the bar. The case presented a threefold opportunity: (1) it fulfilled a lawyer's duty to render pro bono services; (2) it would aid a potential fellow member of the legal profession; and (3) it could assist in reforming a legal institution.[9]

ADOPTING AN ADVOCACY STRATEGY

Our primary goal was to obtain Ms. Doe's prompt admission to the bar. To this end, we identified two individuals who would each write a letter strongly supporting Ms. Doe's admission. One was her treating psychiatrist, the other her former clinical law professor.

Nearly two months of legal and factual research convinced us that we had a strong case if litigation became necessary. But because the December 1995 swearing-in ceremony was fast approaching, we decided that a problem-solving rather than a confrontational approach would permit Ms. Doe to join the ranks of the bar before another year would pass.

In light of her long struggle for admission and our success in utilizing a client-centered approach, Ms. Doe asked us to achieve a more altruistic end, thus making her struggle the first step toward achieving a higher goal. From the outset of the representation, we had agreed to pursue some systemic changes to spare future candidates from related difficulties. After all, more than a year in limbo cost her lost economic opportunities, some embarrassment, and considerable emotional turmoil. More important, we believed that the questionnaire placed would-be applicants in an extremely uncomfortable position. They faced tormenting choices: either divulge information that might be protected from disclosure under the ADA, unilaterally interpret ambiguous terms to shield themselves from disclosing disability conditions and treatment, or give evasive, if not untruthful, answers.

From informal conversations with such applicants as well as with a well-respected member of the bar who had not disclosed past treatment, the author knew that these terrible dilemmas were real. As one federal judge recently recognized, mental health questions are ineffective in identifying applicants with mental illnesses.[10] In reality, candidates seem to be engaging in mass noncompliance, a form of "questionnaire nullification," as they resist undue governmental scrutiny into their private lives. Thus, to Ms. Doe and her counsel, the time seemed ripe to sharply reduce bar inquiries into the disability conditions and treatments protected by the ADA.

Analysis of precedents from other jurisdictions revealed mixed results where applicants litigated such issues. In contrast, we devised a strategy that we hoped would lead to a relatively rapid negotiated resolution of both Ms. Doe's personal and altruistic objectives. Thus, we sought to identify a common ground between the bar and our client, urging the State Board of Law Examiners to accept our position as "a balance between considerations of public interest, which demand that applicants to the bar be screened for the requisite character and behavior befitting the practice of law, and the rights of persons with disabilities to avoid undue stigma, embarrassment, intrusion on highly personal domains, and financial and psychological costs." In assuming that the board shared this goal, we urged them to move "to eliminate the appearance or actuality of discrimination based on disability in the Bar application process."

Ultimately, this strategy worked. Measured in terms of the time from the Clinical Law Office's intervention to Ms. Doe's admission and to the revisions to the bar's questionnaire, these results occurred more rapidly than in most of the litigated cases. Seven days after our first telephone call to a bar official, and six days after the doctor's letter accompanied by our letter with legal arguments, Jane Doe received a call from the Court of Appeals inviting her to the ceremony. In December 1995, she officially became a member of the Bar of Maryland. It would be another eight months, however, before systemic changes to the bar questionnaire would be achieved.

REVAMPING THE QUESTIONNAIRE

Ms. Doe and her counsel zeroed in on the questionnaire for obvious reasons. Her travails with the bar began when she was obliged to answer the following broad question: "Have you within the past ten years, ever been a patient in any sanitarium, hospital or mental institution for the treatment of mental illness?"[11] She was also required to execute a very broad authorization and release, thus permitting the character committee and the State Board of Law Examiners to "inspect and make copies of . . . any and all medical reports, laboratory reports, X-rays, or clinical abstracts which may have been made or prepared" by medical doctors and other persons involved in her treatment.[12] This release was not a mere formality. The character committee interviewer had requested and received a large number of Ms. Doe's confidential medical records. None of these intrusions would have occurred if the questionnaire had focused on a candidate's present fitness to practice law rather than his or her past medical status.

By 1995 the board had revised the questionnaire, but the revisions would not help Ms. Doe or other similarly situated candidates, although the revisions did reduce the length of the period subject to inquiry to five years. The questions, however, were still framed around diagnostic labels and past conditions rather than focused on the candidate's current fitness to practice law.

Once Ms. Doe was admitted to the bar, we focused on revamping the two questions that involved mental health history. We urged that question 14, pertaining to mental disability and substance abuse, be scaled back. On the issue of substance abuse, we argued that the ADA protected an individual like Ms. Doe who had successfully completed a program of alcohol treatment and had no current drinking problem.

The focus of the clinic's argument was on the unnecessary differential treatment of candidates with disabilities and the public policy rationales for eliminating or narrowing the disputed questions. Using the force of the ADA, we reasoned that the board, as a public entity, could not impose eligibility criteria that could screen out individuals with disabilities without showing that the board's criteria and questions were "necessary for the provision of that service, program, or activity being offered."[13] With respect to issues of alcohol and substance abuse, we recommended that only questions narrowly drawn to identify current abuse affecting fitness to practice were consistent with the ADA. Similarly, we challenged questions on the diagnoses or treatment of specifically named mental illnesses, or "mental, emotional, nervous, or behavior disorders or conditions" as discriminatory because of their failure to focus on current capability, conduct, or behavior. An applicant's history of past mental illness, we contended, did not prove that a candidate lacked the present capacity to practice law.

From a public policy perspective, we argued that bar inquiries not only discriminated on the basis of disability but also discriminated on the basis of sex, and had profoundly chilling impacts on the timely use of therapy and counseling. Because women tend to obtain psychological and psychiatric treatment more frequently than men, under the old questionnaires they would have a disproportionate duty to report their treatment to bar examiners (Busfield 1996). For example, women are treated and diagnosed far more than men in response to anxiety, depression, and eating disorders. Women are also twice as likely as men to receive prescriptions for psychotropic medication as "treatment," thus making it harder for them to deny the fact of mental health treatment. Furthermore, women seek treatment episodically, often in response to deep personal traumas such as rape, incest, battering, or past abuse.[14] Advocates in Florida and Minnesota had made similar arguments in their respective states, such as the anecdotal accounts presented to the Minnesota Supreme Court when it narrowed the questionnaire on public policy grounds.[15] Finally, we urged the Maryland board to eliminate or narrow the mental health questions since such questions could discourage candidates from seeking early, or any, counseling or treatment out of fear that bar authorities might view such treatment negatively (Rothstein 1994).

To pinpoint a solution to these and other problems with the Maryland questionnaire, we offered a set of revised questions designed to elicit only information regarding a candidate's current mental condition that had a bearing on present fitness to practice. In August 1996, the board decided to revise the questionnaire and adopted many of our recommendations. These reports and recommendations of the Section Council of the Legal Education Section of the Maryland State Bar Association and of the Clinical Law Office, coupled with the board's receptiveness to constructive change, improved the bar's approach to applicants with disabilities or perceived disabilities. For each of the parties, a win–win situation resulted.

IV. Litigation and Other Law Reform Responses

Compared to Maryland's experience, lawsuits elsewhere have had costly and sometimes mixed results. Recent decisions under the ADA curtail the power of state licensing boards to investigate the mental health backgrounds of bar applicants.[16] Courts responding to challenges to mental health questions in professional licensing under the ADA have concluded that broad-based inquiries either violate, or are likely to violate, Title II of the ADA.[17] In *Ellen S. v. Florida Board of Bar Examiners,*[18] the plaintiff challenged questions on the Florida Board of Law Examiners' application that addressed mental health treatment history.[19] She argued that the Florida board's inquiries and investigatory process discriminated against applicants on the basis of their disability in violation of Title II of the ADA.[20] The court agreed with her argument and held that inquiries by the board into mental health treatment and diagnosis violated Title II of the ADA because they "discriminate against Plaintiffs by subjecting them to additional burdens based on their disability."[21] Subsequently, the Florida board narrowed its mental health questions to specifically target individuals who had been treated for certain disabilities.[22]

Supporters of questions about applicants' mental health history often rely on *Applicants v. Texas State Board of Bar Examiners,*[23] which held that the ADA permitted the board to inquire into an applicant's mental health.[24] In this case, however, the court reviewed a revised version of the Texas board questionnaire which addressed only so-called serious mental illnesses—specific disorders of a psychotic nature that it assumed would produce behaviors that could interfere with the practice of law.[25] The earlier broad-based questions, found to be in violation of the ADA in other jurisdictions, had been removed from the Texas Board of Bar Examiners' questionnaire in 1992.[26]

Other authorities have limited or criticized the Texas approach. In *Clark v. Virginia Board of Bar Examiners,*[27] the court argued that the Texas holding had limited application and did not support the claim that broad mental health questions are valid under the ADA.[28] Other supporters of revision have gone further, arguing that even the limited inquiry approved in *Applicants v. Texas*

State Board is invalid under the ADA.[29] The Department of Justice, for example, maintains that questions like those reviewed in *Applicants v. Texas State Board* violate the ADA because they focus on a person's "status" as an individual with a disability instead of the applicant's past behavior (Nicholson and Foran 1995). The United States government takes the position that state boards may inquire about "conduct or behavior" that may be associated with a mental illness. To focus on a person's "status" as disabled or not, however, means that the disability can be used to "singl[e] out persons . . . [and] impos[e] more burdensome requirements on persons with histories of disabilities than on other applicants" (Nicholson and Foran 1995). Even questions like those used in *Applicants v. Texas State Board* "are not focused on actual, current impairments of candidates' abilities or functions, and are not narrowly tailored to determine current fitness to practice the profession" (Nicholson and Foran 1995). Although the Department of Justice presented these arguments to the court in *Clark v. Virginia Board of Bar Examiners,*[30] the court reached its decision without addressing this issue.[31]

In 1996, Rhode Island took an even more impressive step toward bringing disability inquiries on state bar questionnaires into line with the ADA. *In re Questionnaire for Admission to the Rhode Island Bar*[32] found that the procedures for admission to the bar are the "functional equivalent" of the hiring process of a private employer, therefore obliging the Rhode Island bar to follow the ADA when crafting its questionnaire.[33] The Supreme Court of Rhode Island enunciated principles of broad significance to all bar examiners by squarely holding that application questions which ask about "the existence of a disability or treatment . . . may be deemed to violate the ADA, absent a showing of a direct threat to public safety" that would result from an applicant with a disability being admitted to the bar.[34] After noting that the bar must bear the burden of demonstrating actual increased risk to the public from applicants with histories of mental health or substance abuse treatment, the court endorsed findings that showed "no empirical evidence" that lawyers who had received psychiatric help were more prone to disciplinary action than other lawyers.[35] The Rhode Island Supreme Court then exercised its supervisory role over the process by which applicants seek admission to the bar in order to revise questions 26 and 29 of the questionnaire.[36] These newly adopted questions narrow the state's disability inquiry significantly, now focusing exclusively on "current" impairments to practice. The court concluded that questions that do not inquire about the history of a disability, but rather focus on "current" conditions, would allow the state to efficiently "carry out its inquiry into an applicant's background within the constraints imposed by the ADA."[37]

In summary, the case law suggests that broad-based questions into an applicant's mental health history on a bar questionnaire will be strictly reviewed and will usually fail to meet the standards under Title II of the ADA. When a bar questionnaire uses more "narrowly tailored" questions that ask about specific disabilities as they may relate to the practice of law, then at least one court has been willing to uphold the state's inquiry under the ADA. When states employ questions that ask about specific and potentially severe mental disabilities, courts may be tempted to apply a balancing test, similar to the one employed in *Applicants v. Texas State Board*. In theory, this test harmonizes the congressional goals of preventing discrimination against persons with disabilities and integrating them into society with the countervailing goal of protecting the public from harm at the hands of persons holding a public trust. In applying this calculus, courts should pay particular attention to the extent to which the questions employed by different states are as "least intrusive" and as "narrowly tailored" as necessary to accomplish important public safety goals. They should also skeptically examine the relevance of mental health questioning to these goals in light of psychiatry's disclaimers and the growing number of states who have discarded such inquiries.

V. An Agenda for Reform

Professional licensing agencies can avoid proliferating lawsuits and controversies related to the admission of candidates with disabilities if they draw the appropriate lessons from both precedent and the cooperative Maryland experience. The visibility of bar admission activities, the legal training of aggrieved applicants, and the interest of the United States Department of Justice in this subject matter all point to the potential for further litigation. For example, Nevada's protection and advocacy system for individuals with disabilities has recently brought a class action on the issue of enforced disclosure of disabilities by a licensing board (Nisen 1998). Bar officials, however, can and should take preventive action by revamping questionnaires now. As the ABA has recognized, examiners should carefully consider the applicant's "privacy concerns," "narrowly tailor any mental health questions to the practice of law," and ensure that bar processes "do not discourage those who would benefit from seeking professional assistance . . . from doing so."

Unfortunately, despite the 1994 ABA resolution and mounting decisional law on the ADA, many unnecessary questions continue to be asked around the country. Clearly more than broadly phrased resolutions on a national level are needed to bring about change. Reformers drawn from the ranks of disability-related committees of state bar associations, clinical law offices, disability organizations, public interest law firms, or elsewhere will need to work closely with state bar examiners not only to revise questionnaires, but to make improvements in procedures for reviewing applicants who give affirmative answers to questions about disability and for requests for testing accommodations. In developing those state agendas, the following issues should be considered.

THE CASE FOR ELIMINATING DISABILITY QUESTIONS

There is a compelling case that bar examiners should eliminate entirely questions pertaining to mental health and other disabilities to comply with the ADA. In many ways, the argument for elimination is more principled and practical than the argument for incremental change recently advanced in Maryland. First, the ADA does not permit private employers to probe into a job applicant's disability status, even for more sensitive posts.[38] Thus, many disability rights specialists argue that it is inappropriate to ask about an applicant's mental health and treatment, "especially given the possibility that all such questions might be prohibited by the [ADA]" (Turnbull et al. 1994). Second, many law schools and other institutions of higher education for similar reasons no longer inquire into mental illness or other disability in their admissions processes.[39] Third, the bar examiners have the burden of demonstrating that these questions solicit information predictive of fitness to practice law, and thus that such inquiries are necessary for the public's protection. Until scientific proof can be convincingly presented that these inquiries in fact serve this purpose, these questions on disability should be "sunsetted" (Elliott 1991). Fourth, disparities among the states permit social scientists to frame empirical research questions that could help to end the use of disability questions and the resulting geographic inequities. Are the residents of states without disability questions at greater risk of representation by mentally aberrant lawyers than those in states with such questions? Do these queries effectively screen out candidates who are incompetent in the practice of law? Do these queries also effectively identify enough applicants, let alone genuinely risky applicants, to merit exposing the entire candidate pool to these profoundly privacy-denying questions? Fifth, there are grounds for deep skepticism that, even if an appropriately narrow (and legal) question could be framed, applicants would answer it accurately and bar examiners would process and store that information sensitively. In this sense, the jury is still out on the incremental reform adopted in Maryland. Sixth, there is a Fourth Amendment argument that absent "some form of particularized suspicion," general intrusive questions about a candidate's mental health treatment constitute a constitutionally unreasonable search (Salamanca 1999). Finally, the licensing authorities' objective of public protection can be met more effectively through attorney education about seeking help for mental health or substance abuse problems, obtaining rehabilitation for such problems, and imposing attorney discipline for misconduct (Duke 1997). It is time to abandon the costly and intrusive disability inquiries that yield so little protection for the public.

The reality, of course, is that many individuals with disabilities become members of the bar. Very few disclose their conditions in the bar screening process. Most do not. Even for the handful who disclose, the outcome is generally favorable even if the process is stressful. As the Rhode Island Committee on Character and Fitness reassures applicants, the Rhode Island Supreme Court, "consequent upon the Committee's recommendation, regularly admits applicants with a history of mental ill-health, substance abuse, and utilization of the services of mental health professionals."[40] But the so-called low hit rate (i.e., the number of applicants who answer such questions affirmatively) calls the utility — and fairness — of the whole enterprise into question. As Howard Zonana of Yale University's medical and law schools has testified, not only is prior psychiatric treatment not relevant to the question of current impairment,[41] it is a very inefficient screen for detecting individuals who will not be fit lawyers:

> You do this broad screening and, by and large, you come up with nothing, and that's true with most bar examiners across the board. That's why so many states have been willing to drop it, because most people don't see it as producing anything that is useful or that gives any criteria on which you can either deny or make any other judgments about. So you end up collecting all this data that's not useful.[42]

CREATING A SYSTEM TO ASSURE TIMELY, SENSITIVE, AND FAIR PROCESSING

Procedural reforms are needed to make bar questionnaires timely, fair to the applicant, and more sensitive to the mandates of the ADA. As questionnaires evolve during this transitional period, and bar examiners more frequently encounter disability issues, boards should consider changes in interviewer sensitivity, better communication with the applicant with an alleged disability, and avenues for informal redress of grievances.

If there has to be an inquiry into a candidate's mental health or substance abuse record, it should be done by a lawyer with an understanding of disability law, public policy, and the factual context in which treatment issues arise. This suggestion would help to avoid the current practice of having "untrained examiners . . . draw inferences that the mental health community would . . . find highly dubious" (Rhode 1985). Adoption of this recommendation should increase the prospects for a timely and sensitive resolution of a candidate's application for admission to the bar. An interviewer with this expertise (perhaps with credentials in law and medicine) would be able to handle the file with greater efficiency since the relevant law, disability terms, and medical treatments would be more familiar to him or her.

Based on evidence from ADA litigation and anecdotal information, most state bars receive only a small number of applications each year that include an affirmative answer to a disability question. The logistics of recruiting a new qualified interviewer or identifying an interviewer currently sitting on a character committee for such an assignment should not be burdensome.

Another problem in the current process is the risk of undue delay. Currently, the rules on admission to the bar and the board's internal procedures do not provide a time limit as to when a recommendation must be made. In Ms. Doe's case, she spent over a year from the date of passing the bar examination waiting for final action.

Delay of this type in handling an application from a person with a disability may, in and of itself, constitute invidious discrimination. In *Medical Society of New Jersey v. Jacobs*,[43] the United States District Court of New Jersey pointed out that "it is the extra investigations of qualified applicants who answer 'yes' to [questions concerning psychiatric problems] that constitutes invidious discrimination under the Title II regulations."[44] Such delay can also be a great source of inconvenience, distress, economic loss, and even physical harm. Delay may also be a conscious strategy on the part of some examiners. A few have spoken openly about it as a tactic to "scare off" or discourage certain candidates. Others offer a more benign motive: they claim that keeping the candidate's file in "abeyance" allows their condition to improve or their period of sobriety to lengthen.

Another source of injustice is delay in responding to requests for testing accomodations. A board's last-minute denials of all or some requested accommodations can unnerve applicants and produce charges of discrimination (Bahls 1999).

Given the disparity in power in the relationship between the candidate and the character examiner, some candidates with disabilities or perceived disabilities may experience undue difficulty in the interviewing process. An informal

grievance procedure or a monitor to oversee the Character Committee interview process could assist the applicant with a disability (or any applicant) who
feels that he or she has reached an impasse with the interviewer. Although
boards may in theory afford the candidate an opportunity for a formal hearing if
the Character Committee concludes that "there may be grounds for recom-
mending denial of the application,"[45] this provision does not spare the applicant
from harm.

The existence of a publicized grievance process or an intermediary or
specifically named oversight agent offers a better solution. For instance, the
chair of the Character Committee could act in that capacity, or the chair and a
representative of the Board of Law Examiners, acting jointly, could name such
an agent. Aggrieved or confused candidates, in the midst of a disability-related
character review, need information as to how to resolve problems on an informal basis. To assume that they will identify the right person on their own or
design their own informal process is unrealistic. Even if they are clever and
assertive enough to do so, they run the risk of alienating the board officials
whose goodwill they may desperately need.

VI. Conclusion

In many parts of the United States, bar examiners face a long agenda of disability-
related issues in order to satisfy the ADA and the dictates of justice and fair play.
Questions in the phraseology of "are you now, or have you ever been, . . ." with
reference to disabilities are excessive in this context, as were the McCarthy-era
questions directed at ideology and political belief in the 1950s. Rather than adopt
a wait-and-see posture that risks additional litigation, bar and other professional
examiners can act now to eliminate unnecessary questions on disability, as states
such as Hawaii, Illinois, and Pennsylvania have done.

This chapter also reveals that reformers and bar officials can work construc-
tively to remedy intrusive inquiries through dialogue and problem-solving
negotiation. The Maryland model offers a useful case study of how to bring
about incremental change while laying the groundwork for more far-reaching
reform.

The survey data and case law trends suggest that examiners will increasingly narrow, and even phase out, their mental health inquiries. These inquiries
are simply too difficult to defend in light of the speculative and doubtful gains
they provide. If states like Hawaii, Illinois, and Pennsylvania have decided to

discard their mental health questions, why should other states continue to claim a compelling need to ask them? The ADA makes it clear that state agencies may only use criteria that tend to screen out candidates with disabilities, or force such candidates to give up sensitive privacy rights, upon a showing of necessity. The subject of the admission of lawyers with disabilities to the bar demands not further study but decisive action.

In this context, not to act is also to act. With each passing month and year since the enactment of the ADA, the justifications for inertia evaporate. The experience of Jane Doe points to the searing human costs of outdated systems. To spare future Jane Does from suspended professional careers and interrupted dreams of pursuing their calling, her story is told. Her vindication represents progress on the journey from the stigma and discrimination of the past as well as the legal profession's open embrace of all qualified candidates with disabilities in the future. In welcoming her and her peers to a learned profession, licensing authorities can repudiate the darker suspicions of disability and its treatments. The legal profession, as a guardian of employment law, must set its own house in order. With the year 2000 and the tenth anniversary of the ADA as reminders of reforms long overdue, all professions should finally ensure a level playing field for people with disabilities.

Notes

I gratefully acknowledge the research assistance of Booth M. Ripke, former Reuben Shiling Fellow in Mental Disability Law at the University of Maryland School of Law, and of Michael H. Glasser. In my role as supervising attorney in the Clinical Law Office of the University of Maryland School of Law, I represented a client with a disability who sought admission to the bar. To protect the client's confidentiality, this chapter refers to her under the pseudonym "Jane Doe." I would like to express my appreciation to her for giving permission to have this story told. I also acknowledge the outstanding advocacy on the part of Ms. Doe's other cocounsel, then second-year law student and student-attorney Betty S. Diener, and Mary Ann Ryan and Anna M. Coyle of the law firm of Ryan and Coyle. For further details on those efforts, see Stanley S. Herr, Questioning the Questionnaires: Bar Admissions and Candidates with Disabilities, *Villanova L. Rev.* 42 (1997): 635–721.

1. *In re Questionnaire for Admission to the Rhode Island Bar,* 683 A. 2d 1333 (R.I. 1996).

2. See *Bartlett v. New York State Board of Law Examiners,* 970 F. Supp. 1094 (S.D.N.Y. 1997), aff'd. in part, vacated in part, and remanded, 156F3d 321 (2d Cir. 1998) (holding that bar applicant entitled to reasonable accommodations to "take the

examination on a level playing field with other applicants" and board's denial entitled her to compensatory damages).

3. See Americans with Disabilities Act of 1990 (ADA), 42 U.S.C. §§ 12101–12189 (1994).

4. See, e.g., *In re A.T.*, 408 A.2d 1023, 1025, 1028 (Md. 1979) (admitting candidate with history of drug use that led to shoplifting where rehabilitation was "convincing," and last offense occurred thirteen years earlier and last illicit drug use twelve years before board's hearing).

5. See Kentucky Board of Bar Examiners, Application for Admission to the Kentucky Bar 8 (1996).

6. See Committee on Character Appointed by the Supreme Court of New Jersey, Certified Statement of Candidate, Question XV(B), at 13 (Sept. 1996). New York has a similar query. New York Appellate Division (Sup. Ct. Third Dept.), Application Admission, at 9 (Q.17(c)).

7. Pennsylvania Board of Bar Examiners, Application for Permission to Sit for the Pennsylvania Bar Examination and for Character and Fitness Determination, at 3 (Aug. 1996).

8. Hawaii Board of Examiners, Application Information 13 (1996).

9. Model Code of Professional Responsibility EC 2-18 (1983); Maryland Rules of Professional Conduct, Rule 6.1 (1999).

10. *Clark v. Virginia Board of Bar Examiners,* 880 F. Supp. 430, 437 (E.D. Va. 1995) (concluding that, as a practical matter, questions concerning treatment within the last five years were ineffective).

11. State Board of Law Examiners, Application for Admission to the Bar of Maryland, Character Questionnaire, Question 14(a), at 2 (May 3, 1994) (hereafter Maryland Bar Application).

12. Id.

13. 28 C.F.R. § 35.130(b)(8) (1996).

14. *In re Frickey,* 515 N.W.2d 741, 741 (Minn. 1994) (ordering questions in dispute to be removed from Minnesota bar application after receiving evidence of treatment rates by sender).

15. See *Frickey,* 515 N.W.2d at 741.

16. See, e.g., *Clark v. Virginia Board of Bar Examiners,* 880 F. Supp. 430, 444 (E.D. Va. 1995) (holding that question which "discriminates against disabled applicants by imposing additional eligibility criteria" must be deleted and amended).

17. See *Ellen S. v. Florida Board of Examiners,* 859 F. Supp. 1489, 1493 (S.D. Fla. 1994) (holding that broad inquiry into bar applicant's mental health may violate Title II of ADA); *Medical Society of N.J. v. Jacobs,* Civil Action No. 93-3670, 1993 WL 413016, at *7–8 (D.N.J. Oct. 5, 1993) (concluding, in dicta, that licensing agency's investigation associated with affirmative answers to question "have you ever suffered or been treated for any mental illness or psychiatric illness" violates Title II); *In re Underwood,* 1993 WL 649283, at *2 (Me. Dec. 7, 1993) (finding that bar examiner's inquiry into diagnosis and treatment for emotional, nervous, or mental disorders and accompanying medical

authorization form are violations of ADA); see also *Applicants v. Texas State Board of Law Examiners,* No. A 93 CA 740 SS, 1994 WL 776693, at *7 (W.D. Tex. Oct. 11, 1994) (finding that "such a broad-based inquiry violates the ADA").

18. 859 F. Supp. 1489 (S.D. Fla. 1994).

19. Id. at 1491.

20. Id.

21. Id. at 1493–94.

22. Id. at 1494.

23. No. A 93 CA 740 SS, 1994 WL 776693 (W.D. Tex. Oct. 11, 1994).

24. Id. at *9.

25. Id. at *10 n. 5.

26. Id. at *10 nn. 3–4 (explaining earlier versions of questions).

27. 880 F. Supp. 430 (E.D. Va. 1995).

28. Id. at 444.

29. See id. at 444 n. 25 (recognizing that the United States, appearing as amicus curiae before the district court in litigation on the Virginia bar questionnaire, argued that even "limited inquiry" into severe mental disabilities violates Title II of ADA because diagnoses listed are unnecessary classifications).

30. *Clark v. Virginia Board of Bar Examiners,* 880 F. Supp. 430, 4323 (E.D. Va. 1995).

31. Id. at 444 n. 25. In *Doe v. Judicial Nominating Commission,* 906 F. Supp. 1534 (S.D. Fla. 1995), the United States District Court for the Southern District of Florida again found questions that inquire into "any hospital confinement" or "any form of mental illness" or "any form of emotional disorder or disturbance" to be vivid demonstrations of the "over-inclusiveness of the mental health question." Id. at 1544.

32. 683 A.2d 1333 (R.I. 1996).

33. Id. at 1335.

34. Id. at 1336.

35. Id.

36. Id.

37. Id.

38. 42 U.S.C. § 12112(d)(2)(A), (4) (1994) (prohibiting employer from conducting "medical examination or mak[ing] inquiries of a job applicant as to whether such applicant is an individual with a disability or as to the nature or severity of such disability").

39. See, e.g., University of Maryland School of Law, Application for Admission 4 (1996) (containing questions about dismissals from schools, discharges from employment, and criminal charges).

40. Rhode Island Committee on Character and Fitness, Questionnaire for Admission to the Rhode Island Bar, at 14 (1997).

41. Trial Transcript, at 46, *Clark v. Virginia Board of Bar Examiners,* 880 F. Supp. 430 (E.D. Va. 1995) (C.A. No. 94-211-A).

42. Id. at 85–86.

43. Civil Action No. 93-3670, 1993 WL 413016, at *1 (D.N.J. Oct. 5, 1993).

44. Id. at *8.

45. See, e.g., Rules Governing Admission to the Bar of Maryland 5(b)(2) (1996).

References

Adams, Susan Johanne. 1996. Because They're Otherwise Qualified: Accommodating Learning Disabled Law Student Writers. *Journal of Legal Education* 46:189–215.

Aron, Bernard. 1996. Telephone interview by author. Baltimore. November 15.

Bahls, Jane Easter. 1999. Challenging the Bar Exam on Hidden Disabilities. *Student Lawyer* 27 (7): 21–31.

Busfield, Joan. 1996. *Men, Women, and Madness: Understanding Gender and Mental Disorder.* New York: New York University Press.

Commission on Disability Law on Proposed Connecticut Bar Association Application. 1994. *Report of the Section on Human Rights and Responsibilities and the Resolution concerning Inquiries into Mental Health Treatment of Bar Applicants.*

Duke, Hilary. 1997 The Narrowing of State Bar Examiner Inquiries into the Mental Health of Bar Applicants: Bar Examiner Objectives Are Met Better through Attorney Education, Rehabilitation, and Discipline. *Georgetown Journal of Legal Ethics* 11:101–28.

Elliott, Janet. 1991. Senate Softens Licensing Rules; Substance Abusers Would Be Guaranteed Right to Practice. *Texas Lawyer,* May 20.

Ennis, Bruce J., and T. R. Litwack. 1974. Psychiatry and the Presumption of Expertise: Flipping Coins in the Courtroom. *California Law Review* 62:693–752.

Eth, Spencer. 1996. Interview by author. Englewood, N.J. November 23.

Hansen, Thomas E., et al. 1998. Changes in Questions about Psychiatric Illness Asked on Medical Licensure Applications between 1993 and 1996. *Psychiatric Services* 49 (2): 202–6.

Harkin, Tom. 1990. Our Newest Civil Rights Law: The Americans with Disabilities Act. *Trial* 26 (12): 56–61.

Henderson, Cathy. 1995. College Freshmen with Disabilities: A Triennial Statistical Profile. American Council on Education 6–7.

McKenna, John D. 1995. Is the Mental Health History of an Applicant a Legitimate Concern of State Professional Licensing Boards? The Americans with Disabilities Act vs. State Professional Licensing Boards. *Hofstra Labor Law Journal* 12:335–59.

Nicholson, Kate M., and S. M. Foran. 1995. Using the ADA to Open Gateways to the Professions. *Consumer and Personal Rights Litigation Newsletter* 5:5–8.

Nisen, Fred. 1998. Professional Licensing and the ADA. *Nevada Lawyer* 6 (12): 18–20.

Parry, John. 1993. Mental Disabilities under the ADA: A Difficult Path to Follow. *Mental and Physical Disability Law Reporter* 17:100–111.

Rhode, Deborah L. 1985. Moral Character as a Professional Credential. *Yale Law Journal* 94:491–603.

Rothstein, Laura F. 1994. Bar Admissions and the Americans with Disabilities Act. *Houston Lawyer* 32:34–41.

Salamanca, Paul E. 1999. Constitutional Protection for Conversations between Therapists and Clients. *Missouri Law Review* 64:77–122.

Stone, Donald H. 1995. The Bar Admission Process, Gatekeeper or Big Brother? An Empirical Study. *Northern Illinois University Law Review* 15:331–72.

———. 1996. The Impact of the Americans with Disabilities Act on Legal Education and Academic Modifications for Disabled Law Students: An Empirical Study. *University of Kansas Law Review* 44:567–600.

Tucker, Bonnie. 1989. The Americans with Disabilities Act: An Overview. *University of Illinois Law Review* 1989:923–39.

Turnbull, Rutherford H., III, et al. 1994. ABA Bar Admissions Resolution and Report, American Bar Association Bar Admissions Resolution: Narrow Limits Recommended for Questions Related to the Mental Health and Treatment of Bar Applicants. *Mental and Physical Disability Law Reporter* 18:597–99.

Part Three
The Economics of ADA Title I

Chapter VIII

The Economics of the Employment Provisions of the Americans with Disabilities Act

Workplace Accommodations

PETER DAVID BLANCK

I. Introduction

Since its July 26, 1992, effective date, the implementation and effectiveness of Title I of the Americans with Disabilities Act has been the subject of intense debate among employers, courts, policy makers, academics, and persons with and without disabilities (Blanck 1998a; Blanck and Marti 1997). Supporters of the law stress the overarching importance of the civil rights guaranteed by Title I's antidiscrimination provisions. Critics cast the law as overly broad, difficult to interpret, inefficient, and as a preferential treatment initiative. Others question whether the law's economic benefits to employers, to persons with disabilities, and to society outweigh its administrative burdens. These and related issues have fueled the debate about, and some argue a backlash against, Title I.

This chapter examines one aspect of the ongoing evaluation and debate regarding Title I implementation, that is, arguments based primarily in economics. The chapter attempts to examine the economic implications of Title I in ways consistent with cost-benefit analysis of the law suggested by economists (cf. Chirikos, this volume; Baldwin, this volume). As mentioned in the final section, this approach is not meant to suggest that other disciplinary, cultural, or nonutilitarian views of the law are less valid or useful for assessing the impact of the law on employers, persons with disabilities, or society (e.g., Baynton, this volume).

Presently, there exists limited systematic empirical study of Title I implementation in general and of the economic impact of the law on employers and others in particular. This lack of study hinders accurate analysis and interpretation of Title I by both proponents and critics of the law (National Council on Disability 1996, p. 6). This lack of information is troubling in light of findings from the 1992 National Health Interview Survey showing that 19 million working-age adults, roughly 12 percent of the population between the ages of 18 and 69 years old, are restricted in the major life activity of working (Kaye 1998; LaPlante and Carlson 1996).

Section II of this chapter examines the major economic justifications and critiques of Title I in light of existing empirical information on the law's implementation. Section III explores the economics of workplace accommodations required under Title I, in particular as reflective of efficient business practices with applications to persons with and without disabilities.

II. Economic Implications of ADA Title I

There are several economic efficiency justifications linked to the provisions of Title I, each of which may be cast in support or opposition to the purposes of the law and which may impact in significant and measurable ways the American economy (Schwochau and Blanck 1999). This section examines these views with reference to the central provisions of the law and the existing, but limited, empirical study (Blanck 1994d, 1998a). The implications explored relate to the following propositions that are open to empirical verification:

Definition of Disability. Title I's statutory definition of disability affects the value of labor in the American workforce.

Qualified Individual with a Disability. Title I affects employers' ability to hire and retain "qualified" employees and to define essential job functions and production requirements and, thereby, employers' labor market efficiencies.

Reasonable Workplace Accommodations. Title I impacts employers' decisions to provide effective and economically efficient "accommodations" for job applicants and employees with and without disabilities.

Undue Hardship. Title I's economic impact varies for employers of different sizes and in different labor markets.

DEFINITION OF DISABILITY

Proponents and critics of Title I argue that the statutory definition of disability impacts, in either economically efficient or inefficient ways, the "value" of labor to employers in different segments of the American workforce. Worker "value" may be assessed in terms of the net dollar profit to employers of hiring or retaining a worker in a given labor market (Blanck 1997; Baldwin, this volume; Donohue 1994).

In a truly competitive labor market, the value to an employer of a worker's labor should equal or exceed the worker's wage (Collignon 1986; Donohue 1994). Nevertheless, as Donohue has suggested, a worker's value often is "contingent" upon a worker's output and his employers' and relevant consumers' attitudes about the worker (Donohue 1994). Thus, to a given employer, worker value may equal output or productivity plus degree of attitudinal preference or, conversely, disfavoring discrimination, toward the particular worker. Johnson suggests that labor market discrimination against persons with disabilities results more from inadequate information regarding their productivity than from prejudice, and that Title I defines worker value to employers in terms of the productive use of resources (Johnson 1997).

Worker value is linked also to relevant labor market biases or customer attitudes and preferences. A particular geographic market may have a high percentage of persons with disabilities, for example, the elderly or others who value or require physical accessibility to retail establishments. This demand may lead to a preference by these individuals to shop at accessible stores, in addition to the hiring by the stores of individuals with needs similar to those in the relevant market (Wolfe 1996, p. 1E). In such a market there may be increased value to employers (e.g., greater profits) associated with retaining workers and serving customers with disabilities.

In a series of empirical studies discussed in greater detail in section III below, my colleagues and I have illustrated how an employer's sensitivity to disability-related preferences and customer attitudes may lead to enhanced economic efficiency for a particular business (Blanck 1998a, 1996, 1994b). Proponents of Title I argue that the antidiscrimination law promotes economic equality in employment, whether defined in terms of wages or career opportunities, and confronts attitudinal preferences and unjustified discrimination that is faced by qualified employees and job applicants with disabilities in different labor markets. The United States Supreme Court, in *Alexander v. Choate* (1985, p. 295), has recognized that discrimination against people with disabilities is "most often the product, not of invidious animus," but rather of thoughtless and indifferent attitudes.

Under Title I's three-prong definition, a person with a disability covered by the law has a known physical or mental condition or impairment that "substantially limits major life activities," "a record of " a physical or mental condition, or is "regarded as" having such a condition (29 C.F.R. § 1630.2).

The first prong of the definition of disability is directed toward individuals with actual and substantial impairments or conditions, such as those with visual or hearing impairments, cancer, mental illness, physical paralysis, or HIV disease. This prong employs a functional definition of disability that is determined on a case-by-case basis (Burgdorf 1995). This first definition of disability is not only based on the diagnosis of the impairment but also on the effect of the impairment on the individual's life. Nevertheless, physical characteristics, such as hair color or left-handedness, and temporary conditions are not covered disabilities, nor are an individual's economic, environmental, or cultural disadvantages. Several conditions are expressly excluded from coverage as a disability under the statute, including transvestism, homosexuality, and illegal drug use (Burgdorf 1995, pp. 145–46).

During the early years of ADA implementation, some courts held that an employee with a serious but asymptomatic impairment, for instance the early stages of HIV disease, was not "disabled" for purposes of the ADA (for a review, see Blanck 1998a). In 1998, however, the United States Supreme Court resolved the interpretation regarding the ADA's definition of disability in *Bragdon v. Abbott.* In *Bragdon,* the Court concluded that HIV disease, whether symptomatic or asymptomatic, constitutes a disability under the ADA. Writing for the court, Justice Kennedy concluded that HIV disease is an impairment for purposes of the ADA from the moment of infection and during every stage of the disease.

Under the first prong of the definition, disability is interpreted to mean that the individual is substantially limited in a major life activity, for instance, in the ability to work in a class or range of jobs. Thus, in *Gordon v. Hamm* (1996) the court found that while side effects of chemotherapy treatment may be an impairment, they may not always substantially limit an individual's ability to work in a class of jobs or in a broad range of jobs in various classes. Similarly, in *Weiler v. Household Finance Corporation* (1996), the court concluded that an individual did not have a covered disability when he was incapable of satisfying demands of a particular job.

The first definition of disability does not mean, therefore, that a covered individual must work at the job of his choice (Blanck 1998a). Rather, to fall under the first definition, the individual's "access" to the relevant labor market must be substantially limited by the impairment or condition (Baldwin, this volume). Therefore, an impairment must exclude an individual from a wide variety of jobs at the employer in question to be considered a disability under the ADA. However, an individual may show a substantial limitation on a major life activity other than working—for instance, in reproduction, walking, speaking, or thinking—and thereby be a covered person with a disability (*Bragdon v. Abbott* 1998; Burgdorf 1995, pp. 156–57).

Overall, an individual's failure to qualify for one job in a given labor market, even because of a substantial impairment or condition, does not necessarily mean that individual has a covered disability for purposes of Title I analysis. A court must still assess whether the individual's impairment or condition creates a significant barrier to employment or to a particular labor market (*EEOC v. Joslyn Manufacturing Company* 1996).

Factors considered in determining whether an impairment substantially limits the major life activity of work, and therefore is a covered disability, include the individual's access to a geographic area, the number and type of jobs requiring similar training or skills (e.g., class of jobs in the relevant labor market), and the number and type of jobs not requiring similar training and skills (e.g., range of similar jobs in the relevant labor market) (29 C.F.R. § 1630.2).

The access-to-labor-market test associated with the first prong of the definition of disability suggests that in cases where an employer fails to hire a job applicant with an actual impairment that forecloses the individual from working within a broad range of jobs in an industry or in a large company (e.g., a blind person or a person with mental retardation), that individual may have a disability under the first prong of the statutory definition. This determination alone, however, does not indicate that individual is qualified to perform the job in question. Rather, the test focuses on whether the individual's access to the relevant labor market or job is limited due to the substantial nature of his impairment. If limited access to the relevant labor market is demonstrated, then the individual may be disabled for purposes of Title I analysis. A subsequent determination is required of whether he is qualified for the job and whether the employer discriminated against him because of his disability (Blanck 1998a).

Unlike the first prong, the second and third prongs of the definition of disability (i.e., "record of" and "regarded as" having an impairment) are meant to prevent employment discrimination on the basis of biased attitudes toward individuals with perceived yet often presently asymptomatic conditions (e.g., persons with a history of cancer or mental illness) (Blanck and Marti 1997, 1996). As mentioned above, in a discriminatory market, a worker's value sometimes is heavily contingent upon the worker's output and his employers', and relevant coworkers' or consumers', preferential or discriminatory attitudes about the worker (Baldwin, this volume; Donohue 1994).

Arguably, all labor markets are discriminatory in that they reflect, in part, preferences of the relevant employers. Discrimination in labor markets prohibited by Title I, however, is meant to prevent unjustified disfavor or prejudice toward the protected class of covered and qualified individuals with disabilities; for instance, to prevent employment decisions that are not related to worker qualifications and that are based on negative attitudes toward an individual's disability (Baldwin 1997; Johnson 1997).

In a situation where an employment action is made because of an individual's perceived disability, and not on worker output, that is, not on the worker's actual qualifications, the value of the worker to the employer is distorted in a discriminatory manner (*McNely v. Ocala* 1996). This distortion, and, in the aggregate, related market failure, may be reflected in lower wages to the discriminated-against employee or in loss of equal job opportunity. Baldwin finds that the annual losses to workers with disabilities resulting from discrimination in the labor market are substantial, with $28 billion attributed to discrimination in employment and $11 billion attributed to discriminatory wages (Baldwin, this volume). The goal of Title I is to enable qualified workers with perceived disabilities to receive the actual "value of their labor in a nondiscriminatory environment" (Donohue 1994, p. 2585).

Analysis of issues associated with employers' attitudes about perceived and "hidden" disabilities (i.e., conditions that are not immediately obvious, such as Tourette's syndrome or epilepsy) serves several purposes related to the analysis of the statutory definition of disability and its relation to the assessment of the value of labor in the workforce. First, studies suggest that increasing numbers of individuals with perceived disabilities are entering the workforce and are denied equal employment opportunity on the basis of biased attitudes and prejudice about their impairments (Kaye 1998). Some studies find that the most common health impairments associated with disability are "hidden" conditions (Kaye 1998).

Second, the study of attitudes toward persons with hidden or perceived disabilities is illustrative of underlying biases and discrimination unrelated to actual worker value in the relevant labor market (Blanck and Marti 1997, 1996). Thus, diminished worker value reflected in lower wages for comparable work is not related to actual output or to customers' preferences because of unfounded attitudinal discrimination (e.g., biased attitudes toward individuals with physical disfigurements) (Hahn 1996; Krieger 1995). Unlike race or gender employment discrimination, the protected characteristics associated with hidden or perceived disabilities may not be immediately obvious to the employer, either at the time of hiring or during employment (e.g., if the worker is injured on the job) (Blanck and Marti 1997, 1996). Attitudinal bias may be reflected in unconscious or unstated negative views of a worker's ability to perform a job, even though the individual with a perceived disability may be presently asymptomatic and qualified to perform the job in question.

Resultant discrimination by an employer based on animus toward a qualified individual with a perceived disability may result in a loss of productivity or economic value to the employer. Donohue has argued that productivity gains or economic value to employers may be enhanced if antidiscrimination employment laws succeed in reducing such attitudinal discrimination (Donohue 1992). Donohue suggests that the economic benefits of even small gains in worker productivity may largely offset the direct or indirect costs associated with implementation of the particular antidiscrimination law.

A case involving the "regarded as" prong of the definition of disability might involve a qualified asymptomatic individual being denied an employment opportunity because of the employer's negative attitudes toward that individual's predisposition for cancer, genetic illness, HIV disease, psychiatric illness, or any other recognized impairment. In these situations, discriminatory and biased attitudes impact employment decisions, rather than an obvious impairment or the actual market value of the individual's labor. From an economic standpoint, an employer would not be allowed under Title I to consider a presently qualified worker's future lost value or decreased output from actual yet asymptomatic or perceived impairments, such as genetic illness or HIV disease, in making hiring or employment-related decisions.

Title I's three-prong definition of disability is consistent with prior conceptions of employment equality that aim to ensure that "a worker's wage should equal the market-determined value of the individual's labor" (Donohue 1994, p. 2584). The access-to-labor-market tests, increasingly adopted by courts, reflect a high standard to meet for plaintiffs in Title I employment discrimination cases brought under the first prong of the definition of disability. That is because the test is meant to ensure that Title I's definition of disability does not distort the value of labor to employers or alter their rational labor market behavior.

Likewise, an employer's negative attitudes about people with actual or perceived disabilities do not by themselves constitute unjustified discrimination under Title I, unless they form the basis for subsequent discriminatory behavior toward "qualified" individuals (*Gordon v. Hamm* 1996, p. 16). Proof of the link between discriminatory attitudes and behavior, or "discriminatory animus," toward a qualified individual with a covered disability is an essential element of a prima facie ADA Title I case (Blanck 1998a).

Employment decisions based on perceptions of an employee's personality problems, such as a short temper or poor judgment in the workplace, are not prohibited by Title I if the underlying impairment is not "regarded as" a covered disability (Blanck 1998a). For instance, an employee may allege employment discrimination in circumstances where the appropriateness of that employee's workplace behavior is at issue. In one such case, *Fenton v. The Pritchard Corporation* (1996), an employee who was terminated for inappropriate and threatening behavior toward a fellow employee was held to be not qualified and thereby not entitled to Title I protections. The employee contended unsuccessfully that his behavior toward coworkers led his employer to perceive him as a covered person with a mental disability. Cases of this type suggest that an employer's negative attitudes toward an employee resulting in an adverse employment decision still must be based on defined disabilities that fall under the purview of the law.

In addition, employment discrimination under Title I will not be found where the employer does not "know" of, perceive, or treat an employee's impairment as a substantial limitation on the employee's present ability to work (Blanck 1998a). Thus, an employer's economic or humanitarian decision to grant a leave, educational or vocational training, or other workplace accommodations to a worker are not indicative of that employer's perceptions of a defined disability (*Johnson v. Boardman Petroleum* 1996). Likewise, an employer's decision not to hire an individual with an impairment for a position does not demonstrate that it perceives the employee as disabled for purposes of Title I analysis, regardless of whether an accommodation is required (Blanck 1998a; Willborn, this volume).

QUALIFIED INDIVIDUAL WITH A DISABILITY

Proponents and critics of Title I argue that the law affects employers' ability to hire and retain "qualified" employees and thereby distorts labor market efficiencies. Some critics of the law contend that Title I implementation has resulted in economic waste and inefficiency, declines in productivity, and reverse discrimination toward qualified individuals without disabilities (Oi 1996). These arguments often are made by analogy to alleged market inefficiencies associated with Title VII of the Civil Rights Act of 1964 implementation involving issues of race and gender (Blanck 1997).

An individual with a disability is "qualified" for purposes of Title I if he satisfies the prerequisites for the job, such as educational background or employment experience, and can perform essential job functions (Blanck 1998a). The concept of a "qualified individual" with a disability is central to the analysis of the link between improper discriminatory attitudes and behavior, as well as to the portrayal of the economic implications of Title I.

Title I does not require an employer to hire or retain individuals with covered disabilities who are not qualified, or to hire or retain individuals with covered disabilities over equally or more qualified individuals without disabilities (Blanck 1997; Willborn, this volume). Employers are not discouraged from searching for the most qualified individuals with or without disabilities. Nor are employers required to incur burdensome efficiency or productivity losses or opportunity costs, whether defined in terms of economic value in the relevant labor market or in retaining nonqualified workers with or without covered disabilities.

Title I's "qualified individual" requirement is meant to ensure that the value of a worker's labor or productivity should equal or exceed the worker's wage in a given labor market (Donohue 1994). Workers with disabilities are not deemed "equal" by their Title I status to workers without disabilities, nor are they provided preferential treatment in any aspect of employment. The goal of the qualified individual provision is to ensure that a worker with a disability who can perform essential job functions, with or without a reasonable accommodation, receives wages or other compensation that are comparable to his labor market value.

Critics of Title I argue that the definition of employee qualifications artificially constrains employers' ability to define employees' job functions and production requirements, thereby producing economic inefficiencies (Schuman 1995). Yet in establishing employment qualifications (i.e., educational background requirements or essential job functions), Title I only requires that the applicant's or employee's skills are to be considered independent of the purported disability; that is, independent of unfounded attitudes about the relation of disability to current job qualifications or of views about the efficacy or cost of an accommodation for a qualified individual with a disability. Employers are free to determine legitimate essential job functions or production requirements as they see fit (Blanck 1998a).

Several trends in Title I case law support the view that the qualified individual provision of Title I has served to ensure that a worker with a covered disability who can perform essential or fundamental job functions receives a wage that is comparable to his labor market value. First, as mentioned, employers are not required to alter production standards or to shape a job for an individual with a disability. Employers must maintain legitimate job requirements, however, as compared to those that are a subterfuge or pretext to exclude people with disabilities from equal employment.

As Burgdorf has noted, "Employers retain the prerogative . . . to determine what particular jobs need to be performed in their businesses and to establish the functions of those jobs" (Burgdorf 1995, p. 192). ADA Title I expressly distinguishes essential and marginal job functions. Marginal functions are those incidental job requirements that are not necessary to the central performance of the job in question. Employers may not exclude a qualified individual with a covered disability from employment on the basis of inability to perform marginal job functions.

Congress did not intend for ADA Title I to interfere with employers' non-discriminatory rational economic decision making (*Wernick v. Federal Reserve Bank of New York* 1996, p. 384). Nevertheless, businesses of different sizes (only those with fifteen or more employees are covered by the law) or with varying degrees of specialization have different needs with regard to the range of essential functions required of a particular worker. Such economies-of-scale questions are examined under the law on a case-by-case basis, which may have led to initial uncertainty by the small business community about implementation of the law (Blanck 1998a).

Second, as discussed below in the context of Title I's "undue hardship" provision, restructuring job functions as an accommodation to a covered individual with a disability may or may not cause an employer an economic undue hardship (i.e., inefficiencies due to a fundamental alteration of the required job) depending upon relative costs and benefits associated with the specialization of the task, the size and nature of the business, the availability of worker substitutes in the relevant labor market, or cyclical changes in the market or economy that affect labor and production requirements. The determination of the essential or nonessential nature of job functions also is made on a case-by-case basis.

Third, persons with actual, hidden, or perceived disabilities may be deemed "unqualified" for a job in circumstances in which they are shown to pose a direct safety or health threat to themselves or others in the workplace, regardless of their ability to perform essential job functions (Blanck and Marti 1997, 1996). Factors considered in determining whether a direct threat exists include the duration of the risk, nature of potential harm, and likelihood that the harm will occur. Employers are required to make an individualized and objective determination of direct threat, based on the employee's present ability to safely perform essential job functions. This determination must be made on the basis of tests of current medical judgment and not on anticipated lost productivity or predictions about the future impact of a disabling condition (Blanck 1998a; *Bragdon v. Abbott* 1998).

Fourth, pre- and postemployment inquiries regarding medical history or disability have been the subject of controversy in employment discrimination lawsuits involving the assessment of the qualifications of persons with different disabilities (Blanck and Marti 1997). Title I prohibits disability-related preemployment inquiries and medical tests, but such examinations are permitted after a conditional job offer has been made (Blanck and Marti 1997). Medically related employment tests, if used by an employer, must be administered to all employees regardless of disability, and with limited exceptions, the information obtained must be treated as confidential.

Medical results from testing following a conditional offer of employment, or medical results obtained during employment, may not be used to exclude a qualified individual with a covered disability from the job unless the exclusion is job-related, consistent with business necessity, and not amenable to reasonable accommodation (Blanck and Marti 1997, 1996). If an employee alleges discrimination based on an employer's medical test that purports to screen out qualified individuals with disabilities, the employer may rebut the claim by showing that the test accurately measures job skills that are consistent with business necessity, such as workplace safety or security requirements (Blanck 1998a).

REASONABLE WORKPLACE ACCOMMODATIONS

The economic implication that has received the most attention involves Title I's effect on employers' ability to provide workplace accommodations for qualified job applicants and employees with disabilities. As discussed above, an employer may legitimately shape an employee's work or production requirements as long as those requirements are job-related and not a pretext for discrimination against covered persons with disabilities. The employer's right to structure jobs, however, may not violate Title I's requirement that the employer provide "reasonable accommodations" for a qualified employee with a covered disability (Blanck 1998a, 1996, 1994b).

An accommodation is a modification or adjustment to a workplace process or environment that makes it possible for a qualified person with a disability to perform essential job functions, such as physical modifications to a work space, flexible scheduling of duties, or provision of assistive technologies to aid in job performance (Blanck 1998a). To be eligible for an accommodation, an employee must make his disability known to the employer and request an accommodation.

The accommodation requirement places a particular burden on an individual with a hidden and nonobvious disability to disclose in a timely manner the claimed disability and request the employer to provide an accommodation (Blanck 1998a). Once the request is made, the employer retains the right to choose the accommodation, as long as it is effective and the employee has a good faith opportunity to participate in the process (*Bultemeyer v. Fort Wayne Community Schools* 1996). An employee is not "qualified" if he cannot perform the job with or without an accommodation.

Critics of Title I have characterized an employer's obligation to provide accommodations to qualified persons as a form of market distortion leading to economic inefficiencies (Donohue 1994). They claim that the duty of reasonable accommodation creates for persons with disabilities an employment privilege or subsidy, in that it attempts to provide covered workers the wages they would receive in a nondiscriminatory free market (*Vande Zande v. State of Wisconsin Department of Administration* 1995; Weaver 1991). The duty of accommodation is cast as compromising the ideal of free market efficiency by imposing upon employers an affirmative duty to retain less economically efficient workers (Karlan and Rutherglen 1996).

There are at least three simplified hypothetical situations that illustrate the distribution of possible economic implications of the required provision of accommodations for qualified job applicants or employees covered by the law (Blanck 1997). A first example involves two equally qualified workers, that is, workers who are equally productive and of equal economic value to the employer. Donohue has set forth such a hypothetical: "given the choice between two equally productive workers, one requiring the expenditure of significant sums in order to accommodate him, one requiring no such expenditures, the profit-maximizing firm would prefer the worker who is less costly to hire" (Donohue 1994, p. 2608).

Donohue's hypothetical is not problematic for Title I economic impact analysis. Title I does not require the employer to hire or retain a qualified individual with a covered disability, regardless of the need for accommodation, over an equally or more qualified individual without a disability. There is no resultant distortion of labor market or economic efficiencies by Title I's antidiscrimination provisions, nor is there a requirement "to make the disabled equal" (Donohue 1994, p. 2611). Employer prerogative and economic need are not disturbed and the employer is not discouraged from searching for the most qualified worker. Moreover, as discussed in section III, to the extent that many accommodation costs for workers with disabilities are fixed or sunk, the market incentive would be to retain the qualified disabled worker over an equally or less qualified nondisabled worker requiring no accommodation (Blanck 1998a, 1997; Chirikos, this volume).

A similarly simple hypothetical involves two workers whose productivity varies. In this case, one individual with a covered disability is more "qualified" than an individual without a disability, say, by three units of value to the employer. It requires a certain amount of unit value to accommodate this qualified worker with a disability, say, three units of value. In this case, the net cost (including direct and indirect costs) to the employer of employing the individual with a disability is comparable to employing the individual without the disability, and their "value" is identical. Title I would require the employer to hire the legitimately more qualified worker, regardless of disability and require the provision of accommodation. A decision by the employer in this scenario to refuse the provision of accommodation to this qualified individual with a covered disability may constitute discrimination under Title I, assuming no undue hardship is associated with the provision of the accommodation.

The more controversial third hypothetical also involves two workers whose productivity varies. In this case, one individual with a covered disability is more "qualified" than an individual without a disability by three units of value to the employer. However, it requires thirty units of employer value to accommodate effectively the qualified worker with a disability, or ten times the direct cost of the accommodation. In this case, the net cost to the employer of employing the qualified individual with a disability is considerably more than is the cost of employing the less qualified individual without the disability.

In this third scenario, a decision by the employer to refuse to provide an accommodation to the qualified individual with a covered disability may or may not constitute discrimination under Title I. This may be true even though provision of the accommodation may be economically inefficient to the employer, assuming actual direct and indirect costs and benefits of the decision could be calculated. Discrimination may be found if no undue hardship is associated with the provision of an effective accommodation. Alternatively, discrimination may not be found if the element of cost or efficiency is interpreted to be implicit in the concept of a "reasonable" accommodation (*Vande Zande v. State of Wisconsin Department of Administration* 1995). Under this latter view, an employer has no duty to incur even a modest loss in value, because it would not be "reasonable" (i.e., economically rational) to accommodate the disabled employee.

It is this third scenario that critics of Title I use to suggest that the accommodation provision, absent the high evidentiary burden on employers of showing undue hardship discussed below, in effect, is an affirmative subsidy to employees with disabilities (Rosen 1991). Critics argue that the accommodation provision reflects a cost to employers incurred for employees with disabilities that is not spent on other employees without disabilities who arguably are more economically efficient but possibly less qualified or productive to perform the job in question (Schuman 1995). Others argue that Title I provisions reflect a judgment by society that qualified persons with disabilities should be able to work, even when "the value of their output does not equal the cost necessary to accommodate them in the workforce" (Burkhauser 1997, pp. 80–81).

Section III examines in greater detail findings from studies addressing the economic effect on employers of the provision of accommodations. Additional study is required, however, of the costs and benefits associated with accommodations in different businesses, jobs, labor markets, and involving persons with varying disabilities. Study is needed of the frequency of occurrence of the three hypothetical cases highlighted above. This analysis may show that, in practice, accommodating qualified workers with and without disabilities leads to efficient and cost-effective workplace operation. In the alternative, study may reveal that aggregate accommodation costs might rise over time as more severely disabled workers find employment (Chirikos, this volume). In the absence of accurate and reliable measures of worker "value," however, economic efficiency arguments, pro and con, of accommodation implementation may need to be reevaluated.

UNDUE HARDSHIP

A final economic implication involves Title I's economic effect on employers of different sizes and in different labor markets, particularly with regard to the provision of reasonable accommodations. Title I does not require an accommodation if it would impose an "undue hardship" on the employer. An undue hardship requires significant difficulty or expense in relation to the accommodation or the resources of the company (Blanck 1998a, 1997). A common critique is that accommodations for qualified individuals create hardships that are costly and burdensome for employers. Attitudes about the cost-effectiveness of accommodations by employers, however, often have more to do with unfounded beliefs than with the actual qualifications of persons with disabilities or their ability to add to employers' economic value (Blanck 1998a, 1997).

Title I identifies a number of economically based factors to be considered in determining undue hardship, including the nature and net cost of the accommodation, the financial resources of the business, the number of persons employed at the business, the impact of the accommodation on the operation of the business, the geographic separateness of the business facilities affected, and the composition and functions of the workforce of the business. This list of economic impact factors is meant to ensure that business size, type, sales and relevant labor markets are not affected by accommodations that pose a financial hardship to the operation of the business or that fundamentally alter the nature of the business. Although the employer's undue hardship defense is assessed on a case-by-case basis, relevant economic, incremental, and opportunity costs claimed (e.g., measured in terms of lost profits or market value) may vary by industry and will need to be assessed.

The next section examines empirical study on the economics of workplace accommodations. Regardless of such analysis, proponents of Title I suggest that cost-benefit analysis is a secondary justification to the antidiscrimination purposes of the law. Yet, if it is the case that, on average, the benefits and value to employers of effective accommodations implemented exceed the costs, then the accommodation provision is not only consistent with the antidiscrimination purposes of the law but also reflects economically efficient and rational workplace practices that have applications to qualified persons with *and without* disabilities.

III. The Economics of Workplace Accommodations

Answers to questions related to Title I implementation and interpretation must be guided increasingly by systematic empirical study (Blanck 1998a; Kirchner 1996). Collignon has argued that it is crucial to establish baseline data and models of empirical study to help foster an informed dialogue about Title I implementation and effectiveness (Collignon 1997). One area that has received much study, given the ability to quantify associated costs and benefits, has been the analysis of the economic implications to employers of workplace accommodations under Title I (Blanck 1997; Chirikos, this volume). This section examines the ongoing debate regarding the economics of workplace accommodations in light of these emerging studies.

As mentioned above, one common criticism is that the costs of accommodations outweigh the benefits provided to employers and persons with disabilities (Blanck 1997; Collignon 1986). Critics contend that the required provision of reasonable accommodations places financial burdens and administrative costs on the operation of businesses (Barnard 1990). Some argue that the costs of accommodations are especially high for large employers, who may be held accountable for extensive modifications due to their greater financial resources.

A common thread in these critiques is that they are made without reliance on data. In the absence of such information, it is no surprise that the attitudes and behavior of many employers reflect the view that the costs of accommodations outweigh the benefits (Blanck 1997). It is helpful to reiterate that Title I does not require employers to hire individuals with disabilities who are not qualified, or to hire qualified individuals with disabilities over equally or more qualified individuals without disabilities. More than three-quarters of all Title I charges filed with the EEOC have been dismissed because, among other reasons, the plaintiff alleging discrimination failed to show that he was qualified for the position (Blanck 1998a; Moss, this volume).

Many individuals with disabilities currently in the workforce have appropriate job skills, that is, they are "qualified" for purposes of the law and have their accommodation needs met in reasonable and effective ways (Blanck 1997). Findings from the 1989 National Health Interview Survey show that roughly 60 percent of working-age adults with disabilities rate their health as good to excellent (Kaye 1998; LaPlante 1993). Nevertheless, some courts presume that most impairments by definition impact an individual's "ability to perform up to the standards of the workplace" and increase the relative costs to employers of hiring the individual (*Vande Zande v. State of Wisconsin Department of Administration* 1995).

In contrast to this view, surveys show that executives have favorable attitudes toward the employment and accommodation of qualified employees with disabilities. A 1995 Harris poll of business executives found that 79 percent of those surveyed believe that the employment of qualified people with disabilities is a boost to the economy, while only 2 percent believe it poses a "threat to take jobs" from people without disabilities (Louis Harris and Associates 1995).

The developing empirical evidence also does not reflect the view that Title I's accommodation provision is a preferential treatment initiative that forces employers to ignore employee qualifications and economic efficiency (Blanck 1997). To the contrary, studies of accommodations suggest that companies that are effectively implementing the law demonstrate the ability or "corporate culture" to look beyond minimal compliance with the law in ways that enhance economic value (Chirikos, this volume). The low direct costs of accommodations for employees with disabilities have been shown to produce substantial economic benefits to companies, in terms of increased work productivity, injury prevention, reduced workers' compensation costs, and workplace effectiveness and efficiency (Blanck 1997; Daly and Bound 1996; Hall and Hall 1994).

In a series of studies conducted at Sears, Roebuck and Co. from 1978 to 1997, a time period before and after Title I's July 26, 1992, effective date, nearly all of the more than five hundred accommodations sampled required little or no cost—72 percent required no cost, 17 percent cost less than $100, 10 percent cost less than $500, and only 1 percent cost more than $500 but not more than $1,000 (Blanck 1997). During the years 1993 to 1997, the average direct cost for accommodations was less than $45, and from 1978 to 1992, the average direct cost was $121. The Sears studies also show that the direct costs of accommodating employees with hidden disabilities (e.g., emotional and neurological impairments, comprising roughly 15 percent of the cases studied) is even lower than the overall average of $45.

Other studies show that accommodations for employees with disabilities lead to direct and indirect benefits and cost-effective applications that increase the productivity of employees without disabilities. Studies by the Job Accommodation Network (JAN) demonstrate the benefits to employers of accommodations for qualified employees (President's Committee on Employment of People with Disabilities 1994). More than two-thirds of effective accommodations implemented as a result of a JAN consultation cost less than $500. In addition, almost two-thirds of the accommodations studied result in savings to the company in excess of $5,000. The savings associated with accommodations include lower job training costs and insurance claims, increased worker productivity, and reduced rehabilitation costs after injury on the job. JAN reports that for every dollar invested in an effective accommodation, companies sampled realized an average of $50 in benefits. Likewise, the results of a 1995 Harris poll of more than four hundred executives show that more than three-quarters of those surveyed report minimal increases in costs associated with the provision of accommodations (e.g., median direct cost for accommodations was $233 per covered employee), and, from 1986 to 1995, the proportion of companies providing accommodations rose from 51 percent to 81 percent (Blanck 1998a).

Several general implications may be drawn from the existing findings. First, the degree to which many companies comply with the accommodation provisions of Title I appears to have more to do with their corporate cultures, attitudes, and business strategies than with the actual demands of the law. For many companies with a culture of workforce diversity and inclusion, implementation has resulted in economically effective business strategies that transcend minimal compliance with the law and produce economic value (Blanck 1998a). In this regard, studies of accommodation costs at Sears showed that the indirect cost of not retaining qualified workers is high, with the average administrative cost per employee replacement of $1,800 to $2,400—roughly forty times the average of the direct costs and resultant benefits of workplace accommodations (Blanck 1996).

Second, in terms of relative cost, although the direct costs of the accommodations for any particular disability tend to be low, many companies regularly make informal and undocumented accommodations that require minor and cost-free workplace adjustments that are implemented directly by an employee and his supervisor (Blanck 1997). The trend toward the provision of accommodation in the workplace suggests that employers are realizing positive economic returns on the accommodation investment; for instance, by enabling qualified workers with covered disabilities to return to or stay in the workforce and by reducing worker absenteeism (Berven and Blanck, this volume, 1998; Blanck 1997). Chirikos finds that the productivity and job tenure of workers with disabilities is related directly to the provision of effective workplace accommodations (Chirikos, this volume).

Rosen points out, however, that where the benefits of accommodations exceed the costs "there is no inherent reason to expect that labor markets free of government intervention will fail to provide job accommodations in normal job situations" (Rosen 1991, p. 26). Yet, as discussed above, absent a truly competitive labor market, attitudinal discrimination against qualified individuals with disabilities alone may necessitate the required provision of accommodations under Title I, at least for a large segment of the labor force affected by this market failure. This is true given that the value of a worker with a disability often is contingent upon his output and his employers' and others' attitudes about the worker (Donohue 1994). Over time, with the lessening of prejudicial attitudes resulting from effective Title I implementation, and with increased knowledge from empirical study, employers who were formerly "economic discriminators" against qualified persons with disabilities may be less willing or less able to incur lost profits to satisfy their discriminatory tastes or preferences (Becker 1971; Weaver 1991).

Third, accommodations involving universally designed and advanced technology have been shown to enable groups of employees with and without disabilities to perform jobs productively, cost-effectively, and safely (Berven and Blanck, this volume, 1998; Blanck 1997, 1994c). The studies at Sears suggest that the direct costs associated with many technologically based accommodations (e.g., computer voice synthesizers) enabled qualified employees with disabilities to perform essential job functions. That these strategies create an economic "ripple effect" throughout the company, as related applications are developed subsequently that increase the productivity of Sears employees without disabilities (Blanck 1996). These findings suggest that the direct costs attributed to universally designed accommodations may be lower than predicted, particularly when their fixed or sunk costs are amortized over time. In addition, the Sears findings support those of organizational researchers showing that many traditional blue-collar jobs increasingly require workers to use or monitor computers that control equipment performing work tasks, and that workers with disabilities may increasingly and efficiently perform such essential job functions (Yelin 1997; Zuboff 1988).

Future examination is needed of the type, effectiveness, and cost of accommodations at large and small organizations, using standardized means for gathering and analyzing information. Studies must be conducted on the fears and stigmas associated with disclosure of actual and hidden disabilities and the resulting employment consequences; for instance, the extent to which qualified job applicants and employees with hidden disabilities forgo the benefits of accommodations due to fear of disclosure, thereby potentially depriving the labor market and employers of a source of value (Blanck and Marti 1997).

Close examination is needed of direct and indirect costs and benefits of Title I implementation, and of who bears the costs and receives the benefits associated with workplace accommodations for qualified persons with covered disabilities. A study based on over 1,000 observations in the Canadian workforce examined the extent to which the costs of workplace accommodations are shifted by employers to injured workers through wage adjustments upon the injured worker's return to work after a workplace injury (Gunderson and Hyatt 1996). The researchers found that injured workers did not incur the cost of workplace accommodations when they returned to their time-of-accident employer. Presumably, these workers were "qualified" to resume their essential or comparable job duties in ways that added economic value to the employer. Injured workers who returned to the workforce but to a different employer did "pay" for a portion of workplace accommodations by accepting substantially lower wages.

Additional study is required of the extent to which accommodations for workplace injury enable qualified workers with covered disabilities to stay or return to work at their time-of-accident employer or to a different employer, who bears the associated costs, and how these costs vary with job type and other factors such as insurance coverage rates (Chirikos, this volume). Some researchers have suggested that, over time, the provision of Title I accommodations may increase or at least help maintain employment rates by enabling newly disabled workers to retain employment (Mudrick 1997). Other studies show that accommodations for workers' health conditions extends their work life an average of five years (Burkhauser 1997).

Indirect costs associated with Title I implementation include related expenses for administrative, compliance, or legal actions. The Sears study examined all 138 Title I charges filed with the EEOC against Sears from 1990 to mid-1995 (Blanck 1996, 1994b). The findings showed that almost all of the EEOC charges (98 percent) were resolved without resort to trial litigation, and many through informal dispute processes that enabled qualified employees with disabilities to return to productive work. Consistent with the Sears findings, a 1997 study of nationwide trends in Title I charges filed with the EEOC showed that 94 percent of beneficial outcomes were obtained by the charging parties before full EEOC investigations and formal litigation were initiated (Moss, this volume).

Additional analysis is needed on a national scale of the patterns and magnitude of the costs and benefits associated with Title I implementation, compliance, and related litigation. Karlan and Rutherglen (1996) have suggested a variety of factors involving Title I implementation and compliance that may help guide future study. They hypothesize that, given the low cost of many accommodations and high costs attendant to litigation, employers and applicants or employees with disabilities create a "bargaining range" within which they negotiate the costs and benefits associated with the minimum accommodation the employee or applicant may accept and the costs and benefits associated with the maximum accommodation the employer may undertake. Analysis of the relative magnitude of direct and indirect costs and benefits associated with the accommodation process, for different employers and for workers with and without disabilities in similar jobs, may enable a more accurate assessment over time of the economic impact of Title I. Moreover, broadly defined, indirect costs and benefits may include the impact of effective accommodations on employee morale, perceptions of the business and its reputation by customers and the community, or relationship to effective implementation of other laws such as the Family Medical Leave Act or workers' compensation laws (Blanck 1997).

IV. Conclusion

Systematic evaluation of the economic implications associated with the emerging and existing workforce of qualified persons with disabilities is needed for several reasons. First, study of the labor force of qualified persons with disabilities may aid in long-term Title I implementation, as well as interpretation of related initiatives such as welfare, health care, and health insurance reform (Blanck 1998a). The Health Insurance Reform Act of 1996 is written to ensure access to portable health insurance for employees with chronic illness or disabilities who lose or change their jobs. Under the law, group health plan premium charges may not be based solely on disability status or the severity of an individual's chronic illness. The combined economic impact of the Health Insurance Reform Act and Title I on reducing employment discrimination facing qualified persons with covered disabilities is a promising area for study.

Second, study limited to the analysis of litigation and the EEOC charges associated with Title I implementation, while necessary, tends to focus discussion on the "failures" of the system, as opposed to economically efficient strategies designed to enhance a productive workforce and identify potential disputes before they arise (Blanck 1997; Karlan and Rutherglen 1996; Moss, this volume; Willborn, this volume). Independent of study of the enforcement of the civil rights guaranteed by Title I, the long-term promise of the law to raise awareness of the promise of equal employment opportunity for qualified persons requires the collection of information on attitudes, behavior, and the related economic implications of the law (Blanck 1998a; Colella, DeNisi, and Varma 1997).

Third, some evidence suggests that Title I implementation has coincided with larger numbers of qualified persons with severe disabilities entering the labor force. In 1996, the U.S. Census Bureau released data showing that the employment to population ratio for persons with severe disabilities has increased from roughly 23 percent in 1991 to 26 percent in 1994, reflecting an increase of approximately 800,000 people with severe disabilities in the workforce (Blanck 1998a). Examination is required of the economic impact of Title I on workplace accommodation costs and benefits against this backdrop of increased labor force participation of qualified workers with disabilities, particularly in the context of the recent reforms to welfare policy.

In this last regard, my colleagues and I have completed an in-depth case study of Manpower Inc., the world's largest staffing employer (Blanck 1998b). Manpower annually provides temporary employment opportunities to more than 2,000,000 people worldwide. The Manpower study examines emerging employment opportunities available to persons with disabilities within the staffing industry. The study explores the importance of these opportunities to reform strategies that provide a bridge from no employment to temporary employment to permanent employment. A critical element of the company's success in hiring and retaining workers with disabilities has been its investment in individualized training, worker assessment, and job-matching tools.

The Manpower study identifies aspects of its corporate culture that foster employment of persons with disabilities, including a belief that there are no unskilled workers, that every individual has skills and aptitudes that can be measured, and that every job may be broken down into essential tasks. The core findings of the study illustrate that for Manpower's employees: (1) individualized training and job placement are available; (2) above minimum wages and health insurance benefits are provided; (3) there is opportunity for career advancement; (4) there is opportunity for transition to full-time competitive employment; and (5) there are opportunities for self-advancement and self-learning. In these ways, Manpower serves as a bridge to the workforce for qualified workers with disabilities. Sixty percent of Manpower employees with disabilities studied moved from no employment to permanent employment as a direct result of temporary assignments.

Despite the encouraging trends found in the Sears and Manpower reports, estimates of unemployment levels for persons with disabilities range as high as 50 percent (Blanck 1998a). Some studies suggest that in the years 1970 to 1992 there was no significant positive change in the labor force participation rate among persons with disabilities (Blanck 1998a). As a result, the continued reality of economic, structural, attitudinal, and behavioral discrimination increasingly may lead qualified individuals to assert their Title I rights in the future. Analysis of job retention, assessment, advancement, disclosure, and accommodation strategies are needed to help qualified individuals keep jobs and achieve their potential. This analysis is particularly important for those qualified individuals with severe disabilities, who may be most susceptible to unfounded negative attitudes about their labor force potential and value.

Future studies must address the social and cultural factors, and the structural and cyclical changes in the labor market and the economy, that influence employment opportunity for persons with and without different disabilities (Baynton, this volume; Harkin 1994). This study may include factors such as types of jobs attained (e.g., entry level, service-related, or production), number of hours worked (e.g., full-time and temporary positions), geographic differences in labor markets and hiring patterns, turnover, productivity, retention, wage, and promotion rates, availability of transportation to work, and provision of accommodations. It may also include analysis of persons with disabilities who are particularly vulnerable to changes in economic conditions, such as those in poverty or those with minimal education or job skills.

Similar analysis is needed of cost-effective workplace accommodation strategies affecting qualified job applicants and employees without disabilities, such as those geared toward employee wellness programs, flexible hours for workers with young children, employer-sponsored child-care centers, job-sharing strategies for workers with limited time availability, or employee assistance programs (EAPs) (Blanck 1997). As Gerry has suggested, many companies already expend large sums of money accommodating the needs of workers without disabilities, which in the aggregate may be substantially greater than the costs associated with accommodations for qualified workers with covered disabilities (Gerry 1991). Analysis of these innovative strategies may show that they effectively and efficiently complement accommodations required by many qualified workers with disabilities.

Studies show that workplace accommodation strategies enhance the productivity and job tenure of those large numbers of qualified workers without disabilities who are injured on the job or who may become impaired in the future (Blanck 1997). In an eight-year study of Coors Brewing Company's health screening program covering almost four thousand employees, the company realized net and direct savings of roughly $2.5 million, in terms of saved payments in short-term disability, temporary worker replacement, and direct medical costs (Greenwood 1996). Given a conservative estimate of $100 average direct cost per employee for workplace accommodations based on the Sears findings described earlier, the savings generated by the Coors study could fund accommodations for 25,000 qualified workers.

Another study of Coors Brewing Company's wellness initiatives (e.g., health screening and education, exercise, stress, and smoking cessation programs) found that the company saves up to $8 for every dollar invested in these programs (Blanck 1997). Likewise, a nine-year study of 28,000 Union Pacific Railroad employees found that its wellness program resulted in net savings of $1.3 million to the company (Blanck 1997). These findings suggest the huge economic implications associated with the development of cost-effective accommodations strategies designed to prevent workplace injury and to help retain the increasing numbers of qualified employees with and without disabilities. Considering that by the end of the year 2000, the costs to employers associated with back injury alone in the workplace are estimated to approach $40 billion, examination of the economic savings related to accommodation strategies, injury prevention, and wellness programs is warranted (Blanck 1994a).

Moreover, the educational side effects associated with Title I implementation and comprehensive accommodation strategies may enhance general employee morale as well as positive attitudes about qualified coworkers with different disabilities or those who are members of other protected groups (Batavia 1997).

In conclusion, this chapter has explored the economics of Title I implementation. Clearly, further empirical study of Title I is needed to address the law's economic, cultural, and symbolic impact on employers and others in society. The economic model has yet to demonstrate empirically the hypothesized labor market inefficiencies associated with the operation of the law, particularly those claimed to be linked to the provision of workplace accommodations (Schwochau and Blanck 1999). Yet independent of economic analysis and related disciplinary study of Title I, definition of the social and moral policies underlying the equal employment of qualified persons with covered disabilities is necessary (Blanck 1998a; Kavka 1992; Scotch and Schriner 1997).

References

Alexander v. Choate, 469 U.S. 287 (1985).

Baldwin, Marjorie L. 1997. Can the ADA Achieve Its Employment Goal? *Annals of the American Academy of Political and Social Science* (hereafter *AAPSS*) 549 (Jan.): 37–52.

Barnard, Thomas H. 1990. The Americans with Disabilities Act: Nightmare for Employers and Dream for Lawyers? *St. John's L. Rev.* 64:229–52.

Batavia, Andrew I. 1997. Ideology and Independent Living: Will Conservatism Harm People with Disabilities? *AAPSS* 549 (Jan.): 10–23.

Becker, Gary S. 1971. *The Economics of Discrimination.* 2d ed. Chicago: University of Chicago Press.

Berven, Heidi M., and Peter David Blanck. 1998. The Economics of the Americans with Disabilities Act: Part II: Patents, Innovations and Assistive Technology. *Notre Dame Journal of Law, Ethics, and Public Policy* 12:9–120.

Blanck, Peter David. 1994a. The Americans with Disabilities Act: Issues for Back and Spine-related Disability. *Spine* 19 (1):103–7.

———. 1994b. Communicating the Americans with Disabilities Act, Transcending Compliance: A Case Report on Sears, Roebuck and Co. *Annenberg Washington Program Reports.* Washington, D.C.

———. 1994c. Communications Technology for Everyone: Implications for the Classroom and Beyond. *Annenberg Washington Program Reports.* Washington, D.C.: Annenberg Washington Program in Communications Policy Studies of Northwestern University.

———. 1994d. Employment Integration, Economic Opportunity, and the Americans with Disabilities Act: Empirical Study from 1990–1993. *Iowa L. Rev.* 79:853–923.

———. 1996. Communicating the Americans with Disabilities Act, Transcending

Compliance: 1996 Follow-up Report on Sears, Roebuck and Co., *Annenberg Washington Program Reports.* Washington, D.C.

————. 1997. The Economics of the Employment Provisions of the Americans with Disabilities Act: Part I: Workplace Accommodations. *DePaul L. Rev.* 46:877–914.

————. 1998a. *The Americans with Disabilities Act and the Emerging Workforce.* Washington, D.C.: American Association on Mental Retardation.

————. 1998b. *The Emerging Role of the Staffing Industry in the Employment of Persons with Disabilities: A Case Report on Manpower Inc.* Iowa Law, Health Policy, and Disability Center Reports, Iowa City, Iowa.

Blanck, Peter David, and Mollie W. Marti. 1996. Genetic Discrimination and the Employment Provisions of the Americans with Disabilities Act: Emerging Legal, Empirical, and Policy Implications. *Behavioral Sci. and L.* 14:411–32.

————. 1997. Attitudes, Behavior, and the Employment Provisions of the Americans with Disabilities Act. *Villanova L. Rev.* 42:345–407.

Bragdon v. Abbott. 524 U.S. 624 (1998).

Bultemeyer v. Fort Wayne Community Schools. 100 F.3d 1281 (7th Cir. 1996).

Burgdorf, Robert L., Jr. 1995. *Disability Discrimination in Employment Law.* Washington, D.C.: Bureau of National Affairs.

Burkhauser, Richard V. 1997. Post-ADA: Are People with Disabilities Expected to Work? *AAPSS* 54 (Jan.): 971–83.

Colella, Adrienne, Angelo DeNisi, and Arup Varma. 1997. Appraising the Performance of Employees with Disabilities: A Review and Model. *Human Resources Management Review* 7 (1): 27–53.

Collignon, Frederick C. 1986. The Role of Reasonable Accommodation in Employing Disabled Persons in Private Industry. In *Disability and the Labor Market,* ed. Monroe Berkowitz and M. Anne Hill, pp. 196–241. Ithaca, N.Y.: ILR Press.

————. 1997. Is the ADA Successful? Indicators for Tracking Gains. *AAPSS* 549 (Jan.): 129–47.

Daly, Mary C., and John Bound. 1996. Worker Adaptation and Employer Accommodation Following the Onset of a Health Impairment. *J. Gerontology* 51B:S53.

Donohue, John J., III. 1992. Advocacy versus Analysis in Assessing Employment Discrimination Law. *Stanford L. Rev.* 44:1583–1614.

————. 1994. Employment Discrimination Law in Perspective: Three Concepts of Equality. *Mich. L. Rev.* 92:2583–612.

EEOC v. Joslyn Manufacturing Co. 1996 U.S. Dist. LEXIS 9882 (N.D. Ill. July 11, 1996).

Fenton v. The Pritchard Corp. 926 F. Supp. 1437 (D. Kan. 1996).

Gerry, Martin H. 1991. Disability and Self-Sufficiency. In *Disability and Work: Incentives, Rights, and Opportunities,* ed. Carolyn L. Weaver, pp. 89–93. Washington, D.C.: AEI Press.

Gordon v. Hamm. 100 F.3d 907 (11th Cir. 1996).

Greenwood, Henritze J. 1996. Coorscreen—a Low Cost, On-site Mammography Screening Program. *Am. J. Health Promotion* 10 (5): 364–70.

Gunderson, Morely, and Douglas Hyatt. 1996. Do Injured Workers Pay for Reasonable Accommodation? *Indus. and Lab. Rel. Rev.* 50 (1): 92–121.

Hahn, Harlan. 1996. Antidiscrimination Laws and Social Research on Disability: The Minority Group Perspective. *Behav. Sci. and Law* 14:41–59.

Hall, Francine S., and Elizabeth L. Hall. 1994. The ADA: Going beyond the Law. *Academy of Management Executive Rev.* 8 (1): 17–26.

Harkin, Tom. 1994. The Americans with Disabilities Act: Four Years Later—Commentary on Blanck. *Iowa L. Rev.* 79:935–39.

Health Insurance Reform Act of 1996. Pub. L. No. 104-191, 110 Stat. 1936 (1996).

Johnson, William G. 1997. The Future of Disability Policy: Benefit Payments or Civil Rights? *AAPSS* 549 (Jan.): 160–72.

Johnson v. Boardman Petroleum. 923 F. Supp. 1563 (S.D. Ga. 1996).

Karlan, Pamela S., and George Rutherglen. 1996. Disabilities, Discrimination, and Reasonable Accommodation. *Duke L. J.* 46:1–41.

Kavka, Gregory S. 1992. Disability and the Right to Work. *Soc. Phil. and Pol.* 9 (1): 262–90.

Kaye, Steve. 1998. *Disability Watch: Status Report on the Condition of People with Disabilities.* Oakland, Calif.: Disability Rights Advocates and Disability Statistics Center.

Kirchner, Corinne. 1996. Looking under the Street Lamp: Inappropriate Uses of Measures Because They Are There. *J. Dis. Pol. Stud.* 7:77–90.

Krieger, Linda Hamilton. 1995. The Content of Our Categories: A Cognitive Bias Approach to Discrimination and Equal Employment Opportunity. *Stanford L. Rev.* 47:1161–248.

LaPlante, Mitchell P. 1993. *Disability, Health Insurance Coverage, and Utilization of Acute Health Services in the United States.* Disability Statistics Report No. 4: U.S. Dept. Ed., National Institute on Disability Research. Washington, D.C.

LaPlante, Mitchell P., and D. Carlson. 1996. *Disability in the United States: Prevalence and Causes, 1992.* Disability Statistics Report No. 7: U.S. Dept. Ed., National Institute on Disability Research. Washington, D.C.

Louis Harris and Associates and National Organization on Disability. 1995. 1995 Survey of Corporate Executives of the ADA. Washington, D.C.

McNely v. Ocala. 99 F.3d 1068 (11th Cir. 1996).

Mudrick, Nancy R. 1997. Employment Discrimination Laws for Disability: Utilization and Outcome. *AAPSS* 549 (Jan.): 53–70.

National Council on Disability. 1996. Achieving Independence: The Challenge for the Twenty-first Century—a Decade of Progress in Disability Policy Setting an Agenda for the Future. Washington, D.C. July 26.

Oi, Walter Y. 1996. Employment and Benefits for People with Diverse Disabilities. In *Disability, Work and Cash Benefits,* ed. Jerry L. Mashaw et al., pp. 103–27.

President's Committee on Employment of People with Disabilities. 1994. *Job Accommodation Network (JAN) Reports.* Washington, D.C. Oct.–Dec.

Rosen, Sherwin. 1991. Disability Accommodation and the Labor Market. In *Disability and Work: Incentives, Rights, and Opportunities,* ed. Carolyn L. Weaver, pp. 18–30. Washington, D.C.: AEI Press.

Schuman, Mark A. 1995. The Wheelchair Ramp to Serfdom: The Americans with Disabilities Act, Liberty, and Markets. *St. John's J. Leg. Comm.* 10:495–96.

Schwochau, Susan, and Peter David Blanck. 1999. The Economics of the Americans with Disabilities Act: Part III—Does the ADA Disable the Disabled? *Berkeley Journal of Employment and Labor Law* 21:271–313.

Scotch, Richard K., and Kay Schriner. 1997. Disability as Human Variation: Implications for Policy. *AAPSS* 549 (Jan.): 148–59.

Vande Zande v. State of Wisconsin Dept. Admin. 44 F.3d 538 (7th Cir. 1995).

Weaver, Carolyn L. 1991. Incentives versus Controls in Federal Disability Policy. In *Disability and Work: Incentives, Rights, and Opportunities,* ed. Carolyn L. Weaver, pp. 3–17. Washington, D.C.: AEI Press.

Weiler v. Household Finance Corp. 101 F.3d 519 (7th Cir. 1996).

Wernick v. Federal Reserve Bank of New York. 91 F.3d 379 (2d Cir. 1996).

Wolfe, Bill. 1996. Shopping Trip-ups: How Accessible Are Local Stores to People with Disabilities? *Courier-Journal,* Dec. 23.

Yelin, Edward H. 1997. The Employment of People with and without Disabilities in an Age of Insecurity. *AAPSS* 549 (Jan.): 117–28.

Zuboff, Shoshana. 1988. *In the Age of the Smart Machine: The Future of Work and Power.* New York: Basic Books.

Chapter IX

Employer Accommodation of Older Workers with Disabilities

Some Empirical Evidence and Policy Lessons

Thomas N. Chirikos

Introduction

Careful monitoring of the progress of the Americans with Disabilities Act (ADA) is a matter of increasing urgency as concern mounts that the act has failed to produce the employment gains for persons with disabilities envisaged at the time it was enacted.[1] This essential task is stymied, however, by the absence of benchmark data and a systematic program of empirical research on the population targeted by the ADA. These lacunae are understandable: the ADA was not initially grounded on much hard data, its implementation was expected to proceed on a case-by-case basis, and disability advocacy groups have generally preferred to use scarce resources for technical assistance instead of policy-related research.[2] Nonetheless, the limited knowledge base constrains the ADA-related policy agenda and probably delays some needed corrective actions in disability programming.[3] Indeed, time may already be running out to establish quantitatively the baseline against which ADA progress will be measured, with the very real possibility that the failure twenty-five years ago to obtain benchmark data for appraising the 1973 Rehabilitation Act will be repeated.[4]

High priority items on the empirical research agenda are additional studies elucidating the costs of employer accommodation of workers with disabilities under the "reasonable accommodation" and "undue hardship" provisions of Title I of the act. The level of, and projected trends in, these costs continue to be at the center of the controversy about the potential effects of the ADA, favorable and unfavorable alike.[5] If, as many specialists suppose, accommodation costs are low or even negligible, then employment of workers with disabilities should increase, economic efficiency should improve generally, and redistributive transfers to the disabled population should decline as the act takes hold. Furthermore, if employer accommodations are subject to scale economies, average costs should be expected to fall as more persons with disabilities join the workforce. If, however, costs of accommodating workers with disabilities are high, then employment effects may be smaller, allocative inefficiencies in some economic sectors may occur, and redistributive subsidies to the population with disabilities may actually increase. If costs are affected by the severity or type of disability, they may be expected to rise as additional persons with different types of disabilities enter the labor market. Thus, policy makers clearly have a stake in understanding whether accommodation costs are high or low, or whether they can be expected to rise or fall as additional workers with disabilities seek gainful employment.

Available empirical evidence clearly favors the view that costs are low and likely to decline.[6] Early studies suggested that most job accommodations cost less than $500 and more recent estimates suggest they average about $260 per worker. Yet, valuable as they may otherwise be, these studies have not laid the cost controversy completely to rest for several reasons. One is that the costs of accommodation in this literature generally have been conceptualized very narrowly. Instead of valuing the full opportunity costs of accommodating the average worker with a disability (net of what it costs to "accommodate" an average nondisabled worker), many studies have simply measured at one point in time the costs of special equipment or hardware needed by individuals with just certain types of impairments. A fuller accounting not only of the value of the time of other employees and managerial personnel in accommodating workers with disabilities, but the value of the time of disabled workers themselves, may show that costs are substantially higher on average than those reported in the literature to date. Longitudinal analyses of the cumulative costs of accommodating workers with continuing need for various types of job assistance may also show them to be higher as well.

More significant perhaps is that past studies have invariably ignored selection factors and the composition (heterogeneity) of the population with disabilities in interpreting cost data. Selectivity issues arise mainly because individuals who can be accommodated at low cost are ipso facto more likely to be accommodated. In an earlier paper, I argued that there may be a queue of individuals with disabilities lined up for employment according to the probable costs of accommodation, with those requiring the least costly accommodation always being at the front of the queue.[7] Since past discriminatory practices meant that only small numbers of persons with disabilities worked, and that these workers probably came from the front of the queue, data collected from employers tended to detect low accommodation costs for those workers. But these observed costs are not at all representative of what it would cost to accommodate individuals farther down the queue who have more severe or multiple impairments. Selectivity means, in other words, that observed costs of currently employed individuals with disabilities are not necessarily predictive of the costs of accommodating those not yet employed.

The heterogeneity of the population with disabilities also bears on whether accommodation costs will rise or fall as more disabled workers join the labor market. Scale economies in accommodations may not be realized if newly hired persons with disabilities need different or more extensive types of accommodations than those already accommodated. Furthermore, because the severity of impairments of workers with disabilities influences not only the accommodations they need but also their productivity, differences in productivity-related characteristics such as education and firm-specific training affect accommodation costs indirectly. If these other characteristics can substitute for impairment-related deficits and thus reduce the cost of accommodation, employers may be induced to accommodate workers, even when they are not required to do so. An implication is that accommodation costs should be reckoned in efficiency-adjusted terms, that is, control for work productivity differences across workers with similar types of impairments.

Additional research designed to overcome these limitations in the available literature on accommodation costs is thus needed. Ideally, new studies would observe both workers who were and were not accommodated as well as the expected costs of accommodating each subgroup. This is a tall order for two reasons. One is that empirical observations on firms (covered entities under the ADA legislation) will almost certainly exclude workers who were not accommodated, because many firms will be unwilling to report such cases and have good reason to overstate the probable costs of accommodation if they did. The other is that observations on workers with disabilities will almost certainly exclude data on the costs incurred by employers in accommodating them. Workers with disabilities themselves may not be able to estimate the actual costs of their accommodations very well and may have reasons to understate them if they did. In the absence of specially designed (and very expensive) two-level surveys of firms and the current and former employees of those firms, employer accommodations can be investigated only indirectly, observing either workers or firms and then drawing inferences about either costs or nonaccommodated persons with disabilities. As a complement to the more conventional approach of the available literature of observing firms and costs directly (but nonaccommodation outcomes only indirectly), studies based on empirical observations of workers with disabilities who were and were not accommodated are needed to advance the state of the art. Empirical analyses of the determinants of job accommodation that also trace employment outcomes of accommodated and nonaccommodated workers are of special interest in this regard.

Until quite recently, studies of accommodated and nonaccommodated workers would have been impossible to carry out for lack of suitably detailed information. This situation has now changed with the start-up of a new longitudinal survey that, for the first time ever, collects such data on a nationally representative sample of American workers, namely, the Health and Retirement Study (HRS) being conducted by the University of Michigan's Survey Research Center under a Cooperative Agreement with the National Institute on Aging.[8] The HRS sample encompasses about 12,650 individuals who were between 51 and 61 years of age at baseline and their spouses, irrespective of age. The HRS survey, especially the extensive 1992 baseline interviews, sought from disabled respondents information about the extent to which their employers provided accommodations, if any at all. Responses to this battery of questions permit not only estimates of the crude probabilities that persons with disabilities will be accommodated, but a general portrait of the nature and scope of the accommodations, for example, whether somebody helped out, whether new time schedules or even work assignments occurred, whether special equipment or transportation were obtained, and so forth. These responses can also be combined with the extensive health and economic data obtained in the HRS to study the outcomes of workers who have and have not been accommodated.[9]

While these unique strengths of the HRS data appear to be offset somewhat by the age restrictions of the panel sample, the accommodation experiences of workers in their sixth decade are nonetheless highly relevant to disability policy generally and the ADA in particular. Work disability probabilities rise with age, and incidence rates for individuals in their fifties, especially men, are higher than all other age groups.[10] Older individuals may be subject to discriminatory job practices as they confront the onset of aging-related health problems. Indeed, the employment effects of the ADA may well depend as much on minimizing losses from labor market withdrawal of these older workers as expanding job opportunities for younger persons with disabilities.

The primary objective of this chapter, then, is to draw on the HRS data set to examine cost-relevant issues about employer accommodations of older workers with disabilities. More specifically, the aims are to summarize baseline and follow-up data on the job accommodation experiences of HRS respondents with disabilities, and to analyze by statistical means both the factors that account for why only some disabled workers are accommodated by their employers and the differences job accommodation makes to the employment outcomes of those workers. The statistical analysis highlights the selectivity and heterogeneity issues discussed above and, in so doing, permits policy-relevant inferences to be drawn about cost trends as more workers with disabilities enter the workforce.

The chapter is organized as follows. The next section sets out the analytic framework as well as some methodological details about the data set, variable construction, and the specification of multivariate regression models used to gauge the impact of key factors on accommodation-related outcomes. The third section presents the main empirical results, beginning with a descriptive account of the prevalence rates of job accommodation by type, and selected health and impairment characteristics of individuals by accommodation experience. This section then turns to the results of specifying and testing several statistical models, the main one designed to explain what factors predict the likelihood that a worker will be accommodated by his or her employer. Then, as a means of ascertaining whether these accommodations make any difference, models of sustained employment are specified and tested. The final section draws some lessons for evaluating the employment effects of the ADA.

Methods

ANALYTIC FRAMEWORK

As noted previously, worker-level data on job accommodations have the advantage of permitting empirical analyses of the determinants of such outcomes, but the disadvantage that costs can only be inferred, not measured directly. It is possible, however, to posit a simple economic model of the accommodation decision process that both guides the specification of empirical models and provides a means of drawing those cost inferences. This model may be summarized briefly as follows: employers will choose to accommodate workers with disabilities when the expected benefits of doing so are at least as great as the expected costs of the accommodation, subject to some randomness (u) in ascertaining the true benefits and costs of the accommodation event. That is, the employer will supply an accommodation (A) when:

$$A = E \text{ (Benefits)} - E \text{ (Costs)} - u > 0 \qquad (1)$$

Despite its simplicity, this model highlights several critical features of employer accommodations. For one thing, it is the interaction between the benefits to be derived by the employer in accommodating a worker and the costs of the accommodation that influences whether the accommodation takes place. Low costs alone may not necessarily lead to a decision to accommodate a worker, whereas high costs may not necessarily lead to the opposite outcome. For another, the model suggests that neither the benefits nor the costs of accommodating the average worker may be known with any degree of certainty and, even if the employer has a reasonable grasp of these expected values, there may still be some randomness in the decision process. The manner in which employer representatives carry out the decision rule, the timing of the decision, the sensitivity of different employers to the costs of noncompliance, their attitudes about why accommodations should be made, their knowledge of the ADA, their knowledge about factors such as tax credits that effectively reduce the costs of accommodation, and the resoluteness with which workers themselves seek accommodations illustrate factors that differ across firms randomly.[11] In empirical applications, many of these factors can be accounted for in the error term (u). The trick is to find useful indicators (proxy variables) of potential benefits and costs, and to measure carefully their influence on accommodation outcomes. Since accommodations occur only when benefits are at least equal to costs, indicators that are positive predictors of accommodation may be interpreted as factors that raise benefits or lower costs; conversely, indicators predictive of nonaccommodation may be interpreted as factors that lower benefits or raise costs. Inferences about costs and cost-related factors in the accommodation process may thus be drawn immediately from such empirical results.

In the analysis reported here, proxy indicators of costs and benefits are constructed in terms of self-reported characteristics of the worker and his or her employer. Multivariate regression techniques are then used to gauge the net effects of these proxies on several accommodation outcomes, particularly the probability of ever being accommodated by an employer. Given the earlier discussion about selectivity and heterogeneity, the regression analysis focuses on the type and severity of workers' health conditions to assess the extent to which these cost-augmenting characteristics lead to lower probabilities of accommodation. Similarly, indicators of worker productivity and the scale of the employing firm are examined to ascertain the extent to which such cost-lowering characteristics raise the chances of accommodation. To the extent that other factors plausibly thought to influence the benefit-cost ratio of accommodation are actually found to predict accommodation in the expected direction, the analysis provides a means of drawing policy-relevant inferences about the costs of employer accommodation.

Because the analysis is based on longitudinal observations of individuals who at some point were or could have been accommodated, it is also possible to examine whether receiving that accommodation makes any difference to those individuals. There are several kinds of differences that ideally would be considered in empirical studies, including the long-term accommodation costs to both the firm and the worker as well as the manner in which these costs are borne by the firm, the accommodated worker, other workers, consumers of the firm's product, and society at large. The analysis here is predicated on the simplifying assumption that the costs of accommodation per se as well as the penalty costs of noncompliance fall mainly on the employer. A more realistic assumption, of course, is that these costs will be shifted to others, including the accommodated worker.[12] Of some interest in this regard would be analyses of career progression and earnings growth patterns for workers by accommodation experience in order to assess whether the economic status of these individuals really improved as a result of the accommodation. Regrettably, sufficiently detailed HRS follow-up data needed to conduct an analysis of this sort were unavailable at the time this chapter was prepared. Preliminary data are used to test simpler models of employment outcomes at follow-up with respect to various characteristics of workers with disabilities, including the accommodation experiences of those workers. Despite their preliminary character, these models complement the statistical analysis of accommodation determinants, and they provide further clues about the benefits and costs of employment accommodation of workers with disabilities.

DATA SET AND VARIABLES

The analysis draws principally on baseline (Wave 1) interview data collected in the 1992 Health and Retirement Study (HRS), though as noted above some preliminary (Wave 2) follow-up data collected in 1994 are also used. As noted earlier, the HRS collects unique information on health conditions and functional impairments of all respondents, irrespective of disability status; it also collects data on disability outcomes, including conditions responsible for the disablement and information on job accommodations, for all respondents reporting a work-limiting health problem. Difficulties arose, as they inevitably do, in dealing with responses to some interview items, each requiring adjustments or operational assumptions before incorporating them into the analysis. Key aspects of what I did in this regard are summarized here briefly; a more detailed account of each variable constructed for the analysis is presented in the appendix table.

JOB ACCOMMODATION MEASURES

The battery of disability-related questions in the baseline survey instrument inquires generally whether the respondent has a work-limiting impairment and, if so, whether his or her employer accommodated the disability by providing someone to help out, more rest periods and breaks, special equipment, and so on; see the appendix table for the full list of items. This battery of questions, however, was posed to different subgroups of respondents depending on whether the impairment started before or after the individual joined the workforce, whether (if working) the respondent left the employer at the onset of the disability, whether the employer at that time or the new employer did anything to accommodate the impairment, and/or whether the current employer was doing so at the time of the baseline interview, and so forth.

These conditional nodes or skip patterns in the survey instrument mean that some individuals respond to one and only one accommodation battery, while others respond to more than one set of questions, depending on their job history and the timing of the disabling condition requiring accommodation. In turn, this means that an analysis of accommodation prevalence and type can be carried out either on the basis of individual respondents or on the basis of what I call here accommodation "events" or both. While in some circumstances one of these analytic bases alone would be used, the work reported here uses both in order to ensure adequate sample sizes. As will be seen below, only about one in five respondents report a disabling health condition, and only about one in five workers with a disability get job-accommodated, so that in a sample of about 12,600 respondents, only about 500 individuals have any job accommodation experience. If this small number is further subdivided among specific accommodation events, the number of degrees of freedom for multivariate statistical analyses are quickly used up.

Accordingly, I delineate several "event" populations. The largest of these is comprised of individuals who reported a work-limiting health problem and who had some opportunity to be accommodated, irrespective of job history or timing of the impairment. Essentially, the denominator term or "event" population in this case comprises all individuals who worked for someone else after their health impairment started. This population is then divided into two subgroups: one comprised of those persons who had *at least one* accommodation experience and the other comprised of individuals who had *never* been accommodated. (I refer to this respondent-based group as the "ever-accommodated" subsample). The other populations are delineated in respect to specific types of events and the corresponding accommodation experiences, that is, an accommodation prevalence rate (probability variable) is computed for each, with each individual experiencing accommodation being assigned a value of one and those not accommodated a value of zero. The most important of these is comprised of workers whose impairments started after they were working and could have been accommodated by their employers *at that time;* see the appendix table for a description of the other event populations.

Individuals who were part of an event population and acknowledged that their employer had "done something special" to keep them on the job were then asked a series of closed-ended questions about the nature of the accommodation as described above; see the appendix table. In every case, moreover, there was an open-ended question about whether the employer did "anything else," which is reported here simply as an "other necessary" category. For a select subset of events, the battery of accommodation items also included open-ended questions about the length of time several of the accommodations continued, that is, "how long did they do this?" and "are they still doing it?" Because duration obviously influences the costs of accommodation, the responses to these questions are quite important. However, duration-related questions were put to only a few of the several "event" populations, thus restricting the use that can be made of them here.

In order to model the extent to which a worker was accommodated, instead of just whether any accommodation at all took place, I created an accommodation experience variable or index by counting the number of different types of accommodations a worker received over the set of relevant possibilities.[13] This variable is truncated at zero, in effect indicating whether any accommodation took place and, if so, how much took place. (I refer below to this variable as the count or simple index.) Clearly, more remains to be done in designing and modeling various dimensions of the accommodation experience, work that can be extended as additional HRS follow-up data become available.

EMPLOYMENT OUTCOMES

Two employment outcome variables are created to test whether employer accommodations make any difference to workers with disabilities. Each of these variables gauges the extent to which work activity continued between the time of the baseline interview and the first follow-up interview. In one case, individuals working at baseline who were still working for the same employer and held the same job title at follow-up are assigned a value of one, zero otherwise. In the other case, individuals working at baseline who were still in the workforce at follow-up, irrespective of whether they were still employed by the same firm or performing the same job assignment are assigned a value of one, zero otherwise. As will be seen, I use these variables to assess whether accommodation prolongs the work lives of individuals with disabilities, a matter of considerable importance to appraising the employment effects of the ADA.

Key Explanatory Variables

Accommodation outcomes are expected to vary systematically with health conditions, economic productivity, and firm size, among others. Variables constructed to reflect these factors are briefly described here; a complete account of all of the explanatory variables used in the statistical analysis below is presented in the appendix table.

Impairment Severity
A number of health-related measures available in the HRS are used to characterize the level and severity of impairments of individuals in various event populations. Of special interest are a battery of questions posed to all respondents at baseline about activities of daily living (ADL), such as the ability to eat or dress without help, and about other types of functional limitations, such as difficulty in walking, reaching, stooping, sitting, and so on. I use this information in several ways, including the construction of two functional impairment indexes that count the number of impaired functions that the individual has lost partially (minor functional impairments) and the number of such functional capacities that have been completely lost (major functional impairment); see the appendix table for details. Although relatively crude, these measures do discriminate

between more and less severely impaired individuals and thus proxy the cost differential of accommodating such individuals.

Health Conditions Subject to Discrimination

Apart from the physical and emotional deficits that may legitimately require more resources to accommodate, there is also reason to suppose that some workers with disabilities will be subject to prejudicial or discriminatory practices by employers who simply devalue their health condition, irrespective of its actual impact on productivity.[14] For straightforward reasons, the likelihood that individuals may be discriminated against in this way has to be indexed for the statistical analysis. I draw on the health conditions reported as the main cause of work-limiting behavior to profile individuals more or less likely to be the subject of discriminatory employment practices. Specifically, I use health conditions found in earlier research to be more likely targets of employer prejudice to create an indicator variable.[15] This variable takes the value of one if the respondent reports having cancer, missing limbs, blindness, deafness, stroke, paralysis, epilepsy, mental retardation, alcohol or drug problems, or mental or emotional problems; zero otherwise. If discriminatory practices are widespread, individuals with these conditions are expected to be accommodated less frequently than those with other health or disease characteristics, all else equal.

Marginal Productivity

The real cost of job accommodation is surely lower for more productive workers than for less productive ones; the desire of workers with health problems themselves to be accommodated also probably varies by their productivity and, thereby, the opportunity cost of leaving their jobs.[16] An indicator of the productive capacity of the individual worker must, as a result, be included in the analysis. I construct a marginal productivity index computed from an auxiliary regression equation (instrument) of the implicit market wage against a large set of individual factors that lead to productivity differentials; see the appendix table. This procedure, which is commonplace in the econometric literature on labor supply, has two advantages: (1) it provides a means of indexing the potential productivity of individuals, including those for whom an hourly wage may not be observable; and (2) it summarizes a substantial amount of information about the respondent without requiring that a large number of explanatory variables be introduced directly into the statistical analysis. Since higher index values reflect higher productivity levels of workers and, by implication, lower real costs of accommodation, the expectation is that this index will vary directly with the probability that an employer accommodates a given worker.

Firm Size

Much has been made of the size of employing establishments and the corresponding issue of undue hardship in accommodating workers with disabilities under the ADA.[17] The fact that small firms (at first those with fewer than twenty-five employees and now those with fewer than fifteen) are exempt from the provisions of Title I appears to suggest that any job accommodation will cause these firms undue hardship. In contrast, large firms are expected to make accommodations without much hardship, in part because scale might be expected to lower the actual costs of job accommodation and in part because large firms would be expected to absorb the cost more easily, that is, they have "deep pockets." The HRS interview schedule includes a set of questions about both the size of the local establishment where the respondent works and the size of the firm nationally with which the local establishment is affiliated. While such employee-reported data are doubtless subject to some error, the survey poses the questions in alternative ways to make guesses somewhat more precise, especially guesses about the size of national parent companies. A vector of dummy variables is created for each size category; the variables used here refer to very small local firms relative to all other local sizes or to very large national sizes (i.e., firms with more than five hundred employees) relative to all other national sizes; see the appendix table. In both cases, but especially the latter, the expectation is that the size of the firm will predict the probability that workers are accommodated, because the cost of providing an accommodation is presumably lower for large firms than for small ones.

MODEL SPECIFICATION

The variables just described are used to estimate two types of multivariate regression models, one designed to account for the likelihood or extent of job accommodation and the other the effects, if any, of such accommodation on future employment outcomes. The first type of model may be represented very generally as:

$$A_{ij} = f(H, X, Y; \beta, u) \tag{2}$$

where A represents the job accommodation of an HRS worker with a disability, i indexes the accommodation indicator ($i = 1,2$) and j indexes the accommodation event population (1,2,6); H is a vector characterizing the impairment severity and disabling health conditions of each member of the jth event population, X is a corresponding vector of individual characteristics of that population, including the marginal productivity index of each individual, and Y is a corresponding vector of characteristics of employers of persons comprising that event population such as industry attachment and firm size; and β is the vector of unknown parameters and u the error variance to be estimated by maximum likelihood methods.

In simple terms, estimating equation (2) tests the extent to which accommodation is explained by factors that are expected to raise or lower the costs of accommodation. Statistically significant negative coefficients on the impairment severity and health condition variables imply higher costs, while significant positive coefficients on the marginal productivity and firm size variables imply lower costs. For reasons suggested above, all of the models estimated in this chapter assume that the error term u is normally distributed. This means that for models designed to explain the probability that an individual is job accommodated, that is, when $i = 1$, I used a probit model to estimate the parameters of equation (2); it also means that for models using accommodation indices that are truncated at zero ($i = 2$), I used the Tobit model to estimate the parameters of (2). In order to make the findings comparable, I report the partial derivatives of the estimating equations evaluated at the means of the regressors.

In addition to equation (2), I also estimate the following type of equation:

$$W_k = g(A_{ij}, H', I'; \beta', U') \tag{3}$$

where W_k represents the kth type of work status at follow–up ($k = 1,2$), and the right-hand side includes a given accommodation indicator as well as slightly altered vectors of health and individual characteristics as defined immediately above. The W_k are in every case dichotomous indicator variables, so that in all versions of equation (3) the unknown parameter vector β' and the error variance U' are estimated by means of the maximum likelihood probit technique.

Empirical Findings

DESCRIPTIVE DATA

As described previously, HRS respondents may report several types of accommodation events depending on when the disability started and what job changes, if any, followed. Table 1 presents a descriptive account of a selected set of these events with sufficient numbers of sample cases to be meaningful.[18] Accommodation events obtained at the baseline interview are presented in the top panel of table 1, including retrospective accounts by individuals who incurred some work-limiting impairment before actually ever working and accounts by individuals whose impairment more commonly started after they were working, sometimes much later in the work life cycle. The lower panel presents preliminary

Table 1: Job Accommodation Frequencies
By Type and Selected Events

Selected Events*	Any	Extra Help	Short Week	More Breaks	Trans-port	Equip-ment	Job Design	Flex Time	New Skills	Other Necessary	N
					% of Event Population by Type of Accommodation						
Impairment Preceded Work											
Employer now	19.3	12.8	6.1	9.6	2.7	4.0	na	na	na	5.0	170
Last employer	14.6	10.7	6.6	5.7	0.5	0.5	na	na	na	7.3	149
Working When Impairment Started											
Employer then	21.2	7.9	6.0	7.3	1.1	1.9	8.8	6.3	3.2	5.3	1314
New employer	19.8	6.7	4.0	9.8	0.6	2.4	6.3	6.1	7.6	2.9	222
Baseline											
employer now	25.7	14.1	8.9	12.2	1.6	6.4	9.6	11.9	7.9	5.6	398
Working When Impairment Started											
Follow-up											
employer then	28.8	10.2	14.3	14.3	1.5	3.8	7.5	14.6	2.3	7.9	224
Follow-up											
employer now	29.6	17.1	7.0	13.5	2.2	8.3	8.3	15.5	6.3	8.5	483

Weighted data was used to compute frequencies.
*For a description of the variables, see the table in this chapter's appendix.

calculations showing what the follow-up employer did at the time the impairment started and what that employer was doing at the time of the follow-up per se. Three general aspects of these computed frequencies are noteworthy.

First, relatively small fractions of each of these event-specific populations were actually job accommodated. Only about one in five individuals at baseline reported that they were in a circumstance wherein they might have been accommodated actually were. For example, 21.2 percent of those respondents who were working at the time their health impairment started were accommodated at that point by their employer at the time. Some of those respondents may actually have left their employer and perhaps even the workforce at the time their impairment started. These individuals might have been accommodated later on by a new employer, though only 19.8 percent of that group received any type of accommodation. Preliminary data from the two-year follow-up suggests that the accommodation prevalence is slightly higher in the event population at the time of the follow-up, namely, about 29 percent. Fewer events are included in the follow-up interview schedule, and, since the sample is now two years older, these slightly higher rates may be artifactual.

Second, the nature of these employer accommodations differs strikingly. To illustrate, while approximately 26 percent of individuals who could have been accommodated by their baseline employer at the time of the baseline interview were actually being accommodated, only one type of accommodation was reported by more than half of these individuals, that is, about 14 percent of the event-specific population reported the employer getting "someone to help out." The second most common type of accommodation in this same event population was a tie between the employer allowing "more breaks and rest periods" (more breaks) and changing the "time [you] came to and left work" (flex time), reported by roughly 12 percent of the event population in each case. Since accommodation experiences are by their nature highly individualistic, closed-end questions may yield a biased picture of what employers do to accommodate workers with disabilities. The "other necessary" column in table 1 aggregates responses to an open-ended question about what "other things" the employer might have done to help out, and about one-quarter of those reporting being accommodated responded in open-ended fashion. An examination of the individual responses to this question, however, does not shed much additional light on the nature of job accommodations. The most common of these is that the employer provided "emotional" support, provided medical care, and/or gave the individual more time off from work.

Finally, the prevalence rates of different types of accommodations appear to vary inversely with their probable cost. Such relatively costly accommodations as arranging for special transportation (transport) and getting special equipment (equipment) have the lowest prevalence rates, all things being equal. But the cost of accommodation depends on the number of different types of help that a given individual receives and the duration of each. The mean number of different types of accommodations for those in the any-event population receiving at least one was 2.5. The problem with a count of this sort is that it implicitly assumes cost is a simple linear function of the number of accommodation types, a doubtful assumption. Computed durations available for selected event populations and a subset of accommodation types provide a more meaningful picture of accommodations and their probable costs. For those with a first-accommodation event (table 1, row 3) the mean length of time that employer accommodations lasted was 247 days in the case of "extra help," 209 days for "more breaks," 141 days for "flex time," 113 days for "short week," and 58 days for "special transportation." There is, of course, dispersion around these means, with standard deviations of about 550 days the norm, and the duration of the accommodation ranging upward of eleven or twelve years. These data suggest that accommodation costs have probably been understated in past studies. I will return to this point momentarily.

Given these descriptive data on employer accommodations, I now turn to the explanatory factors that may account for variations in these outcomes. Table 2 arrays a number of health-related characteristics of individuals in the any-accommodation event population classified by whether they were accommodated or not. Interestingly, health-related profiles of this event population do not differ much between the ever- and never-accommodated subgroups. The top of the table shows the frequency distributions of the diseases and health impairments reported as the "main" cause of work-disability status. Although a few of these disease prevalences differ across the accommodated and never-accommodated subgroups, the differences are never statistically significant. In fact, the similarities in the overall frequency distribution of the detailed list of major disease categories are quite remarkable.[19] Severity indicators in respect to ADLs, other functional impairments, and multiple chronic diseases are also quite similar, with one notable exception. The mean number of major functional impairments, that is, the number of functional capacities that are completely lost, is greater in the never-accommodated subgroup, and statistically significantly so on a simple chi-square test. This suggests perhaps that there is a upper bound on the health status needed to be accommodated in the first place.

Table 2: Selected Health Characteristics
By Job Accommodation Experience, Any Event Population

Characteristics*	Accommodated at Least Once	Never Accommodated
Disease Prevalence	(%)	(%)
Cancer	1.5	2.6
Heart, stroke, and related	17.9	18.9
Endocrine, digestive, and related	4.6	5.6
Musculoskeletal	56.7	50.7
Arthritis and related	12.6	13.8
Back, neck, spine, and related	28.7	23.3
Hip, knee, and related	7.6	7.5
Paralysis, missing limbs, and related	7.8	6.1
Neurologic and sensory conditions	7.0	8.0
Psychological and emotional problems	2.5	2.8
Respiratory diseases and related	7.2	8.4
Other diseases	2.6	3.0
Severity Indicators		
ADL functions		
Complete loss (mean number)	0.1	0.1
Partial loss (mean number)	0.5	0.5
Functional impairments		
Complete loss (mean number)	1.9	2.2
Partial loss (mean number)	3.5	3.3
Multiple chronic diseases		
High mortality diseases (mean number)	1.3	1.3
Low mortality diseases (mean number)	2.8	2.9
N	**527**	**1,382**

See the text for a description of accommodation events and populations. The calculations use weighted survey data.
*For descriptions of the variables, see the table in this chapter's appendix.

ACCOMMODATION MODELS

Given these findings, I turn now to the estimation of the multivariate models described previously. Table 3 sets out the results for the accommodation determinants model (equation 2 above) using observations on the ever-accommodated event population.[20] The first column presents the estimated parameters and test statistics for this model when the dependent variable is dichotomous, taking the value of one if the respondent was ever accommodated, zero otherwise.

Some of the estimated effects confirm the expectations of the simple economic model described above, others do not. Most important from the perspective of this chapter is that the marginal productivity and health-related characteristics of workers with disabilities have estimated effects that are consistent with the model. The statistically significant positive sign on the marginal productivity variable suggests that, all else equal, more productive workers are more likely to be accommodated, and vice versa. Controlling for the severity of the functional capacities of individuals, the estimates also show that health conditions subject to discrimination are, indeed, less likely to be accommodated, confirming the continuing existence of discriminatory practices against workers with disabilities.

The estimated net effects on the functional impairment variables themselves are mixed. The major impairment variable does have a negative sign, but it is statistically indistinguishable from zero. Among other things, this casts doubt on the likelihood that severely disabled persons get accommodated at all, because at this stage of the work life cycle, they may simply drop out of the labor force after the onset of an impairment. Interestingly, the minor impairment variable is significantly positive, suggesting that there may also be a lower bound on the health conditions that will be accommodated. Also consistent with the predictions of the economic model is the statistically significant effect of firm size on the probability of being accommodated. Somewhat unexpectedly, workers covered by a union contract are less likely to be accommodated. This may be attributable to the impact of seniority provisions in union contracts that mitigate against flexibility in work assignments.[21] There is an unexpected gender differential in favor of women workers and an occupational difference in favor of nonprofessional workers. Happily, no racial difference is detected one way or the other.

The right-most column in table 3 presents the estimated net effects of the accommodation model using the simple index or score derived by adding the number of different types of accommodations a worker has received as the

Table 3: Determinants of Job Accommodation
Any Accommodation Event

Determinants*	Net Effects (Absolute t-values)	
	Probability of Event [†]	Count [‡]
Age (years)	0.006	0.017
	(2.850)	(2.740)
Male (= 1)	-0.058	-0.139
	(2.010)	(1.750)
White (= 1)	0.025	0.067
	(0.960)	(0.920)
Professional worker (= 1)	-0.139	-0.346
	(3.240)	(2.910)
Marginal productivity (index)	0.128	0.366
	(2.730)	(2.800)
Functional impairments: complete loss	-0.000	0.009
	(0.080)	(0.630)
Functional impairments: partial loss	0.014	0.048
	(2.480)	(3.010)
Health condition subject to discrimination (= 1)	-0.084	-0.243
	(2.530)	(2.610)
Manufacturing (= 1)	-0.006	-0.038
	(0.210)	(0.490)
Union contract (= 1)	-0.099	-0.292
	(2.040)	(2.210)
Small local firm (= 1)	0.043	0.178
	(1.090)	(1.680)
Large national firm (= 1)	0.125	0.361
	(3.540)	(3.740)
Physically demanding work (index)	0.016	0.050
	(1.500)	(1.680)
Constant	-0.863	–8.463
	(5.390)	(5.400)
σ	—	3.460
		(26.190)
Model chi-squared	93.440	101.220
Dependent variable		
Mean	0.292	0.729
Standard deviation	(0.460)	(0.140)
N	1,615	1,615

* For variable definitions, see the table in this chapter's appendix.
† Dichotomous variable is equal to 1 if the respondent has been work accommodated at some point around or before the Wave 1 survey interview; 0 otherwise. The net effects are partial derivatives calculated as $\beta_i\, f(z)$, where β_i is the maximum likelihood probit coefficient for the ith regressor, and $f(z)$ is the probability density function of the unit normal distribution evaluated at the means of the regressors.
‡ Count or simple work-accommodation index truncated at 0 as described in the text. The net effects are partial derivatives calculated as $\beta_i\, f(z)$, where β_i is the maximum likelihood Tobit coefficient for the ith regressor, F is the cumulative normal distribution function, $z = (\Sigma\, \beta_i X/\sigma)$, σ is the standard error about the Tobit equation, and X represents the means of the regressors.

dependent variable. Since, of course, this sum contains a large number of zeros, I use a slightly different estimating procedure, one that in effect asks whether the respondent has ever been accommodated and, if so, by how much. This model fits the data slightly better, while showing the same pattern of results. The marginal productivity measure, the functional impairment profiles, and the health condition variable are estimated to have the same impacts as those presented in the first column. The robustness of these findings to the specification of the model is quite important to the conclusions derived from this analysis.[22] These results differ from the results in the first column only in three minor ways. The gender variable, the physically demanding work index, and the small local firm variable are each now at the borderline of statistical significance at conventional confidence levels. The latter case suggests that when small firms accommodate, they are likely to do more of it than other sized firms, perhaps because the accommodated worker will inevitably be a more prominent or visible part of the very small firm's workforce.

WORK STATUS MODELS

The results of estimating the follow-up work status models are presented in table 4. The dependent variable for the model in the right-most column is the likelihood that individuals who were working at baseline are still working in the same position for the same employer at follow-up, while in the left-hand column the dependent variable is simply the likelihood that these individuals are still working at all at follow-up. Although I estimated these models for various subsamples, including the event-specific populations used for estimating the accommodation models above, table 4 sets out the results for the entire sample of HRS respondents who were working at baseline and were reinterviewed two years later.[23]

Recall that the purpose here is to assess whether accommodation makes any difference either to the person with a disability or to his or her employer. One way of implicitly reducing the cost of accommodation and even indeed shifting part of the burden of that cost onto the employee is to ensure that the accommodated worker stays in the same job longer than would otherwise be expected. Three of the findings in table 4 are noteworthy in this regard. One is that employer accommodation has a significantly positive effect on the probability that an individual with a disability who was working at baseline will still be in the same job at follow-up, all else being equal. In contrast, the influence of accommodation on work status per se is statistically insignificant, suggesting among other things that accommodations yield employer-specific benefits.

Table 4: Determinants of Work Status at Follow-Up
All Working Respondents at Baseline

Baseline Determinants*	Net Effects† (Absolute t-values)	
	Still Working, Same Employer	Still Working, Any Employer
Any accommodation event (= 1)	0.131	-0.009
	(3.07)	(0.33)
Age (years)	-0.006	-0.015
	(4.60)	(15.22)
Male (= 1)	0.045	-0.006
	(2.84)	(0.47)
White (= 1)	0.011	0.022
	(0.78)	(2.12)
Children at home (number)	-0.001	-0.008
	(0.10)	(1.21)
Professional worker (= 1)	0.196	-0.006
	(9.84)	(0.43)
Manufacturing (= 1)	0.104	-0.007
	(6.55)	(0.59)
Union contract (= 1)	0.284	-0.013
	(17.16)	(1.09)
Work-limiting health condition (= 1)	-0.152	-0.057
	(5.55)	(3.09)
Functional impairments: complete loss	-0.018	-0.020
	(2.09)	(3.42)
Functional impairments: partial loss	-0.002	-0.005
	(0.47)	(1.59)
Chronic diseases: high mortality	-0.006	-0.020
	(0.68)	(3.45)
Chronic diseases: low mortality	-0.006	-0.003
	(1.14)	(0.08)
Marginal productivity (index)	-0.335	0.041
	(12.69)	(2.18)
Physically demanding work (index)	-0.024	-0.001
	(4.72)	(0.36)
Constant	1.073	0.975
	(11.71)	(14.17)
Model chi-squared	504.600	381.57
Dependent variable		
Mean	0.514	0.818
Standard deviation	(0.50)	(0.39)
N	7,309	7,309

*For variable definitions, see this chapter's appendix.
†The dichotomous variable is equal to 1 if a respondent working a baseline was still working either for the same employer or any employer at follow-up; 0 otherwise. As before, the net effects are partial derivatives calculated as $\beta_i\, f(z)$, where β_i is the maximum likelihood probit coefficient for the ith regressor and $f(z)$ is the probability density function of the unit normal distribution evaluated at the means of the regressors.

This may also come somewhat at the expense of the individual being accommodated. Workers with higher productivity appear more likely to change positions, at least as evidenced by the fact that the marginal productivity variable takes a negative sign in the same-employer equation, but a positive one in the any-employer equation. Finally, these effects appear to be independent of the impact of major health events. The estimated effects of the major functional impairment measures suggest that health problems induce many workers in their fifties to leave the workforce, irrespective of what employers may do to enable them to stay on the job.

Policy Lessons

Several important inferences may be drawn from the foregoing empirical analysis, each with some lesson for appraising the effectiveness of the ADA. To begin with, employers do accommodate workers with disabilities, and they do so in a variety of ways. The data suggest that accommodation experiences may be substantially more varied than what has been delineated in previous studies. One of the most common things employers do is to get someone to help out, while the least common accommodations are to provide special transportation or special equipment. The survey frequencies also suggest that some types of accommodation continue for considerable periods of time. From an economic perspective, the resources used for such accommodation purposes have an implicit value (opportunity cost) and thus should not be ignored by policy makers. Costs of accommodation are clearly not zero, probably not even negligible, and most likely greater than any of the published figures suggest. More careful measurement of the type and duration of employer accommodation is needed, as is more detailed information on the imputed costs of these accommodations. Appraising the effectiveness of the ADA will be greatly facilitated by expanding the knowledge base about the characteristics and costs of employer accommodation of workers with disabilities.

The empirical analysis also provides some support for the expectation that accommodation costs will rise as more disabled workers find employment. Paradoxically, this means that costs of accommodation might actually be used as an indicator of program success: higher costs would reflect more extensive accommodation of larger numbers of workers with disabilities in the employment queue, and vice versa. Recall that the analysis assumed that accommodation occurs when the expected benefits of accommodation exceed or are equal to expected costs (subject to some randomness), each as judged by the employer.

Although this is clearly a highly simplified view of the accommodation decision process, the analysis did uncover several key pieces of supporting evidence. The productivity of workers with disabilities was found to be a significant predictor of accommodation and in the expected direction. Similarly, health conditions known to be subjected to employer prejudice were also found to be a significant predictor, and again in the expected opposing direction.

Furthermore, it is worth noting that the model is relatively conservative in the sense that it assumes employers fully command the benefits and incur the costs of any accommodation. It is, of course, certainly possible for the employer to shift part of the cost to the employee, say by adjusting the wages of accommodated workers more slowly over time. Several indicators of such shifting are detected in the empirical results reported above: union workers are less likely to be accommodated, perhaps because it is more difficult to shift accommodation costs to workers subject to negotiated compensation packages; accommodated workers stay longer in the same position, perhaps forgoing career-advancing moves; and individuals with major impairments are just as likely to be accommodated as those without them. These factors, in other words, should improve the benefit-cost ratio and make accommodation more likely.

These findings highlight the special dilemma of the ADA: the productivity of workers with disabilities may not be sufficiently great to tip the benefit-cost calculus in their favor, even when penalty costs of noncompliance are either added to benefits or subtracted from costs. While significant and disturbing evidence adduced here of continuing discrimination against workers with certain kinds of health conditions underscores the need for more intensive efforts under the employment provisions of the ADA, that action alone is unlikely to improve the job accommodation prospects of workers with disabilities. The ADA can be a key element of a comprehensive disability policy, but it alone can never serve as that policy.

Finally, the analysis suggests that work disablement and the need for accommodation are quite common at the latter stages of the work life cycle. For this target group, then, the aim of the ADA should be to minimize the number of workers with disabilities dropping out of the labor force. Even if it is successful in these terms, however, it will not produce measurable or detectable changes in the employment prospects or economic welfare of the population with disabilities. One reason is that many of those affected will be incident cases, so both denominator and numerator terms will change. A more important reason is that departures from the labor force, especially those stemming from the onset of a health impairment, rise geometrically for individuals in this age range even under the best of circumstances. Our ability to detect the impact of the ADA on small net changes in the rate of labor force exits for this sub-group is limited. To do so, moreover, requires a competing risk framework in which the effects of ADA action to keep workers in the labor force offset the opposing inducements of income transfer and pension programs for them to withdraw from the labor force. One element in a more elaborate framework of this sort would be the extent to which workers demand accommodations. The analysis here made the simplifying assumption that all workers otherwise eligible for accommodation would choose to be accommodated if the employer offered it. A more realistic model would estimate both the demand and supply determinants of accommodation of workers with disabilities.

Appendix

Variable Definitions and Summary Statistics

Variable	Mean (Standard Deviation)	Definition
Age	55.60 (5.66)	Age of respondent in years at the baseline interview.
Accommodation: event populations	—	Subsets of respondents with a work-limiting health impairment who might have been job accommodated depending on when the impairment started and the job history that followed its onset. From the baseline interview, 6 event populations are delineated as follows, 5 from specific events and 1 that aggregates those events.
Impaired before work, employer now	0.013 (0.12)	Dummy variable taking the value of 1 if the impairment preceded work and the respondent is currently working; 0 otherwise.
Impaired before work, last employer	0.012 (0.11)	Dummy variable taking the value of 1 if the impairment preceded work and it currently prevents work altogether but the respondent could have been accommodated on the previous or last job; 0 otherwise.
Impaired after working, employer then	0.104 (0.30)	Dummy variable taking the value of 1 if the impairment started after working and the employer at the time could have accommodated the respondent; 0 otherwise. This event population is also referred to in the text as the "first accommodation event."

Variable	Mean (Standard Deviation)	Definition
Impaired after working, new employer	0.018 (0.13)	Dummy variable taking the value of 1 if the impairment started after working, the respondent left the employer at the time and then got a new job; 0 otherwise.
Impaired after working, employer now	0.032 (0.17)	Dummy variable taking the value of 1 if the impairment started after working, the respondent is currently working and could be accommodated on the current job; 0 otherwise.
Any event population	0.151 (0.35)	Dummy variable taking the value if the respondent as assigned a value of 1 in any one of the event-specific populations; 0 otherwise.
Accommodation: type	*	Dummy variable taking the value of 1 if a re-spondent in the ith event population reported that the employer had done "anything special to help [you] out so that [you] could stay at work" to any of the following questions about the type of help provided; 0 otherwise. (Note that in selected cases such a question was followed by the questions: "How long did they continue to do that?" [number of weeks/months/years; "still doing it."] These cases are denoted here as duration follow-up questions.)
Extra help	—	"Did [does] your employer get someone to help you?" (duration follow-up)
Short week	—	"Did [does] your employer shorten your work day?" (duration follow-up)
More breaks	—	"Did [does] your employer allow you more breaks and rest periods?" (duration follow-up)
Flex time	—	"Did your employer allow you to change the time you came to and left work?" (duration follow-up)
Transportation	—	"Did your employer arrange for special transporta-tion?" (duration follow-up)
Equipment	—	"Did your employer get you special equipment for the job?"
Job design	—	"Did your employer change the job to something you could do?"
New skills	—	"Did your employer help you learn new skills?"
Other necessary	—	"Did [does] your employer do any other things to help you out? What other things?"

* See text of table 1 in this chapter for the event-specific means of each accommodation type.

Variable	Mean (Standard Deviation)	Definition
ADL Function: complete loss	0.281 (0.63)	Number of the following activities that the respondent reports are "very difficult/can't do": bathe/shower without help, dress without help, get in and out of bed without help, eat without help, use a map to get around a strange place, or use a calculator to help balance a checkbook.
ADL Function: partial loss	0.441 (0.74)	Number of the following activities that the respondent reports are "a little difficult or somewhat difficult": bathe/shower without help, dress without help, get in and out of bed without help, eat without help, use a map to get around a strange place, or use a calculator to help balance a checkbook.
Children at home	0.395 (0.81)	Number of children under 18 years of age that the respondent reports were still living at home at the time of the baseline interview.
Chronic diseases: high mortality	0.739 (0.91)	Number of the following diseases that a doctor has indicated the respondent has cancer, chronic lung disease such as emphysema, congestive heart failure, coronary heart disease, stroke, hypertension, or diabetes.
Chronic diseases: low mortality	1.550 (1.47)	Number of the following chronic conditions a doctor has indicated the respondent has arthritis or rheumatism, asthma, back problems, problems with feet or legs, head injury, emotional problems, kidney problems, or stomach ulcers.
Firm size: small local	0.126 (0.33)	Dummy variable taking the value of 1 if the firm the respondent works for at that location has fewer than 15 employees; 0 otherwise.
Firm size: large national	0.427 (0.49)	Dummy variable taking the value of 1 if the firm the respondent works for has 500 or more employees at all locations; 0 otherwise.
Functional impairments: complete loss	0.634 (1.46)	Number of the following activities that the respondent reports are "very difficult/can't do": walk several blocks, walk one block, sit for two hours, get up from a chair after sitting for long periods, climb a flight of stairs without resting, lift/carry weights over ten pounds, stoop/kneel/crouch, pick up a dime from a table, or reach/extend arms above shoulder level.

Variable	Mean (Standard Deviation)	Definition
Functional impairments: partial loss	1.92 (1.89)	Number of the following activities that the respondent reports are "a little difficult or somewhat difficult": walk several blocks, walk 1 block, sit for 2 hours, get up from a chair after sitting for long periods, climb a flight of stairs without resting, climb several flights of stairs without resting, lift/carry weights over ten pounds, stoop/kneel/crouch, pick up a dime from a table, or reach/extend arms above shoulder level.
Health subject to discrimination	0.032 (0.18)	Dummy variable taking the value of 1 if the respondent's main health condition causing a work limitation is cancer, missing limbs, blindness, deafness, stroke, paralysis, epilepsy, mental retardation, alcohol or drug problems, or mental/emotional problems; 0 otherwise.
Male	0.464 (0.50)	Dummy variable taking the value of 1 if the respondent is male; 0 otherwise.
Manufacturing	0.178 (0.38)	Dummy variable taking the value of 1 if the respondent's industrial attachment for the current or most recent job was coded as either durable or nondurable manufacturing; 0 otherwise.
Marginal productivity index	2.240 (0.48)	Predicted value of a selection-corrected log hourly wage equation using the following regressor variables: age, male, years of schooling, job tenure, job tenure squared, white, professional worker, sales worker, personal services worker, manufacturing job, trade job, service industry job, union worker, self-employed, and IMR/Heckman correction factor. The selection equation included as regressors: age, male, white, married, number of children at home, self-reported retirement at survey week, self-reported disabled at survey week, no reported work experience, and family income net of respondent's market earnings.
Physically demanding work	1.817 (1.64)	Number of the following tasks that the respondent reports are required by the current job: "all or almost all of the time," "most of the time," or "some of the time:" lots of physical effort, lifting heavy loads, stooping/kneeling/crouching, or good eyesight.

Variable	Mean (Standard Deviation)	Definition
Professional worker	0.254 (0.44)	Dummy variable taking the value of 1 if the respondent's occupational title for the current or most recent job was coded professional, managerial specialty operation, or technical support; 0 otherwise.
Union contract	0.140 (0.35)	Dummy variable taking the value of 1 if the respondent's current job was covered by a union contract; 0 otherwise.
White	0.720 (0.45)	Dummy variable taking the value of 1 if the respondent is white; 0 otherwise.
Work-limiting health condition	0.215 (0.41)	Dummy variable taking the value of 1 if the respondent reports that an "impairment or health problem (that) limits the kind or amount of paid work that can be (done)" at baseline; 0 otherwise.
N	12,624	

Notes

1. See P. D. Blanck, "Employment Integration, Economic Opportunity and the Americans with Disabilities Act," *Iowa Law Review* 79 (May 1994): 853–933, and F. C. Collignon, "Is the ADA Successful? Indicators for Tracking Gains," *Annals of the American Academy of Political and Social Science* 549 (Jan. 1997): 129–47.

2. J. West, *Federal Implementation of the Americans with Disabilities Act, 1991–1994* (New York: Milbank Memorial Fund, 1994).

3. D. A. Martin, R. W. Conley, and J. H. Noble, "The ADA and Disability Benefits Policy: Some Research Topics and Issues," *Journal of Disability Policy Studies* 6, no. 2 (1990): 1–16.

4. S. L. Percy, *Disability, Civil Rights, and Public Policy* (Tuscaloosa: University of Alabama Press, 1989).

5. See, among others, P. D. Blanck, "The Economics of the Employment Provisions of the Americans with Disabilities Act: Workplace Accommodations," this volume; T. N. Chirikos, "The Economics of Employment (Title I of the Americans with Disabilities Act)," *Milbank Quarterly* 69, suppl. 1/2 (1991):150–79; N. Daniels, "Mental Disabilities, Equal Opportunity, and the ADA," in *Mental Disorder, Work Disability, and the Law,* ed. R. J. Bonnie and J. Monahan (Chicago: University of Chicago Press,

1997): 281–97; P. S. Karlan and G. Rutherglen, "Disabilities, Discrimination, and Reasonable Accommodation," *Duke Law Journal* 46, no.1 (1996): 1–41; and S. Rosen, "Disability Accommodation and the Labor Market," in *Disability and Work,* ed. C. Weaver (Washington, D.C.: AEI Press, 1991), 18–30.

6. See P. D. Blanck, "Communicating the Americans with Disabilities Act, Transcending Compliance: 1996 Follow-up Report on Sears, Roebuck and Co.," *Annenberg Washington Program Reports* (1996), 70 pp.; P. D. Blanck, "Communicating the Americans with Disabilities Act, Transcending Compliance: A Case Report on Sears, Roebuck and Co.," *Annenberg Washington Program Reports* (1994), 47 pp.; F. C. Collignon, "The Role of Reasonable Accommodation in Employing Disabled Persons in Private Industry," in *Disability and the Labor Market,* ed. M. Berkowitz and M. A. Hill (Ithaca, N.Y.: ILR Press, 1986), 196–241; and E. J. McGraw, "Compliance Costs of the Americans with Disabilities Act," *Delaware Journal of Corporate Law* 18 (Summer 1993): 521–44.

7. Chirikos, "Economics of Employment."

8. See F. T. Juster and R. Suzman, "An Overview of the Health and Retirement Study," *Journal of Human Resources* 30 (1995 supplement): S7–S56. Also see C. Zwerling et al., "Occupational Injuries among Workers with Disabilities," this volume.

9. Cf. M. C. Daly and J. Bound, "Worker Adaptation and Employer Accommodation following the Onset of a Health Impairment," *Journal of Gerontology* 51B, no. 2 (1996): S53–S60.

10. Although SSDI awards to younger persons have been growing rapidly in the recent past, awards to individuals in their fifties still predominate; see T. N. Chirikos, "An Analysis of Compositional Trends in Social Security Disability Insurance Awards, 1960–1991," *Journal of Disability Policy Studies* 6, no. 1 (1995): 1–22.

11. See the chapters by Moss and Scheid in this volume.

12. Cf. Rosen, "Disability Accommodation and the Labor Market," and M. Gunderson and D. Hyatt, "Do Injured Workers Pay for Reasonable Accommodation?" *Industrial and Labor Relations Review* 50 (Oct. 1996): 92–104.

13. This count, of course, implicitly weights each type of accommodation equally. I also constructed a summary index that used durations in year-equivalents as weights and aggregated over the respective types of accommodations. For the reasons described above, this index could be constructed only for selected accommodation events. For those events, however, the results obtained when this weighted index was used were not appreciably different from those using the simple count index.

14. Cf. K. J. Arrow, "The Theory of Discrimination," in *Discrimination in Labor Markets,* ed. O. Ashenfelter and A. Rees (Princeton, N.J.: Princeton University Press, 1973), 3–33.

15. M. L. Baldwin, "Can the ADA Achieve Its Employment Goals?" *Annals of the American Academy of Political and Social Science* 549 (Jan. 1997): 37–52, and M. Baldwin and W. G. Johnson, "Labor Market Discrimination against Men with Disabilities," *Journal of Human Resources* 29 (Winter 1994): 1–19.

16. T. N. Chirikos and G. Nestel, "Economic Determinants and Consequences of Self-Reported Work Disability," *Journal of Health Economics* 3, no. 2 (1984): 117–36.

17. R. V. Burkhauser, "Morality on the Cheap: The Americans with Disabilities Act," *Regulation* 13 (Summer 1990): 47–56.

18. The HRS oversamples blacks, Hispanics, and Florida residents. Frequencies reported in this section are weighted by the baseline sampling ratios of these subgroups.

19. The frequency distributions of health conditions presented here omit cases of nonresponse, which may affect the results. While the overall distribution is quite similar, the proportion of aggregated cases in prejudice-sensitive categories does differ significantly on a simple chi-square test.

20. The same model was also estimated for each of five other event populations. However, questionable results were obtained in four cases because of extremely small sample sizes. The estimated model for the first-accommodation event population did produce usable results. Since these results are generally akin to those in table 3, they are not reported here in detail.

21. Cf. S. Willborn, "The Nonevolution of Enforcement under the ADA: Discharge Cases and the Hiring Problem," this volume.

22. The accommodation model estimated for the first-accommodation event population shows somewhat the same pattern of results, irrespective of whether the dependent variable is the dichotomous probability variable or the weighted accommodation index described above. Of greatest interest is that the marginal productivity and health condition variables in this model continue to show, respectively, statistically significant positive and negative effects as in table 3. However, while the major functional impairment index is again statistically insignificant, so are the minor functional impairment index and several other regressors, including the firm size variables. Furthermore, these models overall do not fit the data nearly as well as those presented in table 3. This is probably due to the fact that fewer observations are available for estimating the likelihood of the job accommodations of this more specific event population than the any-event population.

23. These results, which are based on unweighted data, exclude censored cases attributable to death and survey attrition.

Chapter X

Estimating the Potential Benefits of the ADA on the Wages and Employment of Persons with Disabilities

MARJORIE L. BALDWIN

I. Introduction

In the years following passage of the Americans with Disabilities Act (ADA), complaints of employment and wage discrimination against workers with disabilities have grown rapidly. By July 1, 1994, the Equal Employment Opportunities Commission (EEOC), charged with enforcement of the employment provisions of the act, had received more than 28,000 disability-related complaints (West 1994). The largest single category of complaints, 20 percent of the total, comes from persons with back impairments. Some disability advocates have expressed surprise at the distribution of complaints by impairment and are concerned that enforcement of the ADA is not sufficiently focused on the "truly disabled."

Estimates of the size and composition of the disabled population vary widely, according to the definition of disability. At the time the ADA was debated, no nationally representative data on the scope of labor market discrimination against persons with disabilities was presented. It was difficult to predict, therefore, who was likely to benefit from the act or what the magnitude and distribution of those gains would be. Without such estimates it is impossible to determine whether or not the act has been successful in helping its target population.

This chapter uses data from the 1990 Survey of Income and Program Participation (SIPP) to estimate the potential benefits of eliminating employment and wage discrimination against workers with disabilities. Separate analyses are provided for six impairment groups to control for the heterogeneous nature of the disabled population. The groups are cardiovascular, mental, musculoskeletal, respiratory, sensory, and other disabling health conditions. Multivariate regression techniques are used to estimate the extent of employment and wage discrimination against each group, controlling for other nondiscriminatory factors that influence employment and wage differentials. Those factors include workers' education and experience, job characteristics, and the impact of health impairments on worker productivity.

The results indicate that men and women with disabilities are subject to labor market discrimination that significantly reduces their earnings capacity. The extent of discrimination varies among impairment groups and between men and women but, in nearly all cases, employment discrimination is a more serious problem than wage discrimination. The annual earnings losses attributed to discrimination against workers with disabilities are substantial but far lower than the estimates presented in support of the ADA. This finding suggests that the gains from the act will be more modest than its proponents had hoped.

II. Definitions

Disability is a measure of limitations in activities, such as working or keeping house, rather than an attribute, such as gender or race. To understand the meaning of the term *disability* it is important to distinguish it from two other terms, *impairment* and *functional limitation,* that are often used synonymously but have different meanings.

An *impairment* is a "physiological or anatomical loss or other abnormality" (Nagi 1969). An impairment may or may not cause a *functional limitation,* that is, a restriction of sensory, mental, or physical capacities. A *disability* occurs when a functional limitation restricts the ability to perform normal daily activities such as working or attending school.[1]

Consider, for example, a worker with an impairment, such as epilepsy. The impairment causes a functional limitation, namely, the inability to walk and perform physical tasks during severe seizures. If seizures are not controlled through medication and restrict the worker's ability to perform his usual job, he has a work disability (Chirikos and Nestel 1984). If seizures are almost completely controlled, which is fairly typical, and never seriously interfere with the worker's job performance, the functional limitation does not result in a work disability, but the worker may still be subject to discrimination.

Economic *discrimination* occurs when groups of workers with equal average productivity have different average wages or different opportunities for employment. Discrimination in employment can be expressed as refusals to hire, differentially high rates of job terminations in response to a decrease in the demand for labor, or refusals to rehire workers following absences caused by illnesses or injuries.

Some disability rights advocates maintain that all differences in average employment and wage rates between disabled and nondisabled persons are evidence of discrimination. Their most extreme opponents argue that the differences are completely explained by health-related limitations on productivity. This chapter maintains that neither of the extreme views is correct and that the methods used to estimate discrimination against other minority groups can be applied to workers with disabilities, taking care to control for the effects of functional limitations on worker productivity. The methods are described in the following section.

III. Data and Methods

DATA

The data come from Wave 3 of the 1990 panel of the SIPP. The SIPP is a nationally representative survey designed to collect detailed information on respondents' amounts and sources of income as well as participation in various cash and noncash government assistance programs. The SIPP is uniquely suited to the study of discrimination against workers with disabilities because a supplemental questionnaire collects information on impairments, functional limitations, and disability status, in addition to the detailed data on employment, earnings, and worker characteristics collected in the main survey. The health measures are self-reported but the questions are similar to questions in other surveys that have been shown to yield reasonably accurate information on health status (Stern 1989). Interviews for Wave 3 of the survey, which includes the supplemental questionnaire on health, were conducted from October 1990 to January 1991, and refer to a four-month reference period between June and December 1990.

The sample is restricted to individuals between ages 16 and 65 who are not members of the U.S. military. Persons who receive social security, welfare, disability, or unemployment payments during the reference period are excluded because the programs generally impose restrictions on recipients' work activity.

The remaining sample includes 12,687 men and 14,230 women. Ten percent of the sample is disabled, based on the criteria described in the following section.

DEFINING IMPAIRMENT GROUPS

Persons who respond that a health impairment limits their ability to work at a job or around the house, or limits their mobility or ability to communicate, are considered disabled. These persons are asked a follow-up question identifying the main impairment causing the limitation. The SIPP questionnaire identifies twenty-nine specific impairments and a miscellaneous category of all other health conditions. I classify the impairments into six groups, each group representing at least 4 percent of the population reporting a disabling health condition in 1984 (GAO 1993). The impairment groups include: musculoskeletal conditions (44 percent of the SIPP sample of persons with disabilities), cardiovascular conditions (10 percent), mental conditions (7 percent), respiratory conditions (8 percent), sensory conditions (4 percent), and other disabling health conditions (26 percent). The specific health conditions in each group are defined in table 1.

Table 1: Impairment Groups

Cardiovascular	Heart attack; arteriosclerosis; hypertension; stroke
Mental	Mental disorder; emotional problems; mental retardation; alcohol problem; drug problem; learning disability
Musculoskeletal	Arthritis; rheumatism; back or spine problems; stiffness or deformity of the foot, leg, arm, or hand; missing legs, feet, arms, hands, or fingers; head or spinal cord injury
Respiratory	Asthma; bronchitis; emphysema; respiratory allergies; tuberculosis; other lung trouble
Sensory	Blindness; vision problems; deafness; serious trouble hearing; speech disorder
Other	AIDS; broken bone/fracture; cancer; cerebral palsy; diabetes; epilepsy; hernia; kidney stones; chronic kidney trouble; paralysis; ulcers; gallbladder condition; liver condition; thyroid trouble; goiter; tumor, cyst, or growth; other

Estimates of discrimination against workers with disabilities are obtained from the coefficients of employment and wage functions estimated separately for men and women. Because the samples of persons in each impairment group are too small to estimate separate equations for each group, the equations are estimated for the full sample of disabled and nondisabled adults, with a set of binary variables identifying persons in each of the impairment groups. One advantage of this approach is that the same method can be used to estimate wage and employment discrimination.

ESTIMATING EMPLOYMENT DISCRIMINATION

The decision to work is determined jointly by an employer, who offers a wage rate based on his assessment of a worker's productivity, and a worker, who accepts the wage if it is sufficient to compensate him for his loss of personal time. Thus, the decision to work is influenced by characteristics that determine worker productivity (such as age and education) and characteristics that determine the relative value of personal time (such as marital status and nonlabor sources of income).

A probit model is used to estimate the effects of such characteristics on the probability of employment.[2] The model is estimated separately for men and women. The binary dependent variable equals one if a worker is employed at any time during the four-month reference period and zero otherwise.

Independent variables in the model represent factors that determine the employment agreement between an employer and worker. One set of variables controls for socioeconomic characteristics of the worker that influence his productivity and the relative value he places on personal time. These variables include race (equals one if African-American), ethnicity (equals one if Hispanic), age, education, marital status, and amounts of nonwage incomes.[3] A second set of variables, defined below, controls for the impact of functional limitations on worker productivity. The final set of variables are the binary variables identifying workers in each of the six impairment groups.

A significant negative coefficient associated with one of the binary variables identifying impairment categories is interpreted as evidence of employment discrimination against persons in that impairment group, under the assumption that other determinants of the employment decision, including the impact of functional limitations on worker productivity, have been controlled by the independent variables in the model. The estimated coefficient of each impairment variable can be converted to an odds ratio that represents the marginal effect of the health condition on the probability of employment, holding other variables constant. Then employment losses attributed to discrimination can be estimated by multiplying the reduction in the probability of employment associated with each impairment category by the weighted population of persons in the impairment group.[4]

ESTIMATING WAGE DISCRIMINATION

The determinants of wages are estimated by applying ordinary least squares regression to a human capital wage function. The sample is restricted to persons who report positive wage rates in the reference period, and the function is estimated separately for men and women.

The dependent variable in the wage function is the natural logarithm of the hourly wage rate of each worker. Independent variables include controls for worker productivity (i.e., human capital), factors that influence the demand for labor, and the binary variables identifying workers in the six impairment groups.

Worker productivity is represented by years of education, the functional limitations variables defined below, and three measures of work experience. The experience variables are "specific experience" (years worked for current employer); "general experience" (years worked for other employers); and "missing experience" (years absent from work after completion of schooling). Specific experience is also included as a square term to control for declining investments in job-specific training over time.

Labor demand variables include two binary variables identifying union members and part-time workers, and the race and ethnicity variables in the employment function. The wage function also includes a set of six occupational dummies.[5]

The coefficients of the impairment variables measure the differences in wages between disabled and nondisabled workers that cannot be explained by differences in productivity. A significant negative coefficient for one of the impairment variables is interpreted as evidence of wage discrimination against workers in that impairment group. Because the equation is in loglinear form, estimated coefficients of the impairment variables (after a simple conversion) represent the percentage wage difference between workers in a particular impairment group and nondisabled workers, holding constant all other variables in the model. Annual wage losses attributed to discrimination can be computed by converting the percentage wage differences to hourly wage losses and multiplying by expected annual hours worked for the population of employed persons in the impairment group.

The problem of estimating employment and wage discrimination against workers with disabilities is complicated by the need to control for the effects of functional limitations on worker productivity. Both the employment and wage functions described above include variables to measure differences in workers' functional limitations. The next section describes how the functional limitation variables are constructed.

CONTROLLING FOR THE EFFECTS OF FUNCTIONAL LIMITATIONS
ON WORKER PRODUCTIVITY

The SIPP collects self-reported data on eighteen functional limitations. One straightforward approach to estimating the impact of functional limitations on productivity is to include all available limitations variables as independent variables in the wage and employment functions. The problem with this approach is that it ignores intercorrelations between the variables and assumes their combined effect is additive. In fact, different functional limitations are often highly correlated because a single impairment, such as arthritic degeneration of the joints, can limit several functions (e.g., climbing, lifting, and walking).

Another possible approach is to use factor analysis to cluster the limitations variables into principal components. Unfortunately, the factor analysis approach loses some useful information and sacrifices the ability to logically interpret the meaning of a component or its coefficient (Baldwin and Johnson 1997).

I use an alternate approach to control for functional limitations that minimizes intercorrelations between the limitations variables without sacrificing meaningful interpretations of the results. First, the limitations variables are collected into groups of logically related elements, namely, communication (see, hear, speak, telephone); cognitive (money); strength and endurance (lift, walk); mobility (move, climb, get around inside or outside); and daily living (eat, bath, bed, toilet, housework, dress, meals).[6] A comparison of the groups to the principal components created by factor analysis reveals that the factors are consistent with the definitions of the communication and daily living groups but the lift, walk, climb variables constitute a group representing strength and endurance while the move, outside, inside variables constitute another group representing mobility. The classifications are revised accordingly to create a variable representing each of five categories of limitations (communication, strength, mobility, cognitive, and daily living).

The value of each variable is the number of functional limitations in that category to which a person is subject. The communication variable, for example, equals three for a person who reports difficulty speaking, hearing, and using the telephone. The severity of an impairment (measured by its impact on the total capacity to function) is assumed to increase as the number of limitations increases. The increase in severity must be interpreted ordinally, however, because the exact relationship between severity, which is not observed, and number of limitations is unknown.

Assuming the functional limitations variables control for the impact of impairments on worker productivity, and all relevant variables are included in the wage and employment functions, the coefficients of the impairment variables can be interpreted as measures of discrimination against each impairment group. That is, the coefficients measure the residual effect of an impairment on employment or wages apart from its effect on productivity. If the limitations variables are inadequate measures of the relationship between impairments and worker productivity, then differences in the employment and wages of disabled and nondisabled workers that can be explained by differences in the average productivity of the two groups may be incorrectly attributed to employer discrimination. This may be the case, for example, if the limitations variables do not fully account for interactions between workers' functional limitations and job demands. The results should be interpreted with this limitation in mind.

It is important to distinguish the roles of the functional limitation and impairment variables in the models. The five functional limitation variables are constructed from eighteen questions on physical and cognitive capacities and control for the (nondiscriminatory) effects of impairments on worker productivity. The six impairment categories are constructed from one question on health conditions and measure discriminatory differences in employment and wages between disabled and nondisabled workers.

ESTIMATING EARNINGS LOSSES

The total earnings losses attributed to discrimination against workers with disabilities are the sum of (1) the losses to not-employed men with disabilities who would be working in the absence of discrimination, and (2) the losses to employed men with disabilities who are working at low discriminatory wage rates. Earnings losses attributed to wage discrimination are estimated by converting the coefficients of the impairment variables in the wage equation to annual wage losses, multiplying by the size of the relevant population of employed disabled workers, and summing across impairment groups. Earnings losses attributed to employment discrimination are estimated by computing changes in the probability of employment attributed to discrimination against each impairment group, multiplying by the size of the relevant population of disabled persons, and evaluating the job losses at the estimated nondiscriminatory wage rate for that impairment group. The combined losses across all impairment groups can then be compared to the estimates presented in support of the ADA.

Several cautions should be kept in mind. The results may overestimate discrimination against workers with disabilities if the independent variables in the model do not control adequately for disabled-nondisabled differences in productivity-related characteristics. One example of this problem, discussed above, occurs if the functional limitation variables do not fully control for the effects of impairments on worker productivity. The problem may also affect other independent variables in the model. If, for example, the quality of education differs between disabled and nondisabled groups because children with disabilities have more absences than nondisabled children, productivity differences related to education may be incorrectly attributed to discrimination.

On the other hand, the results may underestimate discrimination against workers with disabilities if the independent variables in the model are influenced by discrimination prior to entering the labor market. This would be the case if, for example, the quality of education differs between the disabled and nondisabled groups because children with disabilities experience discrimination in the educational system.

Finally, it should be kept in mind that the results are based on a sample that differs in important ways from the population covered by the ADA. The three-pronged ADA definition of disability includes not only persons with a health condition that substantially limits a major life activity (represented by the SIPP sample), but also persons with a history of such a condition, and persons who are regarded as having such a condition. The latter groups cannot be identified in the SIPP data; to the extent that they experience wage and employment discrimination in the labor market, my results will underestimate the total extent of earnings losses for persons with disabilities.

IV. Results

SAMPLE CHARACTERISTICS

The sample consists of 12,687 men, of whom 9 percent are disabled, and 14,230 women, of whom 11 percent are disabled. Table 2 describes the distribution of the disabled samples across impairment groups and compares employment and wage rates for the disabled and nondisabled groups.

The distribution of impairments among disabled groups is similar for men and women: musculoskeletal conditions are most prevalent, representing nearly 45 percent of persons with disabilities, while cardiovascular conditions rank second at approximately 10 percent. Mental conditions are more prevalent among

Table 2: Sample Statistics for Impairment Groups

	Non-disabled	Cardio-vascular	Mental	Musculo-skeletal	Respi-ratory	Sensory	Other
Male (N)	11,530	119	110	510	77	63	278
% of disabled	—	10.3	9.5	44.1	6.7	5.4	24.0
Employment rate	.89	.71	.53	.75	.74	.67	.73
	(.32)	(.45)	(.50)	(.43)	(.44)	(.47)	(.45)
Mean wage	$13.37	$11.06	$8.77	$11.68	$12.24	$10.45	$11.50
	(9.42)	(5.88)	(6.40)	(6.87)	(7.79)	(5.03)	(7 86)
Female (N)	12,707	155	87	667	140	42	432
% of disabled	—	10.2	5.7	43.8	9.2	2.8	28.4
Employment rate	.73	.41	.43	.61	.62	.56	.51
	(.45)	(.49)	(.50)	(.49)	(.49)	(.50)	(.50)
Mean wage	$9.63	$7.94	$7.05	$8.95	$7.88	$7.95	$9.15
	(7.23)	(3.62)	(4.65)	(4.97)	(3.56)	(3.72)	(5.20)

Standard deviations in parentheses. Mean wages for employed persons only.
Source: SIPP 1990 (Wave 3).

men (10 percent vs. 6 percent), and respiratory conditions more prevalent among women (9 percent vs. 7 percent). The sample distributions differ somewhat from the overall distributions of disabling health conditions reported from the 1984 SIPP and 1983–85 National Health Interview Survey (GAO 1993). In the sample, for example, musculoskeletal conditions are overrepresented (45 percent vs. 40 percent), and cardiovascular conditions underrepresented (10 percent vs. 20 percent), relative to their distribution throughout the disabled population. A major reason for these differences is that persons who are completely unable to work because of their health condition are excluded from the sample.

Even among this sample of persons with disabilities who are able to work, employment rates are much lower for disabled men and women than for their nondisabled counterparts. Moreover, there is considerable variation in employment rates across impairment groups. Employment rates are lowest for men with mental (53 percent) or sensory (67 percent) impairments, and for women with mental (43 percent) or cardiovascular impairments (41 percent). Men and women with musculoskeletal or respiratory impairments fare better in employment than other groups, but the gap in employment rates between these impairment groups and nondisabled persons is still more than 10 percentage points.

Compared to the large differences in employment rates between disabled and nondisabled workers, the wage penalties associated with most impairments are relatively small. With the exception of the groups with mental or sensory impairments, mean wage rates for all impairment groups are in the range of 80 to 95 percent of the mean nondisabled wage. There is, however, considerable variation in the disabled–nondisabled wage ratio across impairment groups, and between men and women.[7]

The statistics reported in table 2 cannot be used to predict the potential impact of the ADA on the wages and employment of persons with disabilities, because the observed employment and wage rates do not take account of non-discriminatory differences in the human capital and socioeconomic characteristics of disabled and nondisabled workers. To do so, we turn to evidence from the employment and wage functions reported next.

EMPLOYMENT

Coefficient estimates of the employment function are reported in table 3. The variables of most interest are the functional limitations variables controlling for worker productivity, and the impairment variables measuring discrimination in employment. First, consider the results for functional limitations.

The estimated coefficients of the functional limitation variables generally have the expected negative signs, although the effects are not always significant at the accepted levels.

Among men, limitations on strength and endurance (i.e., lifting, walking, climbing) have a significant negative effect on employment, and this is the only limitation variable that is significant at the 5 percent level or better. The coefficient of mobility limitations (i.e., getting around inside or outside, moving about without an aid) is large and negative but fails significance tests.

Among women, limitations on strength and endurance have a significant negative effect on employment, as do limitations on communication (i.e., seeing, hearing, speaking, using the telephone) and limitations on daily living activities (i.e., taking a bath, getting dressed, eating, using the toilet).

Next, consider the results for the impairment variables. Even after controlling for the effects of functional limitations and socioeconomic characteristics on the employment decision, most of the impairment variables have a negative and significant effect on employment. The results are consistent with the hypothesis that persons with disabilities experience discrimination in employment.

The estimated coefficients imply that the probability of employment for the average nondisabled man is 93 percent. Holding functional limitations and worker characteristics constant, mental impairments reduce the probability of employment to 72 percent, sensory impairments to 73 percent, musculoskeletal impairments to 81 percent, cardiovascular impairments to 79 percent, and other health conditions to 84 percent. (The appendix describes how the marginal

Table 3: Means and Coefficient Estimates of the Employment Function

Variable	Male (N = 12,687) Mean	Male (N = 12,687) Coefficient	Female (N = 14,230) Mean	Female (N = 14,230) Coefficient
Employed	.87	—	.71	—
	(.34)		(.45)	
Education	13.1	.087*	13.1	.113*
	(2.9)	(.01)	(2.6)	(.00)
Black	.09	-.433*	.09	-.003
	(.28)	(.05)	(.29)	(.04)
Hispanic	.08	-.074	.08	-.137*
	(.28)	(.05)	(.27)	(.04)
Age	36.1	.021*	36.9	.004*
	(12.3)	(.00)	(12.3)	(.00)
Communication limi-	.068	-.027	.050	-.096†
tations	(.30)	(.05)	(.26)	(.05)
Mobility limitations	.011	-.176	.021	-.087
	(.13)	(.13)	(.20)	(.08)
Strength limitations	.062	-.285*	.117	-.124*
	(.35)	(.05)	(.48)	(.04)
Daily living limitations	.019	-.030	.041	-.138*
	(.23)	(.07)	(.37)	(.05)
Cognitive limitations	.003	.193	.004	-.154
	(.05)	(.24)	(.06)	(.21)
Mental impairment	.008	-.864*	.006	-.682*
	(.09)	(.13)	(.08)	(.15)
Sensory impairment	.005	-.828*	.003	-.189
	(.07)	(.18)	(.05)	(.21)
Musculoskeletal impair-	.041	-.582*	.049	-.170†
ment	(.20)	(.08)	(.21)	(.07)
Cardiovascular impairment	.010	-.652*	.012	-.633*
	(.10)	(.14)	(.11)	(.12)
Respiratory impairment	.006	-.152	.010	-.112
	(.08)	(.18)	(.10)	(.12)
Other impairment	.022	-.441*	.031	-.377*
	(.15)	(.10)	(.17)	(.07)
Log likelihood	—	-3845.15	—	-7632.83

Standard deviations of means and standard errors of coefficients in parentheses. Model also includes a constant term, nonwage incomes, and marital status dummies. Complete results are available from the author.
* = Significant at .01 level
† = Significant at .05 level
Source: SIPP 1990 (Wave 3).

effects are calculated.) Respiratory impairments have no significant effect on employment among men, after the effects of functional limitations and other worker characteristics are controlled.

Among women, four impairment variables have significant negative effects on employment. The probability of employment for the average nondisabled woman is 74 percent. Mental impairments reduce the probability of employment to 49 percent, musculoskeletal impairments to 69 percent, cardiovascular impairments to 51 percent, and other health conditions to 61 percent. In most cases the control variables in the employment function explain 8 to 10 percentage points of the observed differentials in employment rates between disabled and nondisabled women; the unexplained employment differentials that remain range from 5 to 25 percentage points.

In each case where there are significant effects of an impairment on employment, the differentials in estimated employment rates are smaller than the differentials in observed employment rates, indicating that the control variables in the employment function explain part of the observed differentials. In other words, the effect of discrimination on the employment of men or women with disabilities is smaller than observed differences in employment rates indicate. In the case of men with mental impairments the difference is dramatic: the observed differential in employment rates between nondisabled men and men with mental impairments is 36 percentage points; after controlling for functional limitations and worker characteristics the differential is 21 percentage points. The unexplained gap in employment rates is, however, still large for most impairment groups. The results imply that eliminating employment discrimination would create a substantial number of jobs for men and women with disabilities.

WAGES

Table 4 reports means and coefficient estimates of the wage equation. The coefficient estimates of the functional limitation and impairment variables are generally insignificant in the wage model and the signs are often counterintuitive. The results are consistent with previous studies showing that functional limitations and impairments have a more important effect on employment than on wages (Baldwin and Johnson 1994a).

No limitations variables are significant in the model for men, and only mobility limitations are significant in the model for women. The estimated coefficient implies that women's wages decrease 13 percent, on average, with each mobility limitation. There are, however, a few impairment categories with significant negative relationships to wages, indicating that persons with these

Table 4: Means and Coefficient Estimates of the Wage Equation

Variable	Male (N = 10,985)		Female (N = 10,115)	
	Mean	Coefficient	Mean	Coefficient
Wage	13.21	—	9.55	—
	(9.28)		(7.06)	
Education	13.3	.042*	13.4	.055*
	(2.9)	(.00)	(2.5)	(.00)
Black	.08	-.168*	.09	-.079*
	(.26)	(.02)	(.29)	(.02)
Hispanic	.08	-.068*	.07	.002
	(.27)	(.02)	(.25)	(.02)
Union	.22	.152*	.15	.140*
	(.42)	(.01)	(.36)	(.01)
Part-time	.08	-.321*	.24	-.190*
	(.27)	(.02)	(.43)	(.01)
Communication limi-tations	.06	.004	.04	.030
	(.28)	(.02)	(.22)	(.02)
Mobility limitations	.01	-.077	.01	-.128*
	(.09)	(.06)	(.13)	(.04)
Strength limitations	.04	.020	.08	-.011
	(.29)	(.02)	(.37)	(.02)
Daily living limitations	.01	.051	.02	.016
	(.17)	(.03)	(.20)	(.03)
Cognitive limitations	.002	.041	.002	.026
	(.04)	(.11)	(.04)	(.11)
Mental impairment	.005	-.106	.004	-.148†
	(.07)	(.07)	(.06)	(.07)
Sensory impairment	.004	-.057	.002	-.175
	(.06)	(.07)	(.04)	(.10)
Musculoskeletal impair-ment	.036	-.079*	.042	-.042
	(.19)	(.03)	(.20)	(.03)
Cardiovascular impair-ment	.008	-.176*	.007	-.089
	(.09)	(.05)	(.08)	(.06)
Respiratory impairment	.005	.005	.009	-.049
	(.07)	(.07)	(.09)	(.05)
Other impairment	.018	-.170*	.022	-.004
	(.13)	(.04)	(.15)	(.03)
Sample selection variable	.19	-.240*	.43	.065†
	(.20)	(.03)	(.22)	(.03)
Adjusted r-square	—	.41	—	.35

Standard deviations of means and standard errors of coefficients in parentheses. Model also includes a constant term, experience in current and former jobs, and six occupational categories. Complete results are available from the author.
* = Significant at .01 level
† = Significant at .05 level
Source: SIPP 1990 (Wave 3).

impairments experience wage discrimination. Three impairment variables have a significant negative effect on male wages: musculoskeletal impairments, cardiovascular impairments, and other health impairments. The impairment variables are binary, so the marginal effects can be computed using the method suggested by Halvorsen and Palmquist (1980).[8] The results indicate that, after controlling for workers' human capital, job characteristics, and functional limitations, the mean wages of men with musculoskeletal impairments are 8 percent lower than the mean wages of nondisabled men, while the mean wages of men with cardiovascular impairments or other impairments are 19 percent lower.

The coefficient of mental impairments in the wage model for men is large and negative but only significant at the 11 percent level. The marginally significant coefficient is somewhat surprising because studies of negative attitudes toward persons with disabilities consistently report that mental impairments evoke some of the strongest prejudices (Tringo 1970; Yuker 1987; Royal and Roberts 1987). In previous work using the Oaxaca (1973) decomposition to estimate wage discrimination against persons with disabilities, we find large discriminatory wage differentials for persons with mental impairments (Baldwin and Johnson 1994a). The estimate from the present model, although not precise, implies that after controlling for worker characteristics and functional limitations, the hourly wages of men with mental impairments are 10 percent lower, on average, than the hourly wages of nondisabled men.

In the equation for women, only mental impairments have an effect on wages that is significant at the usual levels. After controlling for human capital, job characteristics, and the effects of functional limitations, the estimated coefficient implies that the hourly wages of women with mental impairments are 16 percent lower, on average, than the hourly wages of nondisabled women. The estimated coefficient for sensory impairments is also large, and implies that women with sensory impairments earn 19 percent less, on average, than nondisabled women. There is less confidence in this conclusion, however, because the estimated coefficient is only significant at the 9 percent level.

One interesting feature of the results is that impairments have different effects on the wages of men and women. The result is not surprising because men and women are typically employed in different occupations, so the interactions between functional limitations and job demands will differ by gender. In previous work using the SIPP data but different impairment groups, Baldwin, Zeager, and Flacco (1994) find that impairments limiting mobility and strength are relatively more disabling for men than for women, while the opposite is true for impairments limiting sensory abilities and appearance.

EARNINGS LOSSES

Tables 5A and 5B present estimates of the annual earnings lost to each impairment group because of employer discrimination against workers with disabilities. The estimates are based on the employment and wage functions described above and represent employment and wage differentials that remain after controlling for differences in the human capital, job characteristics, and functional limitations of disabled and nondisabled workers. In cases where the coefficient of an impairment variable is insignificant (i.e., there are no significant differences in the average wages or employment rates of nondisabled workers and workers in that impairment group or the wage or employment differentials are fully explained by other control variables in the model), no earnings losses are reported.

Table 5A: Employment and Wage Losses Attributed to Discrimination (Male)

Employment Losses	Change in Probability of Employment	Population	Jobs Lost	Total Earnings Lost per Year (billions)
Mental impairments	.21	497,665	104,510	$1.8
Sensory impairments	.20	283,306	56,661	$1.2
Musculoskeletal impairments	.12	2,430,168	291,620	$7.5
Cardiovascular impairments	.14	562,294	78,721	$2.1
Respiratory impairments	—	340,553	—	—
Other health conditions	.09	1,282,102	115,389	$3.2
Total			**646,901**	**$15.8**

Wage Losses	% Wage Loss	Hourly Wage Loss	Employed Population	Total Earnings Lost per Year (billions)
Mental impairments	—	—	262,038	—
Sensory impairments	—	—	188,966	—
Musculoskeletal impairments	8.2	$1.10	1,820,967	$4.0
Cardiovascular impairments	19.3	$2.58	399,094	$2.1
Respiratory impairments	—	—	250,600	—
Other health conditions	18.5	$2.47	932,159	$4.6
Total				**$10.7**

Source: SIPP 1990 (Wave 3).

To see how the earnings losses are computed, consider the results for men with musculoskeletal impairments. The results from the employment function indicate that the unexplained difference in probabilities of employment between nondisabled men and men with musculoskeletal impairments is 12 percentage points; if this difference were eliminated by the employment provisions of the ADA, approximately 292,000 additional men would be employed. Evaluating their potential earnings at the nondiscriminatory wage rate ($12.78), and assuming 2,000 hours worked per year, estimated annual earnings losses for not-employed men with musculoskeletal impairments are $7.5 billion.

The results from the male wage equation indicate that a musculoskeletal impairment reduces wages by 8.2 percent, independent of its impact on workers' functional limitations. If this differential were eliminated by the provisions of the ADA prohibiting wage discrimination against workers with disabilities, the hourly wage increase would be $1.10 (from $11.68 to $12.78). Assuming full-time employment at 2,000 hours per year, and multiplying by the population estimate (1.8 million), estimated annual earnings losses for employed men with musculoskeletal impairments are $4 billion.

The total losses to men with musculoskeletal impairments, at $11.5 billion, represent 43 percent of the total $26.5 billion annual earnings losses attributed to wage and employment discrimination against all men with disabilities. Annual earnings losses for other impairment groups, calculated in a similar manner, are: $1.8 billion for not-employed men with mental impairments (7 percent of total losses), $1.2 billion for not-employed men with sensory impairments (5 percent), $4.2 billion for employed and not-employed men with cardiovascular impairments (16 percent), and $7.8 billion for employed and not-employed men with other health conditions (29 percent).

Estimated earnings losses for women with disabilities are reported in table 5B. Total earnings losses are $12.2 billion annually, $11.7 billion lost to women with disabilities who are not employed and $0.5 billion lost to employed women with mental impairments. Women with other health conditions account for 38 percent of total losses ($4.6 billion), women with musculoskeletal and cardiovascular conditions account for 22 percent each ($2.7 billion), and women with mental impairments account for 18 percent ($2.2 billion).

The results for both men and women show that the impairment groups accounting for the largest proportion of total earnings losses (musculoskeletal impairments and other health conditions) are not the impairment groups that experience the most severe discrimination in the labor market. Rather, they are impairment groups accounting for the largest fraction of the disabled popula-

Table 5B: Employment and Wage Losses Attributed to Discrimination (Female)

Employment Losses	Change in Probability of Employment	Population	Jobs Lost	Total Earnings Lost per Year (billions)
Mental impairments	.25	391,462	97,866	$1.7
Sensory impairments	—	158,765	—	—
Musculoskeletal impairments	.05	3,031,885	151,594	$2.7
Cardiovascular impairments	.23	729,219	167,720	$2.7
Respiratory impairments	—	634,502	—	—
Other health conditions	.13	1,931,890	251,146	$4.6
Total				$11.7

Wage Losses	% Wage Loss	Hourly Wage Loss	Employed Population	Total Earnings Lost per Year (billions)
Mental impairments	16.0	$1.54	169,928	0.5
Sensory impairments	—	—	88,286	—
Musculoskeletal impairments	—	—	1,862,799	—
Cardiovascular impairments	—	—	299,606	—
Respiratory impairments	—	—	390,226	—
Other health conditions	—	—	992,921	—
Total				$0.5

Source: SIPP 1990 (Wave 3).

tion. Total earnings losses are greater for women with musculoskeletal impairments (estimated population of 3 million), for example, than for women with mental impairments (estimated population of 400,000), despite the fact that discrimination reduces the probability of employment for women with musculoskeletal impairments by only 5 percentage points (compared to 25 percentage points for women with mental impairments) and has no significant effect on the wages of women with musculoskeletal impairments (compared to hourly wage losses of $1.54 for women with mental impairments).

Interestingly, the groups estimated to suffer the greatest losses from labor market discrimination are also the groups filing the greatest number of ADA-related charges with the EEOC. Approximately 20 percent of disability-related charges are filed by persons with back impairments. Neurological and mental impairments each account for slightly more than 10 percent of total charges; all other individual categories represent 6 percent or less of the total (West 1994).[9]

V. Policy Implications

No nationally representative data on employment and wage discrimination against persons with disabilities were presented during the legislative debates on the ADA, but the results of this study suggest the basic presumptions on which the act is based are correct. Workers with disabilities are subject to discrimination in the labor market. The losses to the disabled population, expressed in terms of annual earnings, are substantial: $28 billion attributed to discrimination in employment and $11 billion attributed to wage discrimination. The estimates are likely to be lower bounds of the true losses to disabled persons because the sample does not include two of the groups covered by the ADA, and because the employment function does not account for workers with disabilities who are underemployed because of discrimination.

The study does not test the sources of discrimination against workers with disabilities, but the results are consistent with the hypothesis that prejudice is one important factor explaining the low employment and wage rates of persons with disabilities.[10] Studies of negative attitudes toward different impairment groups consistently find mental impairments eliciting the strongest prejudices (Tringo 1970; Yuker 1987; Royal and Roberts 1987). The results presented here are consistent with the hypothesis that negative attitudes toward persons with mental conditions significantly reduce their opportunities in the labor market. Discriminatory employment differentials are greater for men and women with mental impairments than for any other impairment group and, among women, the only significant wage discrimination occurs for the group with mental impairments. The results suggest that policies designed to reduce employer prejudice against persons with mental impairments could significantly improve labor market opportunities for this group.

The study emphasizes the importance of controlling for functional limitations in the models that are used to estimate discrimination against persons with disabilities. Some disability advocates argue that functional limitations should be omitted from the models because, with reasonable accommodations, persons with disabilities can be as productive as nondisabled persons. Nevertheless, the accommodations impose direct or indirect costs on an employer that must be factored into calculations. The fact that, even with the best available controls for functional limitations included in the models, I continue to find evidence of discrimination against workers with disabilities, provides a strong counterargument to those who argue that wage and employment differentials between disabled and nondisabled workers are entirely explained by differences in functional limitations.

The results support much previous research showing that employment discrimination is a more serious problem than wage discrimination for persons with disabilities. The earnings losses attributed to discriminatory employment differentials are nearly triple the earnings losses attributed to low discriminatory wage rates. The results suggest that as the EEOC develops priorities for handling charges under the ADA, it should consider procedures that focus attention on the problems persons with disabilities encounter in gaining access to jobs.

The results on employment, however, also suggest that the magnitude of the problem and, therefore, the potential benefits of the ADA, are substantially smaller than the estimates presented in support of the act. The estimates of discriminatory differences in employment indicate that no more than 650,000 men with disabilities will enter the labor market if the ADA achieves the objective of eliminating disability-related discrimination. The estimates are based on the assumption that recipients of Social Security Disability Insurance (SSDI) have permanently withdrawn from the labor force and are, therefore, excluded from the samples. Even if one allows for the possibility that some persons who are SSDI beneficiaries under current conditions would be employed if discrimination were eliminated, the potential effect of the ADA on employment is much lower than the estimate of 3 to 4 million disabled men entering the labor force presented in congressional hearings on the ADA (Tucker and Goldstein 1991).

The ADA's goals, and the persons protected by the act, are best served by comparing its effects to realistic estimates of the potential benefits of reducing discrimination against persons with disabilities. This chapter provides one set of estimates against which subsequent outcomes can be measured.

Appendix

Derivation of the Employment Function

Assume for each individual there is some positive wage rate that represents the minimum wage at which he or she will be observed working. Call this the reservation wage, where

$$W_r = {}_rZ_r + {}_r \tag{A1}$$

In equation A1 the reservation wage is expressed as a function of observable characteristics, Z_r, a corresponding vector of coefficients $_r$, and an error term, $\sim_r$.

Assume there is some nonnegative wage rate that represents the maximum wage an employer has offered to the individual. Call this the offer wage

$$W_o$$

where

$$W_o = {}_oZ_o + {}_o \tag{A2}$$

The offer wage is a function of observable human capital characteristics Z_o, a corresponding vector of coefficients $_o$, and an error term $\sim_o$.

It follows that the ith individual will be observed working whenever

$$y^*i = W_{oi} - W_{ri} = {}_iZ_i + {}_i \, \text{\AE} \, 0 \tag{A3}$$

where $Z = \{Z_r, Z_o\}$ is a corresponding vector of coefficients, and $\sim = {}_o - \sim_r$ is assumed to have a standard normal distribution.

The continuous variable underlying the employment decision y^*i, is unobservable, but we do observe the binary response

$$y_i = 1 \text{ if } y^*i \, \text{\AE} \, 0 \text{ (employed)}, \; y^i = 0 \text{ otherwise (not employed)} \tag{A4}$$

Then from equation A3, the probability the ith person will be observed working is

$$\text{Prob} \, (y_i = 1) = \text{Prob} \, ({}_i \, \text{\AE} \, - \, Z_i) = 1 - (-Z_i) \tag{A5}$$

where $-$ is the cumulative distribution function of a standard normal random variable. The likelihood function, expressed in log form, is A6. Then estimates of the coefficients, $-$, can be obtained by maximizing equation A6 using probit techniques.

The marginal effect of an impairment on the probability of employment can be computed by substituting coefficient estimates and means of the variables in Z into equation A5, setting a particular impairment variable equal to one and all other impairment variables equal to zero. The predicted probability of employment can then be compared to the probability of employment for comparable nondisabled individuals to obtain the difference in employment rates attributed to discrimination.

Specification of the Wage Function

Loglinear wage equations of the form

$$\ln W_i = {}_1X_i + 2_i + {}_i \tag{A7}$$

are estimated separately for men and women. In equation A7, W_i is the hourly wage rate of the ith worker, X_i is a vector of variables that influence wage rates, i is the sample selection variable, 1 and 2 are corresponding vectors of coefficients, and i is a mean–zero error term.

The sample selection variable, i, is included in the wage equation to control for the bias that occurs because we are unable to observe wages offered to nonworkers (Heckman 1980). That is, workers self-select into the group of employed persons; if this selection is nonrandom, it can bias other coefficients in the model. The selection variable, equal to the inverse of the Mill's ratio, is constructed from coefficient estimates of the employment function A6.*

The error term in the wage function, i, is assumed to have a normal distribution independent of the control variables in the model. Thus, estimates of the coefficients 1 and 2 can be obtained by ordinary least squares regression.

---

*The system is identified by including the following variables in the employment function that are not included in the wage equation: nonwage incomes, marital status, and age. In theory, all variables in the wage equation should also be included in the employment function, but some of the variables in the wage equation, namely occupation, union membership, part-time worker, and work experience, are not observed for nonworkers. This may severely limit the selectivity correction in the model. Nevertheless, the more complete model is preferred because correlations between the impairment categories and an omitted variable could lead to biased estimates of discrimination.

Notes

The author is grateful for helpful comments from William G. Johnson, Edward Schumacher, and participants at the 1997 Obermann Seminar. Any remaining errors are my own.

1. The definitions combine concepts from Nagi (1969) and the World Health Organization (1980). The ADA definition of disability is more comprehensive. It includes anyone with "a physical or mental impairment that substantially limits one or more of the major life activities," anyone with a record of having such an impairment, or anyone who is perceived as having such an impairment. Any individual who satisfies one of the three criteria is protected from wage and employment discrimination by the act.

2. The employment and wage models are described in more technical detail in the appendix.

3. Marital status is represented by a set of four binary variables identifying workers who are married, living with spouse; married, not living with spouse; widowed; separated or divorced. Nonwage income variables include amounts of property income, income from veterans' pensions, unemployment or disability income, retirement income, spouse's earnings, and other nonwage income for the four-month reference period.

4. The employment losses represent only the losses to disabled persons who are not employed. Discrimination may also force some workers with disabilities to accept part-time employment, or employment for which they are overqualified. My estimates of earnings losses are likely to underestimate the true losses associated with employment discrimination against persons with disabilities because they do not account for underemployment among disabled persons who are working.

5. The occupation categories are professional/manager, service, skilled labor, semi-skilled labor, unskilled labor, and clerical/sales.

6. Communication limitations include the ability to see words and letters in ordinary newsprint, hear a normal conversation, have one's speech understood, and use the telephone. Mobility limitations include the ability to climb a flight of stairs; move about without the aid of a cane, crutches, or wheelchair; and get around inside and outside. Limitations on strength and endurance include the ability to lift and carry a ten-pound weight and walk one-quarter mile. Limitations on personal care include the ability to get in and out of bed, take a bath or shower, dress oneself, eat, use the toilet, prepare meals, and do light housework. Cognitive limitations include the ability to keep track of money and bills.

Possible responses to the functional limitation questions on the SIPP are: no difficulty performing the function, some difficulty performing the function, or unable to perform the function without assistance. Such self-reported measures of functional limitations have been shown to be reasonably accurate correlates of the capacity to work (Stern 1989).

7. Baldwin, Zeager, and Flacco (1994) show that the wage losses associated with most impairments are significantly different for men and women.

8. Halvorsen and Palmquist (1980) show that the marginal effects of binary variables in semilogarithmic equations can be computed by taking the antilog of the estimated coefficient and subtracting one.

9. The group with mental impairments includes persons with mental retardation, many of whom are likely to be employed in supported employment at below-minimum wages that are not regarded as discriminatory. Persons with mental retardation represent less than 20 percent of the group with mental impairments; when they are excluded from the sample, there is no substantive change in the results.

10. For specific tests of the correlation between attitudes scales and employer discrimination against workers with disabilities, refer to Baldwin and Johnson (1999, 1994a, 1994b).

References

Baldwin, Marjorie L., and William G. Johnson. 1994a. Labor Market Discrimination against Men with Disabilities. *Journal of Human Resources* 29 (Winter): 1–19.

———. 1994b. The Sources of Employment Discrimination: Prejudice or Poor Information? In *New Approaches to Employee Management,* ed. David M. Saunders. Greenwich, Conn.: JAI Press.

———. 1999. Labor Market Discrimination against Men with Disabilities in the Year of the ADA. *Southern Economic Journal.*

Baldwin, Marjorie L., Lester A. Zeager, and Paul R. Flacco. 1994. Gender Differences in Wage Losses from Impairments. *Journal of Human Resources* 29 (Summer): 865–87.

Chirikos, Thomas N., and Gilbert Nestel. Economic Determinants and Consequences of Self-Reported Work Disability. *Journal of Health Economics* 3 (Aug. 1984): 1117–36.

General Accounting Office (GAO). 1993. *Vocational Rehabilitation: Evidence for Federal Program's Effectiveness Is Mixed.* Washington, D.C.: GAO.

Halvorsen, Robert, and Raymond Palmquist. 1980. The Interpretation of Dummy Variables in Semilogarithmic Equations. *American Economic Review* 70 (June): 474–75.

Heckman, James J. 1980. Sample Selection Bias as a Specification Error with an Application to the Estimation of Labor Supply Functions. In *Female Labor Supply: Theory and Estimation,* ed. James P. Smith. Princeton, N.J.: Princeton University Press.

Nagi, Saad Z. 1969. *Disability and Rehabilitation.* Columbus: Ohio State University.

Oaxaca, Ronald. 1973. Male-Female Wage Differentials in Urban Labor Markets. *International Economic Review* 14 (Oct.): 693–711.

Royal, George P., and Michael C. Roberts. 1987. Students' Perceptions of and Attitudes toward Disabilities: A Comparison of Twenty Conditions. *Journal of Clinical Child Psychology* 16 (June): 122–32.

Stern, Steven. 1989. Measuring the Effect of Disability on Labor Force Participation. *Journal of Human Resources* 24 (Summer): 361–95.

Tringo, John L. 1970. The Hierarchy of Preference toward Disability Groups. *Journal of Special Education* 4 (Summer/Fall): 295–306.

Tucker, Bonnie P., and Bruce A. Goldstein. 1991. *Legal Rights of Persons with Disabilities.* Horsham, Pa.: LRP Publications.

West, Jane. 1994. *Federal Implementation of the Americans with Disabilities Act, 1991–1994.* New York: Milbank Memorial Fund.

World Health Organization. 1980. *International Classification of Impairments, Disabilities and Handicaps.* Geneva: WHO.

Yuker, Harold E. 1987. The Disability Hierarchies: Comparative Reactions to Various Types of Physical and Mental Disabilities. Unpublished manuscript.

Part Four

Research on Implementation of ADA Title I

Chapter XI

Genes in the Workplace

New Frontiers for ADA Law,
Policy, and Research

Robert S. Olick

I. Introduction

If research continues to progress according to plan, scientists working on the Human Genome Project (HGP) will soon have constructed detailed maps of the human genome and determined the nucleotide sequence of human DNA. Rapidly expanding knowledge about the human genome promises to arm physicians with impressive diagnostic tools and to pave the way for new and improved therapeutic and preventive measures. The genetic revolution holds the promise of new predictive powers, foretelling future health and illness and, it is hoped, showing the way to genetic or other interventions to prevent, manage, or even cure serious illness. As architects of the HGP recognized, this same genetic information may be used for a range of other purposes beyond the private confines of the physician–patient relationship, including in employment, insurance, and law enforcement; these are uses with "momentous implications for both individuals and society [that pose] a number of consequential choices for public and professional deliberation."[1] For this reason Congress committed substantial funding to study of the ethical, legal, and social implications of mapping and sequencing the human genome, under the auspices of the Program on the Ethical, Legal, and Social Implications of Human Genome Research (popularly known as the ELSI program) of the National Human Genome Research Institute.

This chapter explores some of the challenges posed by the new genetic frontier for our shared commitment to nondiscrimination in employment. My specific focus is the Americans with Disabilities Act (ADA), enacted in 1990, the same year that the HGP began its work in earnest. Hailed as one of the most important pieces of civil rights legislation of our time, the ADA aspires to the lofty goal of ensuring that all persons have the right to participate in the mainstream of American life regardless of disability. Title I of the act protects individuals from discrimination in employment on the basis of disability, broadly defining disability for purposes of the law as "a physical or mental impairment that substantially limits one or more major life activities, . . . having a record of such impairment, or . . . being regarded as having such an impairment."[2] Yet the ADA is notably silent about genetic discrimination and (as this went to press) the judiciary has yet to be called upon to interpret the law's reach. In this early stage of the ADA's evolution, the legal status of genetic discrimination in the workplace looms as a large open question.

It takes but a moment's reflection to appreciate why this area warrants serious attention. Past instances of employment discrimination on the basis of actual and perceived health and disability have been chronicled.[3] Discriminatory practices have most often been rooted in the corporate fisc, sometimes in concern for the health and well-being of employees, coworkers, or the public. These very same arguments may be voiced with renewed vigor with respect to genetics. If genetic markers are predictors of future illness, they may also be taken as predictors of an employee's future years on the job, need for sick leave, and consumption of health and disability benefits; as indicators of an individual's ability to perform a particular job; as signals of hypersusceptibility to workplace injury (e.g., the employee with respiratory sensitivity to the work environment); or as evidence of a (potential) threat to coworkers or to the public at large (the air traffic controller with the gene for Alzheimer's disease). To the extent the ADA permits medical testing, and therefore genetic testing—putting genetic information in the hands of business—opportunities for genetic discrimination are likely to arise.

Our response to genetic information in the workplace signals a critical juncture for ADA law, policy, and research. At issue is whether the ADA's "regarded as" definition of disability protects asymptomatic, otherwise unimpaired persons diagnosed with genetic predispositions to future illness, disease, and disability. Parsing the three-part statutory definition of disability has been perhaps the most contentious litigated issue in the early years of ADA implementation. Considering its place as a gateway to ADA protection, application of the "regarded as" prong to genetic information will also be of keen interest to current controversy over the law's application to persons with asymptomatic, nongenetically associated conditions whose (prospective) employers choose not to chance future disability in their workforce. ADA construction will likely play a pivotal role as well in the burgeoning moral and policy debate about the just and fair uses of genetic information throughout society as the HGP's inexorable path of discovery reveals a growing body of genetic secrets.

The goals of this chapter are part descriptive, part normative. I will be concerned with the following sorts of questions. What do we know about the incidence and threat of genetic discrimination in employment? What does genetic testing tell us about the future, and what are the normative implications of its predictive powers? Docs the ADA bring within its protective reach instances of genetic discrimination? As a matter of social policy, is genetic discrimination in the workplace ever just? I conclude that although hard evidence of genetic discrimination in employment is limited, there is good reason for the issue to hold a prominent place on the moral and policy agenda. The "regarded as" prong of the ADA's definition of disability should be interpreted to extend the law's protections to instances of genetic discrimination, for it would be unjust to permit differential treatment of persons on the basis of their genetic status. If necessary, the ADA should be amended or complementary legislation enacted. On the current state of the science, the probabilistic nature of genetic prediction of future functional impairment renders highly problematic an employer's potential defense of fair discrimination in particular cases. At the same time, the ADA's scheme for individuated assessment points to a wider set of policy concerns to which evolving disability law, policy, and research can make significant contributions.

The scope of the discussion has two important limitations. First, I do not discuss here the growing patchwork of state laws that address various aspects of genetic discrimination. Some of these laws give important protections against genetic discrimination in the workplace.[4] Second, I do not offer an analysis of genetic discrimination in health insurance. This may seem an important omission, for insofar as the majority of insured Americans obtain health insurance through employer-sponsored group plans, discrimination in employment is closely intertwined with fair access to health insurance. Unfortunately, meaningful analysis of the complex problem of insurance discrimination is beyond the scope of the present inquiry. It should be noted that ADA analysis does not in any event take us very far here, as the act expressly permits conventional underwriting in health insurance plans offered by commercial insurers and self-insured companies and places few limitations on such practices.[5]

II. On "Genetic Discrimination"

To begin, we need a working definition of "genetic discrimination." I will understand genetic discrimination to mean negative differential treatment of an individual based solely on that person's possession of one or more genetic traits that deviate from the "normal" genome, or on the perception that the individual possesses one or more genetic traits that deviate from the "norm," when that person is asymptomatic. Rephrased, genetic discrimination occurs when an asymptomatic individual, or a member of that person's family, is treated differently on the basis of the perception of predicted future disability. Genetic discrimination also occurs when members of a person's family are treated differently based on their actual or perceived possession of a genetic trait. Other commentators have embraced a similar definition for purposes of ADA analysis.[6]

This analytical definition distinguishes instances of discrimination based solely on genes from those where the individual has manifested symptoms of an illness or disability which may in part be attributable to gene expression (or be perceived to be a result of gene expression). The distinction has important implications for the ADA. As noted below, there should be little question that the ADA applies to cases in which discrimination is based, in whole or in part, on genetically associated physical or mental impairments, that is, symptomatic genetic conditions. The harder question is how the ADA and social policy should respond to asymptomatic genetic conditions. On this understanding of genetic discrimination the central question for the ADA is whether those who are "regarded as" disabled based on a genetic test are shielded by the law, or whether protections against discrimination would apply only upon manifestation of an actual impairment. The central question for disability policy is whether differential treatment of individuals on the basis of genetically associated predicted future disability is fair and just.

III. The Use and Abuse of Genetic Information: What Do We Know?

Concerns about genetic discrimination are widely shared. Illustrative is a 1995 Harris poll which found that over 85 percent of those surveyed were "very concerned" or "somewhat concerned" about the potential uses of genetic information by employers or insurers.[7] Public fears are reinforced by high-profile cases capturing media attention, such as the 1997 case of a woman whose insurance company refused to cover breast cancer treatment after deeming a prior genetic test evidence of an excluded preexisting condition.[8]

But how often does genetic discrimination actually occur? Review of existing empirical work offers some significant, though limited, insights. In a frequently cited article, Billings and colleagues report forty-one separate incidents of possible discrimination, all but two involving either insurance (thirty-two) or employment (seven).[9] More recently, researchers at Georgetown University (Lapham and colleagues) conducted a survey of 332 members of genetic support groups nationwide, asking whether they believed that they or a member of their family had been the victim of discrimination in employment or insurance. The authors found that 22 percent of respondents believed they had been refused health insurance and 13 percent believed they had been denied employment or let go from a job.[10] Between 1992 and 1993, another group of researchers (Geller and colleagues) surveyed individuals at risk to develop one of four selected genetic conditions (hemochromatosis, phenylketonuria, mucopolysaccharidoses, and Huntington's disease) and parents of children with one of these conditions. They found that nearly half of respondents (n = 917) reported alleged discrimination by a variety of institutions, including health and life insurers and employers (other instances of reported discrimination involved educational institutions, adoption services, and blood banks).[11]

These data send a powerful message. They should also be received with a modicum of caution. As acknowledged by both the Lapham and Geller teams, their surveys were of self-selected individuals highly sensitized to the implications of genetic information, not of a representative sample of the population as a whole. And for the most part published data report on people's beliefs or rely on anecdotal accounts. Since employers do not ordinarily disclose the reasons for rejecting a job applicant, and health insurers may deny contracts with little or no explanation, verification of an employee's suspicion of genetic discrimination can be a difficult task (again, a limitation noted by the authors of these studies).[12] Geller and colleagues write, for example, of a 24-year-old social worker who claimed she was fired shortly after her employer discovered that a member of her family had Huntington's disease. The employer cited poor job performance as the reason for dismissal, despite the fact that the employee had a record of outstanding performance reviews and had been promoted months prior to discharge. The employee was later informed by a coworker that the employer's real motive was the fear that she might develop Huntington's chorea.[13]

Perceptions and fears are reinforced by self-reported attitudes among employers and insurers. A study conducted by the Congressional Office of

Technology Assessment (OTA) in 1989, shortly before enactment of the ADA, found that among Fortune 500 companies, 42 percent of the 330 responding companies believed an applicant's health insurance risks a relevant consideration in an employment decision. Thirty-six percent of companies stated that they conducted health insurance assessments in the screening of job applicants. The OTA concluded that "growing concern among employers over the rising costs of employee health insurance, and the increased efforts to reduce those costs for the employer, are likely to increase the scope of health insurance screening in the workplace."[14] Although few companies reported that these assessments included genetic monitoring and screening, the report concluded that "[i]f genetic tests could be used to predict risk to subsequent health conditions more reliably than medical histories and nongenetic tests, given the present climate of corporate opinion and practice related to employee screening, one would expect the new technology to be increasingly adopted as it passes a cost-effectiveness review."[15] With advances in genetic technology employers are likely to look in this direction and are perhaps likely to consider cost and reliability "more of a factor than any issue of fairness."[16] The lessons of history attest to this conclusion. A glaring early example of genetic discrimination was visited upon African-Americans thought to carry the trait for sickle-cell anemia, even though often the individuals themselves would not develop the disease. The story of employer-employee relations in the United States is replete with examples of health screening and discrimination, including efforts to restrict employment of smokers, persons with HIV/AIDS, cancer, epilepsy, and other conditions.[17]

In the brief time since inception of the HGP, the potential for discrimination on the basis of genetic information has received considerable scrutiny in federal policy circles, with much of the attention focused on access to health insurance and the privacy of genetic information. A task force on Genetic Information and Insurance, formed under the auspices of the ELSI program in 1991, warned that "[n]ew genetic tests in the context of risk underwriting by health insurers are likely to exacerbate an already severely troubled health care system," and suggested that employers would increasingly look to these new technologies for ways to respond to mounting economic pressures.[18] The prevailing climate is aptly characterized in a July 1997 report from the U.S. Department of Health and Human Services (HHS): "[A]s knowledge grows about the genetic basis of disease, so too does the potential for discrimination and stigmatization based on genetic information. Too many Americans fear that their genetic information will be used to discriminate against them and too often they are right."[19] The secretary of HHS urged legislation to impose a tight and comprehensive ban on genetic discrimination in health insurance and to secure genetic privacy,[20] a position later embraced by President Clinton in his 1998 State of the Union Address.[21] Unfortunately, the HHS report makes only passing mention of discrimination in employment.

In sum, fears about genetic discrimination are widely shared and appear well founded. The prevalence of and opportunities for genetic discrimination in employment, insurance, and elsewhere in society warrant close empirical and policy scrutiny. Future empirical work should examine as well the extent to which genetic discrimination is based upon myths and misperceptions about the nature of genetics, genetic conditions, and the predictive value of genetic tests.

IV. On Genetic Conditions and Gene Expression

Careful analysis of genetic discrimination requires a core understanding of the nature of genetic testing and genetic conditions. There is a popular inclination to think of the genome as one's future coded diary—as a blueprint for life—and to embrace the idea that possession of a genetic marker determines one's future health fate. Genetic diagnosis of serious disease may be thought a harbinger of doom, of impending disability, diminished productivity, or early death. Yet genetic determinism (or something close to it) is true for only a handful of genetic diseases (for example, Huntington's, Tay-Sachs). In the vast majority of instances genetic markers identify *predispositions* to develop certain illnesses, diseases, or conditions. Genetic prediction is "probabilistic . . . not deterministic."[22]

Genetic forecasts rest on calculations of the probability that a gene will express itself and lead to disease or disability, as well as the probability of consequent symptoms, their severity, and the course of the condition's progression. Moreover, because genes have different degrees of "penetrance," manifestation of illness and disability may be mild for one person and more severe for another with the same genetic defect. Consequently, the predictive force of genetic diagnosis can vary among individuals with the same genetic condition. "[W]ide variation in clinical manifestations of a gene-associated disorder—individuality—is common."[23] Complicating the picture, some genetic conditions are multifactorial, meaning that a combination of factors, such as diet, other health conditions, or environmental exposure, may suppress or trigger gene expression; some involve multiple gene expression; and still others are late-onset conditions, meaning that gene expression and manifestation may not occur for years or decades from the time of diagnosis, if at all. In other instances a person may be a carrier of a genetic defect but never become symptomatic. In short, it would be a serious error to paint all genetic conditions, or all persons with the same genetic condition, with the same brush.[24]

A related question concerns the reliability and accuracy of genetic tests themselves. Different tests have different degrees of specificity (the measure of the proportion of negative tests when the disease is absent) and sensitivity (the measure of the proportion of positive tests when the disease is in fact present). Depending on the test, there may be a greater or lesser proportion of false positive and false negative results. Furthermore, genetic testing is a new science with uniform, effective quality assurance mechanisms yet to emerge. In 1994, the Institute of Medicine's (IOM) Committee on Assessing Genetic Risks found that regulatory authority is in place, and "[e]xisting quality assurance in genetic testing is voluntary and has improved laboratory quality in its participants, but . . . current laboratory control programs are inadequate to address the special issues posed by genetic testing primarily because these programs lack essential enforcement authority."[25]

Law and policy must be grounded on sound understanding of the science of genetic diagnosis and prediction. As has been true of the history of disability discrimination, genetic discrimination may be based on myth, misperception, and irrational fears rather than hard data and rational understanding.[26] The concern extends beyond hiring decisions to the workplace environment and beyond. Echoing the social impact of more familiar types of disability, individuals at risk for genetic discrimination have reported "stigmatization by relatives, friends, and other members of their communities," as well as feelings of "loss of self-worth" and "powerlessness" to fight discrimination.[27] A majority of Americans believe that coworkers would treat them differently if their disability became known.[28] These beliefs are unlikely to differ with respect to genetic information.

New genetic knowledge must be used responsibly to dispel myths and fears that may fuel discrimination rather than equal acceptance and compassion. Among the questions to be answered: how certain must we be of the accuracy of genetic testing? The IOM committee concluded that "the magnitude of the personal and clinical decisions that may be made based on [genetic test] results . . . warrant a standard with close to 'zero' chance of error for such tests."[29] Assuming testing accuracy, how accurate must predictions of future impairment be to warrant exclusion from employment? The American Medical Association Council on Ethical and Judicial Affairs concluded in 1991 that genetic tests are "poor predictors of disease and even poorer predictors of disabling disease," and recommended that genetic susceptibility testing not be used as a basis for employment decisions.[30] The developing science of molecular genetics will likely challenge this early assessment.

Against this background, the remainder of this chapter turns to interpretation of the ADA, beginning with a basic description of key provisions of the law of particular relevance to problems of genetic discrimination.

V. Key Provisions of the ADA: An Overview

MEDICAL TESTING AND GENETIC TESTING

An initial query is whether the ADA permits access to genetic information, specifically whether the ADA permits genetic screening of individuals for some range of conditions. Under the law, mandatory medical screening of job applicants is prohibited. Employers may not "conduct a medical examination or make inquiries of a job applicant as to whether such applicant is an individual with a disability or as to the nature or severity of such disability."[31] Other types of inquiries are permitted (for example, asking whether the individual is able to use a computer, to drive, to lift heavy objects) if related to an applicant's job qualifications; and inquiries concerning infectious and communicable diseases, as well as drug and alcohol use, are expressly allowed.[32] Medical examinations are permitted based upon a conditional offer of employment, provided the examination is given to all prospective employees and does not single out individuals or groups with disabilities.[33] Postemployment, further medical examinations, including periodic exams, may be required, but only if "job-related and consistent with business necessity."[34] Medical information is to be kept in separate files with firm obligations to maintain confidentiality.[35]

Genetic testing is not mentioned in the law and is neither expressly permitted nor prohibited. But since a genetic test is a medical test administered by trained clinical personnel, it seems clear that genetic testing in the workplace is permissible, at least in connection with a conditional offer of employment, and subsequently if justified as job-related and necessary to the business. As such, the ADA allows a form of genetic screening of applicants and of employees in some circumstances. (An employer might also obtain genetic information about an applicant or employee from other sources, such as application forms or prior medical, insurance, or employment records.) Access to genetic information creates opportunities for genetic discrimination.

It is worth mentioning that the ADA's silence on genetic testing also means there are no mandated workplace standards and practices concerning the nature and quality of informed consent to genetic testing or the provision of pre- and post-test counseling. Study of developing corporate practice is needed, as is scrutiny of the need for policy initiatives to ensure a quality consent process and appropriate privacy safeguards in an era of longitudinal computerized medical records.

BASIC PROTECTIONS AGAINST DISCRIMINATION

Title I contains broad language prohibiting discrimination against qualified individuals on the basis of disability "in regard to job application procedures, the hiring, advancement, or discharge of employees, employee compensation, job training, and other terms, conditions and privileges of employment."[36] To be eligible for the law's protections, a person's condition must satisfy one of the three statutory criteria defining disability: "[having] a physical or mental impairment that substantially limits one or more major life activities, . . . a record of such impairment, or . . . being regarded as having such an impairment."[37] In addition, the person must be a qualified individual, that is, someone "with a disability who, with or without reasonable accommodation, can perform the essential functions of the employment position that such individual holds or desires."[38] Qualification does not require being able to perform all aspects of the job, including "marginal" ones, only essential functions. As we will see, a critical issue to be resolved is whether qualified persons denied employment on the basis of their genes are legally disabled and shielded against discrimination.

Together with the duty not to discriminate against qualified disabled persons, employers have an affirmative obligation to make "reasonable accommodations" to assist otherwise qualified applicants or employees to perform essential job functions. Reasonable accommodation is not required if it would impose "undue hardship" on the employer, defined as "an action requiring significant difficulty or expense." What counts as reasonable accommodation, and, conversely, what counts as undue hardship, is determined on a case-by-case basis taking into account such factors as the nature and cost of the accommodation relative to the employer's size and resources.[39] Thus the reasonable accommodation/undue hardship provisions strike a balance between individual and business interests, placing limits on the employer's obligations to qualified disabled employees. Contrary to the beliefs of some critics, the law does not require hiring and reasonable accommodation of those who are not qualified, nor does it require that qualified disabled persons be given preference over equally or more qualified nondisabled candidates.[40]

THE "DIRECT THREAT" EXCEPTION

An individual's qualifications for the job "may include a requirement that an individual shall not pose a direct threat to the health or safety of other individuals in the workplace."[41] Regulations issued by the Equal Employment Opportunity Commission (EEOC), the body with oversight and enforcement authority for the ADA, extend this language to include a direct threat to self or to the public, defining "direct threat" as "a significant risk of substantial harm to the health and safety of the individual or others that cannot be eliminated or reduced by reasonable accommodation." Under the regulations, this determination is individuated, based on the person's "present ability to safely perform the essential functions of the job." Whether the individual poses a significant risk of substantial harm is to be based on "the most current medical knowledge and/or the best available objective evidence," taking into account the likelihood, nature, severity, and imminence of the potential harm, the duration of the risk, and other pertinent factors.[42] Here again, there is a balancing of interests. Discrimination is lawful where it would protect the employee, coworkers, or the public; but there is a heavy burden of justification, and reasonable accommodation to eliminate the risk is required, perhaps in the form of job restructuring or reduction of harmful substances in the work environment, subject to the undue burden limitation.[43]

The last section of this chapter identifies some emerging policy and research questions suggested by the brokered compromise between individual rights and prevention of harm to self or others underlying the direct threat exception.

VI. The ADA and Genetic Discrimination: Defining Disability

There should be little question that once gene expression manifests as a medical condition, genetically associated conditions are actual physical or mental impairments that satisfy the first prong of the definition of disability. For legal purposes, disability is defined in terms of substantial impairment of major life activities (walking, seeing, hearing, talking, learning, working), not on the basis of the origin or etiology of the impairment. In fact, the legislative history cites numerous examples of genetically associated disabilities, and courts have previously held manifest disabilities with genetic bases to be covered by the act. The same is true for those who have a prior record of a genetically associated disability, for example, a person recovering from cancer or living with chronic illness.[44] Our concern is whether the ADA's definition of disability encompasses and protects asymptomatic individuals who are *regarded as* disabled on the basis of their genes.

The text of the law makes no mention of genetic information or genetic discrimination. When the issue ultimately comes before the judiciary, courts will look to the legislative history; to regulations and interpretive guidance from the EEOC (though not binding, EEOC guidance carries substantial weight); and to analogous precedent parsing application of the "regarded as" clause to other currently asymptomatic conditions. Among the questions awaiting judicial resolution are whether Congress intended the law to apply to instances of genetic discrimination; whether construing the law to exclude protection would be contrary to the intent and purpose of the ADA; and whether a narrow interpretation would lead to absurd results.[45]

THE LEGISLATIVE HISTORY

Several commentators have reviewed the legislative history.[46] All concur that genetic discrimination received scant attention through the course of legislative deliberations. Positive support may be found in isolated statements from several members of Congress who identified the ADA's protection of carriers of genetic traits as one reason to vote in favor of passage. For example, in congressional debates several representatives stated that one reason to support passage of the ADA was that it would protect carriers of genetic conditions who were regarded as having an impairment substantially limiting a major life activity.[47] Occupational screening of persons with sickle-cell trait was a well-known piece of the historical landscape.[48] But there are also suggestions that at least for many in Congress genetic discrimination was not on the table for debate. Gostin notes, for example, that while some members identified genetic discrimination as a concern, Steny Hoyer, then the floor manager in the House, "informed the Congressional Biomedical Ethics Advisory Committee that genetic discrimination was 'not raised or discussed.'"[49] Rothstein concludes that "Congress enacted the ADA without any serious consideration about the law's effect on individuals with various genetic conditions."[50] We can only surmise that Congress might have been more attentive to problems of genetic discrimination had the state of genetic research been more advanced at the time. Remarkably, less than seven years after enactment of the ADA a bevy of federal bills to prohibit or restrict genetic discrimination — most concerned with health insurance — had been introduced.

THE EEOC'S POSITION

Specific support for ADA coverage can be found in the EEOC amended *Compliance Manual* of 1995. Discussing a hypothetical scenario in which a qualified individual with an asymptomatic genetic susceptibility to colon cancer is refused employment following a conditional job offer, the manual states that the individual is covered by the ADA because he is *regarded as* having a disability.[51] This enforcement guidance was reaffirmed in an EEOC policy statement, "Genetic Information and the Workplace," dated January 20, 1998. At present this policy guidance has not been embraced in regulation and is not binding on a court.[52] It is also worth noting that the 1995 manual reverses an earlier EEOC position adopted in 1991, shortly after enactment of the ADA.[53] At that time the EEOC rejected recommendations from the NIH-DOE task force and working group on genetic information and health insurance that genetic discrimination be prohibited under the ADA.[54] Deputy legal counsel for the EEOC flatly stated that the ADA does not protect those with asymptomatic genetic predispositions to illness or disease who are not otherwise impaired.[55] The contrary positions of the EEOC from past to present presage the central issue for ADA interpretation. Must an individual with a diagnosed genetic trait have a current, actual, and substantial impairment to be protected by the law? Or does the fact that an asymptomatic individual is regarded as having a present or future disability trigger legal protections?

INTERPRETING THE "REGARDED AS" CLAUSE

Strong legal arguments in support of ADA coverage along the lines suggested by the EEOC's 1995 and 1998 pronouncements have been articulated.[56] The "regarded as" clause is expressly designed to address situations in which individuals are treated *as if* they were disabled but have no substantial impairments of major life activities. This third prong of the definition is intended to respond to a history of discrimination on the basis of stigma, irrational fears, and stereotypes. The U.S. Supreme Court made the point emphatically in *School Board of Nassau County v. Arline:*[57] "Congress acknowledged that society's accumulated myths and fears about disability and disease are as handicapping as are the physical limitations that flow from actual impairment." (In *Arline,* the high court was reviewing the precursor and model for the ADA, the Rehabilitation Act of 1973, which contains the identical definition of disability.) Here the law "judges the discriminator through his own subjective perceptions, prejudices, and stereotypes," not the individual's actual abilities.[58] To apply the same reasoning when discrimination is based on unfounded negative attitudes about genetic traits and misperceptions of future ability to work is consonant with the law's intent and purpose to protect against just such prejudicial exclusion.

Failure to bring genetic discrimination within the ADA's reach would create huge and anomalous loopholes in the law, permitting exclusion of those who are asymptomatic but currently healthy and able to work but who may become disabled in the future (including those who are only carriers of a genetic trait but will never have the disease), while protecting those whose genetically associated condition has become manifest and whose functional abilities may be compromised. The cruel irony: a person with a genetic marker would have no claim to protection when healthy and able to work but would be protected when he or she becomes ill, disabled, and is functionally impaired.[59] (A variation on the theme would be the following: "I can't get a job because I have a gene for breast cancer, but my neighbor with colon cancer can claim disability discrimination if she is denied employment for which she is otherwise qualified.") This construction portends another troubling scenario. Faced with the prospect of exclusion, stigma, and prejudice in employment and beyond, many may find not knowing their genetic status a risk worth taking, choosing to reject physician-recommended tests, preferring willful ignorance of family history or settling for lesser jobs (even unemployment). As illustrated by the HIV/AIDS pandemic, a policy that discourages consensual presentation to the health care system decreases opportunities for early diagnosis, intervention, and prevention, undermining public health. By analogy, genetic screening unconstrained by the right to fair treatment undermines the salutary public health goals of the HGP. For all of these reasons, courts may well conclude that a narrow reading of the ADA would legitimate absurd consequences inconsistent with the law's purposes and goals.

On the other hand, it is precisely because the asymptomatic person is typically not impaired in any major life activity (let alone substantially impaired) that this otherwise compelling line of reasoning may not find easy acceptance, and that the EEOC's 1991 pronouncement may find a receptive audience in some courtrooms. A number of recent cases have seemingly rejected the *Arline* precedent, embracing instead a narrow and restrictive interpretation of the definition of disability. These courts have ruled that to qualify as disabled a person must presently have an actual and substantial impairment of a major life activity. If actual impairment cannot be demonstrated, the individual is not disabled; if not disabled, there is no ADA protection.[60] A parallel line of cases has held that medical conditions which do not impair abilities to engage in major life activities when controlled with treatment or medication do not count as disabilities. In several rulings persons with chronic but manageable illnesses, such as diabetes, epilepsy, and heart disease, have been held not impaired, not disabled, and therefore not protected by the ADA.[61] By extension, a person with "bad genes" may well find that "the more likely [he or she] is able to perform the job, the more likely it is that he or she will not be seen as disabled enough to be protected by the ADA."[62]

There is good reason to hold this latter group of opinions to be wrongly decided. Linking the first and third prongs of the definition in this way threatens to eviscerate protections expressly intended to redress misperceptions, stereotypes, and prejudices in the absence of actual impairments. And an unduly narrow construction leads to absurd results. Still, precedent presages an uphill battle for those with asymptomatic genetic conditions who are excluded from employment and who seek redress under the ADA.

As this chapter went to press, the U.S. Supreme Court was poised to decide three cases in which the courts below split over whether the ADA protected against employment discrimination when the person's impairment (disability) is controlled by medication or (in two cases) corrective lenses.[63] In 1998, the U.S. Supreme Court issued its first opinion construing the ADA. In a five-to-four decision, *Bragdon v. Abbott*[64] held that asymptomatic HIV infection constitutes a legally protected disability if as a consequence of infection the affected individual is impaired in the major life activity of reproduction. *Bragdon,* together with the three "mitigating measures" cases before the high court, may quiet some disputations over ADA application to asymptomatic individuals and may offer a building block for applying the ADA to asymptomatic genetic conditions. But a close reading suggests that the decision is likely to be of limited import for the emerging debate over genetic discrimination.

As the *Bragdon* court noted, asymptomatic HIV is an actual, diagnosed condition with a (relatively) known and reasonably predictable clinical course. In fact, the majority found that the HIV-infected person is impaired from the moment of infection due to the immediate assault upon the body's white blood cells and the severity of the disease. In addition, the "regarded as" clause was not at issue and was not before the high court. Still, *Bragdon* may have important implications for a more closely analogous issue—whether persons with inheritable genetic conditions are disabled because they are substantially limited in their reproductive choices. The opinion would seem to suggest that the ADA affords some protections here, for example, where the risks to offspring are significant and substantially limit reproductive choice. In sum, current controversy over the definition of disability as a gateway to ADA protection portends that uniform extension of Title I's umbrella to shield against genetic discrimination may require congressional action to amend the ADA;[65] enactment of complementary legislation (perhaps as part of a genetic privacy package); or an authoritative "all directly on point" ruling from the high court.

While definitional quarrels have considerable legal purchase, the monocle of terminology tends to divert attention from larger concerns that ought to inform future interpretive and policy discourse.[66] The next section stakes out some normative ground, approaching the issues from the standpoint of distributive justice. I posit the framework of a deeper moral and policy argument for extending the reach of antidiscrimination law, drawing out points of connection to other features of the history and purpose of the ADA.

VII. Genes and Justice: Taking the Genetic Lottery Seriously

Antidiscrimination laws like the ADA are grounded in notions of fair (just) access to and distribution of societal goods, such as employment, transportation, public accommodations, and insurance, and seek to establish principled responses to whether differences among persons warrant different treatment in access to such goods. It is a familiar maxim of distributive justice that like cases should be treated alike and different cases differently, in proportion to their differences. Differential treatment must be justified on the basis of morally (or legally) relevant differences between or among affected persons. The measure of justice then depends on whether differences in our genes are morally and policy-relevant differences that warrant unequal treatment.

TWO VIEWS OF GENETIC DIFFERENCE

One way to approach this question is through the lens of crafting a just response to the genetic lottery. The lottery metaphor, strongly identified with John Rawls's seminal work on justice, recognizes that each of us possesses certain natural endowments—skills, abilities and capacities—as a result of our particular parentage, our physiological and genetic composition, and through no choice of our own. In like fashion each is endowed with certain natural tendencies toward health, sickness, and disability.[67] Molecular biology has just begun to reveal the links between a person's genetic status and his or her possible future. Given that we neither choose nor deserve our respective outcomes in the lottery, we must ask whether genetic differences warrant differential treatment.

We might hold two sorts of views about the moral and policy relevance of the genetic lottery. The skeleton of the first view—call it the argument from the free market—has already been suggested and looks something like this. Treating persons with "bad genes" differently is (can be) good business practice. Genetic screening offers (or will offer) a powerful instrument for predicting employees' future performance and productivity, need for sick leave, and consumption of health and disability benefits. In a free market system companies should be at liberty to use available resources to maximize business efficiency; when deemed cost-effective, genetic screening is just another tool for doing so. There is no reason, the argument goes, to understand exclusion from employment as unfair simply because some fare better than others in the gene pool. There is no obligation to neutralize or compensate for genetic inequalities in a competitive marketplace by ignoring genetic differences. Bad luck in the lottery is unfortunate (perhaps tragic), but not unfair. Proponents of this position might add an appeal to equity, asserting that to ignore such differences visits unfairness on those who have genetic luck, for it denies the genetically fortunate the competitive advantages of their good fortune, and ultimately imposes on healthy and productive members of the workforce a greater share of the burden (in workload, compensation, benefits) of their more "costly" counterparts.[68] If deeper roots in a theory of justice are needed, free market proponents would find common ground with libertarian thinkers such as Robert Nozick.[69]

The contrary view — call it the argument from fairness — attaches a very different meaning to the genetic lottery. It holds that it is presumptively unfair to provide unequal treatment to persons based upon their genetic status. Neither those with "good genes" nor those with "bad genes" can be said to deserve their relative outcomes in the lottery. To accord advantages to those with good genes while visiting disadvantages on those with bad genes wrongly distributes important social goods on the basis of biological accident.[70] The Rawlsian argument from fairness appeals as well to the principle of fair equality of opportunity. Fairness imposes, the argument goes, affirmative obligations to neither disfavor those with "disease genes" nor to favor those with "healthy genes" in the competition for employment (at least assuming all candidates to be otherwise qualified to perform the job). To disfavor those with disease genes denies equal opportunity. Taking the genetic lottery seriously means that bad outcomes are not just unfortunate (sometimes tragic), they also warrant affirmative obligations to compensate for or redress unfairness in the allocation of societal goods like employment that otherwise occurs if distribution is left entirely to the free market.[71] According to one version of the fairness argument, an effective means of preventing discrimination would be to proscribe genetic screening in the workplace.

UNDERSTANDING THE ADA

Qua social legislation, the ADA embraces the core tenets of the fairness argument and repudiates the heart of the free market position. But Title I does not adopt the fairness view entirely, nor does current policy implement fairness by banning genetic screening. Rather, disability policy can be understood to pursue a principled compromise.

The ADA was enacted to redress a history of unfair treatment of persons with disabilities in an otherwise free marketplace and casts an especially critical eye on status-based discrimination unrelated to functional ability to perform the job. The "findings and purpose" of the law declare a firm commitment to "equality of opportunity, full participation, independent living, and economic self-sufficiency" for persons with disabilities, affirming that persons with disabilities have been "subjected to a history of purposeful unequal treatment . . . based on characteristics that are beyond [their] control and resulting from stereotypic assumptions not truly indicative of . . . individual ability."[72] In addition, there is a strong parallel drawn to discrimination on the basis of race, color, sex, national origin, religion, or age. In a number of important respects prior civil rights legislation prohibiting these forms of status-based discrimination served as models for and animating forces behind construction of the ADA.[73] Exclusion of qualified disabled individuals has been held analogous to discrimination against capable workers "because of their skin color or other vocationally irrelevant characteristic."[74] Unequal treatment of qualified individuals on the basis of their genes seems equally invidious. It is all the more offensive when rejection and denial are based on membership in an ethnic or racial group in which a genetic trait is more prevalent (e.g., sickle-cell trait among African-Americans, Tay-Sachs among Ashkenazi Jews) or on a family member's genetic predisposition not shared by the (prospective) employee.

The ADA expressly targets the economic efficiency argument. Concerned that permitting discrimination to nurture the corporate fisc would eviscerate disability protections and perpetuate stereotyping of disabled persons, Congress rejected projections of future medical costs or other employee benefits as a ground for refusal to hire, prohibiting use of actual or perceived medical histories as a pretense for adverse employment decisions against qualified persons. (Employers may, however, adjust health benefit packages, provided that doing so is not a subterfuge for discrimination.)[75] Differential treatment motivated by beliefs about future productivity and benefit costs creates standing to sue and has been held unlawful.[76] Dollars and cents have their place in the reasonable accommodation/undue hardship calculus, but only in relation to functional ability and the costs of accommodation itself, not with respect to status alone. (For discerning discussion of various aspects of economic issues under the ADA, see the chapters by Blanck, Chirikos, and Baldwin, this volume.)

Unfettered acceptance of the free market view must confront another troubling charge which warrants brief mention. Unchecked genetic discrimination, it has been said, augurs creation of a "new genetic underclass," comprised of those who are excluded from work, insurance, or other social goods because of their genetic report card.[77] Though the claim requires a high degree of crystal-ball gazing and relies on a number of assumptions—among them profound advances in the predictive power of genetics and an undifferentiated job market characterized by uniform stigmatization and segregation—the prognostication cannot simply be dismissed. The specter of classism sounds a disquieting alarm with historical resonance and bolsters the contention that placing genetic discrimination outside the purview of disability law would create huge loopholes and absurd, unjust results. It also counsels a preemptive, preventive response, rather than one of remediation and restitution. The argument from fairness cuts off such dire consequences, presumptively shielding all from the land of the genetic outcasts.

Still, there are limitations to the fairness argument. The claim that genetic status is the same in relevant respects as race, nationality, gender, and so forth, is less compelling in the employment context than elsewhere, for genes can be associated with ability, disability, and employment qualifications in ways that other accidents of birth clearly cannot. Disability policy does not embrace a more radical egalitarian model of fair and equal opportunity that would eliminate inequalities, giving disabled persons jobs regardless of qualifications. Rather, the ADA integrates strong rejection of status-based discrimination with recognition of the moral and policy relevance of functional limitations and acknowledges the need for individuated assessments under the reasonable accommodation and direct threat provisions. The connection between genes and functional (dis)abilities suggests that in principle genetic distinctions may sometimes be fair; absolute prohibition of discrimination may not be warranted. The final section of this chapter identifies some research and policy issues implicated by the ADA's paradigm of fair discrimination.

VIII. Can Genetic Discrimination Be Fair? Some Emerging Issues and an Agenda for Future Study

Does economic efficiency justify differential treatment on the basis of genes? Can a person be denied a position to protect him or her from harm? To prevent harm to others? As questions such as these are debated both publicly and privately, in boardrooms, legislatures, and ultimately the American courtroom (assuming aggrieved plaintiffs succeed on the threshold definitional issue), some familiar themes will emerge—with a new twist. In important respects future law and policy will be pressed to evaluate familiar values in light of complex problems of risk assessment and allocation, the nature of which will require continued scrutiny as the new genetic frontier marches on.

ECONOMIC EFFICIENCY

It is highly questionable whether dollars and cents alone can ever justify discrimination on the basis of genetic status and "best guesses" about predicted future impairment. Still, whether genetic screening promotes business and societal interests in economic efficiency and, if so, whether the price for such gains is the sacrifice of individual rights are likely to be topics of substantial interest and controversy. One important area for study is how employers' perceptions of genetic information influence beliefs about projected business costs.[78] Another is the impact of new genetic information on group benefit plans, including interaction between the ADA and the Health Insurance Portability and Accountability Act of 1996 (HIPAA).[79] This recent law, designed to ensure continuity of health insurance coverage, prohibits group health plans from using genetic information as a basis for imposition of preexisting condition exclusions.[80] It does not appear, however, to prohibit conventional rate setting on this basis.[81] Insurance industry executives have argued that health insurance costs will rise if genetically based rate setting is proscribed[82] and have also contended that risk adjustments using genetic profiles are unlikely to bring substantial change in group premiums.[83] Empirical study is needed of adjusted costs of health benefits (as well as disability, workers' compensation, and other benefits) in light of developing genetic knowledge and policy, including genetic privacy initiatives.

The more narrow issue in contested cases is whether workplace accommodations would impose undue hardship (significant difficulty and expense). Here claims of economic efficiency would seem to face considerable obstacles. Extant law has been highly critical of discrimination based on perceptions of future disability in the absence of current impairment and has imposed a substantial evidentiary burden on companies. Analogous cases have required proof (by expert testimony) of *reasonable probability* that the person would become disabled, and that the risk was *not speculative, but imminent.*[84] The substantial variability of gene expression and clinical progression pose special challenges for any effort to establish reasonable probability and imminence of disability (putting aside what counts as reasonable and probable). The weak predictive power of genetic testing makes cost-benefit calculations of the burdens of workplace accommodations problematic as well. In fact, unless gene expression and onset of illness *are* imminent, affected individuals are not asking for accommodations (flexible hours, environmental modifications, special equipment, and so forth) at all, only for equal treatment with other qualified persons. Accommodations based on far more tangible considerations have often been found to be reasonable and not to impose an undue burden, both in the courtroom and in private studies of the economic impact of ADA Title I.[85]

OCCUPATIONAL SAFETY AND HEALTH

At present a small number of genetic markers for hypersusceptibility to workplace injury have been identified. To choose three examples: glucose-6 phosphate dehydrogenase (G-6-PD) deficiency is a sex-linked (male) disorder that increases the risk of acute hemolysis (the destruction of red blood cells) from chemical exposures;[86] persons predisposed to alpha antitrypsin deficiency may have greater susceptibility to chronic obstructive lung disease when exposed to respiratory irritants;[87] and individuals with the gene for ankylosing spondylitis may be at greater risk for back injury in positions that require certain forms of physical exertion.[88]

As additional markers of hypersusceptibility are identified, genetic screening promises to open new vistas on a familiar debate about the complex inter-relationships among workplace safety, business efficiency, occupational and public health—and the individual, corporate, and public interests at stake. It is a familiar claim that screening to reduce occupational risk benefits affected individuals (including coworkers) and society alike by reducing workplace injury and promoting a healthier workforce, as well as serving both parochial and collective interests in business efficiency. Hypersusceptibility to workplace hazards is for these reasons, the argument goes, a relevant characteristic that justifies differential treatment. The countervailing concern is that a permissive stance toward occupational screening would result in relaxed attention to workplace safety standards. Rather than provide safer work environments, employers might find it more cost-effective to select a more rigorous workforce.[89] On this view, individual sensitivity to features of the work environment is not necessarily irrelevant or morally neutral, but differential treatment on this basis should be closely scrutinized. Health and safety should not be achieved at the expense of fairness in the competition for employment (Zwerling et al., this volume).

If the OTA's assessment is correct, employers may find that they have considerable incentive to employ predictive genetic screening for predisposition to occupational injury.[90] Future disability rights work will need to carefully examine the ADA's interaction with occupational health and safety laws and the underlying goals and values in play. Assessment of underlying empirical evidence and assumptions regarding genetic predispositions and interface with the workplace, as well as the nature and costs of workplace modifications, should hold a critical place in this discourse. Beneath the surface lies a further question of principle. It is not obvious who should have authority to decide what risks are worth taking—whether commitment to individual autonomy or some version of corporate paternalism is to be preferred. Assessment of Title I's middle course with respect to these values should be part of the unfolding dialogue, together with the social and legal implications of allocating responsibility for the risk of workplace injury (e.g., in tort law).

These policy concerns are writ small in a contested "direct threat" case. Under the direct threat provisions, discriminatory treatment may be justified by appeal to prevention of harm to the employee or coworkers; cost-effectiveness alone does not suffice (though it is frequently a motivating factor). Workplace accommodations to eliminate the threat (risk) will be required if reasonable, so long as they do not impose an undue burden. Significantly, invocation of direct threat carries a heavy burden of proof. Attentive to the foregoing concerns, Congress intended that risks be specifically identified and not based on generalizations or misperceptions, and admonished employers that tests should "reliably predict the substantial, imminent degree of harm required."[91] EEOC regulations implement this directive, requiring the employer to demonstrate a "significant risk of substantial harm" based upon the duration of the risk, and the nature, severity, likelihood, and imminence of the potential harm. As indicated earlier, judgments of direct threat are to be based on the individual's present abilities to work, not speculations about future impairments, and must employ current medical knowledge and pertinent, "best available" objective evidence.[92] (Companies are not required to wait for actual injury to occur before taking action, and proof of actual injury is not required.)

It has been argued that companies will sometimes be able to satisfy this standard, and that "[t]he one kind of genetic discrimination that is likely to be upheld is discrimination on the basis of genotype associated with an increased susceptibility to the effects of workplace toxins."[93] On the other hand, not too long ago the American Medical Association concluded that "there is insufficient evidence to justify the use of any existing test for genetic susceptibility as a basis for employer decisions."[94] One especially close parallel is illustrative. In a case decided under New York law, the court held that the plaintiff, who had a diagnosed but asymptomatic spinal condition, spondylolisthesis, could not be disqualified from service as a police officer where one medical expert testified that plaintiff had a "great likelihood of low back disability developing in the future" and another testified that he had a "statistically higher probability . . . compared to a similar person with normal back x-rays."[95] Architects of the ADA stressed that "high probability of substantial harm" must be based on "valid medical analyses," pointing in particular to the low predictive value of back X rays.[96] Would a positive genetic test for ankylosing spondylitis pose a significant threat, including imminent potential harm to the individual or others, should the applicant undertake the position? Our answer would need to account for the fact that while the test for this genetic marker is highly specific and sensitive, a significant number of affected individuals will not manifest the condition, suggesting the weak predictive value of this particular test.[97]

These are of course to a large degree empirical matters concerning, among other things, the predictive force of genetic tests, the nature and extent of risk for those with genetic susceptibility in a particular work environment, and the nature and costs of accommodations such as workplace modifications (improving the air filtration system) or alternative job placement (moving off the assembly line). But how we weigh and measure the empirical claims rests on value judgments about risks, harms, and the balance between individual and business interests at stake. Eventually, courts will be called to wrestle with these questions. As suggested by the foregoing discussion, it is not apparent that case-by-case adjudication is the best way to judge whether, for example, a 50 percent chance of acute hemolysis from (prolonged?) chemical exposure in (substantial?) concentrations is acceptable; especially so where genetic risk scenarios affect large industries as a whole.

PROTECTING PUBLIC HEALTH

The direct threat exception may also be invoked in the name of prevention of harm to the public, such as consumers of goods or services. Consider, for example, the train conductor with a genetic predisposition to macular degeneration. Predicted, genetically associated functional impairment, it may be argued, is a relevant characteristic justifying exclusion because the (prospective) employee would likely cause harm to others, but no such risks are posed by other candidates for the position. On this sort of paradigm, if the greater good is to be served, the means must be screening and selection of the workforce, not changes in the workplace. (Other scenarios implicating changes to the workplace might be imagined.)

That companies have certain responsibilities to safeguard public health and safety is commonplace. Drafters of the ADA noted a range of areas where those responsibilities might be implicated by the direct threat provisions, including curbing the spread of infectious disease in the food industry and in the screening of firefighters, police officers, and other public safety personnel. Drug and alcohol screening conducted by many U.S. companies has found acceptance both in law (including under the ADA) and society at least in part because of appeals to public health and safety.[98] Courts have shown a willingness to uphold specific discriminatory actions to protect others from serious harm. For example, it has been held that the nature, severity, and imminence of substantial harm merits barring a physician with narcolepsy from surgery[99] and restricting the practice privileges of an HIV-positive surgeon through mandatory patient disclosure of HIV-positive status (a de facto termination of the physician's practice).[100] Discharge of a police officer whose "benign essential tremor" prevented proper use of a firearm has been upheld on grounds of significant risk to others.[101] These precedents are instructive, but their distinguishing feature is an actual diagnosis on which to base judgments of the duration, severity, and imminence of potential harm. The qualified predictive power of genetic tests raises serious questions as to whether the likelihood of harm to others can be shown to be substantial, severe, and imminent. Here again empirical and epistemological shortcomings of genetic testing and prediction are serious obstacles for companies that engage in screening for predicted future disability.

At the same time, it is not obvious that the ADA's adjudicatory scheme is appropriate to the task of parsing the public health interests at stake. The complexity of the challenge is illustrated by the case of a Maryland volunteer firefighter whose medical expert testified that with accommodations there was an approximately 10 percent risk of harm to self or others. The court held (under the Rehabilitation Act) that even assuming accommodation of firefighter Huber's asthmatic condition to be reasonable, "the County does not have to assume such a ten percent risk" of harm to Huber, his fellow firefighters, and the public.[102] If an airline or a taxi company were to institute a carefully considered program of genetic screening for specific job-related impairments (consider the airline pilot with a predisposition — 25 percent likelihood? — of sudden cardiac arrest), plausible moral and policy asseverations could be proffered in the policy's defense. In the case of the airline, must the threat of substantial harm be imminent, or does the potential magnitude of the harm justify a lower threshold of probability?

Whether in the boardroom, the courtroom, or the Congress, disability policy will likely be called to participate in a principled discourse about allocation of risk with substantial public health implications, balancing anew individual rights and the public good. The IOM's counsel that "great care should be taken in performing [genetic] tests and interpreting the results," is surely wise, as is its call for a standard of "close to 'zero' chance of error" when genetic tests are the basis for significant personal decisions.[103] Where matters of occupational and public health are concerned, however, this may prove just a comfortable resting place that delays harder moral and policy choices implicated by the new genetics.

IX. Conclusion

When the ADA was enacted, Congress projected that some 43,000,000 Americans with a physical or mental disability would now have legal standing to combat a history of exclusion, stigma, and isolation, and to pursue equal opportunity and full participation in society.[104] There is scant evidence that those with asymptomatic genetic conditions were counted in this number, but there is no sound reason to deny persons regarded as disabled on the basis of genetically associated predicted future illness, disease, and disability these same protections. Failure to do so would work substantial and widespread injustice.

More than five thousand heritable disorders have been identified.[105] If the prophets of genetics are correct, each of us possesses some small number of "disease genes," and each of us is potentially vulnerable to genetic discrimination. In the years ahead, disability policy will be a critical voice in a larger societal debate about genetic privacy; about individual, corporate, and societal interests, rights, and responsibilities; and about the social and legal construction of disability (Baynton, this volume). As we move forward in these uncharted waters, a rare opportunity lies before us—the opportunity to be proactive rather than reactive in shaping the moral, social, and policy context in which molecular science's new revelations will be used and understood.

Notes

1. http://www.nchgr.nih.gov.
2. 42 U.S.C. § 12102(2) (West 1995).

3. Mark A. Rothstein, *Medical Screening and the Employee Health Cost Crisis* (Washington, D.C.: BNA Books, 1989).

4. Paul Steven Miller, "Genetic Discrimination in the Workplace," *Am. J. Law, Med. and Ethics* 26 (1998): 189–97.

5. 42 U.S.C. § 12201(c)(1) (West 1995).

6. Paul R. Billings et al., "Discrimination as a Consequence of Genetic Testing," *Am. J. Hum. Genet.* 50 (1992): 476–82; Marvin R. Natowicz, Jane K. Alper, and Joseph S. Alper, "Genetic Discrimination and the Law," *Am. J. Hum. Genet.* 50 (1992): 465–75.

7. U.S. Department of Health and Human Services, Report of the Secretary to the President, "Health Insurance in the Age of Genetics" (Washington, D.C., July 1997) (hereafter HHS Report), p. 4.

8. Gina Kolata, "Advent of Testing for Breast Cancer Genes Leads to Fears of Disclosure, Discrimination," *New York Times,* Feb. 4, 1997, p. B9.

9. Billings et al., "Discrimination as a Consequence of Genetic Testing."

10. E. Virginia Lapham, Chahira Kozma, and Joan O. Weiss, "Genetic Discrimination: Perspectives of Consumers," *Science* 274 (Oct. 25, 1996): 621–24.

11. Lisa N. Geller et al., "Individual, Family, and Societal Dimensions of Genetic Discrimination: A Case-Study Analysis," *Science and Engineering Ethics* 2 (1996): 71–88. See also Joseph S. Alper et al., "Genetic Discrimination and Screening for Hemochromatosis," *Journal of Public Health Policy* 15 (Autumn 1994): 345–58.

12. Lapham, Kozma, and Weiss, "Genetic Dsicrimination," pp. 622–23; Geller et al., "Individual, Family, and Societal Dimensions," pp. 82–83.

13. Geller et al., "Individual, Family, and Societal Dimensions," pp. 82–83.

14. U.S. Congress, Office of Technology Assessment, *Medical Monitoring and Screening in the Workplace: Results of a Survey—Background Paper,* OTA-BP-BA-67 (Washington, D.C.: U.S.G.P.O., Oct. 1991), p. 45.

15. Id.

16. Id.; Mark A. Rothstein, "Genetic Discrimination in Employment and the Americans with Disabilities Act," *Houston L. Rev.* 29 (1) (1992): 26–30 (discussing the OTA findings).

17. American Medical Association Council on Ethical and Judicial Affairs, "Use of Genetic Testing by Employers," *Journal of the American Medical Association* 266 (13) (Oct. 2, 1991): 1827–30 (hereafter AMA); Rothstein, *Medical Screening.*

18. Task Force on Genetic Information and Insurance, NIH-DOE Working Group on Ethical, Legal, and Social Implications of Human Genome Research, *Genetic Information and Health Insurance* (NIH Publication No. 93-3686, May 10, 1993), p. 5.

19. HHS Report, p. 1.

20. Id., pp. 9–10.

21. Prepared text of President Clinton's State of the Union Message, *New York Times,* Jan. 28, 1998, p. A19.

22. Institute of Medicine, *Assessing Genetic Risks: Implications for Health and Social Policy* (Washington, D.C.: National Academy Press, 1994), p. 9 (hereafter IOM Report).

23. Billings et al., "Discrimination as a Consequence of Genetic Testing," p. 480.

24. See generally IOM Report; Philip Kitcher, *The Lives to Come: The Genetic Revolution and Genetic Possibilities* (New York: Touchstone, 1996), esp. chap. 2.

25. IOM Report, p. 11.

26. Peter David Blanck and Mollie Weighner Marti, "Genetic Discrimination and the Employment Provisions of the Americans with Disabilities Act: Emerging Legal, Empirical, and Policy Implications," *Behavioral Sciences and the Law* 14 (1996): 411–32.

27. Geller et al., "Individual, Family, and Societal Dimensions," p. 81.

28. 5 BNA ADA Manual 62 (May 23, 1996).

29. IOM Report, p. 11.

30. AMA, "Use of Genetic Testing by Employers," pp. 1827, 1829.

31. 42 U.S.C. § 12112(d)(2)(a) (West 1995).

32. 42 U.S.C. §§ 12113(d); 12114 (West 1995).

33. 42 U.S.C. § 12112(d)(2)(a) (West 1995).

34. 42 U.S.C. § 12112(d)(4)(a) (West 1995).

35. 42 U.S.C. § 12112(d)(3)(b) (West 1995).

36. 42 U.S.C. § 12112(a) (West 1995).

37. 42 U.S.C. § 12102(2) (West 1995).

38. 42 U.S.C. § 1211(8) (West 1995).

39. 42 U.S.C. § 12111(10) (West 1995).

40. Peter David Blanck and Mollie Weighner Marti, "Attitudes, Behavior, and the Employment Provisions of the Americans with Disabilities Act," *Villanova L. Rev.* 42 (2) (1997): 376.

41. 42 U.S.C.A. § 12113(a) (West 1995).

42. 29 C.F.R. § 1630.2(r) (1997).

43. 42 U.S.C.A. § 12111(9)(B) (West 1995); Natowicz, Alper, and Alper, "Genetic Discrimination," p. 469.

44. Larry Gostin, "Genetic Discrimination: The Use of Genetically Based Diagnostic and Prognostic Tests by Employers and Insurers," in *Genes and Human Self-Knowledge: Historical and Philosophical Reflections on Modern Genetics,* ed. Robert F. Weir, Susan Lawrence, and Evan Fales (Iowa City: University of Iowa Press, 1994), pp. 132–33.

45. Stephen Breyer, "On the Uses of Legislative History in Interpreting Statutes," *S. Cal. L. Rev.* 65 (1992): 845–74. Justice Breyer's comments are not directly addressed to ADA interpretation.

46. Rothstein, "Genetic Discrimination"; Gostin, "Genetic Discrimination"; Blanck and Marti, "Genetic Discrimination"; Frances H. Miller and Philip A. Huvos, "Genetic Blueprints, Employer Cost-Cutting, and the Americans with Disabilities Act," *Admin. L. Rev.* 46 (Summer 1994): 369–83.

47. See Natowicz, Alper, and Alper, "Genetic Discrimination," p. 470.

48. See AMA, "Use of Genetic Testing by Employers," pp. 1828–29; Marc Lappe et al., "Ethical and Social Aspects of Screening for Genetic Disease," *New England Journal of Medicine* 206 (1972): 1129–32.

49. Gostin, "Genetic Discrimination," p. 134.

50. Rothstein, "Genetic Discrimination," pp. 49–50. See also Gostin, "Genetic Discrimination," pp. 134–35; Ellen Wright Clayton, "The Dispersion of Genetic Technologies and the Law," *Hastings Center Report* 25 (3) (May–June 1995): S14 ("In drafting the ADA, Congress said very little about genetic testing, an oversight that seems almost stunning now").

51. *EEOC Compliance Manual,* vol. 2, number 915.002 (Mar. 14, 1995), p. 45. See also Blanck and Marti, "Genetic Discrimination," p. 417 (discussing the 1995 *EEOC Compliance Manual*).

52. EEOC, "Genetic Information and the Workplace," www.dol.gov/dol/_sec/public/media/reports/genetics.htm (Jan. 20, 1998).

53. Rothstein, "Genetic Discrimination," pp. 45–47 (discussing the EEOC's 1991 position); Miller and Huvos, "Genetic Blueprints," pp. 373–74 (same).

54. Eric T. Juengst, "Priorities in Professional Ethics and Social Policy for Human Genetics," *Journal of the American Medical Association* 266 (1991): 1835–36.

55. Miller and Huvos, "Genetic Blueprints," p. 374 (quoting an Aug. 1991 letter from Elizabeth M. Thornton, Deputy Legal Counsel, EEOC, to the cochairmen of the NIH-DOE Joint Subcommittee on the Human Genome Project).

56. See Gostin, "Genetic Discrimination"; Rothstein, "Genetic Discrimination"; Blanck and Marti, "Genetic Discrimination."

57. 480 U.S. 273, 284 (1987).

58. Gostin, "Genetic Discrimination," p. 134; 29 C.F.R. § 1630.2(l) (1997).

59. Id.; Rothstein, "Genetic Discrimination," p. 50.

60. Arlene B. Mayerson, "Restoring Regard for the 'Regarded as' Prong: Giving Effect to Congressional Intent," *Villanova L. Rev.* 42 (2) (1997): 587–612 (discussing cases requiring an actual impairment and concluding that they represent a misunderstanding and total disregard of the "regarded as" clause).

61. James P. Frierson, presentation at the Obermann Faculty Research Seminar, "Employment, Disability Policy, and the Americans with Disabilities Act," University of Iowa, June 10–26, 1997. Compare *Schluter v. Industrial Coils,* 6 AD Cases 625 (W.D. Wis. 1996) (insulin-dependent diabetic not legally disabled when condition is controlled by medication) with *Arnold v. United Parcel Service, Inc.,* 7 AD Cases 1489 (1st Cir., Feb. 20, 1998) (whether diabetic employee is disabled under ADA is determined without regard to mitigating medication).

62. Mayerson, "Restoring Regard," p. 587.

63. *Kirkenberg v. Albertson's, Inc.,* 143F. 3d 1228 (9th Cir., 1998); *Sutton and Hinton v. United Air Lines* 130F. 3d 893 (10th Cir., 1997); *Murphy v. United Parcel Service,* 141F. 3d 1185 (10th Cir., 1998), cert. granted 119S.Ct. 791 (1999).

64. 118 S.Ct. 2196 (1998).

65. See Gostin, "Genetic Discrimination," p. 148 (proposing amendment to include in the definition of disability "having a genetic or other medically identified potential of, or predisposition toward, such an impairment").

66. One recent article implies that the "regarded as" definition ought to be interpreted broadly, but reaches the curious conclusion that courts should proceed with

caution because (1) ADA protections could bring a litigation explosion; and (2) other laws—HIPAA and ERISA—provide adequate protection against genetic discrimination. Mark S. Dichter and Sarah E. Sutor, "The New Genetic Age: Do Our Genes Make Us Disabled Individuals under the Americans with Disabilities Act?" *Villanova L. Rev.* 42 (2) (1997): 613-33. While refutation of these contentions cannot be undertaken here, the first claim is both highly speculative and unpersuasive; the second relies on a misplaced reading of these other laws. Neither law provides protections against discrimination on the basis of genetically associated predicted future disability coequal to those afforded by a proper and generous reading of the ADA.

67. John Rawls, *A Theory of Justice* (Cambridge, Mass.: Harvard University Press, 1971), p. 15.

68. For a parallel argument with respect to genetic discrimination in insurance, see Robert J. Pokorski, "Use of Genetic Information by Private Insurers," in *Justice and the Human Genome Project,* ed. Timothy F. Murphy and Marc A. Lappe (Berkeley: University of California Press, 1994), pp. 91-109.

69. Robert Nozick, *Anarchy, State, and Utopia* (New York: Basic Books, 1974).

70. Rawls, *A Theory of Justice,* p. 102.

71. For a parallel argument with respect to genetic discrimination in insurance, see Norman Daniels, "The Genome Project, Individual Differences, and Just Health Care," in *Justice and the Human Genome Project,* ed. Timothy F. Murphy and Marc A. Lappe (Berkeley: University of California Press, 1994), pp. 110-32.

72. 42 U.S.C. § 12101(7), (8).

73. 42 U.S.C. § 12101(4); Pamela S. Karlan and George Rutherglen, "Disabilities, Discrimination, and Reasonable Accommodation," *Duke Law Journal* 46 (1) (1996): 5-14.

74. *Vande Zande v. State of Wis. Dept. of Admin.,* 44 F.3d 538, 541 (7th Cir. 1995).

75. 42 U.S.C. § 12112(c) (1995).

76. See, e.g., Dichter and Sutor, "The New Genetic Age," pp. 630-31 (discussing cases); Natowicz, Alper, and Alper, "Genetic Discrimination," p. 469 (discussing Rehabilitation Act cases).

77. Dorothy Nelkin, "The Social Power of Genetic Information," in *The Code of Codes: Scientific and Social Issues in the Human Genome Project,* ed. Daniel J. Kevles and Leroy Hood (Cambridge, Mass.: Harvard University Press, 1992), pp. 177-90.

78. Blanck and Marti, "Attitudes, Behavior," p. 362.

79. P.L. No. 104-191, 110 Stat. 1936 (1996) (codified as amended in various sections of the United States Code).

80. Id., §§ 701(b)(1)(B) and 702(a)(1)(F).

81. In the summer of 1997 the Department of Health and Human Services suggested a number of weaknesses in HIPAA, and called for new legislation to impose restrictions on rate setting and to secure privacy and confidentiality of genetic information. HHS Report.

82. David Gollaher, "The Paradox of Genetic Privacy," *New York Times,* Jan. 7, 1998.

83. Pokorski, "Use of Genetic Information," pp. 103–4.

84. Natowicz, Alper, and Alper, "Genetic Discrimination," p. 469 (discussing cases).

85. Blanck and Marti, "Attitudes, Behavior," pp. 375–80.

86. Marc Lappe, "Ethical Issues in Testing for Differential Sensitivity to Occupational Hazards," *Journal of Occupational Medicine* 25 (11) (Nov. 1983): 798.

87. AMA, "Use of Genetic Testing by Employers," p. 1829.

88. Marc Lappe, "The Predictive Power of the New Genetics," *Hastings Center Report* 14 (5) (Oct. 1984): 20.

89. See Madison Powers, "Justice and Genetics: Privacy Protection and the Moral Basis of Public Policy," in *Genetic Secrets: Protecting Privacy and Confidentiality in the Genetic Era,* ed. Mark A. Rothstein (New Haven, Conn.: Yale University Press, 1997), p. 360 (discussing the tension between individual rights and workplace safety from the standpoint of genetic privacy).

90. See Marne E. Brom, "Insurers and Genetic Testing: Shopping for That Perfect Pair of Genes," *Drake L. Rev.* (1990/1991): 138 (discussing OTA report).

91. House Educ. and Labor Comm., H.R. Rep. No. 485, 101st Cong., 2d Sess., 51, reprinted in 1990 *U.S.C.C.A.N.* 303, 356 (hereafter House Report).

92. 29 C.F.R. § 1630.2(r) (1997).

93. Natowicz, Alper, and Alper, "Genetic Discrimination," p. 469.

94. AMA, "Use of Genetic Testing by Employers," p. 1829.

95. *Matter of State Division of Human Rights, City of New York (Granelle),* 70 N.Y.2d 100, 510 N.E.2d 799, 800–801 (1987).

96. House Report, p. 356.

97. Lappe, "Ethical Issues in Testing," p. 800.

98. Id. (various places); see Lawrence O. Gostin, "The Americans with Disabilities Act and the U.S. Health System," *Health Affairs* (Fall 1992): 249–56 (discussing communicable disease powers under the ADA).

99. *Ross v. Beaumont Hosp.,* 687 F. Supp. 1115 (E.D. Mich. 1988) (decided under the Rehabilitation Act).

100. *Scoles v. Mercy Health Corp. of Southeastern Pa.,* 887 F. Supp. 765 (E.D. Pa. 1994).

101. *Fussell v. Georgia Ports Authority,* S.D. Ga., 906 F. Supp. 1561, affd., 106 F.3d 417 (1995).

102. *Huber v. Howard County, Md.,* 849 F. Supp. 407, 414–15 (D. Md. 1994).

103. IOM Report, p. 11.

104. 42 U.S.C. § 12101(a)(1) (West 1995).

105. C. Thomas Caskey, "DNA-Based Medicine: Prevention and Therapy," in *The Code of Codes: Scientific and Social Issues in the Human Genome Project,* ed. Daniel J. Kevles and Leroy Hood (Cambridge, Mass.: Harvard University Press, 1992), pp. 114–15.

Chapter XII

Occupational Injuries among Workers with Disabilities

CRAIG ZWERLING, NANCY L. SPRINCE, CHARLES S.
DAVIS, ROBERT B. WALLACE, PAUL S. WHITTEN,
AND STEVEN G. HEERINGA

Introduction

As we begin the new millennium, we can expect that a larger percentage of the United States workforce will consist of workers with a wide variety of disabilities—both because of the aging of the workforce and because of the impact of the Americans with Disabilities Act (ADA).

Over the next decades, our workforce will age significantly as the baby boomers—born between 1946 and 1964—reach their fifties and sixties. The Bureau of Labor Statistics predicts that the mean age of the workforce will increase from 37 in 1992 to 41 in 2005.[1] From 1994 to 2005, the number of working men between 55 and 64 years of age will increase by 43 percent; in that same age group, the number of working women will increase by 63 percent.[2] Most likely, many of these workers will bring significant limitations to the workplace. For example, the 1988 Current Population Survey suggests that 6.9 percent of workers between 55 and 64 years of age have a medical impairment that limits their work in some way.[3]

In addition to the aging of the workforce, the implementation of the ADA can be expected to increase the number of workers with disabilities in the workforce. Passed in 1990, the ADA requires that all employers with fifteen or more employees make reasonable accommodations to allow otherwise qualified workers with disabilities to participate in the workforce. Although there are not yet sufficient data to monitor the impact of this law, one would expect that it

315

would enable some workers with disabilities to enter the workplace for the first time and that it would allow older workers with increasing impairment to remain in the workforce rather than choose disability retirement.

In view of the increasing numbers of workers with disabilities expected in the workforce, we should pay some attention to the performance of these workers and to their risk for occupational injuries. Descriptive studies have suggested that these workers are very productive and that the accommodations they require are usually not costly.[4] However, analytic studies have suggested that these workers may have increased risk for occupational injuries.[5]

In a case-control study of 300 Dutch shipyard workers and 300 matched controls, Moll van Charante and Mulder found that those workers with a greater than 20-decibel hearing loss had an increased odds ratio of 1.90 (95 percent confidence interval 1.64–2.21) of occupational injury. The risk was highest for those workers whose jobs were otherwise the least hazardous with an odds ratio of 3.25 (1.45–7.31). They noted that the workers with increased hearing loss were not at increased risk for injury in the loudest parts of the shipyard, presumably because no one could hear in those parts of the yard. Elsewhere, they suggested that the workers with better hearing were better able to protect themselves from injury.

In a case-control study of 154 postal workers with low back injuries and 942 unmatched controls, Zwerling, Ryan, and Schootman found that workers with a previous history of a disability certified by the Veterans Administration had an increased risk of back injury, with an odds ratio of 2.90 (1.88–4.48). Those with previous disabilities of the back had the highest risk of subsequent back injuries with an odds ratio of 4.16 (1.28–13.52), but those with other disabilities had elevated odds ratios as well—lower extremities, 2.48 (1.27–4.84); upper extremities, 2.07 (0.76–5.65); psychiatric, 2.53 (1.12–5.70); and other, 1.93 (1.06–3.51).

Although these results were limited to specific industries, they are suggestive of a problem. To further explore this issue, we undertook a series of secondary analyses of national databases to ascertain whether or not workers with disabilities are at elevated risk for occupational injuries. These analyses studied the association between self-reported disabilities and occupational injuries. As described below, we sometimes focused on self-reported work disabilities and other times considered more specific self-reported impairments such as blindness and deafness.

Health and Retirement Study

COHORT

The Health and Retirement Study (HRS) is a prospective cohort study of a nationally representative sample of Americans who, at the time of enrollment, were between 51 and 61 years of age. It was designed and carried out by the Institute for Social Research at the University of Michigan to assess the relations between health, economic factors, and retirement.[6] Over forty-five weeks beginning in April 1992, the HRS selected a multistage area probability sample of the continental United States. Blacks and Hispanics were oversampled in order to allow precise estimates of health outcomes in those minority communities. Of the 9,756 subjects aged 51 to 61, we focused on the 7,089 who were employed in the year previous to the injury and, therefore, were at risk for occupational injuries.[7] Since preliminary analyses had suggested that farmers had patterns of risk different from the rest of the population, we excluded the 235 farmers from this analysis.[8]

VARIABLES

The outcome variable, occupational injuries, was measured by the question: "During the last 12 months, that is since [month] of 1991, have you had any injuries at work that required medical attention or treatment or interfered with your work activities?" No further information was obtained concerning the nature, severity, or circumstances of the injury. The study did inquire about the number of occupational injuries in the last year and about the date of the most recent injury.

Because of the cross-sectional design of this study, we evaluated two potential groups of risk factors. First, we considered those risk factors that were likely to have preceded the injuries and might be considered risk factors for occupational injury. Anyone who reported an impairment or health condition that limited their ability to work was considered disabled and compared to the others. Data were also available on specific sensory impairments. Those whose hearing, even with a hearing aid, was poor or fair were compared to others and those whose sight, even with glasses, was poor or fair were compared to others. In addition, we considered seven occupational categories: executives, managers, and professionals; sales personnel; administrative support; service personnel; mechanics and repairers; operators and assemblers; and laborers. We compared those whose work required heavy lifting all or most of the time to the others; those who were self-employed to those who worked for others; and those whose work required good vision to others.

We also considered a second group of potential risk factors for which we could not be sure whether they had preceded the occupational injury and should be evaluated as risk factors or whether they were consequences of the injury. Those whose annual income was \$44,000 or greater were compared to the others. The 30 percent with the most depressive symptoms on the modified scale CES-D[9] were compared to the other 70 percent. Those who reported some difficulty with the specific tasks, getting up after sitting, stooping, pushing large objects, lifting 10 pounds, walking one block, and walking several blocks, were compared with those who had no difficulty with the specific task. Those who reported that their health was worse than it had been a year earlier were compared with those whose health was reported the same or better. Those who reported that their emotional health was fair or poor were compared with the others. Those who reported that they were somewhat or very dissatisfied with their house, neighborhood, health, finances, friendships, marriage, job, family life, or life overall were compared with those who were more satisfied with these life circumstances.

ANALYTIC STRATEGY

First, we evaluated the univariate associations of having had an occupational injury with the potential risk factors. Second, using a modeling strategy following Higgins and Koch,[10] we developed a logistic regression model to show the association of occupational injuries with the potential predictors that preceded the injury. We began this model with occupation because both the literature and our preliminary analyses suggested its importance as a risk factor for occupational injury. We chose subsequent variables using the Mantel-Haenszel chi-square statistics, divided by their degrees of freedom, as measures of the relative importance of variables in the multivariate relationship. The variable with the highest chi-square was chosen next. Then we recalculated the associations with the remaining variables, stratifying by those already in the model. We repeated this iterative process until no remaining variable was associated with occupational injury at a level of significance of $P < 0.1$. We then fit these variables in a logistic regression model using a backward elimination process that eliminated variables that did not contribute at a level of $P > 0.05$. Third, starting with this logistic regression model developed from risk factors that clearly preceded the occupational injuries, we added individually the other potential risk factors for which the temporal sequence was not clear. In order to account for the complex structure of the HRS sampling design, we used SUDAAN to calculate the standard errors.[11]

RESULTS

In this cross-sectional analysis, we examined two separate models, one to assess the risk for occupational injury associated with the general disability variable and a second to assess the risk associated with poor hearing and poor sight. We found that even after controlling for occupation, jobs requiring heavy lifting, self-employment, and jobs requiring good vision, there was an elevated odds ratio indicating an association between having a disability and subsequent occupational injury: odds ratio 2.15 (95 percent confidence interval 1.45–3.20). Replacing disability with specific sensory impairments, we found associations between occupational injury and poor hearing, odds ratio 1.60 (1.11–2.30) as well as between occupational injury and poor sight, odds ratio 1.53 (1.11–2.09).

Discussion

These data suggest that the associations between preexisting disabilities and occupational injuries may extend beyond the shipyards and postal service to other American industries, at least among older workers. This cross-sectional study was based on a nationally representative sample of older American workers. The study had a response rate of 82 percent, supporting its generalizability. However, this study has two major limitations. First, it was a cross-sectional study. The data on the risk factors were collected at the same time as the data on the outcomes raising the possibility of recall bias. It is possible that either the presence of an occupational injury may have increased the likelihood that a worker remembered a preexisting disability or the presence of a preexisting disability may have increased the likelihood that a worker remembered an occupational injury. Second, the study was limited to older workers and the results might not apply to younger workers. To address this first concern, we attempted to validate our models using data from the second wave of HRS interviews.

Health and Retirement Study — Two-Year Follow-up

COHORT

In order to study the retirement process, the HRS was designed to follow its cohort prospectively over the years. Thus, between April and December of

1994, the HRS carried out telephone follow-up interviews with its original cohort. Of our original cohort described above, 5,600 subjects (82 percent) participated in the second interview and had worked either full or part time between the two interviews.[12]

VARIABLES

As an outcome variable, we used a history of "any injuries at work that required special medical attention or treatment or interfered with [the subject's] work activities" since the time of the previous interview.

ANALYTIC STRATEGY

Our analysis was designed to validate the models formulated in the cross-sectional study. First, we calculated the univariate associations between the risk factors measured in the first HRS interview and the injury outcome measured in the second interview. Second, we calculated the two models from our cross-sectional study using the risk factor data from the first interview and the injury outcome data from the second interview. The first model included the following risk factors: occupation, a job requiring heavy lifting, a job requiring good vision, self-employment, and self-reported work disability. The second model replaced the general disability variable with more specific measures of sensory impairment— poor vision and poor hearing.

RESULTS

In both models, the pattern of risk factors in the prospective study was very similar to what we had found in the cross-sectional study. The association between occupational injury and a preexisting work disability was still present but somewhat weaker with an odds ratio of 1.58 (1.14–2.19) compared with an odds ratio of 2.15 in the cross-sectional study. The associations of injury with poor hearing and poor sight were also weaker with odds ratios of 1.35 (0.95–1.93) and 1.45 (0.94–2.22), respectively. Again, these results controlled for occupation, heavy lifting, self-employment, and work requiring good vision.

DISCUSSION

These prospective data lend support to the models developed in the cross-sectional study. In particular, they make recall bias a less likely explanation of the findings because the disability data were collected before the injuries took place and, therefore, could not be influenced by the injury history. However, we still cannot rule out the possibility that workers with disabilities were more likely to report their injuries than were their colleagues without disabilities.

The prospective study may well be subject to misclassification bias that would lead to underestimation of the strength of the association between disability and occupational injury. It is possible that the risk factor changed before the injury occurred. For example, the worker's hearing may have improved because of a new hearing aid or it may have been worsened by disease. Such random misclassification usually leads to an underestimation of the strength of the association. To evaluate the magnitude of this bias, we recalculated the models for those whose hearing and vision did not change over the two years of follow-up, controlling for occupation, heavy lifting, and self-employment. We found no increase in the association of poor sight with occupational injury with an odds ratio of 1.51 (1.00–2.29) compared to 1.52 (0.88–2.63), but substantial increase in the association between poor hearing and occupational injury from 1.40 (1.00–1.97) to 1.91 (1.31–2.80). These results suggest that misclassification bias may have reduced the estimate of the risk associated with poor hearing by more than 50 percent.

National Health Interview Survey — Older Workers

COHORT

To further validate the association between occupational injuries and preexisting work disabilities, we used a second national database — the National Health Interview Survey (NHIS). Each week, the U.S. Bureau of the Census, acting under the direction of the National Center for Health Statistics, interviews a probability sample of the noninstitutionalized population of the United States. The results of these interviews are published annually. The household interviews cover a wide variety of health questions, which are repeated annually. In addition, in 1994, the NHIS contained a disability supplement which included a variety of questions on disabilities and impairments.[13] To validate our previous work, we looked at the 7,530 participants in the 1994 NHIS who were between the ages of 51 and 61 years and who reported that "working" was their primary activity in the year preceding the interview.

VARIABLES

Our main outcome variable in this study was the occurrence of at least one occupational injury in the year preceding the interview. The NHIS defined an injury as any condition with an injury code (800–999) in the ninth edition of the International Classification of Diseases.[14] The injury was considered to have occurred "at work" if the injured person was working at a job or business when the injury occurred. The NHIS tallied only those injuries that required medical care or a decrease in normal activities for at least one day in the two weeks preceding the interview. This contrasted with the HRS that counted all occupational injuries over the last year preceding the interview whether or not any activity restriction persisted in the last two weeks.

To validate our previous analysis, we considered all of the variables from that analysis which were also available in the NHIS.[15] These included occupation in seven categories, self-employment, self-reported disability, self-reported visual impairment even while wearing corrective lenses, and self-reported auditory impairment even while using a hearing aid. Two HRS variables—"job requires good sight" and "job requires heavy lifting"—were not available in the NHIS. In addition, the NHIS hearing and visual impairments were more serious than those in the HRS. The NHIS considered "*serious* difficulty seeing, even when wearing glasses" (emphasis in the original) and "trouble hearing what is said in normal conversation (even when wearing a hearing aid)." In contrast, when we analyzed the HRS, we compared those with "fair" or "poor" eyesight or hearing (even while wearing corrective lenses or a hearing aid) to those with better eyesight or hearing.

ANALYTIC STRATEGY

First, we recalculated the HRS model leaving out the two variables that were not included in the NHIS and compared the parameter estimates and confidence intervals of this new model with those from our original HRS model. Second, we calculated the logistic regression model using the NHIS data and compared the parameter estimates and confidence intervals with those obtained previously using HRS data. Third, to assess the injury risk associated with all impairments, rather than just with sensory impairments, we recalculated the model, replacing the visual and auditory impairments with a more general report of preexisting work disability.

RESULTS

Respecifying the HRS model to exclude the job requirements of heavy lifting and good vision that were not asked in the NHIS significantly increased the importance of occupation in predicting injuries.[16] The heavy lifting occupations such as laborer became much stronger predictors of injury. However, the parameter estimates for self-employment, poor vision, and poor hearing changed very little — less than 10 percent.

Although the NHIS and the HRS had similar cohort sizes, 7,530 and 6,370, respectively, the NHIS cohort contained only 54 injured workers compared with 344 in the HRS cohort because of the more restrictive definition of injury. Similarly, the NHIS cohort contained 143 workers with visual impairments and 380 with auditory impairments compared with 649 with visual impairments and 837 with auditory impairments in the HRS. These numbers imply that the standard errors of the NHIS model will be greater than those of the HRS model and that the power of that cohort will be less than the power of the HRS cohort.

A comparison of the HRS and NHIS models shows this to be the case. Controlling for occupation and self-employment, we found that, in the NHIS, poor hearing was associated with occupational injury with an odds ratio of 1.81 (0.74–4.41), compared with 1.55 (1.08–2.23) in the HRS. Poor vision was associated with occupational injury with an odds ratio of 2.42 (0.77–7.60), compared with 1.48 (1.07–2.06) in the HRS. When we replaced the sensory impairment variables with a more general work disability variable, we found that, in the NHIS cohort, it was associated with occupational injury with an odds ratio of 1.84 (0.68–4.95), compared with 2.01 (1.35–2.98) in the HRS.

DISCUSSION

Even though the NHIS cohort had less power than the HRS cohort did, the fact that the pattern of risk factors is similar in both groups lends additional support to the association between occupational injuries and preexisting disabilities. This validation carries additional weight because it uses data from the NHIS's nationally representative sample of Americans with a 94.1 percent participation rate.

National Health Interview Survey — All Ages

COHORT

To generate a larger cohort with a wider age range, we combined the NHIS samples from 1985 to 1994. Over this period, the NHIS had used the same multistage probability design to sample the civilian, noninstitutionalized population of the United States. Our analysis considered the 459,827 NHIS participants from 1985 to 1994 who were from 18 to 65 years of age, who responded that work was their major activity in the last year, and who had occupations other than farming.[17] We excluded those over 65 because they made up less than 3 percent of our cohort, precluding separate analysis. In addition, we excluded 11,062 farmers because previous work had shown that their risk factors for occupational injury differed from other workers.[18]

VARIABLES

Our outcome variable was the occurrence of at least one injury at work within the last year that caused a residual limitation on the subject's ability to work in the two weeks preceding the interview. Thus, we included both those who had severe injuries with lasting sequelae as well as those with less severe but more recent injuries.

Subjects who reported that they had an impairment or health problem that kept them from working or limited the kind or amount of work they could do and who stated that this impairment had begun at least one year prior to the interview were considered to have a disability and compared to those with no disabilities. In addition, about one-sixth of the subjects were asked about certain specific impairments: visual impairment, hearing impairment, back conditions, upper and lower extremity conditions, diabetes, epilepsy, and arthritis. Those who reported having the condition for at least one year were compared with those who were asked about the condition and denied having it. For blindness and deafness, the respondents often noted the conditions even though they were not specifically asked about them. Here we compared those who reported blindness or deafness to those who did not.

We grouped occupation in seven categories and compared the self-employed to those with employers. For age, we compared the youngest (18 to 31) and middle (32 to 43) terciles to the oldest tercile (44 to 65).

ANALYTIC STRATEGY

We estimated the association between occupational injury and preexisting disability controlling for occupation, self-employment, and age.

RESULTS

We found elevated odds ratios for associations between occupational injuries and a variety of conditions: work disability, 1.36 (1.19–1.56); blindness, 3.21 (1.32–7.85); deafness, 2.19 (1.17–4.12); hearing impairment, 1.55 (1.29–1.87); upper extremity impairment, 1.46 (1.05–2.05); and arthritis, 1.34 (1.07–1.68).

DISCUSSION

Although not immune from recall bias, this large retrospective cohort study lends further support to the hypothesis that workers with a range of disabilities are at increased risk for occupational injuries.

Conclusions

Taken together, these four studies, using different methodologies and two different, nationally representative databases, strongly support the hypothesis suggested by previous work — workers with a range of disabilities are at increased risk for occupational injuries. Still, there are several major issues that are not resolved.

First, neither of these databases contains detailed information on the severity of the occupational injuries. Thus, it is possible that workers with disabilities were at increased risk for minor injuries but not for more serious injuries. Alternatively, workers with disabilities might be at increased risk only for the most serious injuries. These two scenarios would have very different health and economic consequences. Unfortunately, our databases could not distinguish between the alternative scenarios.

Second, even using large national data sets, it is difficult to distinguish the risks associated with specific disabilities. In each of these studies, the categories of impairment were very broad and it is certainly possible that some specific impairments are associated with an increased risk of injury while others are not. When we attempt to focus on specific impairments, such as blindness and deafness, confidence in our results is clouded by small numbers, even when we use a cohort of almost half a million drawn from ten years of the NHIS.

Third, all our measures of disability were self-reported. It is possible that some workers with impairments that were well accommodated in the workplace did not report any limitations on their ability to work. In addition, these self-reported impairments and disabilities might not correlate well with disabilities and impairments defined by specific laws and administrative regulations. For example, people who were legally blind might not report themselves as blind.

Fourth, none of our studies control for the provision of adequate accommodations in the workplace. Most American workplaces are designed to be used by male workers of average size who have no particular impairments.

Often, these workplaces cannot be used safely by workers with specific impairments. The Americans with Disabilities Act mandates that employers provide "reasonable accommodations" to all "qualified workers" with disabilities. One would expect that effective workplace accommodations would enable workers with impairments to function more safely in the workplace. But none of our studies controlled for the presence of effective accommodations.

Our research suggests the need for further study of the accommodation of impairments in the workplace. Currently, we don't know what proportion of workers with disabilities need or receive accommodations. We don't know what types of accommodations are provided. And we don't know how these accommodations vary in different industries and for workers with different skills and different disabilities. Two of the papers in this volume (Baldwin; Chirikos) begin to address these issues.

Some might try to use our data to justify excluding workers with disabilities from the workplace. We do not believe such exclusion appropriate for at least four reasons. First, from a legal perspective, such blanket exclusion would likely not be defensible under the Americans with Disabilities Act, which requires that decisions to deny employment because a worker is a direct threat to his own health and safety be based "on an individualized assessment of the individual's present ability" to perform the job, not "merely because of a slightly elevated risk."[19] Second, from a public health perspective, although an odds ratio of 1.36 corresponds to a 36 percent increased risk of occupational injury among workers with disabilities, it may be of less practical significance. If we assume a 10 percent prevalence of disabilities in the workforce, only 3.5 percent of occupational injuries would be explained by prior disability.[20] Third, from a social perspective, excluding workers with disabilities from the workforce will tend to increase welfare costs. Fourth, from an ethical perspective, if a qualified worker with a disability can work with reasonable accommodations, excluding that worker from the workforce is just plain wrong.

Notes

1. H. N. Fullerton, "Another Look at the Labor Force: The American Workforce, 1992–2005," *Monthly Labor Rev.* 16 (1993): 31–40.

2. H. N. Fullerton, "The 2005 Labor Force: Growing, but Slowly," *Monthly Labor Rev.* 118 (1995): 29–44.

3. L. E. Kraus and S. Stoddard, *Chartbook on Work Disability in the United States* (Washington, D.C.: U. S. National Institute on Disability and Rehabilitation Research, 1991).

4. P. D. Blanck, *Communicating the Americans with Disabilities Act, Transcending Compliance: 1996 Follow-up Report on Sears, Roebuck and Co.* (Iowa City, Iowa, 1996).

5. A. W. Moll van Charante and P. G. W. Mulder, "Perceptual Acuity and the Risk of Industrial Accidents," *Am. J. Epidemiol.* 131 (1990): 652–64; and C. Zwerling, J. Ryan, and M. Schootman, "A Case–Control Study of Risk Factors for Industrial Low Back Injury: The Utility of Preplacement Screening in Defining High-Risk Groups," *Spine* 18 (1993): 1242–47.

6. F. T. Juster and R. Suzman, "An Overview of the Health and Retirement Study," *J. Human Res.* 30S (1995): S7–S56.

7. C. Zwerling et al., "Risk Factors for Occupational Injuries among Older Workers: An Analysis of the Health and Retirement Study," *Am. J. Public Health* 86 (1996): 1306–9.

8. C. Zwerling et al., "Occupational Injuries among Agricultural Workers 51 to 61 Years Old: A National Study," *J. Agricultural Safety Health* 1 (1995): 273–81.

9. L. S. Radloff, "The CES-D Scale: A Self-Report Depression Scale for Research in the General Population," *Appl. Psychological Meas.* 1 (1977): 385–401.

10. J. E. Higgins and G. G. Koch, "Variable Selection and Generalized Chi-Square Analysis of Categorical Data Applied to a Large Cross-sectional Occupational Health Survey," *Int. Stat. Rev.* 45 (1977): 51–62.

11. B. V. Shah et al., *SUDAAN User's Manual: Professional Software for Survey Data Analysis for Multi-Stage Sample Design. Release 6.30.1* (Research Triangle Park, N.C.: Research Triangle Institute, 1992).

12. C. Zwerling et al., "Occupational Injuries among Older Workers with Disabilities: A Prospective Study of the Health and Retirement Survey, 1992 to 1994," *Am. J. Public Health* 88 (1998): 1691–95.

13. P. F. Adams and M. A. Marano, "Current Estimates from the National Health Interview Survey, 1994," National Center for Health Statistics. *Vital Health Statistics* 10:193.

14. World Health Organization, *Manual of the International Statistical Classification of Diseases, Injuries, and Causes of Death, Based on the Recommendations of the Ninth Revision Conference, 1975* (Geneva: World Health Organization).

15. Zwerling et al., "Risk Factors for Occupational Injuries among Older Workers."

16. C. Zwerling et al., "Occupational Injuries among Older Workers with Visual, Auditory, and Other Impairments," *J. Occup. Environmental Med.* 40 (1998): 720–23.

17. C. Zwerling et al., "Occupational Injuries among Workers with Disabilities: The National Health Interview Survey, 1985–94," *JAMA* 278 (1997): 2163–66.

18. Zwerling et al., "Occupational Injuries among Agricultural Workers."

19. Equal Employment Opportunity Commission, *A Technical Assistance Manual on the Employment Provisions (Title 1) of the Americans with Disabilities Act* (Washington, D.C.: Equal Employment Opportunity Commission, 1992), p. B-28.

20. N. E. Breslow and N. E. Day, *Statistical Methods in Cancer Research, I: The Analysis of Case-Control Studies* (Lyon, France: International Agency for Research on Cancer, 1980), p. 74.

Chapter XIII

Assistive Technology in the Workplace and the Americans with Disabilities Act

HEIDI M. BERVEN AND PETER DAVID BLANCK

I. Introduction

The Americans with Disabilities Act (ADA) has been criticized for supposed economic inefficiencies it imposes on markets, for instance, by requiring physical modifications to the working environment, and by requiring employers and covered entities to accommodate individuals with disabilities (Blanck, this volume). Without strong support from research, critics continue to argue that the economic costs outweigh the economic benefits of ADA compliance. Some assert that the costs of hiring, accommodating, and retaining workers with disabilities exceed accrued individual or societal benefits. Although the assertion is insufficiently supported by hard data, criticisms of the ADA rooted in cost-benefit rhetoric are frequent (Schwochau and Blanck 1999).

Estimating the costs and benefits of ADA implementation remains a difficult undertaking (Baldwin, this volume; Chirikos, this volume). In studying the implementation of the ADA, one of our objectives has been to examine some of the unforeseen economic implications of the ADA at the time of the law's enactment. The research summarized in this chapter focuses on one such measurable benefit of the ADA: the stimulation of economic activity in the assistive technology market (Bowe 1995).

Assistive technology (AT) is "any item, piece of equipment or product system whether acquired commercially off the shelf, modified, or customized that is used to increase or improve functional capabilities of individuals with disabilities" (Technology-Related Assistance for Individuals with Disabilities Act,

P.L. 103-218). AT devices include motorized and customized wheelchairs; augmentative communication devices; vehicle modifications; computer equipment; assistive listening devices; home modifications; work-site modifications; and classroom modifications (Cook and Hussey 1996; Galvin and Scherer 1996; Scherer 1996). AT can be anything from simple tools with no moving parts to sophisticated mechanical or electronic systems. AT that can be used by everyone is referred to as universal design. AT for the aging population is called transgenerational design.

There is a strong tie between the goals of the ADA and the development and provision of AT goods and services. The ADA seeks to remove the physical barriers that hinder the inclusion of persons with disabilities in employment and other social contexts. One of the law's goals is to make society's physical environment accessible to people with disabilities as they affirm their civil rights and pursue educational and employment goals. For many persons with mild and severe disabilities, AT plays a fundamental role in support of this mandate.

This chapter discusses the ways in which the economic market for AT may be the context of effective ADA implementation. It describes an ongoing study of patent data from the United States Patent and Trademark Office (PTO) that examines how the ADA may be fostering innovation and economic opportunity for AT developers, manufacturers, and retailers. The findings suggest that evaluations of the ADA based on its perceived costs to society need to be balanced by the full range of societal benefits accruing from the law, including those unanticipated economic benefits presented here.

The chapter is divided into several parts. Part II overviews the provisions of the ADA and related legislative initiatives that are aimed at making the physical environment accessible to persons with disabilities. Part III examines the role that the ADA has played in fostering innovation and commercial activity in the AT market and discusses the results of the patent study. Part IV considers emerging policy implications for ADA stakeholders: AT inventors and producers, employers, and people with disabilities.

II. Assistive Technology Use in the United States

Persons with disabilities historically have played the role of the "other," facing discrimination and barriers to inclusion and participation (Golledge and Stimson 1997). In chapter 14, Marti and Blanck discuss the attitudinal barriers facing persons with mental illness in employment settings. Other contributors to this volume have discussed economic (Blanck, Chirikos, Baldwin), legal (Wilkinson and Frieden, Willborn), and cultural (Baynton, Walz and Boucher) obstacles that continue to disempower persons with disabilities. To this list must be added barriers found in the physical environment — in schools, workplaces, malls, public transportation, and other components of urban and rural environments.

For people with mobility impairments, the barrier might be a door with a round handle rather than a lever, or sidewalks without curb cuts. For people with visual or hearing impairments, the obstacles may exist in accessing and using telecommunications services. Blind people continue to experience limited use of the Internet (Blanck 2000). People who are deaf may have inadequate access to telephone services.

The need for improved AT is becoming more critical, according to a 1994 survey conducted by the National Center for Health Statistics (NCHS) (Russell et al. 1997). The survey indicated that AT use is increasing in the United States. The survey estimated that over 17 million Americans used AT. Approximately 7.4 million used AT devices for mobility impairments; 4.6 million, for orthopedic impairments; 4.5 million, for hearing impairments; and .5 million, for vision impairments. The survey also found that there was a positive correlation between increasing age and the prevalence of device usage (Russell et al. 1997). This observed increase in AT use is due to the aging of the population, advances in technology, and the implementation of various disability rights initiatives.

Interest remains strong in tracking AT use for a number of reasons. First, health plans face financial incentives to control costs and limit the use of expensive services, and AT is usually less expensive to provide than managed care (Bristo, this volume). Second, as the number of persons needing AT grows, the AT industry will need more information about the diversity of AT consumers. Finally, federal laws like the ADA and related disability initiatives foster independence. They rely heavily on AT to help people with disabilities achieve their goals.

FEDERAL ASSISTIVE TECHNOLOGY MANDATES

The need to redesign the physical and information environment to improve accessibility and mobility for persons with disabilities has been the focus of a number of federal enactments. Congress first addressed the need to make society accessible to individuals with disabilities in the Architectural Free Barriers Act (P.L. 90-480). The need for AT goods and services was specifically addressed in the Rehabilitation Act of 1973 (P.L. 93-112). The act mandated reasonable accommodation and least restrictive environments in federally funded employment and higher education and required provision of AT devices and services to individuals with disabilities. The 1986 Amendments to the Rehabilitation Act (P.L. 99-506) required all states to include provision for AT services in plans for each disabled client and mandated equal access to all electronic equipment in federal workplaces.

The Education for All Handicapped Children Act of 1975 (EAHC) (P.L. 94-142) notes that AT plays a major role in gaining access to educational programs in applying the reasonable accommodation and least restrictive environment provision of the Rehabilitation Act to students aged 5-21 in education. The EAHC was modified to increase emphasis on educationally related AT and extended to infants and children up to 5 years old in the Handicapped Infants and Toddlers Act (P.L. 99-457).

The 1988 amendments to the Fair Housing Act focus on accessibility in residential settings by prohibiting renters or sellers of residential space from discriminating against persons on the basis of their disabilities. Under the act, owners of rental space must make reasonable accommodations in their rules and services and adopt accessible design standards and AT for new units to allow people with disabilities equal use opportunities. The standards include accessible light switches and thermostats as well as wheelchair-accessible bathrooms.

Finally, the Technology-Related Assistance for Individuals with Disabilities Act (Tech Act), amended in 1994, supports AT research and development initiatives and provides AT information and funding for persons with disabilities (P.L. 103-218). In passing the act, Congress noted that "[f]or some individuals with disabilities, assistive technology devices are necessary to enable the individuals to . . . have greater control over their lives."

THE ADA AND ASSISTIVE TECHNOLOGY

The ADA builds on and expands the reach of the laws mentioned above in mandating the removal of both physical and social barriers. The law prohibits discrimination against individuals with disabilities in employment settings (Title I) and in the provision of governmental services (Title II), public accommodations (Title III), and telecommunications (Title IV). The law was drafted to ensure flexibility in the implementation of accessibility and accommodation strategies. The regulations interpreting the law provide guidelines and specifications and suggest potential accommodations but do not mandate specific products or devices as accommodations.

Under ADA Title I, employers are charged with providing accommodations that are "reasonable." The reasonable accommodation requirement is a means by which physical, structural, and attitudinal barriers to the equal employment opportunities of individuals with disabilities are removed effectively and efficiently. The regulations interpreting the law identify a range of accommodations, but the obligation to accommodate does not extend to the provision of adjustments or modifications for personal use, such as eyeglasses or hearing aids. Accommodations that are reasonable may include workplace supports such as job coaching or the provision of AT devices such as computer screen magnifiers, sit-stand workstations, or ergonomic keyboards (Blanck 1998a, 1997, 1996).

Under ADA Title II, governmental and municipal entities are required to provide certain kinds of augmentative devices and services. Examples of auxiliary aids and services include telephone handset amplifiers, listening devices, assistive listening systems, telephones compatible with hearing aids, closed caption decoders, open and closed captioning, TDDs, videotext displays, taped texts, audio recordings, Brailled materials, and large print materials. The Department of Justice has emphasized that this list is not exhaustive, and to attempt to provide a complete list would omit devices that will become available through emerging technology.

Title III requires covered entities (places of public accommodation such as restaurants or theaters) to make reasonable modifications in policies, practices, or procedures when they are necessary to accommodate individuals with disabilities. Accommodations include providing auxiliary aids, as under Title II, and removing architectural barriers. Covered entities are charged with implementing available technologies that offer readily achievable solutions for people with limitations (e.g., Internet access), unless doing so would fundamentally alter the nature of the goods or services being offered or would pose an undue burden (Blanck 2000).

Title IV requires local and long-distance telephone companies to provide nationwide telephone relay services to individuals with hearing or speech impairments whose communication needs were not adequately addressed by earlier mandates. Title IV represents the culmination of fifty years of telecommunications legislation aimed at achieving universal service. Nationwide adoption of text telephone technology is central to the goals of Title IV. The goal of Title IV is to encourage the optimal use of existing communications technology for persons with disabilities and to avoid discouraging or impairing the development of improved technology.

III. Overview of the Present Study

Our focus was to examine the extent to which the regulatory shifts ascribed to the ADA may be creating economic opportunities for AT inventors and manufacturers—stakeholders not heretofore mentioned in the literature as beneficiaries of the law. We considered the question of whether the ADA was influencing inventive activity or patenting behavior among AT developers. To probe this issue, we examined patenting trends for AT at the United States Patent and Trademark Office (PTO).

BACKGROUND AND METHOD

Researchers use patent data and statistics to forecast technology trends and to probe innovation activity. In the aggregate, patents and patent statistics are employed as technology and economic indicators. Patent application rates provide one measure of the effectiveness of regulation at stimulating technology innovation. Patent data has been used to gauge the success of "technology-forcing" environmental laws (Gollin 1992; Stevens 1981).

Patents provide a snapshot of inventors and their inventions. They are primarily legal devices, however, whose purpose is to delineate the limits of an inventor's intellectual property rights. As a result, the relationship between patents and the inventions they are supposed to describe is limited (Israel and Rosenberg 1992). But patents are artifacts of how societies view and define the concept of invention. The way a patent describes or depicts a device may transcend legal significance by contributing to enhanced social or cultural understanding of inventors and inventions. How inventors describe AT devices, for example, is significant. Whether an inventor refers to a wheelchair as a "personal mobility device" (as did one inventor in U.S. Patent 4,570,739) or as an "invalid carriage" (as did another in U.S. Patent 4,798,255) reflects, to an extent, how society views and values people with disabilities.

The use of patent data and records to gauge AT development and knowledge diffusion about disability policy is unique. A term word-search strategy of the patent database, available through WestLaw or LEXIS, was adopted to identify relevant AT patents for use by individuals with mobility, hearing, and visual impairments. The search strategy is a variant of coword analysis, involving the assignment of words or keywords to papers or articles. Papers that have the same keywords or sets of words can be linked and mapped. The data may be used to understand how documents and researchers are related (Melkers 1988).

Within this set of AT patents, we next searched for references to federal disability rights legislation. Patentees might mention various laws to meet patentability standards, such as utility (or usefulness) and societal need (Chisum and Jacobs 1998). We found that reference to disability rights legislation in patents is rare, in contrast to the trends identified for environmental legislation, where a number of patents were identified that cite environmental legislation such as the Clean Air Act, the Clean Water Act, the National Environmental Protection Act (NEPA or EPA), and the Occupational Safety and Health Act (OSHA)) (Berven and Blanck 1998). No patents were found that referenced other disability enactments, including the Rehabilitation Act of 1973, the Architectural Free Barriers Act, or the Technology-Related Assistance for Individuals with Disabilities Act of 1994. One hundred twenty-five of the AT patents made direct reference to the ADA.

CORE FINDINGS

Several findings emerged from the study:

1. Assistive technology patent numbers have shown annual increases since 1976.
2. Reference to other civil rights legislation has been atypical of patent records. But from January 1990 until December 1997 the number of patents citing the ADA has increased substantially.
3. The inventors who acknowledge the ADA are a geographically diverse group, many unaffiliated with large corporations.
4. From 1990 to 1997, patents were granted for a wide range of assistive devices with uses for a wide array of consumers with disabilities.
5. Patentees are staking claims in patentable assistive technologies because of the promise of future economic benefits.

The core findings, discussed in greater detail in subsequent sections, suggest that ADA implementation is affecting the AT consumer market in economically positive ways and is creating profit-making opportunities for inventors and manufacturers in the sector. As the regulatory shifts imposed by the ADA expand the market for goods that improve accessibility, inventors and manufacturers appear to be responding rationally to the practical economic consequences of ADA implementation.

1. Increasing Assistive Technology Patenting Rate
The number of patents relating to the needs of consumers with disabilities is increasing. The annual number of patents for use by individuals with physical,

visual, or hearing impairments increased between 1975 and 1997. Figure 1 depicts this data by year. The number of patents relating to hearing impairments increased from about 12 in 1977 to 96 in 1997. Similarly, 4 patents relating to visual impairments issued in 1977, compared to almost 97 in 1997. Finally, 30 patents relating to physical impairments issued in 1977, as compared to 62 in 1997. Local patent number maxima occurred in 1977–78 and 1987–88. It is tempting, but possibly misleading, to compare the maxima to the passage of disability legislation or other factors.

Physical impairment patents increased from 118 during the 1976–80 time period to 250 during the 1991–95 time period, representing more than a twofold increase in the patenting rate. Visual impairment patents increased from 12 to 144 (a twelvefold increase in patenting rate) during the same interval. This was a period of advancement for text-to-speech technology. Hearing impairment patents increased from 38 to 270—more than a sevenfold increase. This result is not surprising, since this was a period of growth for hearing aid, text telephone, and cochlear implant technology.

Figure 1: Patents Issued between 1977 and 1995 Mentioning
Physical, Visual, or Hearing Impairments

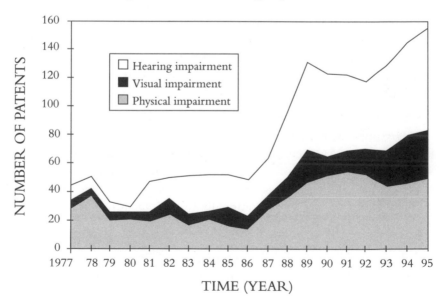

The patents identified by the search strategy were for devices relating to the special needs of people living with impairments. Among physical impairment patents is a new utensil handle more easily held by individuals with arthritis or multiple sclerosis (U.S. Patent 5,680,676). An eye-tracking system allows people without the use of their hands to interact with computers (U.S. Patent 5,481,622). The sensory impairment patents included TDDs (U.S. Patent 5,710,816), hearing aids (U.S. Patent 5,706,351), Braille readers (U.S. Patent 5,685,721), and computer icons (U.S. Patent 5,565,888).

Our observations are consistent with the results of the 1994 NCHS survey. For individuals with disabilities and other AT purchasers, an increasing rate in AT patenting activity well may indicate that design innovations and improvements will continue to characterize and drive market activity in the AT sector. A number of social and economic factors — most notably, those relating to changes in technology policy, technological advances, and consumer demand — might account for the increase. Scholars have argued that technology policy in the United States has shifted focus from industry innovation to technology innovation (Chiang 1993). This shift in focus may have already led to greater levels of innovation for a variety of industries that utilize similar technologies. The process of technological "spillover," from telecommunications and microelectronics technology, made advances in TDD technology possible.

Advances in various fields of technology may be another factor that contributes to the trend. The NCHS survey identified advances in microelectronics, microcomputers, and the development of new composite materials that have led to improved AT design, characterized by devices that are lighter, safer, stronger, easier to use, and, in some cases, less expensive. For example, microelectronic advances have been adopted in hearing aid and cochlear implant technology. More powerful microprocessing architectures have made the advent of text-to-speech machines like the Kurzweil Reader a reality. Finally, the wheelchair industry has moved away from traditional designs to lighter, faster frames by using new materials rather than stainless steel.

The NCHS survey noted that changes in the size and composition of the population have influenced AT use trends. To that end, the rate of device usage among persons aged 65 or older is four times the rate of the total population. Consistent with this finding, we found that patents for devices intended for use by older persons increased dramatically between 1975 and 1995.

2. Proof of Inventive Activity

We identified a number of patents that specifically mentioned the ADA within the assistive technology patent set. In total, 125 patents made direct reference to

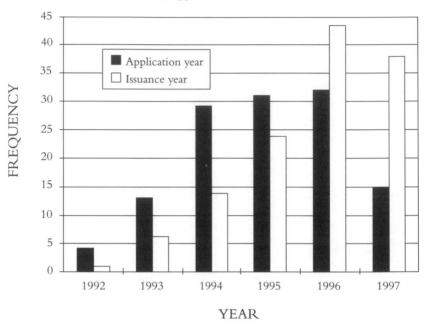

Figure 2: Patents Mentioning the ADA
Classified by Application and Issuance Year

YEAR

the ADA. Descriptive attributes for each of these patents were recorded in a spreadsheet and tabulated. Figure 2 indicates that the number of patents citing the ADA has increased annually since the law was passed in 1990.

Figure 2 records annual numbers of patents by application date and issuance date. Annual issuance numbers rose through 1996. A reduction of patent applications was recorded for the same time period, after maximum application years in 1994 and 1995.

Figure 3 depicts a classification scheme for the inventions. Most of the patents were for "general access" inventions—devices that would improve general accessibility for persons with disabilities in a variety of contexts.

"General access devices" cover a wide range of items and include personal care aids, eating utensils, bathroom fixtures, handrails, handicap-accessible door levers, modular ramps, and universally designed workstations. "Communication devices" include telecommunications components and Braille-coded

Figure 3: Patents Mentioning the ADA
Classified by Type

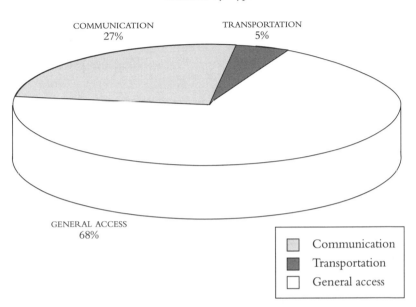

COMMUNICATION
27%

TRANSPORTATION
5%

GENERAL ACCESS
68%

☐ Communication
■ Transportation
☐ General access

signs, among others. "Transportation devices" include vehicle lifts and other mobility-related components. Individual inventors and corporate assignees accounted for approximately equivalent contributions to each category depicted in figure 3.

The AT-ADA patents are significant on a number of levels. At a minimum, the patentees were willing to go through the time and expense of seeking formal patent protection for their inventions. AT inventors initiated the patent process, perhaps because of the promise of future economic returns based on consumer demand.

On another level, the notion of "induced innovation" or "technology-forcing" that may be operative in the environmental context may be also operative in the disability patent context (Ashford 1994, 1985; Derzko 1996). Generally, innovation occurs because firms respond to consumer demands in the marketplace. In the case of environmental technology, the market for pollution control devices has been created artificially through government regulation. Provisions of the Clean Air Act, the Clean Water Act, the Occupational Safety and Health Act, and the Toxic Substances Control Act detailed incentives for corporate pollution control strategies. In these examples, regulatory shifts demanding compliance were intended to force technological innovation, both directly and through a series of tax incentives (Hamrin 1982).

Whether technology-forcing has encouraged innovation in pollution control technology remains a subject for debate. Studies suggest that regulations can have a positive impact on the process of innovation (Gollin 1992). This finding may extend to AT development. By invoking accommodation and accessibility requirements on covered entities, the ADA and supporting regulations expanded the market for new AT devices.

3. Diversity of Assistive Technology Inventors

For patents in general, over two-thirds of inventors assign their patent rights to their employers — usually corporate or academic entities. Yet individual inventors accounted for over half of the AT-ADA patents. Unfortunately, it was difficult to determine the identity of these entrepreneurs — whether, for instance, they had special knowledge about the needs of persons with disabilities because they or an acquaintance or family member needed AT because of a disability.

Generally, individuals working outside of corporate or university settings face more difficulty in commercializing their inventions. To foster commercialization of new AT, companies such as the Buffalo, New York–based Aztech help individual inventors bring their products to the marketplace. Aztech began as a collaborative effort between University of Buffalo researchers and the Center for Independent Living. To date, Aztech has helped nine inventors to license or commercialize their AT ideas (Drury 1998).

The lower proportion of corporate inventors might indicate a lack of interest in AT, perhaps because potential market growth and profitability are perceived to be limited. Yet some large corporations have identified new market opportunities that arose because of the ADA. For instance, 3-M holds a number of patents for making tactile signs for people who are blind or visually impaired. Schalge holds patents for door levers that can be manipulated by people with mobility impairments.

Other companies not part of the patent study are beginning to address the needs of computer and Internet consumers with sensory impairments. IBM, Microsoft, and Apple recently have expressed their commitment to improving accessibility for people with disabilities. For example, Apple incorporated "Mouse

Keys" in its Macintosh computers that allow users to move the cursor one pixel at a time in any direction. This feature allows individuals with mobility impairments to precisely position the mouse on the screen. The Mouse Key feature is an example of an accessible or universal design that has the added feature of increasing the functionality of users who are not disabled. In general, when products or environments are made more accessible to persons with disabilities, they become easier for everyone to use (Vanderheiden 1990).

In addition, a number of small firms have sprung up that specifically cater to the needs of consumers with disabilities. Estimates suggest that there are approximately two to three thousand businesses that manufacture assistive technology devices (Mraz 1992). Many of these are small operations or sole inventors, marketing a maximum of one or two devices. Some, like Henter-Joyce or LC Technologies, market computer technology exclusively for disabled consumers. Henter-Joyce has tripled its workforce since it was formed several years ago (Felton 1997). LC Technologies has recorded sharp increases in orders in the last six months. The market for some assistive technology products — for instance, for speech-to-text products — continues to grow. The market was projected to reach $410 million in 1997. It should exceed $4.3 billion by 2001.

4. Diversity of Assistive Technology Consumers

The AT-ADA patents were for devices designed to help persons with a range of impairments navigate home, office, and school environments. The inventions ranged from sit-stand stations to ergonomically designed disposable tableware to tactile sign displays and nonslip surfaces.

The results indicate that the ADA is helping inventors and manufacturers identify other potential consumers of AT besides people with disabilities. Prior to the passage and implementation of the ADA, persons with disabilities may have been considered the sole direct consumers for AT. The elderly and the chronically ill are recognized as participating as direct consumers in the AT market (Wylde 1995a, 1995b).

After implementation of the ADA in 1992, employers, property owners, and municipal transport authorities became indirect AT consumers. Engineering trade journals and popular literature reflect an understanding of the implications of ADA implementation. Some view the ADA program of national accessibility compliance with the law as a potential source of profit (Mraz 1992; Henry 1993; Blackman 1991; Cutler 1993; Tompkins 1993; Waldrop 1990; Matthews 1997).

Because AT has strong ties to each ADA title and plays a critical role in achieving ADA goals, federal regulations requiring ADA compliance appear to be having a beneficial effect on AT purchasing by covered entities (Button and Wobschall 1994). Title I employers charged with providing accommodations have purchased a wide variety of work-related products, for instance. The effect of the ADA has thus been to encourage AT firms to innovate in order to compete in the Title I market. The flexibility of EEOC regulations and accommodation guidelines may be positively impacting the innovation process (Bowe 1995).

The effects of ADA passage also are noteworthy for entities covered by Titles II and III. As indicated in an earlier section, Department of Justice (DOJ) guidelines for Title II and III entities call for certain kinds of services but do not detail product specifications. Title III requires covered entities to implement available technologies that offer "readily achievable" solutions for people with limitations. The result has been to encourage the search for commercially viable technologies to meet Title III requirements. One author has noted that Title III has stimulated research in captioning technology for movie theaters — a full fifteen years after captioning technology was developed for television (Bowe 1995).

5. Promise of Economic Benefits for Assistive Technology Inventors

The present study documents a range of findings regarding AT inventors. First, inventors have successfully guided their inventions through the patent process. In many cases, they have carried them to the consumer market, where demand for assistive technology continues to grow. The "push-pull" of disability policy may be fostering the research initiatives of individual and corporate inventors. The regulatory "push" introduced by the ADA expanded the market for AT to include a range of consumer groups, including persons with disabilities, their employers, and other public, municipal, and governmental entities. At the same time, financial incentives (the "pull") provided research and development opportunities to AT inventors and producers.

The findings suggest that the patent system may not need to be modified to encourage AT patenting (Verzani 1995). AT patenting rates are not disproportionately small relative to general utility patenting rates. To the contrary, AT patenting appears to be increasing at a substantial rate. The data support the notion that the patent process is "working" for AT: inventors are patenting their inventions and marketing their goods.

IV. Emerging Policy Implications

A shortage of empirical data continues to hinder balanced evaluation of the ADA. The present study illustrates that a range of viewpoints from multiple disciplines are needed to gauge the successes and failures of ADA implementation and to correct prior conclusions regarding ADA cost-effectiveness that have been based on incomplete data or misinformation (Olsen 1997).

Taken with other factors, the ADA patenting data suggest that unanticipated economic benefits are accruing from the law. AT market growth is one positive economic benefit that heretofore has been overlooked by ADA critics. Inventors are attempting to meet the needs of AT consumers.

More and better AT does not necessarily mean greater participation for people with disabilities, however. Work remains in removing the societal and attitudinal barriers that individuals with disabilities still face. State and national policy initiatives must continue to support universal design technology strategies. Including individuals with disabilities in the assistive technology research and design process will lead to more user-friendly products. Funding and consumer protections also are needed for AT users.

THE ECONOMIC FEASIBILITY OF THE ADA

Unforeseen economic benefits are arising from ADA implementation. These include gains: (1) to AT inventors and producers as increased profits because of demand in the highly diversified and rapidly expanding AT market, and (2) to direct and indirect AT consumers (individuals with disabilities, the elderly, operators of public facilities, schools, and employers) who enjoy more choice and pay less for AT because of interfirm competition.

The law is generating economic benefits to other ADA stakeholders. Employers benefit economically by drawing on a largely untapped productive workforce. Taxpayers benefit when capable workers are taken off the welfare rolls. These direct and indirect economic benefits should be reflected in cost-benefit evaluations of the ADA.

1. Incorporating Unforeseen Economic Benefits in Title I
ADA Cost-Benefit Evaluations

Scholars argue that the economic costs of ADA implementation far outweigh economic benefits accruing to society (Blanck 1998a). This is particularly true for the ADA's Title I employment provisions. Title I seeks to ensure that "qualified individuals with disabilities" will have equal access to the job market, and, where appropriate, that employers provide reasonable accommodations to individual workers who can perform essential job functions.

Cost-benefit analysis has become the dominant method to evaluate a range of government programs and policies, including civil rights laws like the ADA. Using the method as a decision-making tool presents a number of shortcomings. In practice, it is not well suited to measure social policy effects, particularly those relating to quality of life factors. In addition, preexisting market imperfections are generally reflected in market-based cost-benefit estimates. Cost-benefit analysis also is subject to bias and politicization (Ashford and Caldart 1996).

These shortcomings are reflected in some judicially constructed evaluations of the ADA and its Title I. Some courts focus on a narrow range of cost-benefit factors, in the sense that they emphasize direct costs and benefits to employers rather than the full range of indirect costs and benefits. As applied to the "reasonable accommodation" provision found in ADA Title I, the cost-benefit scale adopted by some courts allows employers to weigh the direct costs of providing accommodations for qualified disabled individuals against the benefits associated with the accommodation (Fram 1997). For instance, in *Vande Zande v. Wisconsin Department of Administration,* the court concluded that the cost of accommodation should "not be disproportionate to the benefit."

Similarly, some courts apply the reasonableness standard to cost-benefit determinations in analyzing Title I "undue hardship" questions. Under Title I, covered entities are not required to provide accommodations that impose undue hardships. Employers invoking the Title I's undue hardship defense have argued that the costs of reasonable accommodations are too high relative to an employee's salary. By tying reasonableness to cost-benefit determinations, some courts potentially are opening the door to judicial interpretations of the ADA's undue hardship provision favoring employers who argue that accommodation costs should be limited by an employee's salary. This would make it easier for an employer to show that providing a high-tech, high-cost AT accommodation for a minimum wage worker poses an undue hardship.

This result would stand contrary to congressional intent behind the ADA. In passing the ADA, Congress considered and then rejected an amendment that would have placed a 10 percent ceiling on reasonable accommodation costs based on an employee's salary. The EEOC has stipulated that the employer's resources—not the employee's salary, position, or status in the company—determine the cost that must be spent on reasonable accommodations.

2. Benefits Accruing to Title I Stakeholders

The study indicates that patent and innovative activity are evidence of direct and indirect economic benefits accruing to AT inventors and consumers. For employers, the gains may include the addition of effective, productive employees to their workforce because of the adoption of AT and universal design strategies.

Yet some employers have been unwilling to make accommodations because of perceived or actual expense. They argue that the cost of supplying AT as an accommodation to a worker with a disability places financial burdens and administrative costs on business operations (Gostin and Beyer 1993). The costs of accommodations may be especially high for large employers who are held accountable for extensive modifications due to their greater financial resources (Barnard 1990; Chirikos, this volume). These arguments often are made without reliance on data.

The findings of the patent study suggest that ATs were typically "low tech," inexpensive, and represent "capital improvements" from which all employees may benefit. The low direct costs of accommodations for employees with disabilities have been shown to produce substantial economic benefits to companies, in terms of increased work productivity, injury prevention, reduced workers' compensation costs, and workplace effectiveness and efficiency (Blanck, this volume; Hall and Hall 1994).

One research group has found that a number of factors influence corporate willingness to adopt AT, universal design, and related accommodation strategies. In a study cosponsored by the U.S. Department of Education and the National Institute on Disability and Rehabilitation Research (NIDRR), the Trace Research Institute at the University of Wisconsin surveyed twenty-two companies about universal design implementation. The study found that corporate size is not predictive of universal design adoption, although firms subject to state or federal regulation like the ADA Title I are more likely to adopt accessibility and universal design strategies. Firms were also concerned about AT cost (Vanderheiden 1990).

This trend is also reflected in data collected from a series of studies conducted at Sears, Roebuck and Co. from 1978 to 1997 (Blanck 1996). Nearly all of the five hundred accommodations sampled at Sears required little or no cost. Effective accommodations included AT, improved physical access (such as closer parking spaces), changed schedules, assistance by others, and changed job duties (Daly and Bound 1996). During the years 1990 to 1997, the average direct cost for accommodations was less than $45.

Accommodations involving universally designed and advanced technology have been shown to enable groups of employees with and without disabilities to perform jobs productively, cost-effectively, and safely (Vanderheiden 1990). The studies at Sears suggest that the direct costs associated with many technologically based accommodations (e.g., computer voice synthesizers) enabled qualified employees with disabilities to perform essential job functions. These strategies created an economic "ripple effect" throughout the company (Blanck 1996).

The Sears findings suggest that the direct costs attributed to universally designed accommodations may be lower than predicted, particularly when their fixed costs are amortized over time (Blanck 1998b). They also suggest that the costs and benefits of workplace accommodation require continued examination in a number of contexts, including the type, effectiveness, and cost of accommodations at large and small organizations; the direct and indirect costs and benefits of accommodations; and accommodation patterns in the national aggregate (Blanck 1996).

REMOVING BARRIERS

AT plays a fundamental role in achieving the ADA's goal of reshaping employment, public accommodations, and public attitudes. Continuing to develop AT for home, school, and work will help abolish the physical and communication barriers facing many individuals with disabilities. Consistent with the 1994 NCHS survey, a recent report by the National Center on Disability concludes that as the population ages, state and national initiatives will need to continue to further the universal design of technology, particularly in the communications realm.

1. Legislative Initiatives

The Telecommunications Act of 1996 requires telecommunications equipment to be accessible to individuals with disabilities. Under the law, the Federal Communications Commission is required to issue accessibility guidelines for telecommunications equipment. The act mandates the continued development of telemedicine systems and services. Telemedicine programming will help meet the health care delivery needs and options of people with disabilities, particularly in rural areas (Blanck 1994c). Telemedicine relies on telecommunications for medical diagnosis and patient care.

The act also mandates the adoption of advanced telecommunications technology to improve the classroom experiences of students with and without disabilities. Electronic media, based in computer and video technology, can offer alternative access systems that have strong appeal to students, with and without disabilities (Blanck 1994c). Creating "schools without walls" using advanced telecommunications technology will help to prepare students with disabilities for employment.

To improve Internet access for people with disabilities, the Web Accessibility Initiative (WAI) was launched in early 1997 (Blanck 2000). In support of WAI goals, IBM and Sun Microsystems are developing software to make Java-based technology accessible to Internet users who are disabled. Microsoft has released technology that allows Windows applications to communicate with adaptive equipment, including screen readers.

2. AT Research and Development

Continued financial support of research and development is necessary to ensure improvements in AT design. A number of programs that foster AT development currently are in place. These include:

Consumer Assistive Technology Transfer Network (CATN). Funded by the National Institute on Disability and Rehabilitation Research (NIDRR), the program identifies linkages to resources for consumers regarding difficult-to-solve AT needs and problems. CATN also helps researchers and engineers to identify development and commercialization resources for AT prototypes and technology applications.

Rehabilitation Engineering Research Centers Program. The program is funded by the National Institute on Disability and Rehabilitation Research (NIDRR) and the U.S. Department of Education. The program focuses on research and development of new AT as well as information dissemination and educational activities.

NIDRR Utilization Projects. The programs support activities that will ensure that rehabilitation knowledge generated from projects and centers funded by the NIDRR will be utilized to improve the lives of individuals with disabilities.

NIDRR Tech Act Program. Funded by the NIDRR as part of the Technology-Related Assistance Act (Tech Act), the programs focus on improving public awareness, public access to information, funding for AT devices and services, training and technical assistance, and coordination of statewide activities.

National Science Foundation Programs. The National Science Foundation sponsors a number of programs focusing on people with disabilities.

3. Participatory Design Strategies

In the past, the social and historical context for disability was characterized by a dominant society that created a clear distinction between normal and abnormal. The abnormal identity could be subhuman, satanic/sinful, impaired/sick, or infantile, depending on the stereotype. Public officials may have employed stereotypes to deny AT resources. People with disabilities may have incorporated these stereotypes into their identities (Marti and Blanck, this volume). The technologies justified by disability stereotypes include life-ending technology, restraining technology, punishing technology, cure technology, medical technology, and simple and safe technology (Seelman 1993).

Technologies that are justified by disability stereotypes have been described in some patent disclosures, for example, U.S. Patent No. 851,851, issued in 1977 for "a preventive apron, used to control human sexual conduct, especially among the mentally retarded." The patentee equated mental retardation with sexual deviancy and violence in describing the invention:

> There are presently a large number of retarded people in the United States. The degree of mental retardation varies but there is a substantial number who have IQs in the range of idiot, moron, and imbecile. . . . It has been difficult to control the sexual conduct of such people in social settings. . . . The presence of such conduct is undesirable, and of course is disruptive when it occurs in a group setting, and can be dangerous when an individual is attacked by a retarded person.

Ultimately, if assistive technology devices are effective but carry the aura of stigma and thus create interpersonal barriers for the people who use them, they are design failures (Norman 1988).

Individuals with disabilities were excluded from the AT design process and usually found themselves dependent on public programs for decisions regarding technology. This may have actually impeded AT innovation (Scherer 1996; Galvin and Scherer 1996). In addition, dominant models and definitions of disability, based on medical, economic, and minority paradigms, characterized disability in the context of particular institutional systems and affected the design process. Each provided an incomplete picture of the meaning and consequences of disability (Seelman 1993).

Technology developers are attempting to incorporate social knowledge (i.e., the experiences of persons with disabilities) more frequently in their development practices prior to innovation and market establishment. Inventors like Raymond Kurzweil sought knowledge from blind readers early in the design process (Hauger 1995). The inclusion of persons with disabilities in the design process is a significant indicator of changing attitudes about disability and technology within engineering research and development sectors.

Historical disability models are giving way to less stigmatizing, more proactive variants. In the "human variation" model of disability, problems faced by disabled individuals are seen as a consequence of the failure of social institutions to consider the full range of variation within a population (Minaire 1992; Cook and Hussey 1996; Scotch and Schriner 1997; Seelman 1993). Thus, "individuals whose mobility, communication, medical needs, or cognition differ from social norms find themselves confronting institutions not well suited to their abilities and potential"(Scotch and Schriner 1997).

Viewing disability as an issue of human variation has contributed to improved AT design and practice. For instance, the Human Adaption Assistive Technology (HAAT) model tries to take into account social and cultural factors as well as environmental and physical conditions (Cook and Hussey 1996). The rise of human factors engineering and the development of universal and transgenerational design principles to meet the needs of an aging population have led to improved AT for persons with disabilities as well as the general population (Petroski 1991; Henry 1993; Mraz 1992).

4. Assistive Technology Funding

According to a 1992 needs survey, of the 2.5 million persons who had an unmet need for assistive technology, about 1.2 million persons were of working age (25–64) (LaPlante, Hendershot, and Moss 1992). Poor people were about twice as likely as nonpoor people to say they needed an AT device.

Consumers who can afford AT will continue to have a choice between different products and designs. For these individuals, a competitive assistive technology market should continue to lead to improved quality and lower prices. Individuals who live in poverty, including persons with disabilities, the elderly, and the chronically ill, are shadow consumers of advanced AT (Sheldon and Hager 1997).

Sources of funding for AT are inadequate. People who need and would benefit from AT often must self-finance or go without. This means that most individuals who live in poverty function without the benefit of AT. The fact that many must pay for their own assistive devices discloses the inadequacies of existing AT delivery systems, including third-party insurance carriers who refuse to cover assistive technology. Although the Technology-Related Assistance for

Individuals with Disabilities Act was reauthorized in 1994 to address many of these failings, work still remains.

Current AT policy continues to raise a host of equity issues. Who has access to technology? Which technology is available? Who decides on the technology? Who controls or determines allocation of assistive technology? Despite the existence of numerous important problems related to developing technologies, the more serious problems are still social ones. Governmental agencies, including the Health Care Financing Administration, need to address the shortage of publicly subsidized assistive technology.

5. AT Consumer Protection

Over twenty states have passed lemon laws to protect AT consumers. For instance, Nebraska's AT Regulation Act covers any device that assists a person with a disability to perform one or several major life activities, including moving, hearing, seeing, speaking, breathing, learning, or working. Examples include manual or motorized wheelchairs or other mobility aids; assistive listening devices, hearing aids, text telephones (TTY), or other aids that enhance an individual's ability to hear; voice-synthesized computer modules, optical scanners, Braille printers, talking software, or other devices that enhance visual communication; and environmental control devices, including wheelchair lifts and other automation.

The lemon law is designed to protect consumers by requiring manufacturers or dealers to provide one-year warranties for AT. If a device doesn't work, the manufacturer or dealer is required to repair the device, replace it, or provide a refund, assuming it was not abused or used improperly. Consumers may attempt to recover damages in civil court.

ADA IMPLEMENTATION AND ASSISTIVE TECHNOLOGY PROVISION

Effective ADA implementation requires coordination with other disability, welfare, and health policy reforms. Economic incentive programs encourage businesses to hire persons with disabilities and to purchase assistive devices for qualified employees in need. AT provision and service programs through the Tech Act and related programs are designed to meet the AT needs of consumers. Federal support of AT research and development fosters the promise of improved AT design. Small business loans encourage entrepreneurs, many of whom are individuals with disabilities, to carry their AT designs from conception through production to consumers.

As indicated, disability policy requires harmonization with respect to AT funding. A recent needs-assessment survey showed that AT funding was the most significant problem experienced by consumers and service providers, over other need areas (Erhart et al. 1992). Funding for AT devices and services is available through a complex network of federal and state disability programs, including SSDI, SSI, Medicaid, Medicare, and a variety of federal and state vocational rehabilitation and assistive technology programs (Seelman 1993). The interpretation of disability standards under each of these laws varies. Third-party payment of assistive technology is the norm under most of the programs.

According to the 1992 NCHS AT needs survey mentioned above, third-party funders made complete or partial payments for more than half (52 percent) of AT users' devices (LaPlante, Hendershot, and Moss 1992). About 48 percent of the people who used assistive technology or their families paid for devices with no help from social service agencies or third parties. More than three-quarters of the persons with home modifications or accessibility features paid for them out of pocket.

V. Conclusion

In his introduction to this volume, EEOC Commissioner Paul Steven Miller reflects on the exclusion of persons with disabilities from society shortly after reauthorization of the Tech Act. For years the physical environment—including buildings, work sites, public places, and schools—was constructed without regard to people with disabilities. Disabled people were sheltered away from participation in society—not ignored, but invisible (Blanck 1994b).

The invisible community of persons with disabilities numbers over 50 million Americans by Census Bureau estimates. The ADA and related federal legislation seek to provide workers and consumers with disabilities access to the goods and services that would allow them to participate equally in society. AT plays a fundamental role in achieving this goal. As noted by Congress in the findings of the Tech Act, "For some individuals with disabilities, AT devices are necessary to enable the individuals to . . . have greater control over their lives."

Based on the patenting trends discussed in this chapter, the ADA has had a measurable effect on the activity of AT inventors. AT inventors responded rationally to the passage of the ADA and to the economic opportunities that the law has created through regulatory shifts relating to accessibility. The findings suggest that the ADA is succeeding in unanticipated ways, creating unanticipated benefits for ADA stakeholders and others. Knowledge of the ADA appears to have reached assistive technology inventors and to have influenced their inventive activity.

The words of Stanley Herr still ring true, however: "[F]or all the glamour and the appeal of new technologies, we still need the old virtues of listening, of remedying the injustices that we encounter . . . of communicating with those we hope to help" (Blanck 1994b). The achievement of the ADA's promise of full inclusion and equal participation requires more than advancing AT. It requires careful study of underlying attitudes and behaviors toward individuals with disabilities in all parts of American society.

References

Albert, M., et al. 1991. Direct Validation of Citation Counts as Indicators of Industrially Important Patents. *Research Policy* 20:251–59.

Ashford, N. A. 1985. Using Regulation to Change the Market for Innovation. *Harvard Environmental L. Rev.* 9:419–66.

———. 1994. An Innovation-Based Strategy for the Environment. In *Worst Things First? The Debate over Risk-Based National Environmental Priorities,* ed. A. M. Finkel and D. Golding, pp. 275–314. Washington, D.C.: Resources Future.

Ashford, N. A., and C. C. Caldart. 1996. *Technology, Law, and the Working Environment.* New York: Island Press.

Barnard, T. H. 1990. The Americans with Disabilities Act: Nightmare for Employers and Dream for Lawyers? *St. John's L. Rev.* 64:229–52.

Berven, H. M., and P. D. Blanck. 1998. The Economics of the Americans with Disabilities Act: Part II—Patents and Innovations in Assistive Technology. *Notre Dame Journal of Law, Philosophy, and Public Policy* 12:9–120.

Blackman, A. 1991. Machines That Work Miracles. *Washington Post,* Feb. 18, p. 70.

Blanck, P. D. 1994a. Celebrating Communications Technology for Everyone. *Federal Communications Law Journal* 45:185–91.

———. 1994b. Communicating the Americans with Disabilities Act, Transcending Compliance: A Case Report on Sears, Roebuck and Co. *Annenberg Washington Program Reports.*

———. 1994c. Communications Technology for Everyone: Implications for the Classroom and Beyond. *Annenberg Washington Program Reports.*

———. 1996. Communicating the Americans with Disabilities Act, Transcending Compliance: 1996 Follow-up Report on Sears, Roebuck and Co. *Annenberg Washington Program Reports.*

———. 1997. The Economics of the Americans with Disabilities Act: Part I—Reasonable Accommodation. *DePaul L. Rev.* 46:877–914.

————. 1998a. *The Americans with Disabilities Act and the Emerging Workforce of the Twenty-First Century.* Washington, D.C.: American Association on Mental Retardation.

————. 1998b. The Emerging of the Staffing Industry in the Employment of Persons with Disabilities. *University of Iowa Law, Health Policy, and Disability Center Reports.*

————. 2000. ADA Title III and the Internet: Technology and Civil Rights. Forthcoming.

Borkowski v. Valley Central School District. 63 F.3d 131 (2d Cir. 1995).

Bowe, F. G. 1995. Is It Medically Necessary? The Political and Economic Issues That Drive and Derail Assistive Technology Development. *Generations* 19:37–40.

Button, C., and R. Wobschall. 1994. The Americans with Disabilities Act and Assistive Technology. *Journal of Vocational Rehabilitation* 4:196.

Chandler, S. K., T. Czerlinski, and P. Wehman. 1993. Provisions of Assistive Technology: Bridging the Gap to Accessibility. In *The ADA Mandate for Social Change,* ed. P. Wehman. New York: Brooks.

Chiang, J. T. 1993. From Industry Targeting to Technology Targeting: A Policy Paradigm Shift in the 1980's. *Technology in Society* 15:341–57.

Chisum, D. S., and M. Jacobs. 1998. *Understanding Intellectual Property Law.* New York: Irwin.

Cook, A. M., and S. M. Hussey. 1996. *Assistive Technologies: Principles and Practice.* St. Louis: Mosby.

Cutler, B. 1993. Hot Gadgets for Disabled Workers. *American Demographics* (Jan.).

Daly, M. C., and J. Bound. 1996. Worker Adaptation and Employer Accommodation Following the Onset of a Health Impairment. *Journal of Gerontology* 51B:S53.

Derzko, N. M. 1996. Using Intellectual Property Law and Regulatory Processes to Foster the Innovation and Diffusion of Environmental Technologies. *Harvard Environmental L. Rev.* 20:3–58.

Drury, T. 1998. Aztech Braces for Change as Focus Shifts to Marketing. *Business First of Buffalo* (Jan. 26): 16.

Erhart, L. M., et al. 1992. Technical Assistance Needs Survey: Virginia Assistive Technology System. *Journal of Vocational Rehabilitation* 2:84–87.

Felton, B. 1997. Technologies That Enable the Disabled. *New York Times,* Sept. 14, p. C11.

Fram, D. K. 1997. Complex Reasonable Accommodation Issues under the ADA. National Employment Law Institute Report for the Industry Labor Council. Chicago.

Galvin, J. C., and M. J. Scherer. 1996. *Evaluating, Selecting, and Using Appropriate Assistive Technology.* New York: Aspen.

Golledge, R. G., and R. J. Stimson. 1997. *Spatial Behavior: A Geographic Perspective.* New York: Guilford.

Gollin, M. A. 1992. Using Intellectual Property to Improve Environmental Protection. *Harvard Journal of Law and Technology* 4:193–235.

Gostin, L. O., and H. A. Beyer, eds. 1993. *Implementing the Americans with Disabilities Act*. Baltimore: Brookes.

Hall, F. S., and E. L. Hall. 1994. The ADA: Going beyond the Law. *Academy Management Executive Review* 8:17–26.

Hamrin, R. 1982. Environmental Regulations and Technological Innovation. In *Managing Innovation*, ed. S. B. Lundstedt and E. W. Colglazier, p. 148. New York: Pergamon.

Hauger, J. S. 1995. Reading Machines for the Blind: Federally Supported Technology Development and Innovation. 56/05-A Dissertation Abstracts Online International, p. 1954.

Henry, A. 1993. A Universal Approach to an Ever-changing Universe. *Appliance* 50:34.

Israel, P., and R. Rosenberg. 1992. Patent Office Records as an Historical Source: The Case of Thomas Edison. *Technology and Culture* 32:1094.

LaPlante, M. A., G. E. Hendershot, and A. J. Moss. 1992. Assistive Technology Devices and Home Accessibility Features: Prevalence, Payment, Needs, and Trends. *Advance Data from Vital and Health Statistics of the Centers for Disease Control/National Center for Health Statistics* 217 (Sept. 16).

Matthews, J. 1997. Opening Doors by Enabling the Disabled: Entrepreneurs Find a Niche in Providing Services to Meet the Demands of the Disabilities Act. *Washington Post*, Mar. 3, p. A5.

Melkers, J. 1988. Bibliometrics as a Tool for Analysis of R and D Impacts. In *Evaluating R and D Impacts: Methods and Practice*, ed. B. Bozeman and J. Melkers, pp. 43–57. Boston: Kluwer Academic.

Minaire, P. 1992. Disease, Illness, and Health: Theoretical Models of the Disablement Process. *World Health Organization Bulletin* 40:373.

Monette v. Electronic Data Systems. 90 F.3d 1173 (6th Cir. 1996).

Mraz, S. J. 1992. Designing around Disabilities. *Machine Design* 64:60.

Narin, F. 1994. Patent Bibliometrics. *Scientometrics* 30:147–55.

Norman, D. 1988. *The Psychology of Everyday Things.* New York: HarperCollins.

Olsen, W. K. 1997. *The Excuse Factory.* New York: Martin Kessler.

Parry, J. 1993. Title I—Employment. In *Implementing the Americans with Disabilities Act,* ed. L. O. Gostin and H. A. Beyer, pp. 57–74. Baltimore: Brookes.

Peltz-Strauss, K. P. 1993. Title IV—Telecommunications. In *Implementing the Americans with Disabilities Act,* ed. L. O. Gostin and H. A. Beyer, pp. 155–74. Baltimore: Brookes.

Petroski, H. 1991. *The Evolution of Useful Things.* New York: Knopf.

President's Committee on Employment of People with Disabilities. 1994. *Job Accommodation Network (JAN) Reports.* Washington, D.C. Oct.–Dec.

Russell, J. N., et al.. 1997. Trends and Differential Use of Assistive Technology Devices: United States, 1994. *Advance Data from Vital and Health Statistics of the Centers for Disease Control and Prevention/National Center for Health Statistics* 292 (Nov. 13): 1–10.

Scherer, M. J. 1996. *Living in a State of Stuck: How Technology Impacts the Lives of People with Disabilities.* New York: Brookline.

Schwochau, S., and P. D. Blanck. 1999. The Economics of the Americans with Disabilities Act: Part III: Does the ADA Disable the Disabled? *Berkeley. J. Emp & Lab. L.* 21:271-313.

Scotch, R. K., and K. Schriner. 1997. Disability as Human Variation: Implications for Policy. *Annals of the American Academy of Political and Social Science* 549:148-59.

Seelman, K. D. 1993. Assistive Technology Policy: A Road to Independence for Individuals with Disabilities. *Journal of Social Issues* 49:115-36.

Shapiro, J. 1993. *No Pity: People with Disabilities Forging a New Civil Rights Movement.* New York: Times.

Sheldon, J. R., and R. M. Hager. 1997. Funding Assistive Technology for Persons with Disabilities: The Availability of Assistive Technology through Medicaid, Public School Special Education Programs, and State Vocational Rehabilitation Agencies. *Clearinghouse Review* (May-June): 50-69.

Stevens, R. B. 1981. Regulation, Innovation, and Administrative Law: A Conceptual Framework. *Calif. L. Rev.* 69:1259-377.

Tompkins, N. C. 1993. Tools That Help Performance on the Job: Assistive Technology for the Handicapped in the Workplace. *HR Magazine* 38:84.

United States Department of Commerce Census Bureau. http://www.census.gov/Press-Release/cb97-148.html. Visited Oct. 29, 1997.

Vanderheiden, G. C. 1990. Thirty Something (Million): Should There Be Exceptions? Research paper posted at http://www.trace.wisc.edu/docs/30_some/30_some.htm. Visited July 19, 1998.

Vande Zande v. Wisc. Dept. of Admin. 44 F.3d 538 (7th Cir. 1995).

Verzani, M. 1995. The Orphan Patent Act. *Journal of the Patent and Trademark Office Society* 77:5-15.

Waldrop, J. 1990. From Handicap to Advantage. *American Demographics* 34:132-35.

Wehman, P., ed. 1993. *The ADA Mandate for Social Change.* Baltimore: Brookes.

Wylde, M. A. 1995a. How to Size Up the Current and Future Markets: Technologies and the Older Adult. *Generations* 5:20-24.

———. 1995b. If You Could See It through My Eyes: Perspectives on Technology for Older People. *Generations* 19:15-19.

Chapter XIV

Attitudes, Behavior, and ADA Title I

Mollie Weighner Marti and
Peter David Blanck

Introduction

Title I of the Americans with Disabilities Act of 1990 (ADA) mandates changes in employers' and others' behavior to ensure equal employment opportunities to qualified individuals with disabilities. It also seeks to confront attitudinal barriers and prejudice faced by individuals with disabilities. As noted by the United States Supreme Court when examining the concept of employment discrimination based on attitudes toward disability, "society's accumulated myths and fears about disability and diseases are as handicapping as are the physical limitations that flow from actual impairment" (*School Bd. of Nassau Co. v. Arline* 1987).

This chapter examines research on attitudes toward persons with disabilities in the employment context, the effect of attitudes on Title I implementation, and the role Title I plays in shaping attitudes. This review is needed for several reasons. First, persons with physical and mental disabilities are among those minority groups most stigmatized by society (Goffman 1963; Jones et al. 1984). They are targets of negative stereotypes, are devalued by those sharing mainstream cultural values, and suffer negative interpersonal and economic consequences (Crocker and Major 1989; Katz 1981). Some have theorized that the degree of stigma attached to individuals with disabilities is greater than that attached to ethnic groups, in part due to a lack of cultural identity and pride (Henderson and Bryan 1984).

Second, in our society, employment is valued and is a central part of life. Productive employment for persons with disabilities is essential to independence and self-esteem (Florian 1982; Hantula and Reilly 1996; Havranek 1991; ICD 1986). More than 60 percent of persons with disabilities of working age are unemployed (Kaye 1996; Wehman 1993). The vast majority of these individuals want to work (Kaye 1996; National Academy of Social Insurance 1996; United Cerebral Palsy Associations 1996). Many of these individuals are uninsured, living in poverty, and trapped in segregated lives (Blanck 1998). Negative attitudes and stereotypes that impede employment opportunities for qualified job applicants and employees with disabilities must be assessed and addressed. Study about attitudes toward persons with disabilities in the workforce may guide policy development and assist in the administration of Title I. Improving the efficiency of Title I not only will increase equal employment opportunities but also may help prevent legal disputes before they arise (Blanck 1996, 1994).

Finally, even when individuals with disabilities obtain employment, they face great attitudinal barriers within the workplace (Blanck 1998). Thirty percent of working-age adults surveyed reported that they experienced job discrimination on the basis of disability (National Organization on Disability 1994). Studies show that employer and coworkers' negative attitudes toward persons with disabilities affect the target employee's self-esteem, performance, and job satisfaction (Feuerstein and Thebarge 1991; Havranek 1991). Negative attitudes impede the integration of individuals with disabilities into the workplace and negatively affect the performance of the work group (Marchioro and Bartels 1994; Nathanson and Lambert 1981).

This chapter has three related objectives. First, it surveys the literature on attitudes toward persons with disabilities, with a focus on the employment context. Second, it discusses attitudinal biases associated with the central terms of Title I. Finally, it examines the effect of Title I on shaping attitudes toward qualified job applicants and employees with disabilities.

Attitudes toward Persons with Disabilities in the Workplace

DEFINITION OF QUALIFIED INDIVIDUAL

This chapter commonly refers to a "qualified" job applicant or employee. This term is used as defined by Title I (see Blanck, this volume). An individual with a disability is qualified if he or she satisfies the job prerequisites and can perform essential job functions.

Attitudes about an individual's qualifications based on preconceived, negative biases about disability are not permissible under Title I. Thus, in *Equal Employment Opportunity Commission v. Texas Bus Lines* (1996), the court held that the employer wrongly determined an employee bus driver was unqualified solely on the basis of her obesity, in the absence of job-related weight restrictions.

Attitudes toward individuals with disabilities may be legitimately based on differences in an employee's actual ability to perform essential job functions. Thus, a job applicant or employee may be found to be unqualified when he or she exceeds standards that serve as a reasonable means of insuring the health and safety of employees and the public. In *Hegwer v. Board of Civil Service Commissioners* (1992), the court found that a paramedic whose thyroid condition caused excessive weight gain was not a qualified employee because she exceeded the body-fat-based weight standards for firefighters and emergency medical technicians. According to the court, the standards were a reasonable means of insuring the health and safety of both employees and the public.

THE NATURE OF ATTITUDES TOWARD PERSONS WITH DISABILITIES

In his classic work on stigma, Goffman (1963) discusses three general classes of stigmas: abominations of the body, blemishes of character, and tribal stigmas. Reactions to individuals differ as a function of the nature of the stigma (Goffman 1963; Jones et al. 1984). Although "the disabled," as a group, would be considered a tribal stigma, physical disabilities likely would be classified as abominations of the body, while most psychiatric disabilities would be considered blemishes of character (see Goffman 1963). This heterogeneity in the types of disabilities presents a hurdle when attempting to measure the impact of disabilities in the employment context (see Stone, Stone, and Dipboye 1992; Yuker 1994).

Across broad categories of disabilities, studies have established a fairly uniform hierarchy of reactions to different types of disabilities. Addictive conditions (e.g., alcoholism, drug use), psychological conditions (e.g., mental retardation, mental illness), and neurological conditions (e.g., epilepsy, cerebral palsy) are viewed most negatively, followed by obvious physical conditions (e.g., amputee, dwarf) and then nonobvious physical disabilities (e.g., arthritis, heart disease) (e.g., Horne and Ricciardo 1988; Tringo 1970; Tripp 1988; West-brook, Legge, and Pennay 1993).

Johnson and Baldwin (1993) summarized the rankings obtained from more than forty studies of attitudes toward persons with disabilities. This summary showed that the most positive attitudes were expressed toward physical disabil-ities and the most negative attitudes toward addictions, mental illness, and ner-vous or emotional problems. The study further found that individuals with the most negatively viewed disabilities were rated least employable.

Studies of employers' attitudes (e.g., Combs and Omvig 1986; Johnson, Greenwood, and Schriner 1988; Jones et al. 1991; Stone and Sawatzki 1980) demonstrate similar hierarchies of attitudes toward different disabilities. Like-wise, a study of coworkers' attitudes (Jones and Stone 1995) revealed that the participants viewed working with persons with addictions and mental disabili-ties more negatively than working with those with physical disabilities. Partic-ipants reported that they would feel least comfortable working with persons with drug addictions, mental illness, HIV infection/AIDS, and alcoholism, and would feel most comfortable working with persons with high blood pressure, diabetes, arthritis, and heart disease. Reactions to the more obvious physical disabilities (e.g., facial disfigurement, paraplegic, amputee) were located within the middle of the subjects' comfort zone.

An important factor in explaining hierarchies of attitudes toward different disabilities is the nature of the disability (see Jones et al. 1984; Stone and Colella 1996; Stone, Stone, and Dipboye 1992). Important dimensions of the nature of the disability include obviousness and aesthetics, uncertainty or perceived threat, and causal attributions.

OBVIOUSNESS AND AESTHETICS

Studies have shown that the more obvious a disability is, the more negative the reactions are to the disability (Comer and Piliavin 1972; Gouvier et al. 1991; Tringo 1970). Observers react to the aesthetics of the disability—that is, to the degree to which an individual's appearance differs from our societal standard for attractiveness (Hahn 1988). The more a disability causes a body to deviate from the concept of how a body "should" look and function, the greater prejudice expressed toward the disability (Beuf 1990; Hahn 1988; Livneh 1988, 1982; Olkin and Howson 1994; Tringo 1970). This is not surprising, given that unat-tractive job applicants are viewed more negatively and perceived as less qualified than attractive applicants (Raza and Carpenter 1987; Stone, Stone, and Dipboye 1992).

The influence of aesthetics on attitudes is not limited to attitudes toward individuals with physical disabilities. Psychiatric disabilities are associated with certain characteristics—such as deviant behavior, reduced personal hygiene, and lower socioeconomic status—that affect individual appearance and generate negative attitudes (Farina 1982). A related factor present with certain disabilities (e.g., Tourette's syndrome, schizophrenia) is the extent to which the disability interferes with social interaction (see Stone and Colella 1996). Disruptiveness may cause anxiety and frustration on the part of observers, leading to negative reactions (see Kleck, Ono, and Hastorf 1966; Stone and Colella 1996).

UNCERTAINTY OR PERCEIVED THREAT

Extreme negative attitudes are expressed toward individuals with addictions or psychiatric conditions. This finding cannot be explained solely by the impact of aesthetics on attitudes because these conditions often are hidden or not readily apparent. A better explanation for these attitudes is the perceived uncertainty associated with the disability.

The degree to which a disability impedes employers in predicting the behavior of employees has a large influence on employers' attitudes toward those employees (Diksa and Rogers 1996; see Stone and Colella 1996; Stone, Stone, and Dipboye 1992). Similarly, when the course of a disability is perceived as uncontrollable, it is viewed more negatively than when it is seen as controllable (Meyerowitz, Williams, and Gessner 1987; Triplet and Sugarman 1987). In one study (Meyerowitz, Williams, and Gessner 1987), research participants rated cancer more negatively than a fictitious disease that was described in an identical manner, largely due to beliefs that the disease was difficult to prevent and treat. When circumstances associated with a disability are viewed as controllable, it is likely the perceiver feels empowered to take necessary precautions to reduce negative feelings toward the person with the disability (see Stone and Colella 1996; Stone, Stone, and Dipboye 1992).

CAUSAL ATTRIBUTIONS

One of the most interesting dimensions of the nature of a disability is the extent to which the disability is perceived to be caused by the person with the disability (see Key 1997). When disabilities are attributed to internal causes (i.e., caused by the individuals themselves), they are evaluated more negatively than when attributed to external causes (i.e., caused by factors beyond one's control) (Jones et al. 1984; Weiner 1993; Weiner, Perry, and Magnusson 1988). Thus, people are more likely to have negative attitudes about an obese person when they believe that the obesity was caused by insufficient exercise rather than a thyroid condition (Rodin et al. 1989; Weiner 1993).

Observers have a tendency to attribute the origin of another's disability to internal causes (see Jones and Nisbett 1971; Pettigrew 1979). This may be especially true for stigmatized disabilities, such as mental illness and AIDS (e.g., Triplet and Sugarman 1987; Weiner, Perry, and Magnusson 1988). For instance, people generally perceive individuals with psychiatric disabilities as more responsible for the disability's onset than those with physical disabilities (Campbell and Kaufmann 1997; Weiner, Perry, and Magnusson 1988). These perceptions cause observers to react negatively toward individuals with psychiatric disabilities, expressing anger and less liking, pity, and assistance (Weiner, Perry, and Magnusson 1988).

Making faulty attributions about personal responsibility may serve an ego-protective function by defending one's belief system (e.g., Lerner and Simmons 1966; Lerner and Miller 1978). According to the "just world phenomenon" (Lerner 1980), people tend to believe that the world is just. People get what they deserve and bad things happen only to bad people. This belief may be threatened when meeting individuals with disabilities if they are viewed as good and undeserving of having a disability.

To eliminate this threat, people employ defensive strategies. Some make negative inferences about the person's character by viewing them as "asking" for the disability (see Carli and Leonard 1989; Lerner and Miller 1978) or reinterpret the cause of the disability to conclude that the individual did something wrong to deserve the disability (Jones et al. 1984; Schneider and Anderson 1980; Wright 1983). "Defensive attributions" make the blamer feel less likely to be victimized in a similar way (Blanck and Marti 1996; Finerman and Bennett 1995). Individuals with disabilities often seek to protect their self-esteem from negative attributions by overattributing negative feedback they receive to prejudice on the part of the observer (Crocker and Major 1994).

More research is needed to develop a framework to explain the varying reactions toward different disabilities (see Stone and Colella 1996). Study should measure how and to what extent the different dimensions of the nature of one's disability affect attitudes within the workplace. These dimensions influence the extent to which employers and coworkers rely on stereotypical thinking, set expectations for performance, and treat qualified individuals with disabilities (Stone and Colella 1996). Title I and its definition of disability, discussed in the next section, provide a framework for this research.

The Attitudinal Implications of Title I

This section examines the role of attitudes toward persons with disabilities in the implementation of Title I. It focuses on the provisions of Title I regarding the definition of disability, reasonable accommodations, and the direct threat defense. It discusses "corporate culture" as an example of the interplay between attitudes and Title I implementation.

THE DEFINITION OF DISABILITY

Persons with disabilities traditionally have been institutionalized and physically separated from the rest of society (Shapiro 1994). The medical model, with its emphasis on the physical limitations of disabilities, was the dominant framework through the early 1900s (Hahn 1996, 1985). More recent social transformations, such as the deinstitutionalization movement of the 1970s and increased physical access for persons with disabilities, reflect a new cultural norm of opposition to discrimination against persons with disabilities (Pfeiffer 1994).

The ADA is one of the strongest indicators of this emerging norm of equal rights (see Burris and Moss, this volume). Title I's definition of disability highlights the shift in emphasis from the physical restrictions of disability to the attitudinal restrictions placed on individuals with disabilities by society. Under Title I's three-prong definition of disability, a person (1) must have a known physical or mental condition or impairment that substantially limits a major life activity; (2) must have a record of a physical or mental condition; or (3) be regarded as having such a condition. By providing that a person may be disabled on the basis of an employer's attitudes, Title I recognizes that beyond any physical restrictions of a disability, the attitudinal restrictions placed on individuals with disabilities by society serve as a major impediment to equal employment opportunities.

The first prong of Title I's definition of disability requires that an individual have a known physical or mental condition or impairment that substantially limits a major life activity. Even if an employee has an impairment that is independently covered under the first prong, the impairment may be "disabling" in the workplace as a result of the employer's misperceptions about individual performance capabilities or about the efficacy of certain workplace accommodations (see Blanck and Marti 1997).

The second and third prongs of the definition of disability are particularly relevant to attitudes toward persons with disabilities in the workplace. These prongs prohibit discrimination on the basis of biased attitudes associated with perceived disabilities, even in the absence of actual impairments (see Blanck and Marti 1997; Moberly 1996). In *La Paz v. Henry's Diner, Inc.* (1996), an employer allegedly perceived an employee who was openly gay to have HIV disease and terminated him on that basis. Although the case has not been resolved by a court, the employee would be entitled to relief under Title I if he was fired because of his employer's unjustified attitudes toward the perceived disability of AIDS and not because of an actual impairment or present job abilities.

Title I also prohibits discrimination on the basis of an association with a person with a disability. This provision is warranted in light of studies showing that people who hold negative attitudes toward a group experience negative feelings toward individuals who merely associate with the group. People who have negative attitudes toward homosexuals, for instance, express negative attitudes toward persons who simply associate with homosexuals or express progay sentiments (Neuberg et al. 1994; Russell and Gray 1992). Title I does allow an employer to discharge a nondisabled employee who has a relative or associate with a disability, however, if the relative or associate poses a direct threat to the employer's workplace. Thus, in *Hartog v. Wasatch Academy* (1997), the court held that a boarding school was justified in firing a teacher with over twenty-five years' experience because his adult son, who had bipolar disorder, had threatened and attacked several members of the school community.

Analysis of an employer's attitudes is central to the question of whether the employer discriminated against a qualified person with a disability under Title I. Although researchers are beginning to develop theories of Title I discrimination based on attitudinal bias (see Blanck and Marti 1997; Colella, DeNisi, and Varma 1997; Stone and Colella 1996), additional study is needed. Future research should examine the relation between the nature of an employee's impairment and an employer's tendency to regard the employee as disabled. How do the different dimensions of the nature of an impairment (e.g., aesthetics, perceived threat) affect employers' perceptions of and attitudes toward qualified employees with impairments? The fairly stable hierarchy of attitudes toward persons with disabilities discussed above (e.g., psychological disabilities are viewed more negatively than physical disabilities) suggests that some dimensions—such as uncertainty or perceived threat—are more influential than others.

Study also is needed of employers' knowledge of Title I and the effect of such knowledge on their attitudes toward qualified persons with disabilities. It is unknown to what extent employers assume that employees who exhibit violent behavior within the workplace are entitled to protection under Title I. It is likely that this is a strong presumption on the part of employers (see Campbell and Kaufmann 1997; Diksa and Rogers 1996; Perlin 1993; Sharp 1996). Employers may not be aware that character flaws or common personality traits—such as poor judgment, quick temper, and impulsive behavior—are not impairments under Title I when they are not symptoms of a covered psychological disorder (for a review of cases, see Blanck and Marti 1997). The more familiar an employer is with the actual requirements of Title I, the more positive its attitudes likely will be toward employing qualified persons with disabilities (cf. Blanck 1998; Levy et al. 1991).

Finally, study is needed of attitudes toward Title I itself. Title I was enacted amid great controversy. Persons with disabilities and disability rights advocates embraced the law as a significant civil rights and antidiscrimination law (Ravid 1992; Shapiro 1994). Critics regarded Title I as extending the guarantees of equal employment opportunity beyond the scope of previous antidiscrimination laws (Rosen 1991). The small business community viewed the law with apprehension, fearing costly compliance and an explosion of litigation (Barnard 1990; Willis 1994–95). Some argue that these divergent attitudes are causing a backlash against the ADA (Shapiro 1994). Study is needed to examine the extent to which attitudes toward Title I itself are impeding implementation of the law and the integration of qualified individuals with disabilities into the workforce.

REASONABLE ACCOMMODATIONS

The requirement that employers provide "reasonable accommodations" to enable qualified employees with disabilities to perform essential job functions is a central provision for Title I implementation. This provision represents a shift in emphasis from the limitations of the individual's disability to society's obligation to provide equal employment opportunities (Milstein, Rubenstein, and Cyr 1991; Pollet 1995). The success of the law in improving employment opportunities for persons with disabilities is dependent on employers determining that the cost of accommodation is less than the cost of noncompliance (Blanck, this volume; Johnson and Baldwin 1993).

To be eligible for an accommodation, an employee must make his or her disability "known" to the employer and request an accommodation. Without timely disclosure by the employee of his or her disability, the employer has no obligation to make reasonable accommodations (see Blanck and Marti 1997). This requirement places a burden on individuals with highly stigmatized disabilities, such as psychiatric disabilities. Although disclosure is necessary to obtain accommodations, fear of negative attitudes and discriminatory behavior often prevents qualified workers from disclosing their disabilities (Blanck and Marti 1997; Fisher 1995; Hall 1997).

Workplace accommodations may themselves be stigmatized (Bell 1997; EEOC 1997; Mancuso 1990; Parry 1993). Employers view certain accommodations (such as reasonable time off and restructuring the work environment) as burdensome because they involve modifications of the managerial and social aspects of the workplace rather than the physical aspects (Hantula and Reilly 1996). Prejudiced attitudes may cause employers to perceive employees who utilize such accommodations as being less capable or responsible and as a result less deserving of promotions (Carling 1994; Moore 1995). Coworkers may view employees who take more breaks or who work in private areas as enjoying special privileges (Carling 1994). These perceptions lead to a loss of morale in the workplace (Key 1997).

Negative attitudes about providing reasonable accommodations may overshadow the actual qualifications of persons with disabilities or their ability to contribute to the employer's economic bottom line (Blanck and Marti 1997). Employers are more willing to provide accommodations for persons with physical disabilities than with psychiatric disabilities (Michaels et al. 1993). This decision appears to be fueled more by negative attitudes than by a rational analysis of costs or benefits. Studies show that with support or accommodation, qualified people with psychiatric disabilities perform as well or better than employees without such disabilities (e.g., Howard 1975; Mancuso 1990; McFarlin, Song, and Sonntag 1991; Mintz et al. 1992). Accommodations for psychiatric disabilities also have been found to be less expensive than accommodations for physical disabilities (Blanck 1996).

Information is needed about the relation between knowledge of Title I's provisions, Title I compliance, and attitudes toward persons with disabilities. Several studies have demonstrated that the direct costs of reasonable accommodations are relatively low and are outweighed by the benefits of employing people with disabilities (for a review, see Blanck 1998). Employers who are knowledgeable about the economic benefits of providing accommodations to qualified employees with disabilities are more likely to comply with Title I (see Johnson and Baldwin 1993). Additionally, as discussed in the final section of this chapter, Title I compliance by employers actually may cause employers to have more positive attitudes toward employees with disabilities.

An interesting and overlooked area of study is employers' attitudes and beliefs about what is a "reasonable" accommodation. Employers' attitudes on this subject have a direct impact on persons with disabilities because employers choose what accommodations they will offer. Research is needed on the fears and stigmas associated with disclosure of different disabilities, particularly more stigmatized disabilities, and the resulting consequences for qualified job applicants and employees with disabilities. This study should examine self-perceptions of empowerment by persons with disabilities, which can help maximize the effectiveness of Title I by promoting disclosure of one's disability and increasing self-advocacy in the workplace (see Miller and Keys 1996; Shapiro 1994).

DIRECT THREAT DEFENSE

Employers use Title I's "direct threat" defense to justify the dismissal of employees with disabilities when they pose a significant risk of substantial harm to themselves or others that cannot be reduced by reasonable accommodation. Employers are required to make an individualized and objective determination of direct threat, based on the employee's present ability to safely perform essential job functions. This determination may not be based on biased attitudes.

The significance attached to the direct threat defense highlights the pervasiveness of unjustified biases (see Blanck and Marti 1997). The defense commonly is used by employers with regard to highly stigmatized impairments, such as psychiatric disabilities and AIDS (e.g., Campbell and Kaufmann 1997; McDonald, Kulick, and Ceighton 1995; McIntosh 1996; Miller 1997; Perlin 1993; Sharp 1996). Studies of employer concerns about the employability of persons with psychiatric disabilities (e.g., Fuqua, Rathbun, and Gade 1984; Johnson, Greenwood, and Schriner 1988) suggest that employers are concerned about violence by employees with psychiatric disabilities.

Diksa and Rogers (1996) conducted a factor analysis in an attempt to categorize these concerns about employing persons with psychiatric disabilities. They examined four major areas of employer concerns: (1) symptomatology (e.g., violence, poor memory or judgment, effects of medication); (2) administrative concerns (e.g., discipline, time off, acceptance by coworkers, costs); (3) work performance (e.g., acceptable quality and quantity of work, adequate academic skills, safety); and (4) work personality (e.g., promptness, reliability, communication). The researchers found that these factors accounted for nearly 60 percent of the variance in employers' expressed concerns. It is important that the symptomatology factor accounted for nearly 46 percent of the variance. Employers' fear of employees with psychiatric disabilities becoming violent was the item of greatest concern within the symptomatology factor.

The concern regarding the link between psychiatric disabilities and violence in the workplace is not supported by empirical evidence (see Blanck and Marti 1997; Monahan 1992; Mulvey 1994). Studies suggest that a small subset of mental disorders involving active psychosis (e.g., when irrational thoughts override self-control) is linked directly to violence (Link, Andrews, and Cullen 1992). Substance abuse and a history of violent behavior have been shown to be better predictors than severe mental illness of violent behavior in the workplace (Swanson and Holzer 1991). Moreover, the association between mental illness and violence appears to be context-dependent (Campbell and Kaufmann 1997; Hiday 1995; Link et al. 1992). For example, a person with a psychiatric disability might tend to be more violent when he or she feels threatened (Estroff et al. 1994). Ironically, this might lead to a self-fulfilling prophecy (Rosenthal 1994) where biased attitudes cause observers to treat persons with psychiatric conditions as threatening, thereby making violence more likely.

Study is needed of employers' attitudes associated with the direct threat defense. The focus should be on those impairments that are subject to the most negative attitudes (e.g., addictions, psychological conditions). Information is needed on the relation between employers' knowledge of Title I and their attitudes. For instance, do employers who erroneously believe Title I requires them to retain individuals with disabilities, even though they display violent or inappropriate behavior, have more negative attitudes toward qualified individuals with psychiatric conditions than knowledgeable employers? Research is needed that examines factors that make workplace violence more likely, including insufficient wages, long hours, and reduced job security (Campbell and Kaufmann 1997). Related study should explore the role of external forces, such as the media (e.g., Zuckerman, Debenham, and Moore 1993), in reinforcing negative stereotypes and perpetuating misperceptions.

CORPORATE CULTURE

Most of the studies discussed above focused on the personal attitudes of employers (e.g., Combs and Omvig 1986; Johnson, Greenwood, and Schriner 1988; Louis Harris and Associates, Inc. and National Organization on Disability 1995; Stone and Sawatzki 1980). These attitudes are important and have a great impact on the daily lives of employees with disabilities. Corporate culture is a related and largely overlooked concept.

An organization's corporate culture refers to the norms and values of the organization and the degree of support or hostility toward the employment of individuals with disabilities (see Blanck and Marti 1997). An organization's corporate culture determines the presence of employment opportunities for qualified individuals with disabilities (Jones et al. 1991; Levy et al. 1991).

Organizations with a positive corporate culture are more likely to learn that enhancing equal employment opportunities for qualified individuals with disabilities is consistent with other corporate objectives such as maximizing worker productivity, health, and safety (see Blanck and Marti 1997; Talbert and Karp 1995). Organizations also may realize that these strategies make good economic sense (see Johnson and Baldwin 1993). Workplace accommodations have been shown to produce substantial economic benefits to companies in terms of increased worker efficiency, injury prevention, and reduced workers' compensation costs (e.g., Blanck 1996, 1994; Hall and Hall 1994).

A discussion of corporate culture provides a useful example of the interplay between attitudes and Title I implementation. Although most organizations probably would provide accommodations to qualified job applicants and employees if they were aware of the economic benefits of doing so, an organization with a positive corporate culture toward individuals with disabilities is more likely to realize such opportunities.

Imagine that a hotel decides to undertake renovations not only to comply with ADA requirements but to provide excellent services and accommodations to employees and guests with disabilities. After doing so, several disability organizations select the hotel as a conference site because they wish to patronize such a business. The additional business positively affects the hotel's economic bottom line, providing additional incentives to maintain and enhance the accommodations offered. Yet it was the hotel's initial positive attitude toward accommodating persons with disabilities that made the economic profit possible. Thus, an organization's corporate culture may largely dictate the extent to which the organization embraces Title I.

Researchers have hypothesized that the more an organization espouses values such as egalitarianism and cooperation, the more likely it will view individuals with disabilities as qualified and treat them as an integral part of the organization (Stone and Colella 1996). Limited research has addressed the role of a positive corporate culture in extending equal employment opportunities to qualified employees with disabilities (Blanck 1996, 1994; Jones et al. 1991; Levy et al. 1991). Systematic research is needed to explore the relation between an organization's corporate culture, attitudes toward qualified individuals with disabilities, and Title I implementation.

The Effect of Title I on Attitudes

Identifying attitudes toward persons with disabilities seems a sensible and necessary first step toward changing discriminatory behavior. However, attitudes are not always valid predictors of behavior (see Ajzen and Fishbein 1980; Olson and Zanna 1993; Yuker 1994). Social psychologists have identified several factors that moderate the extent to which attitudes influence behavior. An attitude better predicts behavior when other influences are minimized (Kraus 1995) and the attitude is a strong one (Krosnick et al. 1993; Petkova, Ajzen, and Driver 1995). An attitude that is specific to the action has better predictive value than a more general attitude (Ajzen and Fishbein 1977; Ajzen 1982). When trying to predict coworkers' actions toward an employee with bipolar disorder, a measure of one's attitudes toward working with a person with bipolar disorder would better predict behavior than a broad measure of one's attitudes toward "persons with disabilities."

In addition to establishing that attitudes do not always predict behavior, social psychologists have found that behavior influences the formation of attitudes. It is possible to obtain a desired attitude by requiring a consistent behavior and then attitude formation will follow the behavior (e.g., Eagly and Chaiken 1993; Lalonde and Cameron 1994). This suggests that by requiring that equal employment opportunities be extended to qualified individuals with disabilities, Title I will help positively change employer and coworker attitudes toward employees with disabilities.

ATTITUDES FOLLOW BEHAVIOR

Title I mandates a certain type of behavior on the part of employers and employees. By requiring individuals in the workplace to act in ways that ensure equal employment opportunities to persons with disabilities, the law can help change people's attitudes so that their attitudes are consistent with their behavior (see Edelman 1992). Although this concept has been given little attention in the disability literature, there is a rich social psychological literature establishing that attitudes follow behavior (e.g., Blanchard and Cook 1976; Zimbardo 1972; Higgins and Rholes 1978).

An example of attitudes following behavior involves white Americans' attitudes toward African-Americans. In the years following the Civil Rights

Act of 1964, the percentage of white Americans who experienced more integrative settings and relationships increased, as did the percentage of whites who favored school desegregation and the integration of blacks into white neighborhoods (e.g., Greeley and Sheatsley 1971; Taylor, Sheatsley, and Greeley 1978). The more uniform national standards against racial discrimination were accompanied by a reduction in racial prejudice.

Consistent with this finding, one recent study reported that 96 percent of individuals with disabilities, their friends, and family members surveyed felt that the ADA made a difference in the lives of people with disabilities. Of the individuals surveyed, 46 percent perceived greater acceptance by their communities since the law's enactment, and 24 percent said they have experienced or witnessed increased employment (United Cerebral Palsy Associations 1996; see Pfeiffer 1994). This suggests that, analogous to the role of civil rights laws in increasing racial integration, implementation of the ADA is helping establish positive attitudes toward individuals with disabilities. Study is needed to document changes over time in employers' attitudes toward qualified individuals with disabilities and how these changes relate to Title I implementation.

There are two main theories to explain why people who are induced to act in a positive manner toward qualified individuals with disabilities would change their attitudes to be consistent with their behavior. "Cognitive dissonance" theory (Festinger 1957) predicts that people change their attitudes to reduce the tension they experience when they have an attitude and an action that contradict each other. It acknowledges that people have a need for consistency between their attitudes and their actions and that people experience dissonance when their attitudes and actions do not match (e.g., Aronson and Mills 1959; Gerard and Mathewson 1966).

For example, an employer who has a negative attitude toward individuals with psychiatric disabilities would experience tension after granting a reasonable accommodation to a qualified individual with depression. To reduce this tension, the employer might change his attitude to reflect that qualified individuals with psychiatric disabilities are entitled to reasonable accommodations to ensure equal employment opportunities.

Alternatively, according to "self-perception" theory (Bem 1972, 1967), when people have weak or ambiguous attitudes, they draw the same inferences from perceiving their own actions that others who perceived those actions would draw. People infer their attitudes by examining their own behavior and the circumstances under which it occurs. Studies show that people report feeling angry when they are induced to make facial expressions as if they are frowning, and they feel happier when induced to make a smiling face (Laird 1984, 1974).

Self-perception theory is relevant to employees with weak negative attitudes toward people with disabilities who work in an organization with a positive corporate culture. In an environment that is supportive of qualified employees with disabilities, coworkers would be expected to interact in positive ways with employees with disabilities. Accordingly, the individuals would act this way and perceive themselves doing so. Self-perception theory would predict that the employees then would begin to believe that their actions indicate that they have positive attitudes toward individuals with disabilities.

INCREASING CONTACT BETWEEN INDIVIDUALS
WITH AND WITHOUT DISABILITIES

Another way in which Title I changes attitudes positively in the workplace is by increasing contact between individuals with and without disabilities. Studies demonstrate that certain types of contact between individuals with and without disabilities may be an effective way to promote positive attitudes toward persons with disabilities (e.g., Jones and Stone 1995; Makas 1993; McFarlin, Song, and Sonntag 1991; Yuker 1994, 1988). In contrast to the rich literature on beneficial types of interracial contact (e.g., Allport 1954; Amir 1969; Brewer and Miller 1984), there has not been a concerted effort to conduct such research in the disability area (Makas 1993). The contact variables with likely predictive value include equal status, mutual goals, sustained intimate contact, and institutional support for equality.

Equal Status

Negative attitudes are more likely to be changed when nondisabled individuals and persons with disabilities interact in settings where everyone has equal social status (Donaldson 1980; Yuker 1988). A related concept is that of social roles. Social roles can foster prejudice by subtly teaching people how they are expected to act in society (Eagly 1987; Wolfensberger 1983). Social roles often are based on myths (Levy and Langer 1994).

The social role of persons with disabilities is based, in part, on the myth that such individuals are inferior to and less capable than nondisabled persons of performing essential employment functions. The acceptance of myths may lead to negative, self-fulfilling prophecies (Neuberg 1994), whereby expectations of failure on the part of the person with a disability actually lead to such failure.

Equal employment opportunities help elevate individuals with disabilities from their traditionally devalued role in our society. Employment shifts the emphasis from what the person with a disability cannot do to the individual's capabilities and potential for growth. By assuming the role of employee, qualified individuals with disabilities might elicit more positive attitudes. These positive attitudes may help offset some of the negative attitudes generated by the presence of their disability (Lyons 1991).

Mutual Goals

Intergroup cooperation to achieve mutual goals is another method to reduce prejudice (see Aronson et al. 1978; Sherif et al. 1961). Studies suggest that cooperation is effective because people with and without disabilities cognitively recategorize each other from two separate groups into a new, inclusive group (see Bettencourt et al. 1992; Gaertner et al. 1990). Studies show that cooperative behavior positively affects children's attitudes toward other children with disabilities in a school setting (Armstrong, Johnson, and Balow 1981; Moore and Simpson 1984; Rynders et al. 1980). If these cooperative methods have a lasting effect, they eventually may cause a "ripple effect" in the workplace, whereby children who obtain positive attitudes toward people with disabilities then become adults who embrace individuals with disabilities in the workplace.

Study is needed on the effectiveness of cooperative strategies in the workplace, such as team building, in reducing prejudice based on disability. Cooperative strategies and other intervention programs should emphasize that stereotypes are not always accurate, clarify norms about how to treat persons with disabilities, and attempt to decrease anxiety associated with working with individuals with disabilities (see Stone and Colella 1996). The programs should be tailored to the context, type of disability, and individuals involved (see Berry and Meyer 1995; Grand, Bernier, and Strohmer 1982; Johnson and Baldwin 1993; Tringo 1970). Persons with disabilities should be involved in designing such programs, given that even well-intentioned responses by nondisabled persons may appear to persons with disabilities to be prejudicial (Makas 1988; Shapiro 1994).

Sustained Intimate Contact

Interaction that is personal and sustained over an extended period of time will facilitate the effectiveness of contact in decreasing prejudice against individuals with disabilities (Bogdan and Taylor 1989; Horne 1988). An examination of the driving forces behind the ADA highlights the effectiveness of such contact.

Senator Tom Harkin, cosponsor of the law, has a brother who is deaf. President Bush and former Attorney General Richard Thornburgh have family members with cognitive disabilities. Research is needed on how the presence of family members or close others with disabilities affects one's attitudes toward coworkers or employees with disabilities.

More intimate contact helps to dispel stereotypes about persons with disabilities (see Stone and Colella 1996). Individuals with little or no contact with persons with disabilities hold many negative stereotypes (Fichten and Amsel 1986; Patterson and Witten 1987). Contact that conveys information to help disconfirm stereotypes has a positive effect on attitudes (Evans 1976; Rothbart and John 1985). Consistent with this finding, an important factor in decreasing employers' negative attitudes toward the employment of persons with disabilities is prior experience in hiring persons with disabilities (Diksa and Rogers 1996; Emener and McHargue 1978; Florian 1982; Levy et al. 1991; McCarthy 1988).

In addition to the benefits of intergroup contact, direct experience enables employers to realize that many employees with disabilities perform as well as employees without disabilities. Studies have shown that persons with various disabilities perform as well or better than nondisabled employees in such areas as productivity, safety, absenteeism, promptness, and turnover rates (e.g., Ashcraft 1979; McFarlin, Song, and Sonntag 1991; Parent and Everson 1986).

Institutional Support for Equality

Social norms favoring equality reduce intergroup prejudice where there is a clear social perception that prejudice and discrimination will not be condoned (Blanchard, Lilly, and Vaughn 1991; Cook 1984). The role of group authority figures is central in this process (Cook 1984; Weigel and Howes 1985). Thus, organizations that promote tolerance and make clear that insensitivity and discrimination against individuals with disabilities will not be allowed effectively promote equality in the workplace.

The need for a corporate culture of embracing employees with disabilities as a method of reducing prejudice is clear. An established policy toward hiring persons with a disability has been shown to be an important factor in influencing employers' attitudes (Diksa and Rogers 1996; ICD 1987; Levy et al. 1991). Levy and colleagues (1991) found that 64 percent of companies surveyed who had hiring policies had hired at least one person with a disability compared to only 40 percent of those without such hiring policies. Another study found that companies without a formal policy perceive Title I implementation as more burdensome than do companies with a policy (Jones et al. 1991). A formal policy demonstrates increased awareness of and sensitivity to the issues surrounding employment of persons with disabilities.

Summary

Prejudice on the basis of disability impacts the lives of millions of Americans with disabilities on a daily basis and prevents their integration into the workforce. This chapter examined research on attitudes toward persons with disabilities in the employment context and how these attitudes sometimes impede implementation of ADA Title I. A thorough understanding of attitudes toward persons with disabilities is important because negative attitudes and stereotypes impede employment opportunities for qualified job applicants and employees with disabilities.

At the same time, Title I is a powerful tool not only to help qualified persons with disabilities obtain equality in the workplace but to change negative attitudes toward persons with disabilities. Insufficient attention has been given to the role of Title I in changing attitudes within the workplace by requiring changes in behavior. Title I also helps to dispel myths and stereotypes by increasing contact between people with and without disabilities.

There are many unanswered questions about attitudes toward qualified individuals with disabilities and toward Title I itself. The development of several areas of research is required concerning factors that influence attitudes toward qualified individuals with disabilities, the attitudinal biases associated with the central terms of Title I, and the effect of Title I on attitudes toward qualified individuals with disabilities. This research will provide guidance regarding successful strategies to assist qualified persons in entering the workforce and obtaining equal employment opportunities.

References

Ajzen, I. 1982. On Behaving in Accordance with One's Attitudes. In *Consistency in Social Behavior: The Ontario Symposium,* ed. M. P. Zanna, E. T. Higgins, and C. P. Herman, vol. 2. Hillside, N.J.: Erlbaum.

Ajzen, I., and M. Fishbein. 1977. Attitude-Behavior Relations: A Theoretical Analysis and Review of Empirical Research. *Psychological Bulletin* 84:888–918.

———. 1980. *Understanding Attitudes and Predicting Social Behavior.* Englewood Cliffs, N.J.: Prentice-Hall.

Allport, G. W. 1954. *The Nature of Prejudice*. Reading, Mass.: Addison-Wesley.

Amir, Y. 1969. Contact Hypothesis in Ethnic Relations. *Psychological Bulletin* 71:319–42.

Armstrong, B., D. W. Johnson, and B. Balow. 1981. Effects of Cooperative vs. Individualistic Learning Experiences on Interpersonal Attraction between Learning-Disabled and Normal-Progress Elementary School Students. *Contemporary Educational Psychology* 6:102–10.

Aronson, E., and J. Mills. 1959. The Effect of Severity of Initiation on Liking for a Group. *Journal of Abnormal and Social Psychology* 59:177–81.

Aronson, E., et al. 1978. *The Jigsaw Classroom*. Beverly Hills, Calif.: Sage.

Ashcraft, W. W. 1979. The Disabled: An Untapped Labor Market. *Journal of Contemporary Business* 8:75–83.

Barnard, T. H. 1990. The Americans with Disabilities Act: Nightmare for Employers and Dream for Lawyers? *St. John's L. Rev.* 64:229–52.

Bell, C. G. 1997. The Americans with Disabilities Act, Mental Disability, and Work. In *Mental Disorder, Work Disability, and the Law*, ed. R. J. Bonnie and J. Monahan, pp. 203–19. Chicago: University of Chicago Press.

Bem, D. J. 1967. Self-Perception: An Alternative Explanation of Cognitive Dissonance Phenomena. *Psychological Review* 74:183–200.

———. 1972. Self-Perception Theory. In *Advances in Experimental Social Psychology*, ed. L. Berkowitz, vol. 6. New York: Academic Press.

Berry, J. O., and J. A. Meyer. 1995. Employing Persons with Disabilities: Impact of Attitude and Situation. *Rehabilitation Psychology* 40:211–22.

Bettencourt, B. A., et al. 1992. Cooperation and the Reduction of Intergroup Bias: The Role of Reward Structure and Social Orientation. *Journal of Experimental Social Psychology* 28:301–19.

Beuf, A. H. 1990. *Beauty Is the Beast*. Philadelphia: University of Pennsylvania Press.

Blanchard, F. A., and S. W. Cook. 1976. Effects of Helping a Less Competent Member of a Cooperating Interracial Group on the Development of Interpersonal Attraction. *Journal of Personality and Social Psychology* 34:1245–55.

Blanchard, F. A., T. Lilly, and L. A. Vaughn. 1991. Reducing the Expression of Racial Prejudice. *Psychological Science* 2:101–5.

Blanck, P. D. 1994. Communicating the Americans with Disabilities Act, Transcending Compliance: A Case Report on Sears, Roebuck and Co. *Annenberg Washington Program Reports*.

———. 1996. Communicating the Americans with Disabilities Act, Transcending Compliance: 1996 Follow-up Report on Sears, Roebuck and Co. *Annenberg Washington Program Reports*.

———. 1997. The Economics of the Employment Provisions of the Americans with Disabilities Act: Part I — Workplace Accommodations. *DePaul L. Rev.* 46:877–914.

———. 1998. *The Americans with Disabilities Act and the Emerging Workforce*. Washington, D.C.: American Association on Mental Retardation.

Blanck, P. D., and M. W. Marti. 1996. Genetic Discrimination and the Employment Provisions of the Americans with Disabilities Act: Emerging Legal, Empirical, and Policy Implications. *Behavioral Sciences and the Law* 14:411-32.

———. 1997. Attitudes, Behavior, and the Employment Provisions of the Americans with Disabilities Act. *Villanova L. Rev.* 42:345-407.

Bogdan R., and S. J. Taylor. 1989. Relationships with Severely Disabled People: The Social Construction of Humanness. *Social Problems* 36:135-48.

Brewer, M. B., and N. Miller. 1984. Beyond the Contact Hypothesis: Theoretical Perspectives on Desegregation. In *Groups in Contact: The Psychology of Desegregation*, ed. N. Miller and M. B. Brewer, pp. 281-302. New York: Academic Press.

Campbell, J., and C. L. Kaufmann. 1997. Equality and Difference in the ADA: Unintended Consequences for Employment of People with Mental Health Disabilities. In *Mental Disorder, Work Disability, and the Law*, ed. R. J. Bonnie and J. Monahan, pp. 221-39. Chicago: University of Chicago Press.

Carli, L. L., and J. B. Leonard. 1989. The Effect of Hindsight on Victim Derogation. *Journal of Social and Clinical Psychology* 8:331-43.

Carling, P. 1994. Reasonable Accommodation in the Workplace for Persons with Psychiatric Disabilities. In *Implications of the Americans with Disabilities Act for Psychology*, ed. S. M. Bruyere and J. O'Keefe, pp. 103-36. Washington, D.C.: American Psychological Association.

Colella, A., A. DeNisi, and A. Varma. 1997. Appraising the Performance of Employees with Disabilities: A Review and Model. *Human Resources Management Review* 7:27-53.

Combs, I. H., and C. P. Omvig. 1986. Accommodation of Disabled People into Employment: Perceptions of Employers. *Journal of Rehabilitation* 52:42-45.

Comer, R. J., and J. A. Piliavin. 1972. The Effects of Physical Deviance upon Face-to-Face Interaction: The Other Side. *Journal of Personality and Social Psychology* 23:33-39.

Cook, S. W. 1984. Cooperative Interaction in Multiethnic Contexts. In *Groups in Contact: The Psychology of Desegregation*, ed. N. Miller and M. Brewer, pp. 155-85. New York: Academic Press.

Crocker, J., and B. Major. 1989. Social Stigma and Self-Esteem: The Self-Protective Properties of Stigma. *Psychological Review* 96:608-30.

———. 1994. Reactions to Stigma: The Moderating Role of Justifications. In *The Psychology of Prejudice: The Ontario Symposium*, ed. M. P. Zanna and J. M. Olson, vol. 7. Hillsdale, N.J.: Erlbaum.

Diksa, E., and E. S. Rogers. 1996. Employer Concerns about Hiring Persons with Psychiatric Disability: Results of the Employer Attitude Questionnaire. *Rehabilitation Counseling Bulletin* 40:31-44.

Donaldson, J. 1980. Changing Attitudes towards Handicapped Persons: A Review and Analysis of Research. *Exceptional Children* 46:504-15.

Eagly, A. H. 1987. *Sex Differences in Social Behavior: A Social-Role Interpretation.* Hillsdale, N.J.: Erlbaum.

Eagly, A. H., and S. Chaiken. 1993. *The Psychology of Attitudes.* Fort Worth, Tex.: Harcourt Brace Jovanovich.

Edelman, L. B. 1992. Legal Ambiguity and Symbolic Structures: Organizational Mediation of Civil Rights Law. *American Journal of Sociology* 9:1531-76.

Emener, W. G., and J. M. McHargue. 1978. Employer Attitudes toward the Employment and Placement of the Handicapped. *Journal of Applied Rehabilitation Counseling* 9 (3): 120-25.

Equal Employment Opportunity Commission. 1997. *EEOC Compliance Manual: EEOC Guidance on the ADA and Psychiatric Disabilities. FEP Manual (BNA)* 63, 70:1281.

Equal Employment Opportunity Commission v. Texas Bus Lines. 923 F. Supp. 965 (S.D. Texas 1996).

Estroff, S., et al. 1994. The Influence of Social Networks and Social Support on Violence by Persons with Serious Mental Illness. *Hospital and Community Psychiatry* 45:669-78.

Evans, J. H. 1976. Changing Attitudes towards Disabled Persons: An Experimental Study. *Rehabilitation Counseling Bulletin* 19:572-79.

Farina, A. 1982. The Stigma of Mental Disorders. In *In the Eye of the Beholder: Contemporary Issues in Stereotyping,* ed. A. G. Miller, pp. 305-63. New York: Praeger.

Festinger, L. 1957. *A Theory of Cognitive Dissonance.* Stanford, Calif.: Stanford University Press.

Feuerstein, M., and R. Thebarge. 1991. Perceptions of Disability and Occupational Stress as Discriminators of Work Disability in Patients with Chronic Pain. *Journal of Occupational Rehabilitation* 1 (3): 185-95.

Fichten, C. S., and R. Amsel. 1986. Trait Attributions about College Students with a Physical Disability: Circumplex Analyses and Methodological Issues. *Journal of Applied Social Psychology* 16:410-27.

Finerman, R., and L. A. Bennett. 1995. Overview: Guilt, Blame and Shame in Sickness. *Social Science and Medicine* 40:1-3.

Fisher, D. B. 1995. Disclosure, Discrimination and the ADA. *Journal of the California Alliance for the Mentally Ill* 6:55.

Florian, V. 1982. The Meanings of Work for Physically Disabled Clients Undergoing Vocational Rehabilitation. *International Journal of Rehabilitation Research* 5:375-77.

Fuqua, D. R., M. Rathbun, and E. M. Gade. 1984. A Comparison of Employer Attitudes toward the Worker Problems of Eight Types of Disabled Workers. *Journal of Applied Rehabilitation Counseling* 15 (1): 40-43.

Gaertner, S. L., et al. 1990. How Does Cooperation Reduce Intergroup Bias? *Journal of Personality and Social Psychology* 59:692-704.

Gerard, H. B., and G. C. Mathewson. 1966. The Effects of Severity of Initiation on Liking for a Group: A Replication. *Journal of Experimental Social Psychology* 2:278–87.

Goffman, I. 1963. *Stigma: Notes on the Management of Spoiled Identity.* Englewood Cliffs, N.J.: Prentice-Hall.

Gouvier, W. D., et al. 1991. Employment Discrimination against Handicapped Job Candidates: An Analog Study of the Effects of Neurological Causation, Visibility of Handicap, and Public Contact. *Rehabilitation Psychology* 36:121–29.

Grand, S. A., J. E. Bernier, and D. C. Strohmer. 1982. Attitudes toward Disabled Persons as a Function of Social Context and Specific Disability. *Rehabilitation Psychology* 27:165–74.

Greeley, A. M., and P. B. Sheatsley. 1971. Attitudes toward Racial Integration. *Scientific American* 225 (6): 13–19.

Hahn, H. 1985. Toward a Politics of Disability: Definitions, Disciplines, and Policies. *Social Science Journal* 22:87–105.

———. 1988. The Politics of Physical Differences: Disability and Discrimination. *Journal of Social Issues* 44:39–47.

———. 1996. Antidiscrimination Laws and Social Research on Disability: The Minority Group Perspective. *Behavioral Sciences and the Law* 14:41–59.

Hall, F. S., and E. L. Hall. 1994. The ADA: Going beyond the Law. *Academy Management Executive Review* 8:17–26.

Hall, L. L. 1997. Making the ADA Work for People with Psychiatric Disabilities. In *Mental Disorder, Work Disability, and the Law,* ed. R. J. Bonnie and J. Monahan, pp. 241–80. Chicago: University of Chicago Press.

Hantula, D. A., and N. A. Reilly. 1996. Reasonable Accommodation for Employees with Mental Disabilities: A Mandate for Effective Supervision? *Behavioral Sciences and the Law* 14:107–20.

Hartog v. Wasatch Academy. 129 F.3d 1076 (10th Cir. 1997).

Havranek, J. E. 1991. The Social and Individual Costs of Negative Attitudes toward Persons with Physical Disabilities. *Journal of Applied Rehabilitation Counseling* 22 (1): 15–21.

Hegwer v. Bd. of Civil Serv. Commissioners. 7 Cal. Rptr. 2d 389 (Ct. App. 1992).

Henderson, G., and W. V. Bryan. 1984. *Psychological Aspects of Disability.* Springfield, Ill.: Charles C. Thomas.

Hiday, V. A. 1995. The Social Context of Mental Illness and Violence. *Journal of Health and Social Behavior* 36:122–37.

Higgins, E. T., and W. S. Rholes. 1978. Saying Is Believing: Effects of Message Modification on Memory and Liking for the Person Described. *Journal of Experimental Social Psychology* 14:363–78.

Horne, M. D. 1988. Modifying Peer Attitudes toward the Handicapped: Procedures and Research Issues. In *Attitudes toward Persons with Disabilities,* ed. H. Yuker, pp. 203–22. New York: Springer.

Horne, M. D., and J. L. Ricciardo. 1988. Hierarchy of Response to Handicaps. *Psychological Reports* 62:83–86.

Howard, G. 1975. The Ex-mental Patient as an Employee. *American Journal of Orthopsychiatry* 45:479–83.

ICD-International Center for the Disabled and the National Council on the Handicapped. 1986. *The ICD Survey of Disabled Americans: Bringing Disabled Americans into the Mainstream*. New York: Louis Harris and Associates, Inc.

ICD-International Center for the Disabled, the National Council on the Handicapped, and the President's Committee on Employment of the Handicapped. 1987. *The ICD Survey II: Employing Disabled Americans*. New York: Louis Harris and Associates, Inc.

Johnson, V. A., R. Greenwood, and K. F. Schriner. 1988. Work Performance and Work Personality: Employer Concerns about Workers with Disabilities. *Rehabilitation Counseling Bulletin* 32:50–57.

Johnson, W. G., and M. B. Baldwin. 1993. The Americans with Disability Act: Will It Make a Difference? *Policy Studies Journal* 21:775–88.

Jones, B. J., et al. 1991. A Survey of Fortune 500 Corporate Policies concerning the Psychiatrically Handicapped. *Journal of Rehabilitation* 57 (4): 31–35.

Jones, E. E., et al. 1984. *Social Stigma: The Psychology of Marked Relationships*. New York: W. H. Freeman.

Jones, E. E., and R. E. Nisbett. 1971. *The Actor and the Observer: Divergent Perceptions of the Causes of Behavior*. Morristown, N.J.: General Learning Press.

Jones, G. E., and D. L. Stone. 1995. Perceived Discomfort Associated with Working with Persons with Varying Disabilities. *Perceptual and Motor Skills* 81:911–19.

Katz, I. 1981. *Stigma: A Social Psychological Analysis*. Hillsdale, N.J.: Erlbaum.

Kaye, S. 1996. *Disability Watch: Status Report on the Condition of People with Disabilities*. San Francisco: University of California, Disability Rights Advocates and Disability Statistics Center.

Key, L. E. 1997. Co-worker Morale, Confidentiality, and the ADA. *DePaul L. Rev.* 46:1003–42.

Kleck, R. E., H. Ono, and A. H. Hastorf. 1966. The Effects of Physical Deviance upon Face-to-Face Interaction. *Human Relations* 19:425–36.

Kraus, S. J. 1995. Attitudes and the Prediction of Behavior: A Meta-analysis of the Empirical Literature. *Personality and Social Psychology Bulletin* 21:58–75.

Krosnick, J. A., et al. 1993. Attitude Strength: One Construct or Many Related Constructs? *Journal of Personality and Social Psychology* 65:1132–51.

Laird, J. D. 1974. Self-Attribution of Emotion: The Effects of Expressive Behavior on the Quality of Emotional Experience. *Journal of Personality and Social Psychology* 29:475–86.

———. 1984. The Real Role of Facial Response in the Experience of Emotion: A Reply to Tourangeau and Ellsworth, and Others. *Journal of Personality and Social Psychology* 47:909–17.

Lalonde, R. N., and J. E. Cameron. 1994. Behavioral Responses to Discrimination: A Focus on Action. In *The Psychology of Prejudice: The Ontario Symposium,* ed. M. P. Zanna and J. M. Olson, vol. 7, pp. 257–88. Hillsdale, N.J.: Erlbaum.

La Paz v. Henry's Diner, Inc. 946 F. Supp. 484 (N.D. Tex. 1996).

Lerner, M. J. 1980. *The Belief in a Just World: A Fundamental Delusion.* New York: Plenum.

Lerner, M. R., and C. H. Simmons. 1966. Observer's Reaction to the "Innocent Victim": Compassion or Rejection? *Journal of Personality and Social Psychology* 4:203–10.

Lerner, M. R., and D. T. Miller. 1978. Just World Research and the Attribution Process: Looking Back and Ahead. *Psychological Bulletin* 85:1030–51.

Levy, B., and E. Langer. 1994. Aging Free from Negative Stereotypes: Successful Memory in China and among the American Deaf. *Journal of Personality and Social Psychology* 66:989–97.

Levy, J. M., et al. 1991. Employment of Persons with Severe Disabilities in Large Businesses in the United States. *International Journal of Rehabilitation Research* 14:323–32.

Link, B. G., H. Andrews, and F. T. Cullen. 1992. The Violent and Illegal Behavior of Mental Patients Reconsidered. *American Sociological Review* 57:275–92.

Link, B. G., et al. 1992. The Consequences of Stigma for Persons with Mental Illness: Evidence from the Social Sciences. In *Stigma and Mental Illness,* ed. P. J. Fink and A. Tasman, pp. 87–95. Washington, D.C.: American Psychiatric Press.

Livneh, H. 1982. On the Origins of Negative Attitudes toward People with Disabilities. *Rehabilitation Literature* 43:338–47.

———. 1988. A Dimensional Perspective on the Origin of Negative Attitudes toward Persons with Disabilities. In *Attitudes toward Persons with Disabilities,* ed. H. Yuker, pp. 35–46. New York: Springer.

Louis Harris and Associates, Inc. and National Organization on Disability. 1995. *1995 Survey of Corporate Executives of the ADA.* New York: Louis Harris and Associates, Inc.

Lyons, M. 1991. Enabling or Disabling? Students' Attitudes toward Persons with Disabilities. *American Journal of Occupational Therapy* 45:311–16.

Makas, E. 1988. Positive Attitudes toward Disabled People: Disabled and Nondisabled Persons' Perspectives. *Journal of Social Issues* 44:49–61.

———. 1993. Getting in Touch: The Relationship between Contact with and Attitudes toward People with Disabilities. In *Perspectives on Disability,* ed. M. Nagler, 2d ed., pp. 121–36. Palo Alto, Calif.: Health Markets Research.

Mancuso, L. L. 1990. Reasonable Accommodation for Persons with Psychiatric Disabilities. *Psychosocial Rehabilitation Journal* 14:3–19.

Marchioro, C. A., and L. K. Bartels. 1994. Perceptions of a Job Interviewee with a Disability. *Journal of Social Behavior and Personality* 9 (5): 383–94.

McCarthy, H. 1988. Attitudes that Affect Employment Opportunities for Persons with Disabilities. In *Attitudes toward Persons with Disabilities: Progress and Prospects,* ed. H. E. Yuker, pp. 246–61. New York: Springer.

McDonald, J. J., Jr., F. B. Kulick, and M. K. Ceighton. 1995. Mental Disabilities under the ADA: A Management Rights Approach. *Employer Relations Law Journal* 20:541–69.

McFarlin, D. B., J. Song, and M. Sonntag. 1991. Integrating the Disabled in the Work Force: A Survey of Fortune 500 Company Attitudes and Practices. *Employee Responsibilities and Rights Journal* 4:107–22.

McIntosh, P. L. 1996. When the Surgeon Has HIV: What to Tell Patients about the Risk of Exposure and the Risk of Transmission. *U. Kans. L. Rev.* 44:315–64.

Meyerowitz, B. E., J. G. Williams, and J. Gessner. 1987. Perceptions of Controllability and Attitudes toward Cancer and Cancer Patients. *Journal of Applied Social Psychology* 17:471–92.

Michaels, C., et al. 1993. In *The ADA Mandate for Social Change,* ed. P. Wehman, pp. 89–115. Baltimore: Brookes.

Miller, A. B., and C. B. Keys. 1996. Awareness, Action, and Collaboration: How the Self-Advocacy Movement Is Empowering for Persons with Developmental Disabilities. *Mental Retardation* 34 (5): 312–19.

Miller, S. P. 1997. Keeping the Promise: The Americans with Disabilities Act and Employment Discrimination on the Basis of Psychiatric Disabilities. *Calif. L. Rev.* 85:701–47.

Milstein, B., L. Rubenstein, and R. Cyr. 1991. The Americans with Disabilities Act: A Breathtaking Promise for People with Mental Disabilities. *Clearinghouse Review* 24:1240–49.

Mintz, J., et al. 1992. Treatments of Depression and Functional Capacity to Work. *Archives of General Psychiatry* 49:761–68.

Moberly, M. D. 1996. Perception or Reality? Some Reflections on the Interpretation of Disability Discrimination Statutes. *Hofstra Labor Law Journal* 13:345–79.

Monahan, J. 1992. Mental Disorder and Violent Behavior: Perceptions and Evidence. *American Psychologist* 47:511–21.

Moore, J. A. 1995. Can the ADA Work for People with Mental Illness? *Journal of the California Alliance for the Mentally Ill* 6:25–26.

Moore, S. R., and R. L. Simpson. 1984. Reciprocity in the Teacher-Pupil and Peer Verbal Interactions of Learning Disabled, Behavior-Disordered and Regular Education Students. *Learning Disabled Quarterly* 7:30–38.

Mulvey, E. 1994. Assessing the Evidence of a Link between Mental Illness and Violence. *Hospital and Community* 45:663–68.

Nathanson, R. B., and J. Lambert. 1981. Integrating Disabled Employees into the Workplace. *Personnel Journal* 60 (2): 109–13.

National Academy of Social Insurance. 1996. Balancing Security and Opportunity: The Challenge of Disability Income Policy. Washington, D.C.: National Academy of Social Insurance.

National Organization on Disability. 1994. *Survey of Americans with Disabilities.* New York: Louis Harris and Associates, Inc.

Neuberg, S. L. 1994. Expectancy-Confirmation Processes in Stereotype-Tinged Social Encounters: The Moderating Role of Social Goals. In *The Psychology of Prejudice: The Ontario Symposium,* ed. M. P. Zanna and J. M. Olson, vol. 7, pp. 103–30. Hillsdale, N.J.: Erlbaum.

Neuberg, S. L., et al. 1994. When We Observe Stigmatized and "Normal" Individuals Interacting: Stigma by Association. *Personality and Social Psychology Bulletin* 20:196–209.

Olkin, R., and L. J. Howson. 1994. Attitudes toward and Images of Physical Disability. *Journal of Social Behavior and Personality* 9 (5): 81–96.

Olson, J. M., and M. P. Zanna. 1993. Attitudes and Attitude Change. In *Annual Review of Psychology,* ed. L. W. Perter and M. R. Rosenzweig, vol. 44, pp. 117–54. Palo Alto, Calif.: Annual Reviews Inc.

Parent, W. S., and J. M. Everson. 1986. Competencies of Disabled Workers in Industry: A Review of Business Literature. *Journal of Rehabilitation* 52 (4): 16–23.

Parry, J. W. 1993. Mental Disabilities under the ADA: A Difficult Path to Follow. *Mental and Physical Disability Law Reporter* 17:100–112.

Patterson, J. B., and B. Witten. 1987. Myths concerning People with Disabilities. *Journal of Applied Rehabilitation Counseling* 18 (3): 42–44.

Perlin, M. 1993. The ADA and Persons with Mental Disabilities: Can Sanist Attitudes Be Undone? *Journal of Law and Health* 8:15–45.

Petkova, K. G., I. Ajzen, and B. L. Driver. 1995. Salience of Anti-abortion Beliefs and Commitment to an Attitudinal Position: On the Strength, Structure, and Predictive Validity of Anti-abortion Attitudes. *Journal of Applied Social Psychology* 25:463–83.

Pettigrew, T. F. 1979. The Ultimate Attribution Error: Extending Allport's Cognitive Analysis of Prejudice. *Personality and Social Psychology Bulletin* 5:461–76.

Pfeiffer, D. 1994. Overview of the Disability Movement: History, Legislative Record, and Political Implications. *Policy Studies Journal* 21:724–34.

Pollet, S. 1995. Mental Illness in the Workplace: The Tension between Productivity and Reasonable Accommodation. *Journal of Psychiatry and Law* 23:155–84.

Ravid, R. 1992. Disclosure of Mental Illness to Employers: Legal Recourses and Ramifications. *Journal of Psychiatry and Law* 20:85–102.

Raza, S. M., and B. N. Carpenter. 1987. A Model of Hiring Decisions in Real Employment Interviews. *Journal of Applied Psychology* 72:596–603.

Rodin, M., et al. 1989. Derogation, Exclusion, and Unfair Treatment of Persons with Social Flaws: Controllability of Stigma and the Attribution of Prejudice. *Personality and Social Psychology Bulletin* 15:439–51.

Rosen, S. 1991. Disability Accommodation and the Labor Market. In *Disability and Work: Incentives, Rights, and Opportunities,* ed. C. L. Weaver. Washington, D.C.: AEI Press.

Rosenthal, R. 1994. Interpersonal Expectancy Effects: A Thirty-Year Perspective. *Current Directions in Psychological Science* 3:176–79.

Rothbart, M., and O. P. John. 1985. Social Categorization and Behavioral Episodes: A Cognitive Analysis of the Effects of Intergroup Contact. *Journal of Social Issues* 41:81–104.

Russell, P. A., and C. D. Gray. 1992. Prejudice against a Progay Man in an Everyday Situation: A Scenario Study. *Journal of Applied Social Psychology* 22:1676–87.

Rynders, J. E., et al. 1980. Producing Positive Interaction among Down Syndrome and Nonhandicapped Teenagers through Cooperative Goal Structuring. *American Journal of Mental Deficiency* 85:268–73.

Schneider, D. R., and A. Anderson. 1980. Attitudes toward the Stigmatized: Some Insights from Recent Research. *Rehabilitation Counseling Bulletin* 23:299–313.

School Bd. of Nassau Co. v. Arline. 480 U.S. 273 (1987).

Shapiro, J. P. 1994. *No Pity: People with Disabilities Forging a Civil Rights Movement.* New York: Random House.

Sharp, M. E. 1996. The Hidden Disability That Finds Protection under the Americans with Disabilities Act: Employing the Mentally Impaired. *Georgia State U. L. Rev.* 12:889–927.

Sherif, M., et al. 1961. *Intergroup Conflict and Cooperation: The Robbers' Cave Experiment.* Norman: Oklahoma Book Exchange.

Stone, C. I., and B. Sawatzki. 1980. Hiring Bias and the Disabled Interviewee: Effects of Manipulating Work History and Disability Information of the Disabled Job Applicant. *Journal of Vocational Behavior* 16:96–104.

Stone, D. L., and A. Colella. 1996. A Model of Factors Affecting the Treatment of Disabled Individuals in Organizations. *Academy of Management Review* 21:352–401.

Stone, E. G., D. L. Stone, and R. L. Dipboye. 1992. Stigmas in Organizations: Race, Handicaps, and Physical Unattractiveness. In *Issues, Theory, and Research in Industrial/Organizational Psychology,* ed. K. Kelley, pp. 385–457. New York: Elsevier.

Swanson, J., and C. Holzer. 1991. Violence and the ECA Data. *Hospital and Community Psychiatry* 42:954–55.

Talbert, R., and N. Karp. 1995. Collaborative Approaches: Aging, Discrimination, and Dispute Resolutions. *Clearinghouse Review* 29:638–42.

Taylor, D. G., P. B. Sheatsley, and A. M. Greeley. 1978. Attitudes toward Racial Integration. *Scientific American* 238 (6): 42–49.

Tringo, J. L. 1970. The Hierarchy of Preference toward Disability Groups. *Journal of Special Education* 4:295–306.

Triplet, R. G., and D. B. Sugarman. 1987. Reactions to AIDS Victims: Ambiguity Breeds Contempt. *Personality and Social Psychology Bulletin* 13:265–74.

Tripp, A. 1988. Comparison of Attitudes of Regular and Adapted Physical Educators toward Disabled Individuals. *Perceptual and Motor Skills* 66:425–26.

United Cerebral Palsy Associations. 1996. *1996 ADA "Snapshot of America" Shows Change in Lives of Americans with Disabilities.*

Wehman, P. 1993. Employment Opportunities and Career Development. In *The ADA Mandate for Social Change,* ed. P. Wehman. Baltimore: Brookes.

Weigel, R. H., and P. W. Howes. 1985. Conceptions of Racial Prejudice: Symbolic Racism Reconsidered. *Journal of Social Issues* 41:117–38.

Weiner, B. 1993. On Sin versus Sickness: A Theory of Perceived Responsibility and Social Motivation. *American Psychologist* 48:957–65.

Weiner, B., R. P. Perry, and J. Magnusson. 1988. An Attributional Analysis of Reactions to Stigmas. *Journal of Personality and Social Psychology* 55:738–48.

West, J. 1993. The Evolution of Disability Rights. In *Implementing the Americans with Disabilities Act: Rights and Responsibilities of All Americans,* ed. L. O. Gostin and H. A. Beyer, pp. 3–15. Baltimore: Brookes.

Westbrook, M. T., V. Legge, and M. Pennay. 1993. Attitudes towards Disabilities in a Multicultural Society. *Social Science Medicine* 36:615–23.

Willis, C. J. 1994–95. Title I of the Americans with Disabilities Act: Disabling the Disabled. *Cumberland L. Rev.* 25:715–52.

Wolfensberger, W. 1983. Social Role Valorization: A Proposed New Term for the Principle of Normalization. *Mental Retardation* 21:234–39.

Wright, B. A. 1983. *Physical Disability: A Psychosocial Approach.* 2d ed. New York: Harper and Row.

Yuker, H. E. 1988. The Effects of Contact on Attitudes toward Disabled Persons: Some Empirical Generalizations. In *Attitudes toward Persons with Disabilities: Progress and Prospects,* ed. H. E. Yuker, pp. 262–74. New York: Springer.

———. 1994. Variables That Influence Attitudes toward People with Disabilities: Conclusions from the Data. *Journal of Social Behavior and Personality* 9 (5): 3–22.

Zimbardo, P. G. 1972. The Stanford Prison Experiment (a slide/tape presentation). Stanford, Calif.: Philip G. Zimbardo, Inc.

Zuckerman, D., K. Debenham, and K. Moore. 1993. *The ADA and People with Mental Illness: A Resource Manual for Employers.* Washington, D.C.: American Bar Association.

Part Five

Culture and Policy in ADA Title I

Chapter XV

Bodies and Environments

The Cultural Construction of Disability

DOUGLAS C. BAYNTON

For most people, disability and impairment are synonymous terms. Professionals in disability-related fields, on the other hand, usually distinguish between them: impairment denotes a specific functional limitation while disability refers to a limitation on major life activities. While not treated as synonymous, however, professionals nevertheless generally tie disability closely to impairment. This allows the category of "disabled" to be, if not completely unambiguous in practice, conceptually at least relatively clear and definable. Disabled people are those who are limited in regard to certain kinds of functions and activities. Those without disabilities do not experience these limitations.

The suggestion that disability might be *primarily* a cultural and political matter, a social construction, or that it might fundamentally vary over time and from culture to culture, is hence perplexing to most. Yet activists in the disability rights movement and scholars in the new disability studies increasingly argue that this is the case: that the concept of disability is fraught with ambiguity and based on highly variable cultural rules and values concerning the body, personal competence, social interaction, individual responsibility, dependence and independence. Further, public policies and professional practices not only respond to changing definitions of disability but in turn help to shape and change those definitions. Indeed, disability appears to be similar in this way to the idea of race, another highly problematic, flexible, and ambiguous concept that most people take to be fixed and definite. And, as with race, it is likely that the courts will have an important role in defining it.[1]

Difficulties of interpretation occasioned by the Americans with Disabilities Act (ADA) have demonstrated the ambiguities inherent in the concept of disability, as courts have had to grapple with questions of who is and who is not disabled for the purposes of the act. The ADA defines a disabled person as one who "has a physical or mental impairment that substantially limits one or more of the major life activities." The ADA also includes under its protections the individual who "has a record of such an impairment that is used by the employer to discriminate against the individual, whether or not the individual still has the impairment," as well as one who "is regarded as having a disability, whether or not the individual is impaired at all." While the latter two provisions may be interpreted as recognition that people are often identified as disabled and subject to discrimination regardless of physical impairment, the causal linkage of impairment with disability in the law encourages (though it does not necessitate) a definition that locates disability primarily or solely in the body of the individual (Hahn 1996, p. 44).

Immediate difficulties arise with such a definition. It suggests, for example, that "major life activity" be interpreted as *walking* rather than as *moving about freely.* The former interpretation emphasizes individual impairment, while the latter directs attention to a built environment that impedes mobility for, say, wheelchair users. The former assumes a *normal* means of locomotion, identifying other ways as abnormal, impaired, different, and unexpected. An impairment-centered definition of disability selects walking as a major life activity and rolling on wheels as an inferior substitute necessitated by the inability to engage in a normal life activity.

Of course, arguably walking *is* normal. Locomotion by walking is typical for the species. If we look at disabilities one by one, we can repeat this analysis ad infinitum, identifying each category of disabled persons as a small, abnormal minority. However, if we think of people with disabilities as a whole, as people who experience discrimination because of stigmatized differences from the majority, we have, if still a minority, a considerably larger one. In fact, according to currently accepted definitions of disability, this is the largest minority in America, variously estimated at 35 to 45 million people. If we further think of differentiation as a continuous process—positing that for any function or activity there is a continuum of ability/impairment, that no community ever lacks a broad range of physical, mental, and psychological variation, that such variation is both normal and expected, and indeed that the presence of people deemed "abnormal" is entirely normal and expected in any population—then we begin to think of disability in a different way. (The faith that such variation might *not* be normal or expected at some uncertain, soon-but-always-receding point in the future is, as we shall see, a phenomenon of the modern age with its faith in progress and passion for narratives of a utopian future.) If we think in terms of normal *communities,* as opposed to normal *individuals,* then the presence of people who communicate, move about, and process information in unconventional ways begins to seem quite normal. Furthermore, their relative absence from the streets and businesses of America—their enforced absence—begins to seem disturbingly abnormal.

Since normal variation is continuous and not subject to sharp breaks, the line between disabled and nondisabled is fairly arbitrary. Eyesight, hearing, strength, height, mobility, flexibility, dexterity, mental health, intelligence, and the like are all matters that exist on a continuum. Who has imperfect but normal eyesight, and who has a disability from a vision impairment? We might use the usual functional definition based on whether the impairment is correctable to the point where it does not interfere with major life activities, but clearly this varies with lifestyle and occupation. Further complicating the problem of definition are particular historical or social circumstances: economic structures, residential and occupational patterns, ordinary or necessary daily activities such as automobile driving, as well as cultural ideals and expectations. "Disability," as B. J. Gleeson recently wrote, "is what *may* become of impairment as each society produces itself sociospatially: there is no *necessary* correspondence between impairment and disability" (1997, p. 194). Lois Bragg (1997, pp. 165, 167, 173) argues that while "many conditions that resulted in disability 100 years ago—nearsightedness, epilepsy, harelip—no longer do so," other impairments that are disabling today were not considered so in the past. As one example, in a study of medieval Icelandic sagas she found that what would be severe vision impairments today were treated as relatively inconsequential, and concluded that "what we call disabilities are perhaps always and everywhere exceptionalities, but not always disabilities."

A Minority Group Model

As long ago as 1976 the Union of Physically Impaired against Segregation, in London, was challenging overly simple and essentialist definitions of disability, defining it as "the disadvantage or restriction of activity caused by a contemporary social organisation which takes no or little account of people who have physical impairments and thus excludes them from the mainstream of social activities" (pp. 3–4). In 1988, Michelle Fine and Adrienne Asch, as editors of a special issue of the *Journal of Social Issues* devoted to disability, advocated a minority group model defined in part by "differential power, differential and pejorative treatment, and group awareness" (p. 7). And as Simi Linton argues in her recent book, "*disability* is best understood as a marker of identity" that has now become instrumental in building "a coalition of people with significant impairments, people with behavioral or anatomical characteristics marked as deviant, and people who have or are suspected as having conditions, such as AIDS or emotional illness, that make them targets of discrimination" (Linton 1998, p. 12; see also Shakespeare and Watson 1997; Oliver 1996).[2]

Context clearly looms large in defining disability. For example, should we call disabled a deaf professor fluent in American Sign Language who teaches at Gallaudet University (the university for deaf students in Washington, D.C.), socializes and does business chiefly with others fluent in ASL, and uses an interpreter when that is not possible? The answer depends on whether we interpret "major life activity" to mean *hearing* or *communicating with others in a community.* If the latter, it is hard to imagine what major life activities would be limited for such a person. If the deaf professor worked at a university other than Gallaudet where there were few other deaf people, would he or she then *become* disabled? If interpreters were universally and readily available, or if most people learned American Sign Language in school, would that change the answer?

Communities in which everyone did know sign language have in fact existed, one of them on Martha's Vineyard from the seventeenth to the early twentieth century. An unusually high rate of inherited deafness resulted in a community in which both hearing and deaf islanders knew and used a sign language, the hearing members of the community moving back and forth between speech and sign depending on who was present. Nora Groce, an anthropologist who researched the history of the island and interviewed elderly residents who still remembered that community, was told repeatedly that no one on the island gave much thought to the presence of deaf people—"they were just like everyone else." "I didn't think about the deaf any more than you'd think about anybody with a different voice." "Those people weren't handicapped. They were just deaf." Groce concluded that "the Martha's Vineyard experience suggests strongly that the concept of a handicap is an arbitrary social category. And if it is a question of definition, rather than a universal given, perhaps it can be redefined, and many of the cultural preconceptions summarized in the term 'handicapped,' as it is now used, eliminated" (1985, p. 108).

It may be that the argument for the social construction of disability is easier to make for some disabilities such as deafness than for others. After all, the major impact of deafness is on communication, and since language works visually just as well as it does aurally, the use of a visual language obviates most of the limitations associated with the impairment—at least for those who learn sign language at an early enough age to attain native or near-native fluency in it. Since the disability of deafness results from having to interact with the larger, hearing community, a minority group model seems at least equally appropriate. However, while the same kind of argument perhaps cannot be made quite so easily for all disabilities (or even for those deafened later in life), certainly similar dynamics are at work. For example, would people with mobility impairments who lived in a hypothetical fully accessible city be disabled? Again, it depends on how we define disability: as an inability to walk or as an inability to move about freely. Then of course there are the significant numbers of people with what are largely or entirely formal, as opposed to functional, impairments such as bodily and facial disfigurement, minor speech impairments, limps, involuntary and unusual behaviors and/or movements. Such people may experience little or no functional limitation, yet face discriminatory treatment on the basis of physical or behavioral differences from the majority.

Moreover, the line between an impairment of appearance and one of function is problematic. Harlan Hahn (1996, p. 54) argues that much discrimination against visibly disabled people results from "aesthetic anxiety," a discomfort with unusual and stigmatized physical characteristics. Lennard Davis (1995) points out that in general "disability presents itself to 'normal people' through two main modalities—function and appearance." Not only does the sight of the disabled person commonly evoke such feelings as discomfort, fear, pity, horror, repulsion, disgust, and compassion, but "the disabled object *is produced or constructed by* the strong feelings of repulsion." The result is that "a person with an impairment is turned into a disabled person" (pp. 11-12, emphasis added).

Whether the courts use a definition of disability that assumes a direct and uncomplicated relationship between functional impairment and disability or define disability as largely produced by discrimination has a potentially profound impact upon the future of the ADA. Like other professional discourses concerning disability, most legal discourse has so far rested on a functional impairment paradigm, described by Hahn (1996, pp. 41, 44-45) as one that seeks "to alleviate the physical and economic impact of disability primarily by correcting impairments to the maximum extent possible and by encouraging disabled individuals to strive to approximate standards set by the nondisabled majority." It comprises two related but distinguishable ways of thinking about disability—an economic model that focuses on impairment as a disqualification for employment, and a medical model that focuses on organic impairment. Both are predicated on the notion that disability resides largely or solely in the affected individual. Both "concentrate on the behavioral or vocational restrictions that stem from bodily impairments as the primary issue to be studied and as the principal problem to be solved."

The economic model has resulted in a long succession of government benefit programs, from Revolutionary War pensions for disabled soldiers to Social Security Disability Income today, based on the notion that disability is practically synonymous with inability to work. Deborah Stone (1984, pp. 29–89; see also Berkowitz 1987) argues that the category "disabled" arose with the economic model, as an administrative category designed to determine legitimate reasons for not working and receiving public relief. A model that presumes unemployability is on its face incompatible with a law such as the ADA that forbids employment discrimination.

Many argue that the medical model is equally untenable. Claire Liachowitz (1988, p. xi), among others, has maintained that "much of the inability to function that characterizes physically impaired people is an outcome of political and social decisions rather than medical limitations." The disability rights movement is based in large part on the renunciation of the medical model as a counterproductive approach to disability outside the doctor's office. According to Karen Hirsch (1995, p. 5), the medical model, "with its emphasis on evaluation, diagnosis, prescription, isolation, treatment, cure, and prognosis," is not merely unproductive but oppressive. The disability rights movement "was in part born out of the desire of disabled people to demedicalize their lives and take control over their own destinies." One of the major initiatives of that movement today is to free thousands of disabled people from what is, for all practical purposes, incarceration in nursing homes (Johnson 1998).

ADA research findings, legal arguments, employment strategies, and government policies based on the functional limitations paradigm—if its critics are right—will not address the real problem and indeed will probably exacerbate it. Liachowitz's analysis (1988, p. 1) of the history of public policy regarding disability in Pennsylvania from colonial times to the 1980s led her to conclude that "the cultural practice of translating physical abnormality into social inferiority is so deeply rooted" that it has inevitably affected the implementation of public policies. If disability continues to be viewed primarily as a functional limitation of the individual, the ADA will be merely another rehabilitative act—that is, it will encourage a view of the ADA as mandating goodwill and benevolent actions on the behalf of unfortunate individuals. Such mandates tend to be self-limiting, encouraging verbal support (who has ever spoken against "helping the handicapped") that evaporates when the costs of compliance rise. If, on the other hand, disability is seen as residing primarily in disabling environments and attitudes, then we begin to view disability as a matter of civil rights rather than special assistance for individuals, and costs become a more surmountable, if never easily overcome, objection.

James Frierson's (1997) analysis of recent court decisions in ADA cases is not reassuring. In many cases, plaintiffs who were fired or demoted primarily *because they had certain conditions,* such as multiple sclerosis, diabetes, mental illness, cancer, or asbestosis, were nevertheless found to be not disabled and therefore not qualified for protection. Federal courts have ruled in these cases that individuals are not disabled under the ADA if their impairments are currently controlled by medication or not severe enough to be described as substantially limiting a major life activity. With the focus on plaintiffs' bodies, disabled people are placed in the undignified (to say the least) position of having to impress a judge with the seriousness of their impairment. By locating the crux of the issue in the body of the individual rather than in discriminatory attitudes and practices, people who have experienced discrimination on the basis of a physical, mental, or psychological difference from the majority can nevertheless be excluded from ADA protection.

It is worth pondering in this context the meaningfulness of a distinction between medication that alleviates symptoms and a wheelchair that alleviates the functional limitation of not having the use of one's legs. In a fully accessible environment, without physical barriers, a wheelchair-using paraplegic would not experience significant "functional limitations," just as someone who used medication to alleviate his or her impairment would not, yet both might face similar attitudinal barriers. To courts that define "major life activity" simply as "walking," however, the former will be afforded protection as a disabled person while the latter will not. The distinction at work in these cases seems to be that a person with a condition controlled by medication is not visibly different from others—that is, he or she appears *normal*—while the wheelchair user, though perhaps enjoying unrestricted mobility, does not. Thus, the paraplegic whose mobility has been restored by a wheelchair is disabled and the epileptic whose mobility, so to speak, has been restored by medication is not. Hence the restoration of mobility was not the deciding factor but rather the restoration of normality.

As Liachowitz (1988, p.113) has argued, "the less that physical handicap is thought of in medical terms, and the less that the source of social deviation is thought to be within the physically abnormal person, the more attention can be paid to the socially created factors" that produce disability. The functional limitations model for understanding disability is being increasingly challenged by social, cultural, and political approaches that complicate our notion of disability by relocating it in the relationship between the individual and the environment (broadly defined to include the social as well as architectural and technological environment). Hahn (1996, pp. 45, 53) argues that, "from this perspective, the effects of disability can be attributed primarily to a disabling environment rather than to personal defects or deficiencies." Furthermore the barriers that disabled people face are the result not of passive indifference but of active prejudice. Since public policy reflects those attitudes and shapes the environment, "ultimate responsibility for the inequality of the disabled minority in American society can be found in political decisions that have required or permitted the creation of a disabling environment." If disability is a product of an interaction between an individual and an environment, a result of discrimination, the test ought not to be whether some ill-defined "major life activity" is limited by an impairment but whether an individual suffered discrimination on account of an "abnormal" and stigmatized physical, mental, or psychological characteristic.

Hahn (1996, p. 52) argues that while "there is ample evidence of a widespread and profound antipathy toward visibly disabled persons," still "relatively little research has been conducted on cultural values that reflect an unconscious aversion to people with disabilities." Karen Hirsch (1995, p. 3) also notes that "the disciplines that traditionally have been concerned with disability do not deal well with the impact of cultural contexts, while scholars in the humanities have rarely included 'disability' in their analytical framework." That is beginning to change, however, as scholars in the humanities increasingly use disability as a category of analysis alongside more familiar categories such as race, class, and gender.

Disability Studies in the Humanities

One of the most fruitful areas of disability studies in the humanities has been the analysis of disability images in television, film, and literature. These analyses demonstrate not only that disabled people appear with a frequency of which few viewers are consciously aware, but that disability is so deeply implicated in how people make sense of the world that ending discrimination will entail confronting deeply rooted beliefs. Paul Longmore (1987, pp. 31–32) has written on the remarkable range of mass-media "characters with all sorts of disabilities: handicapped horror 'monsters'; 'crippled' criminals; disabled war veterans . . . ; central characters of television series temporarily disabled for one episode; blind detectives; disabled victims of villains; animated characters like stuttering Porky Pig, speech impaired Elmer Fudd, near-sighted Mr. Magoo, and mentally retarded Dopey." If asked, however, most people would be hard-pressed to think of disabled characters. Longmore explains this as one of the functions of popular film and television: "Disability happens around us more often than we generally recognize or care to notice. What we fear, we often stigmatize and shun and sometimes seek to destroy. Popular entertainments depicting disabled characters allude to these fears and prejudices, or address them obliquely or fragmentarily, seeking to reassure us about ourselves."

Fictional disabled characters show up everywhere: Richard III, Quasimodo, Ahab, Captain Hook, Long John Silver, Lenny in *Of Mice and Men,* Laura in *The Glass Menagerie,* Heidi, Melville's Black Guineau, Hawthorne's Chillingsworth, Freddie Krueger, the Joker and the Penguin in the *Batman* movies, Dr. Strangelove, James Bond villains, and Dick Tracy criminals. Dickens alone brought us Tiny Tim, Daniel Quilp, Barnaby Rudge, blind Stagg, Bertha Plummer, and Mr. Cripples. These are only a few of the better-known examples and, as Rosemarie Thomson (1997, pp. 9–12) points out, most disabled characters are not central characters—the great majority crowding stage, page, and screen are those marginal ones "whose bodily configurations operate as spectacles, eliciting responses from other characters or producing rhetorical effects that depend on disability's cultural resonance." Literary critics have never ignored the existence of disabled characters nor their symbolic power—they could hardly do that, given their prevalence—but they have usually treated them as natural symbols and overlooked their relation to culturally generated and transmitted attitudes toward disabled people.

According to Martin Norden (1994, pp. ix, 3), "mainstream filmmakers have constructed hundreds upon hundreds of cinematic portraits of disabled characters for predominantly able-bodied audiences since the earliest days of the medium." These disabled characters are usually not people who just happen to have disabilities, present for the sake of realism and reflecting the fact that there are people with disabilities in the world. Instead, their disabilities function as potent and easily exploited symbols. The movie industry's most common depictions of disabled people in film, Norden writes, have included "extraordinary (and often initially embittered) individuals whose lonely struggles against incredible odds make for what it considers heart-warming stories of courage

and triumph, violence-prone beasts just asking to be destroyed, comic characters who inadvertently cause trouble for themselves or others, saintly sages who
possess the gift of second sight, and sweet young things whose goodness and
innocence are sufficient currency for a one-way ticket out of isolation in the
form of a miraculous cure."

The new cultural study of disability in the humanities, Thomson (1997,
pp. 5–6) explains, "investigates how representation attaches meanings to bodies," and seeks to frame disability as a "culture-bound physically justified difference to consider along with race, gender, class, ethnicity, and sexuality." One
of Thomson's contributions to that project has been to analyze the cultural
meanings assigned to bodily difference and the uses of those meanings in
fictional literature and the theatrical performance known as the freak show.
Her goal is to "move disability from the realm of medicine into that of political
minorities, to recast it from a form of pathology to a form of ethnicity," to
show how "the 'physically disabled' are produced by way of legal, medical,
political, cultural, and literary narratives that comprise an exclusionary discourse." Against the view of disability as a matter of a damaged, dysfunctional,
or inferior body, Thomson posits disability as an attribution of deviance to
bodily difference, an attribution fraught with coded meanings and instrumental
in the production of social and cultural hierarchies.

Thomson argues for a "universalizing" view of difference as opposed to a
"minoritizing" one: "one minoritizes difference by imagining its significance
and concerns as limited to a narrow, specific, relatively fixed population or area
of inquiry. In contrast, a universalizing view sees issues surrounding a particular
difference as having 'continuing, determinative importance in the lives of people across the spectrum of [identities]'" (Thomson 1997, p. 22). Just as universal design in architecture recognizes natural human variation to create buildings
usable by all, rather than designing for a privileged majority and then adding
"handicapped accessible" features as an afterthought, a universal approach to
disability studies recognizes that when we speak of diversity we are talking not
about this group and that but the human condition. It shifts focus from the consequences of the social construction of difference for one group to the consequences for the whole community. It suggests, for example, that how we think
about and deal with disability is not important just to people with disabilities
but important for us all.

Disability affects everyone, not just in the sense that most people have
some kind of relationship with a disabled person, not merely in the trite but
true sense that most of us will be disabled at some point in our lives — the sense

expressed by the acronym TAB (Temporarily Able Bodied) sometimes used by disabled people to describe the nondisabled—but because all of us conceptualize our world in part based on notions of disability (just as we do with race, class, gender, age, and other such conceptual categories). Yes, when we discover our spouse's hearing is starting to fade, find out our child will be born with Down's syndrome, interview a job applicant with cerebral palsy, teach a class with a learning disabled student, or when we conduct a study, write an article, defend, prosecute, or judge a case in which disability figures, our preconceptions of disability inevitably affect our decisions. Beyond that, however, how we define disabled people also defines people who are not disabled. Just as masculinity is defined by femininity, and whiteness by blackness, "normality" is shaped by the concept of disability. Our understanding of disability enters into crucial decisions we make about our own lives and those of our children and parents, shapes our ideas about health, illness, and death, and affects the kinds of communities and public institutions that we create.

Disability and History

Scholars have not yet scratched the surface of the multiple and complex cultural uses of disability as representation. Joan Scott (1986, p. 1071), in her important essay, "Gender: A Useful Category of Historical Analysis," maintained that the growing body of work on gender in history would remain marginal until feminist historians could show that "gender is a constitutive element of social relationships." To make that argument, Scott focused on political history, at that time a field in which gender was generally considered irrelevant, and in which most scholars today would imagine disability to be unimportant. She pointed out that Edmund Burke's attack on the French Revolution was "built around a contrast between ugly, murderous *sans-culottes* hags ('the furies of hell, in the abused shape of the vilest of women') and the soft femininity of Marie-Antoinette." What Scott and others have overlooked, however, is that in addition to the rhetoric of gender, Burke's argument rested also on a rhetorical contrast between the natural constitution of the body politic and the monstrous (in the eighteenth-century sense of an "unnatural" or "deformed" birth) constitution that the Revolution had brought forth. Burke repeatedly decries "public measures . . . deformed into monsters," "monstrous democratic assemblies," "this monster of a constitution," "unnatural and monstrous activity," and the like. In his response to Burke, Thomas Paine turned to the same metaphor: "exterminate the monster aristocracy," he wrote.

The juxtaposition of the natural versus the monstrous was a common rhetorical strategy in Burke's time. The natural suggested an ostensibly neutral ground beyond politics and culture upon which social and political arrangements could be constructed and cultural mores legitimated. During the nineteenth century, however, the concept of the natural began to be displaced as a central organizing principle by the concept of the *normal*. Previously used by builders to denote a normal or perpendicular angle, medical doctors were the first to expand the meaning of the word—a healthy organ or organism was in its "normal state," an unhealthy one was in its "abnormal state." Sociologists then began to use it analogously to refer to the healthy state of a society, statisticians invented the "normal curve" or "normal distribution," and with its dual definition of *healthy* and *typical,* normality entered popular usage. It became a culturally important idea as a result of several interrelated factors: urbanization accompanied by new demands for the tracking and control of large populations; industrialization with its needs for interchangeable parts, products, and workers; and the rise of the social sciences. By the late nineteenth century normality was on its way to becoming one of the most powerful principles of the modern world (Foucault 1979, pp. 183–84; Canguilhem 1989; Hacking 1990, pp. 160–69; Ewald 1990; Davis 1995; Baynton 1996, pp. 136–48).

Just as the concept of the natural acquired meaning in relation to the monstrous and the deformed in Burke's time, the ever-shifting meanings of the normal were produced in tandem with culturally variable notions of disability. Indeed, as Lennard Davis (1995, p. 2) argues, "the very concept of normalcy by which most people (by definition) shape their existence is in fact tied inexorably to the concept of disability." Throughout its modern career the word has been used to describe how things are *and* to prescribe how they ought to be— often both at once. While the concept of the norm is sometimes synonymous with *average* or *typical,* in most popular usage the concept of abnormality expresses a fear of the *below* average. "Is the child normal?" has never been a question reflecting concern about whether a child has above average intelligence, motor skills, or beauty. Abnormal suggests *sub*normal.[3]

Evolutionary Progress

Normality, then, is an ideal as well as a description. On the one hand, it is an ideal in the present—the normal body is ideal in relation to the disabled body. Having always coexisted with the popular belief in evolutionary progress—the notion that the human race almost inevitably improves physically and mentally over time—normality is also an ideal in the future, a promise to be fulfilled. As Ian Hacking (1990, p. 168) has noted, when Auguste Comte used the word to describe social conditions, "the normal ceased to be the ordinary healthy state; it became the purified state to which we should strive." In Comte's sociology, "progress and the normal state became inextricably linked." Similarly, disability in the modern age has been typically depicted as something that will one day cease to exist in a more perfect future. The conception of disabled bodies as inferior bodies, along with a vision of evolutionary change as progress, meant that normality was from its beginning a temporal idea. Normality was implicitly defined as the condition that advanced progress. Abnormality, conversely, was that which pulled humanity back toward its past, toward its animal origins.

The connection of disability with abnormality and the past has been expressed explicitly in descriptions of congenital physical or mental abnormalities as reversions to earlier stages of evolution. John Langdon Haydon Down, the British physician who in 1866 identified the syndrome that now bears his name, termed the syndrome "Mongolism" or "Mongolian imbecility," because he believed it to be the result of a biological reversion by Caucasians to the Mongol racial type (Kevles 1985, p. 160). Similarly, microcephalism was theorized by some researchers as an atavism, while people with mental retardation were described as having "a mixture of human and simious character, the latter being produced by an arrested development of the foetus *in utero,* forming thus an intermediate stage between ape and man" (Rothfels 1996, p. 166). Down believed that parental tuberculosis might be the cause for the atavistic reversion to a Mongoloid state, but in popular thinking immorality, vice, or unhealthy living could produce similar results. Even more feared than the atavistic reversion of an individual was degeneration, the continuous downward spiral of an entire line of descent or race. For example, as one doctor explained, "alcohol and neurosis in one generation might be followed by hysteria in the next, insanity in the third, then idiocy and sterility" (Russett 1989, p. 67).

The assumption behind these kinds of explanations was that evolutionary change was like climbing a ladder, that there was a single line of development from low to high. Europeans were uppermost on the ladder, but they retained in their physical makeup the constituent elements from lower levels of evolution. Recapitulation theory posited that the evolutionary history of the human race was recapitulated in the development of each individual human (thus, for example, the apparent gill slits and tail that appear in the human fetus at a certain stage of development). Under certain pathological circumstances it was thought possible for these primitive elements to reassert themselves, as when congenital abnormalities were explained as failures in the recapitulation process: "If different parts of the fetus can develop at different rates, then monstrosities will arise when certain parts lag behind and retain, at birth, the character of some lower animal." A standard anthropology text explained that "harelip, polydactilia, microcephaly, are, as it were, hesitations of the principles of evolution, attempts on its part to stop at points where it had rested in anterior forms, or to progress in other previously-followed directions" (Russett 1989, pp. 68–69). As the noted psychologist Henry Maudsley explained:

> When we reflect that every human brain does, in the course of its development, pass through the same stages as the brains of other vertebrate animals, and that its transitional stages resemble the permanent forms of their brains; and when we reflect further, that the stages of its development in the womb may be considered the abstract and brief chronicle of a series of developments that have gone on through countless ages in nature, it does not seem so wonderful, as at the first blush it might do, that it should, when in a condition of arrested development, sometimes display animal instincts. Summing up, as it were, in itself the leading forms of the vertebrate type, there is truly a brute brain within the man's; and when the latter stops short of its characteristic development as *human*—when it remains arrested at or below the level of an orang's brain—it may be presumed that it will manifest its most primitive functions, and no higher functions. (Quoted in Russett 1989, p. 69)

This pairing of disability with the primitive has been quite common. Teachers of the deaf at the turn of the century explicitly described their educational aims in terms of making deaf children more like "normal" people, and less like "savages" and animals, by forbidding them the use of sign language. They contended that sign language was "characteristic of tribes low in the scale of development," and that the sign language of deaf people "resembles the languages of the North American Indian and the Hottentot of South Africa." They proclaimed spoken language the "crown of history" and insisted that to permit deaf children the use of sign language was to "push them back in the world's history to the infancy of our race." Sign language was explicitly associated with not only the lower human but the nonhuman as well. Deaf people were frequently told that "you look like monkeys when you make signs," that sign language was nothing more than "monkey-like grimaces and antics," and that "it is apish to talk on the fingers" (Baynton 1996, pp. 43, 52–53).

In freak shows, where disability and race intersected to illustrate familiar narratives of evolutionary progress, disabled adults were displayed as less-evolved human beings supposedly discovered in far-off jungles. The man featured in P. T. Barnum's American Museum exhibit titled "What Is It?" was promoted as a "missing link" between human and animal, a "man-monkey." At least two different men played the role: a white actor with unusually short legs of uneven length, and a mentally retarded black man with microcephaly who later became well known by the stage name "Zip." The presence of disability (two very different disabilities) was in effect the costume, or at least an important part of the costume, that signified the role of "subhuman" (Cook 1996; Rothfels 1996; Bogdan 1988, pp. 134–42). At the 1904 World's Fair, exhibits of "defectives" alongside exhibits of "primitives" revealed similar and interconnected hierarchical classifications, with both defective individuals and defective races ranked by how "improvable" they were deemed to be — that is, how capable of being educated or civilized (Trent 1996). The theory that congenital disabilities were evolutionary reversions had wide appeal, as when a doctor in 1916 justified allowing a disabled infant to die by describing it as "An inferior animal! A lower form! An imbecile!" (Pernick 1996, p. 79).

Eugenic Progress

The belief in progress has always been accompanied by a fear of decline and, as potent symbols of decline, disabled people have been frequent targets of this fear. The imagined future of the modern world has been typically a place where everyone would be youthful and strong, stand upright and tall, possess a "sound mind and body," and live free from disability and disease. As the dark shadow of this vision of the future, disability has been at the core of the construction of both past and the future. Since the late nineteenth century, progress has been depicted as a process of purification, of ridding the world of contaminants and imperfection. "Eugenic," literally meaning "well-born," implied not just purity of heredity but a more general notion of purity. A Chicago politician in 1915, for example, billed himself as the "eugenic candidate," meaning not that he had superior ancestry or was in favor of eugenics, but that he was pure and uncorrupted. Allowing disabled infants to die was justified early in the century as "the Greater Surgery — the surgery that cuts away the vileness and decay and leaves only the sweet and clean and wholesome in this life of ours" (Pernick 1996, pp. 54, 74).

The linkage between notions of purity and progress led in the United States to eugenic sterilization and euthanasia campaigns, and in Germany to the mass killing of "defective individuals" and "defective races." People with disabilities were the first targets of the Nazi campaign for racial purity. Thousands were sterilized and as many as 275,000 were murdered. Paul Longmore (1987, pp. 146–47), writing of the "handicapped Holocaust," argues that we "mislead ourselves if we regard the Nazi doctors as monsters. Many were well-intentioned, even compassionate men, who were convinced that both society and people with disabilities themselves would be better off if they were relieved of their burdensome lives. Most of these physicians acted not out of a penchant for cruelty, but by carrying intense social prejudice against disabled people to its logical conclusion." The Nazi "final solution" was unique, but the ideas that justified it were not. Just as anti-Semitism was rife throughout Europe and the United States, so was disdain for disabled people. Far from being a phenomenon of the extreme right, eugenics attracted the support of many liberals and socialists as well, and sterilization of the "unfit" took place across Europe. In progressive Sweden, from 1934 to 1974, 62,000 people were sterilized, many of them disabled (Balz 1997). Even the staid *Encyclopaedia Britannica* of 1911 noted that future progress would require "the organic betterment of the race through wise application of the laws of heredity" (Kevles 1985, p. 63).

In the United States, the feminist reformer Elizabeth Cady Stanton among many others called for the state to prevent the marriage of people with physical and mental disabilities, maintaining that only those "who can give the world children with splendid physique, strong intellect, and high moral sentiment" should be permitted to reproduce (quoted in Leach 1980, pp. 31–32, 35). It was generally assumed that these three characteristics—the physical, intellectual, and moral—were closely related and tended to reflect each other. A strong body indicated a strong intellect and morality. Immorality and criminality were both believed to be the direct result of "defective intelligence, defective emotions or a combination of both defects" (Kevles 1985, p. 73). A turn-of-the-century reformer maintained, "we are satisfied that the race is making progress, that as an eminent statesman has well said, 'the frightful number of those unfortunates, whose ranks encumber the march of humanity, the insane, the idiots, the blind, the deaf, the drunkards, the criminals, the paupers, will dwindle away, as the light of knowledge makes clear the laws which govern our existence'" (Brockett 1976, p. 86). The minister and best-selling author Josiah Strong affirmed the strong cultural connections between progress and disability at the turn of the century: "the race cannot be perfected without perfecting the body" (quoted in Takaki 1990, p. 263).

The implications of this constellation of ideas were evident in the 1927

Supreme Court decision in *Buck v. Bell,* that involuntary sterilization on eugenic grounds was constitutional. The eight-justice majority ran the gamut from Louis D. Brandeis to Oliver Wendell Holmes to William Howard Taft, representing a remarkable consensus across the range of political opinion that mental disability obviated the usual rights of citizenship (Kevles 1985, p. 111). By the mid-1930s, forty-one states restricted the marriage of "lunatics," "imbeciles," "idiots," and the "feebleminded"; twenty-seven states had sterilization laws; and about twenty thousand legal sterilizations had been performed in the United States. At the same time, states passed strict miscegenation laws reflecting the belief that race was a matter of biological essence, that miscegenation represented contamination of white blood by a physically, mentally, and morally inferior race, and that racial "hybrids" were constitutionally weaker (Pascoe 1996, pp. 44-69).

The value of disabled lives is still at issue today in discussions of physician-assisted death, the aborting of fetuses likely to be born disabled, euthanasia, genetic counseling, and hospital do-not-resuscitate orders. Courts have been willing to sanction suicide in cases where they would be unlikely to do so if the person involved were not disabled. Although courts have framed their decisions as upholding a "right to refuse treatment" rather than as assisted suicide, critics such as Paul Longmore (1987, p. 157) argue that in these cases the distinction has been specious and achieved only through "tortuous legal and verbal circumlocutions." Longmore (1991, 1987) and others have criticized recent cases in which disabled people who had experienced personal setbacks and traumatic circumstances, and who appear to have been in depression, have asked for and been granted assistance in committing suicide (see also Shapiro 1993, pp. 258-88). When a disabled person expresses a desire to die, nondisabled people are prone to assume that this is reasonable and justified desire, and that assisting in the person's death is merely an enlightened and humane response to individual suffering. So long as we continue to view disability simply as a personal misfortune and an afflicted body, rather than a social, cultural, and political relationship, suicide will continue to seem a rational, understandable, and acceptable response.

Disability as Justification for Discrimination

Our attitudes toward disability have even broader ramifications. Disability has functioned historically as a justification for inequality not just for disabled people, but covertly for women and minority groups as well. It may be the case, in fact, that the concept of disability is implicated to some extent in the production and maintenance of all social hierarchies. Since the social and political revolutions of the eighteenth century, it has been increasingly unacceptable in Western cultures to suggest that inequalities between persons or groups can be taken for granted. If people are accorded differential and unequal treatment, it has been considered incumbent on modern societies to produce a reason. These reasons may not necessarily be seen as good or sufficient by everyone involved, but they are nevertheless generally demanded and produced. A great many reasons have been invoked over the years for inequalities based solely on gender, race, or ethnicity, but ultimately these rest on culturally sanctioned beliefs about impairment and disability. That is, the inequality of women and minorities has been justified by attributing to them physical, psychological, and mental inferiority of one kind or another. In effect, they have been said to possess "functional limitations."

For example, immigration laws at the turn of the century limited the entry of ethnic groups thought to be prone to physical, mental, and moral degeneracy. While exclusion based on national origin was controversial (the Chinese were the only nationality ever specifically barred from entering the country), denying immigration on the basis of disability was not. Thus, legislators found it relatively easy to forbid entry to "all idiots, imbeciles, feeble-minded persons, epileptics, insane persons, and persons who have been insane within five years previous; persons who have had two or more attacks of insanity at any time previously; . . . persons not comprehended within any of the foregoing excluded classes who are found to be . . . mentally or physically defective." While immigration law first included national quotas in 1924, disabilities stood in for nationality well before that. That is, while people with disabilities constituted a distinct category of persons unwelcome in the United States, the concept of disability was also an important ingredient in creating the images of undesirable ethnic groups and justifying their restriction. The first federal immigration laws were inspired by the intersection of cultural beliefs about disability and ethnicity. The assumption that certain ethnic groups were mentally and physically deficient was instrumental in configuring the concept of the undesirable immigrant, and the belief that discriminating on the basis of disability was justifiable was central to the creation of the laws (*U.S. Statutes* 1907, pp. 898–99).

Immigrants at Ellis Island were scrutinized as they carried luggage up the stairs to evaluate their fitness. According to medical officials, "the exertion would reveal deformities and defective posture." Inspectors chalked letters on immigrants' backs to indicate disabilities that might justify exclusion: "L for lameness, K for hernia, G for goiter, X for mental illness and so on" (Kraut 1994, pp. 54–55). An Ellis Island physician, reflecting on his years of service, wrote:

> It is no more difficult to detect poorly built, defective or broken down human beings than to recognize a cheap or defective automobile. . . . The wise man who really wants to find out all he can about an automobile or an immigrant, will want to see both in action, performing as well as at rest, and to watch both at a distance as well as to scrutinize them close at hand. Defects, derangements and symptoms of disease which would not be disclosed by a so-called "careful physical examination," are often recognizable in watching a person twenty-five feet away. (Kraut 1994, p. 63)

A popular collection of essays published in 1930 that advocated immigration restriction based many of its arguments on disability. One writer assumed all would agree that "the necessity of the exclusion of the crippled, the blind, those who are likely to become public charges . . . is self evident" (Eliot 1930, p. 101). Issues of nationality and disability were routinely treated as closely related, as when William Green, president of the American Federation of Labor, argued that immigration restriction was "necessary to the preservation of our national characteristics and to our physical and our mental health." A justice on the New York Supreme Court worried about "adding to that appalling number of our inhabitants who handicap us by reason of their mental and physical disabilities" (Dike 1930, p. 81). A medical doctor succinctly stated the simple equation that undergirded the case for immigration restriction: "if in the future the proportion of people of Grades A and B increases, the nation will prosper; while if the proportion of people of Grades D and E increases, the nation will decay." He added that "eugenic ideals . . . are the sole and final means of keeping a nation from deterioration and decay" (East 1930, pp. 93, 97).

Opponents of civil and political rights for African-Americans made similar claims. Supposed tendencies to feeble-mindedness, mental illness, deafness, blindness, and physical disabilities among races thought inferior were invoked in arguments against racial equality. Nonwhite races were explicitly connected to people with physical or mental disabilities, both of whom were depicted as evolutionary laggards or throwbacks. Some theorized that all whites in a natural state (that is, barring disability) had roughly similar capacities; so did all blacks —but at a much lower level. The views of a New York doctor were typical:

"God has made the negro an inferior being. . . . There never could be a negro equaling the standard Caucasian in natural ability. The same almighty creator made all white men equal—for idiots, insane people, etc., are not exceptions, they are the result of human vices, crimes, or ignorance, immediate or remote." Whites were naturally superior unless lowered in the evolutionary scale by disability (Fredrickson 1971, pp. 93, 250–51). Daryl Michael Scott (1997, pp. xi–xvii), in his recent book, *Contempt and Pity: Social Policy and the Image of the Damaged Black Soul, 1880–1996*, describes how both conservatives and liberals have long used "biological and cultural notions of black inferiority" and an extensive repertory of "damage imagery" to describe African-Americans.

Opponents of women's political equality cited their supposed physical, intellectual, or psychological flaws, deficits, or deviations from the male norm. These flaws—irrationality, excessive emotionality, or physical weakness—are in essence mental, emotional, or physical disabilities, although they are rarely discussed or examined as such. As Cynthia Eagle Russett has noted, "women and savages, together with idiots, criminals, and pathological monstrosities," all of whom were considered to be cases of arrested evolutionary development, or atavism, were "a constant source of anxiety in the late nineteenth century" (Russett 1989, p. 63). Herbert Spencer among a great many others maintained that women were less highly evolved than men and argued against women's suffrage on those grounds. Further, the "onerous burden" of reproduction not only produced a variety of limitations on physical and mental activity for women, but made women psychologically incapable of dealing realistically with social issues. Women were not only intellectually unfit for such activity but emotionally incapable of bearing the strains of political participation (Magner 1992, pp. 118–20).

Furthermore, disability has figured not just in arguments *against* the equality of women and minorities, but also in arguments *for* equality. Such arguments do not deny that disability is an adequate justification for social and political inequality, but rather deny that the groups in question have these disabilities. Thus, a popular theme in British and American women's suffrage posters and articles was to contrast strong, upright women with "degenerate" men identified as "idiots" or "lunatics," and to ask rhetorically whether it is right to treat women as though they belonged in this category—one justifiably denied social and political rights (see, e.g., Tickner 1988, illustration no. 4). Delegates to the 1848 Seneca Falls Woman's Rights Convention resolved that "the equality of human rights results necessarily from the fact of the identity of the race in capabilities and responsibilities." Frederick Douglass proclaimed to the assemblage that "the true basis of rights was the capacity of individuals" (Women's Rights Conventions 1969, pp. 4–5). Arguments in favor of women's suffrage all proceeded from the same premise: equality in capacity justifies political equality. The converse was implicit: differences in capacity, if present, are justification for political inequality.

Oppressed groups have responded angrily to accusations that they might be characterized by physical, mental, or emotional disabilities. Rather than challenging the basic assumptions behind the hierarchy, they instead work to remove themselves from the negatively marked categories—that is, to disassociate themselves from those people who "really are" disabled—knowing that it invites discrimination. For example, a recent proposal in Louisiana to permit pregnant women to use parking spaces reserved for people with mobility impairments was opposed by women's organizations. A lobbyist for the Women's Health Foundation said, "We've spent a long time trying to dispel the myth that pregnancy is a disability, for obvious reasons of discrimination." She added, "I have no problem with it being a courtesy, but not when a legislative mandate provides for pregnancy in the same way as for disabled persons" (Salerno 1997). To be associated with disabled people, or with the accommodations accorded disabled people, is known to be stigmatizing.

Even disabled people have used this strategy to try to deflect discrimination. Thomson (1997, p. 15) notes that "disabled people also often avoid and stereotype one another in attempting to normalize their own social identities." Deaf people throughout the twentieth century have rejected the label of disability, knowing its dangers, while the tendency of those with lesser stigmatized disabilities to distance themselves from those with more highly stigmatized disabilities is a common phenomenon. In 1918, the associate director of what was known as the "Cleveland Cripple Survey" reported that some of those surveyed "were amazed that they should be considered cripples, even though they were without an arm or leg, or perhaps seriously crippled as a result of infantile paralysis. They had never considered themselves handicapped in any way" (Hamburger 1918, p. 39; see also Finkelstein 1993, pp. 13–14).

This tacit and widespread acceptance of the idea that disability is a legitimate reason for stigmatization and inequality is one of the reasons discrimination against people with disabilities is so intractable. As Hahn (1996, p. 43) has noted, "unlike other disadvantaged groups, citizens with disabilities have not yet fully succeeded in refuting the presumption that their subordinate status can be ascribed to an innate biological inferiority." He is perhaps too optimistic about the extent to which women and minority groups have managed to eliminate such presumptions. Nevertheless, it is true that such views do not now meet with the near-universal acceptance they once did, while the same views regarding disability are still widely and openly espoused.

The assumption of a direct, unmediated, causal linkage between impairment and disability, and the conception of disability as largely a matter of individual deficit or limitation, encourages such views, and also ensures a narrow and ineffectual interpretation of the ADA. The functional limitations paradigm provides no tools for understanding the complex social and cultural processes that go into the production and maintenance of concepts of normality and disability. Nor does it provide an effective means of countering the widespread notion that discrimination against disabled people is natural, rational, justified, and acceptable. It has, that is to say, serious functional limitations. The more complex cultural, social, and political approaches to disability move the focus from disabled individuals to where it belongs: disabling cultural beliefs and social practices.

Notes

1. On the role of the courts in fixing the meaning of race and drawing the boundary between "black" and "white" in America, see Pascoe 1996.

2. Some scholars who are generally supportive of the "social model" of disability have recently argued for revisions to it (e.g., see French 1993; Hughes and Paterson 1997).

3. In the late nineteenth century, educators of the deaf began using the term "normal child" as the counterpart to "deaf child," instead of the "hearing" and "deaf" of previous generations. In this case, "normal" *appears* to refer to an average, since the "average" person is hearing. However, since it does not exclude those with extrasensitive hearing, it does not denote the average but only those *above* a certain standard (see Baynton 1996, chap. 6).

References

Balz, D. 1997. Sweden Sterilized Thousands of "Useless" Citizens for Decades. *Washington Post,* Aug. 29.

Baynton, D. C. 1996. *Forbidden Signs: American Culture and the Campaign against Sign Language.* Chicago: University of Chicago Press.

Berkowitz, E. D. 1987. *Disabled Policy: America's Programs for the Handicapped.* Cambridge: Cambridge University Press.

Bogdan, R. 1988. *Freak Show: Exhibiting Human Oddities for Amusement and Profit.* Chicago: University of Chicago Press.

Bragg, L. 1997. From the Mute God to the Lesser God: Disability in Medieval Celtic and Old Norse Literature. *Disability and Society* 12:165–77.

Brockett, L. P. 1976. Idiots and the Efforts for Their Improvement. In *The History of Mental Retardation: Collected Papers,* ed. Marv Rosen et al. Baltimore: University Park Press.

Canguilhem, G. 1989. *The Normal and the Pathological.* New York: Zone Books.

Cook, J. W., Jr. 1996. Of Men, Missing Links, and Nondescripts: The Strange Career of P. T. Barnum's "What Is It?" Exhibition. In *Freakery: Cultural Spectacles of the Extraordinary Body,* ed. R. G. Thomson, pp. 39–57. New York: New York University Press.

Davis, L. J. 1995. *Enforcing Normalcy: Disability, Deafness, and the Body.* London and New York: Verso.

Dike, N. S. 1930. Aliens and Crime. In *The Alien in Our Midst, or Selling Our Birthright for a Mess of Industrial Pottage,* ed. M. Grant and C. S. Davison. New York: Galton Publishing Co.

East, E. M. 1930. Population Pressure and Immigration. In *The Alien in Our Midst, or Selling Our Birthright for a Mess of Industrial Pottage,* ed. M. Grant and C. S. Davison. New York: Galton Publishing Co.

Eliot, E. 1930. Immigration. In *The Alien in Our Midst, or Selling Our Birthright for a Mess of Industrial Pottage,* ed. M. Grant and C. S. Davison, pp. 99–104. New York: Galton Publishing Co.

Ewald, F. 1990. Norms, Discipline, and the Law. *Representations* 30:138–61.

Fine, M., and A. Asch. 1988. Disability beyond Stigma: Social Interaction, Discrimination, and Activism. *Journal of Social Issues* 44:3–21.

Finkelstein, V. 1993. The Commonality of Disability. In *Disabling Barriers—Enabling Environments,* ed. J. Swain et al., pp. 9–16. London: Sage Publications.

Foucault, M. 1979. *Discipline and Punish: The Birth of the Prison.* New York: Vintage Books.

Fredrickson, G. M. 1971. *The Black Image in the White Mind.* New York: Harper and Row.

French, S. 1993. Disability, Impairment, or Something in Between. In *Disabling Barriers— Enabling Environments,* ed. J. Swain et al., pp. 17–25. London: Sage Publications.

Frierson, J. G. 1997. Heads You Lose, Tails You Lose: A Disturbing Judicial Trend in Defining Disability. *Labor Law Journal* 48:419–30.

Gleeson, B. J. 1997. Disability Studies: A Historical Materialist View. *Disability and Society* 12:179–202.

Green, W. 1930. Immigration Should Be Regulated. In *The Alien in Our Midst, or Selling Our Birthright for a Mess of Industrial Pottage,* ed. M. Grant and C. S. Davison. New York: Galton Publishing Co.

Groce, N. E. 1985. *Everyone Here Spoke Sign Language: Hereditary Deafness on Martha's Vineyard.* Cambridge, Mass.: Harvard University Press.

Hacking, I. 1990. *The Taming of Chance.* Cambridge: Cambridge University Press.

Hahn, H. 1996. Antidiscrimination Laws and Social Research on Disability: The Minority Group Perspective. *Behavioral Sciences and the Law* 14:41–59.

Hamburger, A. 1918. The Cripple and His Place in the Community. *Annals of the American Academy of Political and Social Science* 77:36–44.

Hirsch, K. 1995. Culture and Disability: The Role of Oral History. *Oral History Review* 22:1–27.

Hubbard R. 1997. Abortion and Disability: Who Should and Who Should Not Inhabit the World. In *The Disability Studies Reader,* ed. L. Davis, pp. 187–200. London: Routledge.

Hughes, B., and K. Paterson. 1997. The Social Model of Disability and the Disappearing Body: Towards a Sociology of Impairment. *Disability and Society* 12:325–40.

Johnson, M. 1998. The Choice That Nobody's Heard of. *Ragged Edge: The Disability Experience in America* 19 (Jan.–Feb): 22–29.

Kevles, D. J. 1985. *In the Name of Eugenics: Genetics and the Uses of Human Heredity.* Berkeley: University of California Press.

Kraut, A. M. 1994. *Silent Travelers: Germs, Genes, and the "Immigrant Menace."* New York: Basic Books.

Leach, W. 1980. *True Love and Perfect Union: The Feminist Reform of Sex and Society.* New York: Basic Books.

Liachowitz, C. H. 1988. *Disability as a Social Construct: Legislative Roots.* Philadelphia: University of Pennsylvania Press.

Linton, S. 1998. *Claiming Disability: Knowledge and Identity.* New York: New York University Press.

Longmore, P. K. 1985. Screening Stereotypes: Images of Disabled People. *Social Policy* 16:31–37.

———. 1987. Elizabeth Bouvia, Assisted Suicide, and Social Prejudice. *Issues in Law and Medicine* 3:141–68.

———. 1991. The Strange Death of David Rivlin. *Western Journal of Medicine* 154:615–16.

Magner, L. N. 1992. Darwinism and the Woman Question: The Evolving Views of Charlotte Perkins Gilman. In *Critical Essays on Charlotte Perkins Gilman,* ed. J. Karpinski. New York: G. K. Hall.

Minow, M. 1990. *Making All the Difference: Inclusion, Exclusion, and American Law.* Ithaca, N.Y.: Cornell University Press.

Norden, M. F. 1994. *The Cinema of Isolation: A History of Physical Disability in the Movies.* New Brunswick, N.J.: Rutgers University Press.

Oliver, M. 1996. *Understanding Disability: From Theory to Practice.* New York: St. Martin's Press.

Pascoe, P. 1996. Miscegenation Law, Court Cases, and Ideologies of "Race" in Twentieth-Century America. *Journal of American History* 83:44–69.

Pernick, M. S. 1996. *The Black Stork: Eugenics and the Death of "Defective" Babies in American Medicine and Motion Pictures since 1915.* Oxford: Oxford University Press.

Rothfels, N. A. 1996. Aborigines and Ape-People: Science and Freaks in Germany, 1850–1900. In *Freakery: Cultural Spectacles of the Extraordinary Body,* ed. R. G. Thomson, pp. 158–72. New York: New York University Press.

Russett, C. R. 1989. *Sexual Science: The Victorian Construction of Womanhood*. Cambridge, Mass.: Harvard University Press.

Salerno, H. 1997. Mother's Little Dividend: Parking. *Washington Post*, Sept. 16.

Scott, D. M. 1997. *Contempt and Pity: Social Policy and the Image of the Damaged Black Soul, 1880–1996*. Chapel Hill: University of North Carolina Press.

Scott, J. W. 1986. Gender: A Useful Category of Historical Analysis. *American Historical Review* 91:1053–75.

Shakespeare, T., and N. Watson. 1997. Defending the Social Model. *Disability and Society* 12:293–300.

Shapiro, J. P. 1993. *No Pity: People with Disabilities Forging a New Civil Rights Movement*. New York: Times Books/Random House.

Stone, D. A. 1984. *The Disabled State*. Philadelphia: Temple University Press.

Takaki, R. 1990. *Iron Cages: Race and Culture in Nineteenth-Century America*. Oxford: Oxford University Press.

Thomson, R. G. 1997. *Extraordinary Bodies: Figuring Physical Disability in American Culture and Literature*. New York: Columbia University Press.

Tickner, L. 1988. *The Spectacle of Women: Imagery of the Suffrage Campaign, 1907–14*. Chicago: University of Chicago Press.

Trent. J. W. 1996. Defectives at the Fair: Constructing Disability at the 1904 Saint Louis World's Fair. Unpublished paper presented at meeting of Society for Disability Studies, Washington, D.C.

Union of Physically Impaired against Segregation. 1976. *Fundamental Principles of Disability*. London: Union of Physically Impaired against Segregation.

United States Statutes at Large. 1907. Vol. 34. Washington: Government Printing Office.

Woman's Rights Conventions: Seneca Falls and Rochester, 1848. 1969. New York: Arno Press, Inc. and the *New York Times*. Reprint of *Proceedings of the Woman's Rights Convention, Held at Seneca Falls and Rochester, NY, July and August, 1848*. 1870. New York: Robert J. Johnston, Printer.

Chapter XVI

From Colonization to Civil Rights

People with Disabilities and Gainful Employment

Karen Hirsch

This chapter explores the relationship between potential workers with disabilities and the competitive workplace since World War II, using examples from archival sources as well as life-story interviews with disabled individuals. An examination of this relationship reveals cultural attitudes toward disability that are deeply inscribed in people's minds and acted out in the workplace. The work histories of many disabled individuals demonstrate how the characteristics of the job market and not just the characteristics of the disabled job applicants determine whether they get work or not.

The first section of this chapter briefly describes people with disabilities as a potential addition to the workforce. Next, colonization is introduced as an interpretive analogy which helps explain some of the cultural and historical forces that have delimited the ability of disabled citizens to participate in the competitive employment market. Colonization is also useful in understanding disabled people's struggle for inclusion and self-determination in contrast to segregation and having to live out their lives in family back rooms or nursing homes. Another section provides some examples from recent history of how disabled individuals can contribute valuable work if given the opportunity as well as a forgotten employment discrimination story that is brought back to light by disability historian Paul Longmore.

A cross-disability group identity is emerging in the United States. The ways in which this new disability community is arguing for the right to work and to profit fairly from their efforts are described in the last part of this chapter. Strong voices in the disability community are challenging the common view of people with disabilities as mere financial burdens and argue that they are more often exploited for the economic benefit of others. The final section is a short discussion of how disabled people are redefining who they are. They are beginning to tell their own stories, uncover the disability issues of the past, write their history, and help shape their future.

It is not possible to represent fairly all possible disability perspectives in a single essay. While the thoughts expressed here are informed by a long life of work on various disability issues, my primary perspective comes from personal experience with a mobility disability. It is also informed by my experiences in a remote northern European cultural setting and my sudden move to a liberal academic cultural context in the United States. The empowering messages from the growing, international disability rights movement, however, have spawned the ideas in this essay about colonization and the roles that people with disabilities and many "helping professionals" are destined to play out within existing political, cultural, and economic climates of the world.

Workforce Potential

People with disabilities represent a largely untapped resource of talents and creativity. Data from the 1995 United States Census Bureau estimated that about 17 million Americans aged 16–64 had disabilities that in some way affected their relationship to the world of work. Only 32 percent of these people were participating in the workforce, that is, employed either full or part time or looking for work (LaPlante et al. 1996).

Although there are individuals with disabilities who are *not* potential workers, this group is probably considerably smaller than most people imagine. However, while this chapter describes the struggle of potential workers with disabilities to gain access to jobs and careers, the argument here is not at all intended to link human worth with work or participation in the workforce. All disabled individuals are human beings with the same needs for respect and dignity—potential workers or not.

Changes in the workplace, such as the shift away from manual labor to mental work, have important implications for people with disabilities. With the aid of computers and other assistive technology, physically disabled individuals with high mental capacities can perform at any level. An excellent and frequently cited example is physicist Stephen Hawking. At the same time, it might be more than a coincidence that this shift in workplace opportunities is paralleled by an identification of and a rapid increase in such conditions as "learning disabilities" and "attention deficit disorders." These disabilities are more difficult to handle in jobs that are based on the manipulation of abstract concepts rather than the application of physical strength.

Given that the educational system is responsive to and follows changes in the workplace, the rapid increase in the prevalence of learning disabilities and attention deficit disorders — tagged as emerging high-frequency disabilities — may ultimately be related to the changing nature of adult work. Medical and educational experts see most emerging high-frequency disabilities as physical conditions caused by diet, pollution, drugs, or other environmental factors. From a cultural and historical perspective, however, these emerging disabilities illustrate how the idea of disability is a social construction that changes over time.

The long-term employment situation for people with learning disabilities is not clear. As the following story suggests, an individual can have a successful educational and work history in spite of low expectations. Steve Skolnick had trouble with spelling and writing in school. His teachers did not understand his dyslexia. They thought he was lazy and told him he could do better if he only tried harder. Skolnick dropped out of high school after his principal told him that the only job he thought Steven could do was to work at a gas station. Skolnick went on to an adult learning center, was instructed in how to work around his learning disability, received his GED, and went on to college and law school. Before long, he became a lawyer with the Missouri Commission on Human Rights (Skolnick 1995). Systematic research on the struggle against oppression by those with invisible disabilities is difficult, in part because of the enduring perceived need of many disabled individuals to pass as nondisabled in order to avoid employment discrimination.

Some of the historical and cultural forces that continue to keep people with disabilities poor and powerless as a group are especially played out in the competitive employment market. Life stories from disabled individuals often reveal numerous examples of subtle as well as blatant experiences with discrimination in employment as well as other areas. Only a few years ago, hardly anyone called such treatment of disabled people discriminatory. Today, with the help of the civil rights protection provided by the Americans with Disabilities Act (ADA), people with disabilities are protesting these discriminatory practices and fighting to win access to gainful employment opportunities, promotions, careers, and financial security.

Colonization: An Interpretive Analogy

The analogy of "colonization" is proposed here as an interpretive framework for understanding the experiences of people with disabilities in relation to past and current prevailing attitudes toward disability among the public in general and the "helping professions" in particular. Colonization is defined as the economic, political, and social domination of a powerless people by a powerful nation. Colonized people have lost their independence, have lost their right to define who they are, have lost the power to control their own destinies. They have also lost their history, their sense of a meaningful past, their pride in a collective memory of anterior events. The internal colonization of powerless groups, such as African-Americans and people with disabilities, has caused them to acquire "minority status" within American society because political and economic equality is being achieved too slowly—or not at all.

Simi Linton describes the colonization of disabled people in terms of "containment and control." Although she does not mention directly who the "colonizers" might be, she gives examples of institutions where the colonization of disabled people takes place: asylums and state institutions for people with mental retardation. Ironically, several of these early-twentieth-century institutions were called "The Colony" (Linton 1998).

In the United States, societal attitudes toward people with disabilities have been characterized by paternalism and charity mixed with fear and coercion during most of the period since World War II. It has been only recently, with the emergence of such 1980s disability movements as the "independent living" and the "psychiatric survivor" movements, that a shift from charity to equal opportunities for people with disabilities slowly started to become the valued approach to the "disability problem." Individuals with disabilities are joining a number of other oppressed groups who are beginning to gain momentum in their struggle for equal rights. The competitive employment market represents the stage where the last and longest battles will likely take place. This is because financial security provides opportunities for power and influence, independence and self-determination, and freedom from domination: in other words, an overturning of the colonial social order.

Judy Heumann's life story clearly illustrates the potential overturning of power relationships. Since contracting polio at the age of eighteen months, Heumann has known discrimination firsthand. As a child she was denied access to her neighborhood school in Brooklyn because the principal saw her wheelchair as a fire hazard. When she was finally admitted into the school system, she was offered "special" education in a segregated setting. In the early 1970s she was able to begin her career as a teacher in the New York City school system only after she sued the Board of Education, which had turned her down for a teaching position because she could not walk.

After her career had begun, Heumann quickly moved on from one crucial leadership position to the next within the disability movement. Her abilities and accomplishments eventually led to her nomination by President Clinton as assistant secretary for special education and rehabilitative services in the United States Department of Education. Heumann does not see her success merely as an individual triumph, but rather as an indication that the collective disability movement is making it possible for people with disabilities to overturn old power relationships (Pelka 1993).

In the postmodern world a variety of oppressed classes have challenged the definitions of their groups that arose with modernity. Colonization is a phenomenon that is rooted in the modern worldview—the ideology that colonized people needed to be conquered and educated by the colonizers before they could become part of the modern world. The powerful colonizers saw the native inhabitants of the colonies as incapable of self-government. Only gradually did colonized people all over the world start the struggle to free themselves from the rule(s) of the people who governed them and from the definitions of who they were that the colonizers imposed on them.

Descriptions of medical conditions and behavioral syndromes have been used extensively by the medical professions to define, label, and categorize people with disabilities, often leaving them feeling reduced to objects and stripped of human dignity. Cultural and historical examinations of these experiences have only recently been initiated by disability scholars.

The prevailing notion among professionals has been that a disability was like an illness, something that only the medical and psychological professions needed to deal with. However, disability scholars are beginning to call for a change in the "constricted and myopic thinking that has long characterized the study of disability." Some claim that this thinking is comparable to "confusing gynecology with the study of women in society, or dermatology with the study of racism" (Eisenberg, Griggins, and Duval 1982). The medical model, with its emphasis on evaluation, diagnosis, prescription, isolation, treatment, cure, and prognosis, has dominated theory and practice in all the "helping professions" that deal with disabled people. This model and the concomitant "sick role" have relegated people with disabilities to a passive role which often does not permit them to control crucial aspects of the services they need or even the choices they must make in their own lives (Parsons 1951). Designating such a passive sick role for disabled individuals also made it possible to develop programs that paid for disabled individuals to stay out of the workforce and even labeled the payments "disability" checks; the money and the recipients went by the same designation.

It is only with the emerging field of disability studies that the need for a cultural and historical approach to disability experiences has been recognized. The disability rights movement was in part born out of the desire by disabled people to demedicalize their lives and take control of their own destinies. The level of control many have in mind does not begin and end with choices or control of daily living activities; disabled people are beginning to dream that, just like everyone else, through their labors they will have the opportunity to achieve the American dream.

Like inhabitants of colonized nations of the past, people with disabilities have been expected to take on a passive role in relation to their own destiny while expressing gratitude and appreciation toward their oppressors. As slaves were obliged to show deference and respect to their masters, disabled persons are still assumed to be grateful for every small gesture of kindness, every insignificant improvement in their lives, every demeaning handout. Negotiating these complex social expectancies with a growing understanding of the injustices they manifest becomes a monumental task for many disabled individuals. The additional social roles that must be handled in an employment setting make the workplace a virtual minefield for people with disabilities.

There are growing expectations that people with disabilities will take full advantage of the new technology that is becoming available to them. Research is needed to sort out how disabled people of different ages are dealing with the contradictory expectations of the sick role and the technology consumer. How can significantly disabled individuals, simply through the use of technology, overcome the view of able-bodied people that a disability leads to a lack of physical or mental competence? Surviving ancient cultural assumptions about the relationship between body and mind lead people to believe that it takes a "sound body" to possess a "sound mind." Is it possible that these cultural values are responsible for the pervasively negative attitudes toward people with disabilities? (The question posed here includes psychiatric, sensory, and all kinds of physical disabilities; technology is available as a way of "overcoming" a wide variety of disabilities.) An essentialist notion about a "whole" person as opposed to a "broken" or disabled person is another reason why medical-model thinking is so hard to shake outside of medical contexts, such as in employment settings.

Disabled people, who live their daily lives with the tensions described here, are confronted with a large number of theories about their self-image: adjustments to loss of function, "overcompensations," and expected frustrations caused by environmental and attitudinal barriers. But because there is practically no written disability history, most of these theories, including some formulated by activists in the disability rights movement, are simplistic and not capable of revealing, much less sorting out, the tensions between ancient ideas and modern expectations. Disability history, uncovered from archival sources and the collection of individual narratives in the voices of disabled people themselves, could shed new light on some of these perplexing questions.

The central concern of disability history is the individual and social experience of living with a disability. This accumulative experience is as varied, complex, and shifting as life itself, and it is intimately mixed up with all the human milestones of birth, growth, maturation, procreation, aging, and death. Like women, people with disabilities exist within every other group and have an impact on all societal institutions—the school, the church, the courthouse, the playground, and the workplace. Yet, the experience of disability is largely absent from most examinations of human cultures; it is a subject which has not received much investment of material or intellectual resources. Perhaps the deepest reason for this is fear—individual fear of losing bodily worth and function, and societal fear that a large number of disabled individuals might somehow endanger the future of the human species. In an age when medical advances allow many who used to die to survive instead as people with disabilities, it is increasingly important to overcome the fear of a "different" bodily experience, to uncover the history of disabled people, to explore the cultural meaning of disability, and to end the oppression of disabled people (Hirsch 1995a).

In the wake of the civil rights movement, increasing numbers of oppressed groups are claiming their right to define who they are and what terms should be used to describe them. Individuals with disabilities are largely seen as incapable of exercising self-government and wielding sovereign authority over wealth and power in the modern world, especially by the professionals who are trained to "care for them." Yet, because of the activities of a growing number of disabled activists, the medical model and its paternalistic implications that were imposed upon people with disabilities by the "helping professions" are being rejected and replaced by other models. These new models locate disability in the interaction between an individual and the environment, not merely in a set of medically defined characteristics of human bodies.

A Struggle for Inclusion and Control

If people with disabilities are the "colonized" people and the "helping professionals" are the colonizers, the struggle of the oppressed to free themselves from their colonizers often takes place within institutions that the colonizers established: residential institutions, group homes, nursing homes, special education, vocational rehabilitation. These institutions, run by "helping professionals," are currently being challenged by articulate disability activists, including parents of children with developmental disabilities, who question their value and the validity of their established traditions.

Colonization of the minds of indigenous people was essential to a "successful" politics of domination and obtaining the desired economic benefits to the colonizers. The coercion, exploitation, and loss of dignity that became a fact of daily life for the colonized natives gradually would lead to the internalization of a negative self-image and a prevailing fear of being unfit for equal participation in the modern world. For people with disabilities, internalized oppression is the result of a life outside the disability community and/or inside the colonizing institutions — with only the paternalism of caretakers available as the interpreting framework of the disability experience.

The medical model of disability, while often effective and beneficial for the medical treatment of disabling conditions, usually helps perpetuate stigmatizing cultural conceptions of disability when applied to such other aspects of a disabled person's life as educational, professional, social, economic, recreational, and civic activities and interests. Since the medical model locates the disability solely in the person rather than in the interaction between the person and the environment, a life with limited experiences seems to be the "natural" consequence for a person with a significant disability. As long as this view of disability dominates, the opportunity to work and pursue a well-paid career track, for example, is not even contemplated as an option for disabled people by either the disabled individuals themselves, their families, or other "caregivers."

Teachers and other professionals advocate for segregated educational settings for children with disabilities despite the wishes of many parents of disabled children and students with disabilities. Nora Carr's daughter, Erin, is developmentally disabled. Yet, Erin goes to the neighborhood school a few blocks from her home, attends a YMCA latchkey program after class, and goes horseback riding on Saturdays. Carr wants Erin to have a regular life with meaningful work, a few good friends, a nice place to live with the colors she likes and beautiful things that she cares for. Carr wants her daughter to have a say in what she has for dinner, what clothes she wears on a given day, who she lives with and where. To that end, Carr has fought for inclusion, started a parent training center, chaired a number of national conferences on special education, and advocated for policy changes at every level, from the neighborhood school to the statehouse and Congress.

Carr believes that the biggest challenge she and her daughter are facing is not Erin's disabilities but the overwhelming ignorance, negative attitudes, and prejudice toward people who are different that they encounter each day. She maintains that inciting fear, creating divisions, placing blame, and segregating people by race, ability, gender, religion, or economics represent the politics of oppression. Carr is challenging the politics of oppression and is working to change the institutions that are perpetuating the colonization of disabled people and their families (Carr and Stewart 1994).

Life in a Nursing Home

Until recently, most people with disabilities had few opportunities to view their lives as rich and full of the same options that are available to others. This internalized state of oppression remains unchanged for many disabled individuals. Roger Wood, a polio survivor in the American Midwest, did not see the attitudes and barriers in his environment as limiting agents. He lamented in February 1993 that he felt "sad [about] the last eleven years [that] I've been here [in the nursing home]. I have more freedom than I used to [have] when I lived with my parents and my brother. I do more, but I still feel like I was cheated out of a normal life, I mean, yeah, I have a life, yes, but I wanted what I would have [had] if I hadn't gotten crippled."

Wood believed he would have been a farmer, or perhaps a local businessman, if he had not contracted polio. And he surely would have been married and had children. He assumed there was no work or career and no romance or family relationship available to a person with his level of disability (Wood 1993). This polio survivor died in 1995, believing that it was essentially his disability and not external and internalized oppression that had circumscribed his life.

Nursing homes are disastrous places for working-age disabled people to live their lives. Still, the nursing home is too often the only chance for survival for significantly disabled individuals. Loretta Campbell, born in 1949 with cerebral palsy, grew up as an only child in a small California town. After spending the elementary years in a class for orthopedically disabled children, she was integrated into a regular high school for part of the day. Later she went on to college, but she did not receive support from vocational rehabilitation because she was not able to carry a full load of classes. When her parents retired and moved to rural Missouri, she had no choice but to move along with them. Before long, Campbell's parents became incapable of taking care of themselves, much less her, and all three ended up in nursing homes. In spite of her academic abilities, Campbell lost all opportunities to pursue her education, embark upon a career, find a lover, or start her own family.

Loretta Campbell writes poetry on her computer. Her eyes are failing, however, and she does not have access to readers or any similar supports, so she is not able to read the poetry of other writers or stay in touch with current literature. She has become a local disability activist and a participant in the independent living movement, and her identity as a disabled person is clearly expressed in her poetry. The discriminatory and oppressive aspects of her life in a nursing home, however, keep Campbell from living a full life as a woman and achieving her potential as an artist.

Like Wood's were, Campbell's daily life activities are restricted by the trivial rules of an institution that was not designed to serve her needs. Unlike Wood, Campbell recognizes the inequities inherent in a social system which assigns people with disabilities to live their lives achieving nothing. However, Loretta Campbell will not leave the nursing home as long as her mother is alive and occupies a bed in the same room. This decision is not just caused by internalized oppression but also by a strong personal commitment to a mother who gave love and care beyond conceivable bounds. It is important to note that, as a nursing home resident, Campbell is one of the disabled individuals who is not counted as unemployed or considered a potential worker (Campbell 1995).

Integrated community living, personal friendships, ties with families and neighbors, contacts with disabled peers, and access to information and support from the disability community—these experiences contribute significantly more to the quality of life for a person with a disability than do "services" provided by professionals. There is a growing dissatisfaction among disabled people with the "services" they have received for so long from professionals who are trained, paid, and given the power to "serve" them. People with disabilities are using judicial and political means to gain control over service delivery programs, educational institutions, and public policy developments. The "natives" are rebelling against the colonizers and taking power and control away from them (Hirsch 1995b).

Lessons from Recent History

Many people have constricted and limiting visions of what a person with a disability can expect to experience in life. The characteristics of the individual are seen as the only factors responsible for success or failure in achieving important life ambitions. Lessons from recent history, however, show how conditions of the employment market determine whether people with disabilities are given a chance to participate in the labor force. In the United States, World War II expanded opportunities for work not just to women and African-Americans but also to disabled citizens. People who were blind or deaf, had physical disabilities, or were mentally retarded, for example, worked in factories producing such goods as sheets and blankets for the soldiers. When the war was over, most people with disabilities lost their jobs. Although they had performed well as part of the war effort, disabled individuals were quickly considered incapable of serious and well-compensated work (Wolfe 1995).

It is curious, indeed, how little is known about this wartime employment story. One explanation for the sudden reversal of disabled workers' perceived abilities parallels the experiences of blacks and women. It was a patriotic necessity that justified permitting blacks, women, and disabled citizens to contribute to the war effort and participate in valued work settings. Their employment was seen as a temporary solution that did not challenge the prevailing cultural values or ideologies about African-Americans, women, or people with disabilities and their proper role in relation to the competitive job market.

As soon as the patriotic necessity was gone, the behavior of these groups was expected to return to conformity with pre- and postwar ideologies. One lesson to be learned from this brief period in history is central to the question of how people with disabilities can function in the labor force. If there are jobs in need of being done, there likely are disabled individuals able to do them. Paternalism that serves the needs of the colonizers, coupled with an unbridled spirit of individual competition, tends to support the medical-model view of disabled people as ill suited for the workplace.

Historian Daniel Rodgers describes how the idea of the work ethic has played an important part in American life since the first Puritan colonies were established in New England. He studies the work ethic as a historical construct in regards to identity and the sense of self-worth among women, men, immigrants, and minority groups in America (Rodgers 1974). Scholarly work on self-worth and identity development among people with disabilities, in contrast, is usually focused on psychological factors related to the disabled person's reaction to his or her disability. It is assumed that work is not important to disabled citizens. They are, however, a part of the culture in which they live and share the same cultural values. When given a chance to tell the stories of their lives, people with disabilities reveal how their sense of self-worth is as closely tied to the opportunity to perform useful work as it is for other groups. Throughout history disabled individuals have spent much time and energy applying for work.

A Forgotten Employment Discrimination Story

A group of unemployed East Side New York Jewish job applicants staged a protest against the Works Progress Administration (WPA) in the 1930s. They had found out that they did not get employment with the WPA because they were disabled from polio and used braces and crutches to get around. After successfully making their case public with an article on the front page of the *New York Times,* they got the jobs they wanted. This story was forgotten and overlooked until disability historian Paul Longmore brought it back to light recently. Longmore sees these disabled job-seekers as early activists who aimed at combating discrimination in the workplace (Longmore and Goldberger 1992).

Longmore was able to conduct interviews with members of this group, the League of the Physically Handicapped, who were still alive in the early 1990s. He learned that while these disabled individuals provided great support for each other in their fight for employment, they did not extend their support to individuals who had to use wheelchairs. Members of New York City's League of the Physically Handicapped, using braces and crutches, were convinced that wheelchairs users were not capable of holding down a job as they themselves could. Given the general level of accessibility in the built environment of New York City at that time, this may have been a reasonable, albeit an unreflective position. It seemed clear to Longmore, however, that the walking and disabled members of the 1930s League of the Physically Handicapped did not extend their sense of group belonging to people in wheelchairs (Longmore and Goldberger 1992).

A New Group Identity

An emerging group identity among people with various kinds of disabilities is evolving and can be documented by systematic polls and through subjective anecdotal accounts. A national survey conducted by Louis Harris in 1987 shows that almost half of the disabled individuals polled viewed themselves as members of a disadvantaged minority group (Harris 1987). Young disabled respondents had especially strong feelings about this. Three-fourths of the group polled identified with other disabled people. Although there may not be similar previous surveys to make direct comparisons with, these results differ from the inevitable social reactions to disability described earlier by Erving Goffman, where disabled people often tried to pass as nondisabled while avoiding each other (Goffman 1963).

The shift toward an inclusive disability group identity is demonstrated in this story from the late architect Ron Mace, one of the early leaders of the disability rights movement and the originator of the concept of universal design: "I didn't associate with other people with disabilities. . . . I didn't feel part of any movement. . . . I had a disability and I tried to keep it as quiet as I could and go on with my life." When the Rehabilitation Act was passed, a few people with disabilities were "asked to help educate government employees about disability . . . we decided to tell personal stories. . . . I told my story and I was totally amazed, totally blown away by it, because it was nothing but discrimination from start to finish. It was amazing to me to hear other people talk about their experiences. It's a whole culture of it we all live with and people just can't believe it happens" (Danovitz 1993).

In a time when integration into the mainstream of society is the goal of many people with disabilities, they are discovering that they need each other, and that they can provide community and a positive sense of belonging for each other. There is evidence in the educational and psychological literature supporting the notion that social relationships are negatively affected by disabilities. Most of this literature addresses attitudes of nondisabled subjects toward disabled children and adults. However, because of the experimental nature of this research, the social situations studied often are devised and manipulated in ways that make generalizations to real experiences by disabled people impossible.

Oral history interviews are useful in exploring the different kinds of disability identities that can be found among disabled people from a variety of backgrounds. People with disabilities are engaging in efforts to define themselves as a group with comparable cultural experiences. As they create spaces in which they can share their stories, they are shaping individual and group narratives of disability experiences that make for a shared but not a fixed identity. The language used in these narratives reveals the shift from the medical to the minority group model. In the process of telling their stories, disabled individuals are dismantling essentialist notions about the "handicapped" imposed on them by the "helping professions" and the larger culture.

What many people with disabilities are asking for is a community of peers and a disability identity that is voluntary and constructed by themselves, not one that is prescribed from the outside by others. People with disabilities have begun to signal to each other that a positive disability identity and a sense of belonging to a cross-categorical disability community can represent a wealth of healthy, sustaining, and enriching life experiences that in turn cancel out many of the negative aspects of living with a disability. For many, this positive disability identity includes the right to work.

The Right to Work and Profit

The philosopher Gregory Kavka has argued that people with disabilities have a moral as well as a legal right to employment. He considers gainful employment to be an important factor for the maintenance of positive self-esteem. Kavka argues that society (and he seems to imply that "society" is made up of only able-bodied people) should be willing to sustain some level of cost so that people with disabilities can earn their keep through work rather than be paid not to work (Kavka 1992).

For many potential workers with disabilities the concept of "reasonable accommodations" described in the ADA is becoming an important issue. While integrating society in terms of race does not depend on any extra expenses at all, full integration of people with disabilities is frequently accompanied by some level of expense. How much it costs, and whether or not it is worth it, is a discussion that disabled people find both distasteful and painful. Is there a price on the value of their lives? Why is this not a question of right or wrong rather than money?

Kavka suggests that the costs of providing employment to people with disabilities should be spread as widely as possible across the population — that is, as a tax of some sort; it should not be borne mainly by disabled individuals and their families or the employers who choose to hire them (Kavka 1992). The question remains of whether employment as a moral right for people with disabilities can be considered in isolation from more general human rights of all people. Or perhaps this right can only become a reality in the political atmosphere of a social democracy and not in an atmosphere of "trickle-down" capitalism. Like other social movements, the disability movement is challenging some core values of American society.

Colonialism was clearly based on the desire of the colonizers to gain economic advantages from the colonies. Laws were established that regulated what the colonies could do in order to take advantage of their own resources and their opportunities for economic gain. Compare this to the kind of economic restrictions that have been imposed on disabled United States citizens. In a country where health insurance is a private, for-profit industry, and "preexisting conditions" are invariably excluded from coverage, people with disabilities are obliged to turn to governmental programs for health insurance. The rub is that health insurance from the government is given only to people who do not work or earn any money on their own. This situation repeatedly generates typical stories of oppression:

I Want to Work: Why Won't the Government Let Me?

Because of childhood polio, I have no use of my arms and a severe spinal curvature. I sleep with a ventilator. I earned my Ph.D. in American history, intending to become a college teacher. Next month the University of California Press will publish my first book, "The Invention of George Washington." My disability has not prevented me from working and working hard, but it does incur enormous expenses. I employ aides in my home to do housekeeping chores and to assist me with such activities as showering and dressing. Their wages plus the rental of my ventilators total $20,000 a year. Realistically, I am unlikely ever to earn enough in a scholarly career to cover such costs.

My situation is not unusual. Millions of Americans with major disabilities grapple with high disability-related expenses. They too could work but could never earn enough to pay for the services and devices they need. . . . What blocks many of us is not our disabilities, but discriminatory government policies that penalize us for working. We want those unfair rules changed. . . . We want to work. We want to know why the government won't let us? (Longmore 1988)

While he eventually worked out an agreement with the government so that he is employed as an historian, new chapters in Paul Longmore's story are still being written as he continues to struggle against remaining work disincentives built into support programs for people with disabilities. It is ironic, indeed, that in the current political climate, when work is being required from other welfare recipients, many people with disabilities who would like to work are risking the loss of benefits if they do.

Stories like Longmore's suggest that changes are needed on many fronts, such as ensuring the availability of affordable medical insurance and personal assistant services, in order to make employment and the pursuit of a career a possibility for most individuals with disabilities. Most nondisabled people can take for granted that their lives will be manageable, that they will be able to get back and forth to work, be well compensated for their efforts, keep up with household chores and self-care activities, and own property — they even seek wealth, have access to political processes, expect to be heard by elected officials and other people who govern, and have the right to protect and maintain their dignity. In the current economic, social, and political climate of the United States, when a person becomes disabled, many of these things are lost; they cannot be taken for granted anymore. Increasingly, disabled people are fighting to gain access to such inalienable rights as sustenance, shelter, safety, relationships, political influence, and participation in the labor force. Too many people with disabilities still tolerate inequities because they have internalized their oppression and implicitly accepted the status of second-class citizens.

Challenging the Master Narrative

Outspoken voices in the disability press describe existing inequities in order to mobilize the community and garner collective strength in the struggle to decolonize disabled people as a group. Psychologist Carol Gill, for example, published an article in *Mainstream* in 1992 entitled "Who Gets the Profits? Workplace Oppression Devalues the Disability Experience." Gill argues that many disabled people "receive token wages for oppressive work that companies exploit for big profits" (p. 12). Because of the persistent ideology that describes disabled people as unfit for the labor force, employees with disabilities, like Gill, are often expected to work harder than others in order to prove their worth in the workplace.

As a disabled psychologist, Gill has chosen to spend much of her life learning about the disability experience, analyzing this knowledge in relation to psychological theories, talking, thinking, and writing about it. She maintains that

> the subject of disability is a lot more complex than most people realize. It takes hard work and a great deal of insight and information to grasp disability issues. In understanding disability, it helps to have lived it. . . . Yet when a situation calls for an expert on disability, in an overwhelming proportion of the cases, a non-disabled person gets the job. . . . When experts with disabilities are recruited for a position or project, it is common for us to receive token pay and lesser titles than non-disabled experts. . . . While we remain shackled by oppression, non-disabled people . . . publish disability books and magazines,

profit from the sale and repair of disability equipment . . . jump on our political issues, conduct disability research, and provide consultation regarding our issues to a wide variety of markets. Disability is big business. . . . The flow of disability-related profits and power seems to go from us to non-disabled people at a fairly steady rate. (Gill 1992)

The realities Gill describes represent quintessential aspects of the dominating role that "helping" professionals often play in relationship to people with disabilities under the system of colonization. Economic exploitation remains a fundamental cornerstone to the maintenance of a colonial social order in which disabled people occupy the lowest positions. The only people who will even try to succeed in overturning this particular social hierarchy are people with disabilities themselves. By telling her story and asking "who profits?" Gill is challenging the master narrative created by the colonizers.

We Are the Stories We Tell

Disability as a positive identity is a recent phenomenon that has become possible in the postmodern, post–civil rights movement era. Claiming to be "proud and disabled" and expressing community bonds with other categories of disabled people, claiming the rights of all citizens to participate in the economic and political life of their communities, people with disabilities are becoming involved in a new use of language, the telling of new stories, a different discourse on disability experiences. As they develop narratives that communicate their issues and concerns, they are working to establish the cultural meanings of disability. They are attempting to understand the cultural values that have shaped their lives in the past and to create new cultural disability images, to gain self-determination and personal self-worth by redefining who they are and how the disability side of their identities relates to such other aspects of identity as gender, class, racial background, and sexual orientation.

An emerging history of disability experiences demonstrates that people with disabilities are in the process of becoming a more cohesive group than before: a minority group with shared political goals, similar educational experiences, a shared desire to contribute meaningful work, and common emotional bonds and concerns. Self-defining narratives are seen as important tools in the process of political empowerment and in the effort to redefine the cultural meaning of disability. People with disabilities have stories to tell that the world has not listened to before. Some of the stories are challenging the comfortable social order of dividing people into two separate camps: those who provide care and those who need it, those who define the roles to be played by disabled people and those who must accept these definitions. Disabled people are beginning to tell their own stories, stories that do not always end with a general feeling of comfort and reassurance depicting the disabled person as an inspiration or a distant and therefore safe other. Instead, people with disabilities tell stories about discrimination in education, in transportation, in housing, and in the workplace, stories about how they seldom get a chance to even join the workforce.

Oral history interviews with disabled people are adding a new viewpoint that has been ignored partly because it has been assumed that disabled people do not have an articulate view of their circumstances that differs from other views. People with disabilities are upsetting the old colonial social order because, by "refusing to be reduced to 'clinical material' in the construction of the medical text, they are claiming voices" (Frank 1995). Scholars in the humanities are beginning to discover that disabled people have a unique perspective on life that is informed by their disability experiences. There are, of course, some disabled individuals who are not able to generate articulate statements about their disability experiences. Some, like Chris, the son of Steve Thunder-McGuire (see Thunder-McGuire, this volume), and Erin, Nora Carr's daughter (Carr and Stewart 1994), are lucky to have people in their lives who can give voice to their stories. The important point is that the lives of all disabled individuals, regardless of disability, have a place in the narratives that describe the disability experience.

Conclusion

The master narrative about people with disabilities and competitive employment that dominates the discourse relevant to public policy and economic agendas still discriminates against disabled workers. While the implementation of the ADA of 1990 has led to a sharp increase in disability-related complaints filed with the Equal Employment Opportunities Commission (EEOC), it is not clear that people with disabilities are better treated or more welcomed in the competitive employment market. Many disabled workers have employment experiences that show why passing—denying or hiding the disability as much as possible—is still the best choice when a career and a respectable income are important goals. Their stories show that people with disabilities have the same attitudes toward work as other people. The American work ethic, the desire to be useful and contribute meaningful work, is shared by disabled and nondisabled citizens.

One goal of the disability community is for individuals with disabilities to be able to disclose any kind of disability, including mental illness, while having equal access to gainful employment, meaningful work, a challenging and satisfying career. This goal can only be accomplished if it becomes socially intolerable to use disability as a justification for inequality. Historian Douglas Baynton has argued that disability is still being used extensively as an accepted reason for inequality and discrimination in many settings (see Baynton, this volume). While the American public is beginning to accept that it is socially inappropriate to discriminate against women, African-Americans, homosexuals, and seniors, it is perfectly fine for respectable, sensitive, and liberal-minded people to be prejudiced at worst, or ignorant at best, about people with disabilities and the negative social images with which they often have to live.

To change the master narrative about disability and employment that is largely accepted without reflection by the general public as well as most professionals and policy makers, people with disabilities must develop more effective stories that convey a new perspective on disability in the workplace. The idea of internal colonization, the ancillary view that many professionals dominate rather than empower disabled individuals, and the concomitant claim that people with disabilities are subject to economic exploitation all suggest ways to change the existing master narrative about disability and work. Individual stories from the lives of disabled citizens—some already written or told, many forgotten, others waiting to be heard and written down—support this new perspective.

References

Campbell, L. 1995. Unpublished oral history interview by author.

Carr, N., and B. Stewart. 1994. Commentary: Disabled Kids Deserve Chance in School. *St. Louis Post Dispatch*. Feb. 28.

Danovitz, S. 1993. The Disability Movement: From Caste to Class. Paper presented at the Oral History Association Annual Meeting.

Eisenberg, M. G., C. Griggins, and R. J. Duval. 1982. *Disabled People as Second-Class Citizens*. New York: Springer.

Frank, A. W. 1995. *The Wounded Storyteller: Body, Illness, and Ethics*. Chicago: University of Chicago Press.

Gill, C. 1992. Who Gets the Profits? Workplace Oppression Devalues the Disability Experience. *Mainstream* (Nov.): 12–17.

Goffman, E. 1963. *Stigma: Notes on the Management of Spoiled Identity.* Englewood Cliffs, N.J.: Prentice-Hall.

Harris, L. H. 1987. *Inside America.* New York: Vintage Books.

Hirsch, K. 1995a. Culture and Disability: The Role of Oral History. *Oral History Review* 22:1–27.

————. 1995b. Self-Defining Narratives: Disability Identity in the Postmodern Era. *Disability Studies Quarterly* 15:21–27.

Kavka, G. 1992. Disability and the Right to Work. *Social Philosophy and Policy* 9 (1): 262–90.

LaPlante, M. P., et al. 1996. Disability and Employment. *Disability Statistics Abstract* (Jan.): 11.

Linton, S. 1998. *Claiming Disability: Knowledge and Identity.* New York: New York University Press.

Longmore, P. 1988. Op-ed page. *New York Times,* Nov. 26.

Longmore, P., and D. Goldberger. 1992. Jobs, Not Tin Cups: New York City's League of the Physically Handicapped and the Definition of Disability Identity. Paper presented at the Oral History Association Annual Meeting.

Parsons, T. 1951. *The Social System.* Glencoe, Ill.: Free Press of Glencoe.

Pelka, F. 1993. Judy Heumann: Advocate Carries the Disability Rights Agenda to a Top Job in Washington. *Mainstream* (June–July): 4–5.

Rodgers, D. 1974. *The Work Ethic in Industrial America, 1859–1920.* Chicago: University of Chicago Press.

Skolnick, S. 1995. Unpublished autobiographical life story.

Wolfe, K. 1995. War Work. *Mainstream* (Aug.): 17–21.

Wood, R. 1993. Unpublished oral history interview by Jena Jetmore.

Chapter XVII

Avoiding Iron-Door Barriers to the Employment of Persons with Developmental Disabilities

TOM WALZ AND LEA ANNE BOUCHER

Introduction

A persistent theme in American social welfare policy has been "upside-down welfarism," the situation where those in greatest need get the least and those with lesser needs get the most (Walz 1984). Elman (1968) spoke of this phenomenon as a welfare state for upper-income persons and a poorhouse state for lower-income persons. Arguments can be made that most federal social welfare policy, including civil rights policy, can be interpreted in this light. The allocation of public resources, rights, or statuses fails to spread evenly among those who qualify and is rarely biased in favor of those in greatest need.

Some believe a hidden principle governs most welfare policy making that is essentially classist (Stoesz and Karger 1992), though at times it may be expressed as one of the other "isms" (i.e., racism, sexism, etc.). Historically, the hidden principle has been that government support should be invested to serve the interests of the market. According to this principle, various kinds of public assistance, support, and civil protections go to persons who best fit the current market economy (Piven and Cloward 1972) or to those who, for whatever mix of reasons, are felt to be most worthy by policy makers (Halachmi 1981; Rawls 1971).

Another explanation of the failure of public social welfare policy to reach the "hard core" disadvantaged is the theory that much of social welfare policy is illusionary (Estes 1984). In effect, Congress knowingly passes legislation that is more virtual reality than reality, rhetoric without appropriations. A current example is the selling of welfare reform as a way of enhancing the income sufficiency and social status of poor families. The critics argue this is more illusion than reality. The welfare poor simply become the working poor with no measurable improvement in either their income or their social status. As much a beneficiary of such welfare reform are service corporations in need of low-wage, unskilled workers.

One could argue that civil rights legislation suffers the same fate. The rhetoric of civil rights legislation is vigorous, but the implementation and the resources to enact the laudable purposes of the legislation are often lacking. Legislators may resist being opposed to antidiscrimination measures in a public forum, when in fact they are not in favor of them. Lack of enthusiasm is then repackaged in a weak appropriations bill, spelled out in ambiguous language, with other measures designed to insure that not too much is accomplished.

A review of congressional intent in civil rights legislation seems to be to do something, but not too much; to do it in ways that minimize criticism and backlash; and to do it first for persons of the "discriminated" group in question in the ways most acceptable to majority interests or attitudes. This is clearly evident in the congressional support given to the Equal Employment Opportunity Commission (EEOC).

A reading of the Americans with Disabilities Act (ADA) and a review of the case law decisions that have followed suggest this law has been written and is being implemented in ways suited to business interests. This observation is neither surprising nor meant as a wholesale criticism of the ADA. The ADA appears to be following a path of political expediency. Yet, in so doing, the ADA has opened the door to employment for some persons with disabilities, has served as the catalyst for some limited measures of accommodations in the workplace, and has fostered some changed attitudes with respect to disabled workers in the workplace.

The Problem Statement

Given this short preface, it is our view that there is a preferred and privileged group being served (first) by the ADA and a group systematically slighted by the legislation. The preferred group appears to be relatively competitive for conventional employment, with or without accommodation. They are typically the better educated, more work experienced, higher social class persons within the disability community. We consider this group to be of "lesser need" for employment assistance.

Those "systematically slighted" are persons with substantial disabling conditions who share certain lower social class characteristics, have less acceptable disabilities (i.e., mental illness, mental retardation, etc.), have more limited work experience, and tend to require a wider range of accommodations. These are persons for whom the clause "unqualified for employment" and for whom needed accommodations would create "an undue hardship" for employers turn into an "iron door" to employment.

Most systematically slighted persons have one or more developmental disabilities. Included are persons who have experienced moderate to severe mental retardation or autism, mental illness, and physical impairments, or dual diagnoses of the aforementioned. They tend to be persons who are not highly competitive for conventional employment and persons whom public policy has tended to divert into social service sheltered employment (e.g., Goodwill Industries). As "clients" of sheltered employment, they typically earn a substandard wage, have little to no choice in their vocational rehabilitation, and are under constant supervision (Conte 1983; Vash 1980; Murphy and Rogan 1995).

Employers and policy makers generally consider the persons described unemployable and noncompetitive. The policy choices have been to provide them some form of a disability transfer payment and/or to relegate them to a segregated, protective work site (sheltered employment workshops).

Problem Analysis

Policy makers and the general public tend to think of employment in fairly conventional ways (i.e., in terms of competitiveness and productivity). Rational employment decisions, even those with civil rights accommodations, are expected to be "economically" sound. A person who cannot be competitively productive with reasonable accommodations has no claim to employment. Daniel Bell (1976) referred to the rationale that underlies such beliefs as the application of the "economizing principle," one of a trio of driving forces behind the postindustrial revolution.

Bell (1976) also identified the copresence of a "human rights" principle as a catalyst for postindustrial changes occurring in society. In this instance the change was in the direction of greater political equity among persons in the political minority. The explosion of civil rights movements beginning in the 1960s demonstrated its presence, while resulting statutory civil protections documented the outcomes. The ADA is among the last of the efforts to expand civil rights protections to a previously discriminated-against population.

Unfortunately, the effort to extend civil rights protections to persons with disabilities comes at a time of a major shift in power between the state and the market economy. The shift has been toward an increase in the power of the market economy, especially in its influence over government. This change in the political economy could make equity achievement for disabled persons more difficult than was the case with civil protections of people of color and women.

At the time of the 1960s round of civil rights legislation, government was the power center in society. Expansion of civil liberties was seen as an extension of civil authority. Extending civil liberties was not perceived as coming at the expense of government. However, in extending civil rights protection in employment at the current time, the employment discrimination features of the law may challenge the self interest of the market economy. With private sector influence over public policy, this can impact any employment-related legislation. Consequently, there may be little enthusiasm for implementing the ADA, especially its employment discrimination features.

The power shift between government and the market economy has been noted by a number of social power theorists (McDermott 1980; Boulding 1989; Domhoff 1990). They believe the influence of today's market economy in society to be pervasive. One aspect of the power shift is the ability of the private sector to infuse its vision and values on the other institutions in society. An example would be the corporatizing and privatizing behaviors of public and private universities and the professions that serve them (Walz, editorial). Market values have become the dominant cultural values and, ironically, take on the character of moral values.

These observations make the latest civil rights measure (ADA) suspect—an anomaly. It would be difficult for legislative bodies to outright deny civil rights protections to disabled persons. Only through employing a variety of political maneuvers (underfunding, careful political appointments) and legal stratagems (stacking the courts, subsequent court decisions) can the movement be "controlled" (limited). As a result of the way the ADA is written and implemented, for some persons with disabilities there is an open door, for others a glass ceiling (Braddock and Bachelder 1994), and, for others still, an iron door.

Some policy makers and even some disability advocates may see the effort to remove barriers to employment for some disabled persons and to push others toward sheltered work as a reasonable course of action. It fits both the paradigm of economizing behavior and the intent of Congress. While we do not find such reactions surprising, we nonetheless challenge them. It would seem that employment rights should be more than the right of freedom from employment discrimination among persons with differing social characteristics. Workers are not only competing with each other; they are also competing with decisions about the mode of production over which they have no control.

When one looks at the history of civil rights in the twentieth century, one sees a degree of optimism about the future of democracy and its contribution to fostering human rights. However, recent events give pause for concern. One such concern is the "loss of public assistance entitlements" through welfare reform, which in effect reduced the civil rights of poor families. This could signal not only a slowdown in civil rights expansion but also its reversal (Walz and Theisen 1997). It is also cause for concern about the future of the ADA.

With many disabled considered unemployable and facing an iron door to employment in the conventional job market, what course of action remains? Given the assumption that every person with disabilities is to a greater or lesser extent employable, if work is designed to fit their needs, interests, and limitations, how could employment opportunities be provided to less competitive workers?

Exploring Alternatives

A continuing concern of advocates of developmentally disabled persons is employment opportunities for persons with severe disabilities. In a tight and tough labor market any compromised condition or situation places a person with disabilities at a competitive disadvantage (Greenwood 1991; Link 1982). No affirmative action laws promote the employment of the developmentally disabled. Nondiscrimination laws are welcome but limited in their impact on actual employment of the less competitive, more severely disabled worker. In fact, participation in the labor force by persons with disabilities has decreased since the enactment of P.L. 94-142 (Greenwood 1991).

The limited data available, much of it qualitative, documents the struggle developmentally disabled persons have in securing employment (Link 1982; Weisgerber 1991; Walker 1982). Unlike the glass ceiling faced by the more preferred disabled workers, this group faces an iron door barring access to employment. It is estimated that among those with developmental disabilities, approximately 61 percent are unemployed (U.S. Dept. of Commerce 1996), with most of those who are working being underemployed (Donovan 1991). Those most likely to be struggling in finding work opportunities are persons with cognitive impairments or gross physical motor impairment (Wehman et al. 1990).

The employability of those with developmental disabilities varies greatly by the nature and extent of the disability. Still, the conditions of employment and the working environment play a significant role in who gains entry into the workforce. As noted, virtually everyone is employable when cost and productivity issues are set aside. The exceptions would be the few adult disabled in vegetative states.

The Policy Picture

Public policy has not been generous in facilitating employment for the developmentally disabled population. Title I of the Education Act, the Americans with Disabilities Act, and the Vocational Rehabilitation Act have been a welcomed advance, but their impact on furthering mainstream employability of developmentally disabled persons could be questioned. Further assistance, such as federally funded school-to-work programs or programs that promote the hiring of persons with disabilities, is required for encouraging workplace accommodations.

Gaining access to a building, unfortunately, is not getting a job; being mainstreamed through early education guarantees little with respect to future employment (Wall and Culhane 1991). Being referred to vocational rehabilitation yields limited benefits unless one has definite potential for competitive employment.

Welfare reform, with its vigorous pursuit of economic self-sufficiency for clients, has contributed even less toward the employment of the developmentally disabled. Even when the welfare population overlaps with persons with disabilities, workfare seldom produces work opportunities at a living wage for disabled persons. If anything, welfare reform has hurt the developmentally disabled client by its cutbacks and reductions in in-kind services and social supports (Walz, editorial).

Government jobs programs designed to serve the unemployed and underemployed noncategorically have produced few employment opportunities for persons with disabilities. From the Comprehensive Employment Training Act (CETA) to the Joint Partnership Training Act (JPTA), the focus of these employment programs has been on numbers of placements (working with those easiest to place), particularly on regular workers who are involuntarily unemployed.

Falling outside of employment policy, many developmentally disabled persons end up in the safety net of social service policy. The less competitive persons with disabilities show up as referrals to sheltered employment, where the "accommodations" are made and paid for by government subsidy or through private nonprofit funding sources.

The costs and benefits of sheltered work alternatives are questionable. Goodwill, for example, provides work for a relatively large number of developmentally disabled persons whose employment rarely produces income self-sufficiency. And sheltered employment tends to segregate its worker-clients from the social mainstream. According to the New York State Office of Vocational Rehabilitation, people labeled blind in these programs earn about $1.96 per hour, while those labeled mentally retarded earn about $.85 per hour (Murphy and Rogan 1992).

Some sheltered work is viewed more as training than a true job, the goal presumably being to move the client into conventional employment. When and if this does happen, the agency still has to provide job-search skill training and/or job coaching. These are both costly services, especially when the job in question usually offers only a poverty wage.

Those with moderate to severe congenital or early onset impairments tend to be excused from employment and allowed entitlement benefits. It is assumed they are unemployable or uninterested in employment and, at best, candidates for sheltered employment. As a consequence, these persons rarely surface as "discriminated workers" and, hence, fail to come under the protection of the ADA.

The premise of the ADA is that the person with disabilities, if given opportunity and accommodations, can compete with the abled. This, of course, is true for the better educated and those whose disabilities lend themselves to reasonable accommodation. Unfortunately, these are not the characteristics of a large number of developmentally disabled persons, particularly persons with brain injury, retardation, severe chronic mental illness or autism, and severe neuromuscular damage (e.g., cerebral palsy, multiple sclerosis, etc.). Nonetheless, many within this population want to work, even when they know they cannot work competitively, and would prefer to work in mainstream sectors outside the sheltered workshop environments (Murphy and Rogan 1995).

The ADA has a conspicuous absence of proactive features that would promote job opportunities for persons with disabilities, perhaps a necessary consequence of its being a civil rights law and not a social service or affirmative action law. The ADA appears to operate within the conventional definition of work and employment and stays within these parameters in its efforts to level the playing field for disabled persons. From our perspective this is one of its limitations. The ADA offers no vision of employment beyond that of a competitive income producing exchange of skills for wages.

As the economy becomes more capital intensive it alters the nature, distribution, and availability of work. It also establishes another form of competitiveness. The worker must now prove cost efficient to a technological alternative. Once one of FDR's four freedoms, the right to work has been relegated to the policy wastebasket. The contemporary capitalist economy has little commitment to meaningful and productive work for persons in society unless they fit the current mode of production and contribute to the efficiency of that system.

Society would be better served by making full use of human productive capacities, even when and where they are not cost effective. This is a value that the ADA could have spoken to in Title I but did not for a variety of reasons. Many of these have to do with the current conservative political environment.

It could be argued that both welfare reform and the ADA are being used to respond to a labor shortage in the low-wage service sectors by recruiting welfare clients and the disabled into part-time/no benefit employment. This observation is not meant to cloud the success of the ADA in protecting competitive workers with disabilities from discriminatory practices by employers.

A Model for Small Enterprise Development

So what can be done to make satisfying employment available to the population of persons with moderate to severe developmental disabilities?

In this chapter we discuss an approach for increasing employment on behalf of persons with developmental disabilities. This approach we refer to as the "small enterprise employment development model." By small enterprise employment we are referring to either self-employment or employment in a small business. In this instance, small enterprise development refers to promoting self-employment or work opportunities in small businesses for persons with moderate to severe developmental disabilities. We would expect either type of employment or business to be located in the social mainstream (i.e., the worker is not segregated nor does the work serve a segregated market). Employment, however, would not necessarily have to be in the formal economy.

The proposed employment model represents a more or less middle-ground position. It neither takes an overly protective stance (e.g., sheltered employment) nor does it make income self-sufficiency (competitive employment) the end goal. The goal of the small enterprise model for persons with disabilities is satisfying and creative work in an open (integrated, mainstream) environment.

Small enterprise development is enjoying somewhat of a renaissance. One area where efforts are being made to promote small enterprise development is in the third world, where economic and political chaos inhibit anything approaching full employment in the formal sector of the economy (Walz and McFadden). Here many nongovernmental agencies have made the decision to help individuals and families work around the institutional chaos by assisting them into some sort of family- or cottage-based self-employment. Often, however, it is through the initiative and creativity of the workers themselves that their informal street employment is developed.

A recently completed study of the street economy in Mexico showed that nearly 60 percent of the working population found employment in small enterprises (Walz and McFadden). Most were niche work opportunities, not profitable enough for large merchants or corporate enterprises to bother with. In this study there was no evidence of discrimination against disabled workers in the Mexican informal economy. Physically and mentally disabled persons were found operating street vending services at their own pace and energy level, either as self-employed individuals or as part of a family business. They earned what they could and/or contributed what they were able to family income. Most important, they saw themselves as part of the social and economic life of the society.

On the domestic front is the government-sponsored Small Business Administration. As an agency, however, it has had limited involvement with persons with disabilities. Closer to the model we are proposing are the experiments with small enterprise development on behalf of poverty or welfare client groups. An example is the work of the Institute of Social and Economic Development (ISED) in Iowa City, Iowa. This organization, now in its tenth year, has managed to assist between eighty and one hundred individuals annually to some form of self-employment. ISED's goal, influenced by its grant-driven funding source, has been to help its clients achieve income self-sufficiency through self-developed employment.

In the proposed small enterprise development model, concern for income self-sufficiency is not a primary program goal. The proposed model speaks more to the achievement of work satisfaction and social mainstreaming than it does to achieving full income self-support.

The core operating principles that characterize the employment model being proposed are the following:

1. Persons with developmental disabilities would work for themselves or in micro industries involving only a relatively small number of employees.
2. Persons would work in settings or with markets that are "mainstreamed," providing a fully integrated work and social experience.
3. Income self-sufficiency would not be essential, though maximum self-

support through employment would be desirable. Most workers would continue to receive a disability benefit.

4. Workers would own or have a strong management voice in whatever micro enterprise they worked.
5. Micro enterprises based on the above principles would be promoted, developed, and assisted by advocacy agencies serving adult disabled persons.

These principles would guide the expansion of employment opportunities for the developmentally disabled. The goal would be to provide employment opportunities for noncompetitive disabled employees in work that is satisfying and in locations where they are not segregated from the social mainstream. The workplace could be within or outside the formal economy and the work could but would not have to yield total self-support.

Case Study of the International Bill Foundation

The above model is a derivative of nearly a quarter century's experimentation with small enterprise developments involving the employment of developmentally disabled adults by a university department. The first of these projects was an experiment called Wild Bill's CoffeeShop. The project developed in response to the employment needs of an elderly mentally retarded man.

The need to find the elderly man a job was occasioned by the recruitment of a staff member to the university department. The staff person was the legal guardian of the old man whose name was Bill. Bill had spent most of life, forty-six years in all, institutionalized in a state hospital. Given his illiteracy and lack of work experience, Bill faced an iron-door barrier to conventional employment. At the suggestion of his guardian, a job running a small coffee service was created for Bill in the university department.

In the course of his employment, Bill's popularity grew first with department students and faculty and then spread throughout the university and into the community. Bill's coffee service, as a result, expanded into a full-scale coffee shop that eventually carried his name ("Wild Bill's"). Over the final eight years of Bill's life, the coffee shop became a local Alice's Restaurant. Bill's story became legendary and was made into a television movie. *Bill* premiered on CBS in 1981.

The popularity of the movie led to the filming of a sequel, a rare event in television movie history. More than 130 million people viewed the *Bill* movies.

The films are credited with opening up a whole new genre of films with persons with disabilities as central characters being portrayed in a positive light.

When Bill died at age 70, the university department was left with the question of what to do about the coffee shop. The faculty and staff chose not to shut it down. They voted to expand it to afford other developmentally disabled adults opportunity for employment. The department, at the same time, recognized that in making this decision it was expanding educational opportunities for its students. The department was a professional program training persons for social work. Wild Bill's CoffeeShop became part of the curriculum for students, while providing work opportunities for adults with major disabilities.

Wild Bill's CoffeeShop expanded as a micro enterprise to provide employment for up to a dozen employees at a time. The nature of the work and work environment, with its mainstreaming, produced remarkable stability among client workers. Many of the original employees in the post–Bill era still remain. For them work has become a way of life or at least a meaningful extension to their lives. The university department has integrated coffee shop employees into most of their social functions, and they, in turn, almost always include some departmental faculty, staff, and students in their social events. Students are commonly assigned to Wild Bill's CoffeeShop for field experience.

Most of the persons employed in the coffee shop project fall into the category of persons with moderate to profound disability. Included are several who are wheelchair-bound, one with cerebral palsy, and one with multiple sclerosis. Another has brain damage and hemiplegia; several others have struggled with major mental illness.

Over time the coffee shop project has expanded as a result of the success of its original venture. New developments include an independent coffeehouse; a small antique, curio, and student furniture shop; a graphic design service; and a web master service. Each of these work/service projects has developed around the interests and talents of particular developmentally disabled individuals.

For example, a new small business, Mr. Ed's Supergraphics, was started with the help of a state economic development grant. The state grants were designed to assist disabled persons to start small businesses. Mr. Ed is a man whose disabilities include cerebral palsy coupled with deafness. Yet he had developed facility with the computer and, as was discovered, had a good sense of design. With the equipment purchased through grant funds, he has been able to develop a small graphics business. This business, given his profound physical impairments, does not allow him to work at a speed that would normally allow him to compete with abled workers. However, he can do the work if given time. In his own business Ed is able to schedule his work to meet the needs of his clients. While not allowing him to become income independent, his work has given him work satisfaction and his clients a quality product. Through being the owner/manager of his own business, Ed gets plenty of positive recognition. He was the lead story in the Iowa business news magazine recently.

Bill's Coffeehouse is the project of a severely disabled man with quadriplegia who serves as impresario for local folk musicians. The coffee shop has been turned over to him on weekends for his coffeehouse programs. While this former musician gains no personal revenue from this activity, he earns community recognition and the satisfaction of helping new musicians establish themselves.

The man who has taken on the web master position, working from his home, is a person with serious chronic mental illness. Over half of his life has been spent in institutions. Like Bill, he had been institutionalized at age 7 and was not discharged until two decades later. His illness kept him from completing any real formal education; yet brightness and self-taught computer skills, along with a subsidy to supply him with an upgraded computer and connect him to the web, allowed him to become an expert and consultant on the web. He consults with faculty and students on web page designs and on surfing techniques.

Another man, whose mental illness is less severe, has been able to secure a similar position with a university department. The department spotted his talents during his several years of employment at Wild Bill's CoffeeShop. Both men are examples of persons who have the ability to function in a mainstream capacity at something they love to do. Tailoring their work experience to fit their talents was what they needed.

The quarter-century experience of a coffee shop run by developmentally disabled adults has produced replications of the project. Typically these have been started by persons familiar with the project as former students in the university department. One of the most interesting copies is a downtown restaurant in Rock Island, Illinois, established over a decade ago to provide employment for chronically mentally ill persons. This long-standing project now employs ninety people in its restaurant and catering service. All share the characteristic of suffering from chronic mental illness. Interestingly, the restaurant also serves as a drop-in center for clients in the evening hours after serving an upscale business clientele during the lunch hour.

Policy Implications

Based on the apparent success of micro enterprise developments for this group of moderately to severely developmentally disabled persons as well as arguments against shelter services (Murphy and Rogan 1995; Albin and Rhodes 1993; Wehman 1994; Mank 1994), we would propose a new national policy initiative. This policy initiative should provide start-up capital and technical assistance for individuals and/or agency sponsors to start niche enterprises tailored to the abilities and capacities of developmentally disabled persons.

The program could be modeled on the current Iowa Economic Development and State Vocational Rehabilitation program, although we would argue for less emphasis on making the policy goal income self-sufficiency. The federal counterparts for these two agencies would be the preferred location for administering the policy.

Both individuals and/or advocacy agencies should be able to apply for start-up grants to cover capital costs and training associated with becoming ready for business. The federal Vocational Rehabilitation agency would be charged with conducting a market analysis to identify the types of small enterprise niches that would be most economically viable and best suited to the capacities of the moderate to severe developmentally disabled persons. The agency also would be charged with identifying sponsors and semiprotected locations for business start-ups.

One concept that we would propose is to work with downtown redevelopment programs to provide for protected small enterprise zones for the self-employment or small businesses of persons with disabilities. The concept would include seeking larger downtown businesses to serve as sponsors for the smaller micro enterprises run by disabled persons. For example, the larger businesses could contract with the micro enterprises to help them with technical assistance and/or use them for outsourcing.

The intent of the policy is not to reduce the employment of the developmentally disabled within the formal economy or private corporations but to open up employment alternatives where the severely disabled are not forced to compete with abled workers. The effort is to open up new forms of employment which go beyond the usual low-wage service employment and which offer clients greater voice and status.

A further policy consideration is the need to develop an international network of small enterprise projects involving persons with disabilities. Such a network would serve the need to share experiences and to recognize the work being done by persons with disabilities. Recently Wild Bill's CoffeeShop was reorganized as the International Bill Foundation, and it added as one of its missions the goal of building a worldwide network among employment programs for disabled persons. Several such projects now share a computer bulletin board and have their own web pages. The International Bill Foundation can be found at http://www.uiowa.edu/~socialwk/bills.

Conclusions

It is uncertain what role the ADA could play in policy formation of this kind. Certainly, through tracking the employment experiences of moderately to severely developmentally disabled persons, it could help to build a case for the employment rights of the noncompetitive worker as well as for nondiscrimination in employment for the competitive worker with a disability.

What is certain is that there is a need for policy that directly addresses the employment interests and needs of persons with more severe disabilities. Obviously this will require more than removal of barriers to employment as found in Title I. Future policy must address the promotion of job opportunities in a noncompetitive but non-social service sector of the society: an economic small enterprise development zone for the developmentally disabled worker.

References

Albin, J., and L. Rhodes. 1993. Changeover to Community Employment: The Problem of Realigning Organizational Culture, Resources, and Community Roles. Eugene: University of Oregon, Specialized Training Program.

Bell, D. 1976. *The Coming of Post-industrial Society: A Venture in Social Forecasting.* New York: Basic Books.

Boulding, K. E. 1989. *Three Faces of Power.* Newbury Park, Calif.: Sage Publications.

Braddock, D., and L. Bachelder. 1994. The Glass Ceiling and Persons with Disabilities. Chicago: Institute on Disability and Human Development, College of Associated Health Professions, University of Illinois at Chicago.

Conte, L. 1983. Sheltered Employment Services and Programs. Washington, D.C.: National Rehabilitation Information Center.

Domhoff, G. W. 1990. *The Power Elite and the State: How Policy Is Made in America.* New York: Aldine De Gruyter.

Donovan, M. 1991. Help Wanted: People with Disabilities Needed. OSERS News in Print, pp. 22-25. Washington, D.C.: U.S. Department of Education.

Elman, R. M. 1968. *The Poorhouse State: The American Way of Life on Public Assistance.* New York: Dell.

Estes, R. J. 1984. *Health Care and the Social Services: Social Work Practice in Health Care.* St. Louis: W. H.

Greenwood, R. 1991. Employment and Workers with Disabilities. OSERS News in Print, pp. 25–28. Washington, D.C.: U.S. Department of Education.

Halachmi, A. 1981. Disability in America: Paradoxes and Public Policy. In *Administration for the Disabled: Policy and Organizational Issues,* ed. T. N. Chaturee. New Delhi: Indian Institute of Public Administration.

Link, B. 1982. Mental Patient Status, Work, and Income: An Examination of the Effects of a Psychiatric Label. *American Sociological Review* 47 (2): 202–15.

Mank, D. 1994. The Underachievement of Supported Employment: A Call for Reinvestment. *Journal of Disability Policy Studies* 5 (2): 1–24.

McDermott, J. 1980. *Crisis in the Working Class and Some Arguments for a New Labor Movement.* Boston: South End Press.

Murphy, S., and P. Rogan. 1992. Closing the Sheltered Workshop: A Case Study of Agency Change. OSERS News in Print, pp. 29–33. Washington, D.C.: U.S. Department of Education.

Murphy, S. T., and M. M. Rogan. 1995. *Closing the Shop: Conversion from Sheltered to Integrated Work.* Baltimore: Brookes.

Piven, F. F., and R. A. Cloward. 1972. *Regulating the Poor: The Functions of Public Welfare.* New York: Vintage Books.

Rawls, J. 1971. *A Theory of Justice.* Oxford: Oxford University Press.

Stoesz, D., and H. J. Karger. 1992. *Reconstructing the Welfare State.* Lanham, Md: Rowman and Littlefield.

U.S. Department of Commerce. 1996. Economics and Statistics Administration C3.272: CQ C-18. April.

Vash, C. 1980. Sheltered Industrial Employment. In *Annual Review of Rehabilitation*, ed. E. Pan, T. Backer, and C. Vash. New York: Springer Verlag.

Walker, A. 1982. *Unqualified and Underemployed: Handicapped Young People and the Labour Market.* Hong Kong: Macmillan.

Wall, C., and H. Culhane. 1991. Project Employment: A Model for Change. OSERS News in Print, pp. 17–21. Washington, D.C.: U.S. Department of Education.

Walz, T., and J. McFadden. The Informal Economy in a Post-capitalistic Society: The Mexican Experience.

Walz, T., and W. Theisen. 1997. The Political Economy of the American Family: Implications for Human Service Providers.

Wehman, P. 1994. Toward a National Agenda for Supported Employment. *Advance* 5 (2): 1–3.

Wehman, P., et al., 1990. The National Supported Employment Initiative: Expanding Employment Opportunities for Persons with Severe Disabilities. OSERS News in Print, pp. 7–13. Washington, D.C.: U.S. Department of Education.

Weisgerber, R. A. 1991. *Quality of Life for Persons with Disabilities.* Gaithersburg, Md.: Aspen Publications.

Chapter XVIII
Completing Stories

Steve Thunder-McGuire

I recall once wondering where my scholarly research on interpretation crossed my work as a storyteller. And then, one afternoon after telling a story that included my son Chris, who has cerebral palsy, to a number of people gathered on disability policy, there came a question: "Do you ever write these stories down?" And then a member of the audience spoke up, and by telling what she did, tried to provide a context for her question. The person, Karen Hirsch, explained she had spent much time within the realm of stories told by people with disabilities. In her essay "Culture and Disability: The Role of Oral History," she considers the "use of oral history interviews to shed light on past events still alive in the memories of people" with disabilities (Hirsch 1995, p. 2).

The special charm of that question at that moment with that audience was that behind it lay an implicit assumption: that as a storyteller with a son with cerebral palsy, I was especially interested in the telling of stories because doing so was the best way to pay the closest heed to the meaning of his and my experience. This assumption centers on an interesting, inscrutable, and yet very ordinary reality about the moral energy of storytelling. One way or another we need to comprehend our lives and the lives of others in terms of their meaning, because this is how we accommodate more fully each other's and our own being in the world.

In a sense I was being challenged to take measure of the use of narrative, beyond my storytelling performance. While I am a contemporary traditional storyteller, I have also surveyed the use of narrative as an interpretative tool, tried to draw on some of the broader philosophical grounding of "narrative understanding" in the work of Paul Ricoeur (1984, p. 67), and written on the evaluative role of "reflective judgment" in the composition of stories.

On my way home that afternoon, I reflected on the request that I write down the story I had told. I was searching for an explanation that would account for this sudden happenstance: my creative work as an artist and my role as a parent actually grounding an appraisal of the function of narrative, for this seemed to be the challenge. I found an explanation easily: even as an artist, in that story, I was affirming the insight that Chris's cerebral palsy makes me see what to do differently than I would if I were not the father of a son experiencing cerebral palsy.

Later I will tell what are, in a sense, two companion stories. I have tried to connect the moral energy of the story I told that afternoon with a story I told in an individualized educational plan meeting for Chris at the school he attends, a story whose telling rises out of the moral energy of a parent's responsibility. Needless to say, readers will recognize that together the stories convey two different but generatively related summonses.

Being Narrator

How do we regard the additions of the newfound commitment to storytelling, narrative, and oral history in the vocation of work with people experiencing disabilities? Hirsch writes, "Oral history interviews with disabled people are adding a viewpoint that has been ignored partly because it has been assumed that disabled people do not have an articulate view of their circumstances that differs from other views" (1995, p. 6). Hirsch appears to imply something more than the epistemological reality that telling stories, telling oral histories, enables getting knowledge otherwise unattainable.

Our capacity to create pictures of what our lives should be and how we are involved in others' lives oftentimes comes down to telling stories. This is what Maxine Greene has in mind in her book, *The Dialectic of Freedom* (1988). She writes:

> To tell the truth . . . is to articulate a life story that enables a [person] to know perhaps for the first time how she has encountered the world and what she desires to do and be. . . . Where freedom is concerned, it is taken to signify either liberation from domination or the provision of spaces where choices can be made. There is a general acknowledgment that the opening of such spaces depends on support and connectedness. . . . It is to interpret from as

many vantage points as possible lived experience, the ways there are of being in the world. (pp. 570, 120)

While working on an essay, "A Liberatory Story" (1997), I reflected on the work of Green (1995), who argues that we understand the reasons people find for doing what they do, the way they do it, in the complex narratives of their lives.

For Hirsch what matters is that protagonists of autobiographical stories and oral histories want, one way or another, to be comprehended in terms of the purpose, meaning, and context of their experience, because being understood leverages more completely being in the world. Needless to say, this is what Engel and Munger (1996) are especially interested in:

> Individual life stories weave in and out of the fabric of public events and social history. Autobiographical narrations by ordinary people reflect the influence of political change, of cultural transformations—and, at times, of legal innovation. Yet the threads of individual lives also constitute this fabric: Through the choices and struggles of individuals in their everyday lives, events are channeled in particular directions and history is carried forward. The telling of life stories becomes part of this process. By drawing selectively on elements of the remembered past, the autobiographical narrators create an identity and a destiny for their protagonist. (p. 8)

When I read this opening statement in Engel and Munger's essay "Rights, Remembrance, and the Reconciliation of Difference," I understood what they were suggesting within the context of Greene. Greene believes "John Dewey saw the relation between freedom and experienced resistance" (1988, p. 6). And clearly Greene recognizes that resistances require naming. Naming experienced resistance is a product of the generative praxis developed between being narrator and taking action—the dialectic of freedom. I mention Greene here because Engel and Munger's insistence on the use of constitutive narratives is an affirmation of the necessity to learn the origins of meaningful human actions and their connections to aspirations. These authors' turn to autobiography appears to be grounded not only in political action but also in the ontological pertinence of making narratives.

I often hearken back to the philosophical writing of Paul Ricoeur because much of what the social sciences now understand about the ontological pertinence of making narratives—stories—is informed by his version of hermeneutical ontology: narrative understanding. As I read through the compelling stories in

Engel and Munger's work, I kept thinking of Ricoeur's essay "Life: A Story in Search of a Narrator" (1991). In this essay, Ricoeur's thesis is "that the process of composition, of configuration, . . . realizes itself in . . . the reader, and under this configuration makes possible reconfiguration of life by way of the narrative" (p. 430). Reading is the crucial moment of storymaking.

The synthetic act of imagination, which grasps together events and experiences into a temporal whole, underlies the autobiographies of the storytellers in Engel and Munger's research as well as autobiography and storytelling in general. Ricoeur compared characteristics of the configurational act that underpins both oral history and autobiography with two Kantian conceptions: reflective judgment and productive imagination. "The labor of productive imagination" orders events according to their "causal connections" so that a universal meaning emerges in the narrative (1984, p. 69). Ricoeur wrote, "To understand the story is to understand how and why the successive episodes led to this conclusion, which, far from foreseeable, must finally be acceptable, as congruent with the episodes brought together by the story" (p. 67). Telling stories is the practice of unraveling the connections and direction of human action. It involves recovering meaning by putting events and experiences into a story, events that would otherwise be unrelated. The integrating function of oral history and autobiography allow the teller to bring about, beyond the grasping together of incidents, a mediation between "what happened" and the meaning of what happened. Ricoeur (1984) maintained that this kind of judgment, which seeks to establish direction, bearing, and continuity—an integrating judgment—required the author to be the reader of her or his story.

Ricoeur suggested that in the act of being the reader of our stories, as we compose or tell them, we necessarily transform the self as well. "It is only in reading," Ricoeur wrote, "that the dynamism of configuration completes its course. And, it is beyond reading in effective action . . . that the configuration of the text is transformed into refiguration . . . [reading] makes the intersection between the world configured and . . . the world in which effective action is unfolded and itself unfolds" (1988, p. 159). Put simply, we become more when we tell stories because meanings of events and experiences become evident to us as we unfold our stories.

My Story

Every so often someone asks me if I've written down a particular story they heard me tell. "Well," I'll say, "telling a story to an audience is really very different than writing a story." What I mean when I say this is that the audience with whom a particular story happens matters to the success of the story, the ability of the story being able to arrive at a definitely situated meaning. And, following this, a story told is often a story that can't be the same in writing.

I had not written down the story I told that afternoon to people gathered on disability policy. But when I finished that story, as so often happens, I learned something from telling it. And I did write down what I had learned, which was actually a kind of refrain that guided me as I told it: "We help complete each others' stories." It was, I thought, what I do with my son Chris.

For a second time I tell this story, only now I write it. This is how it happened.

I came up over the crest of the first steep hill on Sugarbottom Road, outside of Solon, Iowa, on my bicycle, my son Chris, who is 12, riding in a trailer behind me. Chris was much heavier than when I last pulled him.

Chris was riding with me on the final day of a thirty-eight-day trip—riding my bicycle back from Fairbanks, Alaska, to Iowa City, Iowa, 3,473 miles. I rode to raise both awareness and money for Close Encounters Art Workshop, a two-week summer residency program for high school students with developmental disabilities. Because, as it turned out, a number of collaborative partnerships—schools and community service organizations—were formed with the project, we received a good deal of media coverage.

At that moment on the hills, I struggled pulling Chris in ninety-plus-degree heat, even though I had crossed the Canadian Rockies on my bike with seventy pounds of gear. In fact, the temperature was hard on both of us. I stopped frequently to give Chris drinks of water, and when I did I always worried we might be getting further off our scheduled arrival and celebration in Iowa City. By now a number of people had joined us—themselves more effortlessly climbing the Sugarbottom hills. As I reached the top of the hill, where media were positioned with their cameras, I concentrated on not looking exhausted. But I was wiped out. When I saw Chris in my rearview mirror, looking intently ahead at two cameramen waving to him, I knew they had the photo they wanted, the one they had tried to get the past twenty-eight miles they'd followed us. And as I watched Chris, the fire truck approaching from behind signaled its inclusion in the now formed procession, as our escort, by turning on its siren. Chris arched around to see and screamed with delight at the sound. And as all this happened photographs were taken.

When I saw Chris through the rearview mirror, I got a picture in my head of his photograph as it might appear the next day in the newspaper.

Sometimes, right when we take note of a situation and conclude a matter-of-fact understanding of the event, we find ourselves drawn instantly deeper into the experience. All we can do then is follow one experience to another as they line up side by side in our memories, completing and, yet, generating the meaning of each experience. This is what I thought at that moment: "Chris will like to see his picture in the paper. The smile on his face, the arching of his back and neck to reach a glimpse of the fire truck whose sound animated him with pure exuberance is something I love. And his mom will recognize the purposeful determination in his body's gesture when she sees the photograph."

I remembered when I was 12, I was at the halfway house across the street, the House of Agape, with Anne. Anne taught at the Kansas City Art Institute. I looked up when she asked me the question, "Steve, what do you want to paint?" When she asked me that question I saw two canvases both about twenty-four by thirty-six inches sitting across the room in the corner.

Even at the age of 12 I was quite skilled at drawing things and people as they looked, because my grandfather—in an ordinary but roundabout way— himself had become an artist. My grandfather, because he was deaf, at an early age did not receive the education that he otherwise might have. But a man whom he worked for as a custodian saw that he was a tremendous drawer and took it upon himself to send my grandfather back to school at the Kansas City Art Institute. To this day my mom reminds me, "Steve, don't forget your grandfather had Thomas Hart Benton for a teacher."

When I was young I stayed three or four days a week at my grandparents' because it made going to the store for my grandmother, who was also deaf, a little easier. And when I stayed with my grandparents, I, of course, did what my grandfather did—painted and drew. So at an early age I became quite good at drawing.

When Anne asked me what I wanted to paint, the first thing I thought was, "This is my chance to be a real artist," because, well, real artists paint with oil paint on canvas. This was the invitation. I also knew from my grandfather that oil paint and canvas were expensive; I had never painted with them.

Then I asked Anne if I could run home. I went across the street to our house and up the stairs and back to my room. From under my bed I pulled a metal lunch box with Hotwheels pictured on it. Inside were sixteen plastic compartments. From the upper left-hand compartment I pulled my Demon Hotwheel.

Now what you have to know is this: that previous Wednesday I called down to Gateway Sporting Goods on the Plaza with a question. The woman answered the phone and I asked, "Ma'am, do you have any new Hotwheels in this week?" She put down the phone on a glass case and returned in about two minutes. She said, "We have one new car this week. It's a Demon Hotwheel."

When she said that, a picture came to my head. The Demon Hotwheel was pictured on the back of my Hotwheel boxes, lined up side by side with the other Hotwheels, the Cheetah, the Silhouette. The Demon was the car pictured on my box of Hotwheel Track—jumping through the air, wheels spinning into action, ready to land on the orange ramp and track. When she said, "We have a Demon Hotwheel," I could picture myself holding it.

Setting the phone down, I ran into the kitchen. "Mom," I said, "you've got to let me go to Gateway. They've got a Demon Hotwheel." My mom said, "Steve, you know the rule. It's a school night. Wait 'til Saturday." "But, Mom, if I don't go now, someone is going to buy that car. Please." My mom said, "You can go, but remember Gateway closes at 5:30."

Outside of Gateway I opened the box with my Demon Hotwheel. I held the Demon up in the position it was pictured on the box of Hotwheel Track—a view from the side and underneath. As I walked I played with it, moving it through the air, capturing the pose on the box of Hotwheel Track.

The only thing that disappointed me about this car was that it was burgundy, a color I did not find attractive. As I walked I also considered painting it Day-Glo orange, a color that was popular and that I was particularly taken with. But then I remembered other previous attempts at painting my cars. I would get a little paint—no matter how hard I tried not to—on the windshield, try to take it off with turpentine, and melt the windshield. No, I wasn't going to make that mistake with possibly the only Demon Hotwheel I might have.

That day, when Anne asked me what I wanted to paint, I knew what I wanted to paint. It was an image that was demanding. It was an image I wanted to accomplish. That day I painted my Demon Hotwheel, bright orange against a blue sky, jumping through the air, like the image on my box of Hotwheel Track.

That Demon Hotwheel painting was a kind of story I wanted to complete.

It's kind of like something Chris does. Chris converses with others about his interests through images he selects and has taped to his hands. The images can be anything from collectors' cards to stickers. Chris is quadriplegic and has no fine or gross motor development. He communicates with eye gaze. More recently Chris has taken to finding pictures in magazines, the newspaper, or on boxes. Once taped to his hand, they remain there for upward of an entire day. What Chris has learned is that people will ask him about what he has "taped."

This is what Elliana, Chris's classmate, had learned. Chris sang to Elliana the most excited notes of their play with the action figures on his tray. They were all about the jumps of a Power Ranger as he leaped over the Power Ranger Elliana held. Chris had an almost constant scream of excitement. And when Elliana couldn't figure what Chris was thinking, as he moved his action figure, she just made up something she thought he might be thinking. "Now that's a high jump, Christopher," she said. Chris couldn't disagree and smiled. "Draw Power Rangers with me," Chris told Elliana, looking at the pencil and crayon box. Elliana put a crayon in his hand and began to draw with him a Power Ranger mask. It was a sticker of a Power Ranger mask Chris had taped to his hand.

Because the painting of my Demon Hotwheel was oil, I hung it to dry in my room on the chimney painted white. For the next few weeks I played intently with that Demon Hotwheel on the floor under the painting. When I played I would get down so close to my car that I could block off the view of the rest of the room and picture myself in the Demon, as if I were driving.

Later that summer two new Hotwheels were issued, replicas of the funny cars of drag racing superstars Don "The Snake" Prudhomme and Tom "Mongoose" McEwen. I played just as intently with those two cars under that oil painting of my Demon Hotwheel. In my head I imagined myself driving the Demon Hotwheel to the drag strip, where I would then climb into Don Prudhomme's car and race, shooting down the drag strip at 250 miles an hour. It was a magnificent image.

Some years later, in August 1995, I was in the Prairie Lights bookstore in Iowa City. My wife, Lore, was looking for books on volcanoes for her seventh-grade earth science class. I was paging through a book on bicycling when I came across a photograph of a man on his bike in what appeared, from his attire, to be extreme winter conditions. The caption under the photograph explained: "The Idita-bike, already half the participants have pulled out from frostbite and hypothermia. Billed as the 'world's toughest human powered ultra-marathon' the race takes place annually on the Idita-Rod Trail in the Alaskan bush where temperatures frequently reach 40 below zero."

I took the book over to my wife and said, "Look at this, Lore!" After she read the caption, she said, "Don't think about it, because it is not going to happen!"

Wouldn't you know, some months later, on February 19, I found myself on my back at three o'clock in the morning. The thermometer on my jacket was buried at 35 degrees below zero. The Idita-Rod Trail, Alaska.

I quickly got my wits about me and slipped my foot back into my boot, recovering from a moment of stupidity. I'd taken my foot out because the tops of my toes had been rubbed raw from the ridge on my sock liners. Every step I took was painful. And I'd taken a lot of steps because I'd pushed my bike the past 19 miles. I had pushed my bike because the trail was moose-rutted—chewed up from the hooves of moose using the trail in late winter to better negotiate deep snow in the Alaskan bush—and impossible to pedal on.

As I lay on my back I asked myself, "What was I thinking when I saw that photograph?" As I lay on my back, above the Northern Lights cascaded green like a waterfall. And I thought, "Isn't that a magnificent image? Isn't that an image that's demanding?"

I stood up and began to gather the Nutty-Butty bars that had spilled from the bag on my handlebars as I leaned my bike over to take off my boot. I'd bought forty-seven boxes for this race. I noticed, then, a light off in the distance approaching. Instantly it was upon me and swallowed me up. So bright and intense I had to cover my eyes and look down. And then I heard a voice. And the voice said, "Are your feet cold? Are your hands warm? Have you had enough to eat? How often do you have something to drink?" All these questions I had been asking myself for the past three miles, since I'd come upon a man standing in the trail with his feet so cold he could not step forward and his hands too numb to turn the dial on his stove.

Click. The light went off. In front of me a cloud of breath hovered four feet above the ground and trailed nearly twenty feet back, at the end of which stood a kind of hero—Martin Buser. Martin Buser had, at that time, already won the Idita-Rod Sled Dog Race two times. He's since won it again. He looked at me and said, "You should make it to Skwentna by sunup. Good luck." And he left.

I made it to Skwentna by sunup and ate moose stew and reindeer sausage at the checkpoint. And then, I don't know if it was a mistake, but I kept on riding. My mind was rolling on its own, so I pedaled.

I had ridden seventeen miles, away from Skwentna, down the frozen Yentna River at a pace of about seven miles an hour, when I rounded the corner into a kind of futility I had never come upon before. In a heartbeat I was torn from my bicycle and tossed end over end by the wind. I tried to stand back up and was knocked back down. Even crawling on all fours resulted in tumbling disorder. I lay on my stomach, sprawled out on the Yentna River, a spontaneous human wind gauge being cast about.

The wind lasted no more than a few minutes. And when it stopped, everything about this race I feared rushed out to meet the crisp, instant stillness of the wind's departure. I tried desperately to catch the glimmer of the reflective tape on my bicycle with the light mounted to my helmet. My light caught the reflective tape of my bicycle two hundred feet away. I stood up, wobbled a couple of steps forward and made my way to my bike. Instinctively I climbed on and began to pedal. I don't know why, but I actually felt a sense of liberation.

Twenty hours later, fifty-one hours after the race began, I stood at the finish line. Jeff, a man from Connecticut I'd walked much of the race with, took my photograph.

When I showed my father that photograph he asked me, "What were you thinking at that moment?" I replied, "Do you remember the summer I painted a picture of my Demon Hotwheel?"

When the camera flashed I remembered of all things this:

Later that summer in 1970, I was so taken with the image in my head of racing the Snake—the actual car of my replica Hotwheel—that when I saw, in the Kansas City Star, an advertisement to sell Cokes at the drag strip, I went to my father with a request. I asked, "Dad, do you think I could get this job selling Cokes at Kansas City International Raceway?" My dad said, "Steve, Blue Springs is twenty-three miles away. We don't even have a car. How are you, at the age of 12, going to get a job at the drag strip?" But on that Thursday my father put together a series of bus routes and I got a job selling Cokes at the drag strip.

Fate should have it so wonderful. The weekend before school started that September, the Summer Nationals were held at Kansas City International Raceway. The previous Wednesday I heard on WHB Radio an advertisement that announced that Don "The Snake" Prudhomme and Tom "The Mongoose" McEwen would be there. On Saturday when I rounded the corner into the pits, the fastest drag-racing cars in the world were spread out over two square miles. As I carried my Cokes, I visually scanned the area for Don Prudhomme, who was advertised on the radio to be there. And then I spotted that yellow 1970 Barracuda, body raised, the Hotwheel emblem flashing across the side. Don Prudhomme was standing next to his car.

I walked up and said, "Mr. Prudhomme, do you think I could take your picture with your car?" "Sure," he said. I set down my Cokes and with my grandpa's camera took his picture.

And then, as I bent over to pick the Cokes back up, I asked the question that I had probably been working on all summer as I played with my Hotwheels under my painting of the Demon. I asked, "Mr. Prudhomme, do you think you could take a picture of me sitting in your car?" He looked to his mechanic, who shrugged his shoulders quizzically. I could see that they had not been asked this question before. "Why not?" he said.

I handed Don Prudhomme my grandpa's camera and with the help of his mechanic climbed into the seat of the Snake. As the seatbelts were clasped, I reached and held the steering wheel. They lowered the body down so that now

I was looking out the windshield of the car over the blower. Don Prudhomme backed up to an appropriate distance with my grandpa's camera. When he clicked my photograph I could actually see myself shooting down the drag strip in his car, just like the picture in my head formed that summer as I rolled his car on the floor in my room. It was a story I was completing.

Now, I tell you this because as I stood at the finish line of the Idita-Bike, I realized that a long time ago I had learned a lesson from a hidden teacher: if you pay attention to the images in your head and follow them all the way through, you will always be heading in the right direction.

When the media photographed Chris and me riding the Sugarbottom hills, coming back into Iowa City, I thought in a more concentrated way about this lesson. And I remembered an anecdote once told me.

A woman, who was participating in a conference I was speaking at, came up during a break and said, "When you talked about how your son uses pictures taped to his wrist to initiate stories, well, I thought about this boy I met once." She explained:

> Three years ago I was visiting a special education classroom. I brought with me, at the request of the teacher, one of the potbelly pigs my husband and I rescued, Rose. Potbelly pigs are good tempered but can sometimes have bad manners. As I walked Rose through the room amongst the children, she nipped the hand of a boy who had cerebral palsy. His hand was hanging alongside his wheelchair and apparently Rose imagined he was holding food for her. Of course, I was alarmed and thanked God that Rose only nipped him and that he was not upset. As I drove home after my visit I was mad at myself for not anticipating something like this.
>
> Some months passed and I was being seated in a restaurant when I noticed this same boy. I walked over to his table. He remembered me and smiled. I introduced myself to his father. And then the boy looked at me, and then to his father, trying to tell me something. He could not vocalize words. Of course, the thing I remembered was the story of Rose nipping him in the hand. I asked, Did you tell your father about Rose, the potbelly pig? The smile on his face grew until he screamed with delight and again looked directly at me and then to his father. Do you want me to tell your dad about Rose? With tremendous enthusiasm he nodded his head, Yes. I told the story. And he loved it.
>
> It occurred to me that he had waited a long time for this story to be told and that telling it mattered tremendously to him. How many other stories was he waiting and wanting to tell?

When I came over the crest of the hill at Sugarbottom and Chris's and my pictures were taken, I thought back to that moment at the finish line of the Idita-bike, to sitting in Don Prudhomme's funny car, and to the woman's story: what matters most is that we complete each other's stories.

Substance of Stories Told

Not least, this story is prompted by a clarifying wonder for Chris's idiosyncratic approach to participating in stories of his life: he works his eyes and images with others to tell, to complete, his stories. Eventually I learned this more fully by telling this story.

For me telling this story is a way of affirming the insight that Chris's disability makes me see what I've done in the past, am doing now, and imagine, in ways that I would not otherwise, if he vocalized words. I didn't have to try to connect Chris's eye-gaze to a thread of meaning in events of my life that, in fact, predate him. But rather, how Chris uses his eyes in place of voice makes me realize the link between experiences that were otherwise disparate. Telling this story is a means of glimpsing and comprehending not only Chris, but the world.

The Function of Telling Anecdotes

At other times the tug of trying to involve Chris in the world with others — situations where there is the promise of better things — I offer stories of Chris to others in a very ordinary but definitely strategic way. And so does his mom. And so does his brother, Daniel. Eventually I learned that there was plenty of necessity to compose stories of Chris's being in the world.

In response to overcoming the perceived inability to "measure" Chris similarly to other students and then more fully include him in the wider curriculum of the school he attends, Chris's mother and I tried the best we could to present to the therapist, counselors, and teachers what he really does with the images taped to his hand. To tell how Chris composes, I told everyone assembled at an Individualized Educational Plan (IEP) meeting an anecdote I actually used in the story I have previously mentioned. I draw your attention to it again: Chris sang to Elliana the most excited notes of their play with the action figures on his tray. They were all about the jumps of a Power Ranger as he leaped over the Power Ranger Elliana held. Chris had an almost constant scream of excitement. And when Elliana couldn't figure what Chris was thinking, as he moved his action figure, she just made up something she thought he might be thinking. "Now that's a high jump, Christopher," she said. Chris couldn't disagree and smiled. "Draw Power Rangers with me," Chris told Elliana, looking at the pencil and crayon box. Elliana put a crayon in his hand and began to draw with him a Power Ranger mask. It was a sticker of a Power Ranger mask Chris had taped to his hand.

As the reader will see, I draw from anecdotes I tell about Chris that explain better to others my interpretation of his involvement with his disability, in broader stories whose situated meanings are contingent upon what I learned from considering things from Chris's perspective. This is to say, anecdotes of Chris inform my autobiography as surely as telling them can also function to help others understand Chris.

What I wanted to do, though, in the IEP meeting, was get everyone to understand Chris's stubborn use of eye-gaze, the pursuit of composing meaning that characterized his fictive play with images. And this anecdote spoke to this truth. When Chris's teacher mentioned the distinct presence of hockey cards taped to his hand in school, I remembered Chris and Elliana playing Power Rangers and a moment two weeks earlier when I showed Chris a photograph, from the newspaper, of five dogs dressed in sheets, looking like ghosts. I told him that I cut it out since I knew he would enjoy it. Chris urged me to tape the picture on his hand, because, I am sure, he wanted to talk with other people about the content of the photograph. These two experiences connected solidly, and I told Chris's teacher and others in the IEP meeting the anecdote of Elliana and Chris and then the following anecdote:

Recently I was with Chris, and spread open on the tray of his wheelchair was a book, *Plane Song*. I started to turn the pages, remembering to look him in the eyes, so that he could direct me with his gaze. Once our eyes met he let me know he was looking for something in the book. I turned the pages slowly. This required Chris to visually analyze the drawn images on each page and started him picking definite points of interest, which I knew by him looking directly at my eyes and then looking directly back at the picture. Even when we are viewing the same thing, though, I am not certain what he is interested in until he answers yes to one of my inquiries. Chris answers yes by looking me straight in the eyes and blinking when I have guessed right. The up and down of his eyelids is a kind of shorthand for the nodding of his head, which for him is not necessarily quick or automatic.

Until I went through the whole book with him, performing this exercise of page turning, I did not understand as fully as Chris wanted me to understand why he chose this book. It is important to Chris that I not only perform page turning but be intent on knowing what he is interested in. There is, absolutely, nothing more lively than discovering in detail (which is hard interpretative work for both Chris and me) his idea. Chris literally screamed with enthusiasm when, after a few questions, I figured out why he is so interested in this book. Chris was particularly taken with an image of a jet fighter pilot thrust back in his seat, looking, with his full flight gear, very much like an insect.

I was not happy, though, that Chris was upset that I would not cut out the picture from the library book so that it could be taped on his hand. What I did, when Chris insisted continuously that I pick up the scissors and cut out the picture, was say, "No, we are not going to cut anything out of a library book." Chris did not resort to demanding, but he stared at the image and then repeatedly nodded with his eyes in the direction of the drawing for me to look at it too. He had something in mind. He waited solemnly for me to resolve this interpretative dilemma: "You want that picture and you know I won't cut it out of the book?" Chris can manage a silent conversation this way with his eyes.

I resorted first to asking what he wanted to do since we couldn't cut it out, and then to the usual questioning and entreaties. But Chris turned silent and began looking around and, I thought, had given up on this picture. He seemed to change the subject. Chris did not respond to my asking if he wanted me to draw the picture, and he looked at the photocopy of the ghost dogs, now located under the Plexiglas sheet covering his tray. But he hadn't changed his intention after all. Chris wanted me to photocopy the image. He imagined himself to be the fighter pilot pictured in the same way I pictured myself inside my Hotwheel when I was his age. I am sure of this!

I simply wanted to relate that "story" and "play" are what come to people's minds when they are working with Chris and trying to explain what he is doing with images and eye-gaze. Again, this is what Elliana had learned. As I sat there in the meeting and told both this anecdote and the one of Elliana and Chris playing, I began trying to explain, even as I spoke, this moment to myself, also trying to explain to others what I understood was going on. Another anecdote, of a different boy doing something similar to Chris, entered my head. And I used this to illustrate an understanding, as it were to measure Chris in the world of other children.

"Once," I said, "a third-grade boy told me about why he was using his G.I. Joes for his art project in school." He told me:

I always make up scenes for my G.I. Joe Action Figures when I play with them. I thought, I'll just write down what my G.I. Joes say and do. You see, on the weekends I have battles with them that take different lengths of time. All week long, I think about how to position different guys and how things could turn out. So, in my book I wrote down what was going on in the battles.

From here Ryan went on to create drawings of his G.I. Joes and their vehicles. Doing drawings of vehicles invigorated Ryan's play by engaging him in a reflective encounter with specific images from memories of particular "battles" he had set up in his room.

Story: Context, Meaning, and Purpose

My point is that an inventory, not of products, but of the context, meaning, and purpose of what Chris and Ryan do, bears a remarkable similarity. That is, Chris has an elaborate pursuit of fictive play that involves images, such as cards and stickers taped to his hands, action figures, and other people drawing with him, often on his hands. Accomplishing fictive play, which is utmost to many children's art-making, is precisely the stuff of Chris's strategy for accomplishing images, although it is packaged differently.

From observing the centrality of images in Chris's play with Elliana, it becomes clear that Chris has adapted an interpretative process of picturing, where picturing is used as a tool to configure meaning and help individuals understand his personal constructs. To be sure, this is what this story about Chris suggested. What kinds of things can Chris's teachers have knowledge of if they approach, as Elliana does, the images on his hands as invitations for interpretation, as poems?

Both the occasion and the story itself, that afternoon in the IEP, were ordinary enough. But upon reflection I realized how telling the story was essential to leveraging Chris's inclusion. Perhaps the most important contribution a parent makes is configuring a liberatory story. And of course that liberatory story is very much contingent upon the completion of many other autobiographical and biographical stories.

References

Engel, D., and F. Munger. 1996. Rights, Remembrance, and the Reconciliation of Difference. *Law and Society Review* 1:7–53.

Greene, Maxine. 1988. *The Dialectic of Freedom*. New York: Teachers College Press.

———. 1995. *Releasing the Imagination*. San Francisco: Jossey-Bass.

Hirsch, Karen. 1995. Culture and Disability: The Role of Oral History. *Journal of the Oral History Association.* 1:1–27.

Ricoeur, Paul. 1984–88. *Time and Narrative.* Trans. K. McLaughlin and D. Pellauer. Vols. 1–3. Chicago: University of Chicago Press.

———. 1991. Life: A Story in Search of a Narrator. In *Reflection and Imagination,* ed. M. J. Valdes. Toronto: University of Toronto Press.

Thunder-McGuire, Steve. 1997. Liberatory Story. *Visual Arts Research* 1:36–40.

Conclusion

ADA at a Crossroads

MARCA BRISTO

W e stand at a crossroads in what we know about and what we expect from our citizens with disabilities. Research can help to elucidate the path to progress, and it can be used to undermine progress. The contributions in this volume reflect an important call to action for researchers, policy makers, and others from many disciplines to bring their efforts into line with the visions and goals of the Americans with Disabilities Act (ADA).

After the tenth anniversary of the signing of the ADA, on July 26, 2000, many scholars and researchers are attempting to evaluate the true impact that the law has had on the lives of the over 54 million people with disabilities living in the United States. This presents a challenge for researchers in a variety of disciplines, from law to labor market economics to social theory. The multidisciplinary approach reflected in this volume is critical for describing an accurate picture of the progress and continuing challenges faced by the disability community in the new millennium.

Reorienting Research on Disability

In April 1998, the National Council on Disability (NCD) released a report called "Reorienting Disability Research." The report synthesizes recommendations by researchers and consumers toward a disability statistics policy that is more meaningful and useful in light of the paradigm shift precipitated by the ADA, which the NCD originally proposed. For many years, research on disability has appeared to be essentially a scientific exercise, based on academic procedures applied in a medical context and the provision of health care. People with disabilities have learned, however, that underlying values and assumptions have guided research in ways that are not necessarily important or helpful to them as the ultimate beneficiaries (see, e.g., Baynton; Hirsch; Thunder-McGuire, this volume).

Choices are made, either consciously or not, at each stage of research design, collection, and dissemination that significantly affect the utility of the research to individuals with disabilities, to policy makers, to employers, and others. In addition, given limited federal resources, issues arise such as: which questions should be studied? what disciplines and methods should be used in study? and how should the research findings be disseminated and applied by policy makers and others?

The 1998 NCD report recommended several specific "action steps" to help reorient the answers to these and other questions based on the view that disability is a natural part of the human experience; that people *with* disabilities should participate in the production and consumption of research about disability; and that disability data should be an integral part of regularly collected federal population statistics and socioeconomic measures of progress. While the NCD report does not purport to represent consensus among the disability community, researchers, and policy makers, it does offer a synthesis of recent viewpoints on this topic.

Research on Employment, Disability, and the ADA

With the enactment of the ADA, a new paradigm about conceptions of disability was established in law and policy. Moving away from the so-called medical model that historically formed the foundation of disability policy, the new paradigm offered a civil rights orientation that focused on societal barriers to full participation rather than the functional impairments of individuals. The disability community has embraced ADA as its declaration of independence, one that articulates a vision of an accessible and equitable society.

Unfortunately, the vast majority of data collection activities of the federal, state, and local governments and from the private sector have retained the medical bias, not yet adopting the new paradigm. Examples of medical bias are found in questions about work in population-based surveys such as the Decennial Census and the Current Population Survey (CPS). Questions in such surveys focus on the individual's impairment and functional level. For instance, they do not identify barriers in society and the environment—such as discrimination and lack of accommodations in the workplace—that are often obstacles to employment. In addition, they assume that obstacles to employment reside solely with the individual as a result of the impairment itself.

Disability measures must inform employers and others about participation with and without accommodations (see, e.g., Blanck, this volume). The ADA recognizes the need for and emphasizes the use of accommodations to enable people with disabilities to participate fully in employment and other activities of daily life. Measuring the use of accommodations will not only indicate the overall level of need, but it is the best indicator of how our society is meeting the ADA's goals.

With the enactment of the ADA, people with disabilities established themselves as a minority group with civil rights protections, comparable to those available to other protected groups, such as ethnic and racial minorities, women, and the elderly. As a minority group, people with disabilities increasingly seek to have data about themselves that are comparable to data collected about other protected groups. For example, through the CPS, the Bureau of Labor Statistics collects and disseminates data each month about the employment rate of other protected groups. Yet these same data are collected and disseminated only yearly about people with disabilities

Action Steps

At the Obermann conference and elsewhere I have articulated several action steps to infuse the disability paradigm embodied in the ADA into federal data collection activities.

1. *Use the ADA as the basis for the definition of disability in federal surveys.* The ADA requires viewing disability as a dynamic rather than static attribute, as an interaction between an individual with an impairment and the environment rather than as a deficit of an individual. Legal and research definitions of disability need to be changed to reflect this orientation. In addition, questions about disability issues need to be integrated into questions being asked of all respondents. For example, disability-related support needs may be included in a list of support needs in a question asked of all respondents, not just those who have identified themselves as having an impairment.
2. *Operationalize the nation's goals for people with disabilities, as articulated in the ADA, so that data may be collected about the extent to which society is moving toward reaching those goals.* The ADA states that the nation's proper goals for

people with disabilities are (1) equality of opportunity, (2) full participation, (3) independent living, and (4) economic self-sufficiency. Statistical measures should be developed for each of these goals. Data should be collected regularly to determine whether the nation is moving toward these goals. The government and the private sector should dedicate resources to this effort.

3. *Breakdowns by disability should be included in all federal data collections that collect data on gender and race/ethnicity; and disability data should include breakdowns by rate/ethnicity and gender.* Where data are collected, analyzed, and reported about other protected groups, these should also be collected, analyzed, and reported about people with disabilities. Similarly, disability data should include breakdowns by race, ethnicity, and gender, so that subpopulations of the community can be studied and have their needs assessed. These research and data collection activities are a matter of equity and sound research. Of course, there are unique issues involved in obtaining adequate samples of people with disabilities, but they are often resolvable with techniques such as careful sampling, larger samples, or both.

4. *Research on the methodology of the development of national survey definitions of disability and its definitional subtypes, on sampling issues, and on research participation criteria must be ongoing.* Disability data collection is an evolving field (e.g., Miller, this volume). A formidable amount of work remains to improve the validity and accuracy of disability statistics. The multidisciplinary research reflected in the volume in fields such as economics, sociology, law, and medicine is invaluable for improving research results in those fields. Equal attention should be given to disability-related research in the voices of those with disabilities to ensure that upcoming substantive research will be conducted appropriately (see, e.g., Hirsch, this volume).

5. *Ensure that people with disabilities are included in the planning, development, and implementation of disability-related data collection activities at all levels, from local to national to international.* People with disabilities should be a part of designing and refining data collection instruments, determining questions that will guide analysis, and developing dissemination strategies. Too often, data are generated that are irrelevant or unusable by people with disabilities. Moreover, people with disabilities often are unaware of the importance of research methods and dissemination of the findings. People with disabilities should be provided financial support for their participation in the provision of data (e.g., responding to surveys and requests for information), the development of data activities, and the utilization of data. Infor-

mation should be available in accessible formats in all phases of data collection activities.

6. *Ensure that researchers in an array of disciplines have an understanding of the research and policy priorities of the disability community.* Federal policy is rife with inconsistent messages and unrealistic requirements. For people with disabilities to accomplish the vision of the ADA and achieve independence, empowerment, and inclusion, it is critical that researchers understand and support a disability policy agenda that enables people with disabilities to work and pay taxes but does not economically punish people with disabilities when they are unable to work or find a job.

Toward a Research Agenda

The action steps I have highlighted and the broader disability agenda, which might be framed as an opportunity agenda for all people, must address the numerous barriers to employment and self-sufficiency for people with disabilities. In addressing these barriers, the agenda would include:

- complete and timely data about people with disabilities and a need for a new research agenda grounded in the ADA paradigm;
- return-to-work legislation for Social Security disability benefit recipients that addresses health care, makes work pay, and provides recipients a choice in vocational rehabilitation and other employment and training services;
- an unwavering commitment to accommodate people with disabilities who are seeking to leave the welfare and social security rolls in the workplace and elsewhere;
- renewed efforts to expand family supports for individuals with disabilities, including appropriate child-care and related strategies;
- a reexamination of the recent cuts in the children's SSI program and immigrant programs to ensure that federal policy is applied consistently and not hindered with respect to these vulnerable populations;
- a concentrated effort to bring immigrants, minorities, and rural residents with disabilities into the mainstream of disability policy through outreach, educational, technical assistance, and inclusion programs;
- an examination of the 1997 reauthorization of the Individuals with Disabilities Education Act to maximize outcomes and integration for students with disabilities, including the issues facing deaf students, blind students, and minority students, and without diluting civil rights protections in the name of discipline;

- examination and study of the assistive technology agenda that ensures access to the information superhighway for all people (e.g., Berven and Blanck, this volume);
- a coordinated and well-funded ADA enforcement and implementation strategy that addresses disturbing trends in the case law and educates underserved groups about their rights under ADA;
- a transportation agenda that addresses accessibility, cost, and enforcement in air travel, bus travel, and all other forms of mass transit;
- a housing agenda that creates real choice for people with disabilities within their budgets and does not force them to live in group settings to receive services;
- examination of long-term services-and-supports legislation that replaces a prior bias toward life in institutions for persons with disabilities, a bias that has long existed in our publicly administered long-term care programs;
- ongoing attempts to enhance a quality health care system so that people with disabilities are not forced to accept publicly funded second-rate health care, to enroll in inappropriate managed care arrangements, or to forgo employment to have access to health coverage at all;
- an international agenda that empowers people with disabilities throughout the world and makes ADA's message global; and
- a flexible approach to emerging issues such as physician-assisted suicide, genetic discrimination, wilderness accessibility, and currency accessibility in a manner that is consistent with the vision of the ADA.

This volume illustrates that the ADA may be a beacon for showing where our society is headed in disability policy. Yet, as Paul Miller articulated in his introduction, the ADA does not self-enforce. All of us have a responsibility to assure that research from multiple points of view is consistent with the ADA's vision of inclusion, independence, and empowerment, and to ensure that this effort is supported by sound and realistic data that are not used to undermine the law's success. Working together, people with disabilities, researchers from many disciplines, policy makers, and others may build on the foundation that the ADA provides so that Americans will continue to provide a model for citizens with disabilities throughout the world.

Author Index to the Chapters

References are to chapter numbers, not page numbers.

Subject Index to the Chapters

References are to chapter numbers, not page numbers.

Notes on Contributors

Peter David Blanck (editor) is a professor of law, psychology, and preventive medicine at the University of Iowa. He received his doctorate in psychology from Harvard University and his J.D. from Stanford Law School, where he served as president of the *Stanford Law Review*. Blanck is the director of the Law, Health Policy, and Disability Center at the Iowa College of Law. He is a member of the President's Committee on the Employment of People with Disabilities and has been a senior fellow of the Annenberg Washington Program, in which capacity he explored the implementation of the Americans with Disabilities Act.

Marjorie L. Baldwin is an associate professor in the Department of Economics at East Carolina University. She is the author or coauthor of more than two dozen articles on work disability, return to work following a job-related injury, and labor market discrimination against workers with disabilities. She has presented her work on discrimination at the Equal Employment Opportunity Commission, the National Institute on Disability and Rehabilitation Research, and the Social Security Administration. Her current research includes a two-year prospective study of the relative cost-effectiveness of chiropractic and physician care for work-related back pain.

Douglas C. Baynton is an assistant professor of history and American Sign Language at the University of Iowa. He is the author of *Forbidden Signs: American Culture and the Campaign against Sign Language*. His current project is a history of the concept of disability in the making of American immigration policy since the late nineteenth century. He urges any disabled person with an immigration story to contact him.

Heidi M. Berven received her doctorate from Pennsylvania State University, her J.D. from the University of Iowa College of Law, and was a postdoctoral research fellow at the Law, Health Policy, and Disability Center. She is a patent attorney in a Minneapolis law firm.

Lea Anne Boucher is a social worker at the Veterans Administration Hospital in Iowa City. She is a former director of Wild Bill's Coffee Shop at the University of Iowa, a special project serving persons with developmental disabilities.

Marca Bristo is chairperson of the National Council on Disability (NCD), an independent federal agency making recommendations to the president and Congress on issues affecting 54 million Americans with disabilities. In its 1986 report *Toward Independence,* NCD first proposed that Congress should enact a civil rights law for people with disabilities. In 1990 the Americans with Disabilities Act was signed into law. NCD's overall purpose is to promote policies, programs, practices, and procedures that guarantee equal opportunity for all individuals with disabilities, regardless of the nature or severity of the disability, and to empower individuals with disabilities to achieve economic self-sufficiency, independent living, and inclusion and integration into all aspects of society. NCD is currently coordinating a multiyear study on the implementation and enforcement of the Americans with Disabilities Act and other civil rights laws. Bristo is also the president and chief executive officer of Access Living of Metropolitan Chicago. She co-founded and served a two-term presidency for the National Council on Independent Living.

Scott Burris is a professor of law at the Beasley School of Law, Temple University, in Philadelphia.

Thomas N. Chirikos is a member-in-residence at the H. Lee Moffitt Cancer Center and Research Institute and a professor of health policy and management at the College of Public Health, University of South Florida at Tampa. He received a doctorate in economics from Ohio State University and has conducted research on the economics of health and medical care.

Charles S. Davis is a professor in the Department of Biostatistics at the University of Iowa. His research and teaching interests include categorical data analysis, methods for the analysis of repeated measurements, and clinical trials.

Lex Frieden, a quadriplegic due to a spinal-cord injury, is the author of books and papers on independent living; the senior vice president of the Institute for Rehabilitation and Research; a professor of physical medicine and rehabilitation at Baylor College of Medicine; the North American vice president of Rehabilitation International; a member of the United Nations Panel of Experts on the Standard Rules for Disability; and the chairman of the American Association of People with Disabilities. A former executive director of the National Council on the Handicapped, he was instrumental in the creation of the Americans with Disabilities Act.

Steven G. Heeringa is the director of the Division of Surveys and Technologies at the University of Michigan's Institute for Social Research (ISR). He has over twenty-four years of statistical design experience directing the development of ISR's national sample design as well as sample designs for ISR's major longitudinal and cross-sectional survey programs. He has been actively involved in research and publication on sample design methods and procedures such as weighting, variance estimation, and the imputation of missing data that are required in the analysis of sample survey data. He has been a teacher of survey sampling methods in the United States and abroad and has served as a sample design consultant to a wide variety of international research programs.

Stanley S. Herr is a professor of law at the University of Maryland School of Law and directs the Clinical Law Office program in disability rights. He is also a Mary Switzer Distinguished Research Fellow with the National Institute on Disability and Rehabilitation Research, senior research fellow at the Yale Law School's Center for International Human Rights, and president of the American Association on Mental Retardation. He was formerly a Fulbright Senior Scholar at Tel Aviv University and Hebrew University. A graduate of Yale College, Yale Law School, and Oxford University, where he received his doctorate, Herr is also a commissioner on the American Bar Association Commission on Mental and Physical Disability Law and the author of five books and numerous articles on disability rights.

Karen Hirsch received her doctorate in special education from the University of North Carolina in Chapel Hill in 1984. She has started two centers for independent living and has taught in the Division of Education at Truman State University, Kirksville, Missouri. Hirsch is a National Association of State Mental Health Program Directors Fellow at the Missouri Institute of Mental Health in St. Louis. She is working to promote the study of disability history within the academy; her pathbreaking article "Culture and Disability: The Role of Oral History" was published in *Oral History Review* in the summer of 1995.

Mollie Weighner Marti is an assistant in instruction in the University of Iowa Department of Psychology. She practices law part time and consults in the area of law and psychology. She received her doctorate in psychology from the University of Iowa and her J.D. from the Iowa College of Law, where she served as senior articles editor of the *Iowa Law Review.*

Paul Steven Miller is a commissioner of the U.S. Equal Opportunity Commission. In addition, he serves on the Executive Committee of the President's Committee on the Employment of People with Disabilities and on the Presidential Task Force on Employment of Adults with Disabilities, a government-wide presidential task force created to develop a national policy to raise the employment rate of adults with disabilities. Prior to his confirmation to the EEOC, Miller served as the deputy director of the United States Office of Consumer Affairs and the White House liaison to the disability community. Earlier, Miller was the director of litigation for the Western Law Center for Disability Rights, a nonprofit legal services center specializing in disability rights issues; he has also been a law professor. He received his J.D. from the Harvard Law School.

Kathryn Moss is a senior research fellow at the Jordan Institute for Families in the School of Social Work at the University of North Carolina at Chapel Hill and a research fellow at the Cecil G. Sheps Center for Health Services Research at the University of North Carolina at Chapel Hill.

Robert S. Olick is an associate professor in the Program in Biomedical Ethics and Medical Humanities and in the Department of Family Medicine, University of Iowa College of Medicine, and at the University of Iowa College of Law.

Teresa L. Scheid is an associate professor of sociology at the University of North Carolina and a member of the local Mental Health Association. She has published on the work experiences of consumers in supported employment as well as on the effects of unemployment in producing stress and hindering community adjustment. She has also published widely on various types of organization processes within mental health centers. She continues to investigate the response of businesses to the ADA and is especially interested in how organizations can be more responsive to the unique abilities and needs of consumers.

Nancy L. Sprince is a professor of occupational and environmental health and internal medicine at the University of Iowa and directs the Occupational Medicine Residency Program. She is an occupational medicine physician with research interests in epidemiology and prevention of occupational injury and occupational lung diseases.

Michael Ashley Stein received his doctorate from the University of Cambridge and his J.D. from Harvard Law School, where he was the first physically disabled member of the *Harvard Law Review.* Stein is currently a consulting assistant professor at Stanford Law School, where he teaches disability law and federal litigation.

Steve Thunder-McGuire is an associate professor in curriculum and instruction and program coordinator of art education at the University of Iowa, where he teaches "What Is Storytelling For?" He is a contemporary traditional storyteller who has performed across the United States and in Mexico and Canada. His art education research on acts of interpretation has been published widely.

Robert B. Wallace is professor of epidemiology and internal medicine at the University of Iowa's College of Public Health and Medicine. He has been a member of the U.S. Preventive Serivces Task Force (USPSTF) and the National Advisory Council on Aging of the National Institutes of Health. He is currently a member of the Health Promotion and Disease Prevention Board of the Institute of Medicine, National Academy of Sciences, and a senior advisor to the USPSTF. His research focuses on the causes and prevention of disabling conditions of older persons.

Tom Walz is a professor emeritus of social work at the University of Iowa. He is a faculty liaison to Wild Bill's CoffeeShop, a special-service learning project for adult persons with disabilities, which he founded in 1974. He was featured in two television movies in the early 1980s that told the story of a mentally challenged elderly man who became something of a celebrity before his death. His most recent book is *The Unlikely Celebrity: Bill Sackter's Triumph over Disability.*

Paul S. Whitten has worked as a data analyst in the College of Medicine at the University of Iowa since 1981.

Wendy Wilkinson is an attorney, the project director of the Southwest Disability and Business and Technical Assistance Center, and a principal investigator on Legal Protections for People with Disabilities for the Research and Training

Center on Managed Care and Disability. Both are projects of the Independent Living Research Utilization Program, which is based at the Institute for Rehabilitation and Research. She has published articles on the Americans with Disabilities Act and other disability-related issues. In 1995 she was appointed clinical assistant professor in the Department of Physical Medicine and Rehabilitation at the Baylor College of Medicine.

Steven L. Willborn is the Cline Williams Professor of Law at the University of Nebraska–Lincoln, where he has been on the faculty since 1979. He has been a Fulbright Scholar at the University of London and a visiting professor at Australian National University, the University of Michigan, and Oxford University. He has written several books and articles on discrimination law, employment law, and the law of pensions and employee benefits.

Craig Zwerling is an occupational physician and injury epidemiologist. He is the head of the Department of Occupational and Environmental Health at the University of Iowa College of Public Health and the director of the University of Iowa Injury Prevention Research Center.